Best Practices and Conceptual Innovations in Information Resources Management:
Utilizing Technologies to Enable Global Progressions

Mehdi Khosrow-Pour
Information Resources Management Association, USA

Information Science REFERENCE
INFORMATION SCIENCE REFERENCE
Hershey · New York

Director of Editorial Content: Kristin Klinger
Director of Production: Jennifer Neidig
Managing Editor: Jamie Snavely
Assistant Managing Editor: Carole Coulson
Typesetter: Sean Woznicki
Cover Design: Lisa Tosheff
Printed at: Yurchak Printing Inc.

Published in the United States of America by
Information Science Reference (an imprint of IGI Global)
701 E. Chocolate Avenue, Suite 200
Hershey PA 17033
Tel: 717-533-8845
Fax: 717-533-8661
E-mail: cust@igi-global.com
Web site: http://www.igi-global.com

and in the United Kingdom by
Information Science Reference (an imprint of IGI Global)
3 Henrietta Street
Covent Garden
London WC2E 8LU
Tel: 44 20 7240 0856
Fax: 44 20 7379 0609
Web site: http://www.eurospanbookstore.com

Library of Congress Cataloging-in-Publication Data

Best practices and conceptual innovations in information resources management : utilizing technologies to enable global progressions / Mehdi Khosrow-Pour, editor.

p. cm. -- (Advances in information resources management book series)
Includes bibliographical references and index.
Summary: "This book offers insight into emerging developments in information resources management and how these technologies are shaping the way the world does business, creates policies, and advances organizational practices"--Provided by publisher.

ISBN 978-1-60566-128-5 (hardcover) -- ISBN 978-1-60566-129-2 (ebook)
1. Information resources management. I. Khosrowpour, Mehdi, 1951-
T58.64.B47 2009
658.4'038--dc22
2008022538

British Cataloguing in Publication Data
A Cataloguing in Publication record for this book is available from the British Library.

Best Practices and Conceptual Innovations in Information Resources Management: Utilizing Technologies to Enable Global Progressions is part of the IGI Global series named *Advances in Information Resources Management (AIRM)* Series, ISBN: 1537-3367

Table of Contents

Detailed Table of Contents

This chapter is concerned with methodological issues. In particular, it addresses the question of how is it possible to align the design of management information systems with the structure of an organization. The method proposed is built upon the Cybersin method developed by Stafford Beer (1975) and Raul Espejo (1992). The chapter shows a way to intersect three complementary organizational fields: management information systems, management control systems, and organizational learning when studied from a systemic perspective; in this case from the point of view of management cybernetics (Beer 1959, 1979, 1981, 1985).

This chapter seeks to address the dearth of practical examples of research in the area by proposing that critical realism be adopted as the underlying research philosophy for enterprise systems evaluation. We address some of the implications of adopting such an approach by discussing the evaluation and implementation of a number of automated performance measurement systems (APMS). Such systems are a recent evolution within the context of enterprise information systems. They collect operational data from integrated systems to generate values for key performance indicators, which are delivered directly to senior management. The creation and delivery of these data are fully automated, precluding manual intervention by middle or line management. Whilst these systems appear to be a logical progression in the exploitation of the available rich, real-time data, the statistics for APMS projects are disappointing. An understanding of the reasons is elusive and little researched. We describe how critical realism can provide a useful "underlabourer" for such research, by "clearing the ground a little ... removing some of the rubbish that lies in the way of knowledge" (Locke, 1894, p. 14). The implications of such an underlabouring role are investigated. Whilst the research is still underway, the article indicates how a critical realist foundation is assisting the research process.

As organizations strive to expand system capabilities through the development of system-of-systems (SoS) architectures, they want to know "how much effort" and "how long" to implement the SoS. In order to answer these questions, it is important to first understand the types of activities performed in SoS architecture development and integration and how these vary across different SoS implementations.

This article provides results of research conducted to determine types of SoS lead system integrator (LSI) activities and how these differ from the more traditional system engineering activities described in Electronic Industries Alliance (EIA) 632 ("Processes for Engineering a System"). This research further analyzed effort and schedule issues on "very large" SoS programs to more clearly identify and profile the types of activities performed by the typical LSI and to determine organizational characteristics that significantly impact overall success and productivity of the LSI effort. The results of this effort have been captured in a reduced-parameter version of the constructive SoS integration cost model (COSOSIMO) that estimates LSI SoS engineering (SoSE) effort.

The chapter provides an action research account of formulating and applying a new business process modeling framework to a manufacturing processes to guide software development. It is based on a mix of soft systems methodology (SSM) and the Unified Modeling Language (UML) business process modeling extensions suggested by Eriksson and Penker. The combination of SSM and UML is justified through the ideas on Multimethodology by Mingers. The Multimethodology framework is used to reason about the combination of methods from different paradigms in a single intervention. The proposed framework was applied to modeling the production process in an aluminum rolling plant as a step in the development of a new information system for it. The reflections on the intervention give details on how actual learning and appreciation is facilitated using SSM leading to better UML models of business processes.

An email system is a critical business tool and an essential part of organisational communication. Many organisations have experienced negative impacts from email and have responded by electronically monitoring and restricting email system use. However, electronic monitoring of email can be contentious. Staff can react to these controls by dissent, protest and potentially transformative action. This chapter presents the results of a single case study investigation of staff reactions to electronic monitoring and control of an email system in a company based in Ireland. The findings highlight the variations in staff reactions through multiple time frames of electronic monitoring and control, and the chapter identifies the key concerns of staff which need to be addressed by management and consultants advocating the implementation of email system monitoring and control.

This chapter provides an overview of perspectives associated with information and knowledge resource management in systems engineering and systems management in accomplishing enterprise resource planning for enhanced innovation and productivity. Accordingly, we discuss economic concepts involving information and knowledge, and the important role of network effects and path dependencies in influencing enterprise transformation through enterprise resource planning.

This chapter works out a method on how information resources in organizations can be turned into a knowledge sharing (KS) information culture, which can further feed business success. This process is complicated, and the value chain can be broken in many places. In this study this process is viewed in the light of resource-based theory. A KS-model is developed where the hard information resources of time, people and computers are defined. When wisely used, these make communication a core competence for the company. As the soft information resources are added, that is the intellectual capital, KS, and willingness to learn, a knowledge sharing culture is developed, which feeds business success. This model is empirically discussed through a case study of fifteen Finnish insurance companies. The overall KS capability of a company corresponds positively to the different dimensions applied in the model. KS is an interactive process where organizations must work on both hard information resources, the basic cornerstones of any knowledge sharing, and makes constant investment into soft information resources, learning, intellectual capital and process design in order to manage their information resources effectively.

Escalation is a serious management problem, and sunk costs are believed to be a key factor in promoting escalation behavior. While many laboratory experiments have been conducted to examine the effect of sunk costs on escalation, there has been no effort to examine these studies as a group in order to determine the effect size associated with the so-called "sunk cost effect." Using meta-analysis, we analyzed the results of 20 sunk cost experiments and found: (1) a large effect size associated with sunk costs, and (2) stronger effects in experiments involving information technology (IT) projects as opposed to non-IT projects. Implications of the results and future research directions are discussed.

E-learning markets have been expanding very rapidly. As a result, the involved senior managers are increasingly being confronted with the need to make significant investment decisions related to the e-learning business activities. Real options applications to risk management and investment evaluation of Information and Communication Technologies (ICT) have mainly focused on a single and a-priori known option. However, these options are not inherent in any ICT investment. Actually, they must be carefully planned and intentionally embedded in the ICT investment in order to mitigate its risks and increase its return. Moreover, when an ICT investment involves multiple risks, by adopting different series of cascading options we may achieve risk mitigation and enhance investment performance. In this paper, we apply real options to the e-learning investments evaluation. Given the investment's requirements, assumptions and risks, the goal is to maximize the investment's value by identifying a good way to structure it using carefully chosen real options.

Research on online shopping has taken three broad and divergent approaches viz, human-computer interaction, behavioral, and consumerist approaches to examine online consumer behavior. Assimilating these three approaches, this study proposes an integrated model of online shopping behavior, with four major antecedents influencing online purchase intent: Web site quality, customer concerns in online shopping, self-efficacy, and past online shopping experience. These antecedents were modeled as second-order constructs with subsuming first-order constituent factors. The model was tested using data from a questionnaire survey of 214 online shoppers. Statistical analyses using structural equation modeling was used to validate the model, and identify the relative importance of the key antecedents to online purchase intent. Past online shopping experience was found to have the strongest association with online purchase intent, followed by customer concerns, Web site quality, and computer self efficacy. The findings and their implications are discussed.

This chapter combines disruptive innovation strategy (DIS) theory with the system dynamics (SD) modeling method. It presents a simulation model of the hard-disk (HD) maker population overshoot and collapse dynamics, showing that DIS can crucially affect the dynamics of the IT industry. Data from the HD maker industry help calibrate the parameters of the SD model and replicate the HD makers' overshoot and collapse dynamics, which DIS allegedly caused from 1973 through 1993. SD model analysis entails articulating exactly how the structure of feedback relations among variables in a system determines its performance through time. The HD maker population model analysis shows that, over five distinct time phases, four different feedback loops might have been most prominent in generating the HD maker population dynamics. The chapter shows the benefits of using SD modeling software, such as iThink®, and SD model analysis software, such as Digest®. The latter helps detect exactly how changes in loop polarity and prominence determine system performance through time. Strategic scenarios computed with the model also show the relevance of using SD for information system management and research in areas where dynamic complexity rules.

and IS employees for technology management, interpersonal, and business skills to determine if their perceptions can serve to predict user satisfaction. Simple gap measures are dismissed as inadequate because weights on the individual expectations are not equal and predictive properties low. Exploratory results from polynomial regression models indicate that the problems in defining a predictive model extend beyond the weighting difficulties, as results differ by each skill type. Compound this with inherent problems in the selection of a success measure, and we only begin to understand the complexities in the relationships that may be required in an adequate predictive model relating skills to success.

James Jiang, University of Central Florida, USA
Gary Klein, University of Colorado in Colorado Springs, USA
Phil Beck, Southwest Airlines, USA
Eric T.G. Wang, National Central University, Taiwan

To improve the performance of software projects, a number of practices are encouraged that serve to control certain risks in the development process, including the risk of limited competences related to the application domain and system development process. A potential mediating variable between this lack of skill and project performance is the ability of an organization to acquire the essential domain knowledge and technology skills through learning, specifically organizational technology learning. However, the same lack of knowledge that hinders good project performance may also inhibit learning since a base of knowledge is essential in developing new skills and retaining lessons learned. This study examines the relationship between information system personnel skills and domain knowledge, organizational technology learning, and software project performance with a sample of professional software developers. Indications are that the relationship between information systems (IS) personnel skills and project performance is partially mediated by organizational technology learning.

Leigh Jin, San Francisco State University, USA
Daniel Robey, Georgia State University, USA
Marie-Claude Boudreau, University of Georgia, USA

Open source software has rapidly become a popular area of study within the information systems research community. Most of the research conducted so far has focused on the phenomenon of open source software development, rather than use. We argue for the importance of studying open source software use and propose a framework to guide research in this area. The framework describes four main areas of investigation: the creation of OSS user communities, their characteristics, their contributions and how they change. For each area of the framework, we suggest several research questions that deserve attention.

In the literature of electronic meetings, few studies have investigated the effects of topic-related variables on group processes. This chapter explores the effects of an individual's perception of topics on process gains or process losses using a sample of 110 students in 14 electronic meetings. The results of the study showed that topic characteristics variables, individual knowledge, and individual self-efficacy had a significant influence on the number of relevant comments generated in an electronic meeting.

Text documents are the most common means for exchanging formal knowledge among people. Text is a rich medium that can contain a vast range of information, but text can be difficult to decipher automatically. Many organizations have vast repositories of textual data but with few means of automatically mining that text. Text mining methods seek to use an understanding of natural language text to extract information relevant to user needs. This article evaluates a new text mining methodology: prototype-matching for text clustering, developed by the authors' research group. The methodology was applied to four applications: clustering documents based on their abstracts, analyzing financial data, distinguishing authorship, and evaluating multiple translation similarity. The results are discussed in terms of common business applications and possible future research.

Using March and Smith's taxonomy of information systems (IS) research activities and outputs and Newman's method of pro forma abstracting, this research mapped the current space of IS research and identified research activities and outputs that have received very little or no attention in the top IS publishing outlets. We reviewed and classified 1,157 articles published in some of the top IS journals and the ICIS proceedings for the period 1998–2002. The results demonstrate the efficacy of March and

Preface

In the time of constant technological and managerial advancement, organizations of the 21st century are faced with an ongoing quest for implementing more effective strategies and methodologies to remain at the apex of the information resources management industry. Considering this, researchers and the pioneers of academia are continuously in search of innovative solutions to increase efficacy within technological and information resources management, as well as identify the emerging technologies and trends. ***Best Practices and Conceptual Innovations in Information Resources Management: Utilizing Technologies to Enable Global Progressions***, part of the *Advances in Information Resources Management Book Series,* supplies the industry leaders, practicing managers, researchers, experts, and educators with the most current findings on undertaking the operation of the latest information technology reforms, developments, and changes. This publication presents the issues facing modern organizations and provides the most recent strategies in overcoming the obstacles of the ever-evolving information management and utilization industry.

Chapter I, "Integrating the Fragmented Pieces of IS Research Paradigms and Frameworks: A Systems Approach" *by Manuel Mora, Autonomous University of Aguascalientes, Mexico, Ovsei Gelman, National Autonomous University of Mexico, Mexico, Guisseppi Forgionne, Maryland University Baltimore County, USA, Doncho Petvok, Eastern State Connecticut University, USA, and Jeimy Cano, Los Andes University, Colombia,* presents a formal conceptualization of the original concept of system and its related concepts from the original Systems Approach movement to facilitate the understanding of information systems (IS). This paper develops a critique integrative of the main IS research paradigms and frameworks reported in the IS literature using a Systems Approach. The effort seeks to reduce or dissolve some current research conflicts on the foci and the underlying paradigms of the IS discipline.

Chapter II, "Could the Work System Method Embrace Systems Concepts More Fully?" *by Steven Alter, University of San Francisco, USA,* discusses how the work system method was developed iteratively with the overarching goal of helping business professionals understand IT-reliant systems in organizations. It uses general systems concepts selectively, and sometimes implicitly. For example, a work system has a boundary, but its inputs are treated implicitly rather than explicitly. This paper asks whether the further development of the work system method might benefit from integrating general systems concepts more completely. After summarizing aspects of the work system method, it dissects some of the underlying ideas and questions how thoroughly even basic systems concepts are applied. It also asks whether and how additional systems concepts might be incorporated beneficially. The inquiry about how to use additional system ideas is of potential interest to people who study systems in general and information systems in particular because it deals with bridging the gap between highly abstract concepts and practical applications.

Chapter III, "The Distribution of a Management Control System in an Organization" *by Alfonso Reyes A., Universidad de los Andes, Colombia,* is concerned with methodological issues. In particular, it addresses the question of how is it possible to align the design of management information systems with the structure of an organization. The method proposed is built upon the Cybersin method developed by Stafford Beer (1975) and Raul Espejo (1992). The paper shows a way to intersect three complementary organizational fields: management information systems, management control systems, and organizational learning when studied from a systemic perspective; in this case from the point of view of management cybernetics (Beer 1959, 1979, 1981, 1985).

Chapter IV, "Making the Case for Critical Realism: Examining the Implementation of Automated Performance Management Systems" *by Phillip Dobson, Edith Cowan University, Perth Western Australia, J. Myles, Edith Cowan University, Perth Western Australia, and Paul Jackson, Edith Cowan University, Perth Western Australia,* explores how although there have been a number of calls for an increased use of critical realism in Information Systems Research, this approach has been little used to date. This paper seeks to address the dearth of practical examples of research in the area by proposing that critical realism be adopted as the underlying research philosophy for enterprise systems evaluation. The authors address some of the implications of adopting such an approach by discussing the evaluation and implementation of a number of Automated Performance Measurement Systems (APMS). Such systems are a recent evolution within the context of enterprise information systems. They collect operational data from integrated systems to generate values for key performance indicators which are delivered directly to senior management. The creation and delivery of these data are fully automated, precluding manual intervention by middle or line management. Whilst these systems appear to be a logical progression in the exploitation of the available rich, real-time data, the statistics for APMS projects are disappointing. An understanding of the reasons is elusive and little researched. The authors examine a number of such implementations and seek to understand the implementation issues involved. The authors describe how critical realism can provide a useful "underlabourer" for such research, by "clearing the ground a little... removing some of the rubbish that lies in the way of knowledge" (Locke, 1894, p. 14). The implications of such an underlabouring role are investigated. Whilst the research is still underway the paper indicates how a critical realist foundation is assisting the research process.

Chapter V, "System-of-Systems Cost Estimation: Analysis of Lead System Integrator Engineering Activities" *by Jo Ann Lane, University of Southern California, USA and Barry Boehm, University of Southern California, USA,* examines how as organizations strive to expand system capabilities through the development of system-of-systems (SoS) architectures, they want to know "how much effort" and "how long" to implement the SoS. In order to answer these questions, it is important to first understand the types of activities performed in SoS architecture development and integration and how these vary across different SoS implementations. This paper provides results of research conducted to determine types of SoS Lead System Integrator (LSI) activities and how these differ from the more traditional system engineering activities described in Electronic Industries Alliance (EIA) 632 ("Processes for Engineering a System"). This research further analyzed effort and schedule issues on "very large" SoS programs to more clearly identify and profile the types of activities performed by the typical LSI and to determine organizational characteristics that significantly impact overall success and productivity of the LSI effort. The results of this effort have been captured in a reduced-parameter version of the Constructive SoS Integration Cost Model (COSOSIMO) that estimates LSI SoS Engineering (SoSE) effort.

Chapter VI, "Mixing Soft Systems Methodology and UML in Business Process Modeling" *by Kosheek Sewchurran, University of Cape Town, South Africa and Doncho Petkov, Eastern Connecticut State University, USA,* provides an action research account of formulating and applying a new business process modeling framework to manufacturing processes to guide software development. It is based on a mix of soft systems methodology (SSM) and the Unified Modeling Language (UML) business process modeling extensions suggested by Eriksson and Penker. The combination of SSM and UML is justified through the ideas on Multimethodology by Mingers. The Multimethodology framework is used to reason about the combination of methods from different paradigms in a single intervention. The proposed framework was applied to modeling the production process in an aluminum rolling plant as a step in the development of a new information system for it. The reflections on the intervention give details on how actual learning and appreciation is facilitated using SSM leading to better UML models of business processes.

Chapter VII, "Managing E-Mail Systems: An Exploration of Electronic Monitoring and Control in Practice" *by Aidan Duane, Waterford Institute of Technology (WIT), Ireland and Patrick Finnegan, University College Cork (UCC), Ireland,* examines how an e-mail system is a critical business tool and an essential part of organisational communication. Many organisations have experienced negative impacts from e-mail and have responded by electronically monitoring and restricting email system use. However, electronic monitoring of email can be contentious. Staff can react to these controls by dissent, protest and potentially transformative action. This paper presents the results of a single case study investigation of staff reactions to electronic monitoring and control of an e-mail system in a company based in Ireland. The findings highlight the variations in staff reactions through multiple time frames of electronic monitoring and control, and this paper identifies the key concerns of staff which need to be addressed by management and consultants advocating the implementation of e-mail system monitoring and control.

Chapter VIII, "Information and Knowledge Perspectives in Systems Engineering and Management for Innovation and Productivity through Enterprise Resource Planning" *by Stephen V. Stephenson, Dell Computer Corporation, USA and Andrew P. Sage, George Mason University, USA,* provides an overview of perspectives associated with information and knowledge resource management in systems engineering and systems management in accomplishing enterprise resource planning for enhanced innovation and productivity. Accordingly, the authors discuss economic concepts involving information and knowledge, the important role of network effects and path dependencies in influencing enterprise transformation through enterprise resource planning.

Chapter IX, "The Knowledge Sharing Model: Stressing the Importance of Social Ties and Capital" *by Gunilla Widén-Wulff, Åbo Akademi University, Finland and Reima Suomi, Turku School of Economics, Finland,* works out a method on how information resources in organizations can be turned into a knowledge sharing (KS) information culture, which can further feed business success. This process is complicated, and the value chain can be broken in many places. In this study this process is viewed in the light of resource-based theory. A KS-model is developed where the hard information resources of time, people and computers are defined. When wisely used, these make communication a core competence for the company. As the soft information resources are added, that is the intellectual capital, KS, and willingness to learn, a knowledge sharing culture is developed, which feeds business success. This model is empirically discussed through a case study of fifteen Finnish insurance companies. The overall KS capability of a company corresponds positively to the different dimensions applied in the model. KS is an interactive process where organizations must work on both hard information resources, the basic cornerstones of any knowledge sharing, and make constant investment into soft information resources, learning, intellectual capital and process design in order to manage their information resources effectively.

Chapter X, "A Meta-Analysis Comparing the Sunk Cost Effect For IT and Non-IT Projects" *by Jijie Wang, Georgia State University, USA and Mark Keil, Georgia State University, USA,* investigates why escalation is a serious management problem and why sunk costs are believed to be a key factor in promoting escalation behavior. While many laboratory experiments have been conducted to examine the effect of sunk costs on escalation, there has been no effort to examine these studies as a group in order to determine the effect size associated with the so-called "sunk cost effect." Using meta-analysis, the authors analyzed the results of 20 sunk cost experiments and found: (1) a large effect size associated with sunk costs, and (2) stronger effects in experiments involving IT projects as opposed to non-IT projects. Implications of the results and future research directions are discussed.

Chapter XI, "E-Learning Business Risk Management with Real Options" *by Georgios N. Angelou, University of Macedonia, Greece and Anastasios A. Economides, University of Macedonia, Greece*, explores the rapid expansion of e-learning markets. As a result, the involved senior managers are increasingly being confronted with the need to make significant investment decisions related to the e-learning business activities. Real options applications to risk management and investment evaluation of Information and Communication Technologies (ICT) have mainly focused on a single and a-priori known option. However, these options are not inherent in any ICT investment. Actually, they must be carefully planned and intentionally embedded in the ICT investment in order to mitigate its risks and increase its return. Moreover, when an ICT investment involves multiple risks, by adopting different series of cascading options we may achieve risk mitigation and enhance investment performance. In this paper, the authors apply real options to the e-learning investments evaluation. Given the investment's requirements, assumptions and risks, the goal is to maximize the investment's value by identifying a good way to structure it using carefully chosen real options.

Chapter XII, "Examining Online Purchase Intentions in B2C E-Commerce: Testing an Integrated Model" *by C. Ranganathan, University of Illinois at Chicago, USA and Sanjeev Jha, University of Illinois at Chicago, USA,* discusses how the research on online shopping has taken three broad and divergent approaches viz., human-computer interaction, behavioral, and consumerist approaches to examine online consumer behavior. Assimilating these three approaches, this study proposes an integrated model of online shopping behavior, with four major antecedents influencing online purchase intent: web site quality, customer concerns in online shopping, self-efficacy, and past online shopping experience. These antecedents were modeled as second-order constructs with subsuming first-order constituent factors. The model was tested using data from a questionnaire survey of 214 online shoppers. Statistical analyses using structural equation modeling were used to validate the model and identify the relative importance of the key antecedents to online purchase intent. Past online shopping experience was found to have the strongest association with online purchase intent, followed by customer concerns, web site quality, and computer self efficacy. The findings and their implications are discussed.

Chapter XIII, "Information Technology Industry Dynamics: Impact of Disruptive Innovation Strategy" *by Nicholas C. Georgantzas , Fordham University Business Schools, USA and Evangelos Katsamakas , Fordham University Business Schools, USA,* combines disruptive innovation strategy (DIS) theory with the system dynamics (SD) modeling method. It presents a simulation model of the hard-disk (HD) maker population overshoot and collapse dynamics, showing that DIS can crucially affect the dynamics of the IT industry. Data from the HD maker industry help calibrate the parameters of the SD model and replicate the HD makers' overshoot and collapse dynamics, which DIS allegedly caused from 1973 through 1993. SD model analysis entails articulating exactly how the structure of feedback relations among variables in a system determines its performance through time. The HD maker population model analysis shows that, over five distinct time phases, four different feedback loops might have been most prominent in generating the HD maker population dynamics. The chapter shows the benefits of using SD modeling software, such as iThink®, and SD model analysis software, such as Digest®. The latter helps detect exactly how changes in loop polarity and prominence determine system performance through time. Strategic scenarios computed with the model also show the relevance of using SD for information system management and research in areas where dynamic complexity rules.

Chapter XIV, "Modeling Customer-Related IT Diffusion," *by Shana L. Dardan, Susquehanna University, USA, Ram L. Kumar, University of North Carolina at Charlotte, USA, and Antonis C. Stylianou, University of North Carolina at Charlotte, USA* presents a diffusion model of customer-related IT (CRIT) based on stock market announcements of investments in those technologies. Customer-related IT investments are defined in this work as information technology investments made with the intention of improving or enhancing the customer experience. The diffusion model developed in our study is based on data for the companies of the S&P 500 and S&P MidCap 400 for the years of 1996-2001. The authors find empirical support for a sigmoid diffusion model. Further, the authors find that both the size and industry of the company affect the path of CRIT diffusion. Another contribution of this study is to illustrate how data collection techniques typically used for financial event studies can be used to study information technology diffusion. Finally, the data collected for this study can serve as a Bayesian prior for future diffusion forecasting studies of CRIT.

Chapter XV, "The Impact of Computer Self-Efficacy and System Complexity on Acceptance of Information Technologies" *by Bassam Hasan, The University of Toledo, USA, and Jafar M. Ali, Kuwait University, Kuwait,* investigates the acceptance and use of information technologies by target users. Building on past research and integrating computer self-efficacy (CSE) and perceived system complexity (SC) as external variables to the technology acceptance model (TAM), this study examines the direct and indirect effects of these two factors on system eventual acceptance and use. Overall, both CSE and SC demonstrated significant direct effects on perceived usefulness and perceived ease of use as well as indirect effects on attitude and behavioral intention. With respect to TAM's variables, perceived ease of use demonstrated a stronger effect on attitude than that of perceived usefulness. Finally, attitude demonstrated a non-significant impact on behavioral intention. Several implications for research and practice can be drawn from the results of this study.

Chapter XVI, "Determining User Satisfaction from the Gaps in Skill Expectations Between IS Employees and Their Managers" *by James Jiang, University of Central Florida, USA, Gary Klein, University of Colorado, USA*, and *Eric T.G. Wang, National Central University, Taiwan,* explores how the skills held by information system professionals clearly impact the outcome of a project. However, the perceptions of just what skills are expected of information systems (IS) employees have not been found to be a reliable predictor of eventual success in the literature. Though relationships to success have been identified, the results broadly reported in the literature are often ambiguous or conflicting, presenting difficulties in developing predictive models of success. The authors examine the perceptions of IS managers and IS employees for technology management, interpersonal, and business skills to determine if their perceptions can serve to predict user satisfaction. Simple gap measures are dismissed as inadequate because weights on the individual expectations are not equal and predictive properties low. Exploratory results from polynomial regression models indicate that the problems in defining a predictive model extend beyond the weighting difficulties, as results differ by each skill type. Compound this with inherent problems in the selection of a success measure, and we only begin to understand the complexities in the relationships that may be required in an adequate predictive model relating skills to success.

Chapter XVII, "The Impact of Missing Skills on Learning and Project Performance" *by James Jiang, University of Central Florida, USA, Gary Klein, University of Colorado in Colorado Springs, USA, Phil Beck, Southwest Airlines, USA, and Eric T.G. Wang, National Central University, Taiwan,* investigate methods to improve the performance of software projects. A number of practices are encouraged that serve to control certain risks in the development process, including the risk of limited competences related to the application domain and system development process. A potential mediating variable between this lack of skill and project performance is the ability of an organization to acquire the essential domain knowledge and technology skills through learning, specifically organizational technology learning. However, the same lack of knowledge that hinders good project performance may also inhibit learning since a base of knowledge is essential in developing new skills and retaining lessons learned. This study examines the relationship between information system personnel skills and domain knowledge, organizational technology learning, and software project performance with a sample of professional software developers. Indications are that the relationship between information systems (IS) personnel skills and project performance is partially mediated by organizational technology learning.

Chapter XVIII, "Beyond Development: A Research Agenda for Investigating Open Source Software User Communities" *by Leigh Jin, San Francisco State University, USA, Daniel Robey, Georgia State University, USA, and Marie-Claude Boudreau, University of Georgia, USA*, explores the use of open source software. Most of the research conducted so far has focused on the phenomenon of open source software development, rather than use. The authors argue for the importance of studying open source software use and propose a framework to guide research in this area. The framework describes four main areas of investigation: the creation of OSS user communities, their characteristics, their contributions, and how they change. For each area of the framework, the authors suggest several research questions that deserve attention.

Chpater XIX, "Electronic Meeting Topic Effects" *by Milam Aiken, University of Mississippi, USA, Linwu Gu, Indiana University of Pennsylvania, USA, and Jianfeng Wang, Indiana University of Pennsylvania, USA,* explores the effects of an individual's perception of topics on process gains or process losses using a sample of 110 students in 14 electronic meetings. The results of the study showed that topic characteristics variables, individual knowledge, and individual self-efficacy had a significant influence on the number of relevant comments generated in an electronic meeting.

Chapter XX, "Mining Text with the Prototype-Matching Method" *by A. Durfee, Appalachian State University, USA , A. Visa, Tampere University of Technology, Finland, H. Vanharanta, Tampere University of Technology, Finland, S. Schneberger, Appalachian State University, USA, and B. Back, Åbo Akademi University, Finland,* evaluates a new text mining methodology: prototype-matching for text clustering, developed by the authors' research group. Text mining methods seek to use an understanding of natural language text to extract information relevant to user needs. The methodology was applied to four applications: clustering documents based on their abstracts, analyzing financial data, distinguishing authorship, and evaluating multiple translation similarity. The results are discussed in terms of common business applications and possible future research.

Chapter XXI, "A Review of IS Research Activities and Outputs Using Pro Forma Abstracts" *by Francis Kofi Andoh-Baidoo, State University of New York at Brockport, USA, Elizabeth White Baker, Virginia Military Institute, USA, Santa R. Susarapu, Virginia Commonwealth University, USA, and George M. Kasper, Virginia Commonwealth University, USA,* evaluates research using March and Smith's taxonomy of information systems (IS) research activities and outputs and Newman's method of pro forma abstracting, which maps the current space of IS research and identifies research activities and outputs that have received very little or no attention in the top IS publishing outlets. Eleven-hundred-fifty-seven (1,157) articles published in some of the top IS journals and the ICIS proceedings for the period 1998-2002 were reviewed and classified. The results demonstrate the efficacy of March and Smith's taxonomy for summarizing the state of IS research and for identifying activity-output categories that have received little or no attention. Examples of published research occupying cells of the taxonomy are cited, and research is posited to populate the one empty cell. The results also affirm the need to balance theorizing with building and evaluating systems because the latter two provide unique feedback that encourage those theories that are the most promising in practice.

In the competing business environment of today, strategically managing information resources is at the forefront for organizations worldwide. The adaptation of technological advance has become the key agenda for firms who desire the greatest effectiveness and efficiency of information resources management. Technology, and all it facilitates, has become the axis of the modern world, and thus, having access to the most current findings allows firms the vehicle for the next echelon of success. By investigating transpiring technological movements, researchers, experts, and practitioners alike have the opportunity to implement the highest of emerging standards and grow from that execution. ***Best Practices and Conceptual Innovations in Information Resources Management: Utilizing Technologies to Enable Global Progressions*** comprises the most current findings associated with utilizing these advancements and applying their latest solutions.

Mehdi Khosrow-Pour, D.B.A.
Editor-in-Chief
Best Practices and Conceptual Innovations in Information Resources Management:
Utilizing Technologies to Enable Global Progressions
Advances in Information Resources Management Book Series

Chapter I
Integrating the Fragmented Pieces of IS Research Paradigms and Frameworks:
A Systems Approach

Manuel Mora
Autonomous University of Aguascalientes, Mexico

Ovsei Gelman
National Autonomous University of Mexico, Mexico

Guisseppi Forgionne
Maryland University, Baltimore County, USA

Doncho Petkov
Eastern State Connecticut University, USA

Jeimy Cano
Los Andes University, Colombia

ABSTRACT

A formal conceptualization of the original concept of system and related concepts—from the original systems approach movement—can facilitate the understanding of information systems (IS). This article develops a critique integrative of the main IS research paradigms and frameworks reported in the IS literature using a systems approach. The effort seeks to reduce or dissolve some current research conflicts on the foci and the underlying paradigms of the IS discipline.

INTRODUCTION

The concept of management information systems (MIS) in particular, or information systems (IS) in general, has been studied intensively since the 1950s (Adam & Fitzgerald, 2000). These investigations have been conducted largely by behavioral-trained scientists to study the emergent phenomena caused by the deployment and utilization of computers in organizations.

This discipline, from its conception as a potential scientific field, has been driven by a dual research perspective: technical (design engineering oriented) or social (behavioral focused). This duality of man-made non-living (hardware, software, data, and procedures) and living systems (human-beings, teams, organizations, and societies), the multiple interrelationships among these elements, and the socio-cultural-economic-politic and physical-natural environment, make IS a complex field of inquiry.

The complexity of the IS field has attracted researchers from disparate disciplines—operations research, accounting, organizational behavior, management, and computer science, among others. This disciplinary disparity has generated the utilization of several isolated research paradigms and lenses (e.g., positivist, interpretative, or critical-based underlying research methodologies). The result has been the lack of a generally accepted IS research framework or broad theory (Hirchheim & Klein, 2003) and has produced: (i) a vast body of disconnected micro-theories (Barkhi & Sheetz, 2001); (ii) multiple self-identities perceived by the different stakeholders (*e.g.*, IS researchers, IS practitioners, and IS users); and (iii) partial, disparate and incomplete IS conceptualizations (Benbazat & Zmud, 2003; Galliers, 2004; Orlikowski & Iacono, 2001).

Despite scholastic indicators[1] of maturity, IS, then, has been assessed as: (1) highly fragmented (Larsen & Levine, 2005), (2) with little cumulative tradition (Weber, 1987), (3) deficient of a formal and standard set of fundamental well-defined and accepted concepts (Alter, 2001, p. 3; Banville & Landry, 1989, p. 56; Wand & Weber, 1990, p. 1282) and (4) with an informal, conflicting and ambiguous communicational system (Banville & Landry, 1989; Hirschheim & Klein, 2003). Such findings provide insights for a plausible explanation of the delayed maturation of the field and the conflictive current perspectives on information systems (Farhoomand, 1987; Wand & Weber, 1990).

This article illustrates how systems theory can be used to alleviate the difficulties. First, there is a review of basic *system* and related concepts relevant to information systems (Ackoff, 1960; Bertalanffy, 1950, 1968, 1972; Boulding, 1956; Checkland, 1983; Forrester, 1958; Jackson, 2000; Klir, 1969; Midgley, 1996; Mingers, 2000, 2001; Rapoport, 1968). Next, these systems approach concepts are used to formulate a critique integrative of the main paradigms and frameworks suggested for IS research. Then, a theoretical scheme is developed to integrate holistically and coherently the fragmented pieces of IS research paradigms and frameworks. To end, this article presents future research directions on potential conflictive conclusions presented.

THE SYSTEMS APPROACH: PRINCIPLES AND PARADIGMS

The Principles of the Systems Approach

The systems approach is an intellectual movement originated by the biologist Ludwig von Bertalanffy[2] (1950, 1968, 1972), the economist Kenneth Boulding (1956), and the mathematicians Anatoly Rapoport (1968) and George Klir (1969) that proposes a complementary paradigm (e.g., a worldview and a framework of ideas, methodologies, and tools) to study complex natural, artificial, and socio-politic cultural phenomena.

Lazlo and Lazlo (1997) interpret the modern conceptualization of the systems approach as a worldview shift from chaos to an organized complexity. Boulding (1956) argues that the systems approach—labeled as general systems theory (GST)—is about an adequate trade-off between the scope and confidence in valid theories from several disciplines. In the former case the greater the level of scope the lesser the level of confidence and vice versa. For Rapoport (1968), the systems approach should be conceptualized as a philosophical strategy or direction for doing science. Klir (1969), in turn, considers that GST should contain general methodological principles for all systems as well as particular principles for specific types of systems. Bertalanffy (1972) quotes himself (Bertalanffy, 1950 (reprinted in Bertalanffy, 1968, p. 32)) to explain that GST's "...task is the formulation and derivation of those general principles that are applicable to systems in general."

According to these systems thinkers and additional seminal contributors to this intellectual movement (Ackoff[3] in particular, 1960, 1973, 1981), the systems approach complements the reductionism, analytic, and mechanic worldview with an expansionist, synthetic, and teleological view.

Reductionism implies that the phenomena are isolated or disconnected from wider systems or the environment, while expansionism claims that each phenomenon can be delimited—objectively, subjectively, or coercively—into a central object of interest (e.g., the system under study) and its wider system and/or environment. The analytic view holds that we need only investigate the internal parts and their interrelationships of the phenomenon to understand its behavior. A synthetic view accepts and uses the analytical view but incorporates the interrelationships between the whole and its environment. Furthermore, the synthetic view holds that some events and attributes of the parts are lost when these are not part of the whole and vice versa (e.g., events and attributes emerge in the whole but are not owned by the parts). The mechanist view holds that the phenomena happen by the occurrence of disconnected and simple linear cause-effect networks, and the systems approach complements this view through a teleological perspective that claims that the phenomena happens via a complex interaction of connected non-linear feed-back networks. Causes or independent constructs are affected by lagged effects.

Under the systems approach, the *systems* own core general properties: *wholeness*, *purposefulness*, *emergence*, *organization*, *hierarchical order*, *interconnectedness*, *competence*, *information-based controllability*, *progressive mechanization*, and *centralization*. *Wholeness* refers to the unitary functional view and existence of a system. *Purposefulness* refers to the extent of a system has predefined or self-generated goals as well as the set of intentional behaviors to reach these targets. *Emergence* involves the actions and/or properties owned solely by the whole and not by their parts. The property *organization* implies a non-random arrangement of its components and *hierarchical order* the existence of multi-level layers of components. *Interconnectedness* accounts for the degree of interdependence effects of components on other components and subgroups. *Competence* implies that the inflows of energy, material, and information toward the system will be distributed in the parts in a competitive manner, and this property also accounts for the conflicts between system, subsystems, and suprasystem's objectives. Finally, the *information-based controllability*, *progressive mechanization*, and *centralization* are properties which involve the transference of information and control fluxes between components that are required to regulate and govern the relationships. In particular, *progressive mechanization* refers to the extent to which the parts of a system act independently and *centralization* to the extent to which changes in the system result from a particular component.

Research Paradigms of the Systems Approach

Many researchers have shaped the systems approach. These researchers include the hard/functionalist/positivist stream (Forrester, 1958, 1991) supported by a positivist/pragmatist philosophy (Jackson, 2000), the soft/interpretative stream (Checkland, 1983, 2000) linked to Husserl's phenomenology and appreciative philosophy

(Checkland, 2000), the critical/emancipative stream (Flood, Norman, & Romm, 1996; Jackson, 2000) underpinned in a critical philosophy from Habermas (referenced by Jackson, 2000) and the emergent critical realism systemic stance (Mingers, 2000, 2002) endorsed by Bhaskar's philosophy (Bhaskar, 1975, quoted by Mingers).

These four main streams can be associated respectively to the following general philosophical principles:

- *P.1* *the intelligible world is an organized complexity comprised of a variety of natural, man-made, and social systems that own a real existence*
- *P.2* *the intelligible world can be studied freely through systemic lenses and under an intersubjective social construction*
- *P.3* *the intelligible world can be uniquely understood when it is studied freely from restrictive social human relationships and a variety of theoretically coherent systemic lenses are used.*
- *P.4* *the world is intelligible*[4a] *for human beings because of its stratified hierarchy of organized complexities—the widest container is the* ***real domain*** *that comprises a multistrata of natural, man-made and social structures*[4b] *as well as of event-generative processes that are manifested in the* ***actual domain*** *that in turn contains to the* ***empirical domain*** *where the generated events can or cannot be dectected-*

The hard/functionalist/positivist systems approach is based on P.1. The soft/interpretative approach rejects P.1 but supports P.2. The critical/emancipative approach is neutral to P.1, rejects P.2, and endorses P.3. Finally, the emergent critical realism systems approach endorses P.4 and automatically includes P.1 through P.3.

The first three systems paradigms have been extensively studied and applied, However, according to several authors (Dobson, 2003; Mingers, 2001; Mora, Gelman, Forgionne, & Cervantes, 2004), Bhaskar's critical realism has emerged to dissolve theoretical contradictions in the different systems approaches and offer an original expected holistic view of the discipline. Critical realism has been suggested as a common underlying philosophy for management sciences/operations research (Mingers, 2000, 2003) and also recently for information systems research (Carlsson, 2003; Dobson, 2001, 2002; Mingers, 2002). According to Mingers (2002):

> *Critical realism does not have a commitment to a single form of research, rather it involves particular attitudes toward its purpose and practice. First, the critical realist is never content just with description, whether it is qualitative or quantitative. No matter how complex a statistical analysis, or rich an ethnographic interpretation, this is only the first step. CR wants to get beneath the surface to understand and explain why things are as they are, to hypothesize the structures and mechanisms that shape observable events. Second, CR recognizes the existence of a variety of objects of knowledge—material, conceptual, social, psychological—each of which requires different research methods to come to understand them. And, CR emphasizes the holistic interaction of these different objects. Thus it is to be expected that understanding in any particular situation will require a variety of research methods (multimethodology [Mingers 2001]), both extensive and intensive. Third, CR recognizes the inevitable fallibility of observation, especially in the social world, and therefore requires the researcher to be particularly aware of the assumptions and limitation of their research.* (p. 302)

Based on Checkland (2000), Jackson's (2000) interpretations of Checkland (1981), Ackoff, Gupta, and Minas (1962), Ackoff (1981), and Midgley (1996), a systemic view of the problem can be articulated with three essential components and five purposes. These components are: (1) the framework **F** of ideas, initial theories, theoretical problems, and models that compose a discipline, (2) the set of philosophical research paradigms and methodologies **M** that define the ontological definitions of the world to be studied as well as the epistemological principles and tools regarding how it can be studied, and (3) the situational area **A** of the reality that contains well-defined or messy situations of interest.

According to Midgley[5] (1996), a science can have the following purposes: (1) to predict and control well-defined objects or situations of study as in the hard/positivist/functionalist systems paradigm, (2) to increase a shared and mutual understanding of messy real situations as in the soft/interpretative systems paradigm, and (3) to increase the quality of work and life of human beings in organizations and societies through an emancipation of power relations between dominant and dominated groups as in the critical systems paradigm. Ackoff et al. (1962) and Ackoff (1981) suggest two main purposes for science: (1) to respond to inquiries and (2) to resolve, solve or dissolve problems.

The integration of these core concepts of the systems research paradigms and the underlying philosophies and research strategies (adapted from Gregory, 1996) leads to the holistic proposal presented in Table 1.

REVIEW AND DISCUSSION OF A CRITICAL REALIST INTEGRATION OF IS RESEARCH PARADIGMS AND FRAMEWORKS

Systemic Integration of the Information Systems Research Paradigms

Six IS research paradigms are reviewed in this section: Weber (1987), Orlikowski and Iacono (2001), Benbazat and Zmud (2003), Hirschheim and Klein (2003), Galliers (2004), and Larsen and Levine (2005), and arguments are articulated for a systemic integration of them.

Weber (1987) critiques the proliferation of research frameworks that have lead to a random and non-selective set of worthy research questions (e.g., a hypothesis generator). Then novel researchers could infer that every relationship is useful to be studied. Weber also asserts that technology-driven research can produce a fragile discipline with a lack of sound theoretical principles. A paradigm is proposed with three required conditions: (i) a set of objects of interest that other disciplines cannot study adequately, (ii) the objects must exhibit an observable behavior, and (iii) a possible underlying order is associated with the object's behaviors. For Weber, two sets of objects are candidates: objects that externally interact with an information system and objects that internally compose the system. The behaviors of interest are performance variables and interrelationships of the two set of objects. Weber claims that an internal order of the second set of objects can and must be assumed to pursue research based on the paradigm. No argument is reported for the first set of objects. Weber also suggests that the IS discipline can have several paradigms. He proposes *static, comparative static,* and *dynamic* paradigms. The articulated paradigm is not the same as a research framework where a definitive set of variables is fixed: "*instead, it provides a way of thinking about the world of IS behavior and the types of research that might be done*" (ibid, p. 16). With such a paradigm, a piecemeal, methodological dominant-oriented and event-day driven research can be avoided.

Orlikowski & Iacono (2001) suggest that IS research should focus on the information technology (IT) artifact as much as its context, effects, and capabilities. According to their study, IT artifacts have been analyzed only as monolithic black-boxes or disconnected from their context, effects, or capabilities. IT artifacts are defined in five different modes: as a *tool*, as a *proxy*, as

Table 1. Systems research paradigms

		Hard/Positivist/ Functionalist System Paradigm	Soft/Interpretative System Paradigm	Critical System Paradigm	Emergent Critical Realism System Paradigm
Framework of Ideas, Theories, Theoretical Problems and Models		- systems and their underlying structures exist in reality (a systemic ontology) and can be studied, predicted and controlled using systems approach (a systemic epistemology)	- the reality and their underlying structures can be studied systemically (a systemic epistemology) but systems do not have a real existence (non systemic ontology)	- the social reality and their underlying structures can be studied systemically when restrictive power relationships are uncovered (a systemic epistemology) but systems can be contingently considered to be real (a conditioned systemic ontology)	- all reality (natural, designed and social) has real underlying mechanisms and structures (real domain) that generate events observed (empirical domain) as well as non observed (the actual domain including the empirical one), but social reality (concepts, meanings, categories) are socially built and thereby rely on the existence of human beings and a communication language (a systemic ontology) - research involves the underlying mechanisms and structures of the observed events (a systemic epistemology)
Methodology (research strategies and methods)		- systems methods are used with an isolated (just a sole research method is required), an imperialist (just a sole research method is required and superior to others but some features of latter can be added) or a pragmatism (any research tool perceived as useful can be used and combined with others despite theoretical inconsistencies) strategy		- systems methods are used in a pluralist and complementarist view with theoretical and practical coherency	
Areas of Study in the Reality		- natural and designed systems	- social systems (including human activity systems)	- social systems	- all systems
Research Purposes	**Response inquiries (understand reality)**	- to predict the behavior of the phenomena of interest	- to formulate interpretative theories and models on the phenomena of interest	- to formulate critical theories and models on the phenomena of interest	- to know the correct underlying mechanisms and structures that causes the actual domain
	Solve, resolve or dissolve problems (intervene and modify reality)	-to control the behavior of the phenomena of interest	- to achieve a shared and mutual understanding of conflictive views of the phenomena	- to foster the emancipation of human beings from restrictive power work , life and societal relationships	- to use knowledge to intervene in the phenomena of interest

an ensemble, as a *computational resource*, and as a *nominal concept*. The IT artifact can be studied as a *tool* for labor substitution, productivity enhancement, information processing, or to alter social relationships. As a *proxy*, the IT artifact refers to the study of some essential attributes such as individual perceptions, diffusion rates and money spent. As an *ensemble*, the IT artifact is associated with development projects, embedded systems, social structures, and production networks. IT artifacts as *computational resources* can be algorithms or models, and then the interactions of the IT artifact with its social context or its effects on dependent variables are not of interest. Finally, IT artifacts as *nominal concepts* imply that no specific technology is referenced, for example, the IT artifact is omitted in such studies. This *nominal* view was found most common next to the *computational* view (e.g., a computer science-oriented perspective of the IT artifact). Next common view is of IT artifacts as *tools* that affect dependent variables. The *ensemble* view was the least frequently reported. According to the authors, the researchers' original research paradigms or lenses bias the IT artifact conceptualization. *Nominal, tool,* or *proxy* views are used for management and social scientists, while computer scientists consider the *computational* view.

Such disparate views indicate a need to develop conceptualizations and theories on the IT artifacts that could be used in every IS study. Otherwise, IS research will be a fragmented field where its core object is not a "*major player in its own playing field*" (ibid, p. 130). However, for Orlikowski & Iacono (2001), the development of a single grand theory for IT artifacts that accommodates all their context-specificities is not adequate.

Benbazat and Zmud's (2003) suggest that the IS discipline's central identity is ambiguous due to an *under-investigation* of core IS issues and *over-investigation* of related and potentially relevant organizational or technical issues. These authors use Aldrich's (1999) theory of formation of organizations to explain that the IS discipline will be considered a mature discipline when a learning/cognitive and sociopolitical legitimacy is achieved. For this maturity to occur, methodological and theoretical rigor and relevance must in turn be achieved. A dominant design, for example, a central core of properties of what must be studied in the IS phenomena, is suggested to accommodate the topical diversity. For Benbazat and Zmud, this dominant identifying design for the IS discipline does not preclude the utilization of an interdisciplinary effort. In this view, the central character for the IS discipline is defined as the composition of the IT artifact that enables/supports some task(s), into structures and later into contexts, and its *nomological* network of IT managerial, technological, methodological, operational, and behavioral capabilities and practices of the pre- and post-core activities to the existence of some IT artifacts. Like Orlokowski and Iacono (2001), Benbazat and Zmud (2003) reject the IS research based in the black-box IT concept.

Hirschheim and Klein's (2003) thesis is that the IS discipline is fragmented with structural deficiencies manifested in a missing and generally accepted body of knowledge and in internal and external communication gaps. These authors build on Habermas' theory of communication (and of knowledge) to pose that any inquiry has two cognitive purposes[6]: a rationale for IS design and the communication for mutual understanding and agreement of disparate perceptions and interpretations (called *technical* and *practical* originally by Habermas). Hirschheim and Klein accept that the technical purpose seeks the prediction and control of the law-based IS phenomena, while the practical seeks the accommodation of disparate viewpoints underpinned in different norms, values, and contexts. They also agree that IS frameworks, called *categorization schemes*, are useful to start a shared body of knowledge (BoK) but fail to indicate how the IS knowledge as a whole—for example, as a system—can be articulated. Also, they accept theoretical and methodological diversity in the discipline. Like others, Hirschheim and Klein suggest that the lack of a shared core set of underlying knowledge weakens the IS discipline. They identify four challenges for the IS community: to accept and understand through clear communication the theoretical and methodological pluralist status, to develop a common general theoretical base, and to conduct research with methodological rigor and relevancy for IS research stakeholders. For the second challenge, they encourage the development of studies that take fragmented pieces of evidence and put them in a broader theoretical framework, as in Ives, Hamilton, and Davis study (1980). In their view, the IS BoK should be integrated with four types of knowledge with similar relevance: theoretical, technical, ethical, and applicative.

Galliers (2004) disagrees with the current evaluation of the IS discipline as a field in crisis. According to Galliers, Kuhn's ideas on paradigms can be interpreted as an *evolution* rather than a *revolution*. Core ideas, then, should not be abandoned but complemented, as in the organizational sciences (Gellner, 1993). For Galliers, the concepts of information and information system must be uncovered to understand the IS discipline. Supporting Land and Kennedy-McGregor's view (1987, quoted by Galliers, 2004), Galliers considers IS as a system that comprises formal and informal human, computer and external systems. In Galliers' view, Benbazat and Zmud's IT artifact is not conceptually sufficient to embrace these elements and thereby the "*essentially human activity of data interpretation and communication, and knowledge sharing and creation*" (2003, p. 342) could be diminished. In addition, Galliers rejects the notion of an IS as solely a generic social system with a strong technological component. Instead, Galliers considers IS a complex, multi-faceted and multi-leveled phenomenon that requires a trans-disciplinary research effort. Gallier's thesis for a mature discipline is the acceptance of a dynamic and evolutionary field in research focus, boundaries, and diversity/pluralism versus a prefixed set of core concepts with a monolithic, and dominant, perspective of the discipline. As a tentative strategy, Galliers uses Checkland's (1981) definition of a system's boundary and environment and its dependence on the observer's research purposes.

In summary, Galliers disagrees with the limited concept of the IT artifact and notes "*inclusion errors*" resulting from the closed boundaries of the IT artifact. Galliers also notes the IT artifact concept ignores relevant topics such as EDI, inter-organizational IS, knowledge management systems, and the digital divide concept.

For Larsen and Levine (2005), the crisis in the field has been over-assessed. While these authors accept the lack of coherence, the paucity of a cumulative tradition, and the loss of relevant research, they blame the university education and disciplinary knowledge aggravated by the effects of a rapid evolution of ITs. Based on Kuhn's field concept, Larsen and Levine suggest that the IS discipline can be considered pre-paradigmatic: "*a common set of theories derived from a paradigmatic platform do not exist in MIS*" (p. 361). They suggest that Kuhn's ideas, built on natural sciences, could be inadequate. Instead, they propose the socio-political Frickel and Gross' (2005, referenced by Larsen & Levine, 2005) concept of scientific/intellectual movement (SIM) in which several SIMs tied to multiple research approaches can co-exist under a common umbrella and compete for recognition and status.

Larsen and Levine use a novel co-word analysis technique (Monarch, 2000; quoted by authors) to identify networks of associated concepts, represented by *leximaps* (Monarch, 2000; quoted by Larsen & Levine), and measure the associative strength of pairs of concepts. Concepts highly connected are considered the center of coherence. A total of 1,325 research articles from five top IS journals in the 1990-2000 period are the dataset. The researchers divide this dataset in two sub-periods: 1990-1994 and 1995-2000. A key finding is that in both sub-periods the center of coherence related to IS generic concepts, like system, information, and management, is present. However, in the *leximap* of 1995-2000, new concepts appear, such as model, process, technology, user, and research. The number of centers of coherence related with identified theories is minimal. Furthermore, four selective pairs of concepts were used to trace a building theory activity. The scarce evidence and the minimal number of centers of coherence for theories are interpreted by Larsen and Levine as a lack of cumulative tradition where innovation is more appreciated than building on the work of others.

The previous studies provide the alternative proposals to establish a framework **F** of ideas, theories, theoretical problems, and models that are suggested to define the distinctive identity of the IS discipline. Table 2 summarizes the key findings from this research.

From the diverse systems paradigms exhibited in Table 1, this article argues that a critical realism systems approach is ontologically and epistemologically valid and comprehensive to integrate with theoretical and pragmatic coherence the shared ideas, theories, theoretical problems, and models from such studies.

Table 3 exhibits a summarized systemic proposal of integration. There are two competitive research paradigms: the IS discipline as a classic Kuhn's imperialist or dominant framework of ideas, theories, and models, and the IS discipline as a post-Kuhnian paradigm, as a dynamic body of knowledge and a diversified intellectual movement under one umbrella. The first includes the approaches of Weber (1987) and Benbazat and Zmud (2003) and partially Orlikowski and Iacono (2001), while second incorporates the work of Galliers (2004) and Larsen and Levine (2005), and partially the paradigm proposed by Hirschheim and Klein (2003).

The critical realism approach claims that the IS discipline can have a framework **F** based in permanent and shared generic knowledge structures on systems, as well as of dynamic or changing concepts that will emerge as in any systemic structure. Also, it supports the utilization of a set of methodologies **M** that are theoretical and pragmatically coherent according to the purpose of a specific research study (Midgley, 1996; Mingers, 2000) and consequently offers a pluralist-complementarist research strategy. The central theme is information systems conceptualized as *systems* (Gelman & Garcia, 1989; Gelman, Mora, Forgionne, & Cervantes, 2005; Mora, Gelman, Cervantes, Mejia, & Weitzenfeld, 2003; Mora, Gelman, Cano, Cervantes, & Forgionne, 2006; Mora, Gelman, Cervantes, & Forgionne, in press). Such an approach incorporates the different components and interrelationships of the system as well as of the lower (subsystems and so on) and upper (suprasystems and wider systems) systemic levels, including the environment. The specific components, attributes, events, and interrelationships and levels of lower and upper systemic layers depend on the specific research purposes, resources, and schedules required.

This critical realism stance can accommodate the two competitive approaches posed for the IS discipline through the acknowledgement of the complexity and diversity of the phenomenon. Weber's (1987) foci of IS research is identified as systemically founded: its components and its environment are based on Miller's living systems model (1978). Also, Benbazat and Zmud's (2003) IT artifact and its nomological network can be accommodated in a systemic structure. As Galliers (2004) suggests implicitly, the nomological network should be considered a dynamic rather than static set of concepts. Additional research could extend the inside and outside elements, attributes, events, and interrelationships according their specific purposes. The systems approach provides the methodological tools for this extended analysis. Since Orlikowski and Iacono's (2001) framework of ideas is a subset of Benbazat and Zmud (2003), the previous arguments apply also for this framework.

Table 2. Analysis of main IS research paradigms

IS Research Paradigm or Framework	Main weaknesses identified in the IS Discipline	Maturity Criteria	Foci for IS Research	Concept of what an Information System is	Underlying System Theories Used
Weber (1987)	- lack of a research paradigm - little cumulative tradition - lack of grand stream direction - fashion event-day driven research	- existence of at least one Kuhn's Paradigm (used as a grand theory) - pattern of literature citations in the field	- set of objects that interacts with an information system - set of objects that comprises an information system	- not reported	- Milller's Living Systems Theory - Simon's concept of Complex Systems
Orlikowski & Iacono (2001)	- not engaged with the central object for IS: the IT artifact - thus the IT artifact is not studied per se but is studied within its context or as it affectsthe dependent variable - IT as a monolithic black-box or even absent - IT artifacts are conceptualized in multiple ways by management, social and computer scientists - lack of theories on IT artifacts	- IT artifact is included in every IS research in any of its multiple views	- the IT artifact, its context, effects and capabilities	- IT artifact as a software-hardware package with cultural and material properties - IT artifacts are not natural, neutral, universal and given - IT artifacts are embedded in some time, place, discourse and community - IT artifacts involve an arrangement of components - IT artifacts are not fixed, static, or independent from context	- no explicit theory of systems - pluralism and multi-methodology is encouraged
Benbazat & Zmud (2003)	- lack of a core collective identity - errors of inclusion by doing research on non IS issues and of omission by not studying core IS issues	- central character, claimed distinctiveness and claimed temporal continuity (based on the central identify concept for organizations of Albert & Whetten, 1985) - cognitive legitimacy	- the IT artifact (any application of IT to support tasks, embedded in structures and latter in contexts) and its nomological network (IT managerial, technological, methodological , operational and behavioral capabilities) and practices for pre and post core activities of an IT existence	- IT artifacts related with tasks, inserted in structures and latter in contexts	- no explicit theory of systems - interdisciplinary research is encouraged

continued on following page

Table 2. continued

Hirschheim & Klein (2003)	- IS field is fragmented - internal and external communication gap - intellectually rigid and lack of fruitful communication - disagreement about the nature of IS field includes - lack of a shared core set of underlying knowledge - a high strategic task uncertainty	- an accepted IS body of knowledge is available	- the IS body of knowledge	- not defined but implicitly inferred as instruments for process and organizational efficiency and effectiveness	- partial use of Habermas' philosophy - no other systems theory but it is accepted that IS are systems (pp. 282)
Galliers (2004)	- change and new challenges as opportunities for field evolution instead of a crisis status	- a field that evolves dynamically in research focus and boundaries - a trans-disciplinary criteria - practice improved through research - IS interaction with other disciplines	- organizations, individuals and information systems	- an IS is composed of six elements: formal and informal human, computer and external systems (based on Land and Kennedy-McGregory, 1981)	- based on Checkland's soft systems view - trans-disciplinary holistic-systemic approach encouraged - Asbhy's Law of Variety of Requisite - methodological, theoretical and topical diversity and pluralism encouraged
Larsen & Levine (2005)	- lack of cumulative tradition - weak coherence in the field - affected by the current intellectual anxiety on the role of university education and disciplinary knowledge and augmented by the rapid change of IT - a Kuhnian pre-paradigm status - ambiguity, fragmentation and change patterns as most frequent	- Kuhn's field in its own right manifested by an shared exemplar study as base, an image of the subject matter, theories, and methods and instruments or - scientific/intellectual movement umbrella (based on Frickel & Gross, 2005)	- centers of coherence linked to the concepts of system, information, management, process, model, user, research, technology mainly.	(Lee's (1999) definitions supported) - MIS includes an information system and its organizational context - MIS includes information technology and its instantiation - MIS includes the activities of a corporative function	- the system of systems (SoS) concept is subtly endorsed from Systems Engineering discipline

Galliers' (2004) conceptualization for the IS discipline focused on information systems, organizations and their individuals; that is, philosophically supported by the soft/interpretative systemic approach (Checkland, 2000), can be also accommodated in the critical realism stance by the arguments reported in Table 1. Larsen & Levine's (2005) framework of ideas, based in a subtle concept of *system of systems* and the empirical evidence to keep as center of coherence the concept of information systems with some dynamic concepts, also can be accommodated in the critical realism stance as follows: the underlying mechanisms and structures of the real domain become the permanent center of coherence to be searched and the dynamic elements of knowledge are located in the empirical domain of the events observed. Then, according to the specific research purposes, tools, resources, and schedules, some events generated in the actual domain will be observed in the empirical domain. In this way, the permanent and dynamic central themes are linked to a critical realism view of the world.

Hirschheim and Klein (2003) admit the usefulness of a broad underlying structure for the IS discipline that can organize the fragmented pieces of the IS knowledge in a coherent whole (e.g., a conceptual *system)*. This IS body of knowledge initiative relies on a systemic approach. Furthermore, its philosophical support, based in Habermas' theory of knowledge, links their ideas automatically with the systems intellectual movement.

Hence, we claim that competitive and conflictive perspectives posed for the IS discipline can be dissolved under a critical realism view as articulated in Table 3.

A Systemic Integration of the Information Systems Research Frameworks

Ives, Hamilton, and Davis' study (1980) can be considered the first effort to develop a comprehensive IS research framework. According to Ives et al. (1980), the previous five similar studies were dimensionally incomplete (e.g. capture a partial view of the IS field). These previous studies do not account for the overall processes and environments to develop, operate, and evolve the IS artifact, are focused on specific types of IS, or omit the organizational environment except by the type of managerial levels related with the IS artifact. Based on Mora et al. (2006), Ives et al.'s (1980) IS research framework contributes to the integration of the disparate dimensions and provides a structured framework to organize and classify IS research. However, Mora et al. (2006) suggest that Ives et al. (1980) do not articulate a correct systemic organization (e.g. a hierarchical definition of <system, subsystems, environment> and the conceptual differentiation of system's outcomes with systems elements in the model), and the concept of <organization> and <organizational environment> are not well differentiated.

A second IS research framework is reported by Nolan and Wetherbe (1980). This framework also draws on the same five past studies analyzed by Ives et al (1980). However, Nolan and Wetherbe build on a more fundamental conceptualization of the theory of systems (Boulding, 1956). As result, the IS research framework is more congruent with the formal concept of *system*. According to Mora et al. (2006), this framework is composed of:

a <MIS Technology System> that is part of an < Organization> and it of its < Organizational Environment >. The <MIS Technology system> is conceptualized as a system composed of the following subsystems: <hardware>, <software>, <data base>, <personnel> and <procedures>. In turn, the <Organization>, as the wider system for the <MIS Technology system> is conceptualized in five subsystems: <goals and values>, <psychosocial>, <structural>, <technical> and <managerial>.

Nolan and Wetherbe's contribution can be identified as a more coherent articulation of the main theory of system elements of interest to be studied in the IS discipline. Nonetheless, Mora et al. (2006, p. 3) report the following deficiencies: (1) the outputs of the <MIS Technology system> are only conceptualized in terms of types of IS, omitting other outcomes that it can generate such as <IT audits>, <IT proposal assessments>

Table 3. Systemic integration of main IS research paradigms.

Key Systemic Issues for Integrating IS Research Paradigms	IS discipline toward a well-defined Kuhnian's Paradigm	IS discipline toward a Kuhnian's Evolution of the discipline	IS discipline toward a holistic and critical realism integration
F: ***Framework of fundamental concepts***	- a central character manifested by a core set of concepts linked to the IT artifact and nomological network based in contexts, effects and capabilities (inferred from Weber (1987); Orlikowski & Iacono (2001); Benbazat & Zmud (2003))	- a dynamic IS body of knowledge – with centers of coherence varying in time that considers the formal and informal human, organizational and technical components of IS (inferred from Hirschheim & Klein (2003), Galliers (2004) and Larsen & Levine (2005)	- a broad systems view of the field with permanent and shared generic constructs and dynamic and emergent system properties
M: ***Methodological research tools***	- monolithic research approach (hard/ quantitative or soft/interpretative tools)	- multi-methodology research approach but limited to some dominant tools/lenses	- real multi-methodology research approach not limited to dominant tools/lenses (all variety of hard/quantitative, soft/interpretative or critical/intervention tools) (inferred from Midgley (1996), Mingers (2000))
A: ***Areas/situations of study in the world***	- IT artifact (internal view) and its nomological network based on contexts, effects and capabilities (inferred from Weber (1987); Orlikowski & Iacono (2001); Benbazat & Zmud (2003))	- Information systems, individual, organizations and society and future centers of coherence (inferred from Galliers (2004) and Larsen & Levine (2005))	- Information systems as *systems* (and automatically includes both perspectives) (inferred from Gelman & Garcia (1989) and Mora et al (2003))
Research Strategy	- an imperialist paradigm that integrates other paradigms that strengthen the dominant paradigm (inferred from Weber (1987), Benbazat & Zmud (2003))	- pluralist paradigm under the concept of scientific/intellectual movement umbrellas (inferred from Orlikowski & Iacono (2001), Galliers (2004) and Larsen & Levine (2005). Hirschheim & Klein (2003) holds a neutral position.	- pluralist paradigm with theoretical and practical coherence between different philosophical paradigms (Mingers, 2001, 2002).
Philosophy of Science	Kuhn's imperialist or paradigmatic stance	Post-Kuhnian imperialist or paradigmatic stance	- Critical realism: all reality (natural, designed and social) has real underlying mechanisms and structures (real domain) that generate observable events (empirical domain) as well as non observable events (the actual domain including the empirical one), but social reality (concepts, meanings, categories) are socially built and thereby rely in the existence of human beings and a communication language (a systemic ontology).

and <IT services> in general; (2) the model does not conceptualize the interactions between the systems considered as wholes and the systems considered as a set of components—e.g. the system type I and type II views respectively defined in Gelman and García (1989) and updated in Mora, Gelman et al (2003)- and then influences like <IT suppliers>, <IT trends> or the conceptualization of an <Inter-organizational IS> cannot be modeled; and (3) the time dimension that is critical for some of the 33 cases reported—e.g., on system's evolutions- is implicitly assumed and not related with the state ω(t) of the system, subsystem or environment.

In a third IS framework (Silver & Markus, 1995), the researchers quote an MBA student's claim: "*I understand the pieces but I don't see how to fit together*" (p. 361). Based on Bertlanffy's (1951) ideas and using Ackoff's (1993) recommendations to study a phenomenon from a systems view, the researchers recognize that the study of an IS as a *system* implies the need to identify its supersystem—e.g. its suprasystem—as well as its subsystems. The Silver and Markus' model places the IS as the central object of learning into a supersystem: the organization, and this in its wider environment. In the organization as a *system*, the following elements are identified: firm strategy, business processes, structure and culture, and the IT infrastructure. Also, additional elements for the model are included: IS features and IS implementation process. For each category, a list of sub-elements are also identified. Yet the three levels of systems, suprasystem, and subsystems are inconsistently structured from a formal systemic perspective (Johnson, Kast, & Rosenzweig, 1964). Conceptual categories for subsystems are mixed with system outcomes, actions, and attributes. For example, firm strategy can be categorized as a system's outcome instead of a subsystem, and the IS implementation process is disconnected from the subsystem of business processes.

Furthermore, the initial systemic views for IS and for organization—exhibited in Figures 1 and 2 (ibid, p. 364)—are disconnected from the final model. The IT infrastructure element —viewed as a subsystem of the organization —affects the component, but it is not part of the IS system, and the people component—also an initial subsystem of the organization— is lost or transformed in the structure and culture element. Then the formal utilization of the Systems Approach is incomplete.

In a fourth IS research framework (Bacon & Fitzgerald, 2001), the researchers contrast arguments on the advantages and disadvantages of frameworks and conclude that the potential benefits exceed the potential limitations. The researchers also support empirically the academic and practical need to have and use frameworks for the IS discipline. This evidence is based on a survey of 52 prominent IS individuals from 15 representative countries in North-America, Europe and Oceania. However, given the current philosophical and methodological debate, it is noted that a general IS research framework could be not totally possible but it is highly encouraged to be pursued (Bacon & Fitzgerald, 2001, pp. 51). According to the researchers, previous related studies fail to describe a holistic—e.g.integrated, overall, and systemic (ibid, pp. 47)—view of the discipline.

Through a grounded theory research method and after an extensive review of concepts from the literature, IS syllabus, IS curricula proposals and opinions of IS academicians, Bacon and Fitzgerald induce five categories for IS research framework: (a) information for knowledge work, customer satisfaction, and business performance, (b) IS development, acquisition, and support activities, (c) information and communication technologies, (d) operations and network management activities, and (e) people and organizations issues.

Despite four references to recognized systems researchers (Checkland & Howell, 1995; Mason & Mitroff, 1973; Stowell & Mingers, 1997; van Gich & Pipino, 1983), no specific systems model or approach is used to structure the conceptual system posed. Then its framework is not systemically articulated. A formal systemic analysis reveals that this systemic model lacks: (a) a coherent set of subsystems, (b) a description of its subsystems as systems, and (c) an environment for the system.

Hence the four comprehensive IS research frameworks posited, despite their theoretical and practical contributions, are incomplete and non-comprehensive from a formal systems-based view. A framework with systemic theoretical soundness that is able to integrate holistically all dimensions considered in past frameworks and the few dimensions omitted is still required. Mora et al. (2006) report a framework that can be useful for such purposes. This systems-founded IS research framework is based on formal definitions of *systems*[7] (Gelman & Garcia, 1989) and formal definitions of *organization, business process* and *information systems* (Gelman et al., 2005; Mora et al., 2003, 2006, in press).

According to Gelman and Garcia (1989), Gelman et al. (2005), and Mora et al. (2003, 2006, in press), to define an object of study as a ***system-I*** implies to specify it as a whole composed by *attributes, events,* and *domains* for *attributes.* For the case of ***system-II***, the formal definition offers the classic view of a *system* as a set of interrelated components. Furthermore, the definition used here also considers the *output/input* relationships between any *subsystem* and the whole *system.* In turn, the auxiliary definitions — reported in Mora et al. (2006, in press)—help to support the expansionist systemic perspective that indicates that every *system* always belongs to another larger *system* (Ackoff, 1971). Figure 1—borrowed from Mora et al. (in press)—exhibits a graphical interpretation of the *system-II* view. In turn, Figure 2 exhibits a diagram of the concept *organization O(X)* as *system* with its *high-level, low-level,* and *socio-political business processes* as *subsystems.*

Mora et al.'s (2006) framework uses an integrative cybernetic, as well as interpretative socio-political systemic paradigm theoretically coherent through a critical realism stance, where $S_{II}(X.1)$ and $S_{II}(X.2)$ are conceptualized as a *driving-org-subsystem* and a *driven-org-subsystem,* respectively, $S_{II}(X.3)$ = *HLBP(X.3)* as a *information-org-subsystem*, and $S_{II}(X.4)$ = *SSBP(X.4)*

Figure 1. A diagram of the multilevel layers of the concept system and related terms

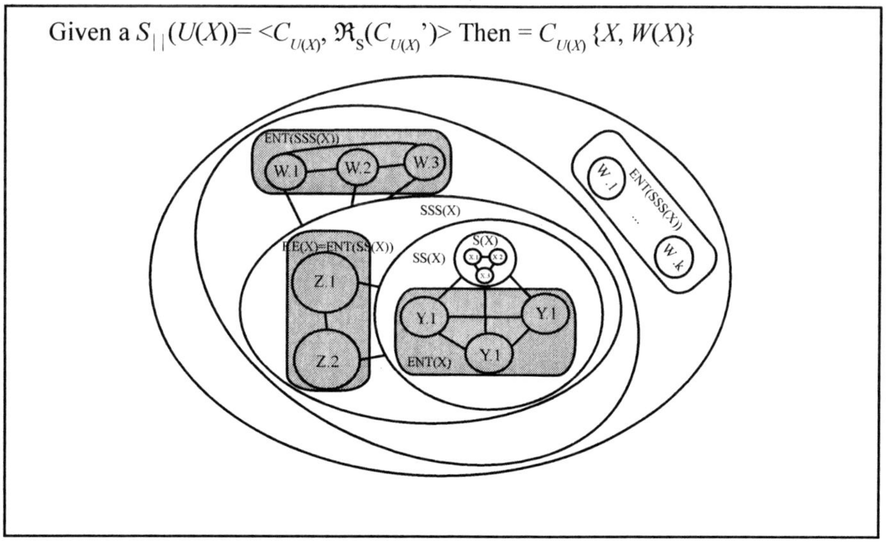

Figure 2. A schematic view of an organization as a system

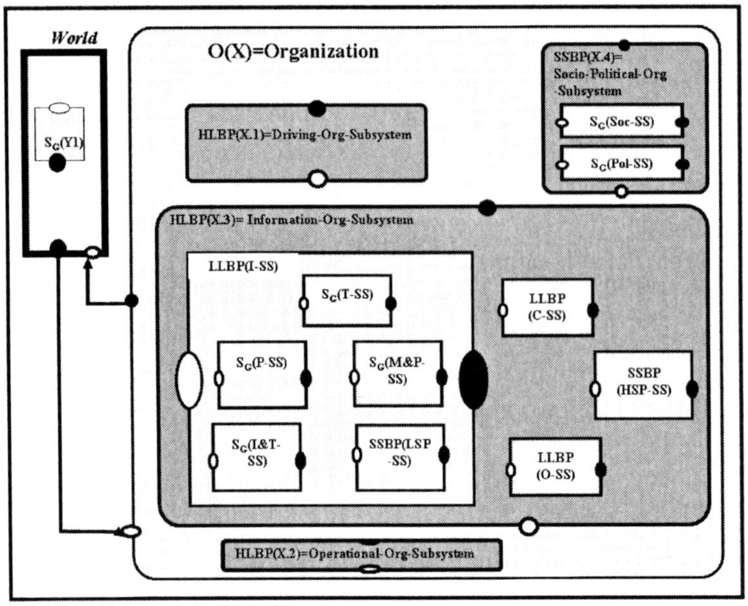

as a *socio-political-org-subsystem*. The Figure 3[8]—also borrowed from Mora et al. (2006)—exhibits the systemic articulation of the concepts: *organization* and *information systems*, as well as of its wider *systems* and *subsystems*.

Finally, Table 4 exhibits a mapping of the concepts posited in the previous four frameworks onto the systemic framework. It can be inferred from the formal definitions of *system-I*, *system-II*, and *general system*, *organization*, *suprasystem*, *supra-suprasystem*, *envelop*, *entourage* and *world*, *high-level process*, *low-level high process*, *socio-political process*, and *information systems* that previous frameworks are systemically incomplete.

CONCLUSION

We have reviewed the main IS research paradigms and frameworks reported in the IS literature by using a Systems Approach. This review has identified that previous studies have been developed using no, informal or few, systemic concepts from the formal spectrum of systemic concepts developed by the systems approach intellectual movement. Then, through the acceptance of a critical realist view, an IS research framework has been developed to integrate theoretically these disparate and conflictive views of IS as objects of study as well as a discipline.

We claim that this systemic framework: (1) is congruent with formal definitions of *system;* (2) permits the modeling of all variables reported in previous IS research frameworks as sub-systems or attributes and relationships of sub-systems as well as of the wider systems; (3) permits the study of static or dynamic IS phenomenon through the consideration of the concept of state of the *system*; (4) integrates theoretically the different positivist, interpretative, and emancipative paradigms through a critical realism stance; and (5) provides a systemic-holistic backbone and main ramifications to start the building of the required IS BoK.

We admit that this framework must be considered a research starting point rather than an end point in the long-term aim to have a non-

Figure 3. The articulation of the concepts of organization and information systems

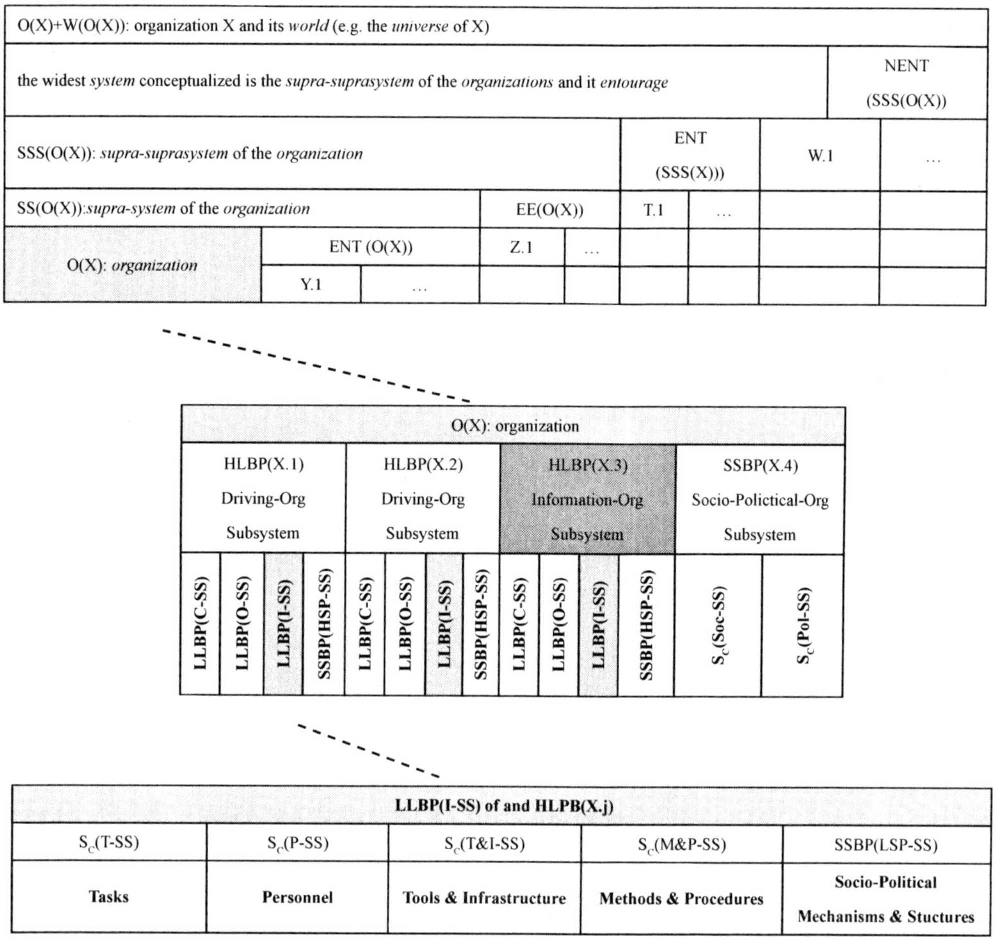

fragmented discipline with a strong cumulative tradition. Davis' (1974) seminal ideas for IS were related with general systems theory. Back to the basics could be useful to coherently organize the discipline.

REFERENCES

Ackoff, R. (1960). Systems, organizations and interdisciplinary research. *General System Yearbook, 5*, 1-8.

Ackoff, R., Gupta, S., & Minas, J. (1962). *Scientific method: Optimizing applied research decisions*. New York: Wiley.

Ackoff, R. (1971). Towards a system of systems concepts. *Management Science, 17*(11), 661-671.

Ackoff, R. (1973). Science in the systems age: Beyond IE, OR and MS. *Operations Research, 21*(3), 661-671.

Ackoff, R. (1981). The art and science of mess management. *Interfaces, 11*(1), 20-26.

Ackoff, R. (1993, November). From mechanistic to social systems thinking. In *Proceedings of Systems Thinking Action Conference*, Cambridge, MA.

Table 4. Systemic map of the concepts for IS Research in the five frameworks

The Critical Integrative IS Research Framework				
Ives, Hamilton & Davis' Framework	**Nolan & Wetherbe's Framework**	**Mora, Gelman, Cano, Cervantes & Forgionne's Framework**	**Bacon & Fitzgerald's Framework**	**Silver & Markus' Framework**
<external environment> : legal social, cultural, economic, educational, resource and industry/trade systems	**this is not explicitly considered**	**EE(O(X))** : (the systems to be modeled at this level of analysis are determined by the researcher)	**this is not explicitly considered**	**this is not explicitly considered**
<organizational environment>	**<environment of the organization>**	**ENT(O(X))**	**Environment**	**External Environment**
The concept of **<organizational environment>** used by Ives et al, does not consider the environment of an organization, but the organization's attributes per se such as: goals, tasks, structure, volatility and management philosophy/style	competitors, government, suppliers, customers, etc.	(the systems to be modeled at this level of analysis are determined by the researcher)	**this is not explicitly considered**	**five Porter's forces model**
	<organization>	**O(X)**	**<organization>**	**<the organization>**
	The 5 subsystems of <organization>: goals and value SS, psychosocial SS, managerial SS, structural SS and technical SS	**Goals & Value SS, psychosocial SS, and structural SS,** are considered in the **SSBP(X.4)** and the **SSBP(HSP-SS)** for any **HLBP(X.j).** The **managerial** and **technical SS** respectively corresponds to the **HLBP(X.1) (e.g. the driving-org subsystem)** and to **HLBP(X.2) (e.g. the driven-org subsystem).** Ives' et al such as: **goals, tasks, volatility and management philosophy/style,** as well as <**organization**> issues of others can be also modeled.	**<organization & people>** are considered in the same component	**Firm strategy, business processes, structure & culture**
<user environment> + <use process>	**this is not explicitly considered but is implicit in the 5 subsystems**	Any **HLBP(X.j)** and **SSBP(X.4)** of the **O(X)**		
IS as function is implicit in the framework		**HLBP(X.3) = The IS function as system**	**IS Function**	**IT infrastructure**
<IS development environment> + <IS development process>	**Development, operations** and **maintenance** aspects are considered in this concept of **<MIS Technology>**	**LLBP(O-SS)** and **SSBP(HSP-SS)** of the **HLBP(X.3) accounts for any IS operation and process to be considered.**	**<IS development, acquisition & support>**	**Resources of the firm to generate IT applications and <Implementation Process>**
<IS operations environment> + <IS operations process>			**<Operations & Network management>**	
IS as <properties and effects>	**IS as <<MIS Technology>**	**LLBP(I-SS) = The IS artifact as system**	**IS as ICT + Impacts**	**IS as core element**
<Information Subsystem> (attributes of content, presentation, time, etc)	**(hardware, software, data base, procedures and personnel)**	**LLBP(I-SS)** of any **HLBP(X.j)** comprised of the **SG(T-SS) +SG(P-SS) + SG(T&I-SS) + SG(M&P-SS) + SSBP(LSP-SS)** (e.g. **the low-level business process** that corresponds to the **<informational subsystem>** of any **high-level business process** in an **O(X)**)	**<Information for KW, CS & BP> + <ICT>**	**(hardware, software, procedures, data and people)**

Adam, F., & Fitzgerald, B. (2000). The status of the information systems field: Historical perspective and practical orientation. *Information Research, 5*(4), 1-16.

Aldrich, H. (1999). *Organizations evolving.* Thousand Oaks, CA: Sage.

Alter, S. (2001). Are the fundamental concepts of information systems mostly about work systems? *CAIS*, 5(11), 1-67.

Alter, S. (2003). 18 reasons why IT-reliant work systems should replace "The IT Artifact" as the core subject matter of the IS field. *CAIS, 12*(23), 366-395.

Bacon, J., & Fitzgerald, B. (2001) A systemic Framework for the Field of Informaiton Systems. *The DATA BASE for Adavances in Informaion Systems, 32(2)*, 46-67.

Banville, C., & Landry, M. (1989). Can the field of MIS be disciplined? *Communications of the ACM, 32*(1), 48-60.

Barkhi, R., & Sheetz, S. (2001). The state of theoretical diversity of information systems. *CAIS, 7*(6), 1-19.

Benbazat, I., & Zmud, R. (2003). The crisis identity within the IS discipline: Defining and communicating the discipline's core properties. *MIS Quarterly, 27*(2), 187-194.

Beer, S. (1966). *Decision and control.* Chichester: Wiley.

Bertalanffy, L. von. (1950). An outline of general systems theory. *British Journal of the Philosophy of Science, 1*, 134-164 (reprinted in Bertalanffy (1968)).

Bertalanffy, L. von. (1951). The theory of open systems in physics and biology. *Science, 111*, 23-29.

Bertalanffy, L. von. (1968). *General systems theory–foundations, developments, applications.* New York: G. Brazillier.

Bertalanffy, L. von. (1972). The history and status of general systems theory. *Academy of Management Journal, December*, 407-426.

Bhaskar, R. (1975). *A realist theory of science.* Sussex: Harvester Press.

Boulding, K. (1956). General systems theory – the skeleton of the science. *Management Science, 2*(3), 197-208.

Carlsson, S. (2003, June 16-21). Critical realism: A way forward in IS research. In *Proceedings of the ECIS 2003 Conference* Naples, Italy.

Checkland, P. (1981). *Systems thinking, systems practice.* Chichester: John Wiley.

Checkland, P. (1983). O.R. and the systems movement: mappings and conflicts. *Journal of the Operational Research Society, 34*(8), pp. 661-675.

Checkland, P. (2000). Soft systems methodology: A thirty year retrospective. *Systems Research and Behavioral Science, 17*, S11–S58.

Checkland, P., & Holwell, S. (1995). Information systems: What's the big idea?. *Systemist, 7*(1), 7-13.

Davis, G. (1974). *Management information systems: Conceptual foundations, structure and development.* New York: McGraw-Hill.

Dobson, P. (2001). The philosophy of critical realism -- An opportunity for information systems research. *Information Systems Frontiers, 3*(2), 199-210.

Dobson, P. (2002). Critical realism and information systems research: Why bother with philosophy? *Information Systems Research,* 7(2). Retrieved from http://InformationR.net/ir/7-2/paper124,html.

Dobson, P. (2003). The SoSM revisited – A critical realist perspective. In Cano, J. (Ed). *Critical reflections of information systems: A systemic approach* (pp. 122-135). Hershey, PA: Idea Group Publishing.

Farhoomand, A. (1987). Scientific progress of management information systems. *Database, Summer*, 48-57.

Farhoomand, A., & Drury, D. (2001). Diversity and scientific progress in the information systems discipline. *CAIS, 5*(12), 1-22.

Flood, R., & Jackson, M. (1991). *Creative problem solving: Total systems intervention.* New York: Wiley.

Flood, R., & Romm, N. (Eds). (1996) *Critical Systems Thinking.* New York: Plenum Press.

Forrester, J. (1958). Industrial dynamics – A major breakthrough for decision makers. *Harvard Business Review, 36*, 37-66.

Forrester, J. (1991). *Systems dynamics and the lessons of 35 years.* (Tech. Rep. D-4224-4). Retrieved from http://sysdyn.mit.edu/sd-group/home.html

Frickel, S., & Gross, N. (2005). A general theory of scientific/intellectual movements. *American Sociological Review, 70*, 204-232.

Galliers, R. (2004). Change as crisis or growth? Toward a trans-disciplinary view of information systems as a field of study: A response to Benbasat and Zmud's call for returning to the IT artifact. *JAIS, 4*(7), 337-351.

Gellner, E. (1993). What do we need now? Social anthropology and its new global context. *The Times Literary Supplement, 16*, July, 3-4.

Gelman, O., & Garcia, J. (1989). Formulation and axiomatization of the concept of general system. *Outlet IMPOS (Mexican Institute of Planning and Systems Operation), 19*(92), 1-81.

Gelman, O., Mora, M., Forgionne, G., & Cervantes, F. (2005). M. Khosrow-Pour (Ed.) Information Systems and Systems Theory. In *Encyclopedia of Information Science and Technology* (1491-1496). Hershey, PA: IGR.

Gigch, van J., & Pipino, L. (1986). In search of a paradigm for the discipline of information systems. *Future Computer Systems, 1*(1), 71-97.

Gregory, W. (1996). Dealing with diversity. In R. Flood & N. Romm (Eds.), *Critical Systems Thinking* (37-61). New York: Plenum Press.

Habermas, J. (1978). Knowledge and human interests. London: Heinemann.

Hirschheim, R., & Klein, H. (2003). Crisis in the IS field? A critical reflection on the state of the discipline. *JAIS, 4*(10), 237-293.

Hoffer, J., George, J., & Valachi, J. (1996). *Modern systems analysis and design.* Menlo Park, CA: Benjamin/Cummings.

Ives, B., Hamilton, S., & Davis, G. (1980). A framework for research in computer-based management information systems. *Management Science, 26*(9), 910-934.

Jackson, M. (2000). *Systems approaches to management.* New York: Kluwer.

Johnson, R., Kast, F., & Rosenzweig, J. (1964). Systems theory and management. *Management Science, 10*(2), 367-384.

Klir, G. (1969). *An approach to general systems theory.* New York: Van Nostrand.

Kuhn, T. (1970). *The structure of scientific revolutions.* Chicago: Chicago University Press.

Land, F., & Kennedy-McGregor, M. (1987). Information and information systems: Concepts and perspectives. In R. Galliers (Ed.), *Information analysis: Selected readings* (pp. 63-91). Sydney: Wesely.

Larson, T., & Levine, J. (2005). Serching for Management Information Systems: Coherence and Change in the Discipline. *Information Systems Journal, 15*, pp. 357-381.

Lazlo, E., & Krippner, S. (1998). In J.S. Jordan (Ed.), *Systems theories and apriori aspects of perception* (47-74). Amsterdam: Elsevier Science.

Lazlo, E., & Lazlo, A. (1997). The contribution of the systems sciences to the humanities. *Systems Research & Behavioral Science, 14*(1), 5-19.

Leavitt, H., & Whisler, T. (1958). Management in the 80's. *Harvard Business Review, 36*(6), 41-48.

Mason, R., & Mitroff, I. (1973). A program of research on MIS. *Management Science, 19*(5), 475-485.

Midgley, G. (1996). What is this thing called CST? In R. Flood & N. Romm (Eds.), *Critical systems thinking* (11-24). New York: Plenum Press.

Miller, J. (1978). *Living systems.* New York: McGraw-Hill.

Mingers, J. (2000). The contributions of critical realism as an underpinning philosophy for OR/MS and systems. *Journal of the Operational Research Society 51*,1256-1270.

Mingers, J. (2001). Combining IS research methods: Towards a pluralist methodology. *Information Systems Research, 12*(3), 240-253.

Mingers, J. (2002). Realizing information systems: Critical realism as an underpinning philosophy for information systems. In *Proceedings of the 23rd International Conference in Information Systems, 295-303.*

Mingers, J. (2003). A classification of the philosophical assumptions of management science methodologies. *Journal of the Operational Research Society, 54*(6), 559-570.

Monarch, I. (2000). Information science and information systems: Converging or diverging? In *Proceedings of the 28th Annual Conference of the Canadian Association in Information Systems*, Alberta.

Mora, M., Gelman, O., Cano, J., Cervantes, F., & Forgionne, G. (2006, July 9-14). Theory of systems and information systems research frameworks. In *Proceedings of the International Society for the Systems Sciences 50th Annual Conference*, Rohnert Park, CA.

Mora, M., Gelman, O., Cervantes, F., Mejia, M., & Weitzenfeld, A. (2003). A systemic approach for the formalization of the information system concept: why information systems are systems? In J. Cano (Ed), *Critical reflections of information systems: A systemic approach* (1-29). Hershey, PA: Idea Group Publishing.

Mora, M., Gelman, O., Forgionne, G., & Cervantes, F. (2004, May 19-21). Integrating the soft and the hard systems approaches: A critical realism based methodology for studying soft systems dynamics (CRM-SSD). In *Proceedings of the 3rd. International Conference on Systems Thinking in Management (ICSTM 2004)*, Philadelphia, PA.

Mora, M., Gelman, O., Forgionne, G., & Cervantes, F. (in press). Information Systems: a systemic view. M. Khosrow-Pour (Ed.) In *Encyclopedia of information science and technology, 2nd ed.* Hershey, PA: IGR.

Nolan, R., & Wetherbe J. (1980). Toward a comprehensive framework for MIS research. *MIS Quarterly, June*, 1, 1-20.

Orlikowski, W., & Iacono, S. (2001). Desperately Seeking the IT in IT research. *Information Systems Research, 7*(4), 400-408.

Rapoport, A. (1968). Systems Analysis: General systems theory. *International Encyclopedia of the Social Sciences, 14*, 452-458.

Silver, M., Markus, M., & Beath, C. (1995) The Information Techonlogy Interation Model: a Foundation of the MBA Course. *MIS Quarterly, 19(3)*, pp. 361-369.

Stowell, F., & Mingers, J. (1997). Introduction. In J. Mingers, & F. Stowell (Eds.), *Information systems: An emerging discipline?* London: Mc-Graw-Hill.

Vickers, G. (1965). *The art of judgment.* London: Chapman & Hall.

Wand, Y., & Weber, R. (1990). An ontological model of an information system. *IEEE Transactions on Software Engineering, 16*(11), 1282-1292.

Weber, R. (1987). Toward a theory of artifacts: A paradigmatic basis for information systems research. *Journal of Information Systems, 2*, 3-19.

ENDNOTES

1 Such as: (1) a vast set of undergraduate, master, and doctoral programs; (2) a network of research centers focused on IS topics; (3) 100 relevant specialized conferences and journals; and (4) the existence of professional and academic associations.

2 According to Lazlo and Lazlo (1997), Bertalanffy's ideas were also influenced by the mathematician Alfred Whitehead and the also biologist Paul Weiss.

3 Ackoff (1973) describes the machine age as useful for some kind of problems but not sufficient for studying the complex phenomena of the present age, hence the emergence of a systems age.

4a Bhaskar (1975, p. 30) explains that "*it is not the character of science that imposes a determinate pattern or order in the world; but the order of the world that, under certain determinate conditions, makes possible the cluster of activities we call science.*"

4b For Bhaskar (1975), the reality exists per se independently of the existence of human beings: "*a law governed world independently of man*" p. 26. However, the social structures and mechanisms are conditioned to the existence of human beings at first and then these have a real existence that can be studied and intervened.

5 Midgley reports his interpretation from Flood and Jackson 's ideas (1991) on Habermas' theory of knowledge.

6 The emancipative Habermas' third purpose is not considered by the authors.

7 Gelman and Garcia analyzed the formal definitions of the concept *system* from Ackoff, Arbib, Bertalanffy, Kalman, Lange, Mesarovic, Rapoport and Zadeh.

8 Interactions between subsystems are not diagrammed.

This work was previously published in the Information Resources Management Journal, Vol. 20, Issue 2, edited by M. Khosrow-Pour, pp. 1-22, copyright 2007 by IGI Publishing, formerly known as Idea Group Publishing (an imprint of IGI Global).

Chapter II
Could the Work System Method Embrace Systems Concepts More Fully?

Steven Alter
University of San Francisco, USA

ABSTRACT

The ***work system method*** *was developed iteratively with the overarching goal of helping business professionals understand IT-reliant systems in organizations. It uses general systems concepts selectively, and sometimes implicitly. For example, a work system has a boundary, but its inputs are treated implicitly rather than explicitly. This chapter asks whether the further development of the work system method might benefit from integrating general systems concepts more completely. After summarizing aspects of the work system method, it dissects some of the underlying ideas and questions how thoroughly even basic systems concepts are applied. It also asks whether and how additional systems concepts might be incorporated beneficially. The inquiry about how to use additional system ideas is of potential interest to people who study systems in general and information systems in particular because it deals with bridging the gap between highly abstract concepts and practical applications.*

BACKGROUND

The idea of using the concept of **work system** as the core of a systems analysis method for business professionals was first published in Alter (2002), although the ideas had percolated for over a decade. Experience as vice president of a manufacturing software company in the 1980s convinced me that many business professionals need a simple, yet organized approach for thinking about systems without getting swamped in details. Such an approach would have helped our customers gain greater benefits from our software and consulting, and would have helped us serve them more effectively across our entire relationship. A return to academia and production of an

IS textbook provided an impetus to develop a set of ideas that might help. Starting in the mid-1990s I required employed MBA and EMBA students to use the ideas in an introductory IS course to do a preliminary analysis of an information system in their own organizations. The main goal was to consolidate their learning; a secondary benefit was insight into whether the course content could actually help people understand systems in business organizations.

To date over 300 group and individual papers have contributed to the development of the **work system method** (WSM). At each stage, the papers attempted to use the then current version of WSM. With each succeeding semester and each succeeding cycle of papers, I tried to identify which confusions and omissions were the students' fault and which were mine because I had not expressed the ideas completely or clearly enough.

Around 1997 I suddenly realized that I, the professor and textbook author, had been confused about what system the students should be analyzing. Unless they are focusing on software or hardware details, business professionals thinking about information systems should not start by describing or analyzing the information system or the technology it uses. Instead, they should start by identifying the work system and summarizing its performance gaps, opportunities, and goals for improvement. Their analysis should focus on improving work system performance, not on fixing information systems. The necessary changes in the information system would emerge from the analysis, as would other work system changes separate from the information system but necessary before information system improvements could have the desired impact.

After additional publications (available for download at www.stevenalter.com) helped develop various aspects of WSM, the overall approach became mature enough to warrant publication of a book (Alter, 2006) that combines and extends the main ideas from the various papers, creating a coherent approach that is organized, flexible, and based on well-defined concepts. Use to date by MBA and EMBA students (early career business professionals) indicates that WSM might be quite useful in practice. Recent developments motivated by widespread interest and concern about services and the service economy led to an attempt to extend the work system approach to incorporate the unique characteristics of services. The main products to date of those efforts are the service value chain framework and service responsibility tables. (Alter, 2007, 2008) Further development of WSM might proceed in many directions, including improving the concepts, testing specific versions in real world settings, and developing online tools that make WSM easier to use and more valuable.

WSM uses system concepts, but the priority in developing WSM always focused on practicality. System concepts and system-related methods that seemed awkward or difficult to apply were not included in WSM. For example, WSM might have incorporated certain aspects of soft system methodology (SSM) developed over several decades by the British researcher Peter Checkland (1999). An area of similarity is SSM's identification of 6 key aspects of a "**human activity system**." Those include customers, actors, transformations, worldview, owner, and environment. Based on an unproven belief that SSM is too abstract and too philosophical to be used effectively by most (American) MBA and EMBA students, WSM was designed to be very flexible but also much more prescriptive than SSM and much more direct about suggesting topics and issues that are often relevant for understanding IT-reliant work systems.

At this point in the development of WSM it is worthwhile to ask whether additional systems concepts might be incorporated beneficially and might contribute to its value for practitioners. Searching for possibilities is a bit awkward because there is very little agreement about what constitutes general systems theory and general systems thinking.

General Systems Theory *(GST) integrates a broad range of special system theories by naming and identifying patterns and processes common to all of them. By use of an overarching terminology, it tries to explain their origin, stability and evolution. While special systems theory explains the particular system, GST explains the systemness itself, regardless of class or level.* (Skyttner, 1996)

A **system** is not something presented to the observer, it is something to be recognized by him. Most often the word does not refer to existing things in the real world but rather to a way of organizing our thoughts about the real world." ... 'A system is anything unitary enough to deserve a name.' (Weiss, 1971) ... 'A system is anything that is not chaos' (Boulding, 1964) ...[A] system is 'a structure that has organized components.' (Churchman, 1979)." (Skyttner, 2001)

One of the problems in trying to incorporate general system ideas is that so many different types of systems fit under the GST umbrella (Larses and El-khoury, 2005):

- Concrete (living, non-living), conceptual, or abstract
- Open, closed, or isolated
- Decomposable, near-decomposable, or non-decomposable
- Static or dynamic
- Black, gray, or white box

This chapter dissects some of the ideas underlying WSM and questions how faithfully even basic systems concepts are incorporated into it. This chapter proceeds as follows. After summarizing WSM, it summarizes four work systems to illustrate the range of systems that WSM addresses (and conversely, the types of systems it does not address). Building on this clarification of the context, the chapter looks at typical concepts from writings about the systems approach or general systems. In each case it discusses whether those ideas already appear in WSM and whether they might be incorporated to a greater extent. The goal is two-fold, to find directions for improving WSM and to reflect on whether typical general systems ideas are truly useful for understanding information systems and other work systems from a business professional's viewpoint.

THE WORK SYSTEM METHOD

WSM focuses on work systems rather than the information systems that support them and often overlap with them. WSM is designed to produce shared understandings that can lead to better technical specifications needed to develop software. It does not produce the type of specification that might be converted mechanically into software. Although WSM can be used for totally new systems, its basic form assumes that a set of problems or opportunities motivate the analysis of an existing work system. The structure and content of WSM attempt to provide both conceptual and procedural knowledge in a readily usable form, and try to express that knowledge in everyday business language.

- **Definition of work system:** A **work system** is a system in which human participants and/or machines perform work using information, technology, and other resources to produce products and/or services for internal or external customers. Typical business organizations contain work systems that procure materials from suppliers, produce products, deliver products to customers, find customers, create financial reports, hire employees, coordinate work across departments, and perform many other functions. Almost all significant work systems in business and governmental organizations employing more than a few people cannot operate efficiently or effectively without using IT. Most practical IS research is about the development, operation, and maintenance of such systems and their components. In effect, the IS field is basically about IT-reliant work systems. (Alter, 2003)

- **Work system framework:** The nine elements of the **work system framework** (Alter, 2003, 2006) are the basis for describing and analyzing an IT-reliant work system in an organization. Even a rudimentary understanding of a work system requires awareness of each of the nine elements. Four of these elements (work practices, participants, information, and technologies) constitute the work system. The other five elements that fill out a basic understanding of the work system include the products and services produced, customers, environment, infrastructure, and strategies (see Figure 1).
- **Work system life cycle model:** WSM's other basic framework describes how work systems change over time. Unlike the system development life cycle (SDLC), which is basically a project model rather than a system life cycle, the work system life cycle model (WSLC) is an iterative model based on the assumption that a work system evolves through a combination of planned and unplanned changes. (Alter, 2003, 2006, 2008) Consistent with Markus and Mao's (2004) emphasis on the distinction between system development and system implementation, the planned changes occur through formal projects with initiation, development, and implementation phases. The unplanned changes are ongoing adaptations and experimentation that adjust details of the work system without performing formal projects. In contrast to control-oriented versions of the SDLC, the WSLC treats unplanned changes as part of a work system's natural evolution. Ideas in WSM can be used by any business or IT professional at any point in the WSLC. The steps in WSM (summarized later) are most pertinent in the initiation phase as individuals think about the situation and as the project team negotiates the project's scope and goals.
- **Information systems as a special case of work systems:** Work system is a general case of systems operating within or across organizations. Special cases of work systems include **information systems**, projects, supply chains, e-commerce web sites, and totally automated work systems. For example, an information system is a work system whose work practices are devoted to processing information, i.e., capturing, transmitting, storing, retrieving, manipulating, and displaying information. Similarly, a project is a work system designed to produce a product and then go out of existence. The relationship between the general case and the special cases is useful because it implies that the special cases should inherit vocabulary and other properties of work systems in general. (Alter, 2005) Based on this hierarchy of cases, an analysis method that applies to work systems in general should also apply to information systems and projects.

Examples of Information Systems

A common problem in reading general discussions of information systems is the lack of clarity about which types of information systems are being discussed and which are being ignored. Similarly, discussions of general systems theory are often unclear about the types of systems for which specific concepts or principles are relevant. WSM is designed for situations in which an information system is viewed as an IT-reliant work system devoted to processing information. WSM is less applicable if the information system is viewed as a technical artifact that operates on a computer and is used by "users" who are external to the system. The following four examples from Alter (2006) illustrate the types of information systems to which WSM applies:

Figure 1. The Work System Framework, slightly updated (Source: S. Alter, The Work System Method: Connecting People, Processes, and IT for Business Results, Larkspur, CA: Work System Press, 2006).

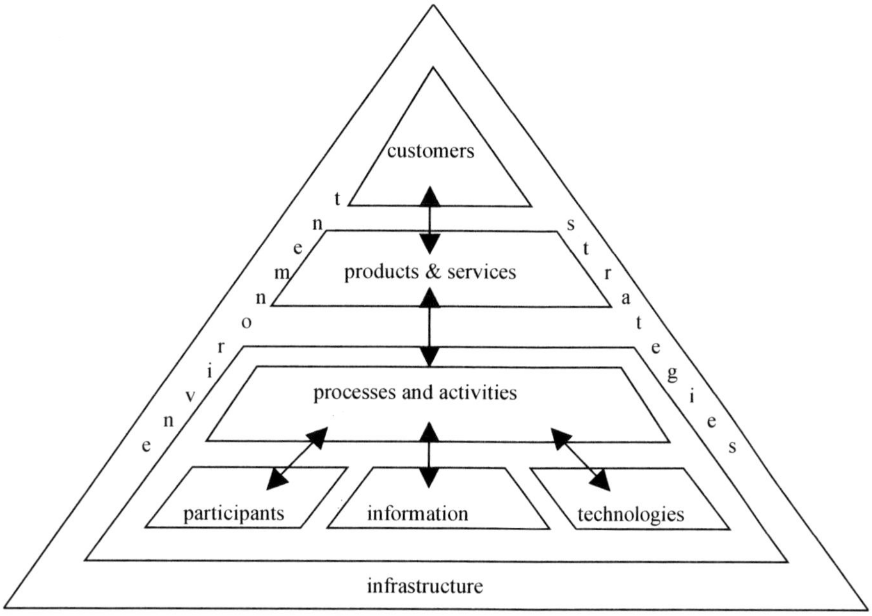

- ***Work system #1: How a bank approves commercial loans***: A large bank's executives believe that its current methods for approving commercial loans have resulted in a substandard loan portfolio. They are under pressure to increase the bank's productivity and profitability. The work system for approving loan applications from new clients starts when a loan officer helps identify a prospect's financing needs. The loan officer helps the client compile a loan application including financial history and projections. A credit analyst prepares a "loan write-up" summarizing the applicant's financial history, projecting sources of funds for loan payments, and discussing market conditions and the applicant's reputation. Each loan is ranked for riskiness based on history and projections. Senior credit officers approve or deny loans of less than $400,000; a loan committee or executive loan committee approves larger loans. The loan officer informs the loan applicant of the decision.
- ***Work system #2: How a software vendor tries to find and qualify sales prospects***: A software vendor sells HR software to small and medium sized enterprises. It receives initial expressions of interest through inquiries from magazine ads, web advertising, and other sources. A specialized sales group contacts leads from other sources and asks questions to qualify them as potential clients. A separate outside sales force contacts qualified prospects, discusses software capabilities, and negotiates a purchase or usage deal. Management is concerned that the sales process is inefficient, that it misses many good leads, and that the outside sales group receives too many unqualified prospects.
- ***Work system #3: How consumers buy gifts using an ecommerce web site***: The web site of a manufacturer of informal clothing for

teenagers has not produced the anticipated level of sales. Surveys and logs of web site usage reveal that customers who know exactly what they want quickly find the product on the web site and make the purchase. Customers who are not sure what they want, such as parents buying gifts for teenagers, often find it awkward to use the site, often leave without making a purchase, and have a high rate of after purchase returns. The company wants to extend existing sales channels. Its managers want to improve the level of sales by improving the customer experience.

- ***Work system #4: How an IT group develops software***: The IT group buys commercial application software whenever possible, but also produces home-grown software when necessary. Many of the IT group's software projects miss schedule deadlines, go over budget, and/or fail to produce what their internal customers want. Software developers often complain that users can't say exactly what they want and often change their minds after programming has begun. Users complain that the programmers are arrogant and unresponsive. Use of the company's computer aided software engineering (CASE) software is uneven. Enthusiasts think it is helpful, but other programmers think it interferes with creativity. The IT group's managers believe that failure to attain greater success within several years could result in outsourcing much of the group's work.

Several features of the four examples should be noted. First, each example concerns an IT-reliant work system, and each of these work systems is an information system. (Yes, software development, work system #4, is basically an information system). In addition, as the analysis proceeds in each case, the system to be analyzed will be defined based on the problem or opportunity posed by management. The system will not be defined based on the software that happens to be used as a part of the system.

Three Levels for Using the Work System Method

The current version of WSM (Alter, 2006) consists of three problem-solving steps (SP, AP, and RJ) related to systems in organizations:

- **SP - Identify the System and Problems:** Identify the work system that has the problems that launched the analysis. The system's size and scope depend on the purpose of the analysis.
- **AP - Analyze the system and identify Possibilities:** Understand current issues and find possibilities for improving the work system.
- **RJ - Recommend and Justify changes:** Specify proposed changes and sanity-check the recommendation.

Recognizing the varied nature of analysis situations and goals, WSM can be used at three levels of detail and depth. The level to use depends on the user's particular situation:

- **Level One (Define):** Be sure to remember the three main steps when thinking about a system in an organization.
- **Level Two (Probe):** Within each main step, ask questions that are typically important. These questions include:
  - *Five SP questions* (What is the system? What is the problem? What are the constraints? And so on)
  - *Ten AP questions* (One question about how well each work system element is performing, and one question about the work system as a whole)
  - *Ten RJ questions* (What is the recommendation? How does it compare to an ideal system? Was the original problem

solved? What new problems will the recommendation cause? How favorable is the balance of costs and benefits? And so on).

- **Level Three (Drill Down):** For each question within each step, apply guidelines, concepts, and checklists that are often useful.

The most recent version of WSM uses an electronic questionnaire, the first page of which is basically a Level One outline of the executive summary of a typical business analysis and recommendation. The next pages present the 25 questions in Level Two, with space to fill in answers. Vocabulary and concepts identified throughout Alter (2006) and arrayed in checklists, templates, and tabular forms provide additional (Level Three) support for the analysis. These tools help in identifying common topics that might be considered, providing hints about common issues, and providing blank tables that might be used to summarize specific topics or perspectives.

WSM is built on the assumption that an organized structure combining flexibility with considerable depth can be effective in helping business professionals pursue whatever amount of detail and depth is appropriate. Because WSM is designed to support a business professional's analysis, even Level Three does not approach the amount of detail or technical content that must be analyzed and documented to produce computerized information systems.

WORK SYSTEM METHOD AS A SYSTEMS APPROACH

At a superficial level WSM surely represents a systems approach because it describes a situation as a system consisting of interacting components that operate together to accomplish a purpose. A closer look is worthwhile, however, because some aspects of WSM use systems concepts in an idiosyncratic manner. In particular, a careful look at the four examples (beyond the scope of this article) would show that each is a system but that describing each as a set of interacting components operating together to accomplish a purpose might miss some insights related to the type of system WSM studies. To reflect on how WSM applies a systems approach, it is possible to look at the form and prominence of basic system concepts within the current version of WSM:

- ***Identification of the system*:** WSM users start their analysis by defining the work system. As a general guideline, the system is the smallest work system that has the problem or opportunity that launched the analysis. The system's scope is revealed by identifying the work practices (typically a business process, but possibly other activities as well) and participants who perform the work.
- ***The observer*:** Systems thinking recognizes that system is a mental construct imposed on a situation in order to understand it. Different observers have different system views of the same situation. Part of WSM's value is as a way to help people come to agreement about what system they are trying to improve.
- ***Boundary and environment*:** The identification of the work system in the initial part of WSM automatically sets the boundaries. The work system framework includes some elements that are part of the work system and some that are outside of the work system. The four elements inside the work system are work practices, people, information, and technologies. The other five elements are not part of the work system but are included in the framework because it tries to identify the components of even a rudimentary understanding of a work system.

Mora et al (2002) noted several logical problems with treatment of the system concept *context* in an earlier version of the work system framework that was used in 2001. (*Context* appeared where *environment* now appears.) They also noted that the customers are not included in the box called context (now environment). These observations are accurate from a definitional viewpoint, but the priority in creating WSM is to combine system-related ideas in a way that makes WSM as useful as possible for typical business professionals. Explicitly saying that a work system exists to produce products and services for customers encourages the WSM user to pay special attention to the products and services and customers. Various aspects of the environment such as culture and political issues may matter greatly in some situations and may be unimportant in other situations, but products and services and customers are always important for understanding work systems (including information systems) in organizations.

The term **infrastructure** is also problematic in relation to boundaries. Real world work systems could not operate without infrastructure owned and managed by the surrounding organization and external organizations. Infrastructure is included as one of the elements for understanding a work system because ignoring external infrastructure may be disastrous. However, it is awkward to treat computer networks, programming languages, IT personnel, and other shared resources as internal parts of the work systems they serve. If these components of infrastructure were treated as internal components of the work system, even small work systems involving a few people and several activities would become gigantic. They would be like an iceberg, with visible aspects of the work system above the water and an enormous mass of shared infrastructure largely invisible below the waterline. To discourage unnecessary attention to distinctions between technology and infrastructure early in the analysis, WSM users creating a 'work system snapshot" for summarizing a work system should assume that the difference between technology and technical infrastructure is unimportant for the initial summary. The distinction should be explored only if it is important for understanding the work system in greater depth.

Inputs and Outputs

The work system framework contains neither the term *inputs* nor the term *outputs*. The term output is not used because it sounds too mechanistic and is associated too much with computer programs. In terms of logic and structure, there is no problem in calling a work system's outputs products and services. Also, that terminology helps focus attention on the work system's goal of providing products and services customers want, rather than just producing whatever outputs it is programmed to produce. Even the terms products and services are occasionally problematic. For example, consider a work system that produces entertainment. The product might be described as a temporally sequenced information flow that is sensed and interpreted by viewers (the customers). It also might be viewed as the customer's stimulation, peace of mind, or enjoyment. At minimum there is question about whether the customer plays an active role as a participant in the work system. As the nature of the product becomes more ambiguous, the boundary of the system also becomes more ambiguous.

The work system framework ignores inputs altogether because it assumes that important inputs will be understood implicitly. The first step in the work practices typically will describe something about receiving, transforming, or responding to something that comes from outside of the work system. (If important inputs are not mentioned anywhere in the work practices, it is likely that the summary of work practices will be insufficient.) Also, information from external sources is often listed under the information used or produced by the work system. And what about other inputs, such as the air the participants breathe, the food they metabolize as they do their work, or the skills they received from a training course last year? It is easy to say in general that systems have inputs, but substantially more difficult to identify which inputs are worth mentioning in an analysis. The work system framework lacks a slot for inputs because it is easier to infer important inputs from the steps listed in the work practices.

Transformations

The term transformation is particularly meaningful in physical systems such as assembling a set of tangible components to produce an automobile. Transformation is less meaningful for various aspects of each of the work system examples mentioned earlier. For example, it doesn't feel natural to say that the loan approval system transforms loan applications into approvals or denials; nor does it feel natural to say that the ecommerce web site transforms customer desires into purchase decisions. Thus, the term transformation is often unsatisfactory for summarizing the activities that occur within the work system. During the development of WSM, alternatives to the term transformation included activities, actions, business process, and work practices. Work practices was selected because it includes business process and other perspectives for thinking about activities, such as communication, decision making, and coordination.

Goals, Controls, and Feedback

Most observers say that purposive systems contain control mechanisms that help the system stay on track or help the system move toward equilibrium (as with a thermostat). A thermostat-like goal and feedback metaphor is appropriate for heating a house, but doesn't fit well for many information systems. For example, the role of feedback control in the use of the ecommerce web site is not apparent. Similarly, the software development system may or may not have formal feedback mechanisms. Those mechanisms will be more apparent in a highly structured software development environment, and much less apparent in an agile development environment that proceeds through a series of incremental changes that receive individual feedback but may or may not lead to a larger goal. WSM treats control as one of the perspectives for thinking about work practices. The basic question is whether controls are built into existing or proposed work practices, and whether a different type or different amount of control effort would likely generate better results.

Wholeness

One of the major premises of the system approach is that systems should be treated as wholes, not just as a set of components. The structure of WSM is designed to recognize systemic issues, but WSM certainly doesn't favor wholeness over analysis of components. The structure of WSM calls for looking at each element separately and drilling down to understand the elements in enough depth to spot problems within each element. Simultaneously, however, the work system framework contains explicit links between elements, showing the main routes through which they interact in the operation of the work system as a whole.

An interesting issue with wholeness is that many components of work systems are not wholly dedicated to those work systems. The work practices are the activities within the work system, but the participants may be involved in many other work systems. Their activities within a particular work system may absorb only an hour a day or an hour a week. Similarly, the information and technologies may be used in other work systems. In the real world, the wholeness of the work system is often challenged when work system participants feel torn about their responsibilities in multiple work systems.

Emergent Properties

Users of WSM automatically observe emergent properties when they look at how a system operates as a whole. However, the level of detail and broad-brush modeling used in WSM is usually insufficient to reveal the types of counterintuitive system behaviors (Forrester, 1971) that are sometimes revealed and understood by system modelers using techniques such as systems dynamics.

Hierarchy, Subsystems and Supersystems

Systems in organizations are typically viewed as subsystems of larger systems. Relationships between information systems and the work systems they support have changed over recent decades. Before real time computing, computerized tracking systems and transaction processing systems were often separate from the manual processes they served or reported. As real time computing became commonplace, information systems became an integral part of the work systems they served. Remove the work system and the information system has no meaning. Turn off the information system and the work system grinds to a halt. All four of the work systems mentioned earlier have some aspect of this feature. All were selected as information systems that are somewhat independent of other work systems, yet major failures in any of these systems would have significant impacts on larger systems or organizations that they serve.

System Elements

Even the idea of system elements can be called into question. The nine elements of the work system framework are different types of things. For example, work practices are different from people (participants) and are different from information. Compare that view of work system elements to Ackoff's (1981) definition of a system as a set of two or more elements that satisfies the following three conditions:

- The behavior of each element has an effect on the behavior of the whole.
- The behavior of the elements and their effects on the whole are interdependent.
- However subgroups of the elements are formed, all have an effect on the behavior of the whole but none has an independent effect on it(cited by Skyttner, 2001).

In Ackoff's view, each element is a separate component that has the capability of behaving. In contrast, the work system framework says that the work practices are the behaviors and the work system participants and in some highly automated cases the technologies have the capability of behaving. In other words, each work system is basically a separate element in Ackoff's terms. The implication for future development of the work system method is that it might be possible to include explicit forms of interaction between work systems. Currently the only form of interaction included in WSM is the potential use of one work system's products and services in the work practices of another work system.

System Evolution

General system theory is primarily concerned with how systems operate, and somewhat less concerned with how they evolve over time. Patterns through which work systems evolve through planned and unplanned change are extremely important in WSM because the justification of a proposed system change includes preliminary ideas about how the system can be converted from its current configuration to a desired future configuration. As explained in substantial detail in Alter (2006), the work system life cycle model says much more about the evolution of a work system than is implied by most general system discussions. As WSM develops further it will surely absorb more ideas and principles related to system change, but most of these will probably come from the IS literature and the organizational behavior and innovation literatures rather than from the general systems literature. On the other hand, it is possible that some aspect of Beer's (1981) viable systems model might be incorporated in future explanations or explorations of the work system life cycle model.

Chaos, Complexity, Entropy, Self-Organization

Concepts such as chaos, complexity, entropy, and self-organization are often part of sophisticated discussions of systems. Although these ideas are sometimes tossed around at a rather non-specific, metaphoric level (the chaos of everyday management, the complexity of our lives, etc.), bringing these concepts into WSM while maintaining their deeper, more precise meanings in sophisticated discussions of systems seems impractical at this point. Attaining insightful analysis when using the existing WSM vocabulary is challenging enough.

The use of the term complexity in WSM illustrates the challenge of moving toward more advanced concepts. Within the current version of WSM, complexity is applied with its every day meaning and is treated as one of many strategy choices for work practices. Simpler work practices deal with fewer variables and are easier to understand and control; the opposite is true for complex work practices. Even with that simple definition, MBA and EMBA students have shown little inclination to use that term when evaluating a work system (i.e., it is too simple or too complex) and little inclination to use it to describe proposed improvements. If they shy away from relatively simple usage of that type, it is unlikely that they would be willing or able to apply advanced understandings of complexity that require insight at a very abstract level.

CONCLUSION

This reflection on WSM's use of general system concepts is highly subjective because different authors use different definitions of terms and have different views of which terms belong under the umbrella of general systems concepts. Evaluation of WSM in relation to general systems theory is all the more difficult because WSM was not developed as an application of general systems theory. It was developed to provide a set of ideas and tools that business professionals can use when trying to understand and analyze systems from a business viewpoint. At every stage in its development, every choice between maximizing ease of use and maximizing conceptual purity was decided in favor of ease of use.

The review of the relationship between typical system concepts and concepts within WSM showed that WSM uses a system approach and system concepts, but sometimes uses those terms idiosyncratically. Consistent with its practical goal of helping business professionals understand and analyze IT-reliant work systems, WSM adapts system concepts within a framework that is easier to understand and apply than any of the frameworks typically associated with general system theory (at least in my opinion).

Real world examples were introduced in this article as a reality check because general systems theory tends to include under one umbrella many different types of systems at vastly different levels (e.g., Miller's (1978) inclusion of cells, organs, organisms, groups, organizations, communities, societies, and supranational systems within the category of living systems). Potential changes in WSM concepts and process should be tested against realistic examples of IT-reliant work systems. If a change would make typical examples clearer to typical business professionals, then it might be appropriate within the spirit of WSM, especially if it could also co-exist with the rest of WSM or if it would make an existing part of WSM unnecessary.

It is unclear whether a detailed review of general system theory and its sophisticated extensions related to concepts such as chaos, complexity, entropy and self-organization might lead to useful improvements in WSM. Although this is a possibility, the path would probably be long. The first step would involve finding real situations in which sophisticated use of these concepts would help in evaluating, analyzing, and designing the types of systems that WSM addresses. It seems likely that sophisticated applications of concepts such as chaos, complexity, entropy, and self-organization are less pertinent to in typical work systems and more pertinent to physical and mathematical systems whose components and component interactions are more amenable to mathematical analysis.

The original question was "Could the work system method embrace systems concepts more fully?" At this point the answer to that question is a weak maybe. WSM is mature enough that its value to business and IT professionals can be tested in a number of different settings. Informal results thus far show that many users find it useful, and imply that at least some future users will suggest ways to make it easier to use in general or easier to apply to specific types of situations.

If I had to guess, I would say that the suggestions most directly associated with general systems concepts would be related to subset/ superset relationships and supplier/customer (output/input) relationships between separate work systems. The current form of WSM focuses on a single work system and says that it may be convenient to subdivide one work system into several or combine several work systems into one. An effective way to handle relationships between separate work systems without making the analysis too awkward probably would be a very useful extension of the current version of WSM.

At a more theoretical level, it also would be interesting to look at general systems concepts and principles at much greater depth than was possible in this brief chapter. For example, Skyttner (2001, pp. 61-64) lists 39 different "widely known laws, principles, theorems, and hypotheses). It would be interesting to look at each in turn and to decide whether it says anything that is both non-obvious about IT-reliant work systems and useful in understanding them in real world situations.

REFERENCES

Ackoff, R. (1981). *Creating the corporate future.* New York: John Wiley & Sons.

Alter, S. (2002). The work system method for understanding information systems and information system research. *Communications of the AIS, 9* (6), 90-104.

Alter, S. (2003). 18 reasons why IT-reliant work systems should replace the IT artifact as the core subject matter of the IS field. *Communications of the AIS, 12* (23), 365-394.

Alter, S. (2005). Architecture of Sysperanto - A model-based ontology of the IS field. *Communications of the AIS, 15* (1), 1-40.

Alter, S (2006). *The work system method: Connecting people, processes, and IT for business results.* Larkspur CA: Work System Press.

Alter, S. (2007). *Service responsibility tables: A new tool for analyzing and designing systems.* Paper presented at the 13th Americas Conference on Information Systems, Keystone, CO.

Alter, S. (2008). Service system fundamentals: work system, value chain, and life cycle. *IBM Systems Journal,* 47(1), 2008, 71-85. Available at http://www.research.ibm.com/journal/sj/471/alter.html

Beer, S. (1981). *Brain of the firm,* 2nd ed. Chichester, UK and New York: John Wiley.

Boulding, K. (1964). General systems as a point of view. In J. Mesarovic (Ed), *Views on general systems theory.* New York: John Wiley.

Checkland, P. (1999). *Systems thinking, systems practice* (Includes a 30-year retrospective). Chichester, UK: John Wiley.

Churchman, C. W. (1979). *The design of inquiring systems: Basic concepts of systems and organizations*. New York, Basic Books.

Forrester, J. (1971). Counterintuitive Behavior of Social Systems. *Technology Review, 73* (3), January.

Larses, O., and El-Khoury, J. (2005). *Review of Skyttner (2001) in O. Larses and J. El-Khoury, "Views on General Systems Theory."* Technical Report TRITA-MMK 2005:10, Royal Institute of Technology, Stockholm, Sweden. Retrieved June 30, 2006 on the World Wide Web: http://apps.md.kth.se/publication_item/web.phtml?ss_brand=MMKResearchPublications&department_id='Damek'

Markus, M.L. and Mao, J.Y. (2004). Participation in development and implementation – updating an old, tired concept for today's IS contexts. *Journal of the Association for Information Systems, 5* (11: 14).

Miller, J. G. (1978). *Living systems*. New York: McGraw-Hill.

Mora, M., Gelman, O., Cervantes, F., Mejía, M., and Weitzenfeld, A. (2002). A Systemic Approach for the Formalization of the Information Systems Concept: Why Information Systems are Systems. In J.J. Cano, (Ed.), *Critical reflections on information systems: A systemic approach*. Hershey, PA: Idea Group Publishing, 1-29.

Skyttner, L. (2001). *General systems theory*. Singapore: World Scientific Publishing

Skyttner, L, (1996). General systems theory: Origin and hallmarks. *Kybernetes, 25* (6), 16, 7 pp.

Weiss, P. (1971). *Hierarchically organized systems in theory and practice*. New York: Hafner.

Chapter III
The Distribution of a Management Control System in an Organization

Alfonso Reyes A.
Universidad de los Andes, Colombia

ABSTRACT

This chapter is concerned with methodological issues. In particular, it addresses the question of how is it possible to align the design of management information systems with the structure of an organization. The method proposed is built upon the Cybersin method developed by Stafford Beer (1975) and Raul Espejo (1992). The chapter shows a way to intersect three complementary organizational fields: management information systems, management control systems, and organizational learning when studied from a systemic perspective; in this case from the point of view of management cybernetics (Beer 1959, 1979, 1981, 1985).

UNDERSTANDING CONTROL IN AN ORGANIZATIONAL CONTEXT

When Norbert Wiener defined cybernetics as the science of control and communication in the animal and the machine (Wiener 1948) he was using the Greek word κυβερνητηζ, or steersman, as his main inspiration. Indeed, he was recalling the ancient practice of steering a ship towards a previously agreed destination regardless of changing conditions of currents and winds. This simple idea of connecting communication (at that time used as a synonymous of information flow) and control by a continuous feedback process opened up a huge space of possibilities to explain physical, biological and social phenomena related to self-regulation (Heims 1991). This is the case, for instance, of a heater in a physical domain, or the homeostatic mechanism to regulate body temperature in mammals (Ashby 1956). In all these cases, however, it is important to notice that control is far from its naïve interpretation as a crude process of coercion, but instead it refers to self-regulation. This is the meaning of control used in this chapter.

Cybernetics has evolved in many branches since its early years (Espejo & Reyes 2000). One of these variations has focused on the study of communication and control processes in organizations; this is the topic of management cybernetics (Beer 1959, 1966, 1979) and is the conceptual underpinning of this chapter.

Given the close relation between information and control in self-regulating systems (as organizations) this chapter addresses the question of how information should be distributed across the structure of an organization in order to allow self-regulation to be effective. In order to achieve this, we would like to show a way of relating three organizational fields: management information systems, management control systems and organizational learning. This is done from a methodological point of view by describing a step-by-step method (although it is not intended to be linear) to build a network of homeostatic mechanisms. But before describing the method, it is important to clarify with more detail the meaning of control used herein.

In an organizational context controlling a system is a process intended to close the gap between the observed outcomes produced by the organization and the expectations previously agreed among relevant stakeholders. It is, therefore, a self-regulating process.

An organization, on the other hand, is understood in this context as a closed network of relationships constituted by the recurrent interplay of roles and resources in a daily basis. In other words, people in organizations play formally defined roles that underpin the working relations they carry out with other organizational members. When these relations allow them to create, regulate and produce the goods and services they want to offer, an organization with a particular identity emerges; a *human interaction system* (Espejo 1994). This is an operational way to distinguish between a group of people that meets regularly to do something (as fans that used to meet at football matches) and an organization (when those fans constitute a club).

There are different ways to describe what an organization is doing; one way is to make explicit the transformation process by which this organization is producing the goods or services it is offering. Figure 1 shows a simple representation of such description. Notice that this description is suitable not only for an organization as a whole (like an insurance company that transforms information into specific products) but also to any other organizational processes like those carry out by the human resource department of a bank or those constituting the quality system of a company.

Figure 1. A representation of a system-in-focus as a transformation process

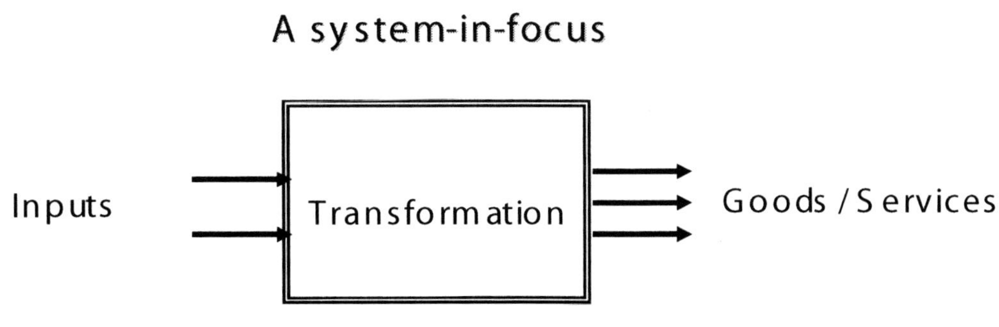

Our concern is to model the self-regulating (or control) process of any organizational system that could be described as a transformation process. From now on we will call an instance of these processes a system-in-focus.

Figure 2 describes a self-regulating mechanism for a system-in-focus. This control cycle starts by observing the behavior of the system, that is, by looking at a set of indices that measure the critical success factors of its operation. If the state of these indices does not match a set of expected values, then the system is out of control. The manager (or any organizational member) that is responsible for its operation has to address the reasons of such an undesirable behavior and as a result of this inquiry design a set of strategic or operational actions to intervene on the system. Once this decision is agreed and carried out by relevant organizational agents the cycle starts over again.

Notice how this self-regulating mechanism allows us to explain the intertwined relation between several organizational fields. First, the need to define a set of critical success factors (CSF) for the system-in-focus and a corresponding set of indices to measure them, along with the regular reports needed to inform management about the behavior of the system are the basis of a management information system. Secondly, inquiring for the reasons underpinning an unexpected behavior of the system-in-focus, designing a strategic and operational action and directing its execution through the doing of other organizational members are at the core of a management control system. And finally, the control loop itself can be related with the continuous operation of four stages: *observing* the state of a system; *assessing* the mismatch with expected outcomes; *designing* a set of actions; and *implementing* them to close the loop. These four stages are characteristics of an individual learning loop usually known as the OADI learning model (Kim 1993). When the loop is designed in such a way that it operates for a particular role (instead of a particular individual) we are entering in the field of organizational learning (Argyris 1993); we will go back to this point later on.

So far we have shown a model that allows the conceptual integration of (management) information systems, (management) control systems and

Figure 2. A general model for a self-regulating mechanism in an organizational system

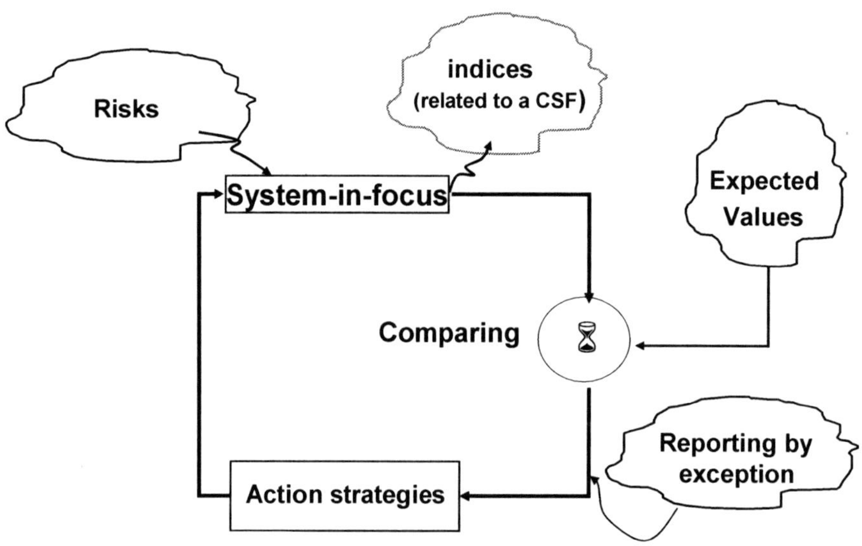

organizational learning; all of them related to self-regulation of a system-in-focus. The methodological problem now is how we can define an integrated set of these self-regulating mechanisms given a particular organization.

A METHOD TO DISTRIBUTE CONTROL IN AN ORGANIZATION

Our goal is to identify a complete set of control loops distributed across the structure of the organization. The steps presented here are based on the Viplan method (Espejo 1989; Espejo et al 1999).

Step 1: Naming a System-in-Focus

The first step of the method consists of identifying precisely the organizational system that will be the focus of control. This could be an organization as a whole, a strategic business unit of an organization, an area of such organization or a support process. In every case what is important is to name the system as a transformation process (see Figure 1). A canonic form to name this transformation is as follows: the system-in-focus S produces *X* by means of the activities *Y* with the purpose *Z*. In short, we are answering three main questions related to the system: ¿What is produced? ¿How is it produced? and ¿with what purpose is it produced?

Next follows the identification of the stakeholders of the system-in-focus. To do this notice that from the elements shown in Figure 1 it is possible to differentiate five stakeholders (see Figure 3): those who supply the inputs to the transformation (called ***suppliers***); those carrying out the activities of the transformation (called generically ***actors***); those who receive the goods/services of the transformation (usually called ***clients***) and those responsible for the management of the transformation (normally called ***owners***). It is also important to take into account the larger organizational context in which the system is operating; this consideration allows us to identify what are called the ***interveners*** of the system. They are stakeholders that although do not belong to the system-in-focus their organizational role may directly affect the system's transformation. This is, for instance, the case of both the competitors and the regulators of the system.

Figure 3. Stakeholders of a system-in-focus

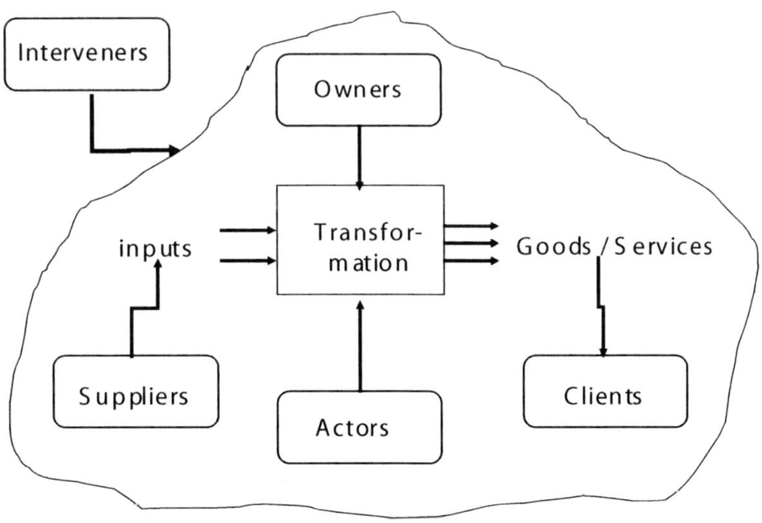

Viplan provides the mnemonic TASCOI to facilitate this process of naming the system-in-focus; certainly T(ransformation), A(ctors), S(uppliers), C(lients), O(wner), and I(nterveners).

Step 2: Unfolding of Complexity

Once the system-in-focus has been named what follows is to recognize the way this system organizes its resources to carry out its transformation. There are four complexity drivers that normally guide an organization to distribute its activities: technology, geography, market segmentation and time (Espejo et al 1999).

The first one refers to the way the activities constituting the transformation are organized according to the technology selected. We can use different technologies to produce the same transformation. For instance, Banks at the beginning of the 20th century used a technology based on the use of books and manual calculations to deliver its services to clients. Nowadays Internet is the main technological driver to deliver these services. The roles, resources used and the way activities are carried out have changed dramatically over this period in the banking industry. Therefore, choosing the appropriate technology to produce a given transformation is crucial to organize the primary activities of an organization. The other way around, given a particular system-in-focus, it is always possible to describe the primary activities implied (and carried out) by the selected technology. To describe these activities and their relations we used technological models (Espejo et al 1999).

A technological model is a macro flow diagram showing the activities needed to produce the transformation of the system-in-focus. Figure 4 shows an example for SATENA, a Colombian airline company.

The second complexity driver for structuring an organizational system refers to the distribution of activities in geographically diverse locations. Indeed, sometimes we need to take into account

Figure 4. An example of a technological model for SATENA, a Colombian airline company

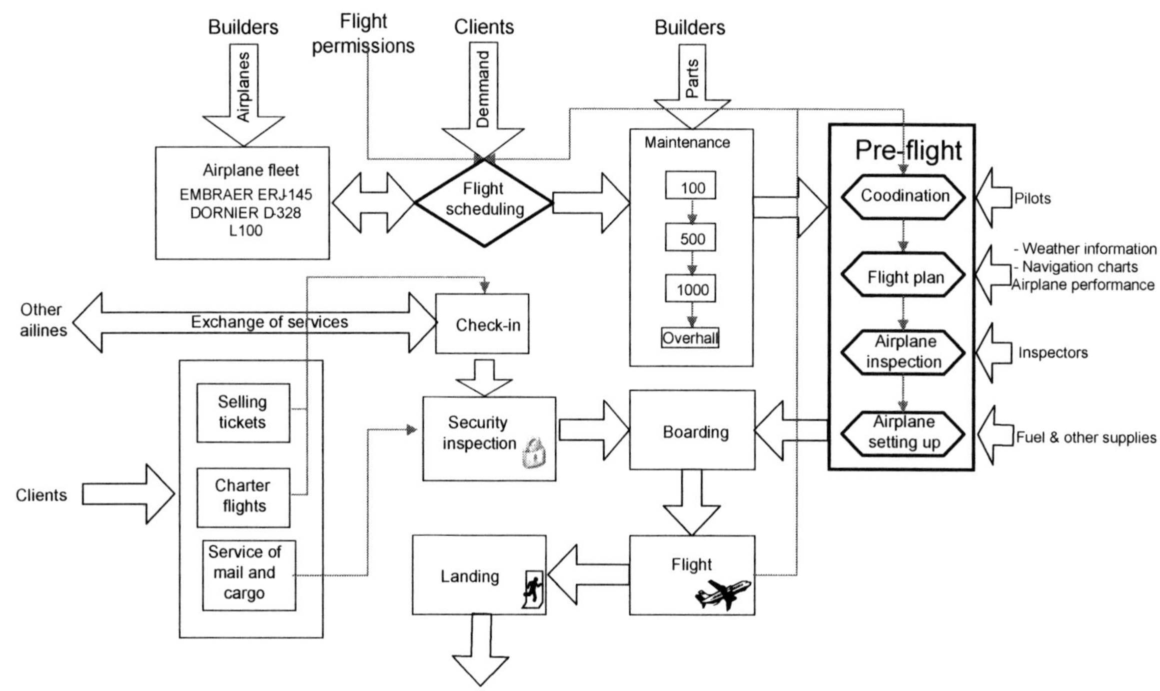

the best location of actors, suppliers and clients in order to organize activities of a transformation. For instance, if a company produces pavement-related products, it makes sense to have activities related to the production process near the quarries whereas its sales division will be near its clients. In the same way, and for economic reasons, some companies do prefer to have their manufacturing processes distributed in different countries (according to the cost of raw materials and salaries of the local work-force) while the assembly of final products could be located in another country. Similarly, a multinational company may group its primary activities according to geographical criteria to distribute its products and services. In all these cases geographical models are used to describe this distribution of activities. Figure 5 shows an example for SATENA, we can see how their resources are distributed across the country and inside each particular city where it operates.

The third driver refers to the grouping of activities that are necessary to produce, in a differentiated way, the goods or services offered to a segmented market. Market segmentation is a good practice to increase market share for many products and services. In this case, each new product/service will respond to more specific needs of potential clients and, therefore, it is probable that the company has to incorporate a further specialization of activities in its production process (or into the design of customize services). This, in turn, may affect the relations with suppliers (to get new raw material) and the relations with clients (to tackle the newly differentiated market).

Client-supplier models are helpful to describe the way a company groups its activities according to this segmentation strategy. Figure 6 shows

Figure 5. An example of a geographical model for SATENA

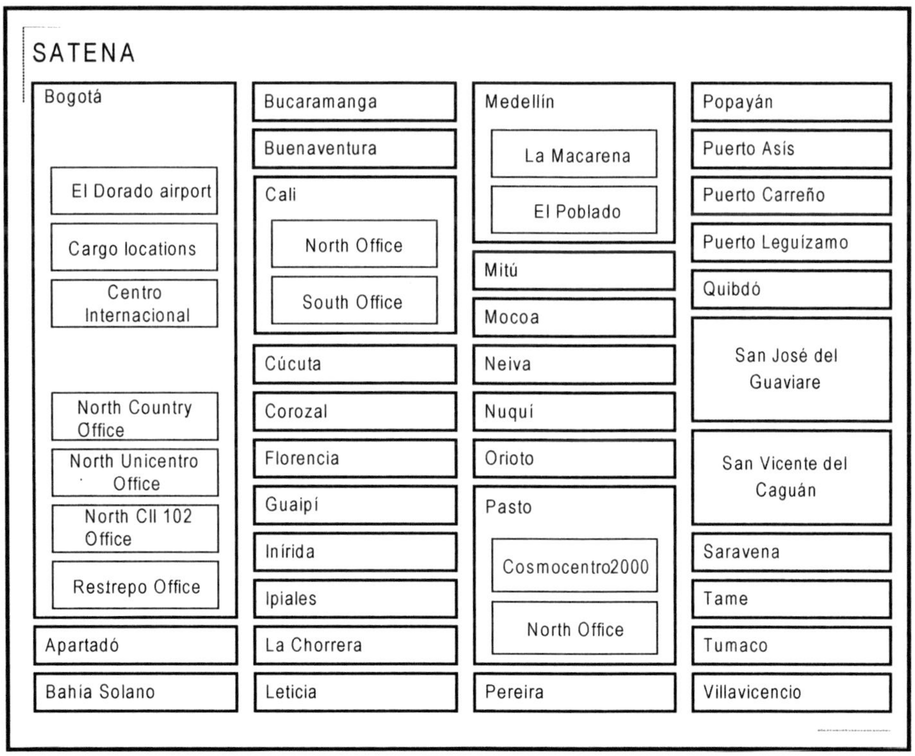

an example of this kind of models for SATENA. Here we have that this company offers two main services: air transportation and plain maintenance to other companies. The first service, in turn, is divided into four sub-services: passenger transportation, packages delivery, charter flights, and planes renting. The model shows the relations between suppliers, services and clients taking into account this market segmentation.

Finally, the last driver refers to the need of differentiating activities according to time chunks. This is usually the case of an organization that has several turns to carry out its activities. For instance that happens when a company is using the same production line to produce different products following a cyclic time-pattern during a month. Figure 7 shows a good example from another company (SATENA does not operate in shifts). Here the company's production cycle is divided into 12 weeks. Each week the company uses its line production structure to produce different products in four shifts (am shift, pm, evening and weekend shift). In this sense, time could be an important aspect to take into account when designing how to group activities in a company. In a similar way, given a system-in-focus, we can use time-models to describe the way time is participating in the structuring of activities of the system.

Once we have described the organization of the system-in-focus from these four perspectives using the structural models (technological, geographical, client-supplier and time) we can go on to summarize the organization's structure of

Figure 6. An example of a client-supplier model for SATENA

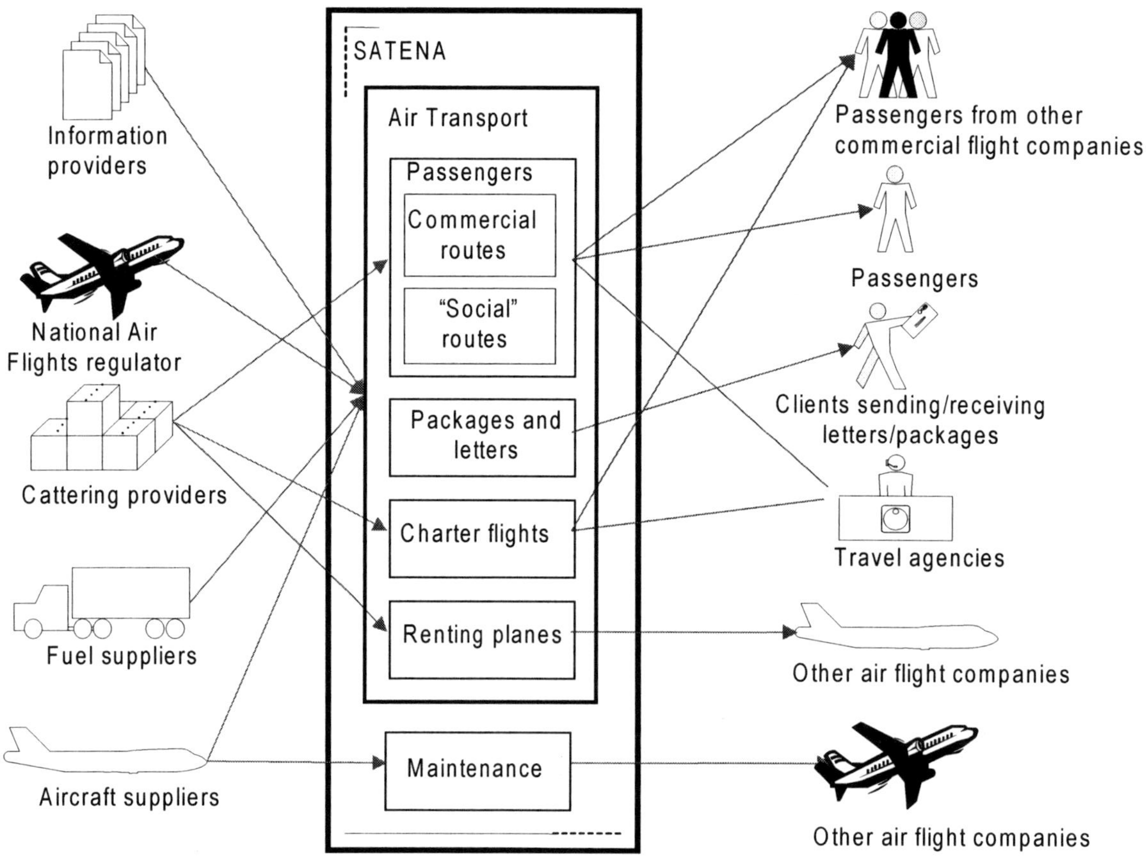

Figure 7. An instance of a Time-Model

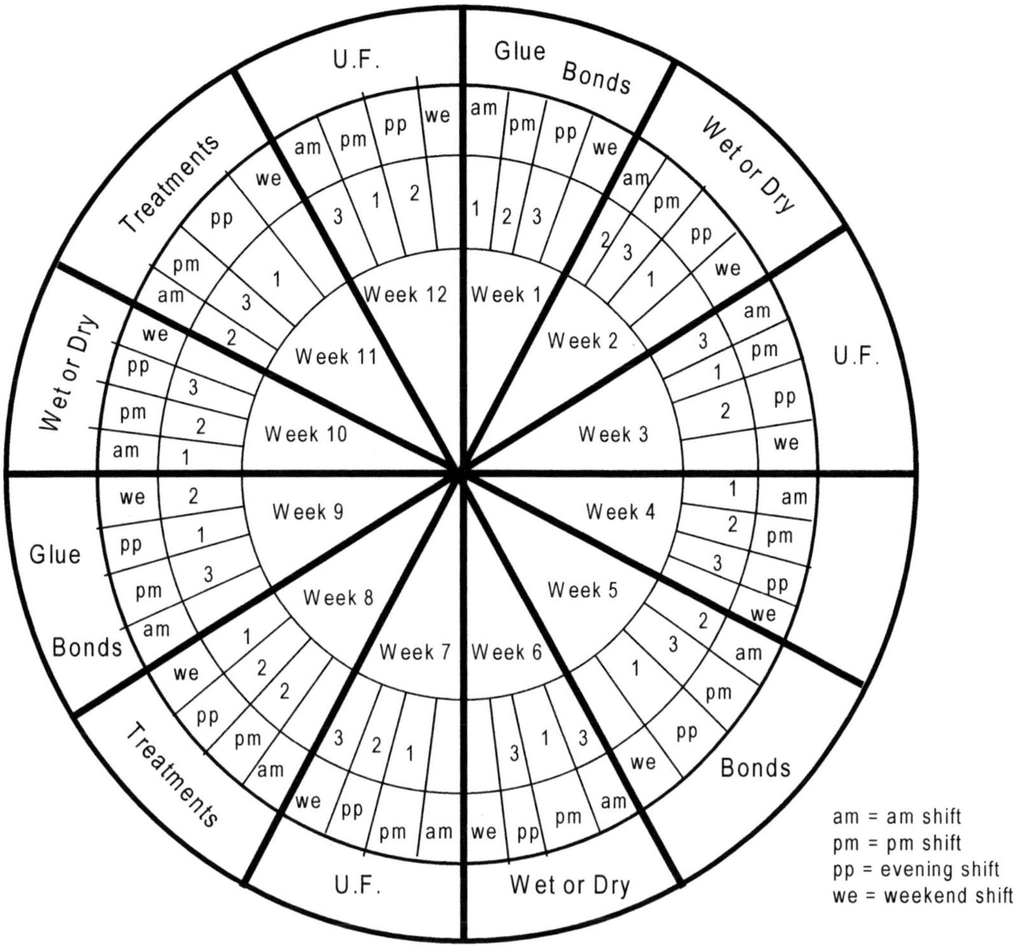

the system by depicting the logical ordering of its primary activities.

A primary activity is an activity that produces an organization's task (i.e., its goods or services). Normally, it is made up of a set of sub-(primary) activities along with some regulatory functions (Espejo 1999). Therefore, the relation of all primary activities will describe the way the system-in-focus performs its mission.

The unfolding of complexity (Espejo 1999) is a diagram that precisely shows the operational structure of an organizational system. It is build up from the primary activities taken from all the structural models used to describe the grouping of activities of the system. Figure 8 shows an example of an unfolding of complexity for SATENA. Here we can see that the second level corresponds to the geographical model whereas subsequent levels come from the client-supplier model indicating the way SATENA groups activities according to particular services. Notice that all services are not provided in all cities, for instance maintenance of planes to other companies is only provided in Bogotá. We can continue doing the unfolding by depicting in the last level activities taken from the technological model. However, for the sake of simplicity we are leaving aside this level in Figure 8.

Figure 8. An example of a complexity unfolding for SATENA

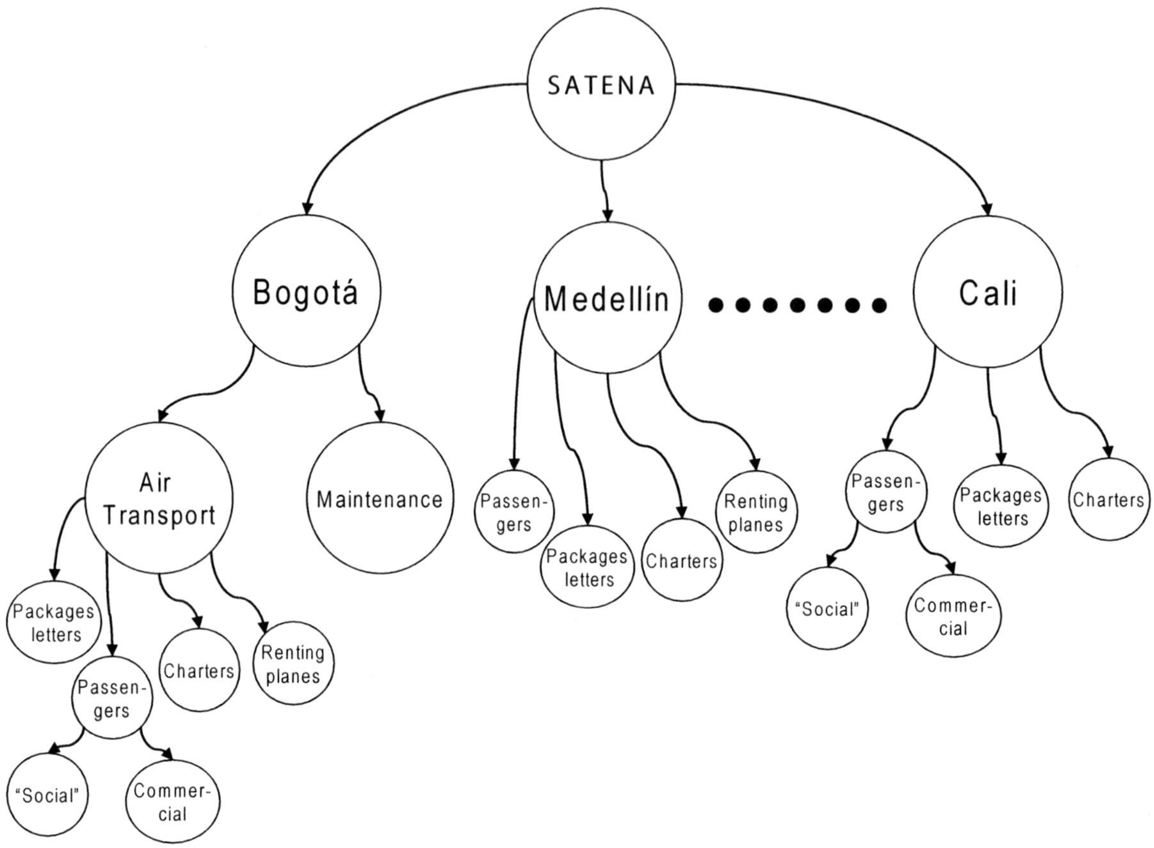

The unfolding of complexity is a means to depict the *operational structure* of an organization. The operational structure refers to the set of interrelated primary activities that produces the organization goods/services. By contrast, the *supporting structure* is the set of interrelated activities that regulate the primary activities. This distinction is similar to one between missional processes and supporting processes normally used in ISO certification projects. This is a systemic way of describing the structure of an organization in which we can simultaneously see the organization as a whole (the first level of the unfolding of complexity) as well as all its primary activities organized in a cascade of subsumed logical levels. Notice that from one level to another there are no hierarchical relations. Indeed, related activities in level n+1 *constitute* the activity they are part of in level n. This is a radically different way of describing the structure of an organization that leaves aside the fragmented view offered by the traditional organization chart.

The unfolding of complexity shows an interrelated set of primary activities autonomously producing, at different structural levels, the organization's goods/services. Each primary activity acts as a "smaller" whole by itself. On the other hand, the organization chart is a functional description of a company that normally difficult a holistic view of the organization by its members.

Step 3: Defining Indices

As mentioned in the previous section, the unfolding of complexity of the system-in-focus shows all primary activities necessary to produce its goods/services. Each of these primary activities can be treated, in turn, as (sub)systems-in-focus at different structural levels and, therefore, they could be named in the same way as explained in step 1. In particular, each one is doing a transformation of inputs to produce specific outputs to clients. So each primary activity has a manager (or an organizational member) who is responsible for its effective performance. Surely the manager, tacitly or explicitly, has chosen a set of critical success factors (CSF) to focus his/her managerial role. Each CSF, in turn, should have associated one or more indices that measure it through time. Figure 9 shows the distribution of CSF and indices across primary activities of a system-in-focus. Of course it is quite possible that several of this CSF were the same for different primary activities.

Notice that this same figure shows the distribution of a managerial information system across this organization. Specifically, it shows what type of reports containing what kind of information (indices) should go to what relevant roles in the organization (in fact, the manager responsible for each particular primary activity). Notice that the higher it goes in the diagram the more aggregate the indices are until we reach the first level in which

Figure 9. Distribution of indices (and CSF) across primary activities of an organization

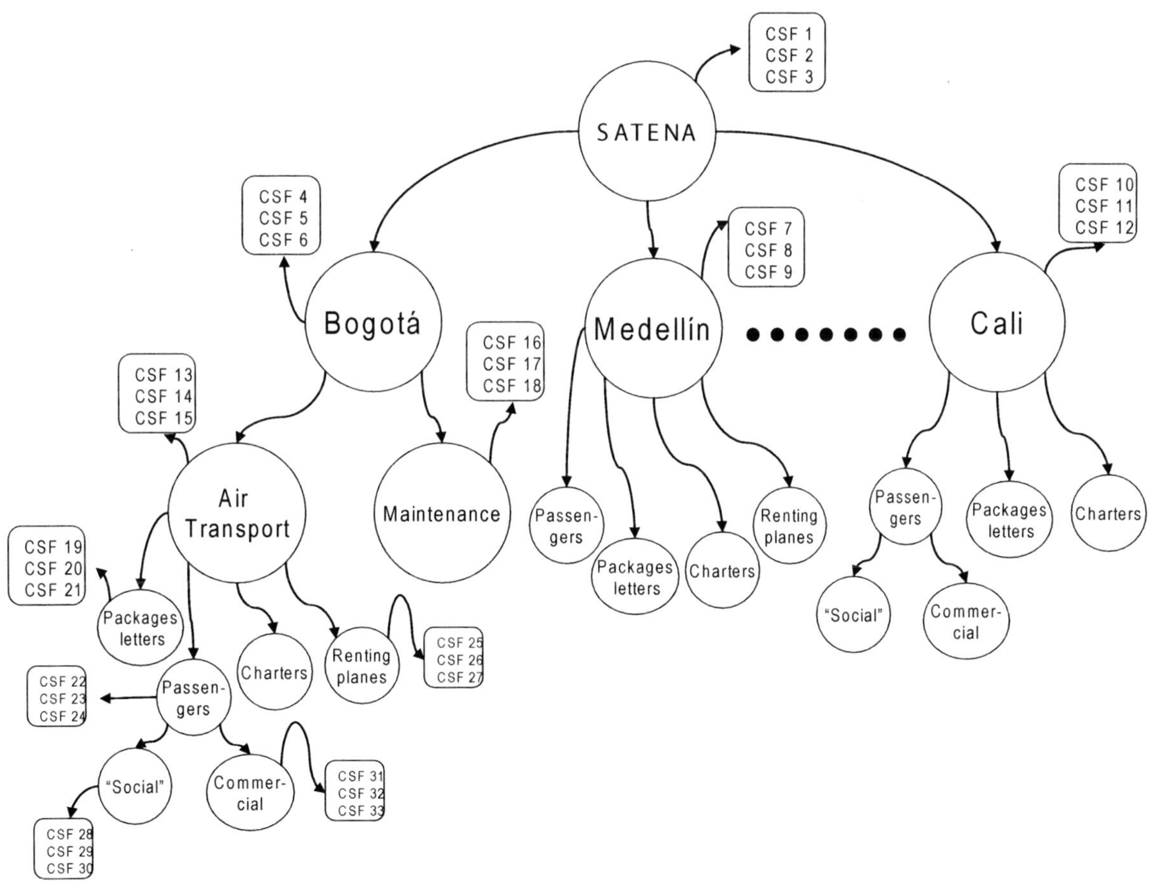

we have indices referring to the performance of the system-in-focus as a whole.

This relationship between the level of aggregation of indices (or information in general) and the structural level of the manager getting the reports is what some authors call the alignment between information systems and organizational structure (Espejo 1993). A mismatch in this alignment implies a manager receiving either information too detailed (in respect to its managerial task) or too aggregated for its actual capabilities. The first one is the case of a manager that is concerned with so much detail that soon losses track of the holistic view of its primary activity and collapses under the pressure of too much information. The second one refers to those managers that are very well informed of such things for which they do not have any capability to take decisions nor mobilize resources to do something about them. In both cases, the information (indices) received by the information system is irrelevant; therefore it make sense to say that the alignment between the two facilitates the effective management of the system-in-focus.

Nowadays many organizations have their own set of indices. So, and independently of its actual relevance, it is quite important to recognize such efforts from the start. Figure 10 shows a table in which it is possible to keep a record of all indices that have been built for the system-in-focus. This table classifies indices in three main categories: efficacy, efficiency and effectiveness, although it can be extended to allow other categories. For each indicator there is a code, a name and an operational definition. But before going any further, it is important to explain the way we understand this taxonomy of indices.

Let us recall that the name of the system-in-focus, using the mnemonic TASCOI, answers three main questions regarding the transformation process: ¿what is produced? ¿how is it produced? and ¿for what purpose it is produced? We say that indices that measure the first question belong to the category of efficacy; those measuring the second question relate to efficiency and those measuring the third one refer to effectiveness. Another way to put this is to say that efficacy measures the relation between what has been produced (or offered, in the case of a service) and what has been planned. Efficiency, in turns, measures the optimal use of resources needed to produce the goods/services of the system-in-focus. Effectiveness, on the other hand, measures to what extend the purpose of the transformation has been accomplished.

Notice that this taxonomy defined in such a way implies that all three categories form an orthogonal set. In other words, none of the indices in one category can be calculated as a function

Figure 10. A table to register the existing indices of a system-in-focus

SYSTEM-IN-FOCUS:

WHAT			HOW			WHAT FOR					
EFFICACY			EFFICIENCY			EFFECTIVENESS /IMPACT			OTHERS		
CODE	NAME OF INDICATOR	OPERATIONAL DEFINITION	CODE	NAME OF INDICATOR	OPERATIONAL DEFINITION	CODE	NAME OF INDICATOR	OPERATIONAL DEFINITION	CODE	NAME OF INDICATOR	DEFINICION OPERACIONAL
E.1			F.1			I.1			0.1		
E.2			F.2			I.2			0.2		
E.3			F.3			I.3			0.3		
E.4			F.4			I.4			0.4		
E.5			F.5			I.5			0.5		

of the other two. In simple terms, it is possible to have a system-in-focus whose indices of efficacy and efficiency (at any moment in time) are high but its effectiveness is low; in the same way it is possible to have a state in which indices of efficiency and effectiveness are high but indices of efficacy are low; and also a state in which while indices of efficacy and effectiveness are high, the system is inefficient.

The following table (Figure 11) shows a distribution of indices used by the system-in-focus according to the primary activities of the unfolding of complexity of such system. Rows in the table correspond to the primary activities of the system-in-focus while columns refer to the indices registered before (using Table in Figure 10).

This table (Figure 11) can be used to show weaknesses of the actual managerial information system of the organization. In fact, an empty third column (for a given primary activity) shows a lack of indices measuring the effectiveness of such primary activity (e.g. most primary activities in SATENA). In other words, the manager will not be aware of the impact of the task s(he) is responsible for in this activity. Similarly, we could point out other managerial problems if other columns are void for a giving primary activity. An empty row is, of course, an extreme case in which a manager is acting by feeling because it lacks any measure (i.e., information) that could guide his/her decisions. This is the case of air transportation of "social" and commercial passengers for SATENA.

Developing an appropriate management (distributed) control system should take care of these weaknesses just mentioned. This means defining new indices (if needed) to measure the efficacy, efficiency and effectiveness of each primary activity of the system-in-focus. Once Table in Figure 11 is filled, we will have the general specifications for a managerial information system (MIS) supporting the distributed control of the system-in-focus.

However, in order to specify more detailed requirements for the MIS, it is quite useful to fill in a form for each indicator (see Figure 12). This form will register, among others, the fol-

Figure 11. A distribution of indices (classified by categories) among primary activities (SATENA)

	EFFICACY					EFFICIENCY				
SATENA	E1	E2				F1	F2	F3		
BogotÆ	E1						F2		F4	
Air transport			E3	E4						F5
Packages and letters					E5					F5
Passengers	E1		E3			F1				
"Social"										
Commercial										
Charters										
Renting planes										
Maintenance			E3			F1				
Medell⊠n	E1						F2		F4	
Passengers	E1		E3			F1				
Packages and letters					E5					F5
Charters										
Renting planes										
⊠										
⊠										
⊠										
⊠										
Cali	E1						F2		F4	
Passengers	E1		E3			F1				
"Social"										
Commercial										
Packages and letters					E5					F5
Charters										

	EFFECTIVENESS					OTHERS				
SATENA	I1					O1				
BogotÆ										
Air transport										
Packages and letters										
Passengers										
"Social"										
Commercial										
Charters										
Renting planes										
Maintenance										
Medell⊠n										
Passengers										
Packages and letters										
Charters										
Renting planes										
⊠										
⊠										
⊠										
⊠										
Cali										
Passengers										
"Social"										
Commercial										
Packages and letters										
Charters										

lowing information: a) Name of the indicator; b) Associated Primary Activity; c) CSF related; d) Type (efficacy, efficiency, effectiveness, other); e) Operational definition, that is the function of variables defining the indicator; f) Relation of variables, indicating for each one its unit, the level of aggregation, its frequency and source (the role responsible for providing or getting the information); g) Level of aggregation of the indicator; h) Goal (that reflects managerial expectations about the CSF associated with the indicator); i) Criteria for interpretation (that facilitates the way to ascribe meaning to the indicator); j) Context for interpretation (that includes other variables or indices that should be looked at in order to understand the behavior of the indicator in a given period); k) the role responsible to produce the indicator (to calculate and generate the report); l) the role responsible to interpret and use the indicator (that usually will be the role responsible for the management of the associated primary activity); and m) Date of definition (that allows a historical tracking of the indicator).

This record should be updated any time an indicator suffers a modification and, in fact, should be part of the MIS itself. This is so because indices are aligned to the strategy of the organization through the CSF of each primary activity. That means that a strategic change in the organization could imply a modification of management priorities. This, in turn, may produce a need to update CSF and, therefore, indices. In other words, as much as an organization is alive and subject to regular changes so should be its distributed control system. This explains the reason to keep track of indices through time.

Figure 12. A form to specify detailed information of indices

INFORMATION OF INDICATORS	Code:
Date of definition:	DD MM YY
1 SYSTEM-IN-FOCUS	
2 Id number:	
3 Primary Activity	
4 Name of indicator	
5 Objective of indicator	*What does it measure? Please, specify related CSF*
6 Classification of INDICATOR (Mark with an "X")	1 Efficacy; 2 Efficiency; 3 Effectiveness; 4 Ecology; 5 Equality; 6 Other
Explain briefly which criterion you used to make this classification:	
¿How it it measured?	
7 OPERATIONAL DEFINITION	*Formula:*
8 MECHANISM USED	

DATA FROM VARIABLES

9 Name of Variable	10 Source	11 Level of Aggregation	12 Frequency	13 Unit of Measurement	14 Responsable

15 Frequency of indicator	
16 RESPONSIBLE of defining Indicador	
17 *WHO* observes the indicator and defines actions to follow?	
18 *HOW is it interpreted?*	
19 WHAT other aspects *(internal or external to the Primary Activity) have to be taking into account for intertreting the indicator?*	
20 Unit of measurement	
OBSERVATIONS:	

Originally designed by: *Soledad Guzmán S.*
Modified by: *Alfonso Reyes A.*
Last version: July 2006

Step 4: Calculating Indexes

Figure 9 shows how indices are distributed through primary activities of the system-in-focus. Each indicator is measuring at least one CSF which reflects management's priorities. These aspects could be of quite different nature: productivity, opportunity, costs/benefits, quality, market share, and so on. Each one, therefore, could have a different unit of measurement: time, quantity, money, percentage, etc. This lack of uniformity, along with the number of indices at any moment in time, could make complex the interpretation of reports produced by the MIS.

In order to reduce such complexity there is a useful method called Ciberfilter (Beer 1975; 1979). This method normalizes any indicator by defining a set of three indexes. The way it works is as follows. First, for each indicator we differentiate three different kinds of values: its *actuality*, its *capability* and its *potentiality*.

The actuality of a given indicator is the value it gets regularly by the MIS; its capability is defined as the maximum value (or the minimum, depending on how the indicator was defined) that the indicator may achieve taking into account all the structural limitations of the corresponding primary activity. If the indicator is defined in such a way that the bigger its value the better (as in the case of measuring productivity or revenue) then capability is the *maximum value* it can get given current structural limitations; on the other hand, if the definition of the indicator implies that the smaller its value the better (as in the case of measuring costs or delays) then capability is the *minimum value* it can get given current structural limitations. Examples of these restrictions could be related to insufficient resources (people, money, etc.), obsolete technology, poor training, and so on. On the other hand, the potentiality of an indicator will be the maximum value that it can achieve (or the minimum) if we invest enough resources in reducing these structural restrictions. Notice that these two types of values are goals defined by recognizing the structural limitations of the primary activity under consideration.

Whereas the capability of a given indicator may be the result of management experience or the output of a benchmarking process, its potentiality is the outcome of a negotiation process. Indeed, the manager responsible for the performance of a primary activity, after recognizing that with its actual resources (people, technology, budget, etc,) s/he could get a (maximum) value for a performance indicator (i.e., its capability), s/he may set for a better goal for this indicator (i.e., its potentiality) as long as s/he can get enough resources to invest in reducing these limitations.

Secondly, once these values (or goals) are set, three indexes can be calculated for each indicator. These indexes are called: *achievement, latency* and *performance* (Beer 1975; 1979). Figure 13 shows the way these indexes are defined. Achievement is the ratio between actuality and capability; latency is the ratio between capability and potentiality; and performance is the ratio between actuality and potentiality (or the product between achievement and latency). Notice that we have to invert these ratios if the indicator is defined in such a way that the smaller its value the better. Indexes should never be greater than unity.

Notice that by definition all indexes are numbers between 0 and 1; in other words, they indicate percentages no matter what is the measurement unit of the corresponding indicator. This is exactly what we were looking for, that is a way to normalize all indicators; therefore, any time a manager gets a report from the MIS, s/he gets an index whose value is always a percentage. How could s/he interpret this value?

Considering that the maximum value that actuality could achieve is capability, then a low level of achievement indicates weaknesses in the management of current resources, whereas a low level of latency indicates that investment is not having an expected effect in reducing the structural limitations of the primary activity. Notice, on the

Figure 13. Three indexes for a given indicator (Beer 1979)

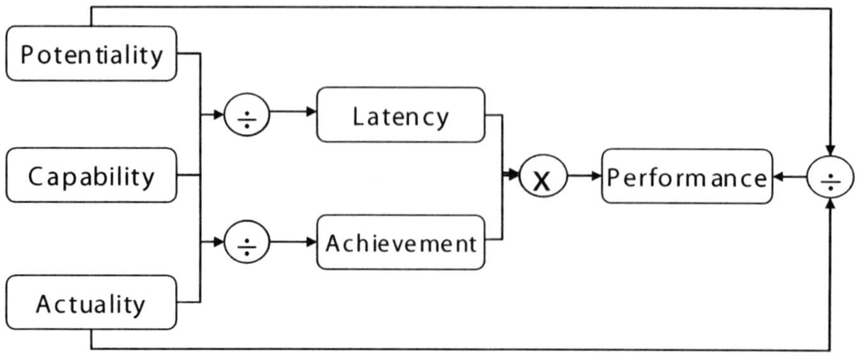

other hand, that performance shows the balance of the other two indexes in the sense that it achieves its maximum value (that is 100%) if and only if simultaneously the indexes of achievement and latency are 100%. In other words, a low level of performance for a given indicator shows that either management of current resources is poor or that we are not investing in improving the primary activity. This is quite important because traditional MIS tends to concentrate in information from the past (measuring and reporting what happened) whereas cyberfilter additionally shows what is the impact of investment over the performance of primary activities. In this way management becomes more proactive.

Finally, managers should fix a range of accepted values for each index so that s/he will get reports from the MIS only by exception. This means that a report is produced only when a given index is falling out of the range previously defined. This setting of the expected values for each index and for each indicator will normally go through a process of tuning until it reaches some stability; this is part of the learning process of managers as part of their structural coupling with the MIS.

Step 5: Setting Control (Learning) Loops

So far, we have shown how indices that are produced by a MIS could be distributed across all primary activities of a system-in-focus. Moreover, each indicator is a way to measure a crucial aspect for the management of each primary activity (indeed, it is a critical success factor). Therefore, Figure 9 is also showing a distributed control system for an organization.

In fact, for each CSF we have a manager responsible to keep this aspect (of a primary activity) under control. In order to do this, as we saw in Figure 2, a manager has to enter into a learning loop in which s/he is able to observe (indices), assess (the reasons of any mismatch with expected values), design (i.e., choose a particular decision), and implement (i.e., transform this decision into effective action). If each one of the organizational members responsible for the management of each primary activity in a system-in-focus has both the capacity and the means to carry out these learning cycles as part of its managerial role, there is a good chance of having an effective control system of primary activities. Notice that in this case a distributed MIS is essential.

But managers not only have to take care (directly or indirectly) of the day-to-day aspects that may affect the performance of their primary activities, they also need to pay attention to those aspects that, although of rare occurrence, may dramatically affect the outcome of the primary activity. These events are usually called *risks*.

Managers not only have to learn how to estimate the probability of risk's occurrences (PRO) but also they have to be able to quantify their impact (IMP). If this impact is measured as a percentage, then the *relevance* of each risk could be calculated as the product (PRO * IMP). This exercise allows managers to establish a priority of risks. At the same time, to determine risks for each primary activity will produce a *risk-map* useful for the management control system as a whole.

Finally, for each one of the top risks identified in each primary activity, it is quite important that managers define in advanced the strategic action and the investment required in order to prevent, diminish or take care of a particular risk occurrence. Figure 14 illustrate this aspect of management.

Learning (i.e., controlling) cycles like these are associated with each CSF of each primary activity of a system-in-focus. This is precisely the way of distributing a control system in an organization. Figure 15 summarizes in a single picture the self-regulating mechanism that has been presented here.

FINAL REMARKS

We have shown a method to a step-by-step building of a distributed control system for a particular organization-in-focus. The method consists of five steps that are mutually interconnected, that is, the process is nonlinear but a cyclical one: outcomes of one step may affect previous steps.

Figure 14. A management of risks as part of a control cycle

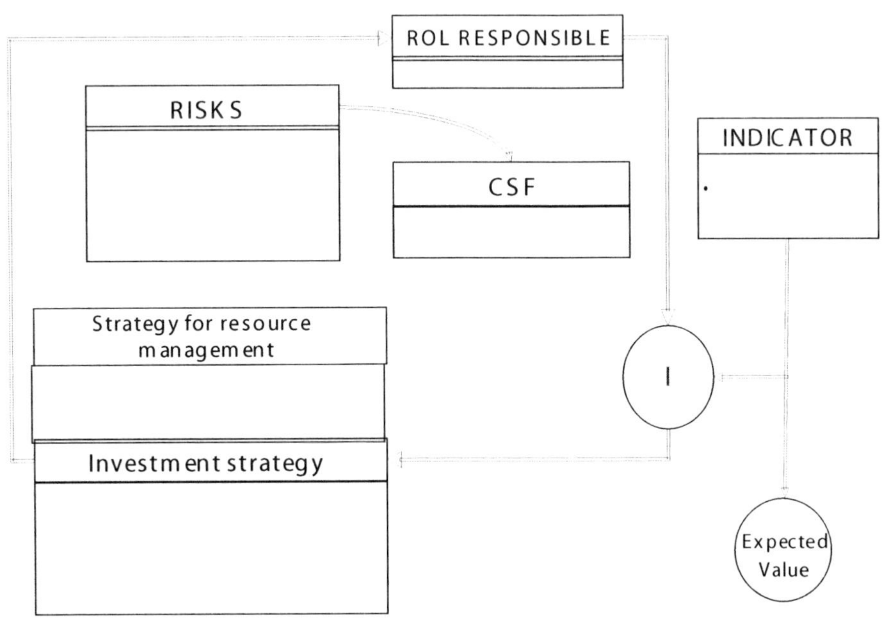

Figure 15. A distributed control system in an organization

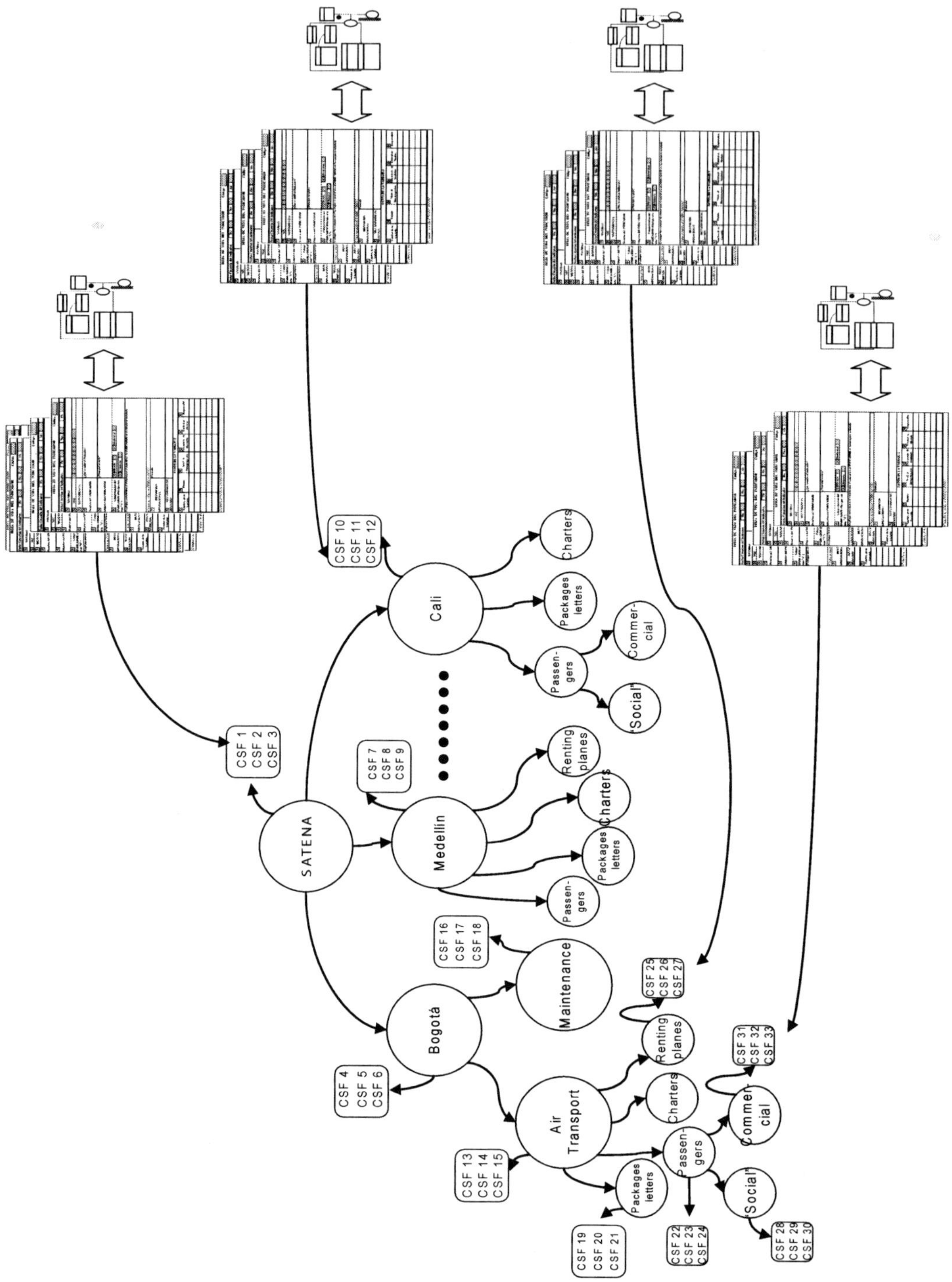

First, we have to explicitly identify the organizational borders of our system-in-focus. The mnemonic TASCOI is the tool used to distinguish the transformation process of this system. Relevant stakeholders of this transformation are Actors, Suppliers, Clients, Owners and Interveners.

Secondly, we used four different structural models (technological, geographical, time and segmentation) in order to describe the way the system-in-focus organizes its primary activities. The whole (systemic) picture is represented by a diagram called an unfolding of complexity.

Thirdly, each primary activity, in the logical hierarchy of the unfolding of complexity, has a manager responsible for its effective performance. To assure this, each manager has to define a set of CSF relevant for its task. Then, it is crucial to define one or more indicators to measure each CSF for each primary activity of the system-in-focus. We presented three main types of indices: efficacy, efficiency and effectiveness defined in such a way that they form an orthogonal space.

Taking into account that we may have many indices with different measurement units, we need a way to normalize them. We showed this in step fourth by identifying three values for each indicator (actuality, capability and potentiality); the last two relate to the structural limitations of their corresponding primary activity. We then built three indexes (achievement, latency and performance) which values are inside the [0,1] range; so they could be interpreted as percentages. By definition a low achievement indicates poor management of actual resources in the primary activity; whereas a low latency points to an ineffective investment plan. The index of performance, in turn, by definition is balancing a short-term tactical management with a medium-term strategic management.

In step 5 we showed how the distribution of control for the system-in-focus means setting a learning loop (observe, asses, design and implement) for each CSF in every primary activity. Indexes are a fundamental part of these learning loops and so are the MIS that provide them. This relation among CSF and indices regarding primary activities shows the way to align a MIS with the organizational structure of the system-in-focus.

Finally, management should be aware not only of daily perturbations that may affect indices but also aware of risks whose occurrence may dramatically impinge upon the performance of CSF. Distributing these learning/control loops across primary activities shows a way to implement a distributed management control system in an organization.

The method has been applied extensively during the last three years in a regular postgraduate course on managerial control systems in the department of industrial engineering in the Universidad de los Andes. Students taking the course have to apply the method in a system-in-focus selected from the organization they work for. About twenty of these applications have actually being implemented.

REFERENCES

Argyris, C. (1993). *On organizational learning.* Cambridge, MA: Blackwell.

Beer, S. (1959). *Cybernetics and management.* London: The English University Press.

Ashby, R. (1956). *An introduction to cybernetics.* London: Chapman & Hall Ltd.

Beer, S. (1966). *Decision and control.* Chichester: Wiley.

Beer, S. (1979). *The heart of enterprise.* Chichester: Wiley.

Beer, S. (1981). *Brain of the firm.* Chichester: Wiley.

Beer, S. (1985). *Diagnosing the system for organisations.* Chichester: Wiley.

Espejo, R. (1989). A cybernetic method to study organisations. In Espejo, R. and Harnden, R. (eds), *The viable system model: interpretations and applications of Stafford Beer's VSM.* Chichester: Wiley.

Espejo, R. (1992). Cyberfilter: A management support system. In Holtham, C.(ed.), *Executive information systems and decision support.* London: Chapman.

Espejo, R. (1993). Strategy, structure and information management. *Journal of Information Systems*, (3), 17-31.

Espejo, R. (1994). ¿What is systemic thinking? *Systems Dynamics Review*, (10), Nos. 2-3 (Summer-Fall), 199-212.

Espejo R., Bowling, D., & Hoverstadt, P. (1999). The viable system model and the viplan software. *Kybernetes*, (28) Number 6/7, 661-678.

Espejo, R, and Reyes, A. (2000). Norbert Wiener. In Malcom Warner (ed), *The international encyclopedia of business and management: The handbook of management thinking.* London: Thompson Business Press.

Heims, S. (1991). *The cybernetics group.* Cambridge, MA: MIT Press.

Kim, D. (1993). The Link between individual and organizational learning. *Sloan Management Review*, Fall, 37-50.

Wiener, N. (1948). *Cybernetics: Or control and communication in the animal and the machine.* New York: Wiley.

Chapter IV
Making the Case for Critical Realism:
Examining the Implementation of Automated Performance Management Systems

Phillip Dobson
Edith Cowan University, Australia

John Myles
Edith Cowan University, Australia

Paul Jackson
Edith Cowan University, Australia

ABSTRACT

This chapter seeks to address the dearth of practical examples of research in the area by proposing that critical realism be adopted as the underlying research philosophy for enterprise systems evaluation. We address some of the implications of adopting such an approach by discussing the evaluation and implementation of a number of automated performance measurement systems (APMS). Such systems are a recent evolution within the context of enterprise information systems. They collect operational data from integrated systems to generate values for key performance indicators, which are delivered directly to senior management. The creation and delivery of these data are fully automated, precluding manual intervention by middle or line management. Whilst these systems appear to be a logical progression in the exploitation of the available rich, real-time data, the statistics for APMS projects are disappointing. An understanding of the reasons is elusive and little researched. We describe how critical realism can provide a useful "underlabourer" for such research, by "clearing the ground a little ... removing some of the rubbish that lies in the way of knowledge" (Locke, 1894, p. 14). The implications of such an underlabouring role are investigated. Whilst the research is still underway, the article indicates how a critical realist foundation is assisting the research process.

INTRODUCTION

Many recent articles from within the information systems (IS) arena present an old-fashioned view of realism. For example, Iivari, Hirschheim, and Klein (1998) see classical realism as seeing "data as describing objective facts, information systems as consisting of technological structures ('hardware'), human beings as subject to causal laws (determinism), and organizations as relatively stable structures" (p. 172). Wilson (1999) sees the realist perspective as relying on "the availability of a set of formal constraints which have the characteristics of abstractness, generality, invariance across contexts." (p. 162)

Fitzgerald and Howcroft (1998) present a realist ontology as one of the foundational elements of positivism in discussing the polarity between hard and soft approaches in IS. Realism is placed alongside positivist and objectivist epistemologies and quantitative, confirmatory, deductive, laboratory-focussed, and nomothetic methodologies. Such a traditional view of realism is perhaps justified within the IS arena as it reflects the historical focus of its use; however, there now needs to be a greater recognition of the newer forms of realism—forms of realism that specifically address all of the positivist leanings emphasised by Fitzgerald and Howcroft (1998). A particular example of this newer form of realism is critical realism. This modern realist approach is primarily founded on the writings of the social sciences philosopher Bhaskar (1978, 1979, 1986, 1989, 1991) and is peculiarly European in its origins.

Critical realism is becoming influential in a range of disciplines including geography (Pratt, 1995), economics (Fleetwood 1999; Lawson, 1997), organization theory (Tsang & Kwan, 1999), accounting (Manicas, 1993), human geography (Sayer, 1985), nursing (Ryan & Porter, 1996; Wainwright, 1997), logistics and network theory (Aastrup 2002), and library science (Spasser, 2002). Critical realism has been proposed as a suitable underlabourer for IS research (Dobson, 2001, 2002; Mingers, 2001, 2002), yet there have been few practical examples of its use in IS research. The application of critical realism within the IS field has been limited to date. Mutch (1999, 2000, 2002) has applied critical realist thinking in the examination of organizational use of information. In so doing, he comments how difficult it is to apply such a wide-ranging and sweeping philosophical position to day-to-day research issues. Mingers (2002) examines the implications of a critical realist approach, particularly in its support for pluralist research. Dobson (2001, 2002) argues for a closer integration of philosophical matters within IS research and suggests a critical realist approach has particular potential for IS research. Carlsson (2003) examines IS evaluation from a critical realist perspective. This chapter seeks to address the dearth of practical examples of critical realist use in IS by proposing the review of APMS implementation from such a perspective.

The Case Example

The Sarbanes-Oxley Act was introduced in 2002 to address high-profile accounting scandals in the U.S. The act requires that senior executives must advise stockholders immediately of any issues that are likely to affect company performance. This liability is personal and thus makes senior executives liable for the effectiveness and immediacy of their internal measurement systems and reporting. Similar legislation has been introduced in many other countries, including Australia, where the Corporations Act was implemented earlier in 2001. The development of effective performance reporting and management tools is one necessary consequence of the Sarbanes-Oxley Act and similar legislation. The resulting requirement for executives to have unimpeded, unmediated access to organizational data suggests that such tools require minimal or no human intervention in the analysis and collection of the data. This automated component in corporate performance management systems will lead to the growth of a new class of monitoring system distinct from traditional business intelligence (BI) and business activity monitoring (BAM) tools—these so-called automated performance management systems can be argued to ultimately rest on a lack of trust or confidence in traditional reporting tools and management structures. The research described in this chapter seeks to understand the issues involved in implementing such performance measurement systems and proposes the adoption of critical realism as a basic underlying philosophical grounding for the research.

Realist Review as a Foundational Platform

The lack of practical examples of critical realist use is perhaps not difficult to understand given the philosophy provides little real methodological guidance. Contemporary realist examination requires precision and contextualized detail, this contextualization being a necessary consequence of an underlying, ontologically bold philosophy (Outhwaite, 1987, p. 34). Along with most realist approaches, critical realism encompasses an external realism in its distinction between the world and our experience of it. This assumption necessarily implies that any knowledge gained of an external world must typically be provisional, fallible, incomplete, and extendable. As Stones (1996) suggests, realist methodologies and writings need to reflect a continual commitment to caution, scepticism, and reflexivity.

In contrast to traditional realist approaches, critical realism also suggests a so-called depth realism and argues for a stratified ontology. This concept suggests that reality is made up of three ontologically distinct realms—first, the empirical, that is, experience; second, the actual, that is, events (i.e., the actual objects of experience); and third, the transcendental, non-actual or deep, that is, structures, mechanisms, and associated powers. Critical realism argues that:

the world is composed not only of events and our experience or impression of them, but also of (irreducible) structures and mechanisms, powers and tendencies, etc. that, although not directly observable, nevertheless underlie actual events that we experience and govern or produce them. (Lawson, 1997, p. 8)

The deep structures and mechanisms that make up the world are the primary focus of such an ontological realism. The realist seeks a deep knowledge and understanding of a social situation. It argues against single concentration on observed events and requires an understanding of the deeper structures and mechanisms that often belie the surface event level observation.

Bhaskar (1979) presents fundamental difficulties with the way that prediction and falsification have been used in the open systems evident within the social arena. For the critical realist, a major issue with social investigation is the inability to create closure—the aim of "experiment" in the natural sciences. Bhaskar argues that this inability implies that theory cannot be used in a predictive manner and can **only** play an explanatory role in social investigations since:

in the absence of spontaneously occurring, and given the impossibility of artificially creating, closed systems , the human sciences must confront the problem of the direct scientific study of phenomena that only manifest themselves in open systems—for which orthodox philosophy of science, with its tacit presupposition of closure, is literally useless. In particular it follows from this condition that criteria for the rational appraisal and development of theories in the social sciences, which are denied (in principle) decisive test situations, **cannot be predictive** *and so must be* **exclusively explanatory**. (Bhaskar, 1979, p. 27)

As Mingers (2002) suggests, such an argument has specific ramifications with respect to the use of statistical reasoning to predict future results. Bhaskar (1979) argues that the primary measure of the "goodness" of a theory is in its explanatory power—from Bhaskar's perspective, predictive use of theories is not possible in open social systems and therefore predictive power cannot be a measure of goodness.

As Sayer (2000) suggests the target for realist research is not the determination of an "objective" or generalisable truth but the achievement of the best we can do at the time, that is, "practically adequate" explanations. This practical focus within critical realism sees knowledge as existing in a "historically specific, symbolically mediated and expressed, practice-dependent form" (Lawson 1997) that is potentially transformable as subsequent deeper knowledge is gained. The realist denies easy generalisability and requires a heavy focus on context.

Implications for APMS Examination

The APMS examined in this study were founded on large-scale data warehousing applications that form a part of various automated business (or corporate) performance measurement systems. All projects were based on SAP's business warehouse product, and the data warehouses sourced their data from SAP's R3 enterprise resource planning (ERP) systems as well as a myriad of other non-SAP production systems. The organisations ranged from a large government business enterprise to a mixture of global commodity companies.

The data warehousing systems had the common objective of producing automatic performance measurement management reporting via a mixture of Microsoft Excel spreadsheets and Web-based reports. The objective of the APMS was for performance measures to be presented directly to senior management in a form that precluded any manual manipulation. In most cases, this was achieved through implementing new security/authorisation layers to protect the reporting document.

Most of the systems examined are languishing as implementation and process change management failed to get traction. Generally these systems have not become embedded within the various organizations as meaningful tools. They are generally used in an ad hoc fashion and are seen by some as just "expensive toys."

In contrast to the general failure, however, two of the APMS are in fact producing useful outcomes with over 60% of managers and information analysts using the tool throughout the business with production benefits being realised. A cursory examination of the different systems has not produced any easy explanation for the differences in implementation success. Given that such systems are expensive and difficult to produce, the organizations were understandably interested in determining the possible reasons for the patchy success.

This widely felt concern prompted a doctoral research study to be conducted by an experienced IS industry consultant. A discussion group involving two academics and the researcher was then formed to analyse and review the critical realist approach being utilised, resulting in this chapter. Figure 1 reflects the approach adopted in the research.

The research stages illustrated in are described below. Each stage number corresponds to the number in a circle on the figure.

1. A literature review was conducted based on the DeLone and McLean I/S Success Model (DeLone & McLean, 1992) by contrasting the DeLone and McLean Ten Year review (DeLone & McLean, 2002) and the Wixon and Watson Data Warehousing Success model (Wixom & Watson, 2001). A consolidated model was proposed based on the information systems literature. This literature review also concentrated on available operations management literature

Figure 1. Research approach

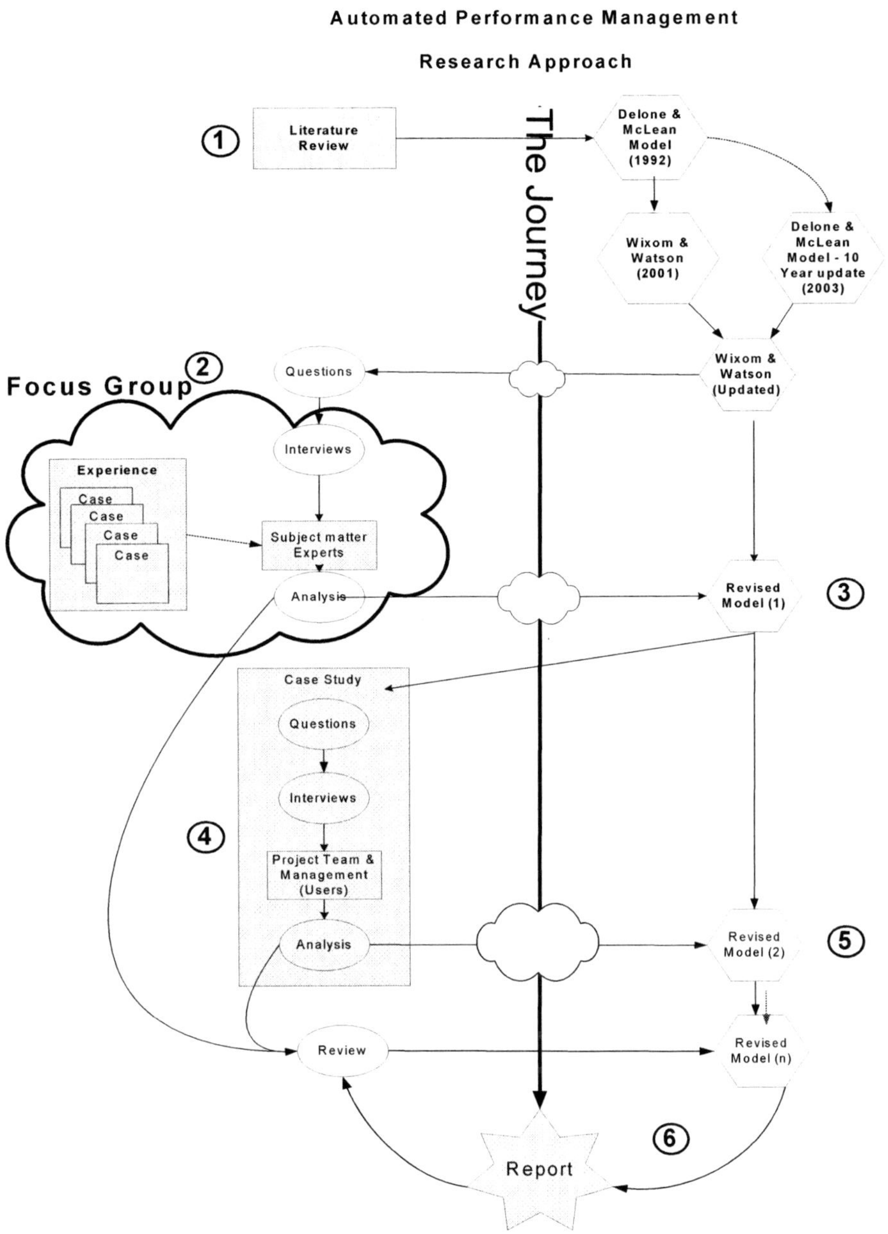

where there have been a number of recent research publications. Through a process of review and consolidation by comparing and contrasting the different domains, a model for performance measurement system success was proposed.

2. This model was then used as the basis for defining a set of questions for semi-structured, qualitative interviews.
3. Once refined, the questions were used in a set of interviews utilising a focus group (Krueger, 1988). This focus group was

composed of I/S industry experts, active in the performance measurement system area. Given the level of organizational interest in the perceived failure of the APMS, recruiting participants was not difficult. Against this data, the results were further analysed and a revised model was produced (Model 1).

4. Model 1 is being tested against a case study (Yin, 1989) with further refinements to the model being made as required. This will result in an updated model (Model 2).
5. Through a number of reviews and case interviews, more refinements to the model will occur (Model 3 & 4).
6. A final model will be synthesised and is to be included in the doctoral thesis to be submitted for examination.

The approach is based upon continual comparison of the data collected in each stage with the developing model. Constant, iterative comparison of the data with the developed model and conceptual categories leads to a continuously refined explanatory model.

Throughout the study, critical realism provided a foundational platform for developing the research. The following realist elements were important in the study development:

The Realist Focus on Context and Setting

Pawson, Greenhalgh, Harvey, and Walshe (2004) describe realist review as "a relatively new strategy for synthesizing research which has an explanatory rather than a judgemental focus. It seeks to unpack the mechanisms of how complex programmes work (or why they fail) in particular contexts and settings" (p. 21). Such methods are becoming more prevalent in the analysis of the effectiveness of social programs. It is the contention of this chapter that a similar approach can be effective in examining the heavily social and contextual nature of complex APMS implementation. Critical realist evaluation moves from the basic evaluative question—*what* works—to *what is it about this implementation that works for whom in what circumstances.*

In the context of the APMS research, it became evident that contextual issues were paramount in explaining the success and failure of the implementations. With the focus group interviews and individual case follow-up, the fundamental discussion is always around the particular circumstances of the implementation. This emphasis on context impacted the underlying research focus. The critical realist focus on retroductive prepositional-type questioning led to a contextual basis for the study seeking to answer "Under what conditions might APMS implementation prove successful?" rather than "What are the (predictive) critical success factors for an APMS implementation?" A simplistic critical success factors approach tends to deny the heavy contextuality and complexity of large-scale systems implementation.

Realist Emphasis on Explanation and Ex-Post Evaluation

The realist focus on explanation rather than prediction necessarily encourages an emphasis on ex-post evaluation. The realist would suggest that ex-ante or predictive evaluation is difficult given the highly complex nature of the implementation environment. Ex-post evaluations after the event are more in keeping with the underlying realist focus on explanation rather than prediction.

The critical realist focus on explanation rather than prediction suggests that the critical realist method involves "the postulation of a possible [structure or] mechanism, the attempt to collect evidence for or against its existence and the elimination of possible alternatives." The realist agrees that we have a good explanation when (1) the postulated mechanism is capable of explaining the phenomenon, (2) we have good reason to believe in its existence, (3) we cannot think of any equally good alternatives. (Outhwaite, 1987). Such an approach has specific impacts on the research process in that it argues for research heavily oriented toward confirming or denying theoretical proposals. For the realist, the initial explanatory focus may be on proposing (i.e., transcending or speculating) non-experienced and perhaps non-observable mechanisms and structures that may well be outside the domain of investigation. As Wad (2001, p. 2) argues:

If we take explanation to be the core purpose of science, critical realism seems to emphasise thinking instead of experiencing, and especially the process of abstraction from the domains of the actual and the empirical world to the transfactual mechanisms of the real world.

For the APMS study, the case examples were of previously implemented systems, and the focus was on confirming or denying a postulated model. The model developed from the focus group interviews is being further refined by examining an actual case study.

The Realist Need for an "Analytical Dualism"

The original Delone and McLean model (1992) of IS success in Figure 2 is realist in focus, as it emphasizes causal factors; however, the critical realist would have difficulty agreeing with the simplistic notion that organizational impacts are solely pre-determined by individual factors. The realist argues for a deeper multi-level analysis that recognizes that individual agency (micro) level impacts are only one of the components. Such an analysis ignores the duality of structure in that agency actions are both constrained and enabled by pre-existing structures.

Any research study founded on critical realism needs to reflect this duality of structure and agency. Archer (1995) proposes that such a duality is difficult to properly examine in social situations and therefore argues for an "analytical" or artificial dualism whereby structure (macro) and agency (micro) are artificially separated in order to properly examine their interaction. Hedström and Swedberg (1998) propose three basic mechanisms:

1. Situational mechanisms (macro-micro level)
2. Action-formation mechanisms (micro-micro level)
3. Transformational mechanisms (micro-macro level)

The typology implies that macro-level events or conditions affect the individual (step 1), the individual assimilates the impact of the macro-level events (step 2), and a number of individuals generate, through their actions and interactions, macro-level outcomes (step 3). Such a critical realist perspective on technology is presented by Smith (2005) when he suggests that:

Figure 2. Delone and Mclean model (1992)

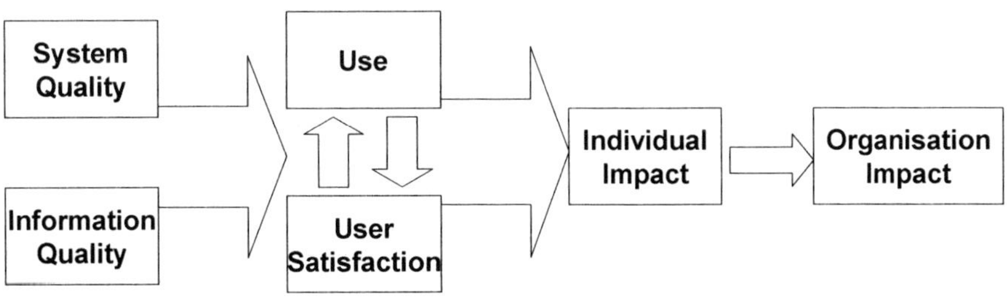

technology introduces resources and ideas (causal mechanisms) that may enable workers to change their practices, but these practices are also constrained and enabled by the structures in which they are embedded ... Thus ... a researcher must try to understand how the generative mechanisms, introduced by the technology into a particular context of structural relations that pre-existed the intervention, provided the resources and ideas that resulted in changes (or not) to individual practices that then either transform or reproduce those original structural relations. (p. 16)

Such a representation highlights the historicity of information technology (IT) implementation and argues for a consideration of the environment prior to IT initiation. The framework also suggests that any study of APMS implementation would need to view the implementation as fundamentally a change of pre-existing *social* practices.

The original Delone and McLean model emphasizes the micro-macro interaction when it suggests individual impacts aggregate to organizational impacts. However, from a realistic perspective, it has no recognition of the macro-micro and micro-micro level interactions.

The 2002 changes made to the original Delone and McLean model (see Figure 3) were the introduction of service quality and two dimensions, organisational and individual impact, being combined into one dimension called net benefits (Delone and McLean, 2002). From a realist perspective, this again moves the model further away from a realist position in that the organizational and individual impacts are conflated. Archer (1995) argues against such conflation when she suggests that "structure and agency can only be linked by examining the interplay between them over time, and that without the proper incorporation of time the problem of structure and agency can never be satisfactorily resolved" (p. 65). The static simplistic representation of Delone and McLean is inconsistent with such a view.

The models did, however, provide guidance as to the various categories that might be used in the grounded theory analysis.

An extension of Delone and McLean's original model developed by Wixom and Watson (2001) to model data warehousing success provided further depth to the analysis. The new model (Figure 4) helped to identify the various levels of analysis needed and associated impacts at each level. The

Figure 3. The reformulated I/S success model (DeLone & McLean, 2002, p. 9)

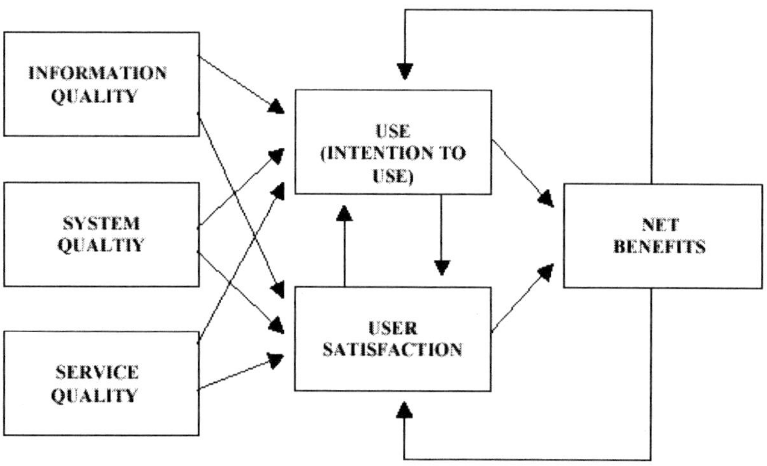

increasing richness of the model suggests a more subtle and differentiated interaction between its elements and reduces the dependence upon a few "critical" success factors.

An Emphasis on the Social Nature of IT Implementation

The defining characteristic of APMS is that it is the automated communication of key performance indicators. As such, the implementation and operation of such a system can be highly political and sensitive. Performance measurement can be defined as the process of quantifying the efficiency and effectiveness of action and a performance measurement system as the set of metrics used to quantify both the efficiency and effectiveness of actions (Bourne, Neely, et al., 2003). The development of any performance management system must adhere to the following definite stages:

- Define the performance to be measured
- Determine and agree on appropriate performance metrics
- Implement systems to monitor performance against these metrics
- Implement systems to communicate these metrics to concerned stakeholders

Each such stage in the development of a performance management system can be expected to be personalised, potentially highly political, possibly controversial, and affect the acceptance of the final management system.

The final communication of performance figures is inherently social. As Pawson et al. (2005) suggest, this collection of performance figures is usually followed by public disclosure of underperforming sectors. Such a public disclosure ideally leads to "sanction instigation" whereby the broader organizational community act to "boycott,

Figure 4. Research model for data ware housing success (Wixom & Watson, 2001)

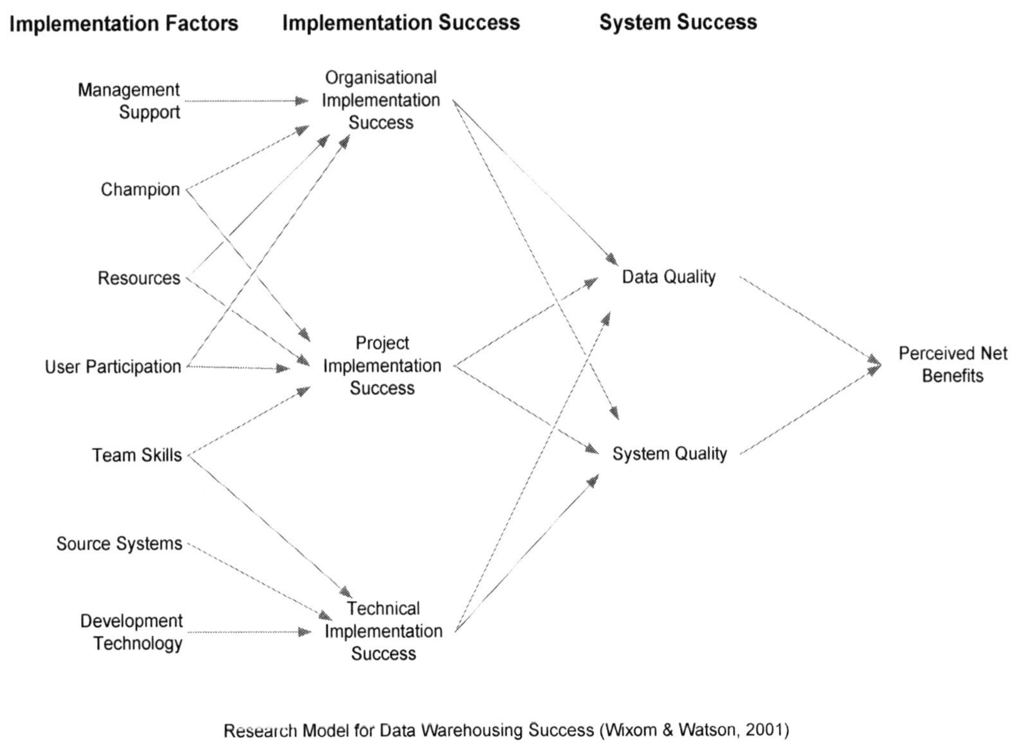

censure, reproach or control the underperforming party." The final phase is termed "miscreant response" in which "failing parties are shamed, chastised, made contrite and so improve performance in order to be reintegrated." As Pawson et al. (2005) argues these social processes are all fallible and can all lead to unintended outcomes. The initial performance metric may be inappropriate or measuring the wrong problem, the dissemination may be inappropriate, public reactions may take the form of apathy or panic rather than reproach, thus leading to attempts to "resist, reject, ignore or actively discredit the official labelling." The potential for active resistance seems more likely given the automated nature of an APMS system. Automated communication may be seen to imply a lack of trust in intervening management structures and could lead to active resistance.

Organizational goals are set by management; high-level requirements are set by management, as are timelines, resources, and objectives. The design solution of APMS, its overarching principles and objectives, depend upon the ideologies, requirements, and principles of these decision makers. These principles are based upon a normative threat (the Sarbanes-Oxley legislation and similar such acts) as well as the drive to maximise productivity through control and early intervention. The ideology of industrialization, that increasing labor productivity is the foundation of increasing wealth and the improvement of social and economic conditions, also makes rational resistance difficult. The solution of APMS is therefore conservative, preserving the power *status quo* and serving the needs of those who need to control, measure, and manipulate. Here we can observe a structure of legitimated management and regulation interacting with the agency of individual and idiosyncratic leaders and subordinates. Critical realism allows that these structures have a causative function, derived from the ontological commitment of protagonists. These causal events may have elements that can be generalized, but their universality needs to be understood in the context of agency and individualism.

Conversely, where there is an emphasis on authority and control, this is antithetical to knowledge commitments and the hostages one gives to fortune, when one gives away knowledge. One of the complicating factors in systems design in particular, as indeed it is in any form of innovation, are the implications of change for participants involved in and stakeholders affected by the change. Innovation of any kind is knowledge intensive and controversial, "uncertain, fragile, political and imperialistic" (Kanter, 1996, p. 95). It crosses boundaries, redefines job descriptions and requires close communication. This leads inexorably to the fact that "Information systems development is also a political process in which various actors stand to gain or lose power as a result of design decisions" (Robey & Markus, 1984, p. 5).

New divisions of labour and requirements for cooperation, a transcendence of current work processes, will break down existing divisions of labour and require extensive cooperation. Particularly in organisations with command and control management paradigms and Fordist conceptions of the structure of work, boundary spanning and the unimpeded flow of information will be perceived as a threat to those whose authority is based upon the existence of boundaries and fiefdoms. The adjustment and threat to power structures defined through knowledge is a high-risk area for projects whose focus and objective is to codify knowledge and ways of doing things and make them freely available. The case of APMS is particularly interesting because it is managers whose knowledge is being codified and commoditized and whose ability to intervene and massage production figures is being withdrawn. It is managers whose fiefs are becoming subject to a super-Panopticon, accessed by the CEO himself, who may ring up at 8 a.m. and complain about the previous day's poor production quality. The stance of critical realism can sensitise researchers not only to the collision of conflicting structures but also to the motivations of the protagonists who inhabit those structures and have careers to build or mortgages to pay.

People in organisations are usually aware of the importance of their knowledge to their position, status, and remuneration, and any reduction may well be met with lack of full cooperation. The implementation of APMS moves this to the next level. Martin (1988) states that "the major resource distribution by technological change is knowledge: groups with knowledge of the old system may lose control of knowledge under the new system." (p. 119) Scarbrough and Corbett (1992) assert that the higher the levels of autonomy and job specialisation, the greater the power of the job holder. If this is correct, then if these two parameters are reduced by technological change, it is more than likely that the change will be resisted at some stage of the technology change project: either in design, implementation, or use. This resistance is a denial of the legitimacy of the technological solution and may have nothing to do with whether the solution is "the best for the company" or even represents a best possible reorganisation of work processes. Critical realism recognises the role of individual agency in the withdrawal of support and legitimation for the normative and regulative structures implied by the "organisation as machine" metaphor in which APMS finds its validation. The *automated* aspect of an APMS has implications for the autonomy of the manager in that the APMS is intended to bypass the manager's intervention. The performance management aspect of the system has implications derived from surveillance and control and the concomitant power structures.

The diverse range of stakeholders, subordinate to the accountable managers, are line staff, whose actions have already been "informated" by the implementation of an operational information system. They are responsible for data entry (which must be timely and accurate for the APMS to succeed). There are the technical personnel who set up and maintain the APMS. They must understand the needs of the other "culture" and be competent in the execution of the technology. There appear to be quite different purposes and value orientations within these groups.

There is a requirement for a high degree of structure and order in the interaction between systems and the delivery of meaningful outcomes. The derivation of a few key numbers from highly complex ERP systems requires the correct functioning of many software and hardware systems and types of components, as well as standardised (highly "structurated") rules, processes, and meta data definitions.

The Ontological Depth of Critical Realism

In line with the recognition of continuing micro/macro interaction and the social implications of IT implementation, Carlsson (2003) proposes a multi-leveled investigation of the research situation. As Figure 5 indicates, the framework includes macro phenomena, like structural and institutional phenomena, as well as micro phenomena, like behaviour and interaction. The framework highlights the importance of wider macro-level issues on individual situated activity. As Carlsson suggests (2003, p. 13), the self and situated activity focus concentrates on "... the way individuals respond to particular features of their social environment and the typical situations associated with this environment" (Layder, 1993).

Critical realism is ontologically bold in the sense that it not only encompasses an external realism in its distinction between the world and our experience of it, but it also suggests a stratified ontology and a so-called depth realism in defining the objects that make up such a world. This concept suggests that reality is made up of three ontologically distinct realms—first, the empirical, that is, experience; second, the actual, that is, events (i.e., the actual objects of experience); and third, the transcendental, non-actual, or deep, that

Figure 5. A realist research map (Carlsson, 2003, p.13, adapted from Layder, 1993)

HISTORY

Element	Focus
CONTEXT	Macro social forms, e.g. gender, national culture, national economic situation
SETTING	Immediate environment of social activity, e.g. organisation, department, team
SITUATED ACTIVITY	Dynamics of face to face interaction
SELF	Biographical experience and social involvements

is structures, mechanisms, and associated powers. The deep structures and mechanisms that make up the world are thus the primary focus of such an ontological realism, *events* as such not being the primary focus. An important element within critical realism is that these deep structures and mechanisms may, in fact, be only observable through their effects and thus a causal criterion for existence is accepted:

Observability may make us more confident about what we think exists, but existence itself is not dependent on it. In virtue of this, then, rather than rely purely upon a criterion of observability for making claims about what exists, realists accept a causal criterion too (Collier, 1994). According to this a plausible case for the existence of unobservable entities can be made by reference to observable effects which can only be explained as the products of such entities.... A crucial implication of this ontology is the recognition of the possibility that powers may exist unexercised, and hence ... the nature of the real objects present at a given time constrains and enables what can happen but does not pre-determine what will happen. (Sayer, 2000, p. 12)

Realist researchers need to be able to account for the underlying ontological richness they implicitly assume and also need to reflect the belief that any knowledge gains are typically provisional, fallible, incomplete, and extendable. Realist methodologies and writings thus must reflect a continual commitment to caution, scepticism, and reflexivity.

DISCUSSION

The focus group meetings with previous APMS project participants confirmed the importance of many of the factors identified in the various models. The study is still ongoing with the in-depth examination of the case study yet to be completed. In the case study, the organization had previously tried to implement automated performance management on at least five occasions with very little success. The final attempt was, however, successful in, that the system is being used to report meaningful data. One of the key aspects being identified is that the successful APMS appears to have a degree of sustainability that other systems did not have. According to Backström, van Eijnatten, & Kira (2002), a sustainable work system can be described as a work system that consciously strives toward simultaneous development at different levels: individual, group/firm, and region/society. The term "sustainability" is also referred to as corporate sustainability (Liyanage & Kumar, 2003) and may convey a difference in meaning to many, but generally it consists of external influences that are not commonly refereed to within the information systems discipline. They can include economy and technology, ecology and demography, and governance and equity.

The notion of timeliness also emerges as an underlying structure. It addresses how quickly, when, or by what date an enhancement or change can be applied to affect the automated performance reporting. The ability to react to a new measure within a reporting cycle is very important. Governments, external regulators, and other *ex machina* bodies do not necessarily wait for a business to be ready to report a particular measure. Sometimes these measures are driven internally due to a need to correct or enhance a particular business process.

From the ongoing study, it is becoming evident that external structures and the constraints and mandates they impose have severely affected APMS implementations. Such a conclusion is consistent with the critical realist view, in that it reveals the evident analytical duality in the way that agents are both constrained and enabled by pre-existing internal and external structures that they transform and reinforce through their ongoing actions.

CONCLUSION

APMS implementation is highly complex, socially and technologically. In a sense, such systems are the pinnacle of enterprise information systems, relying upon the technological success of base systems, the adequacy of their own technology, and the organisational coherence and commitment of a wide range of affected stakeholders. In line with Pawson et al. (2005, p. 22), the use of critical realism as an underlying philosophy for the APMS research appears to offer some particular benefits:

a. It has firm roots in the social sciences and allows one to identify and make salient the external, objectified, social structures that function as causal elements in the success and failure of implementation. Using this paradigm, one is allowed to explore in depth the social aspects of systems use and implementation;
b. It is grounded in the rigor of structured, analytical philosophy, and one can be reasonably confident in its reliability and consistency as a base paradigm for research development;
c. It is not a prescriptive method or formula for developing research but provides a logic of inquiry that is "inherently pluralist and flexible," embracing both "qualitative" and "quantitative," "formative" and "summative," "prospective" and "retrospective," perspectives – it suggests but does not prescribe which "rocks to look under;"
d. It seeks not to judge but to explain and is driven by the question "What works for whom in what circumstances and in what respects?" It supports the pragmatic realization, after many years of information systems failure, that "there is no silver bullet;"
e. It learns from (rather than "controls for") real-world phenomena such as diversity, change, idiosyncrasy, adaptation, cross-contamination, and "programme failure"—its outcomes therefore make a good fit within the context of organisational learning and professional reflection;
f. It engages stakeholders systematically, as experienced but nevertheless fallible

experts whose "insider" understanding of historical reasoning and action needs to be documented, formalised, reflected upon, and validated within complex, multi-level explanatory models.

Realist review does, however, have a number of limitations:

a. It is not an easy foundation on which to build in that it recognizes complexity in social research and requires a pluralist and innovative development process. It is an approach that requires experience, both in research and in subject matter. As Pawson et al. (2004) suggest, realist review is not for the novice.
b. The research generated cannot be taken to be reproducible and has therefore limited generalisability. Expressed differently, this is an honest recognition of the fact that social systems, while they contain real structures, are in fact open-ended and informed with individual agency and situational specificity.
c. Research based around critical realism cannot provide easy answers, as much as users or researchers would like this to be the case. Conclusions reached are always provisional, fallible, incomplete, and extendable and rely upon the reader to draw conclusions about transferability and reuse.

Perhaps the greatest benefit of adopting a critical realist underlabouring is the emphasis on deep understandings and context. The emphasis throughout the study has been to try and understand why particular APMS implementations succeed whereas others did not. The underlying contextual emphasis is always on "what works for whom in what circumstance."

REFERENCES

Aastrup, J. (2002). *Networks producing intermodal transport*. Unpublished doctoral dissertation, Copenhagen Business School.

Archer, M. (1995). *Realist social theory: The morphogenetic approach.* Cambridge: Cambridge University Press.

Backström, T., Eijnatten, F. M. van, & Kira, M. (2002). A complexity perspective on sustainable work systems. In P. Docherty, J. Forslin, & A. B. Shani, (Eds.), *Creating sustainable work systems: Emerging perspectives and practice*. London: Routledge.

Bhaskar, R. (1978). *A realist theory of science*. Sussex: Harvester Press.

Bhaskar, R. (1979). *The possibility of naturalism*. Hemel, Hempstead: Harvester Wheatsheaf.

Bhaskar, R. (1986). *Scientific realism and human emancipation*. Verso: London.

Bhaskar, R. (1989). *Reclaiming reality: A critical introduction to contemporary philosophy.* London: Verso.

Bhaskar, R. (1991). *Philosophy and the idea of freedom*. Oxford: Blackwell.

Bourne, M., Neely, A., et al. (2003). Implementing performance measurement systems: A literature review. *International Journal of Business Performance Management, 5*(1), 1-24.

Carlsson, S. (2003). Advancing information systems evaluation (research): A critical realist approach. *Electronic Journal of Information Systems Evaluation, 6*(2), 11-20.

Collier, A. (1994). *Critical realism: An introduction to the philosophy of Roy Bhaskar*. London: Verso.

DeLone, W. H., & McLean, E. R. (1992). Information systems success: The quest for the dependent variable. *Information Systems Research 3*(1), 60-95.

DeLone, W. H., & McLean, E. R. (2002). Information systems success revisited. *Proceedings of the 35th Hawaii International Conference on System Sciences*, Hawaii.

Dobson, P. (2001). The philosophy of critical realism -- An opportunity for information systems research. *Information Systems Frontiers*.

Dobson, P. (2002). Critical realism and IS research—Why bother with philosophy? *Information Research*, January. Retrieved from http://InformationR.net/ir/

Fitzgerald, B., & Howcroft, D. (1998). Towards dissolution of the IS research debate: From polarization to polarity. *Journal of Information Technology, 13*, 313-326.

Fleetwood, S. (Ed.) (1999). *Critical realism in economics: Development and debate*. London: Routledge.

Hedström, P., & Swedberg, R. (1998). Social mechanisms: An introductory essay. In P. Hedström & R. Swedberg (Eds.), *Social mechanisms: An analytical approach to social theory* (pp. 1-31). Cambridge University Press, New York.

Iivari, J., Hirschheim, R., & Klein, H. K. (1998). A paradigmatic analysis contrasting information systems development approaches and methodologies. *Information Systems Research, 9*(2), 164-193.

Kanter, R. M. (1996). When a thousand flowers bloom: Structural, collective, and social conditions for innovation in organizations. In P. S. Myers (Ed.), *Knowledge management and organizational design*. Newton, MA: Butterworth-Heinemann.

Krueger, R. A. (1988). *Focus groups: A practical guide for applied research*. Newbury Park, CA: Sage Publications.

Lawson, T. (1997). *Economics and reality*. Routledge: London.

Layder, D. (1993). *New strategies in social research: An introduction and guide*. Cambridge: Polity Press.

Liyanage, J. P., & Kumar, U. (2003). Towards a value-based view on operations and maintenance performance management. *Journal of Quality in Maintenance Engineering, 9*(4), 1355-2511.

Locke, J. (1894). An essay concerning human understanding. In A. C. Fraser (Ed.), *vol. 1*. Oxford: Clarendon.

Manicas, P. (1993). Accounting as a human science. *Accounting, Organizations and Society, 18*, 147- 161.

Martin, D. D., (1988). Technological Change and Manual Wiork. In D. Gallie (Ed.), *Employment in Britain* (102-127). Oxford: Basil Balckwell.

Mingers, J. (2001). Combining IS research methods: Towards a pluralist methodology. *Information Systems Research, 12*(3), 240-259.

Mingers, J. (2002). Realizing information systems: Critical realism as an underpinning philosophy for information systems. In *Proceedings Twenty-Third International Conference on Information Systems, 295-303.*

Mutch, A. (1999). Critical realism, managers and information. *British Journal of Management, 10*, 323-333.

Mutch, A. (2000). Managers and information: Agency and structure. *Information Systems Review, 1.*

Mutch, A. (2002). Actors and networks or agents and structures: Towards a realist view of information systems. *Organization, 9*(3), 477-496.

Outhwaite, W. (1987). *New philosophies of social science: Realism, hermeneutics, and critical theory*. New York: St. Martin's Press.

Pawson, R., Greenhalgh, T., Harvey G., & Walshe K. (2004). *Realist synthesis: An introduction* (RMP Methods Paper 2/2004). Manchester, ESRC Research Methods Programme, University of Manchester.

Pawson, R., Greenhalgh, T., Harvey, G., & Walshe K. (2005). Realist review – A new method of systematic review designed for complex policy interventions. *Journal of Health Services Research & Policy 10*(1), 21–34.

Pratt, A. (1995). Putting critical realism to work: The practical implications for geographical research. *Progress in Human Geography 19*(1), 61-74.

Robey, D., & Markus, M.L. (1984). Ritual in information systems design. *MIS Quarterly, 8*, 5-15

Ryan, S., & Porter, S. (1996). Breaking the boundaries between nursing and sociology: A critical realist ethnography of the theory-practice gap. *Journal of Advanced Nursing, 24*, 413-420.

Sayer, A. (1985). Realism in geography. In R. J. Johnston (Ed.), *The future of geography* (pp. 159-173). London: Methuen.

Sayer, A. (2000). *Realism and social science*. London: Sage Publications Ltd.

Sayer, R. A. (1992). *Method in social science: A realist approach*. Routledge: London.

Scarbrough, H., & Corbett, J. M. (1992). *Technology and organization: Power, meaning and design*. Routledge: London.

Smith, M. L. (2005). *Overcoming theory-practice inconsistencies: Critical realism and information systems research*. Unpublished manuscript, Department of Information Systems, London School of Economics and Political Science, working paper 134.

Spasser, M. A. (2002). Realist activity theory for digital library evaluation: Conceptual framework and case study. *Computer Supported Cooperative Work, 11*, 81-110.

Stones, R. (1996). *Sociological reasoning: Towards a past-modern sociology*. MacMillan.

Tsang, E., & Kwan, K., (1999). Replication and theory development in organizational science: A critical realist perspective, Academy of Management Review (24:4), 759-780

Wad, P. (2001, August 17-19). *Critical realism and comparative sociology*. Draft paper for the IACR conference.

Wainwright, S. P. (1997). A new paradigm for nursing: The potential of realism. *Journal of Advanced Nursing, 26*, 1262-1271

Wilson, F. (1999). Flogging a dead horse: The implications of epistemological relativism within information systems methodological practice. *European Journal of Information Systems, 8*(3), 161-169.

Wixom, B. H., & Watson, H. J. (2001). An empirical investigation of the factors affecting data warehousing success. *MIS Quarterly, 25*(1), 17-41.

Yin, R. K. (1989). *Case study research: Design and methods (vol. 5)*. Beverley Hills, CA: SAGE Publications Ltd.

This work was previously published in the Information Resources Management Journal, Vol. 20, Issue 2, edited by M. Khosrow-Pour, pp. 138-152, copyright 2007 by IGI Publishing, formerly known as Idea Group Publishing (an imprint of IGI Global).

Chapter V
System-of-Systems Cost Estimation:
Analysis of Lead System Integrator Engineering Activities

Jo Ann Lane
University of Southern California, USA

Barry Boehm
University of Southern California, USA

ABSTRACT

As organizations strive to expand system capabilities through the development of system-of-systems (SoS) architectures, they want to know "how much effort" and "how long" to implement the SoS. In order to answer these questions, it is important to first understand the types of activities performed in SoS architecture development and integration and how these vary across different SoS implementations. This article provides results of research conducted to determine types of SoS lead system integrator (LSI) activities and how these differ from the more traditional system engineering activities described in Electronic Industries Alliance (EIA) 632 ("Processes for Engineering a System"). This research further analyzed effort and schedule issues on "very large" SoS programs to more clearly identify and profile the types of activities performed by the typical LSI and to determine organizational characteristics that significantly impact overall success and productivity of the LSI effort. The results of this effort have been captured in a reduced-parameter version of the constructive SoS integration cost model (COSOSIMO) that estimates LSI SoS engineering (SoSE) effort.

INTRODUCTION

As organizations strive to expand system capabilities through the development of system-of-systems (SoS) architectures, they want to know "how much effort" and "how long" to implement the SoS. Efforts are currently underway at the University of Southern California (USC) Center for Systems and Software Engineering (CSSE) to develop a cost model to estimate the effort associated with SoS lead system integrator (LSI) activities. The research described in this article is in support of the development of this cost model, the constructive SoS integration cost model (COSOSIMO). Research conducted to date in this area has focused more on technical characteristics of the SoS. However, feedback from USC CSSE industry affiliates indicates that the extreme complexity typically associated with SoS architectures and political issues between participating organizations have a major impact on the LSI effort. This is also supported by surveys of system acquisition managers (Blanchette, 2005) and studies of failed programs (Pressman & Wildavsky, 1973). The focus of this current research is to further investigate effort and schedule issues on "very large" SoS programs and to determine key activities in the development of SoSs and organizational characteristics that significantly impact overall success and productivity of the program.

This article first describes the context for the COSOSIMO cost model, then presents a conceptual view of the cost model that has been developed using expert judgment, describes the methodology being used to develop the model, and summarizes conclusions reached to date.

COSOSIMO CONTEXT

We are seeing a growing trend in industry and the government agencies to "quickly" incorporate new technologies and expand the capabilities of legacy systems by integrating them with other legacy systems, commercial-off-the-shelf (COTS) products, and new systems into a system of systems, generally with the intent to share information from related systems and to create new, emergent capabilities that are not possible with the existing stove-piped systems. With this development approach, we see new activities being performed to define the new architecture, identify sources to either supply or develop the required components, and then to integrate and test these high level components. Along with this "system-of-systems" development approach, we have seen a new role in the development process evolve to perform these activities: that of the LSI. A recent Air Force study (United States Air Force Scientific Advisory Board, 2005) clearly states that the SoS Engineering (SoSE) effort and focus related to LSI activities is considerably different from the more traditional system development projects. According to this report, key areas where LSI activities are more complex or different than traditional systems engineering are the system architecting, especially in the areas of system interoperability and system "ilities;" acquisition and management; and anticipation of needs.

Key to developing a cost model such as COSOSIMO is understanding what a "system-of-systems" is. Early literature research (Jamshidi, 2005) showed that the term "system-of-systems" can mean many things across different organizations. For the purposes of the COSOSIMO cost model development, the research team has focused on the SoS definitions provided in Maier (1999) and Sage and Cuppan (2001): an evolutionary net-centric architecture that allows geographically distributed component systems to exchange information and perform tasks within the framework that they are not capable of performing on their own outside of the framework. This is often referred to as "emergent behaviors." Key issues in developing an SoS are the security of information shared between the various component systems, how to get the right information to the right destinations efficiently without overwhelming users with unnecessary or obsolete information, and how to maintain dynamic networks so that component system "nodes" can enter and leave the SoS.

Today, there are fairly mature tools to support the estimation of the effort and schedule associated with the lower-level SoS component systems (Boehm, Valerdi, Lane, & Brown 2005). However, none of these models supports the estimation of LSI SoSE activities. COSOSIMO, shown in Figure 1, is a parametric model currently under development to compute just this effort. The goal is to support activities for estimating the LSI effort in a way that allows users to develop initial estimates and then conduct tradeoffs based on architecture and development process alternatives.

Recent LSI research conducted by reviewing LSI statements of work identifies the following typical LSI activities:

- Concurrent engineering of requirements, architecture, and plans
- Identification and evaluation of technologies to be integrated
- Source selection of vendors and suppliers
- Management and coordination of supplier activities
- Validation and feasibility assessment of SoS architecture
- Continual integration and test of SoS-level capabilities
- SoS-level implementation planning, preparation, and execution
- On-going change management at the SoS level and across the SoS-related integrated product teams to support the evolution of requirements, interfaces and technology.

With the addition of this new cost model to the constructive cost model (COCOMO) suite of cost models, one can easily develop more comprehensive estimates for the total SoS development, as shown in Figure 2.

LSI EFFORT ESTIMATION APPROACH

As mentioned above, key to an LSI effort estimation model is having a clear understanding of the SoSE activities performed by the organization as well as which activities require the most effort. In addition, it is important to understand how these SoSE activities differ from the more traditional systems engineering activities. Analysis presented in Lane (2005) describes how the typical LSI SoSE activities differ from the more traditional system engineering activities identified in EIA 632 (Electronic Industries Alliance, 1999) and the Software Engineering Institute (SEI) Capability Maturity Model Integration (CMMI) (Software Engineering Institute, 2001). Subsequently, Delphi surveys conducted with USC CSSE industry affiliates have identified key size drivers and cost drivers for LSI effort and are shown in Table 1.

Because there are concerns about the availability of effort data from a sufficient number of SoS programs to support model calibration and validation, current efforts are focusing on

Figure 1. COSOSIMO model structure

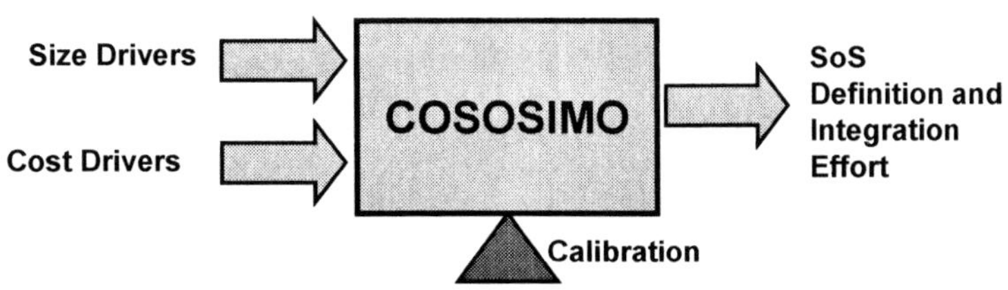

Figure 2. Architecture-based SoS cost estimation

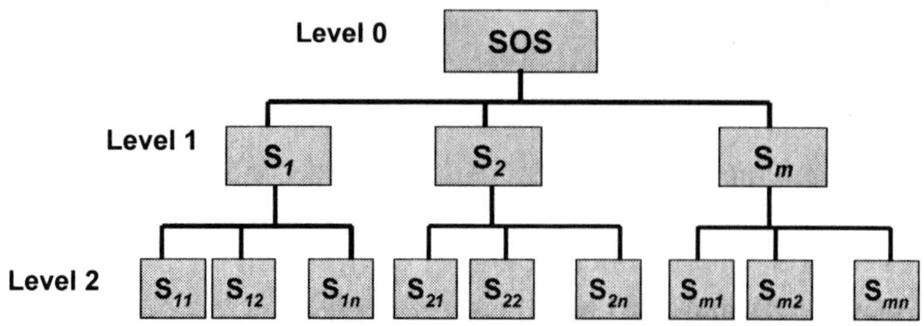

Activity	Levels	Cost Model
SoS Lead System Integrator Effort (SoS scoping, planning, requirements, architecting; source selection; teambuilding, re-architecting, feasibility assurance with selected suppliers; incremental acquisition management; SoS integration and test; transition planning, preparation, and execution; and continuous change, risk, and opportunity management)	Level 0, and other levels if lower level systems components are also SoSs	COSOSIMO
Development of SoS Software-Intensive Infrastructure and Integration Tools	Level 0	COCOMO II
System Engineering for SoS Components	Levels 1-n	COSYSMO
Software Development for Software-Intensive Components	Levels 1-n	COCOMO II
COTS Assessment and Integration for COTS-based Components	Levels 1-n	COCOTS

Table 1. COSOSIMO cost model parameters

Size Drivers	Cost Drivers
• # SoS-related requirements • # SoS interface protocols • # independent component system organizations • # SoS scenarios • # unique component systems	• Requirements understanding • Architecture maturity • Level of service requirements • Stakeholder team cohesion • SoS team capability • Maturity of LSI processes • Tool support • Cost/schedule compatibility • SoS Risk Resolution • Component system maturity and stability • Component system readiness

defining a "reduced parameter set" cost model or ways to estimate parts of the LSI effort using fewer, but more specific, parameters. The following paragraphs present the results of this recent research.

Further observations of LSI organizations indicate that the LSI activities can be grouped into three areas: 1) planning, requirements management, and architecting (PRA), 2) source selection and supplier oversight (SS), and 3) SoS integration and testing (I&T). There are typically different parts of the LSI organization that are responsible for these three areas. Figure 3 illustrates, conceptually, how efforts for these three areas are distributed across the SoS development life cycle phases of inception, elaboration, construction, and transition for a given increment or evolution of SoS development.

Planning, requirements, and architecting begin early in the life cycle. As the requirements are

Figure 3. Conceptual LSI effort profile

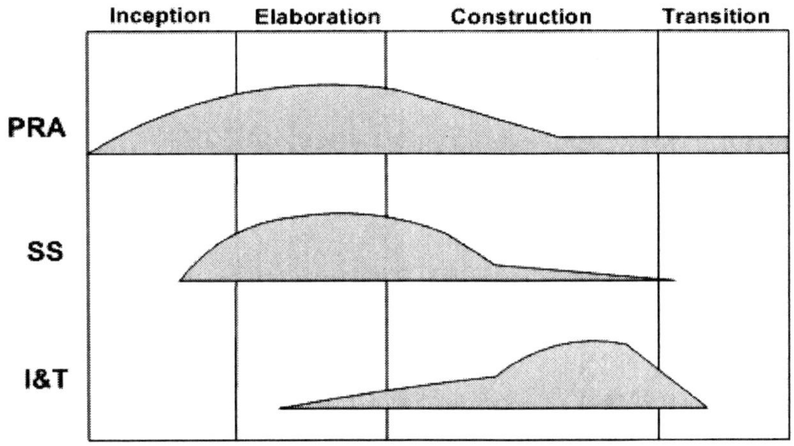

refined and the SoS architecture is defined and matured, source selection activities can begin to identify component system vendors and to issue contracts to incorporate the necessary SoS-enabling capabilities. With a mature SoS architecture and the identification of a set of component systems for the current increment, the integration team can begin the integration and test planning activities. Once an area ramps up, it continues through the transition phase at some nominal level to ensure as smooth a transition as possible and to capture lessons learned to support activities and plans for the next increment. Boehm and Lane (2006) describe how some of these activities directly support the current plan-driven SoS development effort while others are more agile, forward looking, trying to anticipate and resolve problems before they become huge impacts. The goal is to stabilize development for the current increment while deferring as much change as possible to future increments. For example, the planning/requirements/architecture group continues to manage the requirements change traffic that seems to be so common in these large systems, only applying those changes to the current increment that are absolutely necessary and deferring the rest to future increments. The architecture team also monitors current increment activities in order to make necessary adjustments to the architecture to handle cross-cutting technology issues that arise during the component system supplier construction activities. Likewise, the supplier oversight group continues to monitor the suppliers for risks, cost, and schedule issues that arise out of SoS conflicts with the component system stakeholder needs and desires. As the effort ramps down in the transition phase, efforts are typically ramping up for the next increment or evolution.

By decomposing the COSOSIMO cost model into three components that correspond to the three primary areas of LSI SoSE effort, the parameter set for each COSOSIMO component can be reduced from the full set and the applicable cost drivers made more specific to the target area. Table 2 shows the resulting set of size and cost drivers for each of the three primary areas. This approach allows the model developers to calibrate and validate the model components with fewer parameters and data sets. It also allows the collection of data sets from organizations that are only responsible for a part of the LSI SoSE activities. Finally, this approach to LSI SoSE effort estimation allows the cost model to provide estimates for the three areas, as well as a total estimate—a key request from USC CSSE industry affiliates supporting this research effort.

Table 2. COSOSIMO parameters by SoSE area

COSOSIMO Component	Associated Size Drivers	Associated Cost Drivers
PRA	• # SoS-related requirements • # SoS interface protocols	• Requirements understanding • Level of service requirements • Stakeholder team cohesion • SoS PRA capability • Maturity of LSI PRA processes • PRA tool support • Cost/schedule compatibility with PRA processes • SoS PRA risk resolution
SS	• # independent component system organizations	• Requirements understanding • Architecture maturity • Level of service requirements • SoS SS capability • Maturity of LSI SS processes • SS tool support • Cost/schedule compatibility with SS activities • SoS SS risk resolution
I&T	• # SoS interface protocols • # SoS scenarios • # unique component systems	• Requirements understanding • Architecture maturity • Level of service requirements • SoS I&T capability • Maturity of LSI I&T processes • I&T tool support • Cost/schedule compatibility with I&T activities • SoS I&T risk resolution • Component system maturity and stability • Component system readiness

Detailed definitions and proposed ratings for these parameters may be found in Lane (2006). The following provides a brief description of each of the COSOSIMO parameters. Note that several of the COSOSIMO parameters are similar to those defined for the constructive systems engineering cost model (COSYSMO) and are identified in the descriptions below.

COSOSIMO Size Drivers

Number of SoS-Related Requirements[1]

This driver represents the number of requirements for the SoS of interest at the SoS level. Requirements may be functional, performance, feature, or service-oriented in nature depending on the methodology used for specification. They may also be defined by the customer or contractor. SoS requirements can typically be quantified by counting the number of applicable shalls, wills, shoulds, and mays in the SoS or marketing specification. Note: Some work may be required to decompose requirements to a consistent level so that they may be counted accurately for the appropriate SoS-of-interest.

Number of SoS Interface Protocols

The number of distinct net-centric interface protocols to be provided/supported by the SoS framework. Note: This does NOT include interfaces internal to the SoS component systems, but it does include interfaces external to the SoS and between the SoS component systems. Also note that this is not a count of total interfaces (in many SoSs, the total number of interfaces may be very dynamic as component systems come and go in the SoS environment—in addition, there may be multiple instances of a given type of component system), but rather a count of distinct protocols at the SoS level.

Number of Independent Component System Organizations

The number of organizations managed by the LSI that are providing SoS component systems.

Number of Operational Scenarios[1]

This driver represents the number of operational scenarios that an SoS must satisfy. Such scenarios include both the nominal stimulus-response thread plus all of the off-nominal threads resulting from bad or missing data, unavailable processes, network connections, or other exception-handling cases. The number of scenarios can typically be quantified by counting the number of SoS states, modes, and configurations defined in the SoS concept of operations or by counting the number of "sea-level" use cases (Cockburn, 2001), including off-nominal extensions, developed as part of the operational architecture.

Number of Unique Component Systems

The number of types of component systems that are planned to operate within the SoS framework. If there are multiple versions of a given type that have different interfaces, then the different versions should also be included in the count of component systems.

COSOSIMO Cost Drivers

Requirements Understanding[1]

This cost driver rates the level of understanding of the SoS requirements by all of the affected organizations. For the PRA sub-model, it includes the PRA team as well as the SoS customers and sponsors, SoS PRA team members, component system owners, users, and so forth. For the SS sub-model, it is the understanding level between the LSI and the component system suppliers/vendors. For the I&T sub-model, it is the level of understanding between all of the SoS stakeholders with emphasis on the SoS I&T team members.

Level of Service Requirements[1]

This cost driver rates the difficulty and criticality of satisfying the ensemble of level of service requirements or key performance parameters (KPPs), such as security, safety, transaction speed, communication latency, interoperability, flexibility/adaptability, and reliability. This parameter should be evaluated with respect to the scope of the sub-model to which it pertains.

Team Cohesion[1]

Represents a multi-attribute parameter, which includes leadership, shared vision, diversity of stakeholders, approval cycles, group dynamics, integrated product team (IPT) framework, team dynamics, trust, and amount of change in responsibilities. It further represents the heterogeneity in stakeholder community of the end users, customers, implementers, and development team. For each sub-model, this parameter should be evaluated with respect to the appropriate LSI team (e.g., PRA, SS, or I&T).

Team Capability

Represents the anticipated level of team cooperation and cohesion, personnel capability, and continuity, as well as LSI personnel experience with the relevant domains, applications, language, and tools. For each sub-model, this parameter should be evaluated with respect to the appropriate LSI team (e.g., PRA, SS, or I&T).

Process Maturity

A parameter that rates the maturity level and completeness of the LSI's processes and plans. For each sub-model, this parameter should be evaluated with respect to the appropriate LSI team processes (e.g., PRA, SS, or I&T).

Tool Support[1]

Indicates the coverage, integration, and maturity of the tools in the SoS engineering and management environments. For each sub-model, this parameter should be evaluated with respect to the tool support available to appropriate LSI team (e.g., PRA, SS, or I&T).

Cost/Schedule Compatibility

The extent of business or political pressures to reduce the cost and schedule associated with the LSI's activities and processes. For each sub-model, this parameter should be evaluated with respect to the cost/schedule compatibility for appropriate LSI team activities (e.g., PRA, SS, or I&T).

Risk Resolution

A multi-attribute parameter that represents the number of major SoS/LSI risk items, the maturity of the associated risk management and mitigation plan, compatibility of schedules and budgets, expert availability, tool support, and level of uncertainty in the risk areas. For each sub-model, this parameter should be evaluated with respect to the risk resolution activities for the associated LSI team (e.g., PRA, SS, or I&T).

Architecture Maturity

A parameter that represents the level of maturity of the SoS architecture. It includes the level of detail of the interface protocols and the level of understanding of the performance of the protocols in the SoS framework. Two COSOSIMO sub-models use this parameter, and it should be evaluated in each case with respect to the LSI activities covered by the sub-model of interest.

Component System Maturity and Stability

A multi-attribute parameter that indicates the maturity level of the component systems (number of new component systems versus number of component systems currently operational in other environments), overall compatibility of the component systems with each other and the SoS interface protocols, the number of major component system changes being implemented in parallel with the SoS framework changes, and the anticipated change in the component systems during SoS integration activities.

Component System Readiness

This indicates readiness of component systems for integration. User evaluates level of verification and validation (V&V) that has/will be performed prior to integration and the level of subsystem integration activities that will be performed prior to integration into the SoS integration lab.

COSOSIMO COST MODEL DEVELOPMENT METHODOLOGY

The COSOSIMO cost model is being developed using the proven cost model development methodology developed over the last several years at the USC CSSE. This methodology, described in (Boehm, Abts, Brown, Chulani, Clark, & et al., 2002), is illustrated in Figure 4.

For COSOSIMO, the *literature review* has focused on the definitions of SoSs and SoSE; the role and scope of activities typically performed by LSIs; and analysis of cost factors used in related software, systems engineering, and COTS integration cost models, as well as related system dynamics models that investigate candidate SoSE cost factors.

The *behavioral analyses* determine the potential range of values for the candidate cost drivers and the relative impact that each has on the overall effort associated with the relevant SOSE activities. For example, if the stakeholder team cohesion is very high, what is the impact on the PRA effort? Likewise, if the stakeholder team cohesion is very low, what is the resulting impact on PRA effort? The results of the behavioral analyses are then used to *develop a preliminary model form*. The parameters include a set of one or more size drivers, a set of exponential scale factors, and a set of effort multipliers. Cost drivers that are related to economies/diseconomies of scale as size is increased are combined into an exponential factor. Other cost drivers that have a more linear behavior with respect to size drivers are combined into an effort multiplier.

Next, the model parameters, definitions, range of values, rating scales, and behaviors are reviewed with industry and research experts using *a wideband Delphi process*. The consensus of the experts is used to update the preliminary model. In addition to expert judgement, *actual effort data* is collected from successful projects covering the LSI activities of interest. A second model, based on actual data fitting, is then developed. Finally, the expert judgment and actual data *models are combined using Bayesian techniques*. In this process, more weight is given to expert judgement when actual data is not consistent or sparse, and more weight is given to actual data when the data is fairly consistent and experts do not strongly agree.

Figure 4. USC CSE cost model development methodology

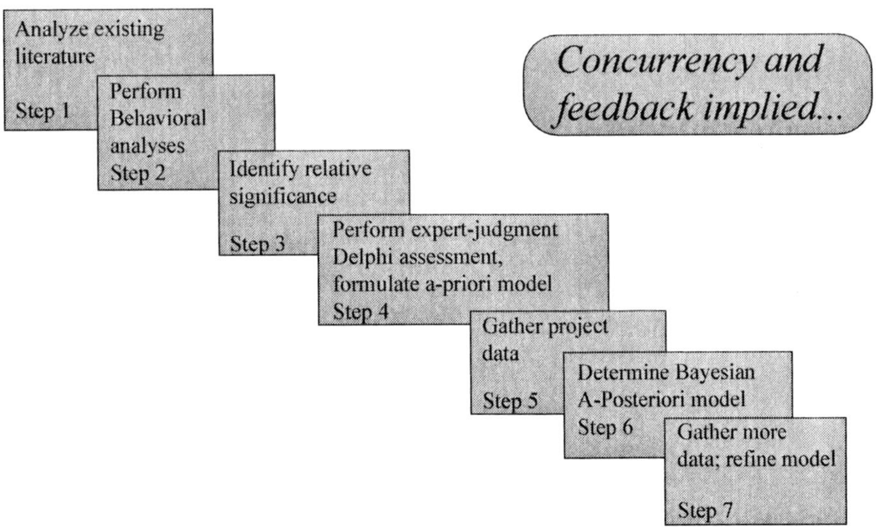

Since technologies and engineering approaches are constantly evolving, it is important to *continue data collection and model analysis* and update the model when appropriate. Historically, this has led to parameters related to older technologies being dropped and new parameters added. In the case of COSOSIMO, it will be important to track the evolution of SoS architectures and integration approaches and the development of convergence protocols.

For COSOSIMO, each of the sub-models will go through this development process. Once the sub-models are calibrated and validated, they may be combined to estimate the total LSI effort for a proposed SoS development program. To date, several expert judgment surveys have been conducted and actual data collection is in process.

CONCLUSION

LSI organizations are realizing that if more traditional processes are used to architect and integrate SoSs, it will take too long and too much effort to find optimal solutions and build them. Preliminary analysis of LSI activities show that while many of the LSI activities are similar to those described in EIA 632 and the SEI's CMMI, LSIs are identifying ways to combine agile processes with traditional processes to increase concurrency, reduce risk, and further compress overall schedules. In addition, effort profiles for the key LSI activities (the up-front effort associated with SoS abstraction, architecting, source selection, systems acquisition, and supplier and vendor oversight during development, as well as the effort associated with the later activities of integration, test, and change management) show that the percentage of time spent on key activities differs considerably from the more traditional system engineering efforts. By capturing the effects of these differences in organizational structure and system engineering processes in a reduced parameter version of COSOSIMO, management will have a tool that will better predict LSI SoSE effort and to conduct "what if" comparisons of different development strategies.

REFERENCES

Blanchette, S. (2005). *U.S. Army acquisition – The program executive officer perspective*, (Special Report CMU/SEI-2005-SR-002). Pittsburgh, PA: Software Engineering Institute.

Boehm, B., Abt, C., Brown, A., Chulani, S., Clark, & et al. (2000). *Software cost estimation with COCOMO II.* Upper Saddle River, NJ: Prentice Hall.

Boehm, B., Valerdi, R., Lane, J., & Brown, A. (2005). COCOMO suite methodology and evolution. *CrossTalk, 18*(4), 20-25.

Boehm, B., & Lane, J. (2006). 21st century processes for acquiring 21st century systems of systems. *CrossTalk, 19*(5), 4-9.

Cockburn, A. (2001). *Writing effective use cases.* Boston: Addison-Wesley.

Electronic Industries Alliance. (1999). EIA Standard 632: Processes for engineering a system.

Jamshidi, M. (2005). System-of-systems engineering - A definition. *Proceedings of IEEE System, Man, and Cybernetics (SMC) Conference.* Retrieved January 29, 2005 from http://ieeesmc2005.unm.edu/SoSE_Defn.htm

Lane, J. (2005). *System of systems lead system integrators: Where do they spend their time and what makes them more/less efficient.* (Tech. Rep. No. 2005-508.) University of Southern California Center for Systems and Software Engineering, Los Angeles, CA.

Lane, J. (2006). *COSOSIMO Parameter Definitions.* (Tech. Rep. No. 2006-606). University of Southern California Center for Systems and Software Engineering, Los Angeles, CA.

Maier, M. (1998). Architecting principles for systems-of-systems. *Systems Engineering, 1*(4), 267-284.

Pressman, J., & Wildavsky, A. (1973). *Implementation: How great expectations in Washington are dashed in Oakland.* Oakland, CA: University of California Press.

Sage, A., and Cuppan, C. (2001). On the systems engineering and management of systems of systems and federations of systems. *Information, Knowledge, and Systems Management 2,* 325-345.

Software Engineering Institute (2001). *Capability maturity model integration* (CMMI) (Special report CMU/SEI-2002-TR-001). Pittsburgh, PA: Software Engineering Institute.

United States Air Force Scientific Advisory Board (2005). *Report on system-of-systems engineering for Air Force capability development.* (Public Release SAB-TR-05-04). Washington, DC: HQUSAF/SB.

Valerdi, R (2005). *The constructive systems engineering cost model (COSYSMO).* Unpublished doctoral dissertation, University of Southern California, Los Angeles.

ENDNOTE

1 Adapted to SoS environment from COSYSMO (Valerdi, 2005).

This work was previously published in the Information Resources Management Journal, Vol. 20, Issue 2, edited by M. Khosrow-Pour, pp. 23-32, copyright 2007 by IGI Publishing, formerly known as Idea Group Publishing (an imprint of IGI Global).

Chapter VI
Mixing Soft Systems Methodology and UML in Business Process Modeling

Kosheek Sewchurran
University of Cape Town, South Africa

Doncho Petkov
Eastern Connecticut State University, USA

ABSTRACT

The chapter provides an action research account of formulating and applying a new business process modeling framework to a manufacturing processes to guide software development. It is based on a mix of soft systems methodology (SSM) and the Unified Modeling Language (UML) business process modeling extensions suggested by Eriksson and Penker. The combination of SSM and UML is justified through the ideas on Multimethodology by Mingers. The Multimethodology framework is used to reason about the combination of methods from different paradigms in a single intervention. The proposed framework was applied to modeling the production process in an aluminum rolling plant as a step in the development of a new information system for it. The reflections on the intervention give details on how actual learning and appreciation is facilitated using SSM leading to better UML models of business processes.

INTRODUCTION

Alter (2006) points the fact that techno-centric analysis of business and Information Technology problems is one of the many causes which contributes to the poor results in information systems development. This underlines the need to bridge the description of business problem contexts with Information Systems (IS) modeling. This requires the application of an interdisciplinary body of knowledge to IS development incorporating the systems approach (see Mora et al., 2007). In calling for greater application of systems thinking in Information Systems, Alter (2006) also emphasized the dangers of promoting single non-systemic approaches, among them Business Process Re-engineering as a panacea for implementation problems. The theoretical motivations for the work on process modeling reported here are of a somewhat similar nature. A recent example of addressing just one aspect of complex problems like enterprise system implementation is a thought provoking paper by Sommer (2002:20). It recognizes that many Enterprise Resource Planning (ERP) implementation failures can be attributable to overzealous implementation cycles, a lack of top management support, traditional scope creep, inadequate requirements definition and a host of other factors but focuses only on the role of middle management in the implementation process. The resulting research model is interesting but it is impossible in our opinion to determine whether middle management or inadequate requirements definition can be taken independently from the other factors affecting IS success. It is hard to ignore the interdependencies between all factors involved. Hence, in line with Alter's (2006) ideas, we conclude that there is a fundamental need for systemic ways of capturing the richness of business processes and expressing their models more adequately for the purposes of building enterprise information systems.

Systems thinking was recently applied to the design of business processes in manufacturing by Clegg (2006). Clegg's (2006) effort was aimed at building process models that can be nested within a hierarchy but without consciously adopting any reductionist principles. Clegg (2006) uses ssystems thinking and input-transformation-output process analyses to produce a new process modeling methodology called process orientated holonic modeling. The paper's value is that it provides a systemic way of building a large scale view of business processes within a company. The effort however does not give indication of how the models can be directly used in the design of information systems. There is no discussion of how one can go from the granularity level of business processes analysis through to a granularity necessary for modeling applications development to reflect the redesigned processes. This is an issue that we attempt to address in this chapter.

The practical reason for the research discussed here emanated from the needs of the employer of the first author which at the time the project took place was an aluminium rolling and extrusion company. In the late nineties, it grappled with understanding the complexities influencing the design of business processes. It is widely accepted that the notion of a business process (see Hammer and Champy, 1993; Kumar and Hillegersberg, 2000:23-25) is central to organisational change and IT development initiatives. In other words the business process serves as the unit of design and the unit of evaluation in change programs. A fundamental activity of all these process-improvement initiatives is business analysis and modeling.

The aluminium semi-fabricator needed to support the complex manufacturing process with suitable information systems and had failed to deliver successful information systems projects using traditional approaches on a number of occasions. The company was looking for better ways of linking process modeling with the development of its information systems. It had already decided on using the Eriksson and Penker (2000) UML business modeling extensions to model business processes which had appeared in an Object Management Group's (OMG) Press book publication. There was however no agreement on how to conceptualise the context of the business situation. Some authors working in business process modeling had suggested the use of soft systems methodology (SSM) to enhance business process analysis and modeling (see Ackermann *et al.* (1999:202) and others). The general theme amongst these researchers seems to be that SSM is advocated in complex management problems because its process provides a rich enquiry process, a problem structuring process, a goal formulation process or sense making devices (Galliers (1994:165); Ormerod (1995:292); Mingers (1995:21); Nuseibeh and Easterbrook (2000:43)). Intuitively, SSM seemed to be a suitable technique to employ in assisting with understanding the problem situation before modeling business processes but it was unclear at the time when the practical need for this project emerged (around 2000) how to combine it effectively with UML in practice in spite of a few publications dealing with the issue on a conceptual level (e.g. see Lane, 1998). The prior experience of the second author, with SSM, see Petkov et al. (2007) was another starting point in the development of the approach which was produced to address the practical problem of the aluminium manufacturer.

The aim of the chapter is to present an innovative systemic framework for modeling business processes, mixing SSM and Eriksson and Penker's (2000) business modeling extensions. Such a combination had not been applied in the same intervention and is not described in the literature before to the best of our knowledge. The contribution of the chapter to the field of Information Systems is in the formulation and justification of the proposed framework following Mingers's (2001) multimethodology concepts and other advances in systems thinking. The proposed framework is applicable with other variants of UML that are currently being developed to improve business modeling. The reflections on the implementation of the framework are another contribution of the chapter. The research had a direct practical contribution through the development of a model of the process of delivery of essential product information to the shop floor during the production process. That helped to resolve subsequently major stumbling blocks in the modeling of the business processes and the development of information systems at the aluminium company.

The following section reviews the problem situation associated with finding more effective techniques to define and communicate information system requirements at the aluminium semi-fabricator. Following this are an overview of business process modeling and a review of the work done in the area of combining SSM with information systems modeling techniques. This is followed by the formulation of the proposed framework combining SSM and UML in the modeling of the production processes, by a brief description how it was applied and by reflections on its implementation. The conclusion summarises the results of this chapter and provides a few directions for future research.

AN OVERVIEW OF THE SITUATION OF CONCERN

The aluminium semi-fabricator, located in South Africa, had embarked on an expansion and transformation of its manufacturing and information systems capabilities in the late 1990s. Prior efforts to meet production information systems requirements with standard Enterprise Resource Planning (ERP) packages were unsuccessful. After several attempts, the ERP approach was abandoned and the company adopted to pursue customised development. The semi-fabricator had a combination of manual and automated machinery. It aimed at integrating, in a better way, shop floor automation with its plant production planning systems. The plant was also unique in that it manufactured diverse products, which were ordered in many specific sizes and features.

Such a flexible business strategy is threatened by fluctuating process conditions and is dependant on constantly having the manufacturing process under control. The most urgent business priority facing the semi-fabricator at the time of this project was eliminating customer complaints. Customers were not satisfied with the erratic quality being supplied. A key factor causing the production of poor products was that operators were not receiving adequate information to set-up, control and monitor the machine. The operators and the traditional manual mechanisms of assimilating new product knowledge gradually became a constraint for the business to continue with its flexible manufacturing strategy. According to management the challenge was to get the right elements of information to the shop floor at the right time, without flooding the operator with excessive details, but making sure the operator gets the critical information that is needed.

Management at the aluminium semi-fabricator had tried in the past to improve the situation through the introduction of technology using traditional approaches to systems analysis and design. According to the plant engineering manager, these attempts were not successful for the following reasons (Torr, 2001):

1. There was a tendency to focus on optimization and automation (technical issues) instead of first measuring, then understanding and finally controlling through IT (learning).
2. There has always been a tendency to be more sophisticated than the users could appreciate or the business was ready to support.
3. Point solutions introduced at particular machine centers were poorly integrated with the remainder of the plant systems and slowly fell into disuse.

In this project we focused particularly on an important production management problem: modeling the process of delivery of essential product information to the shop floor during execution of a customer's order. This process was crucial for improvement of production quality in the plant. The difficulties that the plant was experiencing were related to the distortion of the information by the time it reached the shop floor and were similar to the concerns about the role of middle management discussed in Sommer (2002). The specific problem was that the existing situation of concern was not captured well through a well defined and acceptable human activity system that took into consideration the major issues identified by the stakeholders. Hence there was no starting point to begin thinking about better implementation of information systems to serve the production process.

Mingers (1995:19) along with other researchers argues that related types of failures can ultimately be seen as failures in expectation, i.e. the final information system does not in some way meet the legitimate expectations of the stakeholders. Mingers further states that information system failures ultimately occur as a result of the limitations in conventional (hard) information system analysis and design methodologies. Traditional approaches to information systems design have been attracting a considerable amount of criticism recently because of their lack of attention to social, political and cultural issues. In spite of the fact that some of that criticism has appeared about a decade ago (see Stowell, 1995) there is still very little practical progress to date in the IT field on this issue. Through our work we realized that the positivist, objectivist assumptions with which traditional approaches were underpinned made them inappropriate for the analysis or modeling of production systems at the aluminium semi-fabricator, where there were many stakeholders with potentially divergent interests. Hence we needed to apply relevant interpretive methods together with other existing IS approaches to capture the existing diverse perspectives for modeling the business processes. The latter are briefly reviewed in the next section.

A BRIEF OVERVIEW OF BUSINESS PROCESS RESEARCH

Many business modeling methods have been proposed in the literature. The most important approach that has been receiving attention in recent years is the "process-driven modeling" technique, in which the business is analysed in terms of main business processes (Herzum and Sims, 2000:428). Despite all the effort in this area, business modeling is a poorly understood research area according to Osterwalde, Pigneur and Tucci (2005). They suggest the following definition for business models:

A business model is a conceptual tool that contains a set of elements and their relationships and allows expressing the business logic of a specific firm. It is a description of the value a company offers to one or several segments of customers and of the architecture of the firm and its network of partners for creating, marketing, and delivering this value and relationship capital, to generate profitable and sustainable revenue streams. Osterwalde, Pigneur and Tucci (2005)

The emphasis on business models being conceptual tools is an interesting innovative concept which we adopted as one of the starting points in our work.

Our literature review shows that business process modeling research is reported along three themes. The first theme focuses on the symbology and objective recording of reality as symbols and relationships to other symbols following the stated rules which accompany the symbology. Work done on flow charting, UML modeling, IDEFIX, Petri nets etc can be classified as methods belonging to this first theme (see Peppard and Rowland, 1995; Kettinger, 1997; Osterwalder et al., 2005 and others). It is done typically from a functionalist and reductionist point of view even if the complexity of the problem is acknowledged (Edwards, Braganza and Lambert, 2000). A notable exception is the previously mentioned system approach to modeling business processes suggested by Clegg (2006) which incorporates input-output analysis to structure processes without dealing with the modeling details. The second theme focuses on using modeling for learning about a problematic situation as a social setting. This is the major feature characterizing the application of soft systems thinking (e.g. see Checkland and Holwell, 1998; Checkland and Scholes (1999) and others). The third theme focuses on preceding methods from the first theme with methods from the second theme (see Mingers, 1992; Mingers, 1995; Lane, 1998; Galliers, 1994; and the extensive review in Mathiassen and Nielsen, 2000). Further discussion on business process modeling research may be found in a recent review by Adamides and Karacipidilis (2006), in Barber et al. (2003) and in Pedreira et al. (2007).

Among the methods suggested in the first group an important contribution is the work by Eriksson and Penker (2000). Eriksson and Penker built on the momentum established by the use of UML in software systems design and proposed their extensions with the goal of enabling business modeling with a language that has been used mainly for software systems design. The result is not ground-breaking in terms of business modeling, but presents a synthesis of concepts relevant for modeling business process that are integrated in a UML model and for this reason we found it of interest while working on this project.

Analyzing previous attempts for combining different methods from diverse methodologies in the same operations research intervention, Munro and Mingers (2002) outline a common weakness in them: the combination of these approaches in practice was performed in an ad-hoc manner with no consideration of their theoretical basis linked to interpretive and positivist paradigms. The need to define a business process modeling approach that combines the power of methods from different paradigms and avoids the above criticism was another motivation for our work. The following section gives a review of literature on SSM being linked to Information Systems methodologies.

ON LINKING OF SOFT SYSTEMS METHODOLOFY WITH OTHER INFORMATION SYSTEMS METHODS

Work on Comparing the Foundations of SSM and Information Systems Methods

Publications in the area of information systems show that many researchers have tried to use SSM to improve the requirements determination process in IS development (see Wilson, 1990; Stowell, 1995; Mingers, 1995; Stowell, 1997; Lopes and Bryant, 2004; Al-Humaidan and Rossiter, 2004; and others). These and other sources discuss the benefits and the concerns about how the techniques from two philosophical backgrounds are linked without compromising the advantages the individual techniques provide (see Mingers, 1992). Mingers (1995:45) acknowledges that SSM and information systems analysis and design are philosophically incompatible but also indicates that he does not see how the incompatibility is a serious problem because there must be a path toward greater concreteness, which can result in action being taken. The same author states that although a final design is then used to take action, the design can change through the design process to accommodate new or changed needs. Mingers (1995:45) also explains that, by embedding hard elements into the process, there are advantages to be gained from using SSM as the guiding process for the entire project. According to Mingers, SSM has several advantages over IS approaches because the entire development cycle is based on learning, which is the strength of SSM. In addition to the attempts to improve information systems delivery SSM has also been used to enhance business improvement programs (Ackermann *et al.* 1999:202).

Broad participation is essential to soft systems thinking, philosophically because it provides justification for the objectivity of the results and practically because it generates creativity and ensures acceptance of the proposed system. Although this is recognised by SSM, the processes entailed by SSM do not prescribe a method of encouraging broad participation. Jackson (2003) argues that soft systems thinkers believe in a consensual social world because they take the possibility of participation for granted and see it as a remedy for so many organisation problems. Perhaps because of its significance, soft systems thinkers play down the obstacles to full and effective participation. Although comparing the system model with the reality helps illuminate the assumptions of the participants, there is little in SSM to guide the participants towards taking action and hence there is a need to combine it with other methods to initiate taking action.

The information systems modeling techniques discussed in the IS literature analyse and describe the technical features of information systems instead of the required business architecture, goals, resources, rules and actual work required by the business. A notable exception is the emerging body of knowledge on the Work Systems Method (see Alter, 2006). Therefore, neither structured IS approaches nor Object Oriented Analysis methods like Eriksson and Penker's (2000) business modeling extensions appear to provide a comprehensive enough business modeling approach on their own.

Aspects of linking SSM with information systems development are discussed in Doyle, Wood and Wood-Harper (1993), Lewis (1993), Mathiassen and Nielsen (2000), Petkova and Roode (1999) and others. Although there are different perceptions of the research into ways of linking SSM with information systems analysis and design, the critics do not think the linking is unnecessary, or a bad idea (Mingers, 1995:48). The critics appear to be more concerned with questions about how the techniques are combined. According to the survey by Munro and Mingers (2002) combination arise in most cases without a consideration for the methodological justification of such combinations. This was another motivation behind this research. The next sub-section deals with past attempts at combining SSM and UML leading to a further justification for the approach we propose in this chapter.

On Prior Research on SSM and UML Combinations

Bustard, He and Wilke (2000) present an argument that links SSM with use case analysis. There is no clear distinction in their paper between architectural modeling, analysis models and design models. The authors do not emphasize the difference in the ontological assumptions between SSM and use case analysis. This is precisely the concern this chapter attempts to treat.

Lopes and Bryant (2004) show that there is a connection between patterns, enterprise architecture and SSM. According to them, these techniques aid in unearthing a context to support decisions on further action. Lopes and Bryant (2004) state also that during a particular case study rich pictures were represented as UML diagrams. This implies however that UML diagrams were considered to be sufficiently expressive to be used as rich pictures and in our opinion such an approach prevents the utilization of SSM as a learning framework. Lopes and Bryant (2004) do not offer further comments on what specific UML views were produced. The value of the paper is in the assertion that more work is required on looking at enterprise architecture as a human activity system.

Al-Humaidan and Rossiter (2004) recognize the importance of the ontological challenge in integrating soft(SSM) and hard(UML) techniques. These authors also highlight the potential problems in using the solution proposed by Bustard et al. (2000). Similar to the approach presented in this chapter Al-Humaidan & Rossiter (2004) propose the conceptual primary task model(CPTM). The approach to map each activity from the CPTM directly to a use case is perhaps eradicating the value which business modeling or architectural approaches imply. The research reported in this chapter assumes that a use case is a specific use of a system that is part of a business process. A CPTM is more likely to map to a business process than a specific use of the system. Al-Humaidan and Rossier (2004) state that the UML modeling takes place within SSM but there are no further details provided about how this idea is implemented or formalized. No reasoning is provided on how an SSM analysis is reduced to a CPTM and use case model. Again, as with the effort by Bustard et al. (2000) the real benefit provided by SSM is hard to locate.

Champion, Stowell, & O'Callaghan provide a framework to improve the analysis, modeling and design of IS that is based on interpretive principles (Champion, Stowell, & O'Callaghan, 2005). They offer a solution that appears to emanate from the same concerns as this research but the suggested approach does not show how learning takes place or how their approach compares with the established and proven process of SSM. Their claims of underlying interpretive assumptions are similar to ours but they are not elaborated in detail in their paper.

Prior research on linking SSM and UML modeling gives the impression that the reasoning and feasibility in merging the two methodologies is being judged primarily on the level of continuity offered by moving from SSM to symbolising the desired business process and concepts. If SSM is used for business modeling there is a high probability that the concepts are new to the business and that the software development process has to continue with exploring the needs through the use of exploratory prototyping, evolutionary prototyping or incremental development. It is very unlikely that software development will follow a waterfall like process as implied by the approaches discussed above (Al-Humaidan & Rossiter, 2004; Bustard, He, & Wilkie, 2000). Developers in the 21st century are more likely to follow an agile approach (Ambler, 2005; Cockburn, 2002a, 2002b; Jacobson, 2002). An SSM application should not be trivialised to symbolic representation of objective realities. A lack of underlying theory like Multimethodology (see Mingers, 2001) gives a false sense of linearity, sequence and order, and trivialises the application of SSM. If this happens then the true benefits of using SSM are not being realised. The fundamental flaw evident in previous attempts to offer more comprehensive approaches to business process modeling is that the problem situation is not regarded as a socio-technical system explored as a learning process in order to create a shared understanding of the problem situation. Possibly the only exceptions are the prototype implementation by Adamides and Karacapilidis (2006) and the work by Champion et al. (2006), however in both cases they do not apply UML. The following section presents the implemented approach to mixing SSM and UML modeling in our practical problem and its methodological justification.

THE SYSTEMIC FRAMEWORK FOR BUSINESS PROCESS MODELING

The implemented framework was defined following the foundations of Multimethodology, a recent strand in systems thinking that justifies the mixing of methods from different paradigms. Mingers (2001:251) emphasises that Multimethodology is a regulatory approach guiding suitable combinations of methods in the same managerial intervention. The multi-method approach was used in this research project to ensure that consideration is given to the range of factors that can influence the situation and to critically evaluate the extent to which the proposed techniques add to the richness and validity of results. The decisions on the nature of the framework and the techniques to include were taken by the authors after several meetings with the company managers.

The proposed systemic framework for improved business process modeling comprises SSM (which is used as the overall guiding methodology in the role of a problem sense making tool), and UML business modeling extensions, included for its expressive power in formulating the resulting business processes. The combination of SSM and UML business modeling is structured within the broader scheme of conducting action research suggested by Checkland and Holwell (1998:27). The action research approach was justified by the nature of the problem and by the extensive long work experience of the first author with the company. He was directly involved both as a facilitator and as a middle manager who is affected by the results of the project during the implementation of the framework. Figure 1 shows the proposed framework that was used. As illustrated in figure 1, an analysis of the stakeholders takes place first. The stakeholder analysis is followed by an SSM evaluation of the problem. Once there is agreement on the human activity that will improve the situation, the next step involves the UML modeling, using the Ericsson and Penker's extensions.

Our framework for mixing SSM and UML is different from past attempts of combining methods from the two areas as it is better justified methodologically from the point of view of the underlying current theory on multi-method research in Systems thinking and Operations Research (see Jackson, 2003 and Mingers, 2001). It is also different because it is formulated as an action research approach which is a more likely mode of operation of the systems analyst in the process of uncovering the inherent complexities of business modeling. It is also different because other research has not attempted combinations of SSM with the Ericsson and Penker's extensions to UML for business process modeling

Due to the fact that SSM plays an organizing role in the proposed framework, we can identify such a combination of methods as methodology enhancement within the typology of multimethodology possibilities discussed by Mingers and Brocklesby (1997:491).

Mingers (2001:245) states that any intervention or research is never a discrete event but is a

Figure 1. Proposed Framework for Mixing of SSM and UML for a systemic Business Process Modeling (Based on a generic action research methodology following Checkland and Holwell 1998:27)

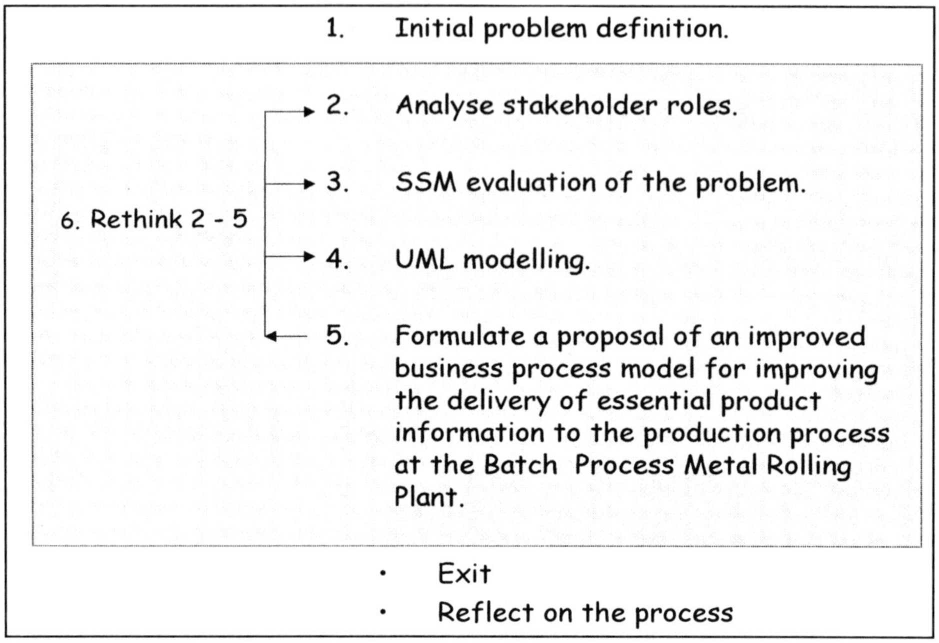

process that has phases requiring different types of activities. Mingers (2001:245) identifies the following four generic phases that comprise a research process:

1. **Appreciation** is concerned with understanding why the problematic situation exists, who the actors are, accepting that the researchers access to the situation and prior experience will influence what is appreciated or observed.
2. **Analysis** is concerned with understanding and explaining the reasons for the information gathered during appreciation.
3. **Assessment** is concerned with evaluating alternatives and assessing the results.
4. **Action** is concerned with reporting the research results in order to bring about change.

Following the above generic model, the content of these four stages as applied to our problem can be formulated in more detail also as shown in Table 1; however their execution is guided through the iterative systemic action research process of mixing SSM and UML in business process modeling as captured in Figure 1. The SSM evaluation of the problem in our framework (see Figure 1) corresponds to the first three stages listed in Table 1 (for details on SSM see Checkland and Scholes, 1999). These equate to the appreciation step, analysis step and assessment step of the problem solving intervention (formulation of a particular business process in our case), as defined by Mingers (2001:245). A known limitation of SSM is the lack of techniques required to initiate taking action. This limitation is overcome in our approach by the use of UML business modeling extensions proposed by Eriksson and Penker (2000). This step equates to the action stage identified by Mingers (2001:246). Thus we have shown here that our framework satisfies the generic process of a managerial intervention suggested by Mingers (2001).

Table 1. Methods used in the four generic stages of applying a mix of SSM and UML business process modeling extensions in a specific modeling intervention.

1. Express the problem situation as experienced, using rich pictures and technical analyses, cultural and political analysis;
2. Model the relevant conceptual systems (holons) using CATWOE analysis, root definitions and conceptual models;
3. Compare the models and real world to arrive at an action that is acceptable to all stakeholders and bring about improvement in the situation. It is defined as an agreed conceptual model of the human activities that will bring about improvement
4. UML business modeling: - expand the conceptual model into a detailed conceptual data flow diagram, - complete a goal model to show goal hierarchy for the production process improvement, - model the important concepts required to improve the production process using a conceptual view (domain class diagram with associations and multiplicity), and - produce the business process view, assembly line diagrams and state transition diagram for sub processes and important business concepts (see Eriksson and Penker (2000).

UML business modeling is initiated by taking the stakeholder approved conceptual model of the human activities that will bring about improvement, and expanding them into a detailed conceptual data flow diagram. The latter and the SSM analysis are used as the basis for the UML models. These included business process views and assembly line diagrams (see Eriksson and Penker (2000). This approach of arriving at the conceptual data flow diagram from the conceptual model is somewhat similar to the steps in the standard seven stages SSM approach (see Checkland and Holwell, 1998). It is necessary to point that Table 1 is useful just as a summary of the techniques relevant for each stage of the generic problem solving process defined by Mingers (2001) but the dynamics of their application in the framework for business process modeling is captured through the iterative systemic process shown in Figure 1.

The Eriksson and Penker (2000) UML business modeling extensions are not discussed here in detail for space reasons. The *goal model* shows goal and sub goal dependencies. The goal model also gives the process model context because it describes the goals that the process model is trying to achieve. The *assembly line diagram* (see Eriksson and Penker, 2000:420) focuses on the connection between the business processes and the domain classes (business objects). According to the same authors, it is the point of connection between the world of business modeling and the world of software engineering. The assembly diagram sets the scene for detailed design of information systems support. A *state machine or state-chart diagram* shows the states transitions of core business objects. If changes result to the goal model, then the changes will have to ripple through the process model, assembly line diagram, domain class diagram and state-machine diagram. Change is seldom linear but iterative.

Mingers (2001:247) identifies the following four levels of problems that can arise when combining methods:

1. **Philosophical** - Particularly the issue of paradigm incommensurability.
2. **Cultural** - the extent to which organisational and academic cultures militate against multi-method work.

3. **Psychological** - the problems of individual researchers who are often only comfortable with a particular type of method.
4. **Practical**.

With regards to paradigm incommensurability, Mingers (2001:247) states that the arguments in support of single paradigm research are overstated and that paradigms are in fact permeable at the edges. In addition to these arguments for a single paradigm being weak, Mingers (2001:248) indicates that reality is more complex than our theories can capture and it is quite wrong to insist on a single paradigm to explain reality. With regards to this research project, SSM is necessary to ensure that the views of stakeholders are considered and the required activities are acceptable to all stakeholders. On the contrary, UML business modelling is necessary to explain the required solutions in a language with which developers are comfortable. The theoretical difficulties of working across paradigms were resolved through an integrative approach addressing the issue of paradigm incommensurability, applied previously in Petkov et al. (2007) and hence will not be discussed here for space reasons.

The issues of cultural feasibility are beyond the scope of this research project, but based on the arguments of Mingers and Brocklesby (1997:498) and Mingers (2001:248) for pluralist methods, it is assumed that the information systems community encourages multi-method research.

Psychological feasibility is concerned with the cognitive feasibility of moving from one paradigm to another. This research project requires that the facilitator learns through SSM about the different systems of meaning that stakeholders attach to the activities they are engaged in. By increasing the stakeholders understanding, the techniques of SSM improve the "appreciative" systems of the stakeholders involved in the process. With improved "appreciative" systems, there is greater probability of a desirable set of activities emerging, which will improve the delivery of critical product information to the production process. A desirable system existing in the form of some objective reality contradicts the philosophical assumptions of SSM, but is necessary in order to specify a state that will lead to improvement.

The cognitive difficulties expressed by Mingers (2001:248) that can be experienced working between paradigms are avoided through the separation of the activities within the SSM and the UML parts of the framework. However the results from one stage continuously were used to feed the next stage in this action research project involving a number of stakeholders from the plant. This basically means that the SSM evaluation of the problem will be at the back of the facilitator's and participants' minds throughout the UML modeling process. This is in line with the ideas for interaction between the various methods involved in a systemic intervention within the actual process as suggested by Jackson (2003) and not at a meta-level. The following section discusses the reflections on the application of the framework to model one of the most important production processes in the plant.

HOW THE FRAMEWORK WAS IMPLEMENTED IN FORMULATING A PROCESS FOR DELIVERY OF ESSENTIAL PRODUCT INFORMATION AT EVERY STAGE OF THE PRODUCTION PROCESS

How SSM was Applied

The issue of delivery essential product information to every stage on the shop floor during the execution of customer orders is extremely complex. The complexity is due to the diverse stakeholders involved at various levels of management, the varying degrees of automation that could be adopted, and the varying levels of expertise and cultural backgrounds of operational staff. In practice their interests were not always aligned with the overall goal of the company, nor were each others perspectives clearly articulated. The communication channels were ineffective and burdened by the traditional organizational structures within the plant. Improving that process was seen as a key to improvement of product quality.

The intervention started after careful planning with the assistance of the chief production manager. The SSM sessions involved brainstorming and rich picture building sessions with different groups of stakeholders in the problem of concern. For each of the recommendations that followed root definitions were compiled to answer three questions: What to do, How to do it, and Why to do it? These were accompanied by corresponding CATWOE analysis from several view points in order to capture the multiple perspectives of the various stakeholders (see Checkland and Scholes, 1999).

A number of root definitions' emerged through the iterations. At the end a root definition was accepted by all stakeholders as a reflection of their integrated views. It was fleshed out into the conceptual model for the desired business process. Both are shown in Figure 2.

The model in Figure 2 is comprised of activities and flows of information and influences between the activities. This makes the conceptual model a closer representation to a dataflow diagram. A similar approach is proposed by Prior (as quoted in Mingers, 1992:83).

According to Checkland (1999) the formal aim of this kind of thinking prior to building a model is to ensure that there is clarity of thought about the purposeful activity. In summary, we used SSM to develop a rich understanding of the issues surrounding the problem of delivery essential information to the shop floor during the production of a customer order and to reach agreement on the activities and concepts that future information systems will need to support.

How UML Was Used for Modeling of the Business Processes

Modeling the business process requirements was the fourth activity of the methodology defined in Figure 1 and Table 1. These models were necessary to communicate the information systems requirements to the software developers to initiate subsequently use-case definitions. The UML views were formulated from the conceptual model and the rich understanding the action researcher acquired. In addition to the SSM workshops, further workshops were needed to clarify detailed aspects of the conceptual and business process views. The subsequent reviews were all done in the spirit of progressive elaboration.

The language and concepts of the Eriksson and Penker (2000) business process modeling extensions provided guidelines for constructing the business process view. It shows primary processes and support processes with dependencies. In addition to sequence and sub-process dependencies, the business process view also indicates inputs, outputs and control information.

The structuring of the production-process-business-process view was achieved through the application of the process layer supply and process layer control patterns suggested by Eriksson and Penker (2000:315-328). The process layer supply pattern assisted in organising the business processes into primary and support processes. The process layer control pattern helped layer the processes to show how certain processes control other processes. The business process view gives a detailed description of the production process activities that are required. A more detailed business process view that also shows the interactions between the processes and concepts of the production process is presented in the assembly line view (following Eriksson and Penker, 2000) that is discussed below. Figure 4 shows the assembly line view of the "Process Lot Operation" activity of the production process.

Figure 2. A root definition and a conceptual model of the business process for the delivery of essential product information to the shop floor in fulfilling customer orders.

***Root definition**: A system is required to present essential product information to operators and sequencers when requested, in the right context without overloading them, to support the sequencers to plan a batch of lots on a specific machine, help the operator create the right conditions before running a product and assist operators in the set-up, control and final releasing of a specific lot to ensure the quality requirements specific to the operation being performed on the product are achieved.*

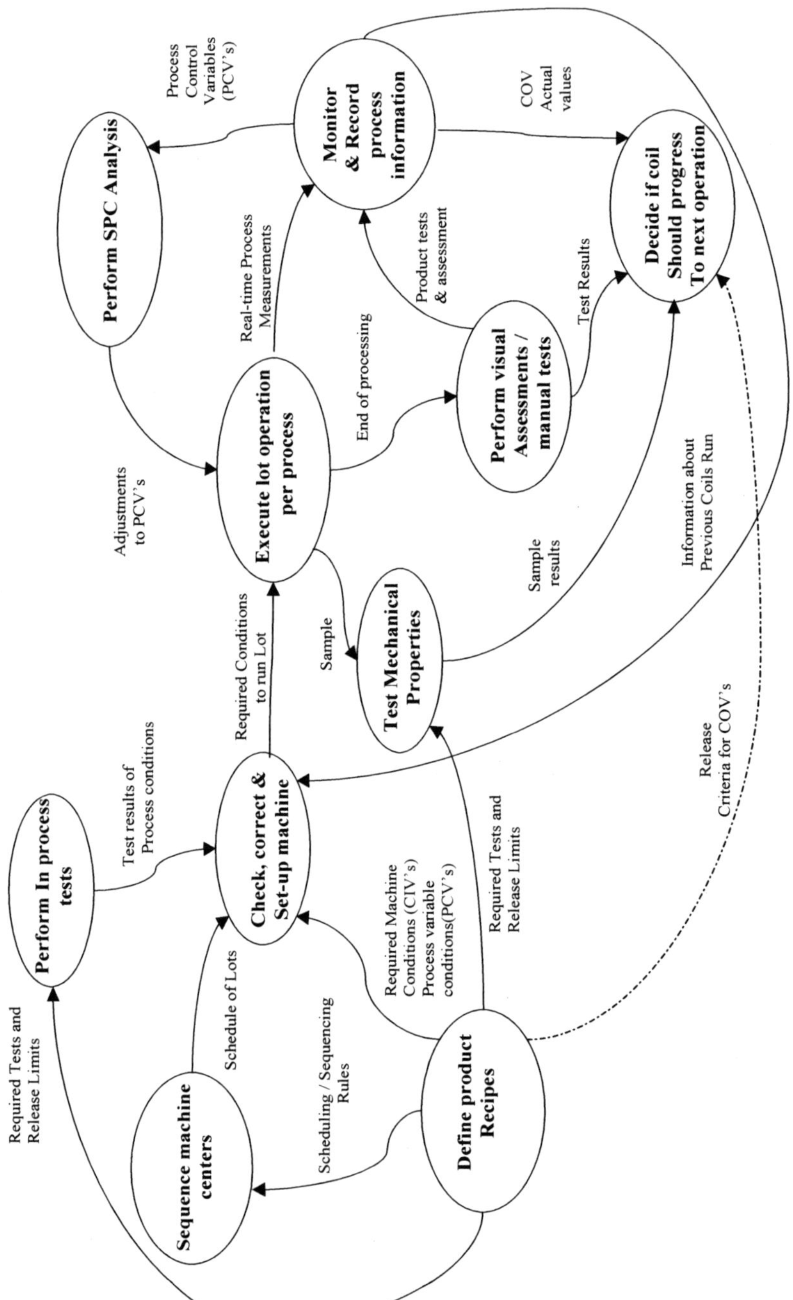

Figure 3. Business process view of the production process of the company

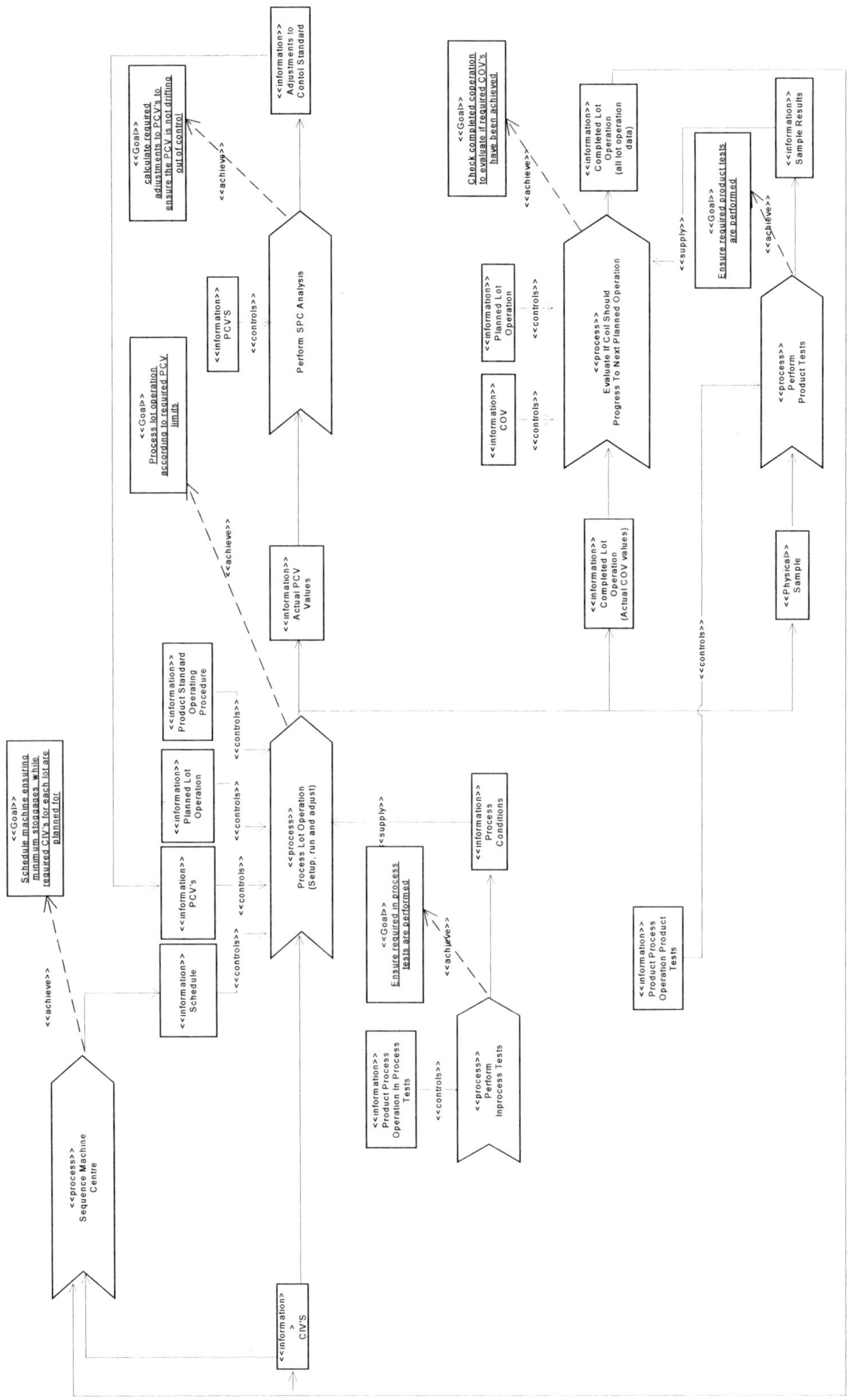

An assembly line diagram was produced for each activity in the business process view. The expanded view has to show information and other resources that are referred to and created during the life cycle of the activity. The interaction is shown using lines drawn from the activity to the resource with an indication of whether the resource is referenced, consumed of created. The dark shaded circles indicate a write while the empty, unfilled circles indicate a read operation. Each read or write operation is described by the type of information that is read or written. Eriksson and Penker (2000:116) propose that the assembly line diagrams provide the connection between business modeling and software requirements modeling with use-cases. This view provided a starting point to begin use case analysis. The developers appreciated the benefit of being able to see in the assembly line view the total set of use-cases that needed to be supported by corresponding information systems.

Once the business analysis and modeling phase was done we typically had the business process model, data architecture model and domain class model. Once these were in place then the development of the software proceeded in iterations. We focussed on delivery of the use-cases in an input, process, and output development order. The assembly line diagram guided choices. No sequence diagrams or extensive explicit modeling was done during the design unless the interaction was complex or a novice developer was working on the project.

REFLECTIONS ON THE APPLICATION OF THE FRAMEWORK

On the Role of SSM in the Development of Understanding of the Problem Situation

The application of the proposed framework afforded the action researcher a deeper understanding of the situation of concern, as experienced by each of the stakeholders. Besides rich pictures we used CATWOE analysis which helps describe the problem from a particular stakeholder perspectiveby elaborating on: Customers; Actors; Transformation; Worldview; Owners and Environment. We found these dimensions of a system description to be crucial in providing a meaningful multifaceted description of the system pursuing purposeful action. The emerging rich understanding of the problem allowed the first author in his role of an action researcher to facilitate the recommendation of a proposed human activity system for delivery of essential product information in every step of the production process. It captured the composite needs of all stakeholders in the overall company drive to improve its operations and information systems.

The use of the SSM techniques made possible delving into sensitive areas of the situation of concern. Although the devices allowed articulation of complex perceptions many iterations were necessary to get to the real interests, world views and expectations each of the stakeholders were consciously latching onto, or unknowingly biased by. The iterations perhaps made the stakeholders conscious of the values they were enacting through the stances they were taking. This is perhaps what Checkland refers to as clarity of thought and learning.

Although we may at this point conclude that the SSM process was used at first somewhat mechanistically during the initial iteration in applying the framework, it is necessary to reiterate that subsequently the action researcher internalized the questioning and manoeuvred the process to address those areas which were directly affecting progress to allow greater learning. Learning took also the tangible form of preparing each of the stakeholders for tolerance of the proposed solution using the sense making devices of SSM. Since the first author has left the company in the second half of 2005, one might expect that the use of SSM there might not be so strongly supported

Figure 4. Assembly line diagram of "Process Lot Operation" activity of the production process.

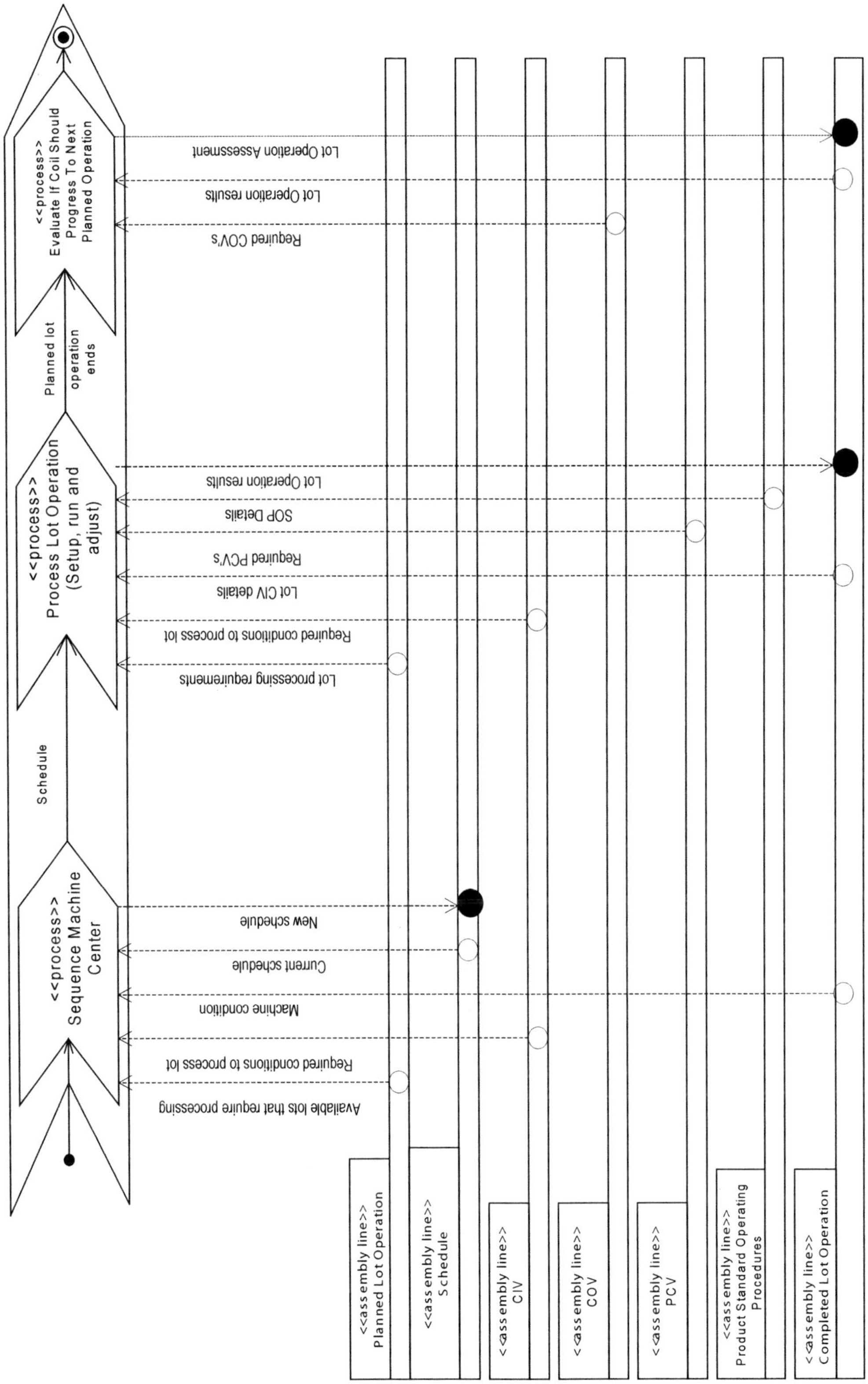

as before but the established ways of consultation between the stakeholders and for questioning the aspects of a problem situation along the principles of SSM are most likely to be sustained as they became part of the standard work practices at the company.

Several factors were influencing the sanction of the proposed human activity system but the use of the SSM sense making devices compelled the stakeholders to consider each perception logically. In a way, acceptance of the solution became so compelling that the stakeholders saw this as an emergent property of the process.

Refelections on the Value of UML Modeling in our Framework

Through the various views, developers were able to understand how the goals of the surrounding business context were being realised. Developers felt that the UML business process views give more information about the business than business process descriptions they had received previously when structured analysis techniques were used for business analysis and modeling.

Generally, the software developers felt that the business rules in the derived UML models were more apparent, and the requirements were defined more precisely. They assessed the models as being capable of guiding them toward the development of required information systems. The response from developers to the results of this project provides supporting evidence to the claims made by Eriksson and Penker (2000, 66-130) about the advantages in having a common language for both the business process model and software models. Those claims are in line with what we achieved in this intervention according to the company management.

Within the project team we knew we were not conforming to the step by step waterfall process and were still delivering adequate quality. We did not use the agile terms to describe what we did but the nature of our activities could be well captured by the concepts raised by the agilest community. However we had to have architectural business models within our project prior to any development starting. Our approach on the project was so architectural centric that we did not even begin any iterations until we knew what the architecture was that needed supporting. Further comments on integrating systems approachs and agile and software engineering models may be found in Boehm (2006) and Petkov et al. (2008).

Although the Eriksson and Penker UML modeling extensions were used in this case, the framework can accommodate other types of IS modeling methods, provided the business process, the interactions with resources and the goals of the models can be represented in the chosen symbology and SSM is used as the integrated sense making mechanism. Since the essence of the proposed framework is not dependent methodologically on the particular UML models, it will be applicable with other emerging variants of UML that aim at improving the business modeling phase.

Lessons Learned from the Application of the Framework for Mixing SSM and UML

If we had to redo this project again we would try to use SSM more widely but less explicitly as a method from the very begining. A less explicit use will make use of the CATWOE and Root definitions to accompany each business process model. Using SSM in that way would clarify the value business processes are designed to yield and would also make goals and purpose assumptions more clear. These would also give direction to more detailed requirements definition and design stages. If SSM is easily interleaved with the typical software techniques and the inclusion of SSM is less of a mechanistic step then there is more of a likelihood that the technique will be used continuously and for the strengths it is noted for.

We would also spend more time delving into the areas of disagreement between the individual stakeholders to see where these disagreements originated from. The resulting information may point to elements of the business process that are candidates for redesign.

We would also like to support the use of the UML standard by trying to use the standard diagrams. Promoting a single modeling standard is important for overall improvement of systems analysis activities. Since the project at the aluminium plant took place, UML has matured significantly and there has been more acceptance of the activity diagram view to model business processes. The assembly line diagram proposed by Ericsson and Penker (2000), however, does not have a matching standard UML view. This view of domain object interaction with business activities is useful according to our experience. In structured analysis techniques the data flow diagram served this purpose. The above discussion can be summarised in the following conclusion.

CONCLUSION

The world of business is imprecise and often characterised by conflicting views of the various stakeholders. On the other side, developers need a view of the world that is precise, consistent and represented by a single model. These differences in assumptions result in information systems delivery being dependant on several types of modeling. This is difficult to achieve in practice following the existing methods for information systems development. This becomes especially obvious when trying to define models suitable for unique situations like the manufacturing process of the aluminium semi-fabricator discussed in this chapter. The motivation for this research project emerged from the limitations of current business process modeling practices. The chapter has presented a systemic integrated framework to business analysis and modeling involving SSM and UML extensions which was not demonstrated before. Its value was demonstrated through the application of our approach to define and model the important process of delivering essential product information at every production stage related a particular customer order in an aluminium semi-fabricator plant.

Our lessons showed that SSM could be used slightly less mechanistically from the start of the project, a manner of use that is a typical of novice applications. The initial weaknesses tend to disappear with more experience in applying it. Nevertheless, the action research approach adopted in this study provided a continuity between the interpretive paradigm of SSM and the functionalist nature of UML. The richness of the appreciation through SSM was not lost. Potential theoretical omissions, implicit assumptions and natural biases can be made explicit and taken into consideration in a practical business modeling activity through the use of our multimethodology framework. The experimental implementation of the framework on a complex production process within the action research reported here provided evidence of the potential benefits that can result from its application.

The practical contribution of this research is that it helped an aluminium semi-fabricator define the required production process activities that will allow shop floor operators to receive sufficient quality information, at the right time and in the right context to enable them to ensure consistent product quality. Another important practical outcome of this research project is the resulting UML definition of the required specific business process. Its purpose is to allow the software developers to pursue the detailed analysis, design construction and implementation of suitable information systems. The management at the aluminium semi-fabricator accepted the solution as a sound approach to guide the subsequent implementation of the various components of the plant production management system. The developers were pleased that the resulting modeling artifacts provided continuity to the subsequent software development activities.

Further work is possible on the verification of the framework in other business settings and for refinement of some of its elements. On the theoretical side, recent developments like the Work Systems Model (Alter, 2006) may require future investigation for possible exploration of incorporating work system modeling analysis techniques in our approach in the strive to enhance business process modeling for information systems analysis and design.

ACKNOWLEDGEMENTS

We would like to express our gratitude to the anonymous referees and the editors for their helpful comments on improving the chapter.

REFERENCES

Ackermann, F., Walls, L., Meer, R. v. d., & Borman, M. (1999). Taking a strategic view of BPR to develop a multidisciplinary framework. *Journal of the Operational Research Society, 50*(1999), 195-204.

Adamides, E.D. and Karacapilidis N., (2006). A knowledge centred framework for collaborative business process modeling. *Business Process Management Journal*, 12(5), 557-575.

Al-Humaidan, F., & Rossiter, N. (2004). Business process modeling with OBPM combining soft and hard approaches. *1st Workshop on Computer Supported Activity Coordination (CSAC)*. Retrieved 13 October 2006, from http://computing.unn.ac.uk/staff/CGNR1/porto%20april%202004%20bus%proc.rtf

Alter, S. (2006). *The work system method: Connecting people, processes and IT for business results*. Larkspur, CA: Work System Press.

Ambler, S. (2005). Quality in an agile world. *Extreme Programming Series, 7*(3), 34-40.

K D Barber; F W Dewhurst; R L D H Burns; J B B Rogers (2003). Business-process modeling and simulation for manufacturing management: a practical way forward. *Business Process Management Journal,* 9(4), 527-543

Bennet, S., McRobb, S., & Farmer, R. (2006). *Object-oriented systems analysis and design* (3rd ed.). Berkshire: McGrawHill.

Boehm, B. (2006). Some future trends and implications for systems and software engineering processes. *Systems Engineering,* 9(1), 1-19.

Burns, T., & Klshner, R. (2005, October 20 -22, 2005). *A cross-collegiate analysis of software development course content.* Paper presented at the SIGITE'05, Newark, NJ, USA.

Bustard, D. W., He, Z., & Wilkie, F. G. (2000). Linking soft systems and use-case modeling through scenarios. *Interacting with Computers,* 13(2000), 97-110.

Champion, D., Stowell, F., & O'Callaghan, A. (2005). Client-led information system creation (CLIC): Navigating the gap. *Information Systems Journal,* (15), 213-231.

Checkland, P. (1999). *Systems thinking, systems practice*. West Sussex, England: Wiley.

Checkland, P., & Holwell, S. (1998). *Information, systems and information systems: Making sense of the field.* West Sussex, England: John Wiley and Sons Ltd

Checkland, P., & Scholes, J. (1999). *Soft systems methodology in action*. Chichester: John Wiley and Sons Ltd.

Clegg, B. (2006), Business process orientated holonic (PrOH) modeling, *Business Process Management Journal,* 12(4), 410-432

Cockburn, A. (2002a). *Agile software development*: Pearson Education, Inc.

Cockburn, A. (2002b). Agile software development joins the "would-be" crowd. *The Journal of Information Technology Management,* 15(1), 6-12.

Edwards, C., Braganza, A., & Lambert, R. (2000). Understanding and managing process initiatives: a framework for developing consensus. *Knowledge and process management,* 7(1), 29-36.

Eriksson, H. E., & Penker, M. (2000). *UML business patterns at work.* New York: John Wiley & Sons Inc.

Esichaikul, V. (2001). Object oriented business process modeling: A case study of a port authority. *Journal of Information Technology: Cases and Applications,* 3(2), 21-41.

Galliers, R. D. (1994). Information systems, operational research and business reengineering. *International Transactions in Operations Research,* 1(2), 159-167.

Hammer, M., & Champy, J. (1993). *Re-engineering the corporation.* London: Harper Business.

Herzum, P., & Sims, O. (2000). *Business component factory.* New York: John Wiley & Sons, Inc.

Jackson, M. C. (1995). Beyond the fads: Systems thinking for managers. *Systems Research,* 12(1), 25-42.

Jackson, M. C. (2003). *Systems thinking, creative holism for managers.* Chichester: Wiley.

Jacobson, I. (2002). A resounding "yes" to agile processes - but also to more. *The Journal of Information Technology Management,* 15(1), 18-24.

Jones, M. (1992). SSM and information systems. *Systemist,* 14(3), 12-125.

Kettinger, W. J. (1997). Business process change: A study of methodologies, techniques, and tools. *MIS Quarterly,* (March), 55-79.

Kumar, K., & Hillegersberg, V. J. (2000). ERP experiences and evolution. *Communications of the ACM,* 43(4), 23-41.

Lane, C. (1998). *Methods for transitioning from soft systems methodology models to object oriented analysis developed to support the army operational architecture and an example of its application.* United Kingdom.: Hi-Q Systems Ltd, The Barn Micheldever Station Winchester S021 3AR.

Lopes, E., & Bryant, A. (2004). SSM: A Pattern and Objet Modeling overview. *ICT+ Conference,* from http://www.leedsmet.ac.uk/ies/redot/Euric%20Lopes.pdf

Mathiassen, L., & Nielsen, P. A. (2000). Interaction and transformation in SSM. *Systems Research and Behavioral Science,* (17), 243-253.

Mingers, J. (1992). SSM and Information Systems: An Overview. *Systemist,* 14(3), 82-87.

Mingers, J. (1995). *Using soft systems methodology in the design of information systems.* London: McGraw-Hill.

Mingers, J. (2001). Combining IS research methods: Towards a pluralist methodology. *Information Systems Research,* 12(3), 240-259.

Mingers, J., & Brocklesby, J. (1997). Multimethodology: Towards a framework for mixing methodologies. *International Journal of Management Science,* 25(5), 489-509.

Mora, M. Gelman, O, Forgionne, G. Petkov D and Cano, J. Integrating the fragmented pieces in IS research paradigms and frameworks – a systems approach. *Information Resource Management Journal,* 20(2), 1-22.

Nuseibeh, B., & Easterbrook, S. (2000). Requirements engineering: A roadmap. *Communications of the ACM,* 35(9), 37-45.

Ormerod, R. (1995). Putting soft OR to work: Information systems strategy development at Sainsbury's. *Journal of the Operational Research Society,* 46, 277-293.

Osterwalder, A., Pigneur, Y., & Tucci, l. C. (2005). Clarifying business models: Origins, present, and future of the concept. *Communications of the Association for Information Systems,* 16, 1-25.

Pedreira, O., Piattini, M., Luaces, M. R., & Brisaboa, N. R. (2007). A systematic review of software process tailoring. *ACM SIGSOFT Software Engineering Notes,* 32(3), 1-6.

Peppard, J., & Rowland, P. (1995). *The essence of business process re-engineering.* New York: Prentice Hall.

Petkov, D. , Petkova, O., Andrew T. and Nepal T. (2007). Mixing multiple criteria decision making with soft systems thinking techniques for decision support in complex situations. *Decision Support Systems,* (43), 1615-1629.

Petkov, D., Edgar-Nevill, D., Madachy, R. and O'Connor, R., (2008). Information systems, software engineering and systems thinking – challenges and opportunities. *International Journal on Information Technologies and Systems Approach,* 1(1), 62-78.

Petkova, O., & Roode, D., R. (1999). A pluralist systemic framework for evaluation of the factors affecting software development productivity. *South African Computer Journal,* 24, 26-32.

Rosenberg, D., & Scott, K. (2004). *Use case driven object modeling with UML.* New York: Addison Wesley.

Sommer, R. (2002). Why is middle management in conflict with ERP? *Journal of International Technology and Information Management,* 11(2), 19-28.

Stowell, F. (1995). *Information systems provision - the contribution of soft systems methodology.* United Kingdom: McGraw-Hill Publishing Co.

Stowell, F. (1997). *Information systems: An emerging discipline?* United Kingdom: McGraw-Hill Publishing Co.

Weston, R. (1999). Model-driven, component-based approach to reconfiguring manufacturing software systems. *International Journal of Operations & Production Management,* 19(8), 834-855.

Chapter VII
Managing E-Mail Systems:
An Exploration of Electronic Monitoring and Control in Practice

Aidan Duane
Waterford Institute of Technology (WIT), Ireland

Patrick Finnegan
University College Cork (UCC), Ireland

ABSTRACT

An email system is a critical business tool and an essential part of organisational communication. Many organisations have experienced negative impacts from email and have responded by electronically monitoring and restricting email system use. However, electronic monitoring of email can be contentious. Staff can react to these controls by dissent, protest and potentially transformative action. This chapter presents the results of a single case study investigation of staff reactions to electronic monitoring and control of an email system in a company based in Ireland. The findings highlight the variations in staff reactions through multiple time frames of electronic monitoring and control, and the chapter identifies the key concerns of staff which need to be addressed by management and consultants advocating the implementation of email system monitoring and control.

INTRODUCTION

The email infrastructure is now a mission critical component of the enterprise information infrastructure and an essential component in all implementations of eCommerce platforms, especially for enterprises striving to become more virtual, resilient and efficient (Graff, 2002a). Email systems have also become heavily integrated with mobile technologies, thus there is an increasing importance on Web or wireless access to central email servers (Graff and Grey, 2002). Mobile email access also increases the pressure on the organisation to maintain and improve the reliability of the core email system infrastructure (Graff and Grey, 2002). The more organisations rely on email, the more reliable it must be, because the risk of business interruption increases dramatically (Graff and Grey, 2002). Organisations must secure, expand and manage this communication medium effectively to meet new challenges (Graff and Grey, 2002; Weber, 2004).

However, the dramatic increase in email usage is commensurate with the rising number of email related workplace incidents and disputes (Simmers, 2002; American Management Association (AMA), 2004; Weber 2004). Personal use of email remains the number one use of email in the workplace (Russell et al., 2007). Organisations are all too aware of the problems associated with email use and are becoming more determined to reduce these threats (Burgess et al., 2005). Organisations must become more focused on stabilising and protecting their email systems, gaining more control over the use of their systems and managing risk associated with these systems (Graff and Grey, 2002).

Some organisations employ technology based solutions to control the email system including electronically monitoring all email activities, electronically filtering and blocking incoming and outgoing emails and restricting email systems for personal use (Sipior and Ward, 2002; Stanton and Stam, 2003). However, organisations can rarely dominate staff with the unilateral imposition of technology (Stanton and Stam, 2003). Although, technical controls are necessary, their effectiveness is questionable if organisations fail to look at the contextual issues of information systems (Dhillon, 1999).

Some organisations do little more than ask their employees to comply with a formal email policy (Simmers, 2002) while other organisations enforce hard-line email policies that exert zero tolerance of personal email use that are so nebulous that every employee could be deemed in violation (Oravec, 2002). However, Simmers (2002) contends that vague, unmonitored, unenforced or absent email policy exposes the organisation to a number of legal, financial and operational risks such as losses of confidential information, network congestion, threats to network integrity, diversion of employee attention, and increased liability.

What is know for certain, is that too much or too little email systems management can be dysfunctional for an organisation (Simmers, 2002). Thus, Weber (2004) argues that 'in our efforts to improve email technology, we need to take care that we do not exacerbate problems with email use'. Weber (2004) suggests that technological developments associated with email use may prove to be ineffective if they are not informed by social science research. Burgess et al. (2005) reveal that training staff on the best practices of email use is a critical factor to reducing email defects within an organisation. Sipior and Ward (2002) argue that it is imperative that organisations formulate a coordinated and comprehensive response to email system management. Stanton and Stam (2003) suggest that this should occur within the context of a negotiatory process involving management, employees and IT professionals.

Weber (2004) contends that we lack a deep understanding of the impacts of email on organisations and our understanding of these impacts remains fragmented and superficial. The majority of the research produced over the past two decades on email systems utilizes quantitative methods to examine the social and technical concerns of email systems. Laboratory-like experiments and mass surveys dominate the literature on email studies. As a result, there has been relatively little published advice on how to take an organisational view of email systems (Ruggeri et al., 2000). As a result, Weber (2004) believes that we still have 'human, technological, and organisational problems to solve' in relation to email systems and calls for 'better ways of managing email and assisting users to deal with the problems it poses'. It is imperative that underlying all uses of email, current and expanded, is careful planning, monitoring and management of the email infrastructure (Graff and Grey, 2002; Simmers, 2002; Sipior and Ward, 2002; Weber, 2004).

This chapter presents the results of a single case study investigation of an Irish-based organisation's strategy to monitor and control an email system. In Ireland, there is no specific legislation addressing email system monitoring and a person has no expressed right to privacy in the Constitution. Ireland's Electronic Commerce Act (2000) indicates that if employees clearly understand that email is a business tool and if the employer has established a clear policy that emails are subject to monitoring and it is conducted in a reasonable manner, it is difficult for employees to object. However, EU law is explicit in stating that email interception is illegal. The next section examines the theoretical grounding for the study and is followed by a discussion of the research method and a presentation of the findings. The chapter reveals a number of key concerns of staff which should be addressed by management or consultants advocating the implementation of email system monitoring and control in its pre, initial, early and latter stages of implementation.

THEORETICAL GROUNDING

Sipior and Ward (2002) propose a strategic response to information systems abuse, consisting of; assessing current operations, implementing proactive measures to reduce potential misuse, formulating a usage policy, providing ongoing training, maintaining awareness of issues, monitoring internal sources, regulating external sources, securing liability insurance, and keeping up-to-date with technological advances, legislative / regulatory initiatives and new areas of vulnerability. Dhillon (1999) argues that the key to an effective control environment is to implement an adequate set of technical, formal and informal controls. Technical control comprises of complex technological control solutions, often mechanistic in fashion. Formal control involves developing controls and rules that reflect the emergent structure and protect against claims of negligent duty and comply with the requirements of data protection legislation. Informal control consists of increasing awareness supplemented with ongoing education and training.

Electronic monitoring extends the scope of control, transforming personal control to systemic control and enabling control over behaviour as well as outcomes (Orlikowski, 1991). However, Dhillon (1999) questions the effectiveness of technical controls if organisations become over-reliant and don't consider the contextual issues of information systems. Furthermore, staff can act to change a control through dissent, protest, and potentially transformative action (Orlikowski, 1991). Failing to fairly apply discipline for email abuse can upset staff, while failing to properly train staff on email system use can lead to its misuse (Attaran, 2000). Furthermore, a poorly designed email policy reduces information exchange, while its poor communication diminishes staff understanding. Email monitoring may also conflict with staff privacy expectations (Sipior and Ward, 2002) and affect staff morale (Hodson et al., 1999). The main dysfunctional effects that can arise from electronic monitoring and control of email systems are outlined in Table 1.

THE RESEARCH METHOD

The objective of this study is to *'investigate the reactions of staff to the implementation of electronic monitoring and control of an email system in a single organisation'.*

The choice of a single case study for this study was based on the arguments put forward by Steinfield (1990), Van den Hooff (1997) and Weber (2004). In particular, Steinfield (1990) suggests that 'case studies of what happens after new media are implemented can help to expand our awareness of the range of possible uses and effects, as well as arm future planners with a broader understanding of the ways in which people adapt technological systems for purposes beyond those envisioned by system designers'.

HealthCo Ireland (pseudonym) was chosen as a suitable case site after multiple site visits and negotiations. HealthCo is a large multinational involved in the manufacturing of well-known healthcare products. It has employees in over thirty countries and sells products in 120 countries. The company has 1,200 employees in Ireland making it one of its largest operations worldwide.

Miles and Huberman (1994) emphasise the importance of 'prestructured theory' when researching areas where some understanding has already been achieved but where more theory building is required before theory testing can be done. They propose that a loose-linkage between induction and deduction is suited for locally focused site sensitive studies. In adopting a loose-linkage inductive and deductive approach, this study utilizes prestructured theory in the form of the main dysfunctional effects that can arise from a strategy of electronic monitoring and control of email systems (see Table 1) to scope of the research.

Data collection took place over a fifteen-month period using a combination of indepth interviews, focus groups, computer monitored data, and other

Table 1. Electronic monitoring and control of an email system and possible dysfunctional effects

Electronic monitoring and control of email		Possible dysfunctional effects
Technical Control	Reconfigure the email system software	Organisations fail to adequately consider the configuration of the email application (Rudy, 1996).
	Implementing email system anti-virus software	Organisations fail to update anti-virus software (Lindquist, 2000).
	Implement email system scanning, filtering and blocking software	Organisations fail to use filtering software effectively (Jackson et al., 2000).
	Implement email system monitoring software	Monitoring is contentious for economic, ethical, legal (Hodson et al., 1999) or health reasons (Markus, 1994); may conflict with staff privacy expectations (Sipior and Ward, 2002) and; may erode the bond of trust between employer and staff (Urbaczewski and Jessup, 2002)
Formal Control	Formulate an email system policy	Policies can be poorly designed (Sproull and Kiesler, 1991).
	Form an email system management team	Organisations fail to appoint an individual or committee to oversee email system management (Sipior et al., 1996).
	Communicate the email policy	Organisations fail to communicate the policy effectively (Sipior and Ward, 2002).
	Audit email system accounts	Organisations fail to assess policy effectiveness and resolve problems (Flood, 2003).
	Discipline staff for email system policy abuse and reward compliance	Organisations fail to consistently and fairly enforce email policies (Flood, 2003).
	Adopt email system pricing structures	Pricing penalises staff with less resources or with more to communicate (Sproull and Kiesler, 1991).
	Establish methods of email system buffering	Buffering separates staff from job critical information or personnel (Sproull and Kiesler, 1991).
Informal Control	Engage in email training	Failing to adequately train staff on email system use can lead to misuse of these systems (Attaran, 2000).
	Maintain awareness of email system policy	Organisations fail to continually raise awareness of the policy, particularly with new staff (Sipior and Ward, 2002).
	Enable self-policing of email system through social forums	Self-policing of email by social forums leads to conflict among staff (Steinfield, 1990).

documents. Data collection was structured using four time frames; (i) pre-implementation; (ii) initial implementation (iii) early implementation, and (iv) latter implementation. Data collection was triangulated throughout the four time frames in order to attain an improved understanding of what was occurring in the organisation.

Semi-structured indepth interviews were used to gain an understanding of management's perceptions of how organisational strategies to control and monitor email use impacted on staff perception and use of email systems. The IT and HR managers were interviewed separately during the four key time frames, and once more upon exiting the organisation. Other managers (the financial controller, the manufacturing managers and the managing director) were also interviewed. Prior to each interview, the interviewee was sent a brief list of questions. Following each interview, the interviewee reviewed a transcript for verification and in some instances, provided additional information or clarification by phone.

Focus groups were conducted with ten interviewees at the initial, early and latter time frames of implementation. The focus groups were conducted after the management interviews had been conducted and the monitoring data had been gathered during each time frame. Focus group participants ranged in age from 27 to 49, and had between 2 to 7 years experience of working in HealthCo in various job functions.

Other documentation analysed included the email policy, corporate records, archival material, staff handbooks, codes of ethics, disciplinary codes, internal communications documentation, policies and other email systems management notifications.

FINDINGS

HealthCo implemented an email system in 1995 but exercised little control over email use at this stage. This approach changed dramatically when HealthCo began to implement numerous controls as a result email monitoring feedback. The IT Manager describes how the decision to monitor and control email was not so much driven by business factors, but because of his preference for 'greater transparency of how email is used'. The IT Manager describes his desire 'to put a bit of a squeeze on email, so that we are ready to move onto the next communication tool whenever that may arrive'. Table 2 outlines the technical, formal and informal controls adopted during the initial, early and latter stages of implementing electronic monitoring and control of the email system, and also illustrates the reactions of staff to electronic monitoring and control of the email system.

Initial Implementation of Electronic Monitoring and Control of the Email System

HealthCo implemented email monitoring software as a result of a decision taken by the EMail Management Group (EMMG), a group specially convened to oversee email monitoring and management. The EMMG initially implemented email monitoring in a covert fashion for a month in order to generate metrics. The IT Manager considered staff to be 'familiar with being monitored electronically' as HealthCo had monitored telephone calls since 1998 and Internet use since 2001. The HR Manager argued that 'as the first months statistics were just used as a benchmark, nobody suffered by not knowing'. Monitoring revealed substantial non-business email use, group-specific information emailed company-wide, excessive email storage, large volumes of undeleted email and disproportionate email volumes for some staff. There were no discussions with staff about the initial covert monitoring as the HR Manager was fearful staff would be suspicious.

Table 2. Electronic monitoring and control of the email system and staff reactions

Category	Control Type	Staff Reactions
Initial implementation of electronic monitoring and control of the email system (July)		
Technical	Covert monitoring begins to generate metrics. Introduction of new email application and basic email filtering for SPAM. Staff requested to forward unsolicited emails to quarantine box.	Staff unaware of covert monitoring. Staff very supportive of SPAM filtering and actively engage in effort to reduce unsolicited email. Staff lack confidence in applying filtering rules.
Formal	An EMail Management Group (EMMG) is formally convened to oversee monitoring and email management. Staff are not formally informed of role. A basic email policy is created using policies from other organisations. No staff disciplined on the basis of covert monitoring data.	Staff suspicious of the EMMG and fear the establishment of a big-brother scenario in the long run.
Informal	Training was not considered necessary	Staff criticise lack of training on email and filtering software.
Early implementation of electronic monitoring and control of the email system (2-7 months - August to January)		
Technical	New anti-virus software implemented.	Despite receiving no training, staff are comfortable with using the anti-virus software.
Formal	A gradual implementation of electronic monitoring and control was chosen in order to set and visibly attain targets. Staff sent the email policy by email and informed about monitoring. Presentation on email policy and monitoring for managers and supervisors. Supervisors requested to enforce the email policy on their subordinates. Policy only available from HR and not included in handbook or on intranet. Some staff formally reprimanded for email abuse. After initial resistance, EMMG sent email to clarify prohibited email use. Email policy not updated to include the clarification.	Initially, staff made no complaints or queries and there were no signs of discontent or trepidation amongst staff. Staff surprised that email wasn't already monitored as telephone and Internet was already monitored. Staff became concerned when some staff were disciplined. Some staff severely curtailed their use of email out of fear. Staff familiar with email policy but email the EMMG seeking clarification of prohibited email use. Staff satisfied with clarification of prohibited email use.
Informal	Staff thanked by email for their efforts to improve email use. Staff emailed to compel relevant email subject headings. All staff reminded by email to read and adhere to policy.	Incentive created to reward staff for good mailbox management. Staff try to circumvent monitoring by omitting and falsifying subject headings for email.
Latter implementation of electronic monitoring and control of the email system (8-15 months - February to September)		
Technical	Filtering software reviewed and extensively reconfigured. Many file attachments blacklisted and communication with web based email addresses blocked. Staff informed by email that this would occur at the end of February to allow alternative arrangements to be made. However, filtering of attachments was inadvertently applied before end of February. After consultation, staff permitted to nominate five family/friends web based email addresses with which to communicate. Automatic online anti-virus software updates.	Staff pleased that filtering reduced their levels of SPAM and that they had been kept informed why certain material was being filtered. The blacklisting and filtering of certain file attachments was resented by staff and they felt they were poorly informed when filtering was applied before the end of February. Staff incensed at the decision to block all communication with web based email addresses. Three hundred members of staff emailed the EMMG to protest. Some staff conduct an online poll to gauge resistance to blacklisting of attachments and blocking of email addresses revealing widespread rejection. EMMG meet with a group of four staff to discuss a compromise. Staff satisfied with the outcome.

continued on following page

Table 2. continued

Formal	Staff informed that business contacts transmitting non-business related content and attachments would be reported to their systems administrator. Email privileges temporarily revoked from twelve staff members for gross violations of email policy. Staff presented with a liability form to accept the contents and any consequences of receiving private attachments. Summer interns are not informed about the email policy, even after been exposed by monitoring. Email privileges revoked for summer interns after network backup failure in second month of placement. Summer interns released from work placement one week later.	The revoking of staff privileges received with an attitude of indifference by staff, feeling staff should be aware of the email policy by now. Staff annoyed after discovering that some staff were exempt from ban on blacklisted file attachments and that IT open all attachments. Mixed reaction from those exempt and subject to the ban. One hundred and sixty staff emails the EMMG to protest at double standards and invasion of privacy. Some staff suggest a liability form to the EMMG to accept the contents of personal attachments. Poor take up of liability form as staff refuse to accept the consequences of rogue attachments. Summer interns misuse the email system in first month of work placement. Some staff find situation with interns amusing, because as engineers the system automatically exempted them from the ban on attachments.
Informal	Staff emailed monthly feedback to encourage continued policy compliance. One day course for managers and supervisors on email management. Staff still do not receive any formal training. Ten staff taken to dinner to reward them for good mailbox management.	Staff circumvent controls by using web based email accounts to send personal email.

Early Implementation of Electronic Monitoring and Control of the Email System

HealthCo chose a gradual implementation of email monitoring and control as 'trying to do too much too quickly would end in failure' according to the HR Manager. One month after implementing monitoring and control, HR/IT notified staff of monitoring and issued a new locally drafted email policy by email. The email policy stated that, *"the email system is to be used for the business purposes of the company and not for the personal purposes of employees unless permission has been granted"*. None of the staff identified any concerns over the introduction of electronic monitoring. An Electrical Engineer explained that 'some people were actually surprised that it wasn't done already because they monitor telephone and Internet use. We haven't had any problems with those so nobody felt email would be any different'. However, the monitoring data from month 2 reveals that in reaction to the implementation of email monitoring and control, the number of non-business emails sent internally declined by 21% and by 24% externally.

As had occurred in month 1, the data for month 2 revealed that the top twenty highest users still accounted for a disproportionate number of emails. Despite a decline in volume by 27% from the baseline metrics, further analysis revealed that many of these emails were non-business related. In month 3, each of the top twenty users were personally admonished for 'misuse of the email system'. HealthCo had never disciplined staff for misuse of the telephone or the Internet, thus the disciplining of staff in month 3 for email misuse was a talking point. A Production Operative commented that 'it reverberated around the company pretty quickly that these guys had been reprimanded for breaching email policy. Everybody wanted to know what they had done wrong'. A Sales Representative contended that 'people were more concerned about the software now'. A Production Operative revealed that he 'didn't use email for anything other than work for several weeks' because he was 'afraid of being fired'. Staff limiting personal use of email in month 3 was very evident in the monitoring data as the total number of non-business email sent internally and externally declined by 30%. A Process Technician described how she 'deleted a lot of stored email because its content was not work related and could be considered a violation of the email policy'. This mass purging of stored email was quite evident in month 3 as the number of emails stored in users accounts fell by 26%.

After the formal reprimands, a number of staff members emailed the EMMG seeking clarification of the email policy. In response, the EMMG emailed all staff encouraging them to read and adhere to the policy while again explaining the need for monitoring. The email policy states that, *"the company reserves and intends to exercise the right to review, audit, intercept and disclose all messages created, filed, received or sent over the email system without the permission of the employee"*. With regard to privacy, the policy contends that *"email communications should not be assumed to be private"* and *"all information and messages that are created, sent, received or stored on the company's email system are the sole property of the company"*. Although month 4 revealed a 3% increase from month 3 in non-business email sent internally and externally, the EMMG emailed staff to thank them for their efforts in improving email management while informing them that the top ten users with the lowest annual percentage non-business email would be taken to dinner.

Staff were reasonably familiar with the email policy having received a copy by email. A Process Technician suggested however that 'the email policy should outline what content and attachments are prohibited as this would increase compliance and eliminate any misunderstandings'. However, the HR Manager stated that 'if you start getting into specific definitions you leave yourself open to oversights and the possibility of definition expiry'. Nevertheless, after discussing requests from staff, the EMMG issued an email stating, *"emails should not contain statements or content that are libelous, offensive, harassing, illegal, derogatory, or discriminatory while foul, inappropriate or offensive messages such as racial, sexual, or religious slurs or jokes are prohibited"* and prohibited use of the email system, *"to solicit for commercial ventures, religious or political causes, outside organisations, or other non-job related solicitations including chain letters"*. Staff were satisfied with the clarification but it was never appended to the email policy.

The EMMG attributed the significant reductions in email use in month 4 to their tough approach to email misuse. The total number of non-business email sent and received internally/externally fell by 27%, the number of unopened email fell by 22%, the average age of unopened email fell by 35%, the number of non-business attachments sent internally had fallen by 22% and the number of deleted emails stored in users accounts fell by 35%. An email was again sent to all staff in month 5 informing them that their efforts were appreciated but that these efforts had to be maintained indefinitely. However, in month 5, a rumour began to circulate amongst staff that if the subject heading was omitted from an email, the monitoring software would not detect if an email was business or non-business. Focus group participants admitted that none of them had ever intentionally omitted or falsified a subject heading from an email but acknowledged the practice amongst staff. The monitoring data supports this as a disproportionate number of emails began to surface with absent or falsified subject headings and the number of non-business attachments forwarded internally increased by 9% on month 4. The number of non-business email sent internally and externally, the average age of unopened email and the number of email stored in users accounts, also showed a slight relapse of 1-2% on the improvements made in month 4. The EMMG believed staff were intentionally trying to circumvent monitoring and in turn, emailed staff in month 6 insisting that all email have a relevant subject heading and that non-business email must be further reduced.

The EMMG believed that 'festive factors' played a significant part in higher email volumes in months 6 and 7 (December and January), as the number of non-business email sent externally rose by 19% above the baseline metrics in month 6. The total number of non-business email sent internally and externally also rose by 26% on month 5. Large volumes of email received during the festive period may have contributed to unopened email increasing by 5% above the baseline metrics. Little improvement occurred in month 7 with a 10% increase in non-business email sent externally compared to the baseline metrics and the total number of non-business email sent internally and externally still 22% higher than month 5. The number of non-business attachments sent internally also rose by 15% on month 5. The HR Manager commented that 'we were riding the crest of a wave after our early success, but you have to remember that email monitoring does not actually control how email is used, it just lets you see how your controls are working'.

Latter Implementation of Electronic Monitoring and Control of the Email System

According to the IT Manager 'after email monitoring software was installed for a few months, we began to get a picture of how poorly the filtering software was working'. He revealed that 'although we found that a lot of these rogue attachments came from web-based email accounts, we also found that a sizeable proportion came from business addresses'. In month 8, the EMMG reconfigured the filtering software, extensively updating the keyword, phrase, the SPAM address library, and the blacklist of attachments. The EMMG emailed staff thanking them for their cooperation to date, but informing them that by the end of month 8, all communications with web-based email accounts would be blocked except for staff handling recruitment or public enquiries and that email filtering had been extensively reconfigured. The EMMG also requested staff to inform all of their business contacts that incoming emails containing questionable content or non-business related attachments would be blocked and reported to their systems administrator.

The decision to blacklist file attachments was not well received as staff felt that they had not being fully briefed. Staff were also incensed at the decision to block web-based email addresses, and were further annoyed when their email contacts immediately began to receive an automated response to some email communications stating *"this email address may not receive this attachment file type"*. The IT Manager explained that the attachment filter had been prematurely implemented but chose not to deactivate the filter despite the EMMG being inundated with complaints. An online poll to determine staff attitudes proved to be overwhelmingly against the changes. Subsequently, over three hundred staff members sent protest emails, resulting in four staff members meeting the EMMG to discuss a compromise. These negotiations led the EMMG to implement a probationary process in month 9 whereby staff were allowed to designate five personal web-based email accounts with which to communicate under the guidance of the email policy. Staff were satisfied with the outcome. A Sales Representative explained 'it's nice to see management listen to reason. Nobody was out to flout the policy or to be confrontational for the sake of it. We just wanted a reasonable solution to the problem'. A Production Operative commented 'they explained to us how these addresses were a problem for our email system because of junk mail and we accept that. However, we explained to them how these addresses were the only way that some of us could keep regular contact with our friends and family'. The impact of the reconfiguration of the filtering and blocking software was clearly evident in the monitoring data in month 9. The average number of email sent by the top 20 email users fell by 35%, the number of non-business email sent internally fell by 39%, the number of non-business attachments sent internally fell by 33%, the average age of unopened email fell by 65% and the number of deleted emails stored in users accounts fell by 46%. In addition the total number of non-business email sent internally and externally matched its highest point of a 30% reduction which had previously been achieved in month 3.

The monitoring data from month 10 was mixed as some measurements showed further or on par improvements with month 9 while other metrics showed some deterioration. The number of non-business attachments sent externally increased by 6% on month 9 while the number sent internally decreased by a further 9%. Further investigation of attachments revealed alternative file types were being used to circumvent blacklists but only to external recipients. The greatest concern to the HR Manager was the nature of some attachments sent to client email addresses. At the end of month 10, twelve staff members had their email access revoked for what the IT Manager described as 'gross violations of email policy'. The IT Manager believed these staff should have been fired as they 'had already received verbal and written warnings'. The email policy states, *"any employee who violates this policy or uses the email system for improper purposes shall be subject to discipline up to and including dismissal"*. Interestingly, the revoking of email access was received with an attitude of indifference by staff. A Sales Representative explained staff 'were aware of what they can and can't do with email, so if they have had their email facilities withdrawn, it must be for a good reason'.

In month 11, staff discovered that some staff could receive blacklisted attachments. The IT Manager reveals 'engineers are exempt from blacklisted attachments because of their jobs'. Other staff members are occasionally allowed to receive these files if IT are supplied with the attachment details and the nature of the contents of the attachment in advance. However, these emails are always opened and checked. A Sales Representative argued that if staff are given permission 'these files should not be opened…as it is an invasion of privacy'. Over one hundred and sixty staff emailed the EMMG to protest about 'double standards' and 'invasion of privacy'. The EMMG adopted a process in month 12 whereby permitted attachments were no longer opened if an electronic liability form was completed. The form required the individual to accept responsibility for any consequential effect the attachment may have on network or business transactions. However, staff would not accept responsibility for rogue attachments. A Process Technician revealed 'it's too risky given the kind of material that comes through our system'. Staff no longer contested their right to receive blacklisted attachments as this reinforced the EMMG's argument that greater control over attachments was needed. Only three staff ever completed the form.

From month 12 the EMMG emailed feedback on the monitoring process to staff at the end of every month and encouraged continued compliance with the email policy. However, in month 13, a failure to communicate the email policy to new staff culminated in what the IT Manager described as 'a systematic failure (in month 13) when a network backup failed. We had six interns (who had only been employed in month 12) with their drive full of Mpegs (movie files)'. Staff believed this highlighted their earlier assertions that engineers were as likely to flout email policy. The IT Manager immediately shut the interns email accounts and one week later all six interns were released from their internship.

Revoking email privileges in month 10 significantly impacted the average number of non-business emails sent by the top twenty email users which fell by 41% from months 11 to 15. The IT Manager believes this demonstrates that enforcing discipline is essential to reducing non-business email use. Furthermore, two staff members rewarded for effective email management in month 14 had been among those initially reprimanded. In the fifteen months, the number of non-business email sent internally fell by 57% while the number of non-business email sent externally fell by 39%. The blocking of attachments had a significant impact on the number of non-business attachments sent internally and externally. Internal non-business attachments fell by 65% from month 10 to month 15 while non-business attachments sent externally fell by 20%.The HR Manager claimed 'this proves monitoring works'. However, one staff member revealed that he now sent personal email by 'a web-based email account' and felt he hadn't reduced his non-business email communication dramatically. The IT Manager suggests 'it is only a small few staff and we will have that eradicated with WebSense very shortly'. Other significant improvements made in the fifteen months of monitoring included reducing the number of unopened email by 53%, the average age of unopened email by 76%, the number of deleted emails in users accounts by 69%, while the total number of non-business email sent was reduced by 49%.

Staff Overview of Electronic Monitoring and Control of the Email System

Staff believed that email monitoring acts as a control, diminishing the likelihood of email being used for non-productive behaviour. However, staff felt that the sudden shift in management attitude to their email use required greater explanation of the rules governing email use. An Electrical Engineer who had initially expressed little concern, reported that 'email monitoring is quite different (from telephone and Internet monitoring) because the information communicated is often more personal and the method by which it is monitored and stored is more invasive'. For these reasons, the engineer admitted to curtailing email use for business and personal use and believes it now takes him longer to write an email.

Staff suggested that tighter control over email use and in particular email monitoring, had created an untrustworthy communication medium because their communications are open to greater scrutiny and staff still felt unsure about the rules of the game. A Manufacturing Engineer believed that email is of far greater value if 'staff have confidence in using the system to voice their opinions, make decisions and group communicate over ideas'. A Sales Representative stated that 'social communication via email is part of decision making and idea generation'. Other staff believe that email use had never negatively affected their productivity. A Process Technician argued that 'email enables more rapid communication because you are more to the point unlike when you are on the phone, but you still need to create personal relationships with the people you communicate with through email'.

Staff are critical of management's efforts to maintain awareness of the email policy, pointing out that the policy is only available by emailing the HR Manager. A Manufacturing Engineer highlighted that 'new staff are never informed of the policy and the problems they create have a direct effect on all other staff'. A Sales Representative believes that 'she shouldn't be 'subject to the same sanctions as those who don't use the email responsibly'.

CONCLUSION

This exploratory study showed that staff can react in a number of negative ways to electronic monitoring and control of email systems. However, it is evident that staff mostly reacted negatively to poor implementation of controls rather than to the controls per se. The study revealed that staff had six primary concerns which should be addressed by management and consultants advocating the implementation of email system monitoring and control:

1. Staff felt that tighter control over email use had created an untrustworthy communication medium and that the social communication necessary for effective business relationships had been negatively affected.
2. Staff felt isolated and under greater scrutiny since the introduction of electronic monitoring and control of the email system.
3. Some staff felt they were punished for policy breaches committed by other staff.
4. Staff believed that email monitoring was more invasive than other forms of monitoring. Although non-business email communication was reduced, staff carefully considered everything they wrote, taking longer to write business emails.
5. Staff attempted to transform and/or circumvent controls if it was perceived to be poorly implemented and/or they felt they had not been adequately consulted or informed. Staff reacted by protesting via email, conducting online polls, removing or falsifying subject headings to circumvent monitoring or using web based email accounts to send non-business communications.
6. Staff were unsure about the rules of the game in the early stages, possibly contributing to greater abuse of the email system. Staff believed that training is essential, and that email policy needs to be more highly visible.

REFERENCES

American Management Association (AMA) (2004) *Workplace E-Mail and Instant Messaging Survey.* New York, USA.

Attaran, M. (2000). Managing Legal Liability of the Net: A Ten Step Guide for IT Managers. *Information Management and Computer Security*, 8, 2, 98-100.

Burgess, A., Jackson, T. & Edwards, J. (2005) Email Training Significantly Reduces Email Defects. *International Journal of Information Management*, 25, 1, 71-83.

Dhillon, G. (1999). Managing and Controlling Computer Misuse. *Information Management and Computer Security*, 7, 4, 171-175.

Flood, L. (2003). Close Monitoring Provides Protection. *Sunday Business Post.* IRL. Feb 9.

Gray and Grey (2002) Email And IM As Essential Platform Components in 2002. *Gartner Group*, 13th December, Note Number SPA-15-0931. Located at Http://www.gl.iit.edu/gartner2/research/103200/103210/103210.html.

Graff, J. (2002a) Building Email: Economy, Resilience and Business Value. *Gartner Group*, 22nd March, Note Number LE-15-6155. Advanced Search of Archived Research. Located At Http://www.Gartner.com

Graff, J. (2002b) Building a High Performance Email Environment. *Gartner Group*, 21st March, Note Number M-15-8182. Advanced Search of Archived Research. Located At Http://www.Gartner.com

Hodson, T.J., Englander, F. and Englander, V. (1999). Ethical, Legal and Economic Aspects of Monitoring of Employee Email. *Journal of Business Ethics*, 19, 99-108.

Jackson, T.W., Dawson, R. and Wilson, D. (2000). The Cost of Email Within Organisations. *Proceedings of the IRMA 2000*, Anchorage, Alaska, May.

Lindquist, C. (2000). You've Got Dirty Mail. *ComputerWorld*, 34, 11, 72-73.

Markus, L.M. (1994). Finding A Happy Medium: Explaining The Negative Effects Of Electronic Communication On Social Life At Work. *ACM Transactions On Information Systems, 12*, 2, Apr, 119-149.

Miles, M.B., And Huberman, M.A. (1994). *An Expanded Sourcebook Of Qualitative Data Analysis.* Sage Publications, California.

Oravec, J.A (2002) Constructive Approaches To Internet Recreation In The Workplace. *Communications Of The ACM*, 45, 1, 60-63.

Orlikowski, W.J. (1991). Integrated Information Environment or Matrix of Control?: The Contradictory Implications of Information Technology. *Accounting, Management and Information Technology*, 1, 1, 9-42.

Rudy, I.A. (1996). A Critical Review of Research on Email. *European Journal of Information Systems*, 4, 4, 198-213.

Ruggeri, G. Stevens and McElhill, J. (2000). A Qualitative Study and Model of the Use of EMail in Organisations. *Internet Research, Special Issue on Electronic Networking Applications and Policy*, 10, 4, 271.

Simmers, C.A. (2002) Aligning Internet Usage With Business Priorities. *Communications Of The ACM*, 45, 1, 71-74.

Sipior, J.C., Ward, B.T. and Rainone, S.M. (1996). The Ethical Dilemma of Employee Email Privacy in the US. *Proceedings of European Conference on Information Systems (ICIS).*

Sipior, J.C. and Ward, B.T. (2002). A Strategic Response to the Broad Spectrum of Internet Abuse. *Information Systems Management*, Fall, 71-79.

Sproull, L. and Kiesler, S. (1991). *Connections: New Ways of Working in the Networked Organisation.* Cambridge, Massachusetts: MIT Press.

Stanton, J.M. and Stam, K.R. (2003). Information Technology, Privacy and Power within Organisations: A View from Boundary Theory and Social Exchange Perspectives. *Surveillance & Society*, 1, 2, 152-190.

Steinfield, C.W. (1990). Computer-Mediated Communications in the Organisation: Using Email at Xerox. In *Case Studies in Organisational Communication*, 282-294, Guilford Press.

Urbaczewski, A. and Jessup, L.M. (2002). Does Electronic Monitoring of Employee Internet Usage Work? *Communications of the ACM*, 45, 1, 80-83.

Van Den Hooff, B. (1997). *Incorporating Email: Adoption, Use and Effects of Email in Organisations.* Universite IT van Amsterdam. ISBN 90-75727-72-0.

Weber, R. (2004). The Grim Reaper: The Curse of Email. Editor's Comments. *MIS Quarterly*, Vol. 28, No.3, iii-xiii, September.

Chapter VIII
Information and Knowledge Perspectives in Systems Engineering and Management for Innovation and Productivity through Enterprise Resource Planning

Stephen V. Stephenson
Dell Computer Corporation, USA

Andrew P. Sage
George Mason University, USA

ABSTRACT

This chapter provides an overview of perspectives associated with information and knowledge resource management in systems engineering and systems management in accomplishing enterprise resource planning for enhanced innovation and productivity. Accordingly, we discuss economic concepts involving information and knowledge, and the important role of network effects and path dependencies in influencing enterprise transformation through enterprise resource planning.

INTRODUCTION

Many have been concerned with the role of information and knowledge and the role of this in enhancing systems engineering and management (Sage, 1995; Sage & Rouse, 1999) principles, practices, and perspectives. Major contemporary attention is being paid to enterprise transformation (Rouse, 2005, 2006) through these efforts. The purpose of this work is to discuss many of these efforts and their role in supporting the definition, development, and deployment of an enterprise resource plan (ERP) that will enhance transformation of existing enterprises and development of new and innovative enterprises.

Economic Concepts Involving Information and Knowledge

Much recent research has been conducted in the general area of information networks and the new economy. Professors Hal R. Varian and Carl Shapiro have published many papers and a seminal text, addressing new economic concepts as they apply to contemporary information networks. These efforts generally illustrate how new economic concepts challenge the traditional model, prevalent during the Industrial Revolution and taught throughout industry and academia over the years. In particular, the book *Information Rules* (Shapiro & Varian, 1999) provides a comprehensive overview of the new economic principles as they relate to today's information and network economy. The book addresses the following key principles:

- Recognizing and exploiting the dynamics of positive feedback
- Understanding the strategic implications of lock-in and switching costs
- Evaluating compatibility choices and standardization efforts
- Developing value-maximizing pricing strategies
- Planning product lines of information goods
- Managing intellectual property rights
- Factoring government policy and regulation into strategy

These concepts have proven their effectiveness in the new information economy and have been fundamental to the success of many information technology enterprises introducing new ideas and innovations into the marketplace. Paramount to an enterprise's success in reaching critical mass for its new product offering is the understanding and implementation of these new economic concepts.

Economides (1996) has also been much concerned with the economics of networks. He and Himmelberg (1994) describe conditions under which a critical mass point exists for a network good. They characterize the existence of critical mass points under various market structures for both durable and non-durable goods. They illustrate how, in the presence of network externalities and high marginal costs, the size of the network is zero until costs eventually decrease sufficiently, thereby causing the network size to increase abruptly. Initially, the network increases to a positive and significant size, and thereafter it continues to increase gradually as costs continue to decline. Odlyzko (2001) expands on the concept of critical mass and describes both the current and future growth rate of the Internet and how proper planning, network budgeting, and engineering are each required. He emphasizes the need for accurate forecasting, since poor planning can lead to poor choices in technology and unnecessary costs.

Economides and White (1996) introduce important concepts with respect to networks and compatibility. They distinguish between direct and indirect externalities, and explore the implications of networks and compatibility for antitrust and regulatory policy in three areas: mergers, joint ventures, and vertical restraints. They also discuss how compatibility and complementarity are linked to provide a framework for analyzing antitrust issues. Strong arguments are made for the beneficial nature of most compatibility and network arrangements, with respect to vertical relationships, and policies are set forth to curb anti-competitive practices and arrangement. Farrell and Katz (2001) introduce concepts of policy formulation in preventing anti-competitive practices and, in addition, explore the logic of predation and rules designed to prevent this in markets that are subject to network effects. This work discusses how the imposition of the leading proposals for rules against predatory pricing may lower or raise consumer welfare, depending on conditions that may be difficult to identify in practice.

Research conducted on these economic concepts establishes a solid foundation and baseline for further research in the area of enterprise resource planning and new technology innovations (Langenwalter, 2000). In this work, he extends the traditional enterprise resource planning (ERP) model to incorporate a total enterprise integration (TEI) framework. He describes TEI as a superset of ERP and also describes how it establishes the communications foundation between customer, manufacturer, and supplier. Each entity is linked internally and externally, allowing the TEI system to enhance performance and to provide process efficiencies that reduce lead times and waste throughout the supply chain. This work illustrates how ERP is uniquely integrated with customers and suppliers into the supply chain using TEI and how it significantly improves customer-driven performance. The model for this includes five major components: executive support, customer integration, engineering integration, manufacturing integration, and support services integration. These components are essential for integrating all information and actions required to fully support a manufacturing company and its supply chain. TEI presents a strategic advantage to an enterprise, rather than just improving operating efficiencies. The TEI framework provides the enterprise a competitive edge by:

- Maximizing speed and throughput of information and materials
- Minimizing response time to customers, suppliers, and decision makers
- Pushing decisions to the appropriate levels of the organization
- Maximizing the information made available to the decision-makers
- Providing direct integration into the supply chain

In addition to the technology, TEI also incorporates stakeholders. People are empowered at all levels of the enterprise to improve the quality of their decision-making. One result of this is MRP II (Manufacturing Resources Planning) systems. MRP II evolved from MRP (Material Requirements Planning), which was a method for materials and capacity planning in a manufacturing environment. Manufacturing plants, to plan and procure the right materials in the right quantities at the right time, used this method. MRP became the core planning module for MRP II and ERP. MRP was later replaced by MRP II, which expanded the MRP component to include integrated material planning, accounting, purchasing of materials for production, and the shop floor. MRP II integrated other functional areas such as order entry, customer service, and cost control. Eventually, MRP II evolved into enterprise resource planning (ERP), integrating even more organizational entities and functions such as human resources, quality management, sales support, and field services. ERPs became richer in functionality and involved a higher degree of integration than their predecessors MRP and MRP II.

Another very well-known contributor to the field of enterprise resource planning is Thomas H. Davenport (2000). In *Mission Critical: Realizing the Promise of Enterprise Systems*, the need to take a customer or product focus when selecting an operational strategy is emphasized. To enable this, a direct connection should exist between the daily operations and the strategic objectives of the enterprise. This is made possible through the use of operational data, that is used to enhance the operational effectiveness of the enterprise. Operational data is defined by the organization seeking to measure the operational effectiveness of its environment. Operational data may be defined in terms of various parameters such as cycle time (CT), customer response time (CRT), or MTTR (mean time to repair). These are only a few of the parameters, and they are contingent on the operational strategy the organization is seeking to adopt. For example, an organization that seeks to reduce cycle time (CT) for processing orders in order to minimize cost may look to capture CT in its operational data. This data is captured over time as process efficiencies are instituted within the existing order process. Operational effectiveness is then determined by comparing the future CT state of the order process with that of its initial CT benchmark. For example, if cycle time to process an order was originally 15 minutes, and after the process efficiencies were instituted, CT was then 5 minutes, then operational effectiveness improved by 10 minutes. Now it takes fewer resources to process orders, thus reducing operational costs.

Davenport (2000) introduces a data-oriented culture and conveys the need for data analysis, data integrity, data synthesis, data completeness, and timely extracts of data. Data is used across organizational boundaries and shared between the various entities in an effort to enhance operational effectiveness. For example, transaction data must be integrated with data from other sources, such as third-party vendors, to support effective management decision-making. One's ability to interpret and analyze data can effect the decisions that are made and the confidence management has in pursuing particular ongoing decisions. Davenport believes that a combination of strategy, technology, data (data that is relevant to the organization), organization, culture, skills and knowledge assist with developing an organization's capabilities for data analysis. When performing data analysis, various organizations may have similar results, but with different meanings. He indicates that a typical corporation may have divisions that have a need to store customer data in different customer profile schemes. Therefore, a common shared master file between the divisions may not be feasible. This approach takes on more of a distributed approach versus a centralized approach to data management. The operational effectiveness of each of these divisions will vary based on the benchmarks and target improvements they have set for themselves.

Christopher Koch (2006) supports Davenport's data concept and elaborates on the value of an ERP and how it can improve the business performance of an enterprise. He demonstrates the value of an ERP by integrating the functions of each organization to serve the needs of all stakeholders. The associated framework attempts to integrate all organizational entities across an enterprise onto a single-systems ERP platform that will serve the needs of the various entities. This single platform replaces the standalone systems prevalent in most functional organizations such as human resources, finance, engineering, and manufacturing, thereby allowing people in the various organizations to access information not only in the most useful manner but also from their own perspectives. This information may be the same shared data used between the organizations or may vary, based on the need of each of the organizations. Each organization in the enterprise and its stakeholders will have their own set of requirements for accessing, viewing and manipulating their data. Data management may even take on a hybrid of a centralized and distributed approach. Some organizations may need a view of the same data, while others may have their own unique data requirements. Koch (2006) indicates that there are five major reasons why an enterprise adopts an ERP strategy:

1. Integrate financial information
2. Integrate customer order information
3. Standardize and speed up manufacturing processes
4. Reduce inventory
5. Standardize human resources (HR) information

Each organization within an enterprise has its own requirements for an ERP. They may share the same ERP solution; however, the ERP may be designed to support the specific business need of each organization. Some organizations may have a need to view the same data. For example, a sales and customer care-focused organization may need to view the same customer profile data to access customer contact information. In comparison, a human resources-focused organization may not need to be privy to this same information. They may be more interested in accessing internal employee personnel records for employee performance monitoring. The senior executive level of an enterprise will also have its own unique data requirements in order to make key strategic and tactical decisions. This executive level may need the capability to access data from each of the organizational units in order to effectively manage the operations of the business. The organizations, within an enterprise each have their own instances of an ERP with respect to accessing data and implementing processes. Some organizations may share a common process such as the order fulfillment process. For example, this process may be shared between organizational entities such as sales, operations, and revenue assurance. Sales would complete a service order, operations would deliver the service, and revenue assurance would bill the customer. However, there are processes that are only unique to a particular organization. For example, the marketing organization may not be interested in the escalation process used by operations to resolve customer issues. This process is unique to operations and, as a result, the ERP would be designed for such uniqueness. The design of an ERP should, of course, take organizational data and process requirements into account and support management of the enterprise and its inter-workings in a transdisciplinary and transinstitutional fashion (Sage 2000, 2006).

William B. Rouse had produced very relevant and important popular work surrounding new technology innovation with respect to the enterprise. In *Strategies for Innovation*, Rouse (1992) addresses four central themes to introduce strategies for innovation in technology-based enterprises. Rouse discusses the importance of strategic thinking and how some enterprises fail to plan long term. This is based on the notion that "while people may want to think strategically, they actually do not know how(p. 3)." He emphasizes the need for stakeholders to understand the solutions offered as a result of new innovation, and how strategies are critical for ensuring successful products and systems. Most importantly, these strategies must also create a successful enterprise for developing, marketing, delivering, and servicing solutions, thus leading to the need for human-centered planning, organization, and control. These are among the approaches needed to stimulate innovation in products and services (Kaufman & Woodhead, 2006).

Rouse (1992) describes the need for applying a human-centered design methodology to the problem of enhancing people's abilities and overcoming their limitations. In the process of planning, organizing, and controlling an enterprise, he illustrates how technology-based enterprises differentiate themselves from each other based on their core product technologies. This strategic strength is based on the unique value that the core product can provide to the marketplace. He indicates that the enterprise should continuously analyze the market and measure core product value to determine the benefits that can be provided. Assessing and balancing the stakeholders' interests will be necessary to ensure success of the core product. Stakeholders consist of both producers and consumers. Each may have a stake in the conceptualization, development, marketing, sales, delivery, servicing, and use of the product. The three key processes highlighted in this work are: strategic planning, operational management, and the engineering/administration, vehicles used by the enterprise to assist stakeholders with pursuing the mission of the enterprise.

Rouse further addresses strategic approaches to innovation in another one of his books. In *Essential Challenges of Strategic Management* (Rouse, 2001), he illustrates the strategic management challenges faced by all enterprises and introduces best practices for addressing these challenges. He disaggregates the process of strategically managing an enterprise into seven fundamental challenges. The essential challenges he describes, which most enterprises are confronted with, are: growth, value, focus, change, future, knowledge, and time. Growth is critical to gaining share in saturated and declining markets and essential to the long-term well-being of an enterprise. A lack of growth results in declining revenues and profits, and, in the case of a new enterprise, there is the possibility of collapse. He describes value as the foundation for growth, the reason an enterprise exists. Matching stakeholders' needs and desires to the competencies of the enterprise, when identifying high-value offerings, will justify the investments needed to bring these offerings to market. While value enhances the relationships of processes to benefits and costs, focus will provide the path for an enterprise to provide value and growth. Focus involves pursuing opportunities and avoiding diversions, that is, making decisions to add value in particular ways and not in others are often involved. For example, allocating too few resources among many projects may lead to inadequate results or possible failure.

The focus path is followed by another path called change. An enterprise challenged with organizational re-engineering, downsizing, and rightsizing often takes this change path. The enterprise will continue to compete creatively while maintaining continuity in its evolution. As the nature of an organization changes rapidly during an enterprise's evolution, managing change becomes an art. According to Rouse (2001), investing in the future involves investing in inherently unpredictable outcomes. He describes the future as uncertain. The intriguing question is, "If we could buy an option on the future, how would we determine what this option is worth(p. 6)?" A new enterprise will be faced with this challange when coming into the marketplace.

The challenge of knowledge is transformation of information from value-driven insights to strategic programs of action. Determining what knowledge would make an impact, and in what ways, is required. This understanding should facilitate determining what information is essential and should provide further elaboration on how it is to be processed and how its use will be supported. The most significant challenge identified is that of time. A lack of time is the most significant challenge facing best use of human resources. Most people spend too much time being reactive and responding to emergencies, attending endless meetings, and addressing an overwhelming number of e-mails, all of which cannibalize time. As a result, there is little time for addressing strategic challenges. Carefully allocating the scarcest resource of an organization is vital to the future of an enterprise. Some of the best practices Rouse (2001) has presented in addressing the seven strategic challenges may be described as follows:

- **Growth:** Buying growth via strategic acquisitions and mergers; fostering growth from existing market offerings via enhanced productivity; and creating growth through innovative new products and brand extensions.
- **Value:** Addressing the nature of value in the market; using market forces in determining the most appropriate business process; and designing cost accounting system to align budgets and expenditures with value streams.
- **Focus:** Deciding what things to invest in and those things to be avoided or stopped; and linking decisions or choices to organizational goals, strategies, and plans.
- **Change:** Instituting cross-functional teams for planning and implementing significant

changes; and redesigning incentive and reward systems in order to ensure that people align their behaviors with desired new directions.

- **Future:** Employing formal and quantitative investment decision processes; and creating mechanisms for recognizing and exploiting unpredictable outcomes.
- **Knowledge:** Ensuring that knowledge acquisition and sharing are driven by business issues in which knowledge has been determined to make a difference; using competitive intelligence and market/customer modeling to provide a valuable means for identifying and compiling knowledge.
- **Time:** Committing top management to devoting time to challenges; and improving time management, executive training, and development programs, in addition to providing increased strategic thinking opportunities.

Gardner (2000) takes a complementary approach to the enterprise and to innovation by focusing on the valuation of information technology. He addresses the difficulties of defining the value of new technologies for company shareholders using integrated analytical techniques in his book *The Valuation of Information Technology*. Gardner presents methodologies for new enterprise business development initiatives and presents techniques for improving investment decisions in new technologies. This 21st-century approach to valuation avoids making investment decisions on an emotional basis only, in favor of predicting shareholder value created by an information technology system before it is built. Determining the contribution an information technology system makes to a company's shareholder value is often challenging and requires a valuation model. Gardner suggests that the primary objective of information technology systems development in business is to increase the wealth of shareholders by adding to the growth premium of their stock. The objective of maximizing shareholder wealth consists of maximizing the value of cash flow generated by operations. This is accomplished by generating future investment in information technology systems. As an example, this could be a state-of-the-art enterprise resource planning system, which could easily maximize what we will call operational velocity and, as a result, maximize shareholder wealth. The process that Gardner suggests using would be to first identify the target opportunity, align the information technology system to provide the features the customer wants in a cost-effective manner, and then to accurately measure the economic value that can be captured through this.

Some of the techniques Gardner uses to compute economic value are net present value (NPV), rate of return (ROR), weighted average cost of capital (WACC), cost of equity, and intrinsic value to shareholders of a system. Each of these techniques may be used to determine aspects of the shareholder value of an information technology system. The results from computing these values will assist an enterprise with making the right decisions with respect to its operations. For example, if the rate of return on capital is high, then time schedule delays in deploying an information technology system can destroy enormous value. Time to market becomes critical in this scenario. Gardner suggests that it may be in the best interest of the company to deploy the system early by mitigating the potential risk and capitalizing on the high rate of return. A risk assessment must be performed to ensure that the customer relationship is not compromised at the expense of implementing the system early. If the primary functionality of the system is ready, then the risk would be minimal, and the other functional capabilities of the system may be phased in at a later time.

If the rate of return is low, however, schedule delays will have a lesser effect on value and deployment of a system does not immediately become crucial to the success of the enterprise.

This approach to predicting value takes a rational approach to decision making by weighing the rewards and risks involved with an information technology system investment. The author suggests moving away from the more intuitive approach of valuation often practiced in the high-tech industry, which is said to be very optimistic, spotty, and driven by unreasonable expectations from management. Gardner describes this intuitive practice as a non-analytical approach to assessing the economic viability of an information technology system. This practice primarily ignores the bare essentials that management must consider in assessing whether the economics of an information technology system are attractive. Gardner has established an analytical framework for analyzing the economics of information technology systems. His process is comprised of the three following steps:

1. Identify the target customer opportunity.
2. Align the information technology system to cost-effectively provide the features the customer wants.
3. Measure the economic value that can be captured.

The result of utilizing the framework is the quantification of the shareholder value created by an information technology system.

Boer (1999) also has much discussion on the subject of valuation in his work on *The Valuation of Technology*. He illustrates links between research and development (R&D) activity and shareholder value. In addition, he identifies the languages and tools used between business executives, scientists, and engineers. The business and scientific/engineering communities are very different environments and are divided by diverse knowledge and interest levels. Bridging the gap between these communities is made possible through the process of valuation, which fosters collaboration and communication between both communities. Boer identifies the link between strategy and value and addresses the mutual relationship between corporate strategy and technology strategy. He introduces tools and approaches used to quantify the link between technological research and commercial payoff within the value model of an enterprise.

This value model is comprised of four elements: operations, financial structure, management, and opportunities. The opportunity element is most critical to the future growth of an enterprise. The options value of an enterprise and how it is addressed strategically will determine the fate of an emerging enterprise. Boer illustrates how productive research and development creates options for the enterprise to grow in profitability and size. He views R&D as a component of operations, since this is the point at which new technology is translated into commercial production. In the competitive marketplace, the enterprise evolves in order to generate opportunity and growth. R&D serves as the vehicle for converting cash into value options for the enterprise. Boer introduces R&D stages (conceptual research, feasibility, development, early commercialization), where the level of risk, spending, and personnel skills vary. Each stage of the R&D process allows management to make effective decisions regarding the technology opportunity and perform levels of risk mitigation. R&D can be instrumental in decreasing capital requirements with results of a very high rate of return on the R&D investment. The art of minimizing capital requirements requires good and effective communication between the scientific/engineering and business communities. This will allow both communities to share their views and foster the need for driving this essential objective.

Some of the methods Boer uses for asset valuation are similar to Rouse's methods. Boer uses discounted cash flow (DCF), NPV, cost of money, weighted average cost of capital, cost of equity, risk-weighted hurdle rates for R&D, and terminal value methods for assessing valuation. In accelerated growth situations, as in the case of an emerging enterprise, Boer emphasizes that the economic value is likely to be derived from the terminal value of the project, not from short-term cash flows. A lack of understanding of terminal value can compromise the analysis of an R&D project. R&D can be a cash drain, and the outcomes are difficult to predict. Boer's techniques provide a vehicle for converting cash into opportunity and creating options for the enterprise.

Another work that addresses valuation is entitled *The Real Options Solution: Finding Total Value in a High-Risk World* (Boer, 2002). Here, the author presents a new approach to the valuation of business and technologies based on options theory. This innovative approach, known as the total value model, applies real options analysis to assessing the validity of a business plan. All business plans are viewed as options. These plans are subject to both unique and market risks. While business plans seem to create no value on a cash flow basis, they do become more appealing once the full merit of all management options is recognized. Since management has much flexibility in execution, the model offers a quantifiable approach to the challenge of determining the strategic premium of a particular business plan. Boer defines total value as "the sum of economic value and the strategic premium created by real options (p. vii)." He presents a six-step method for applying this model in a high-risk environment for evaluating enterprises, R&D-intensive companies, bellwether companies, capital investments, and hypothetical business problems. His method reveals how changes in total value are driven by three major factors: risk, diminishing returns, and innovation.

Boer's option theory efforts provide the enterprise with a vehicle for computing the strategic premium to obtain total value. This six-step method to calculate total value is comprised of:

1. Calculation of the economic value of the enterprise
2. Framing the basic business option
3. Determining the option premium
4. Determining the value of the pro forma business plan
5. Calculating the option value
6. Calculating total value

Options theory approached to valuation leverage on elements of uncertainty such as these afford enterprise managers major investment opportunities. This was not common using more traditional valuation methods such as NPV- and internal rate of return (IRR)-based calculations. As Boer (2002) illustrates, the new options theory emphasizes the link between options, time, and information. Boer states: "Options buy time. Time produces information. Information will eventually validate or invalidate the plan. And information is virtual (p. 106)." This theory and its extensions (Boer, 2004) may well pave the way for a new generation of enterprise evolution and enterprise innovation.

Rouse (2005, 2006) is concerned with the majority of these issues in his development of systems engineering and management approaches to enterprise transformation. According to Rouse, enterprise transformation concerns change, not just routine change but fundamental change that substantially alters an organization's relationships with one or more of its key constituencies: customers, employees, suppliers, and investors. Enterprise transformation can take many forms. It can involve new value propositions in terms of products and services and how the enterprise should be organized to provide these offerings and to support them. Generally, existing or anticipated value deficiencies drive these initiatives. Enterprise transformation initiatives involve addressing the work undertaken by an enterprise and how the work is accomplished. Other important elements of the enterprise that influence this may include market advantage, brand image, employee and customer satisfaction, and many others.

Rouse suggests that enterprise transformation is driven by perceived value deficiencies due to existing or expected downside losses of value; existing or expected failures to meet promised or anticipated gains in value; or desire to achieve new, improved value levels through marketing and/or technological initiatives. He suggests three ways to approach value deficiencies: improve how work is currently performed; perform current work differently; and/or perform different types of work. Central to this work is the notion that enterprise transformation is driven by value deficiencies and is fundamentally associated with investigation and change of current work processes such as to improve the future states of the enterprise. Potential impacts on enterprise states are assessed in terms of value consequences.

Many of the well-known contributors in the field of enterprise resource planning presented had developed their own unique model. Each had established a strategy to address the evolution and growth of the enterprise. Differences between the models varied based on the challenge presented and the final objective to be achieved by the enterprise. A comparison of the ERP models presented is illustrated in Table 1.

Fundamentally, system engineering and system management are inherently transdisciplinary in attempting to find integrated solutions to problems that are of a large scale and scope (Sage, 2000). Enterprise transformation involves fundamental change in terms of reengineering of organizational processes and is also clearly transdisciplinary as that success necessarily requires involvement of management, computing, and engineering, as well as behavioral and social sciences. Enterprises and associated transformation are among the complex systems addressed by systems engineering and management. Rouse's efforts (2005, 2006) provide a foundation for addressing these issues and the transdisciplinary perspective of systems engineering and management provide many potentially competitive advantages to deal with these complex problems and systems.

Network Effects and Their Role in Enterprise Resource Planning

In today's information economy, introducing new technologies into the marketplace has become a significant challenge. The information economy is not driven by the traditional economies of scale and diminishing returns to scale that are prevalent among large traditional production companies. It has been replaced by the existence of network effects (also known as network externalities), increasing returns to scale and path dependence. This is the core economic reality, and not at all a philosophy, which has revolutionized traditional economic theories and practices, resulting in a new approach to economic theory as it pertains to the information economy.

There are a number of market dynamics or external variables that impact the success of any new technology entering the market. The most common variable is the element of network effects. A product exhibits network effects when its value to one user depends on the number of other users. Liebowitz and Margolis (1994) define network effects as the existence of many products for which the utility that a user of them derives from their consumption increases with the number of other agents that are also utilizing the product, and where the utility that a user derives from a product depends upon the number of other users of the product who are in the same network. Network effects are separated into two distinct parts, relative to the value received by the consumer. Liebowitz and Margolis (1994) denote the first component as the autarky value of a technology product, the value generated by the product minus the other users of the network. The second component is the synchronization value, the value associated when interacting with other users of the product. The social value derived from synchronization is far greater than the private value from autarky. This social value leads the way to increasing returns to scale, by creating path dependence (also known as positive

Table 1. Comparison of ERP models

ERP Models				
Contributor	**Model**	**Strategy**	**Challenge**	**Objective**
Gary A. Langenwalter	Total enterprise integration (TEI) framework	• Integrates customer, manufacturer, and supplier • Provides competitive edge by: maximizing speed of information, minimizing response time, pushing decisions to the correct organizational level, maximizing information available to decision-makers, and direct integration of supply chains	• Establishing seamless communication • Multi-functional integration	• Incorporate all stakeholders • Empower people at all levels of the organization • Improve quality of decision-making
Thomas H. Davenport	Operational data model	• Introduces data-oriented culture • Supports a customer and product focus • Uses operational data to measure operational effectiveness	• Defining organizational boundaries • Enhancing operational effectiveness	• Define operational performance parameters • Measure operational effectiveness • Support effective decision-making
Christopher Koch	Business performance framework	• Supports data sharing • Integrates financial information • Integrates customer order information • Standardizes manufacturing process • Reduces inventory • Standardizes HR information	• Centralized and distributed approach to data management • Establishing requirements for accessing, viewing, and manipulating data	• Integrate all organizational entities across a single systems platform • Manage enterprise in transdisciplinary and transinstitutional fashions
William B. Rouse	Strategic innovation model	• Introduces a strategic approach to innovation • Focuses on the need for human-centered planning, organization, and control • Differentiating from the competition based on core product technologies	• Enhancing people's abilities and overcoming their limitations • Essential challenges: growth, value, focus, change, future, knowledge, and time	• Support strategic planning, operational management, and engineering • Ensure the successful innovation of products and systems
Christopher Gardner	Valuation model	• Presents methodologies for new enterprise business development initiatives • Determines the contribution an enterprise system makes to a company's shareholder value	• Defining the value of new technologies • Mitigating the potential risk and capitalizing on the high rate of return	• Increase shareholder wealth • Maximize the value of cash flow generated by operations
Peter F. Boer	Options model	• Bridges the gap between the business and scientific/engineering communities • Introduces research and development that creates options for the enterprise to grow in profitability and size	• Identifying the link between corporate strategy and technology strategy • Minimizing capital requirements • Understanding terminal value of a project	• Introduce research and development stages for assessing technology opportunities • Determine strategic premium created by real options

feedback) and influencing the outcome for network goods. These efforts and others are nicely summarized in Liebowitz (2002) and Liebowitz and Margolis (2002).

Path dependence is essential for a company to reach critical mass when introducing new technologies into the market. As the installed customer base grows, more customers find adoption of a new product or technology of value, resulting in an increase in the number of consumers or users. Consumer choices exhibit path dependence for new products as others realize their value, eventually leading to critical mass. Path dependence is simply an effect whereby the present position is a result of what has happened in the past. The path dependence theory demonstrates that there are a number of stable alternatives, one of which will arise based on the particular initial conditions. Path dependence is evident when there is at least persistence or durability in consumer decision-making. Decisions made by early adopters can exhibit a controlling influence over future decisions or allocations made by late adopters. These product decisions are often based on the individual arbitrary choices of consumers, persistence of certain choices, preferences, states of knowledge, endowments, and compatibility. The outcome may depend on the order in which certain actions occur based on these behavioral determinants.

Network effects, increasing returns, and path dependence can be better illustrated when applied to the concept of a virtual network. The virtual network has similar properties to a physical or real network, such as a communications network. In such networks, there are nodes and links that connect the nodes to each other. In a physical network, such as a hard-wire communications network, the nodes are switching platforms and the links are circuits or telephone wires. Conversely, the virtual network nodes may represent consumers and transparent links represent paths, as driven by network effects and path dependence, that impact consumer behavior. The value of connecting to the network of Microsoft Office users is predicated on the number of people already connected to this virtual network. The strength of the linkages to the virtual network and its future expansion is based on the number of users who will use the same office applications and share files.

Path dependence can easily generate market dominance by a single firm introducing a new technology. This occurs when late adopters latch onto a particular virtual network, because the majority of users already reside on this infrastructure and have accepted the new technology. As more consumers connect to the virtual network, it becomes more valuable to each individual consumer. Consumers benefit from each other as they connect to the infrastructure. The larger network becomes more attractive to the other consumers who eventually become integrated. A communications network can best illustrate this concept. For example, additional users who purchase telephones and connect to a communications infrastructure bring value to the other users on the network, who can now communicate with the newly integrated users. This same concept applies to the virtual network and has the same impact. Real and virtual networks share many of the same properties and, over time, are destined to reach a critical mass of users.

New and emerging startup enterprises seeking to take advantage of network effects and path dependence when launching a new technology or innovation in the marketplace must have a reliable and operationally efficient enterprise resource planning (ERP) solution in place. The ERP solution must be capable of attaining operational velocity to address market demands. Miller and Morris (1999) indicate that traditional methods of managing innovation are no longer adequate. They suggest that as we make the transition to fourth generation R&D, appropriate complex timing for innovations remains a significant challenge. These authors assert that as new technologies and new markets emerge, management must deal with complexity, enormous discontinuities, increasing volatility, and the rapid evolution of industries. The challenge becomes that of linking emerging technologies with emerging markets through methods such as an ERP solution to bridge this link and to allow new emerging enterprises, or established mature enterprises seeking to transform themselves, to adapt quickly to the dynamics of the marketplace. The solution supports both continuous and discontinuous innovation as defined by Miller and Morris (1999). This form of innovation works well when customer needs in a competitive environment can be met within existing organizational structures.

In contrast to this, discontinuous innovation may bring forth conditions emanating from fundamentally different new knowledge in one or more dimensions of a product or service, and offer significantly different performance attributes. Discontinuous change potentially brings about change in a deep and systematic way. It offers a potential lifestyle change to customers that can be dramatic. Miller and Morris (1999) note, for example, the transition from typewriters to personal computers for producing written documents. In part, this occurred because customers no longer were satisfied with the existing framework of capability offered by the typewriter. New knowledge, organizational capabilities, tools, technology, and processes changed the behavior and desires of the customer. In addition to this change was also the change resulting in supporting infrastructure. Miller and Morris (1999) emphasize that discontinuous innovation affects not only products and services but also the infrastructures integral to their use, as well as extensive chains of distribution that may involve a plethora of affiliated and competing organizations.

As the threat of unexpected competition surrounds any new enterprise entering the market, the risk associated with technology shifts and the compression of the sales cycle make successfully managing discontinuous innovation a necessary challenge for success. We must be able to gauge how the market is evolving and what organizational capabilities must exist to sustain competitiveness as a result of this evolution. Because innovation usually requires large capital infusions, decreasing the time for appearance of a positive revenue stream is critical to the success of the enterprise. This decrease in time is made possible through operational velocity attainment, which requires changes in existing implementation strategies and organizational capabilities. This requires a collaborative effort between the various involved organizations to understand what is needed to support new innovations. Responsibility for supporting new innovation is not only supported by internal organizations but by such external organizations as suppliers, customers, and partners. Organizational structure, capabilities, and processes are fundamental to an evolutionary ERP model and serve as the framework for supporting new technology adoption in the marketplace.

The information economy is driven by network effects (also termed demand-side economies of scale or network externalities). Network effects support path dependence and are predicated on Metcalfe's Law, which suggests that the value of a network goes up as the square of the number of users (Shapiro & Varian, 1999), or on recent suggested modifications to this (Briscoe, Odlyzko, & Tilly, 2006). Positive effects occur when the value of one unit increases with an increase in the number of the same unit shared by others. Based on this premise, it is possible to create an enterprise resource planning model that influences positive feedback from human behavior in adopting new technologies and accelerates critical mass early in the deployment phase of the product development lifecycle, by attaining operational velocity. Operational velocity is defined in terms of speed in delivering products or services to market, meeting all customer expectations in a timely manner, and decreasing the time for appearance of a positive revenue stream as much as possible. This ERP model would support the integration of data, standardization of processes, order fulfillment, inventory control, supply-chain management, and customer relationship management (CRM) as critical drivers to result in enterprise transformation.

William B. Rouse, in his work *Strategies for Innovation* (Rouse, 1992), states "A prerequisite for innovation is strategies for making stakeholders aware of enabling technology solutions, delivery of theses solutions in a timely fashion, and providing services that assure the solutions will be successful. These strategies must not only result in successful products or systems, they must also create a successful organization—an enterprise—for developing, marketing, delivering, and serving solutions" (p. 2). His philosophy encompasses the human-centered design approach that takes into account the concerns, values, and perceptions of all stakeholders during a design initiative. This approach entertains the views of all the stakeholders, balancing all human considerations during the design effort.

Traditionally, when designing an enterprise resource planning solution, very few enterprises are easily able to think strategically. Most are only concerned with today's products and services and the financial profits and revenue growth realized in the short term. They often fail to properly forecast future growth and to properly scale their ERP in order to meet the potential consumer demands of the future. An enterprise must be able to plan for and respond to future demands by analyzing the market and evaluating the impact that their core product technologies will have in the marketplace. Market demand will drive consumer needs and desire for these core product technologies, as well as the type of ERP that will be used to support these products. An effective ERP must be capable of assessing and balancing all stakeholders' interests consciously and carefully. The market share that an enterprise is able to acquire for its core product technologies can be tied to how well an ERP is developed, deployed, and implemented in order to provide the operational support infrastructure needed. Many of the traditional success factors for an enterprise have been their position in the marketplace, achievements as innovators, productivity, liquidity and cash flow, and profitability. In order for an enterprise to grow and mature, it must be able to respond to market demand in a timely manner. Responding to market demand includes timely delivery of products and services, immediate attention to customer problem/resolution, and continuous process improvements. Operational velocity attainment becomes the focus and the critical success factor in the execution of an evolutionary ERP strategy, thus supporting the long-term vision of the enterprise by ensuring a strategic advantage for the enterprise.

A well-thought-out ERP strategy will require advanced planning to determine how each of the organizations will be integrated in supporting the long-term objective. Critical to the success of an enterprise is how well its associated organizations can adapt to organizational change, as the company begins to mature and demand increases for the new innovative products and services. Change may include the type of culture that is fostered, tools used, and level of knowledgeable resources required to make the organizational transitions. Most importantly, customer experiences becomes the focus. How fast an enterprise can service customers to meet their expectations may determine how soon it meets revenue expectations. The quality of on-time customer service could impact the number of future sales. A good product or service, combined with excellent customer service, may drive more business to the enterprise, decreasing the time taken to meet revenue forecasts. The mechanism used to drive customer on-time service becomes what we call an evolutionary ERP model. In order for new core technology products to become acceptable to a newly installed base of customers, service delivery and customer response times must be minimized as much as possible. True enterprise growth and profitability can be made possible through this model for emerging enterprises delivering new innovations to the marketplace. The model takes into account the long-term vision of the enterprise, which is a key to its consistent success. Rouse (1992) states this well when he says that many technology-based startup companies are very attracted to learning about new technologies, using these to creating new products, and hiring appropriate staff to accomplish these. Such activities may get the product, resulting from the enterprise vision, into the marketplace. Initial sales and profit goals may be achieved. He appropriately notes that without a long-term vision, plans for getting there, and an appropriate culture; no amount of short-term oriented activity will yield consistent long-term success.

The strategic advantages that a well-defined, developed, and deployed ERP brings to the enterprise are: integration across the enterprise, communication, operating efficiencies, modeling, and supply chain management. These effective strategies assist with bridging the overall corporate strategies with the organizational objectives. Integration across the enterprise supports the following organizational objectives:

- Maximization of speed and throughput of information
- Minimization of customer response times
- Minimization of supplier and partner response times
- Minimization of senior management response times
- Decision-making authority pushed to the appropriate levels within the organization, using work flow management
- Maximization of information to senior management
- Direct integration of the supply chain
- Reduction of inventories
- Reduction in order-to-ship time
- Reduction in customer lead times
- Total quality integration

Communication links the enterprise to both the suppliers and the customers. Good communication between supplier and the enterprise can help reduce design errors, foster good supplier and enterprise relationships, reduce enormous costs, reduce the supplier's time to respond to the enterprise, and improve performance and market adoption of a new core technology product.

Langenwalter (2000) indicates in his work on enterprise resource planning that integrating the design process with customers can surface customer responses with respect to their true needs. He emphasizes the voice of the customer (VOC) as a proven methodology that addresses the true needs and expectations of the customer. VOC serves as basic input to the evolutionary ERP model. Key customer considerations in achieving operational velocity using this model are ranked customer expectations, performance metrics, and customer perceptions of performance.

In *The Valuation of Technology*, Boer (1999) is also concerned with these customer considerations by including the concept of the value proposition from the customer's viewpoint. He emphasizes that stakeholders must find useful ways to determine the value added in every step of the business process from the viewpoint of the customer. The enterprise must exist to deliver value to the extent that it improves operational performance and/or lower costs through new or enhanced products, processes and services. For example, the operations of an enterprise will focus on procuring equipment and materials from vendors and suppliers to produce products on time and within budget. The operations objective is to meet customer demand through scheduling, procurement, implementation, and support, to meet the ever-changing needs of the customer environment. These changes must be measured so that the operations of the enterprise may be able to meet the needs of the marketplace. Such flexibility of operations in the marketplace is essential in keeping up with the dynamic needs of the customer.

In the new technology age, markets are moving much faster than traditional predictive systems suggest. Flexibility therfore becomes an essential and necessary element in achieving operational velocity. To achieve this, Langenwalter (2000) introduces a new measurement system that recognizes the ever-changing dynamics of products, customers, workers, and processes. His approach is based on the assumption that all products have life cycles and should have four key metrics: profitability, time, quality, and company spirit. Encompassing this approach would be the execution of a continuous process improvement initiative, with respect to the operational component of the product lifecycle. He proposes that the enterprise measure each organizational contribution to profit for the entire lifecycle of the product. An ERP can effectively measure the contribution to margin that a sales organization may make on new product releases. Unprofitable products can be immediately identified and retired. In comparison, an ERP can also track the total lifecycle cost that a manufacturing organization incurs when producing a product. Total profit and loss (P&L) responsibilities can be tracked and material procurement and cost strategies can be evaluated to enhance profitability to the extent possible. Other organizational facets such as engineering and marketing can increase profits, by accessing customer profile information from an ERP and trending product demand for various new features and functionality. Incorporating new design considerations in future product releases may also increase potential profitability, as more high-end products are released.

The element of time is an important metric and is truly a measure of process, although process efficiencies can also translate into cost savings. Langenwalter (2000) describes three key time dimensions: time to market, time to customer, and velocity. Each is a component of operational velocity. In achieving operational velocity, time to market is critical for new technology adoption. It is crucial for new enterprises to launch their core technology product(s) on time, in order to sustain long-term product profitability. This is especially true if new technology is involved. Langenwalter (2000) indicates that a study performed by the McKinsey Consulting Group reflects that a six-month delay in entering a market results in a 33% reduction in after-tax profit over the life of the product. In addition, the six-month delay is five times more costly than a 50% development-cost overrun and approximately 30% more costly than having production costs 10% over budget.

An ERP should be capable of monitoring product development and manufacturing processes to ensure timely delivery of products to market. Such items as customer requirements, technical viability, manufacturing costs, production volumes, staffing levels, work order priorities, material requirements, and capacity requirements can be accessible via the ERP, and allow both the engineering and manufacturing components in an organization to respond to product demands quickly. The ERP supports time to market in that these two organizations are able to ensure efficient product development manufacturing processes and organizational communication in launching new products to market. The ERP, so enabled, becomes the common domain and communications intermediary between engineering and manufacturing.

Time to customer is the next most critical dimension, or aspect, of time as described by Langenwalter (2000). This time dimension is focused on reducing lead times to customers. For example, manufacturers look to reduce the lead-time it takes to produce a product, component, or assembly. Although it may have taken weeks to produce a particular component, improved manufacturing capabilities may now enable this process in only two days. This may have been accomplished through the use of an ERP, which made it possible to track performance metrics of the various manufacturing processes. As a result of isolating various inhibiting manufacturing processes and improving these processes, time to customer was reduced significantly, thus supporting the operational velocity objective of the enterprise.

Another good example is customer care, achieved by responding to a product fault scenario and providing technical support capability to the customer for fault resolution. Response to a customer call may have originally taken 72 hours to resolve the problem due to the lack of an effective scheduling tool for the timely dispatching of technical support field resources. With the integration of a resource-scheduling tool within ERP, customer care can now respond perhaps within four hours and provide timely customer support. Velocity, the final dimension that Langenwalter presents, is defined as the total elapsed time consumed by a process divided by the actual value-added time contributed by the same process.

The quality metric of the product life cycle, as described by Langenwalter, focuses on continuous improvement. Quality metrics are very much tied to what may be called an evolutionary enterprise resource planning architecture framework. Operational velocity is only as good as the product and the service that is delivered. Any compromise in quality may translate to potential customer attrition and/or the degradation of market share. A good ERP should be capable of tracking product component failure rates and product design flaws, so that immediate action may be exercised on the part of the enterprise. Speed without quality only becomes a formula for failure. Product failures are not the only inhibitors of quality. A lack of knowledgeable and skilled resources can compromise quality, and this describes Langenwalter's last critical metric – company spirit. He emphasizes the fact that people are the ones who develop relationships with customers and suppliers, eventually leading to new products and processes. This metric goes outside much traditional thinking. However, during the enterprise startup technology revolution, company spirit is generally the most important element of survival and success among enterprises. This leads to a greater sense of ownership and responsibility among the people involved. An enterprise without a healthy team spirit and aggressive workforce has little chance of success.

Rouse (1992) introduces yet another interesting growth strategy that further supports the concept of operational velocity for new technology adoption. He describes a strategy for growth via enhancing productivity through process improvement and information technology. This approach leads to higher quality and lower cost of products and services and, eventually, to greater market share and profits. Enterprise performance is not as visible as product performance, so the money and time saved on process refinements often go unnoticed. Each approach has its own value. Rouse describes product value as the foundation for growth and indicates that the challenge of value concerns matching stakeholders' needs and desires to the enterprise's competencies in the process of identifying high-value offerings that will justify investments needed to bring these to market. Value to the customer is dependent on the particular market domain. The most noticeable form of value comes in the form of new innovations that meet a customer's economics or needs. Customers quickly realize the benefits of a new technology product; however, the real value is determined at the enterprise level, where customer support becomes critical. Technology products are sophisticated and require a high level of customer support when potential problems arise. After the sale of the product, the relative performance of the enterprise becomes the focus of the customer. Lack of timely and quality support can erode consumer confidence and eventually erode market share for an enterprise.

After the launch of its first product, an enterprise is immediately under the scrutiny of the public. Often, early adopters of new technologies can either make or break an emerging enterprise. Early adopters will assess the enterprise on product quality, delivery, and customer support. If the product is reliable and performs well, then delivery and customer support become the two most critical criteria that a customer will evaluate. It is usually the shortfalls in these two areas that diminish consumer confidence and challenge the credibility of a new enterprise. An enterprise that has an ERP strategy to address these criteria is better positioned for success. If the ERP is designed well, it will allow the enterprise to ensure quality delivery and customer support to the end users. The true value to the customer is realized in enterprise performance as opposed to product performance. Historically, customers have been prone to pursue other vendors because of lack of customer support, moreso than with average product performance. The result of a well-executed ERP strategy enables the enterprise to react immediately and consistently, enabling the organizational components to focus their human and financial capital in the right areas.

Rouse describes the challenge of focus as deciding the path whereby the enterprise will provide value and grow. Rouse (2001) introduces some common challenges in and impediments to an organization's decision making, including:

- Assumptions made
- Lack of information
- Prolonged waiting for consensus
- Lack of decision-making mechanisms
- Key stakeholders not involved
- Decisions made but not implemented

An enterprise is capable of addressing these challenges if it institutes an ERP solution during its evolution. The ERP solution will bridge many of the communication gaps common among enterprises that are often organizationally disconnected. A good ERP solution will support information sharing, track performance metrics, and archive information, thus providing methods and tools in supporting rapid decision making and furthering the concept of operational velocity. Many times, senior management is unable to focus on key areas due to lack of information and decision-making tools. This problem can be overcome by integrating these capabilities with the ERP. An ERP can scale easily to meet the business needs. The enterprise that plans for growth through its evolution can scale more easily and adapt to change.

Rouse (2001) states that "given a goal (growth), a foundation (value), and a path (focus), the next challenges concern designing an organization to follow this path, provide this value, and achieve this goal" (pp. 5-6). The climate of the enterprise changes rapidly and dramatically throughout its evolution. As new core technology products are launched, the environment is subject to change. Enterprises find ways to scale their infrastructures to meet growth, fend off competition, restructure, reengineer, and support virtual organizations. The objective of change is to improve quality, delivery, speed, and customer service. All of this is made possible through a well-integrated ERP. An ERP capable of facilitating change allows the enterprise to foster new opportunities for growth and reward. As an enterprise evolves over time into a major corporation, business practices change and a paradigm shift occurs over several phases of maturation. The ERP can assist an enterprise in transitioning new business philosophies and practices and to help pave the way for future growth. There is a major need to anticipate future opportunities and threats, plan for contingencies, and evolve the design of the enterprise so that the plans are successful.

The value of the future is difficult to estimate; this realization has lead to another interesting concept, the option value of an enterprise. As previously mentioned, Boer (2002) is a major proponent of options value as applied to the enterprise. This concept explores investment decisions based on buying an option on the future and determining what that option is worth. An enterprise must plan for future growth and weigh the various investment alternatives available. These include looking at the following:

- Strategic fit
- Financial payoff
- Project risk and probability of success
- Market timing
- Technological capability of the enterprise

The above factors weigh into the decisions made to invest in the future. It is through investments in education, training and organizational development that the enterprise is enabled to meet future objectives through resource allocation.

Other investments in research and development technology make decision-making much more complex. However, they may yield promising future results if planned well and integrated with other decisions taken. Investments in R&D require knowledgeable resources that can influence the abilities of an enterprise to provide value. Knowledge management becomes a key element in the overall ERP strategy. Rouse (2001) indicates that knowledge management and knowledge sharing (Small & Sage, 2006) will promote an integrated approach to identifying, capturing, retrieving, sharing, and evaluating an enterprise's information assets. This may be achieved by applying knowledge management concepts to the ERP strategy. A sound return on investment (ROI) model for an ERP should assess the dynamics of the enterprise, changes needed, and projected savings from these changes. The changes themselves should be measurable. An ERP must be planned carefully and, most importantly, well-executed with all resource considerations made during its evolution. The benefits derived from a well-executed ERP should reveal improvements in task management, automation, information sharing, and process workflow. Each of these components improves the most scarce resources that people face within the enterprise, that of time.

Time is a key ingredient for gaining organizational control. An ERP system with integrated tools and methods for communicating and modeling assists human resources with time management. Time management can be a critical problem and human resources can easily find themselves becoming reactive versus proactive in their day-to-day activities. Rouse (2001) emphasizes that it is important to increase the priority given to various long-term strategic tasks, especially since they too often suffer from demands for time from the many near-term operational tasks. A well-integrated ERP supports time management and allows human resources to gain control of their time and allocate it across the appropriate tasks. It further supports the need for long-term planning by supplying various tools and methods for enhancing strategic thinking. The tools and methods integrated within the ERP should improve both the efficiency and effectiveness of time allocation to tasks. An ERP that is incapable of handling the challenge of time diminishes the true value of the ERP. Time management is a crucial component in achieving operational velocity and must be controlled, in order for the enterprise to respond quickly to customer demands.

The seven challenges to strategic management of Rouse (2001) are all critical elements that need to be considered when designing an ERP. A well-designed ERP helps position the enterprise well in the market and gives it a strategic advantage. The true gauges of success of an enterprise, with a successfully executed ERP, will be reflected in how it is positioned in the marketplace. Rouse (1992) has identified five gauges of success:

1. Standings in your markets
2. Achievements as an innovator
3. Productivity
4. Liquidity and cash flow
5. Profitability

Each of these gauges of success is tied to shareholder value. Gardner (2000) also raises a major consideration about designing an ERP in his book *The Valuation of Information Technology*. He asks the questions:

What contributions will an information technology system make to a company's shareholder value? How can an information technology system be constructed to create shareholder value? In other words, not just determine the effect of a system on shareholder value but guide the activities involved in its construction in the first place. (p. 63)

He emphasizes the need to predict the shareholder value that will be created by an information system before it is actually built. In the context of an ERP, the objective is to increase the wealth of shareholders by adding premium growth to their stock. An ERP can improve the asset utilization of an enterprise by allowing shareholders to increase their returns on invested capital. The traditional approach to increasing shareholder wealth consists of maximizing the value of the cash flow stream generated by an operational ERP. The cash flow generated from the ERP is allocated among the shareholders and debt holders of the enterprise. Shareholder value is traditionally measured by using the DCF method, which is central to the valuation of assets and the return they generate in the future. Boer (1999) addresses the DCF method well in his book *The Valuation of Technology*. He defines the premise of the DCF method "as a dollar received tomorrow is worth less than one in hand today" (p. 63).The question that arises from this premise is how much should one invest today in order to earn a dollar tomorrow. To address this, Boer presents one of the common DCF methods known as net present value.

The NPV method can be used to compute the value of tomorrow's dollar. Boer properly defines NPV as "the present value of a stream of future cash flow less any initial investment (p. 98)." NPV addresses the time value of money, which is essential for developing an ERP strategy, with the objective of attaining operational velocity. Gardner (2000) illustrates how this has a significant effect on the management of ERP systems. If the rate of return is high, schedule delays in deploying an ERP can erode value, which makes time to market critical; and since short product life generates as much value as long product life, there should be little resistance in replacing legacy systems. In comparison, if the rate of return is low, delays have little effect on value, and a longer product lifecycle is feasible, thereby allowing for a more thorough systems development effort. Gardner extends the NPV method to an ERP system and illustrates how shareholder value is created by changes in the present value of the cash flow to shareholders due to the use of the ERP system.

The DCF method illustrated here focuses solely on the economic value of the enterprise. Boer (2002) introduces a concept known as the options value of the enterprise in his book *The Real Options Solution: Finding Total Value in a High-Risk World*. The options method is presented as a means to value the strategic capital of an enterprise. This method is known as the total value model and combines the economic value and strategic value of the enterprise, and also takes into account three major drivers that affect value: risk, diminishing returns, and innovation. Enterprises satisfactorily releasing new technologies into the marketplace normally increase their strategic value if consumers adopt these new technologies to meet their needs. New technology adoption in the marketplace can vary based on need, price, standards, and other related factors. Once the need is recognized, operational velocity becomes critical to answering the customer's needs. How fast customers can be served and cared for will drive the strategic value of the enterprise. A well-designed and executed ERP can assist with operational velocity attainment by improving efficiencies, speed, and time to market. Boer's total value model uses a six-step approach to computing the total value of an enterprise. His practical six-step approach encompasses the following:

- **Step 1.** Calculate the economic value of the enterprise, where free cash flow (FCF) is defined as the actual cash flow minus the amount of cash that must be reinvested: *Economic Value = FCF / (Cost of Capital – Growth Rate).*

- **Step 2.** Frame the basic business option and identify strategic options. For example, leasing space at another site and expanding the enterprise may yield additional future revenue. Here, investment in an ERP system may yield future revenue, as a result of enhancing operational velocity.
- **Step 3.** Determine the option premium, which is the premium paid or expenditures incurred to make the plan actionable. For example, this may include the option cost of technology, people, partners, financing, systems, and R&D.
- **Step 4.** Determine the value of the pro forma business plan, where NPV is computed to determine valuation of the enterprise
- **Step 5.** Calculate the option value. Here, the Black-Scholes option formula is used using five key elements: value of the underlying security, strike price, time period of the option, volatility, and risk-free rate.
- **Step 6.** Calculate total value according to *Total Value = Economic Value + Strategic Value.*

Boer's model computes the true value of the enterprise taking options thinking into consideration, thus reflecting real life and the strategic payoff that can result if an enterprise is successful. To clarify the concept, Boer makes an interesting analogy by illustrating the strategic value of a common family with a low standard of living. The family's principal economic activities concern the income produced. Costs such as mortgage, utilities, and gas are set against this revenue. Any savings are stored away as additional income. The income and expenses mentioned thus far only reflect the economic value of the family. The potential strategic value lies in the education of its children. Education could pay off in the long term and increase the family's standard of living. However, there are also significant market risks. Once the children are educated, the marketplace may not demand their skills, or they may not meet the various job requirements of their profession. In comparison, an enterprise may have potential strategic value in a new technology that it develops. The enterprise may have sufficient venture capital to cover R&D expenses for the next few years. Once the technology goes to marketplace for the first time, the enterprise has first mover advantage in the market if it attracts enough early adopters to build market momentum. Critical mass can be achieved as momentum for the product accelerates. However, there could be the risk of competitors with a similar technology that may go to market during the same time frame. In addition, the competitor may have a similar product with different performance standards, which adds to the competitive nature of the situation. This leads to a race for market share and ultimate establishment of the preferred technology standard between the products.

Strategic value is not always predictable, and the dynamics of the market change constantly. A negative impact on strategic value could result in zero return; this results in a loss of venture capital to cover the R&D expenses. There is evidence during the past five years that a number of startup technology enterprises never arrived at fruition in strategic value. The strategic value represents the potential revenue that could be realized if market conditions are ideal for the enterprise. Gardner (2000) estimates the revenue opportunity for an enterprise using *Annual Revenue = ;Annual Market Segment Size x Annual Likelihood of Purchase x Annual Price*. The terms in this relation are time dependent and are critical to new technology adoption in the marketplace. Forecasting potential annual revenue requires understanding the purchasing decisions and patterns customers will make. Decreasing the time for appearance of a positive revenue stream for an enterprise, a new technology into the marketplace is highly desirable. The mechanism for achieving this objective is the evolutionary enterprise resource planning architecture framework, which will accelerate critical mass early in the deployment phase of the product development lifecycle by achieving operational velocity. Thus , the work established by the early pioneers of ERP and technology valuation methods has laid the foundation for a new ERP paradigm to evolve and support operational velocity attainment.

Network Elements Influencing Path Dependence and Network Effects

Consumers who become completely satisfied with a new technology product or innovation realize the value proposition derived from this new creation. For example, the value of a digital subscriber line (DSL) at home brings value to the home PC user who now has high-speed access to the Internet. The home user is no longer confined to the limiting speed capability of a 56 Kbps dial-up modem. As more users adopt DSL, due to its broadband capabilities, increasing returns to scale and path dependence are achieved. The economy has shifted from the supply-side economies of scale, based on the traditional industrial era of mass production driven by unit costs, to increasing returns to scale (also known as demand-side economies of scale) driven by consumer attitudes and expectations. Strategic timing is vital with respect to demand-side economies of scale. First, introducing an immature technology into the marketplace may result in negative feedback from potential consumers. For example, potential design flaws, functional limitations and constrained feature sets may overshadow the true value of the technology, making it less attractive to potential consumers. In addition, moving too late in the market means not only missing the market entirely but also the opportunity to acquire any significant market share. Moving without an effective ERP strategy compromises new customer acquisition and customer retention.

The marketplace is subject to various network elements that influence path dependence and network effects of new technology adoption. These network elements directly impact consumer decision-making and lead to the formulation of consumer perceptions and expectations of new technology. Network elements can be defined as economic, business, regulatory, market, and technological influences that impact consumer decision making relative to new technology adoption. Understanding what drives consumer behavior and how it can be controlled allows innovators and technologists to achieve better success in launching new products while gaining market acceptance.

In *Information Rules*, Shapiro and Varian (1999) identify 10 primary network elements that influence consumer decision-making. They describe how these network elements impact consumer decision making with respect to new technology adoption. The network elements described are: partnerships, standards, pricing differentials, product differentials, lock-in and switching costs, complementary products, first mover advantage, versioning, government, and competition. Figure 1 reflects these 10 primary network elements that influence consumer decision making over time. These network elements will shape consumer choice, based on the degree of consumer confidence, need, desire, satisfaction, and comfort with adopting a new technology. The degree that these human traits will vary among consumers will determine the speed with which a new technology will be adopted. Consumers will most likely fall into three categories of adoption: early, evolving, and late. As a technology becomes popular, consumer decision-making becomes positive with respect to new product acquisition. Early adopters of the technology will begin to generate demand for the product.

Based on the success of the initial product, more consumers will see and understand the value proposition realized by the early adopters. A large number of consumers begin to evolve connecting

Figure 1. Network elements

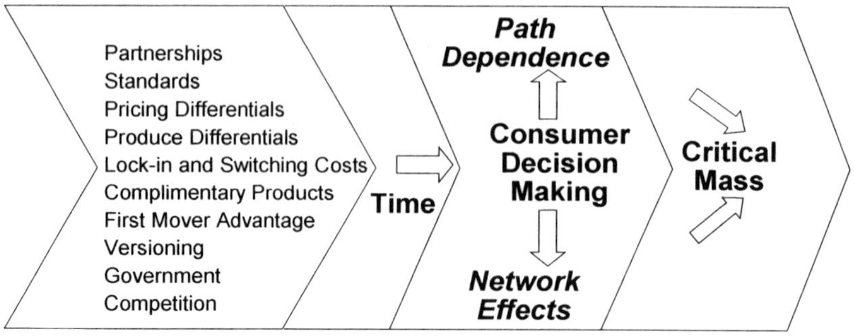

to the network of users. At this stage, consumer choice begins to exhibit path dependence and network effects. As the network of users begins to accelerate, critical mass is realized. Critical mass occurs when a large enough customer-installed base is established, as a result of positive feedback derived from the growing number of adopters. The network continues to expand until these late adopters eventually interconnect and the product reaches maturity in the marketplace. Network elements are also critical to consumer decision-making and can impact the destiny of a new technology if unrecognized. A good illustration of this was the competition between Beta and VHS in the 1970s. Beta was believed by most to be clearly superior to VHS in quality; however, VHS was the de-facto standard among consumers due to its compatibility. Operational velocity is one of the most fundamental critical success factors influencing adoption of new technology the presence of network elements. Operational velocity is a factor that needs the most attention and the one that can easily be controlled by implementing an effective ERP model. Since understanding the influence network elements have on achieving critical mass is essential, a narrative follows describing each one of the elements shown in Figure 1.

The first network element reflects partnerships, which provide a strategic advantage. New technology enterprises, possessing a leading-edge niche product in the marketplace, may find that one or more partnerships, with major players offering a complementary product suite, may be the answer to acquiring critical mass early in the game. An emerging enterprise would have the opportunity to immediately sell its new product to the existing installed customer base of its partner. This existing installed customer base may have taken the partner years to establish and grow, thus offering an advantage to a new enterprise, which has not yet established customer relationships or gained brand name recognition. An opportunity to sell into an existing installed base of customers, by gaining the visibility and credibility via a strong strategic partner, can shorten the sales cycle and accelerate critical mass. Alliances can even be established through suppliers and rivals as a means of accelerating critical mass attainment. It would also be advantageous for the enterprise to offer incentives when possible. Consumer confidence may be won, along with new customer acquisitions, by allowing customers who are undecided over a new technology to sample or test the new product.

The next element reflects standards. Standard setting is one of the major determinants when it comes to new customer acquisitions. Consumer expectations become extremely important when achieving critical mass, especially as each competitor claims they have the leading standard. Standards organizations try to dispel any notions or perceptions as to which company drives the predominant standard; however, most of these standards groups are comprised of industry players, each of whom attempts to market their own agendas. Most will try to influence the direction of standards setting for their own best interests. Standards are necessary for the average consumer, who wants to reduce potential product uncertainties and lock-in (defined as consumers forced to use a non-standard proprietary product). The product that consumers expect to be the standard will eventually become such, as standards organizations and large industry players begin to shape and mold consumer expectations. Standards increase the value of the virtual network and build credibility for new technologies introduced into the market.

One strategy often used among new and aggressive companies in order to gain market momentum is that of pricing differentials. This network element can ignite market momentum by under-pricing competitors and targeting various consumer profiles. Some enterprises may use various pricing strategies to offer incentives to new customers. As a result, this may be an effective strategy, since some customers may be more price sensitive and may not be as influenced by factors such as standards. A common pricing strategy is differential pricing; this may take the form of personalized or group pricing. Personalized pricing takes the form of selling to each consumer at a different price. The focus is in understanding what the consumer wants and tailoring a price to meet the consumer's needs. Group pricing will set targets for various consumer profiles and group them accordingly. This affords flexibility to potential consumers and takes into account various price sensitivities that may impact decision-making. Consumer lock-in may be achieved through pricing strategies by offering incentives such as discounts, promotions, and the absorption of consumer switching costs.

Making product differentials available is another strategy that is very common in the technology industry and that can effectively influence consumer decision-making. Product differentials offer consumers a choice across several product derivatives. By designing a new product from the top down, the company can easily engage any potential competition by introducing the high-end solution first. Once the high-end consumers have been acquired, a low-end solution can be made available to capture the low end of the market. The low-end product also may be used to position the high-end product, when using an up-selling strategy. When introducing a new technology to the market, the market should be segmented based on several factors such as user interface, delay, image resolution, speed, format, capability, flexibility, and features. These factors help target and span various consumer profiles.

As various pricing schemes, product features, and functionality are offered to the consumer, the fears of lock-in and excessive switching costs enter into the decision-making. This network element is one of the most common ones that can halt adoption of a new technology, especially if consumers only deal with one vendor. Most consumers want to deal with two or more vendors in order to maintain a level of integrity among the suppliers offering the product or service. This alleviates the possibility of lock-in with any one particular vendor, as long as they share the same standard. Consumers who deal with only one supplier may face the possibility of lock-in and high switching costs should they decide to select another vendor later. If the existing supplier has not kept up with standards and new technology trends, the consumer may be bound by old legacy infrastructure, which could result in complications if the consumers can no longer scale their environment to meet their own business needs. Some enterprises may absorb the switching costs of a consumer to win their business, if it is in their own best interest, and also if they need to increase their customer base and market share to gain critical mass. New enterprises gaining minimal market momentum with cutting-edge technology product introductions may be more willing to take this approach.

A common competitive strategy used by many high-technology organizations is the selling of complementary products to their installed base of customers. These complementary product offerings can arrive internally within a company by entering new product domains, or externally by offering a partner's complementary product and leveraging on its core competencies.

One of the most challenging network elements that an enterprise faces is having time to market a new innovation, better known as first-mover advantage. First-mover advantage is the best way to gain both market momentum and brand name recognition as the major provider of this new technology. Microsoft, Sun Microsystems, and Netscape serve as good examples of companies that have succeeded in gaining first mover advantage and that have become leaders in their industries (Economides, 2001). An early presence in the market place has allowed these companies to secure leadership positions throughout the years. We note, however, that Netscape has lost considerable market share to Microsoft's Internet Explorer for reasons that are also explainable by this theory.

Over the years, versioning has become a common practice among technology companies. The network element of versioning offers choices to consumers. Companies will offer information products in different versions for different market segments. The intent is to offer versions tailored to the needs of various consumers and to design them to accommodate the needs of different groups of consumers. This strategy allows the company to optimize profitability among the various market segments and to drive consumer requirements. The features and functions of information products can be adjusted to highlight differences and variations of what consumers demand. Companies can offer versions at various prices that appeal to different groups.

As observed with the Microsoft antitrust legislation proceedings, the government can impact the direction of new technology, whether it attempts to control a monopoly or fuel demand for new technologies (Economides, 2001). This network element can be the most restrictive in achieving critical mass. The government, in efforts intending to ensure that there are no illegal predatory practices that violate true competition, scrutinizes mergers and acquisitions involving direct competitors. There is every reason to believe that it will continue to focus on controlling genuine monopoly power and take action where necessary. All mergers and acquisitions are subject to review by the Department of Justice and the Federal Trade Commission. In addition, the government can serve as a large and influential buyer of new technologies. It can become a catalyst by financing, endorsing and adopting new technologies in order to accelerate their development, adoption, and use. Federal government IT spending on emerging technologies over the next several years can potentially aid those enterprises that are struggling for business and survival as a result of downturns in the economy.

Another network element that can restrict critical mass attainment is competition. Competition in the marketplace will continue as new enterprises are entering the market and presenting a challenge to some large established companies that are plagued by inflexibility and bureaucratic challenges. Companies will compete on new innovations, features, functionality, pricing, and, more importantly, standards. Information products are costly to produce but inexpensive to reproduce, pushing pricing toward zero. Companies that are challenged with a negative cash flow, and have limited venture capital, will need to devise creative strategies to keep themselves in the game. Margins begin to diminish as pricing reaches zero; a complementary set of products or services may be necessary or required to maintain a level of profitability. Knowing the customer, owning the customer relationship, and staying ahead of the competition are the major keys to survival.

Operational velocity is the critical success factor, making a much more profound impact on revenue and profit than the individual network elements described and illustrated in Figure 1. This critical mass determinant, which is the key to the success of an enterprise, is often given very little attention due to the organizational dynamics that take place. Operational velocity, as defined earlier, is speed in delivering products or services to market, meeting all customer expectations in a timely manner, and decreasing the time for appearance of a positive revenue stream as much as possible. This may appear to be a simple concept; however, it is very difficult to master. Without an evolutionary ERP approach, it will be quite challenging to scale a business to meet aggressive future customer demands. There exists a direct relationship between an effective evolutionary the ERP model and operational velocity attainment that allows an enterprise to scale its business accordingly while meeting customer demand in a timely manner. More importantly, there is a unique organizational process lifecycle and key behavioral influences that are essential to implementing an effective ERP model. Without these, the model becomes ineffective, in that ERP has not been implemented in an appropriate and effective manner.

Many enterprises lack any initial operations plan or back-office infrastructure to support new product launches in the marketplace. This is a major challenge in the commercial world, where time to market is critical and development of an effective ERP may be neglected in favor of seemingly more pressing and immediate needs. The primary focus of a new technology company is to amass customers immediately at minimal cost. Often a number of senior executives hired to manage a new enterprise come from sales backgrounds and have very little experience in running a company from a strategic IT, operations, and financial perspective. They sometimes lack the associated fundamental technical and non-technical skill sets, which can easily compromise the future of the business. This often stems from senior executives who come from large corporations but who lack the entrepreneurial experience necessary to launch new businesses. For example, they may fail to see the value of hiring a chief operating officer (COO) who has the required operations background and who understands how to run a business in its operational entirety. The importance of the COO role is later recognized, but many times it is too late as much of the infrastructure damage has already occurred.

Many of the chief executive officers (CEO) hired to lead new enterprises are prior senior vice presidents of sales. It is believed that they can bring immediate new business to the enterprise and begin instant revenue-generating activity. The sole focus becomes revenue generation and new customer acquisitions. The common philosophy is that the company will resolve the back-office infrastructure later. This is usually a reactionary approach to developing a back-office versus a proactive approach. The lack of a sound evolutionary approach in developing an ERP from concept to market maturity for new products can result in missed customer opportunities, customer de-bookings, loss of market share, lack of credibility, competitive threats and, most importantly, bankruptcy of the business.

Other potential plaguing factors that can impact implementation of an effective ERP strategy are undefined, or at least under-defined, organizational requirements, sometimes termed business rules, and lack of business process improvement (BPI—also known as workflow management) initiatives and strategies. Organizational requirements and BPI for supporting new product launches should be addressed early in the development phase of the new technology. How a product is supported and the relationship and communication between the respective support organizations will be vital to the success of the product. Quite often, organizational requirements and BPI are lacking due to limited understanding and use of contemporary IT principles and practices. Many of the savvy technologists who have started the enterprise may lack knowledge in formal methods, modeling, systems development, and integration. They may be great internal design engineers who have come across a new innovation or idea; however, they lack infrastructure knowledge for commercializing the new technology. This had been a common problem among a number of new enterprises. Most new enterprises that have succeeded with these challenges have first mover advantage, a positive cash flow to continue hiring unlimited human resources, and, although reacting late in the process, have implemented an infrastructure that could support the business. The infrastructure was a splintered systems environment lending only to a semi-automated environment. The systems migration strategy occured too late in the product launch phase to allow for a seamless automated process.

Another factor that often plagues the enterprise is the lack of IT personnel who have business-specific skills. Personnel in the IT organization who lack business skills in the various vertical markets such as engineering, manufacturing, healthcare, financial, legal, and retail may have a difficult time eliciting internal customer requirements when developing and implementing an ERP. They may also lack the various business skills internally, if they are unfamiliar with the business and technical requirements of the other functional organizational elements such as sales, marketing, finance, operations, engineering, logistics, transportation, manufacturing, human resources, business development, alliances, product development, legal, along with any other relevant enterprise elements.

Finally, not all employees hired into an enterprise come with an entrepreneurial spirit. Some still have a corporate frame of mind and do not become as self-sufficient as is necessary to keep up the pace. They have a tendency to operate in closed groups and do not interact well with other business units. A team philosophy and aggressive work ethic is essential in order to succeed in an enterprise environment.

The approach, suggested here, to achieving operational velocity is to develop an ERP model that meets the following 15 performance criteria:

1. Reduces service delivery intervals
2. Maintains reliable inventory control
3. Reduces mean-time-to-repair (mttr)
4. Enhances customer response time
5. Establishes timely and effective communications mechanism
6. Automates processes
7. Creates tracking mechanisms
8. Maintains continuous business process improvement
9. Supports fault management through problem detection, diagnosis, and correction
10. Manages customer profiles
11. Monitors business performance
12. Establishes best practices
13. Creates forecasting tools
14. Supports supply chain management
15. Integrates all systems within the ERP model such as sales tools, order entry, CRM, billing, and fault management

These performance attributes are ones that companies have adopted to monitor, manage, support, and measure success of their operational environment. Companies are also continuously challenged with developing and implementing an effective model to support these attributes. The challenges stem primarily from a lack of knowledge and limited use of contemporary IT principles and practices. Enterprises must realize the need for appropriate performance metrics in order to measure success criteria and to plan for future growth and expansion.

Of all the network elements impacting the adoption of new technology, operational velocity is the most compelling, since it will influence customer expectations based on how quickly customer needs can be serviced. These needs may consist of rapid customer service response time, product delivery, problem resolution, and maintenance.

Operational velocity, like the network elements, will influence consumer decision making on new technology adoption. If a new technology product has long delays in service delivery or lacks customer support, new customer acquisition and retention eventually become compromised. Under these circumstances, it is possible to lose business to the competition, which may be introducing a similar product into the marketplace. Consumers become disappointed, less patient and quickly begin to look for alternatives. The lack of a reliable operational infrastructure would have been the result of a poorly executed ERP. An effective ERP must be automated, capable of tracking, serve as a communications mechanism, and support various tools. If these criteria are recognized and controlled by the core team of an enterprise, the ERP can provide many benefits as the business begins to scale and the product begins to meet customer expectations. Network elements can influence the outcome of a new technology or the destiny of the product. Understanding the impact that the various network elements have on the enterprise can help position the business in taking on the challenges that prevail. The market timing of the product and the influence on customer decision making will determine the end result of critical mass attainment. An enterprise that prepares and develops strategies, and which takes into account the large number of potential network influences, will accordingly realize this end result. There are a number of complex adaptive system challenges associated with these, and these must be explored as well.

Many of the enterprise resource planning efforts cited in this chapter can be traced to the three basic core elements of an ERP: people, process, and systems. Each of these elements were addressed in the various models and frameworks identified by early contributors in the field. As an ERP architecture evolves, each of the ERP elements goes through a maturity state. The evolution of a fully developed and integrated ERP architecture can be inferred from the phases of a basic systems engineering lifecycle. Table 2 illustrates this inference through a framework of key systems engineering concepts that can be applied to the development of an enterprise resource planning architecture.

This suggested framework could be used to develop an enterprise architecture using six key system engineering concepts. To support the ERP development effort, this 6x3 matrix of Table 2 could be used with the six general system engineering concept areas as rows and the three columns depicting the core components of an ERP. This defines the structural framework for systems engineering concepts and their relevance in developing, designing, and deploying an enterprise architecture. ERP maturity states are represented in each of the quadrants of the 6x3 matrix. As an ERP matures, each of the maturity states is realized and can be directly correlated to its respective systems engineering concept. It can be seen from the framework that the phases of the systems engineering lifecycle can be applied to ERP development. The various ERP models presented in this chapter revealed that a systems engineering paradigm may be inferred. The SE concept framework clearly illustrates a systems engineering orientation with respect to ERP.

SUMMARY

In this chapter we have attempted to summarize the very important effects of contemporary issues surrounding information and knowledge management as they influence systems engineering and management strategies for enhanced innovation and productivity through enterprise resource planning. To this end, we have been especially concerned with economic concepts involving information and knowledge and the important role of network effects and path dependencies in determining efficacious enterprise resource planning strategies. A number of contemporary works were cited. We believe that this provides a

Table 2. Key systems engineering concepts framework

Framework of key systems engineering concepts			
Concept Area	ERP Core Components		
	People	Process	Systems
Requirements definition and management	Organizational requirements elicited	High-level operational processes defined	System functions identified
Systems architecture development	High-level architecture developed by team	Architecture supports organizational processes	Systems defined to address organizational requirements
System, subsystem design	Unique data and functionality criteria addressed for each organization	Operational processes at the organizational level are developed	Organizational system components are designed
Systems integration and interoperability	Shared/segmented data and functionality is designed	Operational processes are fully integrated, seamless, and automated	All organizational system components and interfaces are fully integrated and interoperable
Validation and verification	Organizations benchmark and measure operational performance	Operational process efficiencies and inefficiencies are identified	System response time and performance are benchmarked and measured
System deployment and post deployment	Team launches complete and fully integrated ERP architecture	Operational readiness plan is executed and processes are live	Systems are brought online into production environment and supporting customers

very useful, in fact, a most-needed, background for information resources management using systems engineering and management approaches.

REFERENCES

Boer, P. F. (1999). *The valuation of technology: business and financial issues in R&D.* Hoboken, NJ: Wiley.

Boer, P. F. (2002). *The real options solution: finding total value in a high-risk world.* Hoboken, NJ: Wiley.

Boer, P. F. (2004). *Technology valuation solutions.* Hoboken, NJ: Wiley.

Briscoe, B., Odlyzko, A., & Tilly, B. (2006). Metcalfe's Law is wrong. *IEEE Spectrum*, July, 26-31.

Davenport, T. H. (2000). *Mission critical: Realizing the promise of enterprise systems.* Boston, MA: Harvard Business School Press.

Economides, N. (1996), The economics of networks. *International Journal of Industrial Organization, 14*(6), 673-699.

Economides, N. (2001). The Microsoft antitrust case. *Journal Of Industry, Competition And Trade: From Theory To Policy, 1*(1), 7-39.

Economides, N., & Himmelberg, C. (1994). Critical mass and network evolution in telecommunications. *Proceedings of Telecommunications Policy Research Conference, 1-25*, Retrieved from http://ww.stern.nyu.edu/networks/site.html.

Economides, N., & White, L., J. (1996). One-way networks, two-way networks, compatibility, and antitrust. In D. Gabel & D. Weiman (Eds.), *The regulation and pricing of access.* Kluwer Academic Press.

Farrell, J., & Katz, M. (2001). Competition or predation? Schumpeterian rivalry in network markets. (Working Paper No. E01-306). University of California at Berkeley. Retrieved from http://129.3.20.41/eps/0201/0201003.pdf

Gardner, C. (2000). *The valuation of information technology: A guide for strategy, development, valuation, and financial planning.* Hoboken, NJ: Wiley.

Kaufman, J. J., & Woodhead, R. (2006). *Stimulating innovation in products and services.* Hoboken, NJ: Wiley.

Koch, C. (2006, January). The ABCs of ERP, *CIO Magazine*.

Langenwalter, G. A. (2000). *Enterprise resource planning and beyond: Integrating your entire organization.* Boca Raton, FL: CRC Press, Taylor and Francis.

Liebowitz, S. J. (2002). *Rethinking the networked economy: The true forces driving the digital marketplace.* New York: Amacom Press.

Liebowitz, S. J., & Margolis, S. E. (1994). *Network externality: An uncommon tragedy. Journal of Economic Perspectives, 19*(2), 219-234.

Liebowitz, S. J., & Margolis, S. E. (2002). *Winners, losers & Microsoft.* Oakland, CA: The Independent Institute.

Miller, W. L., & Morris, L. (1999). *Fourth generation R&D: Managing knowledge, technology and innovation.* Hoboken, NJ: Wiley.

Odlyzko, A. (2001). Internet growth: Myth and reality, use and abuse. *Journal of Computer Resource management, 102*, Spring, pp. 23-27.

Rouse, W. B. (1992). *Strategies for innovation: Creating successful products, systems and organizations.* Hoboken, NJ: Wiley.

Rouse, W. B. (2001). *Essential challenges of strategic management.* Hoboken, NJ: Wiley.

Rouse, W. B. (2005). A theory of enterprise transformation. *Systems Engineering, 8*(4) 279-295.

Rouse, W. B. (Ed.). (2006). *Enterprise transformation: Understanding and enabling fundamental change.* Hoboken, NJ: Wiley.

Sage, A. P. (1995). *Systems management for information technology and software engineering.* Hoboken, NJ: John Wiley & Sons.

Sage, A. P. (2000). Transdisciplinarity perspectives in systems engineering and management. In M. A. Somerville & D. Rapport (Eds.) *Transdisciplinarity: Recreating integrated knowledge* (158-169), Oxford, U.K.: EOLSS Publishers Ltd.

Sage, A. P. (2006). The intellectual basis for and content of systems engineering. *INCOSE INSIGHT, 8*(2) 50-53.

Sage, A. P., & Rouse, W. B. (Eds.). (1999). *Handbook of systems engineering and management.* Hoboken, NJ: John Wiley and Sons.

Shapiro, C., & Varian, H. R. (1999). *Information rules – A strategic guide to the network economy.* Boston, MA: Harvard Business School Press.

Small, C. T., & Sage, A. P. (2006). Knowledge management and knowledge sharing: A review. *Information, knowledge, and systems management. 5*(6) 153-169

This work was previously published in the Information Resources Management Journal, Vol. 20, Issue 2, edited by M. Khosrow-Pour, pp. 44-73, copyright 2007 by IGI Publishing, formerly known as Idea Group Publishing (an imprint of IGI Global).

Chapter IX
The Knowledge Sharing Model: Stressing the Importance of Social Ties and Capital

Gunilla Widén-Wulff
Åbo Akademi University, Finland

Reima Suomi
Turku School of Economics, Finland

ABSTRACT

This chapter works out a method on how information resources in organizations can be turned into a knowledge sharing (KS) information culture, which can further feed business success. This process is complicated, and the value chain can be broken in many places. In this study this process is viewed in the light of resource-based theory. A KS-model is developed where the hard information resources of time, people and computers are defined. When wisely used, these make communication a core competence for the company. As the soft information resources are added, that is the intellectual capital, KS, and willingness to learn, a knowledge sharing culture is developed, which feeds business success. This model is empirically discussed through a case study of fifteen Finnish insurance companies. The overall KS capability of a company corresponds positively to the different dimensions applied in the model. KS is an interactive process where organizations must work on both hard information resources, the basic cornerstones of any knowledge sharing, and makes constant investment into soft information resources, learning, intellectual capital and process design in order to manage their information resources effectively.

INTRODUCTION

In the global world with rich information flows coming from many different sources and channels, an organization's ability to manage knowledge effectively becomes a prerequisite for success and innovativeness. This is especially important in information and technology intensive industries.

In these circumstances a greater awareness and a more active debate is needed concerning the creation of internal environments and the organizational ability to support collective knowledge production and knowledge sharing. These information literacy skills are increasingly underlined in different organizational contexts (Abell 2000). An information literate organization has the ability to seek information, but also to understand, evaluate, integrate it into the existing knowledge base, and critically use it (Doyle 1995). However this is not easily done.

In this chapter we will try to illuminate the problematic issues surrounding knowledge sharing in information and communication intensive organizations, based on a study of information cultures in Finnish insurance businesses:

- *How is the internal environment built to support information and knowledge sharing in information intensive companies?*
- *How can information resources in organizations be turned into a knowledge-sharing information culture, which further can feed business success?*

The chapter develops an understanding of the internal structures important to sharing. These structures are important in any organisation and particularly in information-intensive branches. The assumption is that a company with a rich and active information culture and with the different parts of the learning organization integrated also indicates a successful business.

To begin with, some central concepts are defined such as knowledge, knowledge sharing, information culture, and human and intellectual capital. Further, the context of the study is described, that is the insurance business industry. This type of industry represents information intensive organizations. Next, the management of information resources is described from a resource-based approach point of view in order to find out how a company builds a successful knowledge-sharing environment. Based on that a four-step knowledge-sharing model is presented, and a number of case companies are analysed and mirrored into the model. As a part of the analysis the business success is also compared to the existing information cultures within the case companies to see if there is an indication that an emphasis on knowledge work really is worthwhile. Finally, the empirical insights are discussed to see how they support the suggested knowledge-sharing model.

CENTRAL CONCEPTS

In the research question it is asked how the internal environment is built to support knowledge sharing. In order to answer this question it is important to define what knowledge sharing is. Also the internal environment of an organization may include many aspects and perspectives. In the following these concepts are defined and discussed.

Knowledge and Knowledge Sharing

Knowledge is often defined as internalized information (Ingwersen 1992) and understood as blend of explicit and tacit elements (Polanyi 1958; Nonaka 1994). This means that there are many types of knowledge at different levels of the firm. Knowledge lies in human minds and exists only if there is a human mind to do the knowing. This means that knowledge management is about managing the knowledge that the individuals have. Organisational knowledge management means supporting people so that they can use what they know. Furthermore, information and knowledge for the organization is highly specific and every organization must define information and knowledge in the light of their activities and goals (Orna 2004 119).

Knowledge sharing happens in a constant mix of organizational and individual motives, and factors like purpose, timing, and availability play an important role as enablers and barriers to sharing (Sonnenwald and Pierce 2000; Solomon 2002). In this context every individual has his/her own perception of how to make use of their networks and the organisational structures. There is a growing interest looking at individual attitudes affecting motives to knowledge sharing, knowledge donating and collecting, such as enjoyment in helping others and individual benefits of sharing knowledge (Lin 2007; Widén-Wulff 2007; Yang 2007). However, it is important to shape a picture of sharing on the organizational level and then integrate individual profiles into the overall structures.

Internal Environment

When the information and knowledge assets are explained the basis for understanding the information behaviour in a group or organization is the organizational context where the *information culture* forms the communication climate. The actual information use in the workplace is shaped by this environment which is built of institutional, organisational, and personal elements (McDermott and O'Dell 2001; Widén-Wulff 2001; Widén-Wulff 2003; Widén-Wulff 2005). Information culture is difficult to change in a short period, as are other cultures too. Overcoming the cultural barriers to sharing information and knowledge has more to do with how you design and implement your management effort into the culture than with changing the culture (McDermott and O'Dell 2001).

Knowledge aspects in organizations and companies are often also connected to communicative, pedagogical or facilitation skills. *Organisational learning* aspects are about making individual knowledge collective (Srikantaiah 2000). The organisational learning is transferred through the individuals of the organization and therefore also an important aspect (Argyris 2002). The idea with the learning organisation is that an organisation consists of factors that build up a system in which the individual learning, in order to become effective, is anchored in the whole organisational activity. Thus, individual visions are important, and, at the same time, these have to be incorporated into the organisational visions and aims. The learning organisation is constructed from several components such as core competence, co-operation, motivation and communication. It is important that these components create the common base for the organisation. This is considered the starting point for effective information and knowledge use in a business company (Heifez & Laurie 1997; Koenig 1998; Nonaka & Takeuchi 1995; Senge 1994).

Further, organizational learning is built upon *human and intellectual capital*. The human and the intellectual capital are the measures for the different parts of the learning organization. Human capital is the personnel, how it is motivated to effectiveness and creativity. The intellectual capital is about the company's specialties and knowledge creation (Stewart 1998). Innovation, creativity, motivation and learning are processes that need support from many levels in the organization. The support by the management is especially important, but the creation of common strategies, values and getting the personnel's interest for these processes are also underlined in the scientific discussion (Nicholson, Rees and Brookes-Rooney 1990; Andreau and Ciborra 1995; Choo 2001).

THE CONTEXT: THE INFORMATION INTENSIVE INSURANCE BUSINESSES

The amount of information and the development of information technology, have been a great challenge for all business organizations, and, among others, Owens & Wilson (1997) underline the importance of information-related questions integrated in the strategic planning of a business organization.

The concept of information intensity of an industry is well known and documented (Parsons 1983; Harris and Katz 1991; Chou, Dyson and Powell 1998). Financial companies are examples of information intensive enterprises where both processes and products are information intense. In both external and internal intelligence complexity, insurance companies are at a very demanding end. This makes them very dependent on information management skills.

The big challenge for insurance companies is to share information between different insurance lines. Typically, and in many countries demanded by law, insurance lines related to life, pension and indemnity insurance have been kept separate. A full-service insurance company might have up to some 120 different insurance lines. The current trend of customer-orientation however demands that customers must be seen as whole entities. This puts high pressures on the organizational intelligence of insurance companies.

Insurance businesses do not sell concrete products, which means that they are even more affected by qualitative decisions by the personnel who need relevant information. This means that the information is a critical success factor and the cooperation between service, selling, marketing and administration become increasingly important (Codington and Wilson 1994).

THE RESOURCE-BASED APPROACH TO ORGANIZATIONS

One approach to the management of information resources is the resource-based theory, which is one of the current theories enjoying wide acceptance by the scientific community. After a long period of market-oriented theories, for example (Porter 1980; Porter and Millar 1985; Porter 1990), attention has turned to the internal issues of any organization, the assets and resources, which are of permanent character for the organization– on the contrary to the ever changing external world and market. Internal resources are something with which one must live for a long period and of which one must take advantage, "*For managers the challenge is to identify, develop and deploy resources and capabilities in a way that profits the firm with a sustainable competitive advantage and, thereby, a superior return on capital.*" (Amit and Schoemaker 1993).

Clearly we can define labour and information as key resources for any organization. The resource-based theory should give us insights into how to master and foster this resource. One of the weaknesses of the resource-based theory is the complexity of the used concepts. The concepts of capabilities, resources and competences are far from settled (see, for example, (Andreau and Ciborra 1995). However, the conceptual richness of the theory is its main strength and important and interesting concepts can be summarized as follows (Barney 1991):

- Resource mobility and heterogeneity: organizations command over resources of different kinds and qualities. Resources can be very immobile.
- Social complexity: resources may imperfectly be imitable because they are a complex social phenomena, beyond the ability of firms to systematically manage and influence.
- Causal ambiguity: causal ambiguity exists when the link between the resources controlled by a firm and a firm's sustained competitive advantage is not understood or understood only very imperfectly.

Interesting too is the discussion on the strategic potential of resources. A capability has strategic potential if (Barney 1991):

- It is valuable
- It takes advantage of opportunities in the environment and neutralizes risks
- Demand is bigger than supply

- It is difficult to imitate
- It is difficult to get
- It does not have strategically comparable substitutes

The resource-based theory is very reality-oriented. It takes up many concepts of great importance for daily organizational life. The concepts of social complexity and causal ambiguity are particularly relevant in the studies of managing information resources and knowledge sharing in organizations. In this chapter, we will discuss how a company builds a successful business relying on intensive knowledge sharing based on basic (hard) and soft information culture resources.

THE KNOWLEDGE SHARING MODEL

Companies are often aware of the fact that information is an important resource, but only a few concrete measures on how to use this resource effectively exist. Usually the focus of information resources management is fragmented (e.g. information needs analysis, environmental scanning, systems planning, and information resource management). However, a holistic viewpoint is important and knowledge management activities cannot be isolated processes (Hansen, Nohria and Tierney 1999). Information and knowledge management should consider both human and system factors (Choi and Lee 2003) to develop individual knowledge into a collective organisational resource.

In this study this challenge is met in the theoretical contribution, which is an extended version of the Knowledge Sharing Model (Figure 1) (Widén-Wulff and Suomi 2003). In this extended version we strengthen the basis of the model by building connections to the resource-based approach. In addition, the relationship between knowledge sharing and business success is more focused.

The model starts with basic resources, which we call hard information resources.

- Workforce, people (human capital)
- Time (organizational slack)
- Information and communications technology (ICT) infrastructure

As we look at Barney's (1991) definition, none of these resources are strategic as such. ICT resources are most often not rare when it comes to the hardware but some complex software can be difficult to imitate. Time or lack of time is a similar problem to every organization. The workforce can be difficult to imitate in some cases, but usually organizations can hire even persons with deep professionalism from the labour market. One important add-on to human capital is social capital that people can build on in long-term cooperation with each other. Knowledge sharing is a collective phenomenon, and when several persons interact and share information and knowledge for different purposes there is always a social perspective to this process (Solomon 2002; Talja 2002; Hyldegård 2004). Social capital is the collective goal orientation and shared trust, which create value by facilitating successful collective action (Leana and Van Buren 1999). Social capital is also built within an organization and can take time to emerge. All these basic resources are needed if knowledge sharing is a goal (Widén-Wulff and Ginman 2004; Widén-Wulff 2007). With these resources in place, communication can be a core competence for a company. The first step in our KS-model, competence building, represents a process where the hard information resources are present and these resources make it possible to transform communication into a core competence. The operational basis for performing effective communication is established.

The next step is to add the soft information resources. The components in the second phase, adding the soft dimension, are:

Figure 1. An extended knowledge sharing model (Widén-Wulff & Suomi 2003)

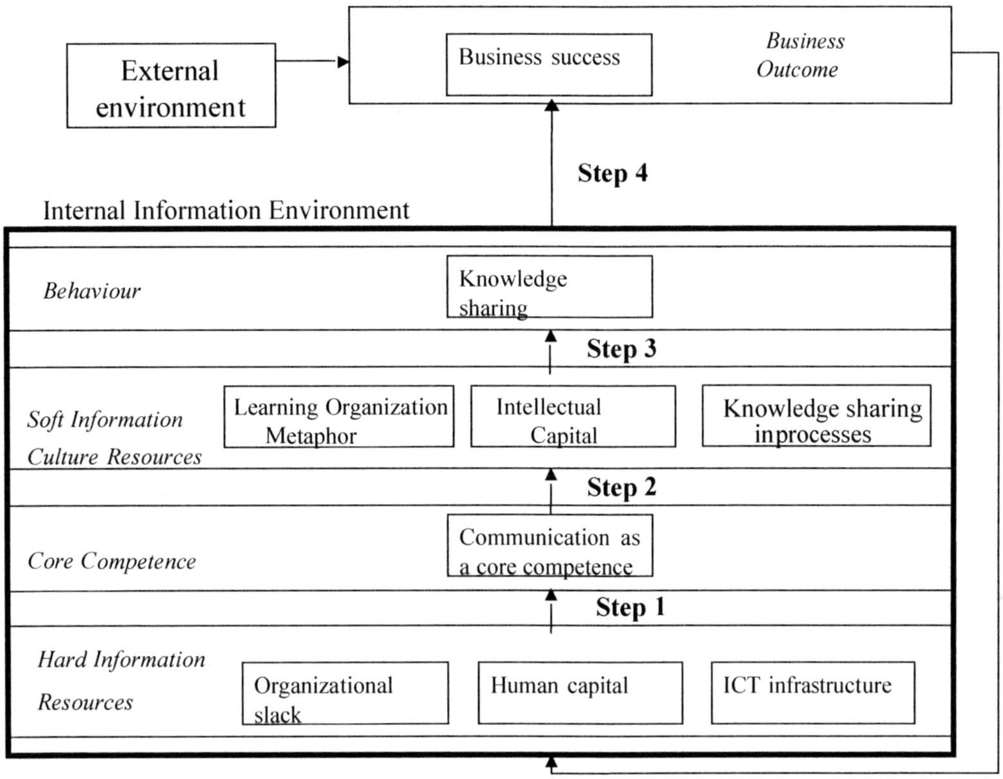

- Utilization of the learning organization metaphor
- Intellectual capital
- Knowledge sharing in processes

In Table 1, we define some basic differences between the "hard" and "soft" information resources. Of our hard concepts time is of most difficult character. Calendar time as such can not of course be purchased, but through adding staff personnel months, also working time, can be increased. Yet the conventional wisdom anyway tells that adding manpower to a group process does not yield a linear benefit (Brooks 1975).

With this set of resources in place, strategic capabilities begin to emerge. The organization starts to utilize the learning organization metaphor, which means that learning is a basic business practice, and where mechanisms to facilitate double loop learning are in order. Further, intellectual capital is the knowledge and knowing capability of a social collectivity, such as an organization, intellectual community, or professional practice (Nahapiet and Ghoshal 1998). Several researchers have shown that intellectual capital grows from social capital (Nahapiet and Ghoshal 1998; Reich and Kaast-Brown 2003). Knowledge sharing happens in processes that have integration, often through computer systems and joint databases. The resources become increasingly rare and more difficult to imitate.

The organization is able to take the third step, called 'utilizing resources'. Here, the company uses the available hard and soft information resources to share knowledge. The total sum of knowledge sharing capabilities and resources of the organization is called the 'internal information environment', or 'information culture', in

Table 1. The differences between hard and soft information resources in our model

	Hard resources	Soft resources
Acquistion	Can be readily purchased	Mature slowly over time
Cost and value	Have clear financial cost and value	Hard to quantify in financial terms
Manageability	Average	Low
Potential strategic advantage	Marginal	High
Operative complexity	Average	High

our model. It is a kind of aggregate parameter indicating the quality of the knowledge sharing capabilities and resources. Finally, there is a last crucial step, where knowledge sharing turns into business success. This step is called 'competitiveness building'. Even the company best in sharing knowledge efficiently may not however encounter business success if the external environment is too difficult or hostile. However, an internal environment that is communication intensive will help in attaining business success (Barney 1991).

In the model, there is also a feedback loop. Strong competitive position – as well as knowledge sharing – allows companies to build their hard information resources, also organizational slack (time), human capital and ICT Infrastructure. Most likely, business success will directly feed core competence building, soft information resources and knowledge sharing behaviour too. In resource-based theory the mobility, social complexity, and the strategic potential and competitive advantage of resources are focused. In our KS-model we try to picture critical resources (both hard and soft resources) with the aim to point out that communicative potential is based on hard resources (ICT, human capital, organizational slack). These resources provide tools for communication upon which the soft resources are built (learning, intellectual capital. knowledge sharing in processes). The social complexity is present in the next stage where knowledge sharing is actualised. These different dimensions of resources are important when knowledge sharing is turned into business success.

To summarize the steps in the model are the following:

- **Step 1:** Competence building – Turning hard information resources into a core competence
- **Step 2:** Adding the soft dimension – Building information culture resources
- **Step 3:** Utilizing the resources – Actualising knowledge sharing
- **Step 4:** Competitiveness building – Turning knowledge sharing into business success.

In the next section the empirical material is presented and the four steps in our KS-model are described based on the data from the studied insurance companies. Our theoretical model is explained through the actual management of information resources and knowledge sharing that took place in our case companies.

THE SAMPLE AND RESEARCH METHOD

Data Collection

This study is based on a survey conducted 1996-2000 in the Finnish insurance industry. The interviews covered aspects on internal knowledge sharing activities and support of these activities on a broad level which means that the material is stable and not affected by new trends in e.g. technology. It is a qualitative study where the interview method is used in order to evolve different angles and a thorough understanding of information behaviour and information cultural aspects (Miller and Glassner 1988). The material was collected qualitatively through 40 in-depth-interviews in fifteen Finnish insurance companies, identified as C1-C15 in our chapter. The insurance companies in our sample are of different sizes and in this material there are mostly medium-sized (100-500 employees), and large (over 500 employees) companies. This sample covers almost of the big Finnish insurance companies, with only two companies turning the study down because of lack of time.

The persons interviewed were managers responsible for strategic planning, marketing, and production to give an overall picture of the knowledge sharing structures in the companies. The interviews were taped and transcribed. In addition, annual reports from each company were analysed, especially as we examine the dimension of financial success. The interview questions covered the themes as in Table 2.

Analysis

The analysis of the empirical material was done by the case study method where the material was categorized and combined in relation to the theoretical framework, which considers aspects on building effective knowledge sharing (ICT, human and intellectual capital, learning, and knowledge sharing). The companies were studied as different cases where the chosen aspects were interpreted within a social complexity. The Knowledge Sharing Model) functions as a basis for the empirical analysis. The proposed four steps of building a knowledge-sharing information culture are presented and discussed on the theoretical basis provided by the KS-model. Earlier research give a picture of how these aspects should be developed in a company and based on that the empirical data is assessed by the researcher on a 5-point scale. This is done in order to give us a possibility to compare the different companies and different components of the KS-model based on quantitative data on an ordinal rank. This would not have been possible based on narrative discussion only. Through these values the companies can better be compared, that is how well the different parts of their information work is developed. Value 1 means that the item is badly developed in the company. Value 5 means that the item is fully developed in the company. The detailed descriptions of the valuation process can be seen in (Widén-Wulff 2001; Widén-Wulff 2005).

A central parameter in this context is the actual performed amount of knowledge sharing in the companies. The analysis of the business activities and their role in the communication process is the basis for this assessment. Table 3 shows how the three groups of different case companies define their communicative and knowledge sharing capability when it comes to strategic planning, marketing, and production.

As knowledge sharers the companies are distributed into three groups. Those companies

Table 2. The interview topics with the insurance company managers

Individuality	Information and communication technology (ICT)
Company aims	Knowledge creation
Motivation	Innovation
Communication	Information resources management

where knowledge sharing is just done between some key persons, and the overall communication of the processes are missing, are assessed as having 1-2 points. The average performers (2, 1-3, 5) have the same problem as the previous group, but the role of different business units in the communication processes is stronger. The good performers (3, 6-5) have a clear aim and genuinely work to improve knowledge sharing processes throughout the organization.

The knowledge sharing parameter is further compared to the other aspects important for building an effective knowledge sharing company; that is aspects on ICT, human and intellectual capital and the learning organization (see tables 4-9, 11). For this comparison the Spearman rank coefficient is used, which is suitable for this purpose where the assessment values are ordinal numbers, and the purpose is to picture the relationship between the variables, both measured by ranking scales. The coefficient tells us the correlation between the items compared.

THE FOURS STEPS BUILDING THE KNOWLEDGE-SHARING MODEL

There are companies in both ends of the performance of the different variables in the four-step model. The active performers (see Table 3) support and take advantage of their information resources and function as good examples on how to build a good knowledge sharing information culture. Therefore, the active performers are mainly described in this context and function as an example of how a good knowledge-sharing information culture can be built.

Step 1: Competence Building – Turning Hard Information Resources into a Core Competence

In this section the analysis is concerned with how the hard information resources are exploited in the studied companies. These are compared to the actual knowledge sharing to see if there is a connection between well-managed information

Table 3. Knowledge sharing capability of the case companies in qualitative terms and in narrative description

Poor performers	C1	1.5	The different business processes involve some key persons, but an overall communication of these processes is missing. The strategic planning is mainly a normative process and involves only the top management.
	C7	2.0	
	C14	2.0	
Average performers	C6	2.3	The middle group has similar difficulties as the poor performers when it comes to communicating business activities. Though these companies underline the role of the units and the departments in the communication and evaluation, strategic planning are the responsibilities of the top management.
	C8	2.3	
	C10	2.8	
	C2	3.3	
	C11	3.3	
	C12	3.3	
	C15	3.3	
Good performers	C13	3.8	The development of the communication of the business activities has existed already for a long period of time. When company guidelines are drawn up, several channels are used in order to involve also the individual level I the planning process. Involving all levels in planning processes is concluded to be difficult where common interest, willingness, and common language are underlined aspects.
	C4	3.9	
	C3	4.0	
	C5	4.0	
	C9	4.0	

resources and knowledge sharing. Further the aim is to explain how these resources are turned into core competencies.

As mentioned earlier, the actual knowledge sharing is measured by how well knowledge is communicated in the different business processes in the company. The evaluated processes are strategic planning, marketing and production (Table 3).

The first part of the hard information resources is to see how the ICT infrastructure can support knowledge sharing. There are great possibilities for ICT to contribute to information intensive organizations. The technology in itself does not bring added value to the organization. However, if ICT merges the different ICT functions in an organization (Huysman and de Wit 2002), and challenges to design incorporated human and information systems (McDermott 1999), it starts to bring positive effects. In the insurance businesses ICT is needed for their activities and ICT is a tool for minimizing the costs and making the administration more effective (Codington and Wilson 1994). In addition, the strategic potential of information technology to the insurance business has been known already for a long time. But of course ICT also is needed for communicative tasks, to help people share knowledge. It is then important to create a functioning infrastructure in order to obtain effective use of ICT with emphasis on both organizational and social structures (Kling 1999; Garrett and Caldwell 2002). Here the top management has an important role (Dixon, Arnold et al. 1994; Koenig 1998).

The ICT infrastructure is evaluated through the following aspects:

- Top management's engagement in developing information technology
- Aims with ICT work as stated by the management
- IT education given by the organization

These aspects are not directly connected to the technical ICT infrastructure, but rather measure the management's relation with and interest in ICT infrastructure. If management is emphasizing the role of ICT, we can indirectly assess that ICT infrastructure is developed in the company. Measuring ICT infrastructure quality and quantity directly in very different organizations is out of the scope of this study.

In the interviews it was shown that all the studied companies have emphasised the technology but they are able to manage this resource very differently. Although they have similar problems with the rapid development in the ICT field, for example, there are problems with several different system- and program-generations within a company, and the demand on different kinds of information skills in the ICT environment is noticed. They emphasize different solutions. Those companies with a more purposeful ICT work and active engagement do not focus solely on the technical problems. Rather they strive to motivate personnel to actively learn new technological solutions.

Table 4 shows that a well-managed ICT infrastructure correlates with active knowledge sharing. In those companies, where the ICT management does not merely occur from the technical perspective, we see more interest in knowledge sharing.

The next basic information resource discussed in the model is the human capital. The role of the individual is very important when the information as a resource is defined. Favourable circumstances for the individual level of the organization are motivating cultures, which support creativity, innovation, and learning (Andreau and Ciborra 1995; Amabile, Conti et al. 1996; Sadler-Smith 1998), which also constitute the measures for the human capital in this study. The aim is to analyse how the organizations identify the human capital as a part of their information culture. Again, human capital is compared to knowledge sharing ability. From Table 5 we can see that the correlation of human

Table 4. Knowledge sharing and ICT infrastructure

	Knowledge sharing	ICT infra-structure	d	d2
C1	1.5	1.7	-0.2	0.04
C7	2	1.7	0.3	0.09
C14	2	3.3	-1.3	1.69
C6	2.3	2.7	-0.4	0.16
C8	2.3	3	-0.7	0.49
C10	2.8	3.7	-0.9	0.81
C2	3.3	2.7	1	1
C11	3.3	2.3	0.6	0.36
C12	3.3	3	0.3	0.09
C15	3.3	3.3	0	0
C13	3.8	3	0.8	0.64
C4	3.9	2.7	1.2	1.44
C3	4	3.7	0.3	0.09
C5	4	4	0	0
C9	4	4	0	0
Sum d2				**6.9**
Spearman r = 0.99				

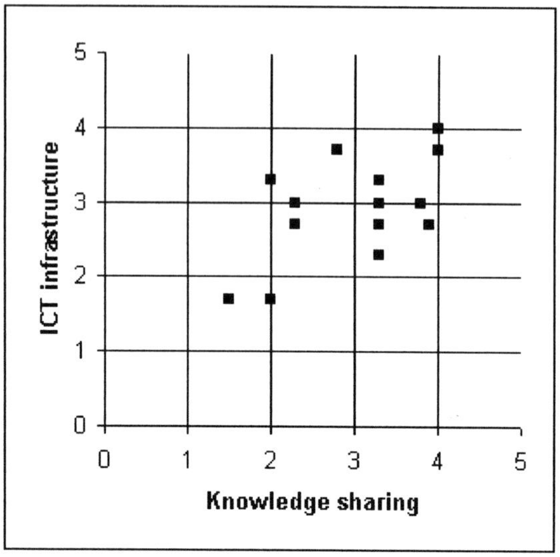

Table 5. Knowledge sharing and human capital

	Knowledge sharing	Human capital	d	d2
C1	1.5	1.8	-0.3	0.06
C7	2	1.8	0.3	0.06
C14	2	2.5	-0.5	0.25
C6	2.3	2.8	-0.5	0.20
C8	2.3	4.0	-1.7	2.89
C10	2.8	3.3	-0.5	0.20
C2	3.3	2.5	0.8	0.64
C11	3.3	2.5	0.8	0.64
C12	3.3	3.3	0.0	0
C15	3.3	2.3	1.0	1
C13	3.8	4.3	-0.5	0.20
C4	3.9	2.0	1.9	3.61
C3	4	4.0	0.0	0
C5	4	4.5	-0.5	0.25
C9	4	4.3	-0.3	0.09
Sum d2				**10.1**
Spearman r = 0.98				

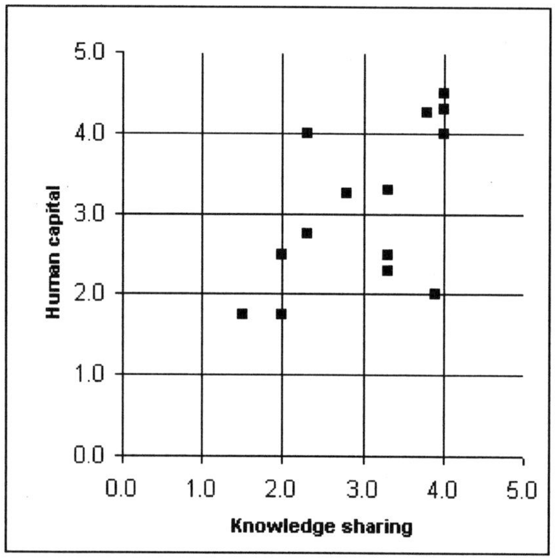

capital with knowledge sharing is high, although less than in the case of ICT infrastructure.

Looking at highly knowledge-sharing companies (C13, C4, C3, C5, C9), it is concluded that creativity is a strong component in these organizational cultures. There are official channels for creativity, but these companies underline the creative atmosphere in the company even more.

We have had creativity as a basic company value. This is a challenge while insurance business is not the most dynamic of businesses. (C9)

Interactivity and active communication support the creativity and motivation processes. This means that the personnel develop an interest in these processes, while the units and the management support the processes. With mutual support the activities are actively integrated into the corporate aims.

Both ICT infrastructure and human capital in knowledge sharing companies are accompanied by strong values of communication with the individual aspect in mind. The motivation for making these resources effectively used lies in a wider perspective of these resources. This is elaborated further in step 2.

The relationship between organizational slack and knowledge sharing was not studied in our empirical data collection. Time was a resource that was added to our model after the data collection phase. In our original plan for data collection, we did not appreciate how an important obstacle lack of time is for knowledge sharing. This aspect comes around first in the first rounds of analysing the data.

Step 2: Adding the Soft Dimension–Building Information Culture Resources

One of the biggest problems with ICT is the fact that there are so many different programs and applications within the organization. Therefore we have established a project that should create a holistic ICT employment, where the different organizational needs are taken into consideration. This should make the whole ICT-use more fluent. (C9)

It was concluded in step 1 that the management of ICT-resources is not only a technical problem issue. This resource is gained by focusing at the learning processes and individual possibilities. Having taken the hard information resources into consideration, the holistic view of how these resources fit into the organizational context, the next step in the building of knowledge-sharing competence. The soft dimension means that the information culture values must be considered on a holistic level. Learning ability and knowledge base utilization are soft resources that are hard to capture. The result of knowledge use is focused at. To this end, we analyse the learning metaphor in the organization more closely, and also the ability to manage the intellectual capital.

To achieve a successful learning process, it is important to eliminate hindrances for learning (Romme and Dillen 1997) and adopt a holistic view of activities and shape a mutual understanding of the values and aims of the company (see further step 3). This study shows that those companies with active knowledge sharing have adopted many of the disciplines involved in organizational learning (Senge 1994). The companies invest in training, which is well planned. Training is seen as a channel for common aims, shared visions and commitment, where the individual's role at the same time is underlined. Overall, it seems that these companies define system (network) thinking strongly and have created an active environment and structure in which to develop this thinking even further. However, it is also important to remember that learning does not always result in positive effects (Holmqvist 2003). Organizational learning aims at formalizing ideas but may generate rules and routines that create traditions not suitable for effective knowledge sharing.

Table 6. Knowledge sharing and application of the learning organization metaphor

	Knowledge sharing	Application of the learning organization metaphor	d	d2
C1	1.5	1.8	-0.3	0.09
C7	2.0	2.0	0.0	0
C14	2.0	2.1	-0.1	0.01
C6	2.3	3.0	-0.7	0.49
C8	2.3	3.1	-0.8	0.64
C10	2.8	3.3	-0.5	0.25
C2	3.3	2.9	0.4	0.16
C11	3.3	3.3	0.0	0
C12	3.3	2.8	0.5	0.25
C15	3.3	3.5	-0.2	0.04
C13	3.8	3.8	0.0	0
C4	3.9	3.0	0.9	0.81
C3	4.0	4.1	-0.1	0.01
C5	4.0	4.3	-0.3	0.09
C9	4.0	3.8	0.2	0.04
Sum d2				**2.88**
Spearman r = 0.99				

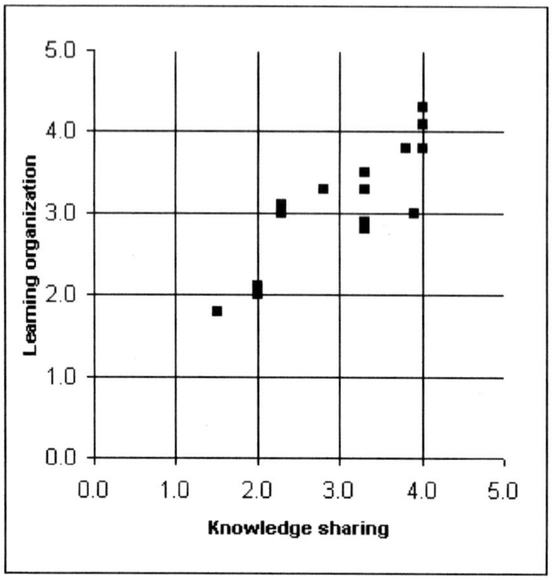

The soft dimension of the information resources is also connected to the knowledge base of the whole organization, the intellectual capital, which is focused on the information user from a cognitive viewpoint. The result of individual knowledge use is the key to understanding intellectual capital (Cronin and Davenport 1993; Nonaka 1994). Especially when communication is a core competence of the organization, it is possible to make effective use of the intellectual capital. In this study, the measures for intellectual capital are assessed by asking the following:

- How is knowledge valued?
- How is the individuality of the company defined and developed?
- What are the prerequisites for knowledge use (teamwork, communicative environment)?

From Table 7 it is obvious that knowledge-sharing companies emphasize the role of intellectual capital. This means that the versatility of knowledge is underlined as well as its content and communication in the company. All the core competencies are well defined and so are the measures for evaluating and developing them. Continuity, technology and the ability to change are the most central factors in this process. The development of the core competencies is a natural activity in those knowledge-sharing companies and does not demand separate attention or special actions. It is a self-evident, integrated part of the basic business activities. The processes in the knowledge creation consist of activities such as teamwork, interactivity by the middle management and integration of new workers. Teamwork is an established way of working, and the aim of

Table 7. Knowledge sharing and intellectual capital

	Knowledge sharing	Intellectual capital	d	d2
C1	1.5	1.9	-0.4	0.16
C7	2.0	1.9	0.1	0.01
C14	2.0	2.9	-0.9	0.81
C6	2.3	2.6	-0.3	0.09
C8	2.3	3.7	-1.4	1.96
C10	2.8	3.9	-1.1	1.21
C2	3.3	2.7	0.6	0.36
C11	3.3	3.0	0.3	0.09
C12	3.3	3.6	-0.3	0.09
C15	3.3	3.7	-0.4	0.16
C13	3.8	3.4	0.4	0.16
C4	3.9	3.3	0.6	0.36
C3	4.0	4.0	0.0	0
C5	4.0	4.1	-0.1	0.01
C9	4.0	4.0	0.0	0
Sum d2				**5.47**
Spearman r=0.99				

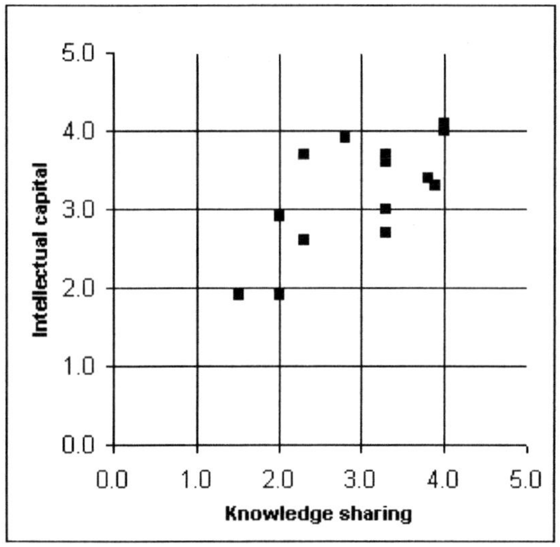

the work is to make internal communication and the circumstances for knowledge transformation more effective. The companies have clear aims concerning knowledge creation but also with the development of the tools that are needed for knowledge creation, that is, those hard information resources such as information technology, and communication networks.

The study shows that when building an information culture there must be a link between the hard and soft information resources, and a consciousness to develop these resources into a functioning entity.

Step 3: Utilizing the Resources – Using Resources to Perform Knowledge Sharing

Having established that the information resources are linked, it is also important to analyse their social complexity (Barney 1991). How the resources are actually used is embedded in the organizational culture, which is the basis on which the organization works. The information culture is a part of the whole organizational culture and, of course, the more specific basis for all information activities. Knowledge organization demands a certain type of environment in order to function well. Earlier studies (Dewhirst 1971; Muchinsky 1977; Samuels and McClure 1983; Hofstede 1991; Blackler 1995; Correia and Wilson 1997) have shown that information and knowledge aspects are best seen in the open vs. closed internal environments dimension. The aim is an open environment where the importance of information awareness is underlined. Flexibility with a focus on the competence of the personnel is important in creating an open internal environment. These are the circumstances that enable cooperation in order to create value from

Table 8. Internal information environment

	ICT infrastructure	Human capital	Application of the learning organization metaphor	Intellectual capital	**Internal information environment**
C1	1.7	1.8	1.8	1.9	1.8
C7	1.7	1.8	2.0	1.9	1.9
C14	3.3	2.5	2.1	2.9	2.7
C6	2.7	2.8	3.0	2.6	2.8
C8	3.0	4.0	3.1	3.7	3.5
C10	3.7	3.3	3.3	3.9	3.6
C2	2.3	2.5	2.9	2.7	2.6
C11	2.7	2.5	3.3	3.0	2.9
C12	3.0	3.3	2.8	3.6	3.2
C15	3.3	2.3	3.5	3.7	3.2
C13	3.0	4.3	3.8	3.4	3.6
C4	2.7	2.0	3.0	3.3	2.8
C3	3.7	4.0	4.1	4.0	4.0
C5	4.0	4.5	4.3	4.1	4.2
C9	4.0	4.3	3.8	4.0	4.0

the information assets (Huotari 1998). The average of the parameters measured in our empirical data, in steps 1-2 (human capital, intellectual capital, ICT infrastructure, and application of the learning organization metaphor), constitutes our measure for the internal information environment, as documented in Table 8.

In this context it is important to look more closely at how the knowledge sharing actually takes place. The interviews showed that work on communication processes is active since the companies need the processes both in the planning stage and in operational implementation. It is typical that the companies with an open environment have worked on developing the communication of their business activities for a long period of time already, the aim of this work is to improve the knowledge of these processes throughout the organization. When the company guidelines are drawn up, several channels are used in order to involve the individual also in this planning. The holistic grip of business processes, which means that all organizational levels should be included, is also underlined in the literature (Abell 2000; Moon 2000). However, the companies in this study conclude that it is very difficult to use the individual level of knowledge in the guidelines and strategic planning process.

How is the challenge of social complexity (Barney 1991) of the information resource management solved? We have seen that knowledge-sharing companies support human capital and ICT. They have also been able to link these resources to a soft dimension of the information resource. These companies also mentioned some ideas about how they thought they could succeed in involving the individual level by considering the fact that every individual is part of a social system. They underline the interest and willingness among the personnel to communicate, which is visible especially in the case of themes of direct interest for the personnel. Further, value discussions and

Table 9. Knowledge sharing and internal information environment

	Knowledge sharing	Internal information environment	d	D2
C1	1.5	1.8	-0.3	0.09
C7	2.0	1.9	0.1	0.01
C14	2.0	2.7	-0.7	0.49
C6	2.3	2.8	-0.5	0.25
C8	2.3	3.5	-1.2	1.44
C10	2.8	3.6	-0.8	0.64
C2	3.3	2.6	0.7	0.49
C11	3.3	2.9	0.4	0.16
C12	3.3	3.2	0.1	0.01
C15	3.3	3.2	0.1	0.01
C13	3.8	3.6	0.2	0.04
C4	3.9	2.8	1.1	1.21
C9	4.0	4.0	0.0	0
C3	4.0	4.2	-0.2	0.04
C5	4.0	4.0	0.0	0
Sum d2				**4.88**
Spearman r= 0.99				

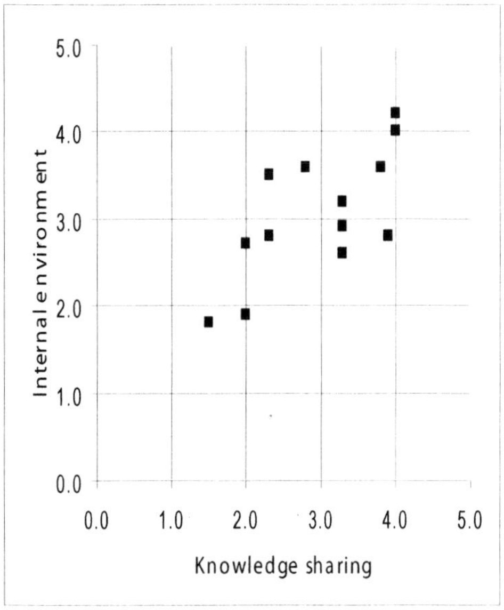

evaluation of the processes are important. Finally, a common language for both management and personnel is needed. These companies have also defined this process as a learning process that is anchored in the real activities, in the overall context. The same idea goes for marketing and production, i.e., the responsibility for communicating the processes throughout the organization. The processes are communicated through several channels and in several different ways. Many different tools are used. The information that is produced in these processes is important for the whole company. The open companies see themselves as expert organizations where everyone is an expert. To mention one example, product development is a part of strategic planning and is also communicated in that way.

Human capital is a key resource for any organization, but in order to gain most added value from this resource, it should be connected to a process which also involves learning, flexibility, and common values (Senge 1994 144-145). In this study, it is clearly shown that a successful utilization of the information resources is connected to an information behaviour that is supported by a suitable internal environment, a rich information culture.

Step 4: Competitiveness Building – Turning Knowledge Sharing into Business Success

We define the total capabilities of the organization to master knowledge sharing the 'internal information environment'. This has some connections to the concept of information culture. The information culture is a form of the entire organizational culture, which is a complex subject with a large

Table 10. Key criteria for the analysis of the business success

1. Market share	The share of the total market for insurance products
2. Solvency	An insurance company should have a solvency position that is sufficient to fulfill its obligations to policyholders and other parties. Regulations to promote solvency include minimum capital and surplus requirements, statutory accounting conventions, limits to insurance company investment and corporate activities, financial ratio tests and financial data disclosure.
3. Expense ratio	The percentage of each premium Euro that goes to insurers' expenses including overheads, marketing and commissions.
4. Net investment income	Income generated by the investment of assets.
5. Difference between current and book values on investment activities	

amount of definitions. In short, its function is to be a source of identity, making it possible to understand and be devoted to the organizational aims. Its function is also to keep the balance in the social system and create meaning and contents (Alvesson 2003). The information culture focuses more specifically on cooperation, communication and information behaviour in general in the organization. In this study, the internal information environment is described as the context in which needed information is communicated so that the company has the largest possible use of the information inside (and also outside) the company. The internal information environment, or information culture, of a company is developed using the 4 steps shown in the KS-model (hard information resources, soft dimension, utilizing resources, building success). It is important to underline how these factors together create the context in which information is communicated (Curry and Moore 2003).

The market feasibility of the Finnish insurance business is generally good, which means that there are not such great differences in the business success of the companies, and thus the critical success factors are not so visible. The measurement of business success is based on the study of companies' annual reports from 1996-98. It is difficult to compare the financial figures between the fifteen different insurance companies exactly because they are quite different in size and insurance trades. We have therefore used five different key criteria for the analysis of the business success as in Table 10.

Again, the key figures are assessed on a 5-point scale. Value 1 means that the criterion company has not been successful in this aspect, whereas value 5 means that the company has been successful in this aspect. In Table 11 the internal information environment is compared to the measures of business success in order to see if there is an indication that emphasis on information and knowledge management is worthwhile.

In Table 11, we see some relation between the quality of the internal information environment and business success. All the best business performers but one have a well-managed internal information environment.

The manageability and especially the cooperation of the factors defined to build the internal information environment seem to be important. An active information culture seems to be an ingredient in financial stability, although it is not possible to clearly say that a developed internal information environment is a given success factor. The external environment plays an important role, and a more passive internal information environment suits a stable external environment, whereas the role of the internal information environment grows in change-intensive environments.

Table 11. Internal information environment and business success

	Internal information environment	Business success	d	d2
C1	1.8	3	-1.2	1.44
C7	1.9	4	-2.1	4.41
C14	2.7	1	1.7	2.89
C6	2.8	2	0.8	0.64
C8	3.5	3	0.5	0.25
C10	3.6	4	-0.4	0.16
C2	2.6	2	0.6	0.36
C11	2.9	3	-0.1	0.01
C12	3.2	2	1.2	1.44
C15	3.2	4	-0.8	0.64
C13	3.6	4	-0.4	0.16
C4	2.8	2	0.8	0.64
C3	4.0	4	0.0	0
C5	4.2	4	0.2	0.04
C9	4.0	4	0.0	0
Sum d2				**13.08**
Spearman r= 0.98				

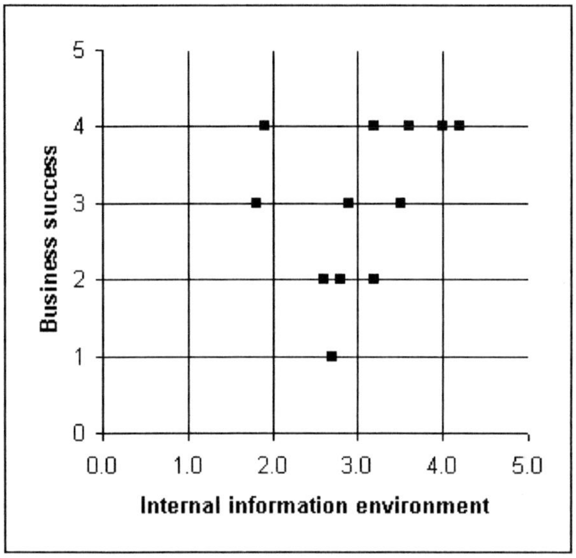

DISCUSSION

We feel that the KS-model relatively effectively explains the process through which knowledge sharing in a company is established. The model is based on the widely accepted resource-based approach and further strengthens its message too. Our empirical data, which was collected prior to the final version of the KS-model, support the ideas behind the model.

We next discuss the results in the light of our original research questions:

- *How is the internal environment built to support information and knowledge sharing in information intensive companies?*
- *How can information resources in organizations be turned into a knowledge-sharing information culture, which further can feed business success?*

In order to answer the questions above we have studied information and knowledge sharing structures, capabilities and use in 15 Finnish insurance companies. The KS-model (Figure 1) constitutes the theoretical framework of this study, built on the resource-based approach. The model is showing how the structural dimension (hard resources) combined with communicative ability turn these resources into soft information resources enabling effective knowledge sharing behaviour. Throughout the empirical analysis it is shown that the active performers of knowledge-sharing capabilities (Table 3) are corresponding positively to the different levels of building a supportive information culture (Tables 4-9, 11). This shows clearly how the internal environment should be built to support information and knowledge sharing in information intensive companies. The link was especially strong in the case of the learning organization metaphor by the organization, also the willingness to learn, and knowledge sharing. If we look at the total summary concept of internal information sharing, the correlation between this and knowledge sharing is strong. Average correlation in our scale could be seen in the cases of ICT infrastructure and intellectual capital. Finally, the correlation between business success and the internal information environment as a whole was there to some extent. The analysis shows that the picture of organisational knowledge sharing needs to be linked by both formal and informal structures.

To answer the second question it can be concluded that the very basic message of the resource-based approach that you have to add value to the existing resources of your organizations in order to cultivate them into capabilities and – finally – sources of competitive advantage, is supported through this study. The approach is well suited to have ramifications for knowledge management studies. In general, knowledge management is a socially complex setting, where the individual level is important to integrate into the organisational level. Active management is needed, but it is difficult to know that every aspect is effectively managed. The conclusions of this study support well those of Cross et al. (2002) who manifest that knowledge and communication networks management is a task which needs constant and intensive engagement. The concept of causal ambiguity manifests itself very clearly in the case of knowledge resources, and our research aims at lessening this state of causal ambiguity. Information and knowledge resources, on different levels of the company, turn into an active knowledge-sharing information culture, supporting business success, by implementing a holistic view to the resource-based approach.

According to the definition, hard information resources are something that can be bought from the market (see Table 1). They are similar to everyone and cannot create competitive advantage as such. In a successful business, you can just use cash to obtain them. The hard part will be of orchestrating them to work together and here the soft information resources step in. Hard information resources need management, but especially intensive is the management task in the case of the soft information resources.

Both in our conceptual and empirical analysis the existence of organizational slack manifested itself as a critical condition for knowledge sharing. If human resources are utilized to a limit, there remains no incentive and power to share knowledge. Allowing for some extra time for the staff is a wise investment from the viewpoint of knowledge sharing. The classical message of Brooks (1975) has not yet come home to knowledge management activities in organizations: work and knowledge sharing in groups demands more time than individual work. The demands of group-work on resources are further documented even in more recent literature (Verner, Overmyer and McCain 1999).

CONCLUSION

Many professionals, managers and policy makers have trouble gaining a reliable understanding of the actual roles of information management, technologies and knowledge sharing as causes, catalysts, facilitators and obstacles in workplaces. Therefore a better comprehension of these mechanisms can improve managerial understanding of the role of KM and knowledge sharing in diverse institutional contexts (Huysman and de Wit 2002). A new challenge in this area is the understanding of motives to knowledge sharing in virtual and online environments (Hew and Hara 2007). Social ties are emphasized but not as easily developed as in offline environments.

The aim with this study was to show the development of knowledge sharing as a process adding value step by step. These are important insights both for knowledge workers in companies as for managers in different areas working with information and knowledge resource aspects. This study integrates both business and information science which gives a broader perspective and a deeper platform to the complex processes of information and knowledge management. The model could preferably be developed to integrate important aspects to knowledge sharing in online environments in the future.

The proposed model shows the components that must exist in order to make knowledge a real resource. The process cannot be performed overnight, but demands years of concentrated work. The message is that the basic premises and resources need to be in place (the lower levels of the Knowledge Sharing Model), after that the upper level conditions can be realized. Focusing the upper levels without having taken the basic level first into consideration results in wasted efforts.

Our recommendations for organizations to master knowledge sharing are:

1. See to it that the basic resources are there. You will need adequate people and time for them to conduct knowledge sharing. A decent ICT infrastructure is a basic requirement for that.
2. See to it that these basic resources are turned into a competence. Competence means that you know how to exploit the resources efficiently. Also a lot of attention has to be paid to the learning on how to use the basic hard resources.
3. Install the metaphor of organizational learning to your organization.
4. Your workforce is not just a collection of expert individuals; emphasise that they must build their intellectual capital, also their skills to adapt and distribute information, in official and unofficial networks. Create an organizational atmosphere that supports and awards knowledge sharing.
5. Do business process re-engineering, and see to it that the processes share information. Technology consultants may want to design your processes with minimal interfaces to other processes, but insist on processes to share information.
6. Understand that knowledge sharing is one important component in your business success, but it cannot alone solve any problems. A business organization has to fulfil customer needs, which is the common aim and purpose of sharing.

We are aware of some shortcomings of our research. Our discussion uses terms that are difficult to define and to make concrete proposals. However, in the development of the terminology here too rests one of our contributions. Further, our sample covers only one industry, and in order to obtain more convincing results, other industries should also be studied. Our assessment of the companies occurs partly on a subjective basis, but in a qualitative analysis like this it is impossible to work out objective operational measures for many of our theoretical concepts. This work functions as a basis for further developments in information culture studies.

REFERENCES

Abell, A. (2000). Creating corporate information literacy: 1-3. *Information Management Report*(April-June): 1-3, 1-3, 1-4.

Alvesson, M. (2003). *Understanding organizational culture*. London, Sage.

Amabile, T. M., Conti, R., et al. (1996). Assessing the work environment for creativity. *Academy of Mangement Journal 39*(5): 1154-1184.

Amit, R. & Schoemaker, P. J. H. (1993). Strategic assets and organizational rent. *Strategic Management Journal 14*: 33-46.

Andreau, R. & Ciborra, C. (1995). Organisational learning and core capabilities development: the role of IT. *Journal of Strategic Information Systems 5*: 111-127.

Argyris, C. (2002). *On organizational learning.* Malden, MA: Blackwell Publishing.

Barney, J. (1991). Firm resources and sustained competitive advantage. *Human Resource Management 36*(1): 39-47.

Blackler, F. (1995). Knowledge, knowledge work and organizations. *Organization Studies 16*(6): 1021-1046.

Brooks, F. (1975). *The Mythical Man-Month.* Reading, MA: Addison Wesley.

Choi, B. & Lee, H. (2003). An Empirical Investigation of KM Styles and Their Effect on Corporate Performance. *Information & Management 40*: 403-417.

Choo, C. W. (2001). Environmental scanning as information seeking and organizational learning. *Information Research: an International Electronic Journal 7*(1).

Chou, T. C., Dyson, R. G. & Powell, P. L. (1998). An empirical study of the impact of information technology intensity in strategic investment decisions. *Technology Analysis & Strategic Management 10*(3): 325-39.

Codington, S. & Wilson, T. D. (1994). Information system strategies in the UK insurance industry. *International Journal of Information Management 14*(3): 188-203.

Correia, Z. & Wilson, T. D. (1997). Scanning the business environment for information: a grounded theory approach. *Information Research: an International Electronic Journal 2*(4).

Cronin, B. & Davenport, E. (1993). Social intelligence. *Annual Review of Information Science and Technology 28*: 3-44.

Curry, A. & Moore, C. (2003). Assessing information culture - an exploratory model. *International Journal of Information Management 23*: 91-110.

Dewhirst, H. D. (1971). Influence of perceived information-sharing norms on communication channel utilization. *Academy of Management Journal 14*(3): 305-315.

Dixon, J. R., Arnold, P., et al. (1994). Business process reengineering: improving in new strategic directions. *California Management Review 36*(4): 93-108.

Doyle, C. S. (1995). Information literacy in an information society. *Emergency Librarian 22*(4): 30-32.

Garrett, S. & Caldwell, B. (2002). Describing functional requirements for knowledge sharing communities. *Behaviour & Information Technology 21*(5): 359-364.

Hansen, M. T., Nohria, N. & Tierney, T. (1999). What's your strategy for managing knowledge. *Harvard Business Review* (March-April): 106-116.

Harris, S. E. & Katz, J. L. (1991). Organizational performance and IT investment intensity in the insurance. *Organization Science 2*(3): 263-95.

Hew, K. F. & Hara, N. (2007). Knowledge sharing in online environments: a qualitative case study. *Journal of the American Society for Information Science and Technology 58*(14): 2310-2324.

Hofstede, G. (1991). *Kulturer og organisationer: overlevelse i en graensoverskridende verden.* Kobenhavn, Schultz.

Holmqvist, M. (2003). Intra- and interorganisational learning processes: an empirical comparison. *Scandinavian Journal of Management 19*: 443-466.

Huotari, M.-L. (1998). Human resource management and information management as a basis for managing knowledge. *Swedish Library Research* (3-4): 53-71.

Huysman, M. & de Wit, D. (2002). *Knowledge sharing in practice.* Dordrecht, Kluwer.

Hyldegård, J. (2004). Collaborative information behaviour - exploring Kuhlthau's Information Search Process model in a group-based educational setting. *Information Processing & Management,* in press.

Ingwersen, P. (1992). *Information retrieval and interaction.* London, Tyler.

Kling, R. (1999). What is social informatics and why does it matter? *D-Lib Magazine 5*(1).

Koenig, M. (1998). *Information Driven management concepts and Themes.* München, Saur.

Leana, C. R. & Van Buren, H. J. (1999). Organizational Social Capital and Employes Practices. *Academy of Management Review 24*(3): 538-555.

Lin, H.-F. (2007). Knowledge sharing and firm innovation capability: an empirical study. *International Journal of Manpower 28*(3/4): 315-332.

McDermott, R. (1999). Why information technology inspired but cannot deliver knolwedge management. *California Management Review 41*(4): 103-117.

McDermott, R. & O'Dell, C. (2001). Overcoming cultural barriers to knowledge sharing. *Journal of Knowledge Management 5*(1): 76-85.

Miller, J. & Glassner, B. (1988). *The 'inside' and 'outside': finding realities in interviews. Qualitative Research.* D. Silverman. London, Sage: 99-112.

Moon, M. (2000). Effective use of information & competitive intelligence. *Information Outlook 4*(2): 17-20.

Muchinsky, P. M. (1977). Organizational communication : relationships to organizational climate and job satisfaction. *Academy of Management Journal 20*(4): 592-607.

Nahapiet, J. & Ghoshal, S. (1998). Social Capital, Intellectual Capital, and the Organizational Advantage. *Academy of Management Review 23*(3): 242-266.

Nicholson, N., Rees, A. & Brookes-Rooney, A. (1990). Strategy, innovation, and performance. *Journal of Management Studies 27*(5): 511-534.

Nonaka, I. (1994). Dynamic theory of organisational knowledge creation. *Organization Science 5*(1): 14-37.

Orna, E. (2004). *Information strategy in practice.* Aldershot, Gower.

Owens, I. & Wilson, T. D. (1997). Information and business performance : a study of information systems and services in high-performing companies. *Journal of Librarianship and Information Science 29*(1): 19-28.

Parsons, G. L. (1983). Information technology: a new competitive weapon. *Sloan Management Review* (Fall): 3-14.

Polanyi, M. (1958). *Personal knowledge: towards a post-critical philosophy.* Chicago, University of Chicago Press.

Porter, M. E. (1980). *Competitive strategy: techniques for analysing industries and competitors.* New York, Free Press.

Porter, M. E. (1990). *The Competitive Advantage of Nations.* New York, Free Press.

Porter, M. E. & Millar, V. E. (1985). How information gives you competitive advantage. *Harvard Business Review 64*(4): 149-160.

Reich, B. H. & Kaast-Brown, M. L. (2003). Creating Social and Intellectual Capital Through IT Career Transitions. *Journal of Strategic Information Systems 12*: 91-109.

Romme, G. & Dillen, R. (1997). Mapping the landscape of organizational learning. *European Management Journal 15*(1): 68-78.

Sadler-Smith, E. (1998). Cognitive style: some human resource implications for managers. *The*

International Journal of Human Resource Management 9(1): 185-199.

Samuels, A. R. & McClure, C. R. (1983). Utilization of information decision making under varying organizational climate conditions in public libraries. *Journal of Library Administration 4*(3): 1-20.

Senge, P. (1994). *The Fifth Discipline: the Art and Practice of Learning Organization.* New York, Currency Doubleday.

Solomon, P. (2002). Discovering information in context. *Annual Review of Information Science and Technology 36*: 229-264.

Sonnenwald, D. H. & Pierce, L. G. (2000). Information behavior in dynamic group work contexts: interwoven situational awareness, dense social networks and contested collaboration in command and control. *Information Processing & Management 36*: 461-479.

Srikantaiah, T. K. (2000). Knowledge Management: a faceted overview. In T. K. Srikantaiah & M. Koenig (Eds.), *Knowledge Management for the information professional.* Medford, NJ, Information Toady: 1-17.

Stewart, T. A. (1998). *Intellectual Capital: the new wealth of organizations.* London, Brealey.

Talja, S. (2002). Information sharing in academic communities: types and levels of collaboration in information seeking and use. *New Review of Information Behaviour Research 3*: 143-159.

Verner, J. M., Overmyer, S. P. & McCain, K. W. (1999). In the 25 years since The Mythical Man-Month what we have learned about project management? *Information and Software Technology 41*: 1021-1026.

Widén-Wulff, G. (2001). *Informationskulturen som drivkraft i företagsorganisationen.* Åbo, Åbo Akademi University Press.

Widén-Wulff, G. (2003). Information as a resource in the insurance business: the impact of structures and processes on organisation information behaviour. *New Review of Information Behaviour Research 4*: 79-94.

Widén-Wulff, G. (2005). Business information culture: a qualitative study of the information culture in the Finnish insurance industry. In E. Maceviciute & T. D. Wilson (Eds), *Introducing Information Management: an Information Research reader.* London, Facet: 31-42.

Widén-Wulff, G. (2007). *Challenges of Knowledge Sharing in Practice: a Social Approach.* Oxford, Chandos Publishing.

Widén-Wulff, G. & Ginman, M. (2004). Explaining knowledge sharing in organizations through the dimensions of social capital. *Journal of Information Science 30*(5): 448-458.

Widén-Wulff, G. & Suomi, R. (2003). Building a knowledge sharing company: evidence from the Finnish insurance industry. *The 36th Hawaii International Conference on System Sciences (HICSS-36)*, Big Island, Hawaii.

Wilson, T. D. (2002). The nonsense of 'knowledge management'. *Information Research: an International Electronic Journal 8*(1).

Yang, J. (2007). Individual attitudes and organisational knowledge sharing. *Tourism Management 29*: 345-353.

Chapter X
A Meta-Analysis Comparing the Sunk Cost Effect for IT and Non-IT Projects

Jijie Wang
Georgia State University, USA

Mark Keil
Georgia State University, USA

ABSTRACT

Escalation is a serious management problem, and sunk costs are believed to be a key factor in promoting escalation behavior. While many laboratory experiments have been conducted to examine the effect of sunk costs on escalation, there has been no effort to examine these studies as a group in order to determine the effect size associated with the so-called "sunk cost effect." Using meta-analysis, we analyzed the results of 20 sunk cost experiments and found: (1) a large effect size associated with sunk costs, and (2) stronger effects in experiments involving information technology (IT) projects as opposed to non-IT projects. Implications of the results and future research directions are discussed.

INTRODUCTION

The amount of money already spent on a project (level of sunk cost), together with other factors, can bias managers' judgment, resulting in "escalation of commitment" behavior (Brockner, 1992) in which failing projects are permitted to continue. Project escalation can absorb valuable resources without producing the intended results. While escalation is a general phenomenon occurring with any type of project, software projects may be particularly susceptible to this problem (Keil et al., 2000a).

Prior research has identified psychological as well as other factors that can promote escalation (Staw & Ross, 1987). The sunk cost effect is a psychological factor that can promote escalation and refers to the notion that people have a greater tendency to continue a project once money, time, and effort have been invested (Arkes & Blumer, 1985).

There are several possible explanations for the sunk cost effect. Chief among these is prospect theory (Brockner, 1992; Kahneman & Tversky, 1979), which suggests that people will choose to engage in risk-seeking behavior when faced with a choice between losses. According to prospect theory, people will prefer to make additional investments (even when the payoff is uncertain) rather than terminating a project and "losing" all of the monies already spent.

In the context of software projects, the intangible nature of the product (Abdel-Hamid & Madnick, 1991) can make it difficult to estimate the amount of work completed. This difficulty manifests itself in the "90% complete syndrome"[1], which may promote the sunk cost effect by giving a false perception that most of the required money, time, and effort have already been expended.

To investigate the sunk cost effect, researchers have conducted many role-playing experiments in which sunk cost levels are manipulated to determine if they have an effect on decision-making (e.g., Garland, 1990;Garland & Newport, 1991). These published experiments suggest that there is broad agreement that sunk cost increases commitment to projects. However, there are a couple of unanswered questions. First, while prior studies have conducted statistical significance testing, they do not provide much information about the magnitude of the sunk cost effect. Second, although there have been claims that IT projects are more prone to the sunk cost effect, there have been no prior studies to determine if the magnitude of the sunk cost effect is larger in an IT project context than it is in a non-IT project context.

Meta-analysis, a literature review method using a quantitative approach, is very good at assessing a stream of research, discovering the consistencies, and accounting for the variability. Therefore, in this study, we conduct a meta-analysis to determine the mean effect size of sunk cost on project escalation and examine variability of effect sizes across experiments. We also examine whether the effect size of the sunk cost effect on project escalation is different for IT vs. non-IT project contexts.

LITERATURE REVIEW

Experiment Studies on Sunk Cost Effect on Project Escalation

Arkes and Blumer (1985) conducted a series of 10 experiments demonstrating that prior investments in an endeavor will motivate people to continue commitment, although rationally people should only consider incremental benefits and costs in decision making. Many researchers have conducted similar experiments based on one of the Arkes and Blumer scenarios (Garland, 1990; Heath, 1995; Moon, 2001; Whyte, 1993). These experiments consistently showed that when facing negative information, subjects with a higher sunk cost level have a greater tendency to continue a project than subjects with a lower sunk cost level. Based on these experiments, escalation has been linked to the level of sunk cost.

Although project escalation is a general phenomenon, IT project escalation has received considerable attention since Keil and his colleagues began studying the phenomenon (Keil et al., 1995a). Survey data suggest that 30 to 40 percent of all IT projects involve some degree of project escalation (Keil et al., 2000a). To study the role of sunk cost in software project escalation, Keil et al. (1995a) conducted a series of lab experiments in which sunk costs were manipulated at various levels, and subjects decided whether or not to continue an IT project facing negative prospects. This IT version of the sunk cost experiment was later replicated across cultures (Keil et al., 2000b), with group decision makers (Boonthanom, 2003) and under different de-escalation situations (Heng et al., 2003). These experiments demonstrated the sunk cost effect to be significant in IT project escalation.

Research Gaps

Many experimental studies have been conducted to investigate the sunk cost effect on project escalation. However, research that summarizes, integrates, and interprets this line of research is still lacking. First, previously published studies all take the approach of statistical significance testing, which only provides information about whether the sunk cost effect is significantly different from zero but does not provide any information about effect size. Is the sunk cost effect a small or moderate effect, or is it a large effect that is really worth noting? Are the results consistent across different experiments? Such questions have not been answered by previous studies. Second, IT projects have been identified as a type of project that may be particularly prone to escalation, but this has not been demonstrated empirically. Therefore, we do not know if the magnitude of the sunk cost effect is truly greater for IT, as opposed to non-IT, projects. In this study, we seek to fill these research gaps.

RESEARCH METHODOLOGY

Meta-Analysis Method

To investigate the above research gaps, we conducted a meta-analysis. Meta-analysis is defined as "the analysis of analysis...the statistical analysis of a large collection of analysis results from individual studies for the purpose of integrating findings" (Glass, 1976). Meta-analysis involves gathering a sample or a population of research reports, reading each research report, coding the appropriate information about the research characteristics and quantitative findings, and analyzing the data using special adaptations of conventional statistical techniques to investigate and describe the pattern of findings in the selected set of studies (Lipsey & Wilson, 2001). Over the years, meta-analysis has become a legitimate statistical tool to integrate empirical research findings in many disciplines, such as medicine, education, and psychology (Hwang, 1996).

Meta-analysis uses effect size as a measure that is "capable of representing the quantitative findings of a set of research studies in a standardized form that permits meaningful numerical comparison and analysis across studies" (Lipsey & Wilson, 2001). In meta-analysis involving experiments, the standardized mean difference between groups is commonly used to compute the effect size (Hunter & Schmidt, 1990). The formula used to compute the effect size depends upon the statistics reported in the study. When descriptive statistics such as the mean and standard deviation are available, the formula used to calculate effect size is:

$$ES_{sm} = \frac{\overline{X}_{G1} - \overline{X}_{G2}}{s_{pool}},$$

where ES_{sm} is effect size, $\overline{X}G1$ is mean of the treatment group, $XG2$ is the mean of the control group, and s_{pool} is the pooled standard deviation of the two groups.

When descriptive statistics such as mean and standard deviations are not available, other reported statistics can be used to derive an estimated effect size. For example, when independent t-test (t) and sample sizes (n) for each group are available, the formula used to calculate effect size is:

$$ES_{sm} = t\sqrt{\frac{n1 + n2}{n1n2}}$$

(Lipsey & Wilson, 2001), where t is the t-test statistic, and n1 and n2 are the sample sizes for the treatment and control group, respectively.

In experiments that use dichotomized dependent measures (e.g., continue the project vs. abandon the project), the proportion of subjects in each group that decided to continue the project is often reported. For example, 80% of the subjects in the treatment group decided to continue the project, while only 30% of the subjects in the control group decided to do so. In such situations, effect size can be estimated by performing an arcsine transformation using the following formula:

$$ES_{sm} = ar\sin e(p_{G1}) - \arcsin e(p_{G2})$$

(Lipsey & Wilson, 2001), where P_{G1} and P_{G2} are the proportions of subjects in the treatment and control group that decided to continue the project.

The two primary functions of meta-analysis are combining and comparing studies (Cooper & Hedges, 1994). Meta-analysis can be used to accumulate empirical results across independent studies and provide a more accurate representation of population characteristics. When effect sizes among studies vary beyond the subject-level sampling errors, moderator analysis can be conducted to find out whether a particular study characteristic causes the variability. Primary studies can be split into subgroups, and findings in different groups can be further tested.

Data Collection and Coding

A literature search was performed primarily on electronic sources (ABI/Inform, EBSCO Business Source Premier, and ScienceDirect), as well as several conference proceedings (ICIS, HICSS, and AMCIS) using the keywords "sunk cost," "project continuation," and "project escalation." After obtaining a list of potentially relevant articles, we scanned the papers' abstracts and retained articles that satisfy the following criteria: (1) It was an experimental study of the sunk cost effect on escalation; (2) The article reported the statistics from which standardized mean differences between groups could be derived; (3) The decision task used in the experiment was a project continuation decision. Based on these criteria, 12 research articles were retained for subsequent analysis. These articles were published from 1985 to 2003. Because IT researchers did not begin to embrace this area until 1995, much of the work was from the psychology and organizational behavior areas. The nature of the 12 articles is summarized in Table A of the appendix.

Some articles contained results from multiple experiments. For example, Keil et al. (2000b) replicated the same experiment across three different countries. Since our unit of analysis was a single experiment, multiple experiments in the same study report are considered statistically independent as long as they use a different subject pool (Hunter & Schmidt, 1990). Thus, we ended up with 20 separate experiments in our sample.

Because the effect size in our study was based on the standardized mean difference between groups, for each experiment we needed to identify one group as the treatment and another as the control group. In the experiments in our sample, the level of sunk cost was manipulated as an independent variable and was used to create multiple treatment levels. In experiments in which sunk costs were manipulated at two levels (for example, 10% vs. 90%), the high sunk cost level group was considered the treatment group and the low sunk cost level group was considered the control group. In experiments in which sunk costs were manipulated at more than two levels, the highest sunk cost group was selected as the experiment group and the lowest sunk cost group as the control group. For example, in some experiments sunk cost were manipulated at 4 levels: 15%, 40%, 60%, and 90%. When such situations arose in our meta-analysis, the sub-group with 90% sunk cost level was considered the treatment group and the sub-group with 10% sunk cost level was considered the control group.

In some experiments, researchers have attempted to independently manipulate sunk cost (e.g., percent of budget already spent) and completion (e.g., percent of project already completed). The problem is that in trying to tease apart the influence of these two factors, confounds can be introduced. For example, when a subject is told that a project is 90% complete, but only 10% of the budgeted funds have been expended, this generates positive feedback (for the project is nearly done, even though only a small fraction of the budget has been spent). To control for this type of confound, we limited ourselves to treatment conditions in which sunk cost and percent completion were jointly manipulated.

In total, 20 experiments were included in our meta-analysis and were coded for statistics that would be used to derive effect sizes, study characteristics such as decision task type, and sunk cost level for both treatment and control groups. The statistics used to derive effect sizes and the effect sizes of the 20 experiments are shown in Table 1. Table B in the appendix lists the formula used to calculate the effect sizes.

Data Analysis and Results

Three analysis steps were taken to address the research gaps identified earlier. First, the mean effect size and confidence interval were calculated for the sunk cost effect. Second, a homogeneity test was performed to determine whether sunk cost effects were consistent across experiments. Third, the type of project involved (IT vs. non-IT) in the decision tasks was used as moderator to explain the variances across studies. The results are shown in Table 2.

- **Step 1:** Calculating the mean effect size and confidence interval

Since standardized mean difference effect size suffers from a slight upward bias when based on small samples (Cooper & Hedges, 1994), each effect size was first corrected before further calculation. The unbiased effect size estimate is

$$ES'_{sm} = \left[1 - \frac{3}{4N-9}\right] ES_{sm}$$

(ES'_{sm} is the corrected effect size, while ES_{sm} is the original effect size, N is the overall sample size). According to Hunter and Schmidt (1990), the best estimate of the population effect size is not the simple mean across studies, but a weighted average in which each effect size is weighted by the number of subjects in a single experiment. Using this method, we calculated the mean effect size and confidence interval for the sunk cost effect. The mean effect size was 0.89. The 95% confidence interval was 0.81-0.97.

- **Step 2:** Testing for homogeneity of effect sizes

Homogeneity analysis of the effect sizes answers one important question: Do the various effect sizes that are averaged into a mean value all come from the same population (Hedges, 1982b; Rosental & Rubin, 1982)? In a homogeneous distribution, the dispersion of the effect sizes around their mean is no greater than that expected from sampling error alone (the sampling error associated with the subject sample upon which the individual effect sizes are based). If the statistical test rejects the null hypothesis of homogeneity, it indicates that variability of the effect sizes is larger than that expected from sampling error alone and thus further analysis is needed to investigate whether there are other systematic factors (e.g., study characteristics) that can explain the heterogeneity among effect sizes (Lipsey & Wilson, 2001).

The homogeneity test is based on the Q statistic, and it was calculated using the following the formula:

$$Q = \sum w_i (ES_i - \overline{ES})^2,$$

where ES_i is the individual effect size for i-1 to k (the number of effect sizes), $\overline{ES}$ is the weighted mean effect size over the k effect sizes, and w_i is the individual weight for ES_i. Q is distributed as a chi-square with k-1 degrees of freedom, where k is the number of effect sizes (Hedges & Olkin, 1985; Lipsey & Wilson, 2001). A statistically significant

Table 1. Data sources and effect sizes

#	Sunk Cost Level in Experiment Group	Sunk Cost Level in Control Group	Context	Effect Size Source	Experiment Group Mean	Experiment Group S.D.	Experiment Group Size	Control Group Mean	Control Group S.D.	Control Group Size	Spool	Other ES Sources	ES	ES'
Arkes and Blumer (1985)	9 million and 90% of budgeted funds	0	non-IT	proportion			48			60	N/A	41 out of 48 subjects in treatment group escalated, while 10 out of 60 subjects in control group escalated	0.8504	0.2021
	9 million and 90% of budgeted funds	0	non-IT	From t value			76			82	N/A	t(156)=2.02, p<0.05	0.3201	0.1602
	9 million and 90% of budgeted funds	0	non-IT	proportion			58			37	N/A	37 out of 58 subjects in treatment group escalated, while 2 out of 37 subjects in control group escalated	0.6326	0.2153
Garland (1990)	9 million	1 million	non-IT	mean and std	76.50	29.36	64	29.00	29.36	64	29.36		1.6178	1.6081
	9 million	1 million	non-IT	mean and std	69.50	29.03	75	36.00	36.00	75	29.36	N/A	1.1540	1.1481
Whyte (1993)	Sunk cost is present (Individual decision makers)	Sunk cost is absent	non-IT	proportion			50			52	N/A		0.4381	0.4348
Conlon and Garland (1993)	9 million/90% complete	1 million/10% complete	non-IT	mean and std	74.57	28.17	35	56.97	28.17	35	28.17	66% of subjects in treatment group escalated, while only 29% in control group escalated	0.6248	0.6178
	9 million/90% complete	1 million/10% complete	non-IT	mean and std	58.03	24.31	53	40.36	24.31	53	24.31	N/A	0.7269	0.7216
Keil et al. (1995a)	90% of budgeted funds	15% of budgeted funds	IT	mean and std	74.87	25.53	39.00	48.21	31.69	39.00	28.77		0.9270	0.9178
Keil, Truex, and Mixon (1995b)	90% of budgeted funds	15% of budgeted funds	IT	mean and std	40.00	25.00	31	40.00	25.00	31	25.00		0.0000	0.0000
	90% of budgeted funds	15% of budgeted funds	IT	mean and std	57.50	25.00	31	40.00	25.00	31	25.00		0.7000	0.6912

continued on following page

Table 1. continued

Garland and Conlon (1998)	8 million/80% complete	2 million/20% complete	non-IT	mean and std	76.00	22.79	24	66.27	22.79	26	22.79		0.4269	0.4206
Arkes and Hutzel (2000)	Sunk cost is present.	Sunk cost is absent.	non-IT	proportion			37			36	N/A	64% of subjects in treatment group escalated, while only 19% in control group escalated	0.5101	0.5047
	Sunk cost is present.	Sunk cost is absent	non-IT	proportion			109			121	N/A	58% of subjects in treatment group escalated, while only 37% in control group escalated	0.2352	0.2344
Keil et al. (2000)	90% of budgeted fund	15% of budgeted fund	IT	mean and std	62.08	22.78	47	44.04	26.76	46	24.95		0.7230	0.7172
	90% of budgeted funds	15% of budgeted fund	IT	mean and std	73.94	22.07	30	37.19	21.14	30	26.20		1.4025	1.3857
	90% of budgeted funds	15% of budgeted fund	IT	mean and std	80.88	14.30	58	57.59	20.55	58	21.73		1.0719	1.0648
Moon (2001)	9 million(90% complete)	1million (10% complete)	non-IT	mean and std	80.73	31.00	170	32.94	31.00	170	31.00		1.5416	1.5382
Heng et al. (2003)	75% of budgeted funds	25% of budgeted funds	IT	mean and std	80.50	14.32	180	57.10	14.32	180	14.32		1.6341	1.6307
Boonthanom (2003)	75% of budgeted funds (75% complete)	25% of budgeted funds (25% complete)	IT	mean and std	60.82	24.10	119	53.90	24.10	116	24.10		0.5423	0.5388

Table 2. Analysis results

Step1: Calculate mean effect size and confidence interval

N	Mean ES	-95%CI	+95%CI	SE	Z	P
20	.89	.81	.97	.04	21.10	.00

Step 2: Homogeneity analysis

Q	df	p
150.88	19	.00

Step 3: Moderator analysis on type of project in decision task

------ Analog ANOVA table (Homogeneity Q) -------

	Q	df	p
Between	7.22	1	.007
Within	143.66	18	.000
Total	150.88	19	.000

------- Q by Group -------

Group	Q	df	p
Non-IT	90.46	11	.00
IT	53.20	7	.00

------- Effect Size Results by Group -------

Group	Mean ES	SE	-95%CI	+95%CI	Z	P	N
Non-IT	.80	.05	.70	.91	15.26	.00	12
IT	1.04	.07	.90	1.18	14.82	.00	8

Q rejects the null hypothesis of homogeneity and thus indicates a heterogeneous distribution.

In our study, a chi-square test was conducted, and the Q statistic was found to be significant at the 0.01 level. A significant Q rejects the assumption of homogeneity. This means that the variability across different experiments is larger than the subject-level sampling error, and thus systematic differences across experiments might cause the variations among effect sizes.

The preceding discussion assumes a fixed effects model, in which effect size observed in a study is assumed to estimate the corresponding population effect with random error that stems only from the chance factors associated with subject-level sampling error in that study (Hedges & Vevea, 1998; Overton, 1998). An alternative is a random effects model, which assumes that there are essentially random differences between studies associated with study-level variations such as study procedures and settings in addition to subject-level sampling error. We used a fixed effects model because the experiments in our analysis followed similar research procedures to study the escalation of commitment.

- **Step 3:** Comparing sunk cost effect sizes for IT projects and Non-IT projects

When the effect sizes are found not to be homogeneous, meta-analysis can proceed with an examination of whether the substantive and methodological study characteristics moderate the effect sizes (Lipsey & Wilson, 2001). In this study, we attempted to detect whether the results of the experiments involving IT projects were different from the results of the experiments involving non-IT projects, so effect sizes were partitioned into two groups according to the project context. A chi square test was conducted to examine the between-group effect size variance and within-group effect size variance. We found that the between-group Q statistic was significant at the 0.01 level, showing that the project context significantly explained part of the variance. However, the within-group statistic was also highly significant, indicating that the variance within each group (IT vs. non-IT projects) still remains heterogeneous. Mean effect sizes and 95% confidence intervals were calculated for each group. The mean effect size for the IT project group was 1.04, and the 95% confidence interval was 0.90-1.18. The mean effect size for non-IT project group was 0.80, and the 95% confidence interval is 0.70-0.91. A t-test revealed that the mean difference was significant at the 0.01 level.

DISCUSSION AND IMPLICATIONS

A widely used convention for appraising the magnitude of effect sizes was established by Cohen (Cohen, 1977; Cohen, 1988). Standard mean difference effect sizes are considered small if less than or equal to 0.20, medium if equal to 0.50, and large if 0.80. In our study, after ruling out subject-level sampling error, the mean effect size associated with the sunk cost effect was 0.89, which qualifies as large. While prior research had already documented the existence of the sunk cost effect, in this study we provide evidence of the strength of the sunk cost effect across a range of experiments that have sought to investigate the phenomenon. The large affect size suggests that decision makers have tremendous difficulty ignoring sunk cost when making project continuance decisions. The implication of such a large effect size is that managers cannot afford to ignore the sunk cost effect and its influence on escalation behavior.

A test of the homogeneity of effect sizes showed that variability in results across experiments goes beyond what one would expect based on subject-level sampling error alone. The project context (IT or non-IT) significantly explains a part of the variance, but the effect sizes remain heterogeneous within each group. Therefore, potentially other substantive or methodological study characteristics moderate the effect sizes.

Our moderator analysis results showed that the magnitude of the sunk cost effect is greater in experiments involving an IT project context than in experiments involving a non-IT project context. While it has previously been claimed that IT projects may be particularly susceptible to escalation (Keil et al., 2000a; Newman and Sabherwal, 1996), there has been no empirical evidence to substantiate this claim. The fact that we observed a difference in effect size between experiments that involved IT project scenarios vs. experiments that involved non-IT project scenarios is intriguing. The implication of this finding is that IT projects may indeed be more susceptible to the sunk cost effect. If this is the case, further research is needed to determine why the magnitude of the sunk cost effect may be greater in IT project settings. One potential explanation is that people are more optimistic about the prospect of IT projects than that of non-IT projects and thus perceive a high likelihood of success even when faced with negative information. While additional research is clearly warranted on this point, in the meantime, IT managers should be particularly sensitive to the impact that sunk costs can have on escalation behavior.

LIMITATIONS

While meta-analysis is a powerful technique for quantitatively integrating and interpreting prior research results, it is not without limitations. One of the limitations of the experimental studies upon which our meta-analysis is based is their external validity, meaning to what extent the results can be generalized to organizational settings. Because the meta-analysis is based on the results from primary studies, it still carries this limitation. Second, effects in published studies tend to be larger and insignificant findings tend to remain unpublished. Meta-analysis, which surveys primary studies, in turn has an upward bias, known as the "file drawer problem" (Begg 1994; Smith, 1980). Third, moderator analysis in meta-analysis is susceptible to confounds. The significant difference observed between the two groups in terms of effect size needs to be interpreted with caution, as it may reflect other experimental differences that do not relate to the type of project. Finally, the sample size of 20 used in this particular meta-analysis was not large. Nonetheless, we were able to have sufficient power to detect significance in our homogeneity test.

CONCLUSION

In spite of the aforementioned limitations, this research represents the first attempt to synthesize, integrate, and interpret the research stream on the sunk cost effect and its influence on project escalation. The study contributes to existing knowledge in two respects. First, through meta-analysis of 20 experiments, we calculated the sunk cost effect size and found that the sunk cost effect is large. Second, we found that the variability of the sunk cost effect is larger than one would expect based on subject-level sampling errors, and part of the variability can be attributed to the context of the experimental scenarios. Specifically, we found that the magnitude of the sunk cost effect was greater in experiments involving IT project contexts than in experiments involving non-IT project contexts.

Our meta-analysis pointed out future research directions in this research stream. Future research can be undertaken in two directions. First, because of the strong magnitude and heterogeneity of effect sizes for the sunk cost effect, we need more primary studies that investigate potential moderators of sunk cost effects. Second, the reasons why IT projects are particularly susceptible to sunk cost effects need to be investigated, and tactics for reducing the influence of sunk costs on decision-making need to be explored.

While more research is needed, prior studies have suggested that the sunk cost effect can be reduced by: (1) avoiding negative framing, (2) encouraging people to focus on alternatives and consider opportunity costs, (3) making negative feedback unambiguous, and (4) increasing the decision-maker's accountability (Garland, Sandefur, & Rogers, 1990; Keil et al., 1995b; Northcraft & Neale, 1986; Simonson & Nye, 1992).

REFERENCES

Abdel-Hamid, T., & Madnick, S. E. (1991). *Software project dynamics: An integrated approach.* Englewood Cliffs, NJ: Prentice Hall.

Arkes, H. R., & Blumer, C. (1985). The psychology of sunk cost. *Organizational Behavior and Human Decision Processes 35*, 124-140.*

Arkes, H. R., & Hutzel, L. (2000). The role of probability of success estimates in the sunk cost effect. *Journal of Behavioral Decision Making 13*(3), 295-306.*

Begg, C. B. (1994). Publication bias. In H. Cooper and L. V. Hedges, *The handbook of research synthesis* (pp. 399-409). New York: Russell Sage Foundation.

Boonthanom, R. (2003). Information technology project escalation: Effects of decision unit and guidance. In *Proceedings of 24th International Conference on Information Systems.**

Brockner, J. (1992). The escalation of commitment to a failing course of action. *Academy of Management Review 17*(1), 39-61.

Brooks, F. P. (1975). *The mythical man-month: Essays on software engineering.* Reading, MA: Addison-Wesley

Cohen, J. (1977). *Statistical power analysis for the behavioral sciences.* New York: Academic Press.

Cohen, J. (1988). *Statistical power analysis for the behavioral sciences (2nd ed.).* Hillsdale, NJ: Erlbaum.

Conlon, D. E., & Garland, H. (1993). The role of project completion information in resource allocation decisions. *Academy of Management Journal 38*(2), 402-413.*

Cooper, H. & Hedges, L. V. (1994). The handbook of research synthesis. New York: Russell Sage Foundation.

Garland, H. (1990). Throwing good money after bad: The effect of sunk costs on the decision to escalate commitment to an ongoing project. *Journal of Applied Psychology 75*(6), 728-731.*

Garland, H. & Conlon, D. E. (1998). Too close to quit: The role of project completion in maintaining commitment. *Journal of Applied Psychology 28*(22), 2025-2048.*

Garland, H., Sandefur, C.A., & Rogers, A.C. (1990) De-escalation of commitment in oil exploration: When sunk costs and negative feedback coincide, *Journal of Applied Psychology 75*(6), 721-727.

Garland, H., & Newport, S. (1991). Effects of absolute and relative sunk costs on the decision to persist with a course of action. *Organizational Behavior and Human Decision Processes 48,* 55-69.

Glass, G. V. (1976). Primary, secondary, secondary, and metaanlaysis. *Educational Researcher 5*, 3-8.

Heath, C. (1995). Escalation and de-escalation of commitment in response to sunk costs: The role of budgeting in mental accounting. *Organizational Behavior and Human Decision Processes 62*(1), 38-54.

Hedges, L. V. (1982). Estimating effect size from a series of independent experiment. *Psychological Bulletin, 92*, 490-499

Hedges, L. V., & Olkin, I. (1985), *Statistical methods for meta-analysis.* Orlando, FL: Academic Press

Hedges, L. V., & Vevea, J. L. (1998). Fixed- and random-effects models in meta-analysis. *Psychological Methods 3*, 486-504.

Heng, C. S., Tan, B. C. Y., & Wei, KK. (2003). De-escalation of commitment in software projects: Who matters? What matters? *Information and Management 41*, 99-110.*

Hunter, J. E., & Schmidt, F. L. (1990). *Methods of meta-analysis, correcting error and bias in research findings.* Sage Publications.

Hwang, M. I. (1996). The use of meta-analysis in MIS research: Promises and problems. *The Data Base for Advances in Information Systems 27*(3), 35-48.

Kahneman, D., & Tversky, A. (1979). Prospect theory: An analysis of decisions under risk. *Econometrica, 47*, 263-291

Keil, M., Mann, J., & Rai, A. (2000a). Why software projects escalate: An empirical analysis and test of four theoretical models. *MIS Quarterly 24*(4), 631-664.

Keil, M., Mixon, R., Saarinen, T., & Tuunainen, V. (1995a). Understanding runaway information technology projects. *Journal of Management Information Systems 11*(3), 65-85.*

Keil, M., Truex, D., & Mixon, R. (1995b). The effects of sunk cost and project completion on information technology project escalation. *IEEE Transactions on Engineering Management, 24*(4), 372-381.*

Keil, M., Tan, B. C. Y., et al. (2000b). A cross-cultural study on escalation of commitment behavior in software projects. *MIS Quarterly 24*(2), 299-325.*

Lipsey, M. W., & Wilson, D. B. (2001). *Practical meta-analysis.* Sage Publications.

Moon, H. (2001). looking forward and looking back: Integrating completion and sunk cost effects within an escalation-of-commitment progress decision. *Journal of Applied Psychology 86*(1), 104-113.*

Newman, M., & Sabherwal, R. (1996). Determinants of commitment to information systems development: A longitudinal investigation. *MIS Quarterly 20*(1), 23-54.

Northcraft, G.B., & Neale, M.A. (1986) Opportunity costs and the framing of resource allocation decisions. *Organizational Behavior and Human Decision Processes* 37(3). 348-356.

Overton, R. C. (1998). A comparison of fixed-effects and mexed (random-effects) models for meta-analysis tests of moderator variable effects. *Psychological Methods 3*, 354-379.

Rosenthal, R., &Rubin, D. B. (1982) Comparing effect sizes of independent studies, *Psychological Bulletin, 92*, 500-504

Simonson, I., & Nye, P. (1992) The effect of accountability on susceptibility to decision errors. *Organizational Behavior and Human Decision Processes (51)*, 416-446.

Smith, M. L. (1980). Publication bias and meta-analysis. *Evaluation in Education 4*, 22-24.

Staw, B. M., & Ross, J. (1987). Behavior in escalation situations: antecedents, prototypes, and solutions. In B. M. Staw and L. L. Cummings, *Research in organizational behavior* (pp. 39-78). Greenwich, CT: JAI Press Inc.

Whyte, G. (1993). Escalating commitment in individual and group decision making: A prospect theory approach. *Organizational Behavior and Human Decision Processes 54*, 430-455.

ENDNOTES

1 This syndrome refers to the tendency for estimates of work completed to increase steadily until a plateau of 90% is reached. Software projects tend to be "90% complete" for half the entire duration (Brooks, 1975).

* The references with * are articles used as primary data sources in the meta-analysis.

APPENDIX

Table A. Summary of the research used in meta-analysis

Paper	Research Focus	Relevant Hypotheses	Sample size	Experimental Design	Reported Results	Conclusion
Arkes and Blumer (1985)	Explore the impact of sunk cost on individuals' decision making Explore the impact of sunk cost on individuals' decision making	No explicit hypotheses	108	Sunk cost was manipulated as either 90% or 0. Subjects made project continuance decision and provided yes/no answers.	chi-square(1, N=108)=50.6, p<0.001	People have difficulty ignoring sunk cost when making decisions.
			158	Sunk cost was manipulated as either 90% or 0. Subjects made project continuance decision and provided yes/no answers. Subjects were also asked to provide the probability of the project's success.	t(156)=2.02, p<0.05	Subjects in sunk cost situation have an inflated estimate of the project success likelihood
		No explicit hypotheses	95	Sunk cost was manipulated as either 90% or 0. Subjects made project continuance decision and provided yes/no answers.	chi-square (1, N=95)=29.5, p<0.01	Sunk cost effect found to be powerful even when one's general opinion is solicited.
Garland (1990)	Study the relationship between the level of the sunk cost and the decision to continue a project.	No explicit hypotheses.	127	Subjects specified the probability that they would invest all the remaining budgeted funds into a failing research and development (R&D) project. Sunk cost and project completion level were jointly manipulated at 4 levels: $1 million (10%), 3m (30%), 5m (50%), 70m (70%), and 9m (90%).	F(4,122)=12.2, p<.0001	Subjects' willingness to continue to invest on a threatened project was positively and linearly related to the proportion of the budget already expended.
			150	Subjects specified the probability that they would invest the next $1 million (of the $10 million budgeted funds) into a failing R&D project. The sunk cost and project completion level were jointly manipulated at 4 levels: 1m (10%), 3m (30%), 5m (50%), 70m (70%), and 9m (90%).	F(4,1145)=6.67, p<.0001	Subjects' willingness to authorize additional resources for a threatened R&D project was positively and linearly related to the proportion of the budget that had already been expended.
Whyte (1993)	Study the sunk cost effect on escalation in individual and group decision making	Escalation will occur for both individuals and groups regardless of personal responsibility.	325	The experimental design involved six project continuance decision making scenarios, three decision frames, and two performing units. Decision frames were manipulated by the presence or absence of sunk cost. Performance units included individual or group decision makers. Subjects were asked to make decisions whether to continue investment on the projects.	The decision frame effect is F(2, 59)=122.6; p<0.001	Escalation occurred at both individual and group levels, and group decision making amplifies this effect.
Conlon and Garland (1993)	Explore whether sunk cost or project completion level leads to escalation	No explicit hypothesis.	554	Sunk cost was manipulated at 1, 5, and 9 million. Project completion levels were manipulated at 10%, 50%, and 90%. Competitor's performance was manipulated at two levels—superior and inferior	Sunk cost effect is F (3, 550) =20.48, p<0.001. The project completion effect is F(3,550)=3.94, p<.01	Both sunk cost and project completion had significant main effects on subjects' willingness to allocate all the money remaining in the budget to complete the project
			226	The experiment was a 2 by 2 by 2 by 2 between subjects factorial design with 2 levels of each of the following: sunk cost (1 million or 9 million), project completion (10% or 90%), knowledge about the budget (known or unknown), and responsibility for initial investment decision (low or high).	Sunk cost effect is insignificant. The project completion effect is significant. F(1, 209), p<.001	The completion effect may dominate the sunk cost effect in terms of promoting escalation behavior.

continued on following page

Table A. continued

Keil, et al. (1995)	Test the impact of sunk cost and completion level within the context of IT project	H1: Willingness to continue with an IT project will be positively correlated with the level of sunk cost and degree of project completion level. H2: Regardless of sunk cost and completion, subjects will exhibit less willingness to continue with a prior course of action given the presence of an alternative course of action that appears equally attractive. H3: In the presence of both sunk cost and completion information, subjects who escalate their commitment to a project will more frequently justify their action on the basis of completion, or proximity to goal, as opposed to sunk cost, or the amount of resources already expended.	322	Sunk cost and completion level were jointly manipulated at 4 levels. An alternative project was manipulated as either present or absent.	Sunk cost/completion was significant at the 0.001 level. The effect of an alternative project was significant at the 0.001 level.	People have difficulty ignoring sunk cost when making project continuation decisions with or without an alternative project. Content analysis shows that sunk cost is the most frequently mentioned factor among people who decide to continue the project. Presence of an alternative project decreases people's willingness to continue a failing project.
Keil et al. (1995)	An initial exploration of sunk costs in an IT project context	No explicit hypotheses	124	The experiment used a scenario of an in-house software development project. Sunk cost level was manipulated as 15%, 40%, 65%, and 90%	The results did not reveal the expected upward sloping sunk cost effect; instead, the results showed a horizontal line with a mean response of approximately 40% to the "willingness to continue" measure	Sunk cost effect was not significant in IT project context.
	Explore the sunk cost effect when projects go over budget	No explicit hypotheses	247	8 levels of sunk cost were manipulated, from 15% to 610%	There appears to be an upward sloping sunk cost effect from 15% to 90% sunk cost level. There was some de-escalation when sunk cost moved from 90% of budget to 10% over budget, but there did not appear to be any further de-escalation as the sunk cost moved from 100% of budget to higher levels.	Subjects did not de-escalate their commitment in the face of extreme budget overruns.
Garland and Conlon (1998)	Replicate Conlon and Garland (1993) with bank managers as subjects	H1: As project completion increases, subjects' willingness to continue investment in the project will increase	106	The experiment was 2 (sunk cost level) by 2 (project completion level) factorial between subjects design. Sunk cost was manipulated at 2 million or 8 million and completion level was manipulated at 20% or 80%	Completion effect is significant $F(1, 102)=11.63$, $p<0.001$. Neither sunk cost effect nor interaction is significant.	The completion effect may dominate the sunk cost effect in promoting escalation behavior.

continued on following page

Table A. continued

Arkes and Hutzel (2000)	Study and the relationship between sunk cost, probability of success(p), and decision to invest. Is p a cause of sunk cost effect, a consequence of the effect or both?	No explicit hypothesis	148	The experimental design is a 2 by 2 design involving sunk cost (90% and no sunk cost) and probability of success (34% or unspecified).	Log-linear analysis shows the sunk cost effect is significant.	The presence of sunk cost significantly increased willingness to invest approximately equally whether or not the project success probability was specified.
		No explicit hypothesis	241	The experimental design was a 2 by 2 design involving sunk cost (10% or 90%) and timing of project success estimate provided by subject (before or after the investment decision).	The sunk cost effect is F(1, 222)=4.61. The effect of the timing of the project success probability on escalation is F(1, 222)=6.43, p<0.02. The sunk cost effect on success rate estimation is F(1, 222)=4.61	When the project success probability estimation followed the investment decision, it was significantly higher than when it preceded the investment decision.
Keil et al. (2000)	Conduct cross-cultural study to examine the impact of sunk cost together with the risk propensity and risk perception of decision makers on their escalation of commitment behaviors	H 2: In all cultures, risk perception will have a significant inverse effect on willingness to continue a project. H 4: In all cultures, level of sunk cost will have a significant inverse effect on risk perception. H4a: The inverse relationship between level of sunk cost and risk perception will be stronger in cultures lower on uncertainty avoidance. H5: In all cultures, level of sunk cost will have a significant direct effect on willingness to continue a project.	185	Subjects were from Finland. In the first part, subjects read an experimental scenario in which sunk cost are manipulated at one of 4 levels (15%, 40%, 60%, 90%) and then indicate the probability they are willing to continue the project. In the second part, subjects complete a questionnaire to provide risk propensity and risk perception information.	The analysis is done using PLS, which uses a jackknifing technique to obtain T values. The relationship between sunk cost and willingness to continue a project was 0.15(T=3.01)*. The relationship between sunk cost level and risk perception was -0.16(T=-1.39). The relationship between risk perception and willingness to continue a project was -0.67(T=-9.04)*	The effect of the level of sunk cost on willingness to continue a project is direct and not mediated by risk perception.
			121	Same as above, but subjects were from the Netherlands.	The relationship between sunk cost and willingness to continue a project was 0.51(T=5.73)*. The relationship between sunk cost level and risk perception was -0.05(T=-0.07). The relationship between risk perception and willingness to continue a project was -0.43(T=-4.19)*	
			230	Same as above, but subjects were from Singapore.	The relationship between sunk cost and willingness to continue a project was 0.37(T=5.12)*. The relationship between sunk cost level and risk perception was -0.10(T=-0.86). The relationship between risk perception and willingness to continue a project was -0.46(T=-6.52)*	

continued on following page

Table A. continued

Moon (2001)	Investigate the main effects of sunk cost and completion level and their interaction effect.	H1: As the level of sunk costs increases, a decision maker will be significantly more willing to invest further into a progress-related project. H1b: The sunk-cost effect on a participant's propensity to continue investment into a project will be curvilinear in nature and shaped similarly to a marginal utility model. H2: As the level of completion increases, a decision maker will be significantly more willing to invest further into a progress-related project. H3a. Sunk cost will be more strongly related to commitment than completion under low-completion conditions but less strongly related to commitment than completion under high completion conditions. H3b. Sunk costs will not be related to commitment under low completions, but sunk costs will be related to commitment under high-completion conditions.	340	2 by 4 factorial design. Completion was manipulated at two levels and sunk cost was manipulated at four levels.	Sunk cost main effect was t (1,338)=2.26, P<.05, R square is 0.01. Completion main effect was significant. The interaction between sunk cost and completion was significant. T(5, 334)=2.00, P<0.05, R square=0.01	Sunk cost effects were present only within situations that were near completion. The shape of sunk cost effects has a curvilinear component.

continued on following page

Table A. continued

Heng et al. (2003)	Investigate the impact of individuals (superior and peers) and approach (shoulder blame and provide assurance) on de-escalation under varying conditions of sunk cost	H1: When sunk cost is low, willingness to terminate software projects with poor prospects (DoC) will be highest with support strategy (superiors provide assurance), followed by the shelter strategy (superiors shoulder blame), and finally no strategy. H2: When sunk cost is high, the willingness to terminate project will be the same with support strategy, shelter strategy, and no strategy. H3. When sunk cost is low, DoC will be highest with the sharing strategy, followed by sympathy strategy and no strategy. H4: When sunk cost is high, DoC will be the same with sharing strategy, the sympathy strategy and no strategy.	360	3 by 2 by 2 design involving: De-escalation approach (shoulder blame, provide assurance, do nothing), individual (superiors, peers), and sunk cost (low, high)	Sunk cost effect was significant at 0.01 level for entire group, for subgroups involving superiors, and for subgroups involving peers.	Under conditions of low sunk cost, several de-escalation strategies are effective. However, under conditions of high sunk cost, these strategies do not appear to facilitate de-escalation.
Boonthanom (2003)	This study investigates escalation of commitment in IT project development. An experiment is conducted to examine the impact of sunk cost, percentage of project completion, de-escalation strategy, and decision unit on the escalation behavior.	H1: Individuals will exhibit more escalation behavior given (a) high level of sunk cost and (b) high percentage of project completion. H2: Individuals will exhibit a relatively equal level of escalation behavior given either: (a) high sunk cost and low percentage of project completion or (b) low sunk cost and high percentage of project completion. H6a: On average, individuals without decisional guidance will exhibit more escalation behavior than individuals receiving decisional guidance.	235	A two-phase 2X2X2X2 lab experiment examining sunk cost (25%, 75%), completion level (25%, 75%), de-escalation strategy (present or absent), and decision unit (individual, group)	For both individuals and groups. The interaction effect between sunk cost level and completion level was significant (p-value=0.007). For individuals, sunk cost effect was only significant when completion level was high. For groups, the main project completion level effect was significant.	For individual escalation behavior, sunk cost effect was evident solely under the high project completion group.

continued on following page

Table B. Formula to calculate effect sizes (adapted from Lipsey & Wilson, 2001)

Formula	Data needed and definition of terms
Derive effect size from mean and standard deviation $ES_{sm} = \frac{\overline{X}_{G1} - \overline{X}_{G2}}{s_{pool}}$ $s_{pool} = \sqrt{\frac{(n_1 - 1)s_1^2 + (n_1 - 1)s_1^2}{n1 + n2 - 2}}$	Means ($\overline{X}G1$, $\overline{X}G2$), standard deviation ($s1$,$s2$), and sample sizes ($n1$, $n2$)
Derive effect size from proportions $ES_{sm} = ar\sin e(p_{G1}) - \arcsin e(p_{G2})$	Arcsine transformation of the proportion (p) in each group. % of people in each group who makes escalation decision(p_{G2}, p_{G2})
Derive effect size from t test $ES_{sm} = t\sqrt{\frac{n1 + n2}{n1n2}}$	Independent t-test (t) and sample sizes ($n1$, $n2$) for each group

This work was previously published in the Information Resources Management Journal, Vol. 20, Issue 3, edited by M. Khosrow-Pour, pp. 1-18, copyright 2007 by IGI Publishing, formerly known as Idea Group Publishing (an imprint of IGI Global).

Chapter XI
E-Learning Business Risk Management with Real Options

Georgios N. Angelou
University of Macedonia, Greece

Anastasios A. Economides
University of Macedonia, Greece

ABSTRACT

E-learning markets have been expanding very rapidly. As a result, the involved senior managers are increasingly being confronted with the need to make significant investment decisions related to the e-learning business activities. Real options applications to risk management and investment evaluation of Information and Communication Technologies (ICT) have mainly focused on a single and a-priori known option. However, these options are not inherent in any ICT investment. Actually, they must be carefully planned and intentionally embedded in the ICT investment in order to mitigate its risks and increase its return. Moreover, when an ICT investment involves multiple risks, by adopting different series of cascading options we may achieve risk mitigation and enhance investment performance. In this paper, we apply real options to the e-learning investments evaluation. Given the investment's requirements, assumptions and risks, the goal is to maximize the investment's value by identifying a good way to structure it using carefully chosen real options.

INTRODUCTION

E-learning is the delivery and management of learning by electronic means. Various devices (workstations, portable computers, handheld devices, smart phones, etc.), networks (wireline, wireless, satellite, etc.) can be used to support e-learning (Wentling et. all., 2000). E-learning may incorporate synchronous or asynchronous communication, multiple senders and receivers (one-to-one, one-to-many, many –to many, etc.), multiple media and format independently of space and time.

Recently the e-learning markets have been expanding very rapidly and led to an unexpected revelation: the forces affecting higher education around the world are strikingly similar. This is true in at least four important areas: expanding enrollments; the growth of new competitors, virtual education and consortia; the global activity of many institutions; and the tendency for policy makers to use market forces as levers for change in higher education. Expansion of enrollments, accompanied by shifts in student demands and expectations, is a global phenomenon. The number of tertiary students worldwide doubled in size in just twenty years, growing from 40.3 million students in 1975 to 80.5 million students in 1995 (Newman and Couturier, 2002).

Previous research on e-learning cost analysis and investment evaluation does not consider the risk inherent in the business activity (Whalen and Wright, 1999; Downes, 1998; Morgan, 2000). In this work we apply a real option model to identify and control the e-learning investments risks in order to achieve a balance between reward and risk.

The real options approach applies methods of financial planning in investment valuation problems. An investment project embeds a real option when it offers to management the opportunity to take some future action (such as abandoning, deferring, or scaling up the project) in response to events occurring within the firm and its business environment (Trigeorgis, 1996). For example, by taking advantage of the option to defer the investment for some time the management can learn whether there are better alternative technologies (Li and Johnson, 2002). This management's flexibility (called active management) to adapt its future actions in response to altered future business conditions expands an investment opportunity's value by improving upside potential and limiting downside losses (Trigeorgis, 1999). Business condition either refers to market conditions or firm conditions depending on where the investment is focusing. For example, an investment of an e-learning infrastructure for providing educational services only inside the premises of a big organization mainly refers to firm conditions. On the other hand, an e-learning application, which mainly focuses on providing services in the market (by a university or other institution), refers to market conditions. Figure 1 is a schematic diagram showing the probability distribution of cash flows for a passively versus actively managed project.

Figure 1. Uncertainty under passive and active management of the investment project, (Trigeorgis, 1996).

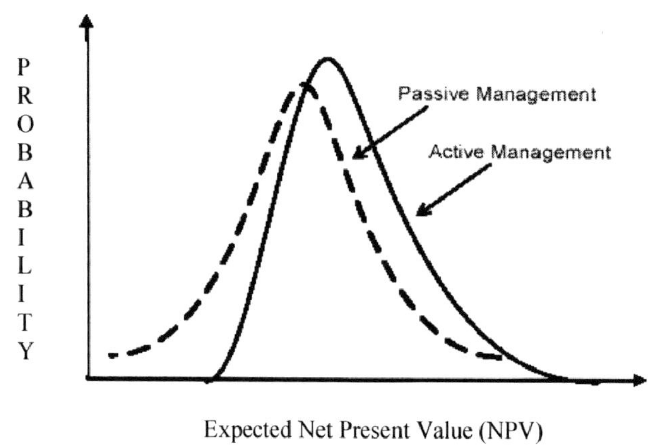

By adopting the active management philosophy we decrease the possibility of experiencing losses while increase the possibility of gaining. This is achieved by deffering the investment's implementation, learning about the changing business conditions, and generally resolving over time part of the overall investment's risk.

Most previous research considers only ICT investment that embeds a single and a-priori known option. However, real options are not inherent in any ICT investment (Benaroch, 2002), and in any case they are not always easily recognizable (Bräutigam and Esche, 2003). In order to optimally configure an ICT investment it may require considering a series of cascading (compound) options that will help to mitigate risk and enhance economic or strategic performance.

Previous research on investment evaluation has applied real options to ICT, pharmaceuticals and petroleum fields (Iatropoulos et. al, 2004; Mun, 2002). In this paper, we apply real options to the e-learning investments risk management and evaluation adopting a framework, which is presented by Benaroch (2002). The target is to configure the investment using real options analysis in such way that risk is minimized while economic performance is maximized.

For valuating series of cascading options, we start with the log-transformed binomial model (LTBM) finding it easy to use for investments plans that contain more than one options. In this model only the revenues uncertainty is considered, while the cost is certain. In addition, we apply for the first time in the ICT literature (to our knowledge) the extended log-transformed binomial model (ELTBM), presented by Gamba and Triggeorgis (2001) for more complex investments involving both stochastic payoffs and stochastic cost and compound options. We investigate the impact of cost's uncertainty in investment's profitability. We perform sensitivity analysis for revenues' and cost's variance and correlation and examine their influence in investment's performance. In appendix A, we briefly introduce the two option pricing models used in our analysis.

We apply the methodology in a case study based on Mantzari and Economides (2004) work. They present a cost model for an e-learning platform investment and analyze the required number of students (customers) in order to start being profitable (break even point analysis).

The remainder of the paper is organized as follows. In Section 2, we offer background material on real options and how they relate to the e-learning business field. In addition, we present the option-based methodology for managing ICT investments' risks as well as explain the concept underlying the methodology. In Section 3 we apply the ROs methodology to justify and extract the optimum deployment strategy for a specific e-learning infrastructure investment. In Section 4, we examine the influence of the cost uncertainty on the options values as well as on the overall investment's profitability. In Section 5, we discuss about the overall applicability of the methodology as well as present key issues for future research. Finally, in Section 6 we offer some concluding remarks.

REAL OPTIONS IN CONTROLLING ICT INVESTMENT RISK

Real Options Review

An option gives its holder the right, but not the obligation, to buy (call option) or sell (put option) an underlying asset in the future. Financial options are options on financial assets (e.g. an option to buy 100 shares of Nokia at 90€ per share on January 2007). Real options approach is the extension of the options concept to real assets. A real option is defined as the right, but not the obligation, to take an investment action on a real asset at a predetermined cost for a predetermined period of time. The real option approach to capital investment has the advantage to capture the value of managerial flexibility, which traditional discount cash flow (DCF) cannot properly address. This value is manifest as a collection of call or put options embedded in capital investment opportunities. These options typically include: option to defer, time-to-build option, option to alter operating scale (expand or contract), option to abandon, option to switch, growth option and multiple interacting options.

Spending money to exploit a business opportunity is analogous to exercising an option on, for example, a share of stock. It gives the right to make an investment's expenditure and receive an investment's asset. Real options' thinking considers that investment's asset fluctuates stochastically. The amount of money spent for investment corresponds to the option's exercise price (X). The present value of the project's asset (total gain of investment) corresponds to the stock price (V). The length of time the company can defer the investment decision without losing the opportunity corresponds to the option's time to expiration (T). The uncertainty about the future value of the project's cash flows (the risk of the project) corresponds to the standard deviation of returns on the stock (σ). Finally, the time value of money is given by the risk-free rate of return (r_f). The project's value as calculated by the real option methodology is the same with the value calculated by the Net Present Value (NPV) methodology when a final decision on the project can no longer be deferred (expiration date of the option). Table 1 summarizes the parameters' correspondence between a call option and an investment project.

The total value of a project that owns one or more options is given by Trigeorgis (1999):

Expanded (Strategic) NPV = Static (Passive) NPV + Value of Options from Active Management (1)

The flexibility value named as option premium is the difference between the NPV value of the project as estimated by the Static or Passive Net Present Value (PNPV) method and the Strategic or Expanded NPV (ENPV) value estimated by the Real Options method. The higher the level of uncertainty, the higher the option value because the flexibility allows for gains in the upside and minimizes the downside potential.

Option valuation models can be categorized in continuous time and discrete time domains. The most widely applied model in continuous time domain is the Black-Scoles formula, while in discrete time domain the Binomial one. However,

Table 1. Parameters' analogy between a call option and an investment opportunity

Investment Opportunity	**Variable**	**Call option**
Present value of a project's assets or Present Value of cash flows from investment (Revenues)	V	Stock price
The amount of money spent for the investment, Investment expenditure required to exercise the option (cost of converting the investment opportunity into the option's underlying asset, i.e., the operational project)	X	Agreed Exercise price of the Option
Length of time where the investment's decision may be deferred	T	Option's time to expiration (i.e., the maximum length of the deferral period).
Time value of money	r_f	Risk-free rate of return
Variance (Riskiness) of the investment's project assets (Costs, Revenues)	σ^2	Variance of returns on stock

continuous time models are not readily applicable for practical valuation purposes or integration with the models in strategic management theory, for example in combining game theory and real options (Smit and Trigeorgis, 2004). For a general overview of real option, Trigeorgis (1996) provides an in-depth review and examples on different real options. For more practical issues the reader is referred to Mun (2002 and 2003). Finally, Angelou and Economides (2004) present an extended survey of real options applications in real life ICT investment analysis.

Risk Management with Real Options in E-Learning Business Field

Virtual learning environments are providing teachers with new tools to manage courses and curricular resources, to communicate with students and to coordinate discussions and assessment tasks. Traditional support services such as libraries are changing dramatically; digital collections are overtaking physical collections with students being able to access their services at any time and from almost anywhere. Administrative systems such as student records are being linked to virtual learning environments making for a seamless linkage across administrative and teaching functions. Wiring and internet connectivity have become business critical to the modern university.

New pedagogical approaches are being developed to capitalise on the opportunities afforded by virtual environments and this is necessitating new forms of preparation and support for students and staff. The scope of these developments are extensive, they cut across all areas of institutional functioning and pose significant challenges to senior managers. How are they to make sense of the range of influence of e-learning developments within their institution and assess the risks associated with these developments? What information will help decision-makers to make strategic choices about where to invest, what to invest and how much to invest? While some institutions have invested heavily in technologies to support learning others have adopted a more cautious approach. These differences in levels of investment depend on a complex mix of internal and external factors – institution's mission, strategic plan, level of technological expertise, staff and student skills in ICT, awareness of the benefits of e-learning and beliefs about what is possible, available funding, attitudes to risk, government policy and funding council initiatives.

The valuation of e-learning business activities is a challenging task since it is characterized by rapidly changing business and technology conditions. Traditional finance theory suggests that firms should use a Discounted Cash Flow (DCF) methodology to analyze capital allocation requests. However, DCF does not properly account the flexibility inherent in most e-learning investment decisions. For example, an e-learning infrastructure project may have a negative Net Present Value (NPV) when evaluated on a stand-alone basis, but it may also provide the option to launch future value-added services if business conditions are favorable. Real options analysis presents an alternative method since it takes into account the managerial flexibility of responding to a change or new situation in business conditions (Trigeorgis, 1996).

ICT investment risks include firm-specific risks, competition risks, market risks, and environmental and technological risks. Firm-specific risks are determined by endogenous factors such as a firm's ability to align its ICT projects portfolio to business strategy and the skill level of its ICT staff. Competition risks include risks posed by competitors who may make preemptive moves to capture market share or make similar investments that may dilute the value of a firm's current ICT project portfolio. Market risks include uncertainty about customer demand for services that are enabled by a firm's ICT projects (Benaroch, 2002). We adopt this analysis for the e-learning investments too. For example, an e-learning project may experience more market risk characteristics while another one more firm risk characteristics. Actually, if a project is focusing more on the open market, for example e-learning services provided by a university, the risks are mainly coming from the market and competition field. On the other hand, when the e-learning service/product is focusing more on internal use by an organisation, the risk is more firm specific.

ICT research on real options recognizes that ICT investments can embed various types of real options, including: defer, stage, explore, alter operating scale, abandon, lease, outsource, and growth (Trigeorgis, 1996). Each type of real option essentially enables the deployment of specific responses to threats and/or enhancement steps, under one of three investment modes. *Defer* investment to learn about risk in the investment recognition stage. Such learning-by-waiting helps to resolve market risk, competition risk, and firm risk. *Partial investment* with active risk exploration in the building stage. If we don't know how serious some risk is, investing on a smaller scale permits to actively explore it. *Dis-investment/ Re-investment* with risk avoidance in the operation stage. If we accept the fact that some risk cannot be actively controlled, two options offer contingency plans for the case it will occur. The option to abandon operations allows redirecting resources if competition, market or organizational risks materialize. The option to contract (partially disinvest) or expand (reinvest) the operational investment in response to unfolding market and firm uncertainties. In general, the greater the risk, the more learning can take place, and the more valuable the option value is (Benaroch, 2001).

Option Based Methodology to Control Market and Competition Risk

The methodology we present next helps to address the question: What are the real options potentially embedded in an ICT investment that can and ought to be exercised in order to maximize the investment's value?

The methodology involves 4 main steps that must be repeated over time. In what follows, we explain these steps and illustrate them in the context of an e-learning investment case study (Matzari and Economides (2004):

1. *Define the investment plan and its risk.* State the investment goals, requirements and assumptions (technological, organizational, economic, etc.), and then identify the risks involved in the investment. After the definition of the business content by the management the specific risk issues and the analysis of the relationship between those issues should be taken place by the evaluation team. The lifecycle of an investment includes 5 stages. It starts at the inception stage, where the investment exists as an implicit opportunity that was probably facilitated by earlier investments. We call investment during this stage as shadow option. At the recognition stage the investment is seen to be a viable opportunity and we call it real option. The building stage follows upon a decision to undertake the investment opportunity. In the operation stage, the investment produces direct, measurable payoffs. Upon retirement, the investment continues to produce indirect payoffs, in the form of spawned investment opportunities that build on the technological assets and capabilities it has yielded. When these assets and capabilities can no longer be reused, the investment reaches the obsoleteness stage, (Benaroch, 2001).
2. *Recognize shadow embedded options based on risk characteristics.* Start by mapping each of the identified investment risks to shadow embedded options that can control them. It may be necessary to reiterate this step to gradually identify compound options, because some options can be the prerequisites or the payoff of some other options.
3. *Choose alternative investment's configurations based on options exercise strategy.*

Upon recognizing the shadow embedded options, use different subsets of these options to generate alternative ways to restructure the investment.

4. *Evaluate investment-structuring alternatives to find a subset of recognized options that maximally contribute to the investment's value.* To choose which of the recognized shadow options to create in order to increase the investment value, assess the value of each shadow option in relations to how it interact with other options, in relation to the risks it controls, and in relation to the cost of converting it into a real options. The project's characteristics are mapped into the option variables. In practice, the DCF projection is rearranged in phases so that the options input values can be isolated. Determine the initial values of the five input variables (V, X, σ, T, r_f), where the variance has to be calculated or estimated. In particular, the variance estimation could be the most difficult task in the overall process. Its estimation can be done either by historical data from other similar projects or by technical estimation such as monte-carlo simulation (Herath and Park, 2002). Investment revenues strongly related to customer demand and product/service price may be results of detailed market survey before final decision. We do not focus on this part of the business analysis and assume that our analysis is starting after obtaining at least partially this information. Starting from the end and going backwards we estimate the option values at each investment stage. We adopt compound option analysis. Finally, we estimate the overall ENPV value, which includes all the embedded options in the selected deployment strategy (selected real options).

The aforementioned steps must be re-applied every new information set arrival when some risks get resolved or new risks surface. Real options analysis assumes that the future is uncertain and the management has the right to change decisions concerning investment deployment strategy when uncertainties become resolved or risks become known. Actually, when some of these risks become known, for example incoming results from a market survey, the analysis should be revisited to incorporate the decisions made or revisiting any input assumptions such as investment variance.

A SPECIFIC E-LEARNING BUSINESS ACTIVITY

Description of a Specific E-Learning Business Activity and NPV Analysis

We examine a business activity to establish an enterprise, which will offer services for learning foreign languages through the World Wide Web (Mantzari and Economides, 2004). The users of our services will be students and adults having access to the Internet. The base scale investment concerns learning English. It is matter of further growth investment opportunity to provide services for other foreign languages. The courses are developed digitally on a special educational software platform that is purchased to cover the needs of our company and it is installed on the collocated server. Afterwards the users of our services submit their own personal passwords and ID's in order to get connected to the server and attend the lessons through the Internet. Competitive advantages of such business model for providing distance-learning services comparing to the conventional syllabus are: i) the absence of traditional classrooms which leads to reduced Operating Costs, ii) the absence of traditional way of teaching which reinforces autonomous learning, iii) offering services 24h a day, 7days a week that leads to maximum exploitation while at the same time it is more convenient for the users, iv) flexible pace of attending the lessons, and v) reduced fees due to the continuous functioning and the reduced operating costs.

Some Investments Assumptions

We examine the investment performance assuming an 11 years period of analysis and assume that all cash inflows and outflows are discounted at the risk-free rate r_f=5%. We consider a risk free rate 5% according to the rate of return on Greeks' Treasury Bills. In addition, we separate the investment's costs, as seen in appendix B in two phases: a) in the initial phase of establishing an e-learning organization, the costs depend mainly on the number of courses (considering a large number of students), b) in the latter phase of operating it, the costs depend on the time duration, on the number of courses and on the number of students, which in addition is divided in fixed and variable cost. We consider as entry time to the market (to implement the investment) when customers (students) demand is such that the operating revenues are equal to the operating costs (Mantzari and Economides 2004).

In appendix C, we present the Cash Flows analysis for the base scale investment. In particular, the base scale investment further to the initial e-learning service provision it mainly contains the infrastructure investment that is able to support up to 1000 students per year. At the entry time in the market to total operating costs are equal to the investment revenues. The computed present value of payoffs expected from the base scale investment becoming operational in time period T=3 is $V_{base\ scale}$, which includes (investment revenues – operating costs). As seen in appendix C the NPV of the e-learning infrastructure investment at T=3 is –3.000 k€, indicating so the non-profitability of the investment.

Methodology Application for an E-Learning Business Activity

Our target is to justify economically the investment of launching e-learning activities in the Greek market. Among others, we have to decide:

1. What is the entry time into the market?
2. What is the scale to enter?
3. What is the optimum way to configure investment in order to minimize risk and maximize profitability (ENPV)?

We follow the aforementioned four steps:

- *Step 1: To define the investment plan and its risk.*

Here we define the investment content, goals and requirements. We start with an initial ICT solution, stating investment assumptions (economic, technological, organizational, etc.), and revealing the investment risks in light of these assumptions. These activities should be carried out relative to each of the stages in the investment lifecycle. In our case, we consider the recognition, building, and operation stages, and the involved risks that fall into these stages, Table 2.

One is environmental risk. There is much uncertainty about the customer demand. Low customer demand can change investment profitability from positive to negative. Another is firm-specific capability risk. There is uncertainty about the firm's capability to integrate efficiently the initially planned scale of the ICT infrastructure with the required applications as well as with the content of them. Finally, the last area is competition risk as a competitor could react by launching improved applications that will erode revenues from future customers.

We initially assume that all these risks affect only the expected revenues and not cost. Actually, cost influences directly the revenues too. Afterwards, we examine the impact of the cost's uncertainty on the investment's profitability.

Table 2. First step of the approach applied to the e-learning investment

Stage	Goals	Risks and Opportunities
Recognition	To establishe an enterprise, which will offer services for learning foreign languages through the World Wide Web	Enviromental (E1) - Low customer/student demand that might not be profitable to let investment pass from the Recognition to Building stage. Firm has to decide when to enter in the market and in what scale.
Building	The initial e-learning solution involves developing an infrastructure platform that will support languages distance learning services	Project (P1)/Organizational (O1) - Firm staff may lack experience with linking ICT technologies with content applications such as educational issues. Functionality (F1) - The firm may build the application right according to the required specifications, but still fail to realize the anticipated benefits because the requirements are wrong to begin with. This could result in poor application functionality
Operation	Support e-learning services for foreign languages	Environmental (E1) – low customer demand could make it non economical to let the investment live long. Enviromental (E2) - demand exceeds expectations (follow-up opportunities exist) Environmental (E3) – too high customer demand could result in an inability of the back office of the firm to handle the extra processing load presented by customers/students Competition (C1) – competitors could react by launching an improved application, and thus erode the extra demand generated produced by the e-learning application

- *Step 2: Recognize shadow options based on risk characteristics.*

In the next step, we recognize shadow options that the investment could embed based on the aforementioned investment risks. The target is to configure the investment plan by using these options in a way that risks are mitigated while overall profitability is maximized. Actually, investments risks can be, at least partially, handled by adopting managerial flexibility, through option analysis. Table 3 shows the main sources of the risks of the e-learning investment that we examine in this paper and the shadow options that we adopt in order to control them.

- *Step 3: Choose alternative investment configurations based on options exercise strategy.*

In the next step we identify alternative ways to configure the e-learning investment using different subsets of the recognized shadow options. Although, it may seem that the number of possible configurations could be large, only configurations involving maximal subsets of shadow (viable) options are worth considering (Benaroch, 2002). We next illustrate plausible investment configuration that considers five of the recognized shadow options, Figure 2.

Business Assumptions

We assume that market entry takes place when demand level reaches the critical number of students and the *Investment Operating Revenues are equal to Operating Costs (we assume that this is reached at year T).*

We start our analysis considering that T is up to 3 years. We also consider that the construction

Table 3. E-learning investment risks mapped to operating options that could mitigate them

Risk Area		Risk Opportunity	Investment Lifecycle Stages - Shadow Options Allocations			
			Recognition	Building	Operation	
			Option to Defer	Option to Contract scale of Investment	Option to Expand	Option to Choose between further Expansion and Contraction
Firm Specific Risks	Project	**P1** staff lacks needed technical skills to successfully intergate and operate ICT infrastructure-applications with content	+	+		
	Functionality	**F1** wrong design (e.g., analysis failed to assess correct requirements)		+		
Market Specific Risks	Competition	**C1** competition's response eliminates the firm's advantage	+	+		+
	Environmental	**E1** low customer demand, with inability to pull out of market	+	+		+
		E2 demand exceeds expectations (follow-up opportunities exist)	+		+	+
		E3 too high customer response may overwhelm the application	+		+	+

phase of our platform is 1 year. Finally, we consider that critical mass for customers is reached at T=3. At the beginning, recognition phase, we face the option to defer investment up to time T in order to resolve market uncertainty concerning customers' demand as well as competition threat. The smaller the T the sooner we should perform investment and the smaller the option value to defer will be, since less amount of uncertainty is resolved. During time period T the firm is facing market uncertainty "clearness" and decides to enter the market when investment starts to become profitable.

Options Presentation

Our configuration considers five of the recognized shadow options (see Figure 2). In this work we consider only this deployment path. Additionally, we could consider other alternatives too, such as the deployment path that includes only the option to explore business activity. The option to explore would facilitate learning-by-doing, through a pilot effort that supports a part of the E-learning services while in case of favorable demand the full scale of the business activity takes place. In our analysis we consider a more complicated deployment path in order to control high number of risks and provide more realistically the applicability of our methodology. Finally, the high number of shadow options that transformed to real ones does not necessarily indicate the maximum investment value since many of the options can control the same type of risks. In this case options are supplementary to the contribution of the overall investment value (Trigeorgis, 1996).

Figure 2. A configuration involving five of the shadow options that the e-learning investment can embed:

1. *The base scale option permits realizing the investment into one cost outlay X1 = 190.000 €, which is deferrable for up to three years, in order to resolve market uncertainty.*
2. *The option to contract the initially planned scope of operations by 20% saving so in cost operations X2' = 30.000 €.*
3. *The option to expand further operations in case of favorable customers demand by 30%, by making a third cost outlay, X3 =55.000 € (it is one third of initial infrastructure investment)*
4. *The options to choose between expand and contract operations. The expand option permits scaling up operations by 40%, by making a fourth cost outlay, X4 =75.000 €, for the base scale. The option to contract scope of operations by 25% saving so in cost operations X5' = 35.000 €. Option exercise costs and revenues to expand – Contract operation presented above concerns base scale operations and single options analysis. In case of compound option analysis expand and contract values as well as option revenues are changing according to predecessor option type.*

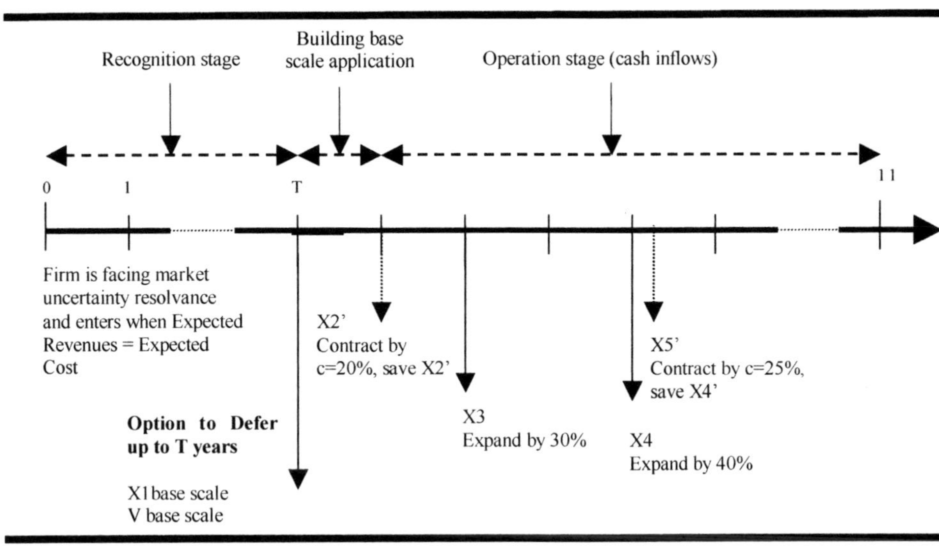

During the Recognition Stage

The first option is to defer the first cost outlay for up to three time periods (assuming that longer deferral would significantly increase the risk of competitive preemption). Deferral permits learning about the levels of demand experienced by other firms with comparable e-learning services, in support of resolving risks E1, E2 and E3. Deferral could also provide the time to get the cooperation of all parties so as to reduce risks F1 and P1. During the deferral period the firm faces the market uncertainty "clearing" especially concerning demand considering the trigger point to start investing when expected revenues becomes equal to investment's operating costs. Finally, competition threat, risk C1, from another firm can be at least partially resolved during deferral period.

During the Building Stage

The building firm's staff may lack experience with linking ICT technologies to content applications such as educational issues. In addition, the firm may build the application right according to the required specifications, but still fail to realize the anticipated benefits because the requirements are wrong to begin with. This could result in poor application functionality, risks F1, P1. In order to control these risks we consider the option to contract, the initially planned, investment scale during the building stage. In addition, competition risk, C1, e.g. a competitor's response eliminates the firm's advantage, is reduced through option to contract the initial planned investment scale. Moreover, customers' uncertainty E1 during the building stage can be mitigated by adopting the contract option. Finally, the aforementioned option to defer enhances possibilities of mitigating such kind of risk during this stage, too.

During the Operating Stage

The next option is the option to expand operations scale by 30% in year T+2 in case of favorable demand and risk mitigation E2 and E3. The last option is actually a combination of one call option and one put option having the same time to maturity. In time T+4 the firm possesses the option to choose between to expand or contract operation scale according to market conditions. Actually, the second option is to contract operations of the investment, by 25%, at time period T+4, in support of hedging risks E1 and E3. At the same time there is the call option to expand operations in case of high demand by making a fourth cost outlay. This option could control demand risk E2. In general a call option is optimally exercised when circumstances become favorable and a put option is exercised when circumstances become unfavorable. Finally, competition risk C2 can be hedged through the option to choose between contracting or expanding the investment scale according to the competitors' actions that could either eliminate firm's market share or just influence the overall market demand for such kind of applications.

- *Step 4. Options evaluation and Investments configurations alternatives profitability.*

In the final step, we evaluate embedded options included in the configuration alternatives. We initially assume that only revenues V are uncertain. We adopt the LTBM because it simplifies the valuation of compound options, Trigeorgis (1996). In addition, we apply for the first time in the ICT literature (to our knowledge), the ELTBM. The ELTBM presented by Gamba and Triggeorgis (2001) is suitable for complex investments involving both stochastic payoffs and stochastic costs and compound options. Actually, we examine the influence of both cost and revenues uncertainty on the overall investment's profitability for base scale e-learning infrastructure investment. We investigate the impact of cost uncertainty in the investment profitability, making sensitivity analysis for Revenues and Costs Variance and Correlation.

Option Analysis and Specific Investments Characteristics Map

For the valuation of options we use the Log-Transformed Binomial Model (LTBM) with 50 steps time resolution (Gamba and Trigeorgis, 2001). Also, the variance of payoffs is considered at $\sigma = 50\%$ adopting similar to the literature values (Oslington, 2004; Angelou and Economides, 2005). The valuation of separate options is given below (Trigeorgis, 1996).

Option to Defer up to T

The option to defer is basically valued as an American call option on the project. The time T for entry in the market is defined as the time when the investment operating cost is equal to the investment revenues. Option Value to Defer, OV(D), is given by:

$$OV(D) = \max(V - X_I, 0) \qquad (2)$$

As seen in Table 4 the managerial flexibility to defer the investment up to three years, in order to wait for the resolvance of the customers demand, is 53,6 k€.

Option to Contract at T+1

During the implementation phase the firm possesses the option to contract the initially planned operation by 20% when the market conditions become unfavorable or the firm's capability to develop the project is inferior to the expected one. The option is valued as European Put option.

Option Value to Contract operations, OV(C) is given by:

$$OV(C) = \max(X_c - c*V,\ 0) \text{ where } c=20\% \quad (3)$$

We consider that contracting the operation by 20% will result in X_c = 30 k€ of operation savings and its option value will be 3,1 k€.

Option to Expand at T+2

In case of favorable demand the firm can expand its operation by 30%. Here, for simplicity we assume that the expected revenues will also increase by 30%. The option value to expand, OV(E), is valued analogously to an European Call option to acquire part of the project by paying an extra outlay as exercise price X_3. It is given by:

$$OV(E) = \max(e*V - X_3,\ 0) \text{ where } e = 30\% \quad (4)$$

while its value is 12,6 k€.

Option to Choose Between to Expand and Contract Operations at T+4

The option to expand (alone) (scale up operations) by e', the initially planned scale of project, is valued analogously to a European call option to acquire part of the project by paying the extra outlay X4 as an exercise price.

The option to contract (alone) (scale down operation) by c' is valued as an European put on part of the project, with exercise price equal to the potential cost savings X5 due to this operation contraction. The option value to choose between contraction and expansion, OV(CH), is given by:

$$OV(CH) = \max(e'*V - X4,\ X5 - c'*V,\ 0) \quad (5)$$

and its value is 34,8 k€.

Value of Option Combinations with Interactions Between Each Other

The value of an option in the presence of other options may differ from its value in isolation because of its strong interaction with these options. Trigeorgis (1993) offers a formal discussion of the factors affecting the non-additivity of options. We follow the compound options valuation process as presented by Herath and Park (2002). However, in our case, only the option to defer is prerequisite for the availability of the following options. This means that in order to posses one or all of the following options we should first adopt the option to defer, fact that is very well understood since this indicates the initiation of the base scale investment. For the rest of the options, each option exercise is not a prerequisite for the possession of the next option.

The valuation of complex options remains a difficult endeavor. Since e-learning investments could be exposed to multiple risks, they may need to be configured using a series of cascading (compound) options. Standard valuation models (e.g., Black-Scholes model) ignore the fact that the value of individual options in a series of cascading options may be lowered or enhanced by interactions with other options. Here, we use the LTBM to simplify the valuation of cascading options. In addition we test the ELTBM in order to consider both revenues and cost uncertainty.

Table 4 shows the value of the project with different combinations of the shadow options. In particular, the higher option value, in isolation,

Table 4. Comparative value contribution of options in the investment alternatives

Option Combination	**Option Value LTBM 50 steps (values in k€)**	**ENPV (overall investment value)**	**Value at**		**Option Name**	**Exercise Price X (for base scale)**	**PV(V) base scale**	**Year to maturity**	**Option Type**
Defer **(D)**	53,6	50,6	t=0		Defer **(D)**	190	161 (187)	up to T=3	Americal Call
Contract **(CN)**	3,1	0,1	t=T		Contract **(CN)** (20%)	30	37	T+1	European Put
Expand **(E)****	12,6	9,6	t=T+1		Expand **(E)** (30%)	55	56	T+2	European Call
Option to Choose **(CH)***** (expand / contract)	34,8	31,8	t=T+1		Option to Choose **(CH)** (expand/contract) (40%/25%)	75/35	74/46	T+4	European Call/ Put
DCN 1	38,3	35,3	t=0		In this case we consider that base scale investment results to V'=0,8V while X'=0,9X				
DE 2	57	54	t=0						
DCH 3	64,2	61,2	t=0						
DCNE 4	42	39	t=0						
DCNCH 5	48	45	t=0						
DECH 6	67	64	t=0						
DCNECH 7	50	47	t=0						
** Option to Expand at time T+2, value at t=T									
*** Option to Choose at time T+4, value at t=T+2									
**** Option to Switch use between T+5 and 11, at t=T+4									
ENPV = Option Value x 1.000 - 3.000									
1 max (0,8V+CN-0,9X, 0)					We consider the Option to Defer and the Option to Contract				
2 max (V+E-X, 0)					We consider the Option to Defer and the Option to Contract				
3 max (V+CH-X, 0)					We consider the Option to Defer and the option to Choose betwee E and CN				
4 max (0,8V+max ((Xc+E-0,2V,E)-0,9Xbasescale, 0)									
5 max (0,8V+max((Xc+CH-0,2V,CH)-0,9Xbasescale, 0),									
6 max (V+max((eV+CH-Xe,CH)-Xbasescale, 0) where e=0,3									
7 max (0,8V+max((Xc+max(eV+CH-Xe, CH)-cV,max(eV+CH-Xe, CH))-0,9Xbasescale, 0)									
To mention here that these expressions do not give the value of three options all together since all are excercised in different time moments.									
With this we want to indicate the logical model that we follow based on nested option analysis as presented by Herath and Park 2002									
Finally, to mention that values for nested options are at times where their predecessor option is exercised.									
In our analysis only option to Defer exercise is prerequisite for the next options									

is the option to defer, which its value is 53,6 k€. We give for comparison the values of the rest of the options, in isolation, at time where the operation stage is starting. The option to choose the strategy between contraction and expansion in year 7 presents the highest value, 34,8 k€ from the rest of the options. Actually, the option to choose between expansion and contraction is the sum of the two separate options, the call option to expand and the put option to contract with the same expiration dates.

In our multioption analysis we consider that the option to Defer is prerequisite for the rest of the options. This means that the option to defer should be included in any of the combinations of the embedded options that we analyze.

Adopting the two-embedded options analysis in the investment plan we can see that the option to Contract contributes negatively to its predecessor option to Defer since their combined value is 38,3 k€. This happens due to the fact that in case of exercising the contract option, the revenues V that correspond to the initially planned base scale investment, will be decreased. We consider that by contracting operation by 20% we have 10% decrease of the initial infrastructure cost, since the infrastructure is the basis and prerequisite for a range of future operating capabilities. On the contrary, the contribution of the option to Choose to the option to Defer is higher giving a value close to 64,2 k€.

In case of three options analysis for more efficient risk handling, the combination of options to Defer, Expand and Choose gives the higher value of about 67 k€. Finally, taking into account the total number of options the overall value is just 50 k€, since the option to contract operations contributes negatively to revenues V base scale of the option to Defer as in the two options analysis.

Hence, the most promising configuration deployment strategy is the combination of the options to DECH that presents the highest value for the investment profitability.

COST & REVENUES UNCERTAINTIES CONSIDERATION

In the following, we apply the ELTBM for more complex investments involving both stochastic payoffs and stochastic costs. We base our analysis on compound options in order to evaluate the highest pay off scenario. We investigate the impact of cost uncertainty in the investment profitability, making sensitivity analysis for various values of revenues' and cost's variance and correlation. It is the first time in ICT literature where both costs and revenues uncertainties are considered in compound ROs analysis. However, the complexity of the model is increasing as the number of steps is increasing. For this reason we examine the case for one time step, as our purpose is to show intuitively the influence of cost uncertainty in investment's performance, Figure 3. Though the complexity of our model is increasing the always increasing computing power can handle this complexity efficiently (Trigeorgis, 1996). In practice, the single-step analysis is appropriate for investments where management has limited opportunity to influence the outcome of the investment and reviews investment status per half or year. On the opposite, in case of large enterprise projects where there is a significant opportunity during the life of the project for management to influence the expected value of the project cash flows, a more realistic solution would use a multiple steps analysis. In this case, management reviews quarterly and even weekly, and risk events will impact the project with a random periodicity. In conclusion, the frequency of management review for the investment status, such as customers demand, indicates the number of steps to be taken into account.

We use the 1 step LTBM to calculate the ENPV and compare it with the ELTBM where both revenues and investment cost uncertainty are considered. However, this is not a problem since, the ELTBM appears to be more stable for small number of steps (here 1 step) compared to the single LTBM and especially for large values of cost's and revenues' variances. In addition, Gamba and Trigeorgis (2001) verify that the correlation between costs and revenues change plays an important role in having positive up and down probabilities for cost's and revenues' assets diffusion process. Actually, if the revenues and costs are uncorrelated then the log-transformed up

Figure 3. Revenues and Cost diffusion process, one time step. Option value at t=0 is given in Appendix A (A3)

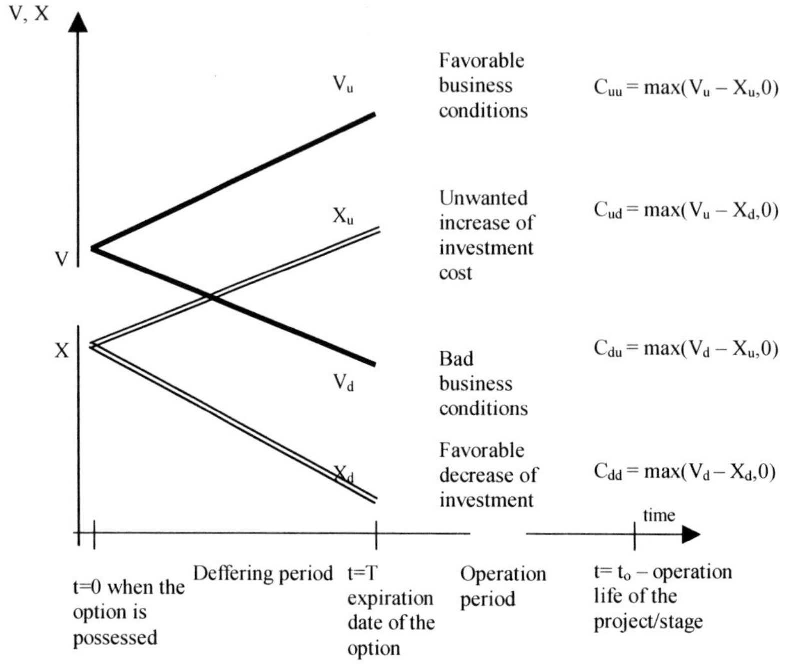

Table 5. Option values comparison between Revenues uncertainty only and Cost-Revenues uncertainty consideration

Options	**Option Value LTBM 50 steps (values in k€)**	**Option Value LTBM 1 step (values in k€)**	**Option Value ELTBM 1 step (values in k€)**
Defer **(D)**	54	65	65
Expand **(E)**	12,6		15,8
Option to Choose **(CH)** (expand/contract)	34,8		47
Optimum Options Combination			
DECH	67	88	77,2
Base case parameters			
Revenuous Variance (Volatility) 50%			
Costs Variance (Volatility) 30%			
Correlation ρvx=-0,2			
The rest of parameters are as before			

and down probabilities in the lattice analysis are strictly positive. In our case, we assume a variance for cost 30% and a correlation between revenues and cost, ρ_{vx} =–0.2. We consider the stochastic changes in the asset value to be correlated with the stochastic changes in the investment cost.

Table 6. Option value to Defer base scale investment for various values of cost-revenues correlation and volatilities

Option to Defer base scale investment	ρvx	Vbase scale variance (volatility) σv (%)	Xbase scale variance (volatility) σx (%)	Comments
13	1	50	30	
35	0,5	50	30	
56,3	0	50	30	
65	-0,2	50	30	
78	-0,5	50	30	
99	-1	50	30	
55,8	-1	50	0	In approximates the LTBM with 50 steps where no cost uncertainty is considered
55,8	-0,2	50	0	
55,8	1	50	0	
55,8	0	50	0	
55,8	0	50	5	
56	0	50	15	
56	0	50	25	
56	0	50	40	
59	0	50	45	
64	0	50	50	
73	0	50	60	
86	0	50	70	
97,4	0	50	80	
57,2	-0,2	50	5	
62	-0,2	50	20	
98	-0,2	50	70	

In particular, a negative ρ_{vx} could represent, for instance, that the inability to control the cost of the development project are associated with lower revenues after the project is completed. In Table 5, we present the results of our analysis for the scenario that involves the options to Defer at t=3, to Expand at t=5 and to Choose between to expand and contract at t=7. As we can see the options values, either in isolation or in combination of the optimum scenario for investment deployment strategy, are higher in case of considering both cost's and revenues' uncertainties.

In addition, we have evaluated the impact of higher or lower variance, higher or lower correlation with respect to the base case, to the option to Defer investment up to the moment where the demand uncertainty will be at least partially resolved. The results are shown in the following Table 6.

As it can be seen, a negative correlation ρ_{vx} contributes to higher option value. In addition, for zero cost uncertainty, the base scale option to defer value, calculated by the one step ELTBM, approaches to the base scale option to defer value calculated by the 50 steps LTBM and no revenues uncertainty. This proves the 1 step ELTBM stability giving comparable results to the 50 steps LTBM. Finally, uncorrelated assets (V,X) give an option value equal to the base case for cost variance less than revenues variance. However, as the cost's variance increases above the revenues' variance the option value increases respectively.

DISCUSSION AND FUTURE RESEARCH

The methodology we presented enables management to optimally configure technology investments. It facilitates a systematic identification of investment's configurations by framing flexibility in terms of risks that real options can control. Otherwise, it supports a solid quantitative configuration valuation for the purpose of identifying the most valuable configuration. This does not mean that the methodology is perfect. One of the main difficulties is the way we estimate the variances of investment's revenues and cost.

The methodology has been applied in an e-learning case study. It can be quite easily extended to other ICT business fields. For example Angelou and Economides (2006) apply ROs analysis to find optimum investment deployment strategy in Broadband investments business field under competition threat that can eliminate part of the business value during deffering period.

In general, the method can be applied in business cases where investments contain wait and see components (deffering periods) as well as risk issues that can be controlled and partially resolved by real options analysis. In case of competition, it is matter of compensation between uncertainty control achieved by the real options analysis and competition threats from other competitors that can enter sooner into the market, while the firm under investigation is waiting, and eliminate the available investment value. Under this analysis, the competitors can arrive randomly following a Poisson distribution (Trigeorgis, 1996). This is more valid in case of high number of competitors (players) where exogenous competition modeling is more practical. In particular, it can be considered that there is an e-learning platform that can support a number of e-learning courses, to similar scientific fields, provided by the firm (institution) of interest. However, other organizations, universities, can also provide similar, courses causing a degradation to the investment opportunity, which is available to the organization of interest.

In case of limited number of competitors (oligopoly) endogenous competition modelling is required adopting the real options with game theory. In this case, each of the players (competitors) will choose their optimum investment deployment strategy. The game equilibrium will be the deployment strategies or real options implementation, which will maximize utility of each of the players. It is subject of further work to consider a real competitive environment and customize or enhance existing real options models evaluation based on compound options analysis under endogenous competition modeling.

Also, the proposed methodology may also be incorporated with other previous studies, such as Scott-Morton's MIT90s framework (Scott Morton, 1991), which it was used to analyse the effects of developments in information technology on business organisations. It has been also used more recently to examine how higher education institutions in Australia were managing the introduction of technology to deliver and administer education (Yetton, 1997). Scott-Morton's MIT90s framework assumes that an institution's effectiveness in the use of ICT for teaching and learning is a function of six inter-related elements:

1. The *external environment* within which the institution is operating

2. The institutional *strategy* in relation to ICT in teaching and learning
3. The way human resources are prepared and deployed *(individuals and their roles)* to support the implementation of ICT in teaching and learning
4. The organisational *structures* that support the application of ICT to teaching and learning
5. The characteristics of the *technology* being applied
6. The *management processes* that facilitate the initiation, sustainability and success of the application of ICT in teaching and learning

Our model can be used for risk recognition and its control with real options in external environment concerning competition, customers demand and technology uncertainty. In addition, management processes, human resources allocation and organizational structure analysis may include real options analysis to optimally configure investment's deployment strategy and control firm's specific uncertainty.

Furthermore, the proposed model and methodology for understanding and hedging risks in ICT projects is based on the finance literature on real options. However, existing real options models are based on quantitative analysis and the required input parameters sometimes may be difficult to be estimated for evaluating real life investment opportunities. Angelou and Economides (2007) adopt a qualitative options thinking for finding the optimum deployment strategy for an ICT project. Analytically, they present a methodology that helps to address the question: "How can we control firm, market and competition risks so as to configure a specific ICT business activity in a way to minimize risk and increase investment performance?" The proposed model contains three perspectives, financial tangible factors (FTF) perspective, risk mitigation (RM) perspective, and intangible factors (IF) perspective.

In addition, the proposed model and methodology can include competition conditions that may decrease or even more eliminate option value. Angelou and Economides (2008a) provide a methodology for finding the optimum deployment strategy of an ICT business activity that is based on an initial infrastructure project, which supports a number of future investment opportunities. They treat these opportunities as real options and assume that there is competition threat that can influence negatively or even worst eliminate their values. They examine the various deployment alternatives for the business activity and consider that each of them embeds a number of growth options. Subject of decision is the implementation time of each growth option comparing step-wise deployment strategies with immediate investment actions without waiting. They relax literature assumptions by considering that the competitors' arrivals rates and competitive erosions during waiting phase for the real options to invest follow a joint-diffusion process with the investments' revenues.

Finally, Angelou and Economides (2008b) combine ROs and the Analytic Hierarchy Process (AHP) into a common decision analysis framework, providing an integrated multi-objective multi-criteria model, called ROAHP, for prioritizing a portfolio of ICT interdependent investments. They combine strategic non-financial and financial tangible goals using a multi-option model for enhancing overall business performance. Our model can be introduced in this decision analysis framework concerning a part of the quantitative factors.

CONCLUSION

In this work, we present a real options methodology for controlling risk and choosing the optimum ICT investment's deployment strategy. We apply it in e-learning infrastructure business field (Mantzari and Economides, 2004). The target is to find the optimal investment's configuration, to handle more efficiently the investment's risk and so to increase its overall performance.

The results of our analysis show that by adopting multioption analysis in a compound basis can enhance investment performance. The specific e-learning investment scenario appears to be more profitable when we adopt real options analysis instead of NPV analysis, taking into account the same business assumptions given by Mantzari and Economides (2004) case study.

In addition, we apply both revenues' and cost's uncertainties modeling estimating the impact of the investment's cost uncertainty to the options' value as well as to the overall economic performance. The e-learning investment's profitability appears even higher. Actually, as the project uncertainty is increasing, the managerial flexibility achieved by adopting real options contributes more to the final economic performance.

It is the subject of further work to consider a real competitive environment and customize or enhance existing real options models evaluation based on compound options analysis. Finally, the proposed methodology can be enhanced by adopting a multicriteria analysis perspective.

REFERENCES

Angelou, G. and Economides, A. (2008a) A Real Options approach for prioritizing ICT business alternatives: A case study from Broadband Technology business field. *Journal of the Operational Research Society*, Forthcoming.

Angelou, G. and Economides, A. (2008b) A decision analysis framework for prioritizing a portfolio of ICT infrastructure projects. *IEEE Transactions on Engineering Management*.

Angelou, G. and Economides A. (2007) Controlling Risks in ICT investments with Real Options thinking. *11th Panhellenic Conference in Informatics (PCI 2007)*, May 18-20, 2007, University of Patras, Patras, Greece

Angelou, G. and Economides, A. (2006). Broadband investments as growth options under competition threat. *FITCE 45th Congress 2006*, Athens, Greece.

Angelou, G. and Economides, A. (2005). Flexible ICT investment analysis using Real Options. *International Journal of Technology, Policy and Management*, 5(2), 146–166

Benaroch, M. (2002). Managing information technology investment risk: A real options Perspective. *Journal of Management Information Systems*, 19(2), 43-84.

Benaroch, M. (2001). Option-based management of technology investment risk. *IEEE Transactions on Engineering Management*, 48(4), 428-444.

Bräutigam, J., and Esche, C. (2003). *Uncertainty as a key value driver of real options*. European Business School, Schloss Reichartshausen, Oestrich-Winkel, Germany Anett Mehler-Bicher University of Applied Science, Mainz, Germany. Working paper, University of Applied Science, 7th Annual Real Options Conference.

Downes S. (1998) *The future of Online Learning*. http://www.downes.ca/future/index.htm

Gamba, A. and Trigeorgis, L., (2001). *A Log-transformed Binomial Lattice Extension for Multi-Dimensional Option Problems*. Paper presented at the 5th Annual Conference on Real Options, Anderson School of Management, UCLA, Los-Angeles.

Herath, H. and Park, C. (2002). Multi-Stage Capital Investment Opportunities as Compound Real Options. *The Engineering Economist*, 47(1), 1-27.

Iatropoulos A., Economides A. and Angelou G., (2004). Broadband investments analysis using real options methodology: A case study for Egnatia Odos S.A.. *Communications and Strategies*, No 55, 3rd quarter 2004, 45-76.

Li, X. and Johnson, J. (2002). Evaluate IT Investment Opportunities Using Real Options Theory. *Information Resource Management Journal*, 15(3), 32-47.

Mantzari, D. and Economides, A. (2004). Cost analysis for e-learning foreign languages. *European Journal of Open and Distance Learning*, November, issue 2, vol 1, http://www.eurodl.org

Morgan, M. (2000). *Is distance learning worth it? Helping to determine the costs of online courses*. ED 446611, http://webpages.marshall.edu/~morgan16/onlinecosts/

Mun, J. (2002) *Real Options Analysis: Tools and Techniques for Valuing Strategic Investments and Decisions*. Wiley Finance.

Mun, J. (2003) *Real Options Analysis Course: Business Cases and Software Applications*. Wiley Finance.

Newman, F. and Couturier, L., (2002). Trading Public Good in the Higher Education Market. *Futures Project: Policy for Higher Education in a Changing World*. January. The observatory on borderless higher education, John Foster House, London UK.

Oslington, P. (2004). The impact of Uncertainty and irreversibility on Investments in Online Learning. *Distance Education*, vol 25, No. 2.

Scott Morton, M. S. (1991). *The Corporation of the 1990s: Information Technology and Organisational Transformation*. Oxford University Press: New York.

Smit H. and Trigeorgis L., (2004). Quantifying The Strategic Option Value of Technology Investments. In *Proceedings of the 8th annual conference in Real Options*. Montréal Canada, June 17-19. (http://www.realoptions.org/papers2004/SmitTrigeorgisAMR.pdf).

Trigeorgis, L., (1999). Real Options: A Primer". In James Alleman and Eli Noam, (Eds), *The New Investment Theory of Real Options and its Implication for Telecommunications Economics*. Kluwer Academic Publishers, Boston, pp. 3-33.

Trigeorgis L. (1996). *Real Options: Managerial Flexibility and Strategy in Resource Allocation*. The MIT Press.

Trigeorgis, L. (1993). The nature of options interactions and the valuation of investments with multiple real options. *Journal of Financial and Quantitative Analysis*. 28(1), 1-20.

Wentling T., Waight C., Gallaher J., Fleur J., Wang C., and Kanfer A., (2000). *E-learning - A Review of Literature*. Knowledge and Learning Systems Group, NCSA, University of Illinois at Urbana-champaign, p.5. http://learning.ncsa.uiuc.edu/papers/elearnlit.pdf

Whalen T. and Wright D.,(1999). Methodology for Cost-Benefit Analysis of Web-based Tele-learning: Case Study of the Bell online Institute. *The American Journal of Distance* Education, 13(1), 26.

Yetton, P. (1997). *Managing the Introduction of Technology in the Delivery and Administration of Higher Education*. Evaluations and Investigations Program; Higher Education Division, Department of Employment, Education, Training and Youth Affairs, Australia. Available at: http://www.dest.gov.au/archive/highered/eippubs/eip9703/front.htm

APPENDIX A

LTBM

LTBM has been proposed to overcome problems of consistency, stability and efficiency encountered in standard binomial model (Gamba and Trigeorgis, 2001). Whereas the binomial model views the behavior of V (the underlying asset or investment value) as being governed by a multiplicative diffusion process, the log-transformed binomial model transforms this process into an additive one. Actually, instead of looking directly at V, the log-transformed binomial model looks at state variable S= logV. The log-transformed binomial algorithm consists of four main steps: parameter value specification, preliminary sequential calculation, determination of terminal values, and backward iterative process.

First, the standard parameters affecting option values (i.e., V, r, σ^2, T, and the set of exercise prices or investment cost outlays X) are specified along with the desired number of subintervals, N. The greater N is chosen, the smaller the number of subintervals and the more accurate the numeric approximation is although at the expense of more computer time (and potentially growing approximation errors).

The second step involves preliminary calculations needed for the rest of the algorithm. Using the values of variables calculated along the way from preceding steps, the algorithm sequentially determines the following key variables:

1. time-step: $k = \sigma^2 T/N$
2. drift: $\mu = (r/\sigma^2)* \frac{1}{2}$
3. state-step: $H = \sqrt{k + (\mu k)^2}$
4. probability: $P = (\frac{1}{2})*(1 + \mu k/H)$

The third step involves the determination of terminal boundary values (at j = N), where j denotes the integer number of time steps with length k. For each state i, the algorithm fills in the underlying asset (project) values from $V(i) = e^{S_0 + iH}$ (since $S \equiv \ln V = S_0 + iH$); and the total investment opportunity values (or expanded NPV) from the terminal condition R(i) = max(V(i), 0). The integer index i of the stage variable S is corresponding to the net number of ups less downs. R(i) denotes the total investment opportunity value (i.e., the combined value for the project and its embedded real options) at state i.

The fourth step follows a backward iterative process for the estimation of total investment value R(i) at state i. Starting from the end (j = N) and working backward for each time-step j (j = N-1, ..., 1) we calculate the total investment opportunity values. Between any two consecutive periods, the value of the opportunity in the earlier period (j) at state i, R(i) is determined iteratively from its expected end-of-period values in the up and down states calculated in the previous time-step (j + 1), discounted back one period of length $\tau = k/\sigma^2$ at the risk-free interest rate r_f:

$$R_{(i)} = \frac{PR_{(i+1)} + (1-P)R_{(i-1)}}{1 + r_f k / \sigma^2} \qquad \text{(A1)}$$

Assuming one-step diffusion process the call option can be written as:

$$C = \frac{PC_u + (1-P)C_d}{1 + r_f k / \sigma^2} =$$

$$= \frac{P \max[uV - X, 0] + (1-P)\max[dV - X, 0]}{1 + r_f k / \sigma^2} \qquad \text{(A2)}$$

where the state rise and fall parameters are $u = e^H$, $d = 1/u$.

ELTBM

The ELTBM values real options whose payoffs depend on several state variables (i.e. cost and revenues diffusion processes). Actually, it is an extension of the LTBM taking into account multi-dimensional diffusion processes for investment's variables such as cost and revenues.

The methodology is similar to the previous one. However, in this case complexity is increasing depending on the number of the diffusion process. In particular, considering a two-dimensional diffusion process the respective parameters are given by:

1. $k_s = \sigma^2 T/N$
2. $\mu_s = (r/\sigma^2)^{\sim} * ½$
3. $H_s = \sqrt{k + (\mu k)^2}$
4. $R_{s,s'} = k_s k_{s'}/(H_s H_{s'})$
5. $Ms = k_s^2 \mu_s / H_s$
6. $s,s' = 1,2$

Note that states rise and fall parameters are $u_s = e^{Hs}$, $d_s = 1/u_s$.

The respective probabilities P are given by the following expressions. We also present their meaning (assuming revenues and costs state variables):

$P_1 = P_{uu} = (1 + (R*\rho + M_1M_2) + M_1 + M2)/4$ (revenues rise, cost rises)
$P_2 = P_{ud} = (1 - (R*\rho + M_1M_2) + M_1 - M2)/4$ (revenues rise, cost falls)
$P_3 = P_{du} = (1 - (R*\rho + M_1M_2) - M_1 + M2)/4$ (revenues fall, cost rises)
$P_4 = P_{dd} = (1 + (R*\rho + M_1M_2) - M_1 - M2)/4$ (revenues fall, cost falls)

where $\rho = \rho_{12}$ is the correlation between revenues and costs and $R = R_{12}$.

Finally, the value of the call option C can be written as:

$$C = \frac{P_{uu}C_{uu} + P_{ud}C_{ud} + P_{du}C_{du} + P_{dd}C_{dd}}{1 + r_f k / \sigma^2} =$$

$$= \frac{P_{uu}\max[uV - uX, 0] + P_{ud}\max[uV - dX, 0] + P_{du}\max[dV - uX, 0] + P_{dd}\max[dV - dX, 0]}{1 + r_f k / \sigma^2} \qquad \text{(A3)}$$

APPENDIX B

Table 7. Cost Structure

Cost Description	Value	Cost Category	Comments	Out Flows Distribution*	Total value**
Switch	385,65 €	LAN & INTERNET CONNECTION COSTS	Infrastructure	At once	385,65 €
Router	154,74 €	LAN & INTERNET CONNECTION COSTS	Infrastructure	At once	154,74 €
UPS	1.050,03 €	LAN & INTERNET CONNECTION COSTS	Infrastructure	At once	1.050,03 €
Server	5.221,27 €	COLLOCATION HOSTING COSTS	Infrastructure	At once	5.221,27 €
Operating System	1.356,90 €	COLLOCATION HOSTING COSTS	Infrastructure	At once	1.356,90 €
Workstations	15.968,00 €	HEADQUARTERS OFFICES COSTS	Infrastructure	At once	15.968,00 €
LAN cards	561,28 €	HEADQUARTERS OFFICES COSTS	Infrastructure	At once	561,28 €
Ms Office Xp	4.418,56 €	HEADQUARTERS OFFICES COSTS	Infrastructure	At once	4.418,56 €
Printers	601,68 €	HEADQUARTERS OFFICES COSTS	Infrastructure	At once	601,68 €
Scanners	359,34 €	HEADQUARTERS OFFICES COSTS	Infrastructure	At once	359,34 €
Zip Drives	1.891,36 €	HEADQUARTERS OFFICES COSTS	Infrastructure	At once	1.891,36 €
Zip Disks	290,56 €	HEADQUARTERS OFFICES COSTS	Infrastructure	At once	290,56 €
Cd-R	37,50 €	HEADQUARTERS OFFICES COSTS	Infrastructure	At once	37,50 €
Cd-RW	16,00 €	HEADQUARTERS OFFICES COSTS	Infrastructure	At once	16,00 €
Office staff	300,00 €	HEADQUARTERS OFFICES COSTS	Infrastructure	At once	300,00 €
Laser Toners	153,00 €	HEADQUARTERS OFFICES COSTS	Infrastructure	At once	153,00 €
Paper for Printers & FAX	94,20 €	HEADQUARTERS OFFICES COSTS	Infrastructure	At once	94,20 €
Desks	3.200,00 €	Fixed equipment costs	Infrastructure	At once	3.200,00 €
Desk Chairs	3.200,00 €	Fixed equipment costs	Infrastructure	At once	3.200,00 €
Chairs	1.600,00 €	Fixed equipment costs	Infrastructure	At once	1.600,00 €
Bookshelves	600,00 €	Fixed equipment costs	Infrastructure	At once	600,00 €
Fax, Copier	2.000,00 €	Fixed equipment costs	Infrastructure	At once	2.000,00 €
Pedagogical & Administrative Training	4.500,00 €	PREPARATION COSTS	Infrastructure	At once	4.500,00 €
Installation on a dedicated server	3.000,00 €	PREPARATION COSTS	Infrastructure	At once	3.000,00 €
Technician's Training	2.000,00 €	PREPARATION COSTS	Infrastructure	At once	2.000,00 €
Educational Software's licenses ***	**55.000,00 €**	**COLLOCATION HOSTING COSTS**	**Variable Cost**	At once	55.000,00 €
Total (infrastructure investment cost)	**107.960,07 €**	**Cost outlayed at once**		**At once**	**107.960,07 €**

Table 7. continued

ADSL (per year)	618,96 €	LAN & INTERNET CONNECTION COSTS	Operating Fixed		
ADSL Internet (per year)	1.140,00 €	LAN & INTERNET CONNECTION COSTS	Operating Fixed		
Collocation Hosting (per year)	13.206,24 €	COLLOCATION HOSTING COSTS	Operating Fixed		
Rent	12.000,00 €	Operating Costs (annual)	Operating Fixed		
Electricity supply	840,00 €	Operating Costs (annual)	Operating Fixed		
Telephone	2.400,00 €	Operating Costs (annual)	Operating Fixed		
Water supply	360,00 €	Operating Costs (annual)	Operating Fixed		
Heating	1.200,00 €	Operating Costs (annual)	Operating Fixed		
Chairman	30.000,00 €	Salaries & wages	Operating Fixed	Yearly	
Financial Manager	36.000,00 €	Salaries & wages	Operating Fixed		
Marketing Manager	30.000,00 €	Salaries & wages	Operating Fixed		
Technical Administrator	6.420,00 €	Salaries & wages	Operating Fixed		
Financial Services Employee	12.000,00 €	Salaries & wages	Operating Fixed		
Help Desk Employee	12.000,00 €	Salaries & wages	Operating Fixed		
Accountant	3.600,00 €	Salaries & wages	Operating Fixed		
Tutors (case 1)	**98.380,80 €**	**Salaries & wages**	**Variable Cost**		
Furniture & Fixed Equipment	2.760,00 €	Amortizations****	Operating Fixed		
Hardware	9.167,67 €	Amortizations****	Operating Fixed		
Total*** (Present Value) Operating cost**	**272.093,67 €**	**Cost outlayed Annually**		**Yearly**	**1.700,00 €**
Total at investment time T	**380.053,74 €**				

APPENDIX C

Table 8. Detailed Cash Flow Analysis for the base case investment (up to 1000 students/customers)

Base scale Cash Flows Analysis												
Year	0	1	2	3	4	5	6	7	8	9	10	11
Infrastracture costs (building stage)	0	0	0	190.000	0	0	0	0	0	0	0	0
Operating fixed costs	0	0	0	0	174.000	182.700	191.835	201.427	211.498	222.073	233.177	244.835
No of students/Customers2	0	0	0	0	585	644	708	779	856	942	950	950
Operating variable costs/student	0	0	0	0	2,15	2,26	2,37	2,49	2,61	2,74	2,88	3,03
Operating variable costs	0	0	0	0	1.258	1.453	1.678	1.938	2.238	2.585	2.737	2.874
Total Costs Cash Flows	0	0	0	190.000	175.258	184.153	193.513	203.365	213.736	224.658	235.914	247.709
Revenues (300€/student initially)	0	0	0	0	175.500	193.050	212.355	233.591	256.950	282.645	285.000	285.000
Annual Operating Cash Flows Summary	0	0	0	0	242	8.897	18.842	30.226	43.213	57.986	49.086	37.291
Total Costs PV	1.320.675 €											
Revenus PV	1.317.823 €											
NPV (Passive Analyses)	-2.853 €											
Xbase scale at t=T	190.000 €											
Vbase scale at t=0	161.276 €											
We consider three years maximum deferral period and 12 years analysis period												
Base scale investment plan to support up to 1000 students and one language. We consider that the operation period is 7 years												
Infrastructure investment includes further to costs described in the detailed table the 60% of the fixed operating cost (preparation cost to lunch activities) of the 1st year operation plus 30.000 € extra Marketing Expenses												
We consider a 10% yearly increase of the customers for the base scale investment plan. The initial planning expects up to 1000 units. For each language there is 2,15 € per student per year. In addition, operating variable cost per student/language/year i												
1 Operating fixed cost is increasing by 5% each year												
2 Break Event Point Analysis performed by Mantzari and Economides 2004 indicates a no of users of about 590. We consider entry in the market when this threshold is reached												
We assume that the Annual Expenses increase by 5% per year. On the opposite, we assume that the Student/customers fees do not change.												

Chapter XII
Examining Online Purchase Intentions in B2C E-Commerce:
Testing an Integrated Model

C. Ranganathan
University of Illinois at Chicago, USA

Sanjeev Jha
University of Illinois at Chicago, USA

ABSTRACT

Research on online shopping has taken three broad and divergent approaches viz, human-computer interaction, behavioral, and consumerist approaches to examine online consumer behavior. Assimilating these three approaches, this study proposes an integrated model of online shopping behavior, with four major antecedents influencing online purchase intent: Web site quality, customer concerns in online shopping, self-efficacy, and past online shopping experience. These antecedents were modeled as second-order constructs with subsuming first-order constituent factors. The model was tested using data from a questionnaire survey of 214 online shoppers. Statistical analyses using structural equation modeling was used to validate the model, and identify the relative importance of the key antecedents to online purchase intent. Past online shopping experience was found to have the strongest association with online purchase intent, followed by customer concerns, Web site quality, and computer self efficacy. The findings and their implications are discussed.

INTRODUCTION

Internet and Web technologies have fundamentally changed the way businesses interacted, transacted and communicated with consumers. As a business medium, the Internet is unique in permitting firms to create interactive online environments that allow consumers to gather and evaluate information, assess purchase options, and directly buy products at their own convenience. Web-based retailing has become a global phenomenon with steady increase in online sales across the globe. The growth in online shopping has been motivated by several reasons—convenience, ease, pricing, comparative analysis, wider selection of products and services, and so forth.

Although online shopping has been on the rise, the challenges associated with Web-based retailing have also increased. First, the growing numbers of traditional merchants and pureplay Internet firms have greatly intensified online competition. With blurring geographical boundaries and reduced barriers to entry, the digital marketplace has become crowded with a large number of players. Second, while the online customer acquisition costs have increased significantly, the switching costs of online consumers have diminished exponentially. Third, despite the growing popularity of online shopping, several factors such as fear of fraud, security concerns, lack of trust have dissuaded consumers to purchase online (Gefen, Karahanna, & Straub, 2003; Kiely, 1997). Several studies have documented the problems associated with attracting and retaining online consumers. For instance, Vatanasombut, Stylianou, and Igbaria (2004) deliberated on the difficulty of retaining online customers and proffered strategies to keep novice and sophisticated users happy and loyal. Chen and Hitt (2002) suggested developing strategies to raise customer switching costs in order to deter them from moving to other Web sites.

Rise in online shopping has generated a growing body of research on online consumer behavior. This research can be grouped into those adopting a technological perspective and others with a marketing perspective. Scholars embracing a technological perspective have focused on technical elements such as Web-site navigation and design (Everard & Galletta, 2005; Liu & Arnett, 2000; Spiller & Lohse, 1997), software tools and technological aids (Heijden, Verhagen, & Creemers, 2003; Salaun & Flores, 2001; Wan, 2000). Researchers adopting a marketing perspective have focused their attention on the decision making process (Gefen, 2000; McKnight, Choudhury, & Kacmar, 2002a), and the marketing elements such as pricing, promotion, branding, reputation and customer attitude (Bart, Shankar, Sultan, & Urban, 2005; Chu, Choi, & Song, 2005; Iwaarden, Wiele, Ball, & Millen, 2004; Urban, Sultan, & Qualls, 2000). These research developments notwithstanding, several significant gaps still remain unaddressed. First, these divergent approaches seem to portray only a partial, yet unclear picture of online consumer behavior. While prior studies have helped identify key issues, lack of an integrated focus has marred the broader applicability of the findings. Second, while past research has identified several technological, behavioral and individual factors as important in influencing online consumer behavior, it is not clear if these factors have a differential impact (i.e., a more clear understanding is required if any of the factors explain or predict online shopping behavior more than the others). Third, a large number of studies have used student samples (Gefen, 2000; Mauldin & Arunachalam, 2002; McKnight, Choudhury, & Kacmar, 2002a, 2002b; Pavlou, 2003), thus raising questions on the generalizability of the findings to a large online consumer community.

In this article, we seek to extend our current knowledge on online shopping behavior in the following ways. Our primary research objective is to combine the key technological, behavioral, and consumer-related constructs identified in prior literature and propose an integrated model of online consumer behavior. Our study directly responds to the research calls to provide an integrated perspective on online consumer behavior (Bart et al., 2005; Heijden, 2003). Further, we test our integrated model using a sample of actual online consumers with prior experience in purchasing goods and services online. We pool together the key technological and behavioral factors and empirically examine the relative importance of these constructs in predicting online purchase intention of consumers.

LITERATURE REVIEW

An analysis of extant literature on online shopping reveals three distinct orientations underlying these studies; viz, Human–Computer Interaction (HCI), behavioral, and consumerist orientations. These three streams have also been identified by Chang, Cheung, and Lai (2005), who reviewed over 45 empirical studies of online consumer behavior. We summarize the essence of these approaches and propose an integrated model that encompasses key elements from all the three streams of research.

HCI research is primarily concerned with design and implementation of user interfaces that are easy to learn, efficient, and pleasant to use. Scholars embracing a HCI orientation have investigated Web-site related characteristics that potentially influence online consumer behavior. These researchers emphasize factors such as information content (Ranganathan & Ganapathy, 2002); visual attractiveness of the Web site (Heijden, 2003); quality of information provided (Salaun & Flores, 2001); ease of navigation, time taken for information search (Evarard & Galletta, 2005; Spiller & Lohse, 1997; Tarafdar & Zhang, 2005); and the overall design of the Web site (Flavin, Guinaliu, & Gurrea, 2006; Huizingh, 2000; G. Lee & Lin, 2005; Zviran, Glezer, & Avni, 2006). This stream of research places technological factors to be at the forefront of factors influencing online consumer shopping behavior.

The second group of scholars has taken a behavioral approach, wherein they have investigated the factors influencing customer concerns in online shopping (CCOS). While a few studies have focused on the trust elements influencing online shopping (Gefen & Straub, 2004; Kaufaris & Hampton-Sosa, 2004; Schlosser, White, & Lloyd, 2006), others have investigated the factors that inhibit or encourage online shopping (Burroughs & Sabherwal, 2002; Brynjolfsson & Smith, 2000). These researchers argue that the primary requirement for the online shopping is a sense of trust between consumers and online merchants (Eastlick, Lotz, & Warrington, 2006; Jarvenpaa, Tractinsky, & Vitale, 2000; Urban et al., 2000). Since the transactions take place in a virtual market and customers do not physically interact with sellers, it is important that customers exude confidence in sellers and are ready to part with personal information to them.

The third group has focused on consumer characteristics and their influence on online shopping behavior. The basic notion underlying this stream is that individual characteristics such as the demographics, personality, and profiles play a larger role in determining the online shopping behavior (De Wulf, Schillewaert, Muylle, & Rangrajan, 2006; Liao & Cheung, 2001; Zhang, Prybutok, & Koh, 2006). Extending the traditional marketing theories, this group argues for consumer characteristics to be dominant in influencing their intention to engage in online purchases. These studies have focused on the variables like technology friendliness of customers and their comfort level in online shopping (Heijden, 2003; Mauldin & Arunachalam, 2002; Pavlou, 2003; Shih, 2004). A few researchers have also looked into the effect of past online shopping experience on future online buying behavior of consumers (Pavlou, 2003; Yoh, Damhorst, Sapp, & Laczniak 2003).

These three broad streams of research place emphasis on divergent technological, attitudinal, and consumer-related elements to provide insights into how these factors affect online shopping behavior. However, our central thesis is that integrating and combining these divergent yet complementary approaches could provide a richer perspective. Online consumer behavior is a multidimensional concept that requires an integrated examination of key elements from all the three research streams (Bart et al., 2005; Heijden, 2003). Integrating insights from these multiple streams, we identify Web-site quality (HCI factor), customer concerns in online shopping (behavioral approach), computer self-efficacy, and past online experience (consumerist variables) to be the key potential predictors of online purchase behavior. Our focus is on examining key variables rather than proposing a comprehensive model with a full set of factors. The conceptual framework for our research is depicted in Figure 1. Our primary research goals are to

a. Empirically examine the association between Web-site quality, customer concerns in online shopping, computer self-efficacy, and past online experience with online purchase intention of consumers.
b. Investigate the relative importance of each of these factors in order to prioritize their significance in predicting online purchase behavior.

Development of Hypotheses

In this section we discuss development of our research model and various hypotheses. To this end, we review pertinent literature from IS, e-commerce, and marketing disciplines to present the operationalization of our research constructs, and the rationale for our hypotheses. The research model is presented in Figure 2 and sources of variables are presented in Table 1.

Web Site Quality

Given that a Web site is the dominant medium of interaction between merchants and consumers in online shopping, it is imperative that the quality of the Web site is given adequate importance. Past research on Web quality can be classified into four complementary approaches (Ethier, Hadaya, Talbot, & Cadieux, in press). The first approach focused on the functional features of the site. Under this approach, scholars examined the content, style, presentation, navigation and other features of the Web site (Tarafdar & Zhang,

Figure 1. Conceptual framework

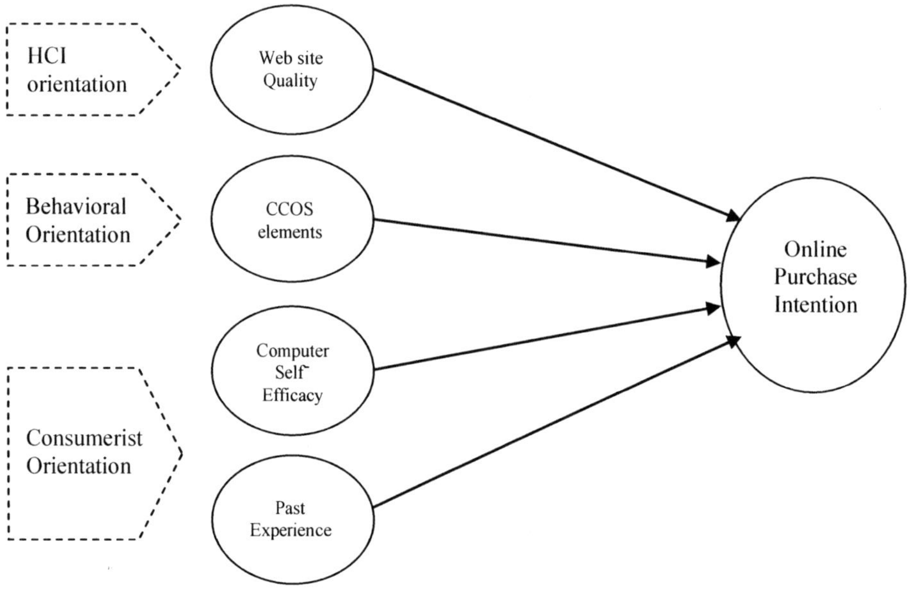

2005). The second approach drew upon the technology acceptance model to view Web quality as an overarching construct that included elements such as information quality, systems quality, and service quality. The third approach emphasized the fundamental service that the business-to-consumer (B2C) Web site provided. Here, Web quality was assessed with subdimensions like reliability, responsiveness, assurance, empathy, and tangibility. The fourth approach viewed Web quality through the lens of the consumer attitudes and perceptions (Aladwani & Palvia, 2002). Extending these approaches, scholars have also proposed multiple instruments for assessing Web quality (e.g., WEBQUAL [Loiacono, Watson, & Goodhue, 2002]; SiteQual [Webb & Webb, 2004]; SERVQUAL [Iwaarden & Wiele, 2003], etc.) that try and incorporate dimensions from one or more of these approaches.

A review of past research on Web site quality reveals little consensus on what constitutes this construct. Multiple terms such as *Web quality, Web site quality, service quality, site usability,* and so forth, have been used to denote different dimensions of Web site quality. Earlier studies adopted a dominant HCI perspective focusing on the quality of the medium through which online commerce was conducted between businesses and consumers. As more behavioral and consumerist studies emerged, multiple lenses were used to assess Web site quality, thus leading to varied terminology and mixed empirical findings. However, there is a broad agreement that quality of a B2C Web site is a multidimensional and a more complex construct (Ethier et al. in press).

In this study, we conceptualize Web site quality as primarily reflecting the content and design functionalities of a B2C site. From a HCI lens, Web site quality simply represents the quality of the online medium, rather than the services or transactions rendered through the Web site. Our approach is consistent with Tarafdar and Zhang (2005), who took a HCI-orientation to

Table 1. Constructs, key variables, and references

Web site quality	
Web-site Content	De Wulf et al. 2006; Huizingh, 2000; Liu and Arnett, 2000; Ranganathan and Ganapathy, 2002; Salaun and Flores, 2001; Spiller and Lohse, 1997
Web-site Design	De Wulf et al. 2006; Heijden, 2003; Huizingh, 2000; Liu and Arnett, 2000; Lohse and Spiller, 1999; Maudlin and Arunachalam, 2002; Ranganathan and Ganapathy, 2002; Spiller and Lohse, 1997; Wan, 2000
Customer Concerns in Online Shopping	
Privacy	Belanger, 2002; Dinev and Hart, 2005–2006; Eastlick et al., 2006; Ranganathan and Ganapathy, 2002; Schlosser et al 2006; Suh and Han, 2003; Vijayasarathy, 2004
Security	Belanger, 2002; Burroughs and Sabherwal, 2002; Koufaris and Hampton-Sosa, 2004; Liao and Cheung, 2001; Ranganathan and Ganapathy, 2002; Scholsser et al., 2006, Vijayasarathy, 2004
Product Delivery & Returns	Bart et al., 2005; Pechtl, 2003; Ranganathan and Ganapathy, 2002; Vijayasarathy, 2004
Computer Self Efficacy	
IT Attitude	Bellman et al., 1999; Liao and Cheung, 2001; Maudlin and Arunachalam, 2002
IT Skills	Burroughs and Sabherwal, 2002; Liao and Cheung, 2001; Maudlin and Arunachalam, 2002; Vijayasarathy, 2004
Past Online Shopping Experience	Bart et al. 2005; Pavlou, 2003; Yoh et al., 2003

Figure 2. Research model

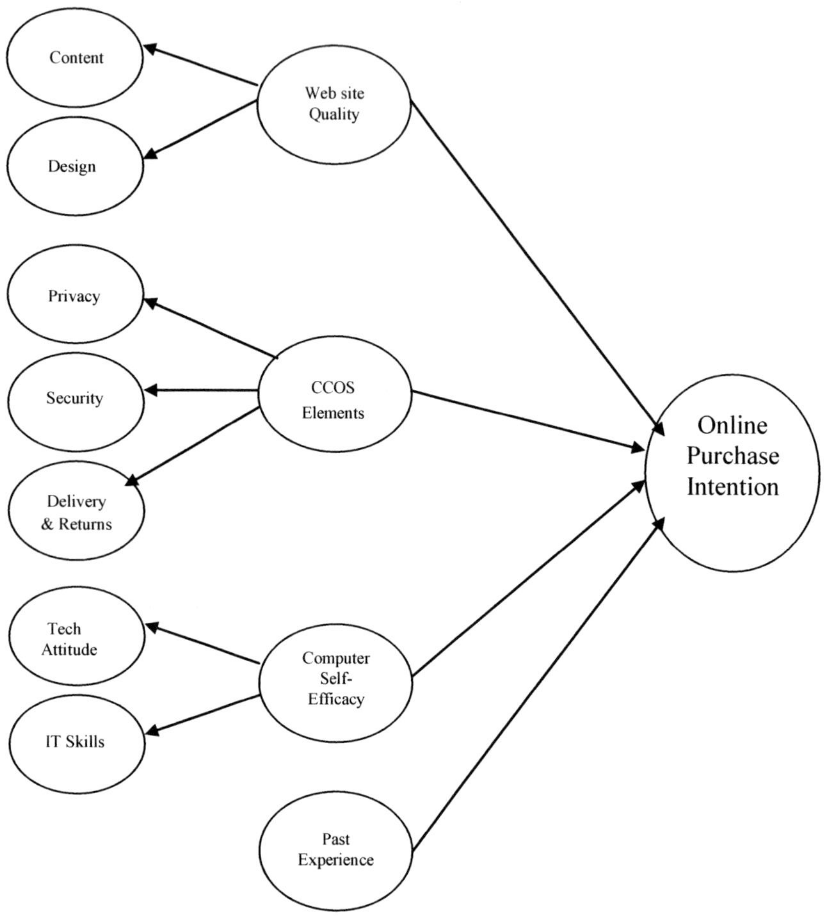

view Web-site usability as reflecting the quality of a B2C Web site.

Within the HCI research stream, Web site quality has been fundamentally assessed using two factors: Web site content and Web site design. Huizingh (2000) stressed on the importance of distinguishing content and design while discussing Web site quality. Ranganathan and Ganapathy (2002) defined content as the information, features or services offered in the Web site and design as the way by which the contents are presented to customers. Spiller and Lohse (1997) reported interface quality as one of the three key qualities on which online stores differed. Everard and Galletta (2005) found that errors, poor style, and incompleteness of information in Web sites negatively impacted online buying intentions. Wan (2000) offered a framework of Web-site design to promote customer values. Based on a study of 271 students, Mauldin & Arunachalam (2002) found strong association between Web site design and intention to purchase online. Using a fairly large sample of online consumers, Heijden (2003) found visual attractiveness of Web sites to significantly influence online consumers. Lee and Lin (2005) surveyed 297 online consumers to find a significant association between Web site design, consumer satisfaction and online purchase intentions. Zviran, Glezer, & Avni (2006) further confirmed the linkage between Web site design and customer satisfaction. Lepkowska-White (2004) found that online buyers and online browsers differed significantly in their evaluation of B2C sites. Online browsers viewed sites more negatively than buyers on various parameters such as site enjoyment, speed of downloads, personalization of information, relevance of information, ease of navigation, and so forth. Flavin et al. (2006) found Web usability (assessed in terms of Web site structure, simplicity, ease of navigation, speed, etc.) to influence buyer satisfaction and loyalty. All these studies point to the importance of content and design elements in Web sites.

Since a Web site forms the primary medium of communication and interaction between merchants and consumers, the quality of the Web site, in terms of the way its contents are structured and the way the Web channel is designed, has the potential to influence the purchase behavior of online consumers. Therefore,

H1: Web site quality will be positively associated with online purchase intent.

Customer Concerns in Online Shopping (CCOS)

The very mechanism of online shopping mandates that customers have faith in Internet sellers. Despite low barriers to entry and almost negligible search costs, not all online firms are successful. Online shoppers have a variety of concerns and they shop where they feel most comfortable doing so. Gefen (2000) conducted a questionnaire survey of 217 students to find that familiarity with Internet vendors and their processes influenced respondents' intention to transact with them. Lee and Turban's (2001) study of Internet shopping emphasized the importance of online merchant's integrity. Online firms that address customers' concerns gain customers confidence and loyalty. Chu et al. (2005) found brand and reputation of online merchants to be significant in determining consumer purchase intentions. Torkzadeh and Dhillon (2002), in a two-phase survey, found trust in online sellers to be one of the major factors influencing the success of the Internet commerce. In other words, although technologically possible, competitors are not a click away and it is important therefore to understand the components of concerns that dissuade customers from shopping online.

Customer concern in online shopping is primarily composed of three important factors: security, privacy of personal information, and assurance of delivery (Suh & Han, 2003). Belanger, Hiller, and Smith (2002) found online shoppers to provide personal information based on their perceptions of trustworthiness of Web merchants. Ranganathan and Ganapathy (2002) empirically validated privacy and security to be significant determinants of online shopping behavior. Vijayasarathy (2004) reported similar results on privacy and security. Koufaris and Hampton-Sosa (2004) also found security control in an online store to significantly affect consumer concerns in purchasing online. Examining online privacy issues, Dinev and Hart (2005–2006) found a strong negative relationship between privacy concerns and consumer intent to conduct online transactions. Eastlick et al. (2006) found strong negative association between privacy concerns and online purchase intentions, with privacy concerns directly and indirectly affecting purchase intent through online trust. Bart et al. (2005) and Schlosser et al. (2006) also found security and privacy concerns to influence online trust that ultimately determined consumer purchase intention. Apart from security and privacy of a Web site, assurances on delivery and returns also form a critical component of consumer concerns. Pechtl (2003) found convenience of a delivery service to have positive influence on the adoption of online shopping. Bart et al. (2005) also found order fulfillment to be a key determinant of online trust and purchase intentions. Based on the previous research findings we believe that customer concerns in terms of security, privacy, delivery and returns in an online store will have a negative influence on the online purchase intentions of customers. Therefore,

H2: Customer concerns in online shopping will be negatively associated with online purchase intent.

Computer Self-Efficacy

Computer self-efficacy reflects the belief in one's capabilities to execute computer-oriented actions to produce desired goal attainments. Individuals with little confidence in using the Internet, dissatisfaction with their Internet skills or uncomfortable using the Web have weak self-efficacy beliefs. Computer self-efficacy influences individual decisions about technology usage, the amount of effort and persistence put forth during obstacles faced, and the overall behavior towards the technology. The linkage between computer self efficacy and IT use has been empirically verified (Compeau & Higgins, 1995).

Computer self-efficacy is a byproduct of the consumer's attitude towards information technology (IT) and the extent of IT skills and knowledge possessed by the consumer. Scholars have argued that an individual's disposition and comfort level towards a specific technology influences the extent of technology usage. Some studies have specifically focused on Internet-specific self-efficacy though the broader construct of computer self-efficacy covers Web related efficacy as well (Hsu & Chiu, 2004). Researchers have identified technology attitude (Maudlin & Arrunachalam, 2002) and skill levels (Vijayasarathy, 2004) to be critical determinants of an individual's disposition towards a specific technology. Moreover, the extent of IT skills especially those related to Internet has been found to augment intentions to conduct online transactions (Dinev & Hart, 2005-2006). Based on the previous research studies we hypothesize computer self-efficacy to have a positive influence on the online purchase intentions of customers. Therefore,

H3: Computer self-efficacy will be positively associated with online purchase intent.

Past Online Shopping Experience

Based on a survey, Yoh et al. (2003) reported customers' prior Internet experience to be a strong determinant of their online shopping behavior. Pavlou (2003) validated that consumers' satisfaction with past online shopping resulted in building trust in the Web merchant, which in turn influenced further online transactions. Based on the above studies we propose that past Web shopping experience will have a strong influence on the online purchase intentions of customers. Therefore,

H4: Past Web shopping experience will be positively associated with online purchase intent.

The complete research model, showing key constructs, operational variables, and hypothesized relationships is shown in Figure 2.

METHODOLOGY

Survey Questionnaire

We identified operational measures for all of our constructs from extant literature. These operational measures were summarized into various items and a survey instrument was created. This questionnaire requested the respondents to rate the level of their agreement with the items in relation to their online shopping experience. The respondents rated each item on a scale of 1 to 7, where 1 represented *strongly disagree*, and 7 represented *strongly agree*. In addition to the above items, we also collected demographic data from the respondents. This included questions regarding their experience in using the Internet, extent and frequency of the Internet usage for different activities, how many purchases they made in last 6 months, and also the amount they spent in shopping online during this period.

The respondents also answered four questions about their online shopping intention. These questions dealt with their likelihood, willingness, likely frequency, and the probability of their making their online purchase. The first three questions were to be answered on a 7-point scale, with 1 equal to *very low* and 7 equal to *very high* probability. The last question was also to be answered on a 7-point scale, with 1 equal to *no chance* of buying to 7 equal to *certain chance* of buying.

After doing a pilot study, we conducted a survey in Illinois over a period of two weeks. Respondents were sought in public places like malls, computer shops, and electronics stores. A total of 409 individuals were administered the survey. Since our intention was to assess the online purchase behavior of consumers, only those individuals with recent prior online shopping experience had to be included as subjects for our study. Out of 409 responses, only 214 individuals had made online purchases in the past 6 months and, therefore, only these responses were considered for analysis.

Sample

We had a diverse sample, with 57% male and 43% female respondents. Nearly 60% of the sample was in the 21 to 30 years of age group. More than 80% of the respondents had more than 1 year of experience in Internet surfing. Over 20% of the respondents in our sample made six or more online purchases in last 6 months. More than 50% of the respondents had spent over US$ 100 in online shopping in the last 6 months. The profile of the respondents suggests that the respondents were considerably exposed to the Internet and online shopping. Table 2 provides some details of the respondents' profile.

DATA ANALYSIS

Validity and Reliability Assessment

Construct validity is the degree to which a measurement scale represents and acts like the concept being measured. In order to assess convergent and discriminant validities, the 29 items used to measure 8 research variables were subjected to principle component analysis. The analysis

Table 2. Profile of respondents (N = 214)

Experience in Internet surfing	
< 3 months	5 (2.3%)
Between 3 and 6 months	8 (3.7%)
Between 6 and 12 months	11 (5.1%)
Between 1 and 2 years	15 (7%)
Between 2 and 3 years	46 (21.5%)
Between 3 and 5 years	85 (39.7%)
> 5 years	44 (20.6%)
Amount spent in online shopping in last 6 months	
< US$ 10	13 (6.1%)
Between US$ 10 and 25	17 (7.9%)
Between US$ 25 and 50	33 (15.4%)
Between US $ 50 and 100	29 (13.6%)
Between US$ 100 and 250	53 (24.8%)
Between US$ 250 and 500	31 (14.5%)
Between US$ 500 and 1000	22 (10.3%)
> US$ 1000	13 (6.1%)

resulted in eight factors, with cumulative 75.85% of variance. Two items were dropped, one from delivery and the other from security, due to poor loadings. The detailed factor loadings are presented in Table 3.

Further, we did reliability analysis using Cronbach's coefficient alpha, to ensure that the items for each of the factors were internally related. The value of the Cronbach's coefficient alpha for seven of the eight variables was much higher than the recommended 0.60 (Table 3). Alpha value for "Delivery & Returns" variable was 0.52. However, we continued with this variable, because this came out as one of the factors with high loadings in our principal component analysis.

Table 3. Validity and reliability analysis

	Loadings	Cronbach's Alpha
Web site quality		
Content		
Information to compare across alternatives	0.81	
Provide decision-making aids (like calculator, comparison charts, calendar, etc.)	0.82	
Complete information about the firms, products and services	0.84	0.88
Opportunities to communicate and interact with the company	0.82	
Design		
Easy to navigate for information	0.85	
Consume less time for finding the information I am looking for	0.88	0.89
Visual presentations enhance the information provided	0.85	
Customer Concerns in Online Shopping		
Privacy		
Concerned about the Web-sites that gather my personal information	0.80	
Don't prefer to shop from sites that ask for my personal information.	0.70	
Think twice before giving personal information online	0.85	0.88
It's important to know how the personal information collected will be used	0.77	
Security		
Secure modes of transactions.	0.74	
Order products on line, but prefer making payments offline	0.79	
Prefer to have an individual account with a logon-id and password.	0.81	0.87
General concern about security of transaction	0.68	
Delivery & Returns		
Delivery concern deter me from purchasing online	0.81	0.52
Concerns about returning the product	0.71	
Computer Self Efficacy		
Tech Attitude		
Technologies such as internet have made me more productive	0.73	
Technologies like internet make it easy to keep in touch with friends and family	0.78	0.83
Technologies like internet have made my life easy and comfortable	0.73	
IT Skills		
Quite comfortable using computers	0.85	
Quite comfortable surfing the Internet	0.86	
Spend considerable time on Internet	0.81	0.91
Consider myself computer and net-savvy	0.82	
Past Online Shopping Experience		
Rate your satisfaction with recent online purchases	0.90	
Rate your experience with recent online purchases	0.91	0.93
Compare your experience in on-line purchasing with retail purchasing	0.89	

Structural Equation Model Analysis

Consistent with our conceptualization, Web site quality, CCOS, and computer self-efficacy were modeled as second order constructs. Web site quality was assessed using two constructs: *Content* and *Design*. For assessing CCOS elements, we used three factors, namely, *Privacy, Security,* and *Delivery & Returns*. Computer self-efficacy was composed of two constructs: *Attitude* towards information technology and *IT Skills*. Past online shopping experience was modeled as a first order construct.

Rather than directly measuring some of our key constructs, our modeling approach involved constructing Web site quality, CCOS and computer self efficacy as second order constructs. We believe Web site quality, CCOS, and computer self-efficacy are latent constructs that are best captured using some of the key dimensions underlying them. This rationale guided us to model them as second order constructs. We assessed these three constructs based on their constituent first order latent constructs.

Structural equation modeling (SEM) using AMOS was used to test and analyze our hypotheses. According to Hair, Anderson, Tatham, & Black (2004), SEM provides an appropriate method of dealing with multiple relationships simultaneously while providing statistical efficiency. SEM evaluates the given model using goodness-of-fit measures to evaluate the model fit and model parsimony. The evaluation of the overall fit of the model is done according to the goodness-of-fit index (GFI), the adjusted goodness-of-fit index (AGFI). The comparative fit index (CFI) and the root-mean-square error of approximation (RMSEA) are also used to assess the model fit. The details of the overall model fit indices along with the recommended values are presented in Table 4. The results of our analysis are shown in Figure 3. Except the GFI, all other indices are as per the recommended value. GFI value of 0.833 suggests a moderate fit of our model to the data collected.

While the overall model was supported ($\chi^2 / df = 1.64, p < 0.01$), the good-of-fit as assessed by GFI and AGFI indicated a moderate fit. However, the CFI and RMSEA scores indicate a good overall fit of the model. These figures provide support for our effort in integrating constructs from HCI, behavioral and consumerist streams of research on online shopping.

Based on the standardized path coefficients shown in Figure 3, all of our hypotheses were supported. Of the key constructs affecting online shopping behavior, past experience with online shopping had a relatively larger association with online purchase intentions as is evident from the high co-efficient (0.518, $p < 0.01$). The next high

Table 4. SEM results

	Score	Recommended Value
Chi-Square	680.104	
p value	0.000	> 0.05
Degrees of freedom	414	
Chi-Square/ Degrees of freedom	1.643	< 3.00
Goodness-of-fit index (GFI)	0.833	> 0.90
Adjusted goodness-of-fit index (AGFI)	0.800	> 0.80
Root mean square error of approximation (RMSEA)	0.055	< 0.10
Comparative fit index (CFI)	0.946	> 0.90

Figure 3. Results of SEM analysis

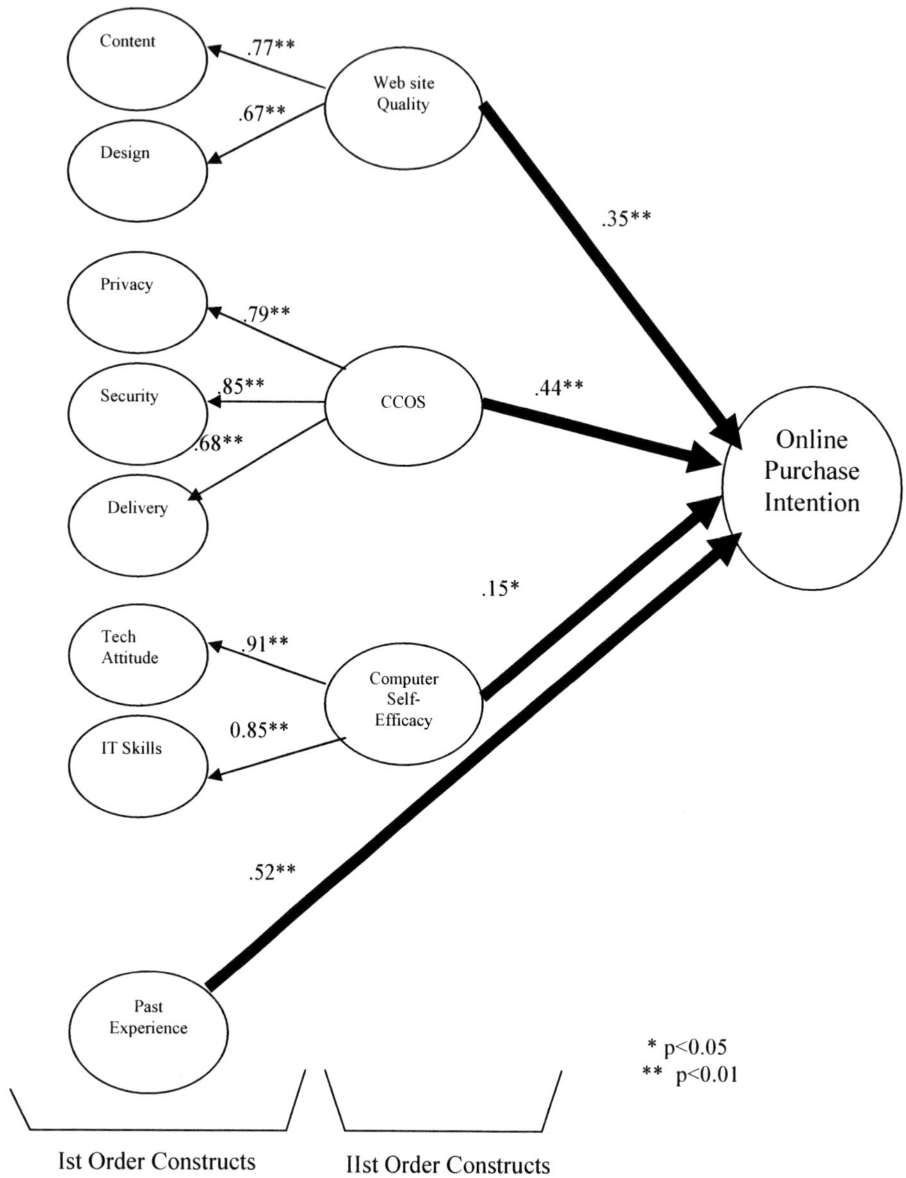

coefficient was for CCOS as assessed by security, privacy and delivery and return assurances (-0.443, $p < 0.01$). Web site quality was also found to be strongly, and positively associated with online purchase intent (0.35, $p < 0.01$), though its influence was relatively lower than those of CCOS and past online shopping experience. Our results also indicate computer self-efficacy to be a significant predictor of online purchase intent (0.153, $p < 0.05$), though the magnitude of its association (assessed by the standardized path coefficient) with online shopping intent is lower than those of other three constructs.

In summary, SEM analysis showed that past online shopping experience had the most dominant effect on online purchase intention, which was followed by CCOS, Web site quality, and computer self-efficacy. The analysis also successfully demonstrated the validity of our proposed integrated model and the efficacy of the multidimensional perspective of online shopping.

DISCUSSION

As Internet technologies continue to proliferate retail and marketing transactions, firms must devise appropriate response mechanisms to assimilate these technologies. Fundamental to such response is a good understanding of online consumer behavior. To address this important research issue, we developed a framework integrating diverse orientations for examining online consumer behavior. Our research had two related goals: (a) to combine the HCI, behavioral and consumerist approaches to propose an integrated model, and (b) to empirically assess the relative importance of the different antecedents on online purchase behavior. Our results highlight the significance of the key predictors, their relative importance and demonstrate the potency of our integrated framework.

We proposed and tested a framework with Web site quality, CCOS, computer self-efficacy, and past online shopping experience as potential antecedents to online purchase intentions. Our results support all of our hypotheses, thus providing evidence for positive association of all these constructs.

Our results reveal a strong negative association between CCOS and online purchase intentions. Although previous studies have studied and operationalized CCOS, the main approach has been to capture trust as a behavioral-attitudinal construct. To obtain contextually meaningful operational items, we captured CCOS through subconstructs; viz, privacy, security, and delivery. These subconstructs emphasize the importance of reducing CCOS through both online and offline mechanisms. By effectively integrating security, privacy and offline delivery and returns, companies can enhance consumer trust, thereby increasing the online purchase intentions. Our findings validate and confirm previous findings on the importance of addressing consumer concerns in online marketing environments (Gefen, 2003; Gefen et al., 2004). As Urban et al. (2000) note, "For the Internet, trust-based marketing is the key to success. Companies can use the Internet to provide customers with a secure, private and calming experience."

We assessed Web site quality through its content and design related aspects, and found site quality to be strongly associated with purchase intentions of customers. Though content and design are basic components of a Web site, the nature of content and the design, and the way in which these two are built can have a major impact on customer perceptions. To enhance Web site quality, online merchants need to provide customers with accurate, up-to-date and complete information on their business, products and services. The Web sites also need to have easy-to-use and smooth navigation that makes searching, comparing, and shopping a pleasure.

While customer concerns and Web site quality could be directly controlled and manipulated by firms trying to engage in B2C e-commerce, computer self-efficacy, and online shopping experience reflect consumer-related variables that are tied to specific consumers. Our study revealed strong positive influence of both self efficacy and past online experience of consumers. Our results also reveal relative influence of both controllable and noncontrollable constructs on online shopping. Research studies have revealed changing attitudes of consumers towards the Internet, with growing use of broadband and Internet connectivity in homes. Consumers have developed more experience with Web over time, though concerns of Internet fraud and privacy violations have not yet been fully addressed.

CONCLUSION

This article makes three main contributions to the research on online shopping. First, we reconcile three different orientations in the literature on online consumer behavior. Extant research typically adopts a single orientation—HCI, behavioral, or consumerist, and rarely integrates all the three facets to assess their overall impact on online purchase intentions. We show that an integrated model provides richer insights rather than relying solely on singular orientations. Only when the three orientations are examined in a composite manner can the effects of these facets be properly assessed. We believe our study nicely complements and extends earlier research, by providing a more holistic and comprehensive picture of key factors affecting online consumer behavior.

Second, we help identify the relative importance of key predictors of online purchase intentions. While some of the factors such as Web site quality and customer concern related factors could be manipulated by online merchants, other factors such as self-efficacy are amenable to change by consumers. Our analysis reveals past online shopping experience to have stronger association with online purchase intent than all the other factors. CCOS factors and Web site quality emerged as the second and third most significant predictors of online purchase intent. Computer self-efficacy had the lowest, yet, significant positive association. Third, the insights from this research are based on responses provided by consumers who have been actively shopping online. Rather than using proxy respondents such as students, we used actual online consumers to test and validate our model.

Our study throws several important implications for online merchants and practitioners. According to our results, past experience in online shopping seems to be a strong determinant of online purchase intention. Therefore, it becomes important for online merchants to carefully plan and execute their online strategies. It is important to plan a rollout of a complete B2C e-commerce strategy rather than trying incremental, ad hoc initiatives to moving online. Moreover, positive online purchase experience seems to cultivate customer loyalty in terms of repeat and multiple purchases. Therefore, rather than experimenting with online sales, it becomes important for online merchants to "get it right" if they are serious about their B2C e-commerce efforts. Treating Internet as a lucrative and additional business channel, merchants need to concentrate on improving their online effectiveness.

Our findings also reinforce the importance of CCOS as a cornerstone of effective online strategy. For mitigating CCOS, companies need to work on allaying consumer concerns on security, privacy, delivery and returns. CCOS is an intangible, yet, powerful factor that could decide the fortunes of online sellers. Every effort must be made by merchants to build mechanisms for building and sustaining consumer trust.

Web merchants need to continuously work on the content and design elements of their Web sites, as they seem to form the building blocks of Web site quality that ultimately influences the purchase intentions of online shoppers. Currency and frequent updates of Web sites, providing pertinent up-to-date information, presented in a user-friendly and customer-centered design is likely to attract and retain a significant portion of online buyers.

Our study also has several limitations that must be kept in mind while interpreting the results. The first limitation pertains to the variables that were included from the three research streams. The variables included in our model were key variables identified from literature—nevertheless, they do not form a comprehensive list of variables affecting online consumer behavior. Recent studies have tried to identify and examine additional variables (e.g., Bart et al., 2005), and future researchers could examine online consumer behavior with a larger set of variables drawn from the three research streams. Moreover, our dataset is relatively small as compared to some of the recent studies that have examined several hundreds of consumers. Other limitations pertain to the measures we used. We relied on simpler measures rather than using lengthy instruments such as SiteQual and WebQual. It should also be noted that our measures were screened and examined for reliability and validity. We also did not test any interaction effects and this is another fruitful avenue for extending the research on this topic.

Though early research studies on online shopping had adopted a specific orientation (HCI, behavioral and consumerist) towards examining online consumer behavior, extant researchers have acknowledged the complementarity among these three research streams. Our study integrates key variables from all the three streams, thus providing a more holistic understanding of online shopping behavior. It should also be emphasized that the variables from different streams could interact with each other, thus exerting a combined influence on the consumer purchase intentions. For instance, computer self-efficacy could allay consumer concerns in online shopping and also help consumers overcome any problems with Web design and usability. Similarly, favorable past online experience could dispel security and privacy concerns and this experience could help consumers overcome any difficulties in Web site navigation and usage. Future researchers could model such interactions to enrich and extend our knowledge on online shopping behavior. In conclusion, our study proposed a more holistic model integrating HCI, behavioral and consumerist approaches to understand online shopping. We developed, tested and validated a pragmatic multidimensional model that Web merchants could adopt to attract and retain online shoppers.

REFERENCES

Aladwani, A. M., & Palvia, P. (2002). Developing and validating an instrument for measuring user-perceived Web quality. *Information & Management, 39,* 467-476.

Bart, Y., Shankar, V., Sultan, F., & Urban, G. L. (2005). Are the drivers and role of online trust the same for all Web sites and consumers? A large-scale exploratory empirical study. *Journal of Marketing, 69*(4), 133-152.

Belanger, F., Hiller, J. S., & Smith, W. J. (2002). Trustworthiness in e-commerce: The role of privacy, security, and site attributes. *Journal of Strategic Information Systems, 11,* 245-270.

Bellman, S., Lohse, G., & Eric, J. (1999). Predictors of online buying behavior. *Communications of the ACM, 42*(12), 32-38.

Brynjolfsson, E., & Smith, M. D. (2000). Frictionless commerce? A comparison of Internet and conventional retailers. *Management Science, 46*(4), 563-585.

Burroughs, R. E., & Sabherwal, R. (2002). Determinants of retail electronic purchasing: A multi-period investigation. *INFOR, 40*(1),.

Chang, M. K., Cheung, W., & Lai,V. S. (2005). Literature derived reference models for the adoption of online shopping. *Information & Management, 42*(4), 543-559.

Chen, P. Y., & Hitt, L. M. (2002). Measuring switching costs and the determinants of customer retention in Internet-enabled businesses: A study of the online brokerage industry. *Information Systems Research, 13*(3), 255-274.

Chu, W., Choi, B., & Song, M. R. (2005). The role of on-line retailer brand and infomediary reputation in increasing consumer purchase intention. *International Journal of Electronic Commerce, 9*(3) 115-127.

Compeau, E. R., & Higgins, C. A. (1995). Computer self-efficacy: Development of a measure and initial test. *MIS Quarterly, 19*(2), 189-211.

De Wulf, K., Schillewaert, N., Muylle, S., & Rangarajan, D. (2006). The role of pleasure in Web site success. *Information & Management, 43*(4), 434-446.

Dinev, T., & Hart, P. (2005–2006). Internet privacy concerns and social awareness as determinants of intention to transact. *International Journal of Electronic Commerce, 10*(2), 7-29.

Eastlick, M., Lotz, S. L., & Warrington, P. (2006). Understanding online B-to-C relationships: An integrated model of privacy concerns, trust, and commitment. *Journal of Business Research, 59*(8), 877-886.

Ethier, J., Hadaya, P., Talbot, J., & Cadieux, J. (in press). B2C Web site quality and emotions during online shopping episodes: An empirical study. *Information & Management.*

Everard, A., & Galletta, D. F. (2005). How presentation flaws affect perceived site quality, trust, and intention to purchase from an online store. *Journal of Management Information Systems, 22*(3), 55-95.

Flavin, C., Guinaliu, M., & Gurrea, R. (2006). The role played by perceived usability, satisfaction, and consumer trust on Web site loyalty. *Information & Management, 43*(1), 1-14.

Gefen, D. (2000). E-commerce: The role of familiarity and trust. *Omega, 28*(6), 725-737.

Gefen, D., Karahanna, E., & Straub, D. W. (2003). Trust and TAM in online shopping: An integrated model. *MIS Quarterly, 27*(1), 51–90.

Gefen, D., & Straub, D. W. (2004). Consumer trust in B2C e-commerce and the importance of social presence: Experiments in e-products and e-services. *Omega, 32*(6), 407-425.

Hair, J. F., Anderson, R. E., Tatham, R. L., & Black, W. C. (1998). *Multivariate data analysis* (5th ed). Upper Saddle River, NJ: Prentice Hall.

Heijden, H. V. D. (2003). Factors Influencing the usage of Websites: The case of a generic portal in the Netherlands. *Information & Management, 40*(6), 541-549.

Heijden, H. V. D., Verhagen, T., & Creemers, M. (2003). Understanding online purchase intentions: Contributions from technology and trust perspectives. *European Journal of Information Systems, 12*(1), 41-49.

Hsu, M., & Chiu, C. (2004). Internet self-efficacy and electronic service acceptance. *Decision Support Systems, 38*(3), 369-381.

Huizingh, E. (2000). The content and design of Web sites: An empirical study. *Information & Management, 37*(3), 123-134.

Iwaarden, J. V., & Wiele, T. V. D. (2003). Applying SERVQUAL to Web sites: An exploratory study. *International Journal of Quality, 20*(8), 919-935.

Iwaarden, J. V., Wiele, T. V. D., Ball, L., & Millen, R. (2004). Perceptions about the quality of Websites: A survey amongst students at Northeastern University and Erasmus University. *Information & Management, 41*(8), 947–959.

Jarvenpaa, S. L., Tractinsky, N., & Vitale, M. (2000). Consumer trust in an Internet store. *Information Technology and Management, 1*(2), 45-71.

Kiely, T. (1997). The Internet: Fear and shopping in cyberspace. *Harvard Business Review, 75*(4), 13-14.

Koufaris, M., & Hampton-Sosa, W. (2004). The development of initial trust in an online company by new customers. *Information & Management, 41*(3), 377-397.

Lee, G., & Lin, H. (2005). Customer perceptions of e-service quality in online shopping. *International Journal of Retail & Distribution Management, 33*(2), 161-176.

Lee, M., & Turban, E. A. (2001). Trust model for consumer Internet shopping. *International Journal of Electronic Commerce, 6*(1), 75-91.

Lepkowska-White, E. (2004). Online store perceptions: How to turn browsers into buyers. *Journal of Marketing Theory and Practice, 12*(3), 36-48.

Liao, Z., & Cheung, T. (2001). Internet-based e-shopping and consumer attitudes: An empirical study. *Information & Management, 38*(5), 299-306.

Liu, C., & Arnett, K. P. (2000). Exploring the factors associated with Web site success in the context of e-commerce. *Information & Management, 38*(1), 23-33.

Lohse, G. L., & Spiller, P. (1999). Internet retail store design: How the user interface influences traffic and sales. *Journal of Computer Mediated Communication, 5*(2). Retrieved from www.ascusc.org/jcmc/vol5/issue2/

Loiacono, E., Watson, R., & Goodhue, D. (2002). WebQual: A Web site quality instrument. *American marketing association. Winter Marketing Educators' Conference, Austin, TX,* 432-438.

Mauldin, E., & Arunachalam, V. (2002). An experimental examination of alternative forms of Web assurance for business-to-consumer e-commerce. *Journal of Information Systems, 16,* 33-54.

McKnight, H. D., Choudhury, V., & Kacmar, C. (2002a). Developing and validating trust measures for e-commerce: An integrative typology. *Information Systems Research, 13*(3), 334-359.

McKnight, H. D., Choudhury, V., & Kacmar, C. (2002b). The impact of initial consumer trust on intentions to transact with a Web site: A trust building model. *Journal of Strategic Information Systems, 11,* 297-323.

Pavlou, P. A. (2003). Consumer acceptance of electronic commerce integrating trust and risk with the technology acceptance model. *International Journal of Electronic Commerce, 7*(3), 101-134.

Pechtl, H. (2003). Adoption of online shopping by German grocery shoppers. *The International Review of Retail, Distribution and Consumer Research, 13*(2), 145-159.

Ranganathan, C., & Ganapathy, S. (2002). Key dimensions of business-to-consumer Web sites. *Information & Management, 39*(6), 457-465.

Salaun, Y., & Flores, K. (2001). Information quality: Meeting the needs of the consumer. *International Journal of Information Management, 21,* 21-37.

Schlosser, A. E., White, T. B., & Lloyd, S. M. (2006). Converting Web site visitors into buyers: How Web site investment increases consumer trusting beliefs and online purchase intentions. *Journal of Marketing, 70*(2), 133-148.

Shih, H. P. (2004). An empirical study on predicting user acceptance of e-shopping on the Web. *Information & Management, 41*(3), 351-368.

Spiller, P., & Lohse, G. L. (1997). A classification of Internet retail stores. *International Journal of Electronic Commerce, 2*(2), 29-56.

Suh, B., & Han, I. (2003). The impact of customer trust and perception of security control on the acceptance of electronic commerce. *International Journal of Electronic Commerce, 7*(3), 135-161.

Tarafdar, M., & Zhang, J. (2005). Analyzing the influence of Web site design parameters on Web site usability. *Information Resources Management Journal, 18*(4), 62-80.

Torkzadeh, G., & Dhillon, G. (2002). Measuring factors that influence the success of Internet commerce. *Information Systems Research, 13*(2), 187-207.

Urban, G. L., Sultan, F., & Qualls, W. J. (2000). Placing trust at the center of your Internet strategy. *Sloan Management Review, 42*(1), 39-48.

Vatanasombut, B., Stylianou, A.C., & Igbaria, M. (2004). How to retain online customers. *Communications of the ACM, 47*(6), 64-70.

Vijayasarathy, L. R. (2004). Predicting consumer intentions to use on-line shopping: The case for an augmented technology acceptance model. *Information & Management, 41*(6), 747-762.

Wan, H. A. (2000). Opportunities to enhance a commercial Website. *Information & Management, 38*(1), 15-21.

Webb, H. W., & Webb, L. A. (2004). SiteQual: An integrated measure of Web site quality. *Journal of Enterprise Information Management, 17*(6), 430-440.

Yoh, E., Damhorst, M. L., Sapp, S., & Laczniak, R. (2003). Consumer adoption of the Internet: The case of apparel shopping. *Psychology & Marketing, 20*(12), 1095–1118.

Zhang, X., Prybutok, V. R., & Koh, C. E. (2006). The role of impulsiveness in TAM-based online purchasing behavior. *Information Resources Management Journal, 19*(2), 54-68.

Zviran, M., Glezer, C., & Avni, I. (2006). User satisfaction from commercial Web sites: The effect of design and use. *Information & Management, 43*(2), 157-178.

This work was previously published in the Information Resources Management Journal, Vol. 20, Issue 4, edited by M. Khosrow-Pour, pp. 48-64, copyright 2007 by IGI Publishing, formerly known as Idea Group Publishing (an imprint of IGI Global).

Chapter XIII
Information Technology Industry Dynamics:
Impact of Disruptive Innovation Strategy

Nicholas C. Georgantzas
Fordham University Business Schools, USA

Evangelos Katsamakas
Fordham University Business Schools, USA

ABSTRACT

This chapter combines disruptive innovation strategy (DIS) theory with the system dynamics (SD) modeling method. It presents a simulation model of the hard-disk (HD) maker population overshoot and collapse dynamics, showing that DIS can crucially affect the dynamics of the IT industry. Data from the HD maker industry help calibrate the parameters of the SD model and replicate the HD makers' overshoot and collapse dynamics, which DIS allegedly caused from 1973 through 1993. SD model analysis entails articulating exactly how the structure of feedback relations among variables in a system determines its performance through time. The HD maker population model analysis shows that, over five distinct time phases, four different feedback loops might have been most prominent in generating the HD maker population dynamics. The chapter shows the benefits of using SD modeling software, such as iThink®, and SD model analysis software, such as Digest®. The latter helps detect exactly how changes in loop polarity and prominence determine system performance through time. Strategic scenarios computed with the model also show the relevance of using SD for information system management and research in areas where dynamic complexity rules.

INTRODUCTION

In challenging business environments, where even the best thought-of and executed strategies can fail dramatically (Raynor, 2007), disruptive innovation is emerging as a mainstream strategy that firms use first to create and subsequently to sustain growth in many industries (Bower & Christensen, 1995; Christensen, 1997; Christensen, et al 2002; Christensen & Raynor, 2003). Honda's small off-road motorcycles of the 60s, for example, personal computers and Intuit's accounting software initially under-performed established product offers. But such innovations bring new value propositions to new users, who do not need all the performance incumbent firms offer. After establishing themselves in a simple application or user niche, potentially disruptive products (goods or services) improve until they "change the game" (Gharajedaghi, 1999), driving incumbent firms to the sidelines.

Christensen and Raynor (2003) see disruptive innovation strategy (DIS) not as the product of random events, but as a repeatable process that managers can design and replicate with sufficient regularity and success, once they understand the circumstances associated with the genesis and distinct dynamics a DIS entails. Similarly, Christensen et al (2002, p. 42) urge technology managers, adept in developing new business processes, to design robust, replicable DIS for creating and nurturing new growth business areas. In so doing, they must (a) seek to balance resources that sustain short-term profit and investments in high-growth opportunities and (b) use both separate screening processes and separate criteria for judging sustaining and disruptive innovation projects.

DIS can crucially affect the dynamics of IT, causing turbulence and industry shake-outs. Anthony and Christensen (2004) and Christensen *et al.* (2002) argue that is extremely important for technology managers to understand DIS. To help them make it so, this chapter shows a system dynamics (SD) model that replicates Christensen's (1992) data on hard-disk (HD) maker population dynamics. The model draws on archetypal SD overshoot and collapse work (Alfeld & Graham, 1974; Mojtahedzadeh, Andersen & Richardson 2004), which covers SD models in many areas with similarities in the structure of causal processes.

Cast as a methodological IS industry case, the chapter also shows the use and benefits of model analysis with Mojtahedzadeh's (1996) pathway participation metric (PPM), implemented in his *Digest®* software (Mojtahedzadeh et al, 2004). Shown here is a small part of a modeling project that combined DIS theory with SD to answer specific client concerns about the dynamic consequences of implementing disruptive innovation strategies in established high-technology markets, which contain over- and under-served (current and potential) users.

By definition, DIS is a dynamic process. Any model that purports to explain the evolution of a dynamic process also defines a dynamic system either explicitly or implicitly (Repenning, 2002). A crucial aspect of model building in any domain is that any claim a model makes about the nature and structure of relations among variables in a system must follow as a logical consequence of its assumptions about the system. And attaining logical consistency requires checking if the dynamic system the model defines can generate the real-life performance of the dynamic process the model tries to explain.

But most existing DIS models are merely textual and diagrammatic in nature. Given a particular disruptive innovation situation, in order to determine if a prescribed DIS idea can generate superior performance, which only 'systemic leverage' endows (Georgantzas & Ritchie-Dunham, 2003), managers must mentally solve a complex system of differential or difference equations. Alas, relying on intuition for testing logical consistency in dynamic business processes might contrast sharply with the long-certified human cognitive limits (Morecroft, 1985; Paich & Sterman 1993; Sterman 1989; Sastry 1997).

Aware of these limits, the chapter makes multiple contributions. *One* is the culmination of the early disruptive innovation literature into a generic model of the hard-disk makers' overshoot and collapse. Using a generic structure from prior SD overshoot and collapse work, the model contains assumptions common to seemingly diverse theories in economics, epidemiology, marketing and sociology. *Two* is the translation of these seemingly diverse components into a simulation model that allows addressing the specific concerns of a real-life client, by generating the overshoot and collapse dynamics of the hard-disk makers' population.

Furthermore, the chapter aims at expanding the relatively scarce but insightful IS research using the SD modeling method (Dutta & Roy, 2005; Kanungo, 2003; Abdel-Hamid & Madnick 1989). By describing the SD method and demonstrating its value, the chapter encourages a wider adoption of the SD modeling method in information systems research.

The model analysis results show that, over five distinct time phases, four different feedback loops become prominent in generating the HD maker population dynamics from 1973 through 1993. The chapter does not merely translate Christensen's DIS work into a SD model to replicate his results. It dares to ask *how* and *why* the model produces the results it does. With the help of *Digest*®, the chapter ventures beyond *dynamic* and *operational thinking*, seeks insight from system structure and thereby accelerates *circular causality thinking* (Richmond, 1993). *Digest*® helps detect exactly how changes in loop prominence determine system performance.

Following are a review of the disruptive innovation strategy literature and an overview of the SD modeling method. Then the chapter proceeds with model description and discussion of the simulation and model analysis results.

DISRUPTIVE INNOVATION STRATEGY (DIS) THEORY

The management innovation literature has delineated multiple ways to dichotomize innovation, such as radical vs. incremental, competency destroying vs. competency enhancing, and component vs. architectural (Hill & Jones, 1998; Christensen, 1997; Tushman & Anderson, 1986). The DIS theory offers a new dichotomy of innovation: *sustaining* vs. *disruptive* (Christensen, 1997). The defining feature of DIS is that it emphasizes new performance virtues or dimensions, which are not the primary performance dimensions of the mainstream market. Conversely, sustaining innovation emphasizes the improvement of extant product performance dimensions.

Typically, DIS or *disrupter* firms start out small and operate on the fringes of existing markets for a while, growing and establishing a foothold under incumbents' radar screens. At the heart of DIS, with the potential to disrupt a mature industry, perhaps even to overtake and to displace incumbent firms through time, is a technology and a good or service platform that marks a departure from sustaining innovation, in the form of product extensions and add-ons to existing goods and services. Such a technology fills a previously unidentified or unaddressed niche with a value proposition aligned with user needs or 'jobs to do' (Christensen & Raynor, 2003).

A disrupter firm offers new choices in the form of stripped down functionality at a lower price, i.e., a 'less for less' offering. Adapted from Christensen and Raynor (2003, p. 44), Figure 1 shows the low-end and non-consumption markets disrupters exploit. The sustaining innovations of established firms often over-supply users with technological functionality or services that users do not actually need. The broken straight lines of Figure 1 show the trajectories of increasing user requirements for a given good or service. The sustaining innovations solid line on the front panel of Figure 1 is the increasing performance the good or service offers, which is steeper than the user requirements broken line. For example, mainframe and mini-computers in the late 1980s offered users higher levels of performance, features and capability than they could use. This oversupply left a vacuum at the low end of the market for a 'simpler' product offering: the personal computer (PC).

Once introduced, along the solid, low-end disruption line on Figure 1, PCs had offered lower performance to users than mainstream mainframe and mini computers did. But a niche of users valued PCs and, through time, PC technological performance improved along the trajectory of the low-end disruption line. At some point, PC performance equaled that demanded by the average mainstream users of mainframes and minicomputers. So users started to switch, causing a widespread disruption of the established computer market, thereby driving many incumbent firms out of business. Depending on the performance ranges users can use or absorb to get a job done (i.e., to fulfill a need), new goods and services continually improve, usually faster than the average user's requirements, leaving space for new-market disruption waves among non-users on the back panel of Figure 1. Potentially, for example, the fast evolving personal digital assistant (PDA) and related mobile devices might next disrupt the PC market further in the future.

Disrupter firms typically target market segments currently unable to purchase a good or service or to fill a specific need. In effect, they create new markets by addressing non-user needs. Each disrupter firm exploits its ability to appeal to incumbent firms' low-end markets, i.e., over-served users facing a good or a service, with functionality that far exceeds their needs, at a price they only pay reluctantly for lack of alternatives. Contrary to fitly served users, users in such markets cannot absorb sustaining performance improvements that exceed the range of utility they need or know how to exploit.

Once a disrupter firm becomes successful at penetrating non-consumption and low-end tiers, and has been on the market long enough to improve service delivery, to strengthen core business processes and to achieve a reasonable level of profitability, then the DIS firm is poised for an up-market march. This entails going after incumbent firms' high-end segments with an improved or expanded good/service offering and

Figure 1. Low-end and non-consumption market disruption (adapted from Christensen and Raynor, 2003, p.44)

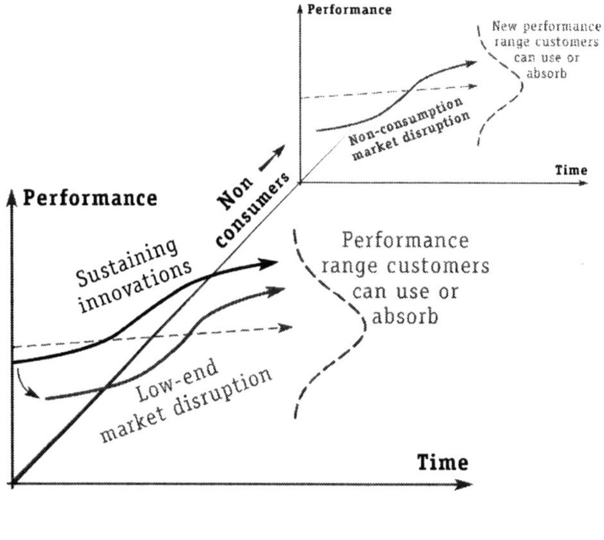

enhanced functionality at higher price points. The disrupter must be aware that moving up market to contest an incumbent firm's lock-in of lucrative users might trigger a wave of retaliation. So disrupters must ensure sufficient readiness to address the competitive response prior to embarking on their up-market march.

Disrupter firms exploit incumbents' exclusive focus on sustaining innovations and improved presence in the high-end, most profitable market segments (Christensen, 1997). As incumbents pay little attention to new and lower-end markets, they allow DIS entrants to move in and position themselves to eventually move up-market and to begin carving paths into the very markets established players serve. Incumbents begin to compromise long-term growth by allowing disrupters to eat into the lower-end segments and undermine their competitive position. Often, incumbents face a cost disadvantage compared to the typically light DIS cost structure. This limits when and how incumbents can respond to the DIS threat. Taking a long-term view might well suggest retaliating early and with great force.

Disrupters are typically ideally positioned to take advantage of the time lag to retaliation. They strengthen their presence and improve the quality and functionality of their offering and its overall value proposition as they prepare to embark upon an up-market march. A successful up-market march can spell a prolonged period of upset and transformation for entire industries. Old ways of doing business and serving users give way to superior ways of addressing user needs or jobs to do, at a more granular level and at a lower price.

This chapter provides insights in industry transformation, focusing on the effects of DIS on the number of firms operating in IT industry. It shows that DIS may crucially affect the dynamics of the IT industry, causing turbulence and consolidation of firms operating in the industry. The number of firms is a core aspect of industry structure because it affects product price and variety, as well as firm profitability and the value enjoyed by technology users (Tirole, 1988). The chapter also contributes to the emerging IS literature on disruptive innovation (e.g. Lyytinen & Rose, 2003a,b; Katsamakas & Georgantzas, 2008; Georgantzas & Katsamakas, 2008). Much of that literature focuses on the organizational impact of disruptive innovations (e.g., Lyytinen & Rose, 2003a,b), but pays little attention on the explanation of industry dynamics.

THE SYSTEM DYNAMICS (SD) MODELING METHOD

Client-driven, the entire SD modeling process aims at helping managers articulate exactly how the structure of circular feedback relations among variables in the system they manage determines its performance through time (Forrester & Senge, 1980). In the endless hunt for superior performance, SD's basic tenet is that the structure of feedback loop relations in a system gives rise to its dynamics (Meadows, 1989; Sterman, 2000, p. 16).

SD moves beyond mere *systems thinking* (Gharajedaghi, 1999; Senge, et. al, 1994) to systems formal modeling. Pioneered by MIT's Forrester (1961) and influenced by engineering control theory, SD calls for formal simulation modeling that provides a rigorous understanding of system behavior. Formal simulation modeling is an essential tool because "people's intuitive predictions about the dynamics of complex systems are systematically flawed" (Sterman, 1994, p. 178), mostly because of human's bounded rationality. Fontana (2006) sees SD as a most coherent modeling method, with high descriptive ability and theory building potential.

Two types of diagrams help formalize system structure: causal loop diagrams (CLDs) and stock and flow diagrams. CLDs depict relations among variables (e.g., Figure 5b). Arrows show the direction of causality and '+' and '–' signs the polarity of

Figure 2. Eight archetypal performance (P) dynamics (i.e., behavior patterns through time) might exist within a single phase of behavior for a single variable (adapted from Mojtahedzadeh et al 2004)

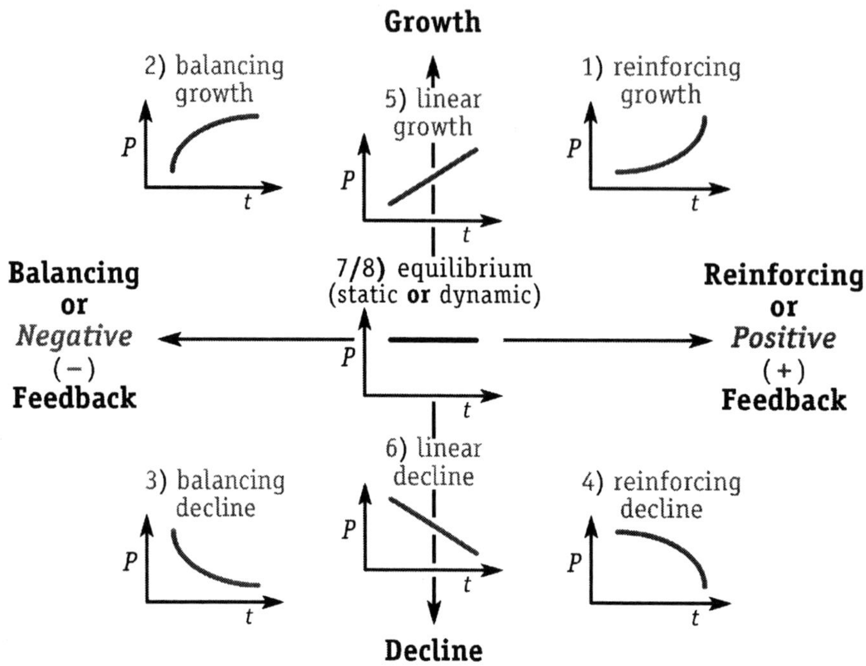

relations, i.e., how an increase in a variable affects change in a related variable. The culmination of all variable relations describes a set of positive or reinforcing and negative or balancing feedback loops characterizing a system.

Complementary to CLDs (Sterman, 2000), stock and flow diagrams depict how flow variables accumulate into stock variables, i.e., how stocks integrate the flows and how the flows differentiate the stocks (e.g., Figure 3). Stock and flow diagrams include causal loops, and provide the system with useful features such as memory and inertia. So they are essential in determining the dynamic behavior of the system under study. Figure 2 shows possible system behavior patterns through time. At the right level of abstraction, SD researchers encounter similar causal processes that underlie *seemingly* highly diverse phenomena (Forrester, 1961).

Model Analysis in the SD Modeling Method

Both as an inquiry and as a coherent problem-solving method, SD can attain its spectacular Darwinian sweep (Atkinson, 2004) as long as it formally links system structure and performance. In order to help academics and managers see exactly what part of system structure affects performance through time, i.e., detect shifting loop polarity and dominance (Richardson, 1995), SD researchers use tools from discrete mathematics and graph theory first to simplify and then to automate model analysis (Gonçalves, Lerpattarapong, & Hines, 2000; Kampmann, 1996; Mojtahedzadeh, 1996; Mojtahedzadeh, et al 2004; Oliva, 2004; Oliva & Mojtahedzadeh, 2004). Mostly, they build on Nathan Forrester's (1983) idea to link loop strength to system eigenvalues.

Mojtahedzadeh's *Digest*® software plays a crucial role in the analysis of this chapter's model. The pathway participation metric inside *Digest®* detects and displays prominent causal paths and loop structures by computing each selected variable's dynamics from its slope and curvature, i.e., its first and second time derivatives. Without computer simulation, even experienced modelers find it hard to test their intuition about the connection between circular causality and SD (Oliva, 2004; Mojtahedzadeh *et al* 2004). Using *Digest®* is, however, a necessary but insufficient condition for insight. Insightful articulations that link performance to system structure integrate insight from dynamic, operational and feedback loop thinking (Mojtahedzadeh *et al* 2004; Richmond, 1993).

Linked to eigenvalue and dominant loop research, Mojtahedzadeh's (1996) PPM is most promising in formally linking performance to system structure. Mojtahedzadeh *et al* (2004) give an extensive overview of PPM that shows its conceptual underpinnings and mathematical definition, exactly how it relates to system eigenvalues and concrete examples to illustrate its merits. Very briefly, the pathway participation metric sees a model's individual causal links or paths among variables as the basic building blocks of structure. PPM can identify dominant loops, but does not start with them as its basic building blocks. Using a recursive heuristic approach, PPM detects compact structures of chief causal paths and loops that contribute the most to the performance of a selected variable through time.

Mojtahedzadeh *et al* (2004, pp. 7-11) also present *Digest®* software. *Digest®* detects the causal paths that contribute the most to generating the dynamics a selected variable shows. It first slices a selected variable's time path or trajectory into discrete phases, each corresponding to one of eight possible behavior patterns through time (Figure 2). Once the selected variable's time trajectory is cut into phases, PPM decides which pathway is most prominent in generating that variable's performance within each phase. As causal paths combine to form loops, combinations of such circular paths shape the most influential or prominent loops within each phase.

Mojtahedzadeh is testing PPM with a multitude of classic SD models, such as, for example, Alfeld and Graham's (1976) urban dynamics model (*cf* Mojtahedzadeh *et al* 2004). Similarly, Oliva and Mojtahedzadeh (2004) use *Digest®* to show that the shortest independent loop set (SILS), which Oliva (2004) structurally derived via an algorithm for model partition and automatic calibration, does contain the most influential or prominent causal paths that *Digest®* detects. Methodologically, this chapter contributes to this line of work.

MODEL DESCRIPTION

The SD model consists of two major components or sectors. First, we describe the hard-disk makers' population and user ***jobs to do*** sector, and then the behavior reproduction testing sector. The SD simulation model was developed using the *iThink®* SD software (Richmond 2006).

Hard-Disk (HD) Maker Population and User Jobs to do Sector

Figure 4 shows the model's hard-disk (HD) makers' population and user jobs to do sector. Listed in the Appendix, Table 1 shows the equations of the model. There is a one-to-one association between the model diagram of Figure 3 and its equations on Table 1. Building a model entails diagramming system structure and then specifying differential equations and parameter values. The software enforces consistency between model diagrams and equations, while its built-in functions help quantify parameters and variables pertinent to the HD Makers' overshoot and collapse dynamics.

Rectangles represent stocks or level variables that accumulate in SD, such as the population of HD Makers (Figure 3 and Eq. 1, Table 1). Emanating from cloud-like *sources* and ebbing into cloud-like *sinks*, the double-line, pipe-and-valvelike icons that fill and drain the stocks represent flows or rate variables that cause the stocks to change. The exit outflow of Figure 3 and Eq. 5, for example, bleeds the HD Makers stock, initialized (INIT) with 18 hard-disk maker firms (Eq. 1.1, Table 1) per Christensen's (1992) data. Single-line arrows represent information connectors, while circular icons depict auxiliary converters where constants, behavioral relations or decision points convert information into decisions.

The enter inflow (Eq. 4), which fills the HD Makers stock, depends, for example, on the HD Makers population itself, multiplied by the industry's empirical growth fraction, an exogenous auxiliary constant parameter (Eq. 7), and by the annual shortage of jobs effect (Eq. 16), a graphical table function (gtf).

The stock and flow diagram on Figure 3 shows accumulations and flows essential in generating the performance dynamics of the hard-disk maker

Figure 3. Hard-disk (HD) makers' population and users' jobs to do sector

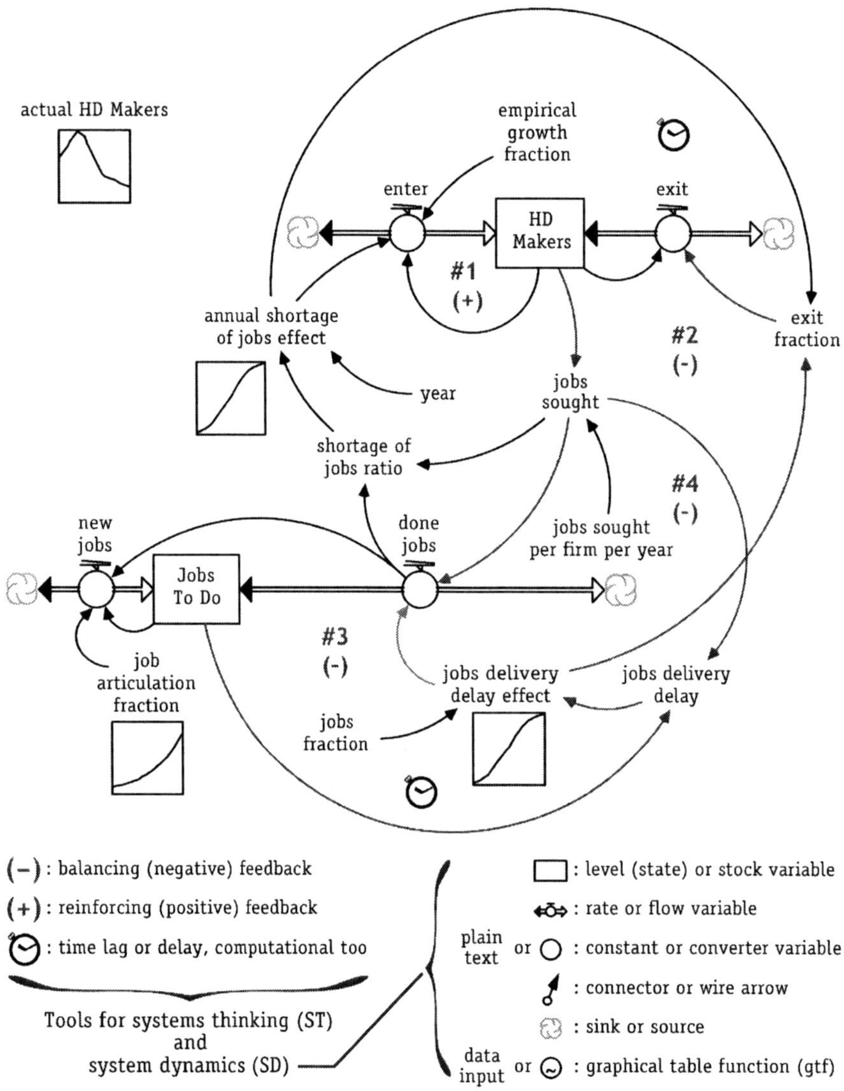

population. The fate of this population was determined by the disruptive innovation diffusion process (Christensen, 1992). This diagram also tells, with the help of the equations on Tables 1, what drives the flows in the system. In the context of systems thinking (ST), stock and flow diagrams like the one on Figure 3 help accelerate what Richmond (1993) calls *operational thinking.*

The model on Figure 3 and Table 1 is based on a classic structure that illustrates how the population of firms in a particular industry grows through time until the resources needed to support its growth are depleted (Alfeld & Graham, 1976; Mojtahedzadeh et al 2004). The model captures real-world processes as feedback loops that might cause the performance dynamics of its pertinent variables. Caught in a web of eleven feedback loops, the HD Makers' population, for example, grows when, *ceteris paribus*, new hard-disk makers enter through a reinforcing or positive (+) loop and declines when, again ceteris paribus, they exit through a balancing or negative (–) loop (Figure 3). Once new firms join the hard-disk makers' population, they immediately begin to deplete the users' Jobs To Do stock (Eq. 2), a vital resource for HD Makers to stay in business.

The shortage of jobs ratio (Eq. 12), i.e., the ratio of done jobs (Eq. 3) to jobs sought (Eq. 13), also affects new firm entry and exit indirectly. Last but not least, the users' Jobs To Do stock controls its own depletion rate, i.e., done jobs, by modulating the jobs delivery delay (Eq. 12), i.e., the ratio of Jobs To Do to jobs sought (Eq. 13).

Given its specific set of parameters and initial values, to explain the dynamics the model generates, the question is: which of the eleven feedback loops HD Makers are caught in are most influential or prominent in generating the HD Makers' behavior Christensen (1992) observed. For example, what made the users' Jobs To Do decline rapidly? What drove HD Makers to grow rapidly in the first few years? What part of the structure is responsible for the decline of the hard-disk makers' population followed by its growth? Those familiar with this archetypal model structure might easily explain the growth and declining phases. It might not be as easy, however, to distinguish which part of the model contributes most to the dynamics of HD Makers in the transition from reinforcing (+) growth to a balancing (–) decline. Using *Digest®* allows detecting the most prominent or influential feedback loops as the HD Makers dynamics unfolds.

Behavior Reproduction Testing Sector

To replicate the DIS-caused overshoot and collapse dynamics of the HD Makers' population that Christensen (1992) reports, the model's specific set of parameters and initial values were set to minimize the mean square error (MSE) between actual and simulation data. Shown on Figure 4, Theil's (1966) inequality statistics (TIS) subsequently decompose MSE on Figure 7.

TIS provide an elegant decomposition of the MSE into three components: bias (U^M), unequal variance (U^S) and unequal covariance (U^C), so that $U^M + U^S + U^C = 1$ (Oliva, 1995; Sterman, 1984 and 2000; Theil, 1966). Briefly, bias arises when competing data have different means. Unequal variance implies that the variances of two time series differ. Unequal covariance means imperfectly correlated data that differ point by point. Dividing each component by the MSE gives the MSE fraction due to bias (U^M), due to unequal variance (U^S) and due to unequal covariance (U^C). A large U^M reveals a potentially serious systematic error. U^S errors can be systematic too. When unequal variation dominates the MSE, the data match on average and is highly correlated but the variation in two time series around their common mean differs. One variable is a stretched out version of the other. U^S may be large either because of trend differences, or because the data have the same phasing but different amplitude fluctuations (Sterman, 2000, p. 876). If most of the error is concentrated in unequal covariance, then the data means and trends match but individual data points differ point by point. When U^C is large, then most of the error is unsystematic and, according to Sterman: "a model should not be faulted for failing to match the random component of the data" (2000, p. 877).

Figure 4 shows the stock and flow diagram of the behavior reproduction testing model sector and Table 2 the sector's equations, complete with explanatory comments included for this TIS implementation. Worth noting, however, on Figure 4 and Table 2 are the estimated hard-disk makers stock (Est HD Makers, Eq. 19), along with its associated in and out flows (Eqs 34 and 35). These last three model components help replicate Christensen's (1992) data exactly, with zero error, using the built-in *STEP* function of *iThink*®. This may seem like a futile exercise at the outset, but it helped convince the client of the much larger modeling project than what is shown here that replicating real-life data does not necessarily produce much insight, nor does it help one appreciate a dynamically complex system.

RESULTS

To be useful, model analysis must create insight via coherent explanations of how influential pieces of system structure give rise to performance through time. Figure 6 shows the simulation results for the hard-disk maker population performance, with

Figure 4. Behavior reproduction testing sector

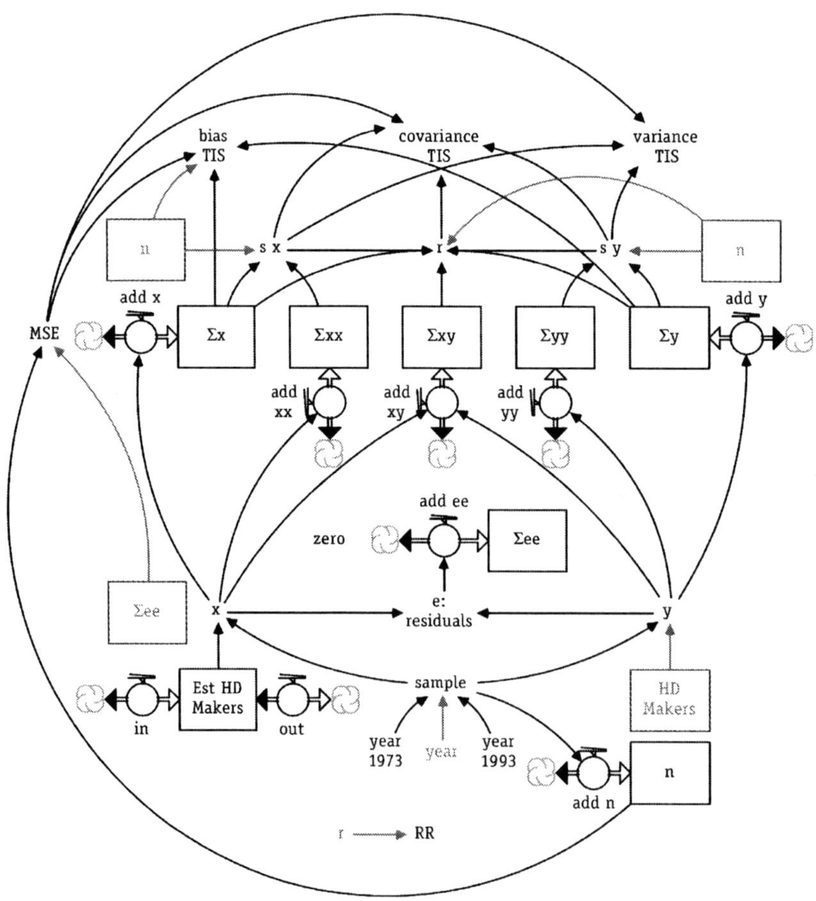

time phases and prominent feedback loops. The Est HD Makers behavior faithfully reproduces the actual HD Makers dynamics without error (Figure 5a). But zero error in behavior pattern reproduction can also mean zero insight for appreciating a dynamically complex system. The HD Makers behavior (line #3 on Figure 5a) provides a less impressive data fit, but the feedback loop web behind its dynamics is where insight lives.

The vertical lines on the time domain output of Figure 5a show five distinct time phases in the HD Makers dynamics, which *Digest®* identified by detecting behavior pattern shifts. Phase I of the HD Makers dynamics on Figure 5a shows reinforcing growth (Figure 2), which lasts for about 4 years. During this time, both the slope (first time derivative) and the curvature (second

Figure 5. Simulation results with time phases and prominent feedback loops

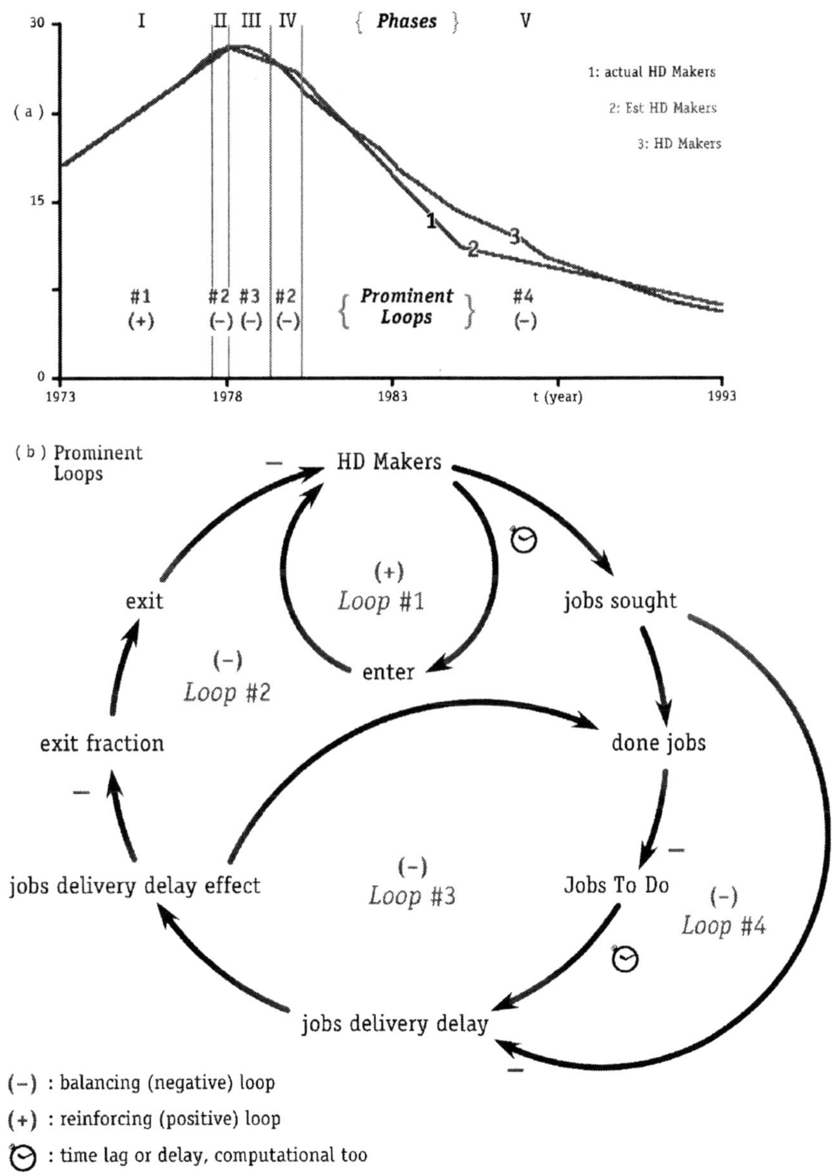

time derivative) of the variable of interest, HD Makers, remain positive. Phase II on Figure 5a shows balancing growth. The slope and curvature of HD Makers have opposite signs in this phase. Phases III and IV show reinforcing decline. And lastly, in its fifth distinct phase (Figure 5a) the HD Makers dynamics shows balancing decline (Figure 2).

In addition to discerning distinct time phases in the dynamics of a variable of interest, *Digest*® also detects and displays the most influential or prominent structures that contribute the most to the selected behavior pattern in each phase. Corresponding to the first phase of the behavior of HD Makers is reinforcing feedback loop #1 of Figure 5b which, according to *Digest*®, is the most prominent loop in generating the reinforcing growth in the HD maker population. Initially, HD Makers attract new hard-disk makers to enter the industry, increasing HD Makers further. By inspecting the model structure on Figure 3, one could identify eleven feedback loops surrounding HD Makers. Using its pathway participation metric, *Digest*® automatically selects reinforcing feedback loop #1 as the most prominent one among all the other loops in the model.

In phase II of the HD Makers dynamics, system control shifts from reinforcing loop #1 to the most influential structure or balancing feedback loop #2 of Figure 5b, associated with the users' Jobs To Do stock. Initially plenty in phase I, users' Jobs To Do now begin to fall, along the pathway that carries the effect of balancing loop #2 to HD Makers. This same structure is also most prominent in phase IV of HD Makers' dynamics.

In phase III of the HD Makers behavior, balancing loop #3 becomes the most influential structure of Figure 5b, associated with the users' Jobs To Do stock and the delivery delay. By phase III, the large HD Makers population causes the done jobs rate to deplete the users' articulated Jobs To Do faster. And the more job delivery delay decreases because of the–by now–large hard-disk maker population, the more it causes the exit fraction to increase, thereby forcing some HD Makers to exit, while preventing new ones from entry.

In phase IV, prominent loop #2 takes over again, now from loop #3, while keeping the users' Jobs To Do stock in focus. In phase V, however, with HD Makers already dropping, prominent loop #4 bypasses the Jobs to Do stock, increasing the jobs delivery delay directly, indirectly causing the exit fraction, and thereby the exit rate of HD Makers, to slow down. Prominent loop #4 remains most influential until the end of the simulation.

In phase II of Figure 5, while trying to explain why HD Makers is generating a balancing growth, it may be easy to spot the role of the balancing

Figure 6. Phase plots of relations among pertinent variables

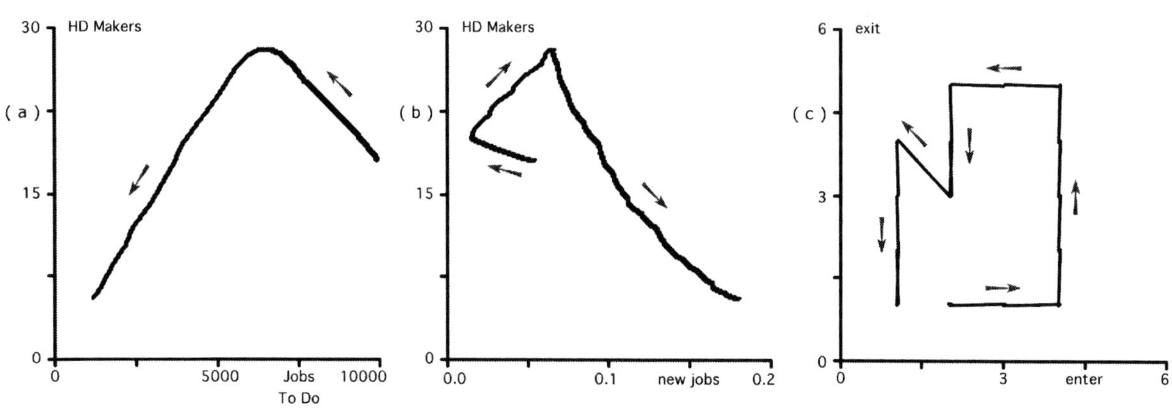

feedback loop that controls the Jobs To Do stock depletion. The users' articulated Jobs To Do is dropping, thereby preventing new hard-disk makers from entry. The subtlety in explaining the behavior of the HD Makers is the subsequent reinforcing decline in HD Makers' dynamics in phase IV. Some novices may even look for reinforcing feedback to explain the reinforcing decline dynamics. But *Digest*® tells that what forces HD Makers to fall faster and faster is exactly the same process that keeps their population at bay. Balancing loop #2, which controls Jobs To Do, prevents new hard-disk makers from entering and, once new entries fall behind those who exit, the HD Makers stock goes into a reinforcing decline.

The relations among select pertinent variables on the phase plots of Figure 6 confirm the above. Polarity changes in all three cases, making it rather impossible to assess such relations with correlation statistics. On Figure 6a, for example, as the users' articulated Jobs To Do decline, HD Makers initially rise and subsequently fall. On Figure 6b, new jobs gradually decrease as the HD Makes stock grows exponentially, then they begin to grow once the HD maker population slows down, i.e., begins to increase at a declining rate but, lastly, they increase even more rapidly once the HD Makes stock decreases.

Behavior Reproduction Test Results

The coefficient of determination, R^2, which measures the variance in the data explained by the model as a dimensionless fraction, is a common statistic used to assess a model's ability to reproduce system behavior. The coefficient of determination is the square of the correlation coefficient, r, which measures the degree to which two series co-vary.

Although widely reported because audiences expect it (Figure 7), R^2 is actually not very useful. Two series with the same error can generate very different R^2 values depending on their trend (Sterman 2000, p. 874). Conversely, Theil's (1966) inequality statistics (TIS) use the mean square error (MSE), which measures the average error between competing data series in the same units as the variable itself and weights large errors more heavily than small ones.

The residual plot of Figure 7a shows an uneven pattern of serially autocorrelated errors, but both the r and the R^2 values are high. And Theil's inequality statistics (Figure 7b and c) do support the model's usefulness. The unequal covariance TIS, U^C, dominates throughout the simulation (Figure 7b), and Figure 7c shows the end TIS values on a vertical bar graph. Most of the MSE fraction is concentrated above U^C, showing that the model captures the mean and trends in the actual data rather well, differing mostly point by point.

Computed Strategic Scenarios

Both academics and managers can benefit from the leading interpretive instruments used in SD model analysis, such as eigenvalues, Theil's (1966) inequality statistics (Oliva, 1995; Sterman, 1984 and 2000) and the pathway participation metric, implemented in the *Digest*® software (Mojtahedzadeh, 1996; Mojtahedzadeh, et al 2004). But SD models also allow computing strategic scenarios of what might happen in the future as well as of what might have been in the past. Both academics and managers again can benefit from the insight such scenarios provide, with respect to the potential effects that changes in environmental and policy parameters and variables might have or might have had on chosen performance variables of interest.

Back to the time domain of Figure 8, the computed strategic scenarios of Figure 8a show, for example, what might have been the effect of increasing the available Jobs To Do stock, i.e., the HD Makers' market size, on the hard-disk maker population. *Ceteris paribus*, a larger market size back in 1973 might have prolonged the reinforcing growth phase of HD Makers, perhaps giving enough time to some of them to respond

Figure 7. Dynamic behavior reproduction test results

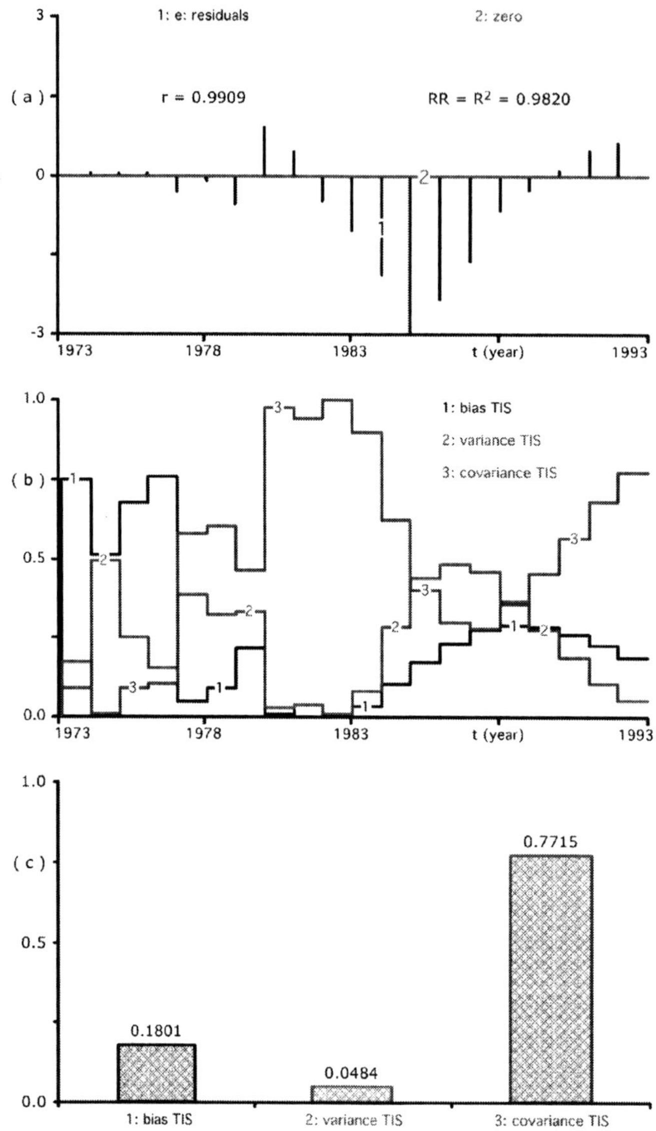

more timely to new entrant firm's DIS. But the assumed structure of relations among variables in the system would still render inevitable the balancing growth phase that followed (Phase II, Figure 5a).

Again *all other things being equal*, less greed on HD Maker's behalf, in terms of the sought-jobs-per-firm-per-year policy parameter (Figure 8b), might have similarly prolonged the Phase I reinforcing growth of Figure 5a, giving time to some HD Makers to develop an effective disruptive innovation response strategy (DIRS). The computed strategic scenarios of Figure 8 show but one example of how academics and managers can benefit from the insight SD models can give them, about the strategic leverage of pertinent strategic performance variables and policy parameters or strategy levers. Choosing which lever to push or pull on and when is crucial for both DIS and DIRS design in IS research and practice.

Figure 8. Strategic scenarios computed with the SD model

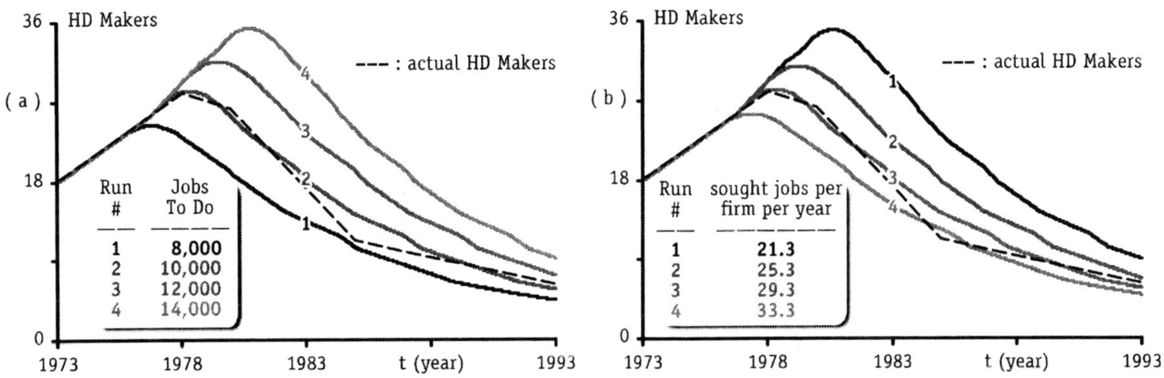

CONCLUSION

In business processes and systems, "randomness is a measure of our ignorance" (Sterman, 2000, p. 127). And Christensen and Raynor (2003) might be right to see disruptive innovation strategies as repeatable processes and not as the products of random events. But have the DIS and DIRS theory proponents used the right tools to help managers understand the circumstances associated with the genesis and distinct dynamics that DIS and DIRS entail?

Purely deterministic, this chapter's SD model is rather useful in explaining the HD Makers dynamics. With four different feedback loops becoming prominent along five distinct time phases, the chapter demonstrates the indispensable role of SD modeling in explaining the hard-disk makers' rise and fall between 1973 and 1993.

It is Mojtahedzadeh's *Digest*®, with its analysis of shifting prominent structure and polarity phases that has helped reveal the model analysis results. Indeed, tools such as PPM can help make sense of the dynamically complex structure of SD models, even if Oliva (2004, p. 331) finds SD keen in understanding system performance, "not structure *per se*", in lieu of its core tenet that system structure causes performance. Undeniably, while looking for *systemic leverage* in strategy making (Georgantzas & Ritchie-Dunham, 2003), modelers do play with structural changes for superior performance. Model analysis tools such as *Digest*® help articulate structural complexity and thereby enable both effective and efficient strategy designs.

The SD model behavior might resemble IS technology industry dynamics beyond the DIS effects in the hard-disk industry. For example, industry overshoot and collapse dynamics have been observed in e-commerce early in this century, when a large number of Internet firms entered the industry and then went out of business (Oliva, Sterman & Giese, 2003). The SD modeling method and tools described here can be extended and used equally well in these diverse contexts and that should be a fruitful direction for future research.

The SD modeling method can provide dynamic leverage insights in the dynamic complexity of information technology markets, and the design, development, implementation and management of IS, DIS and DIRS within organizations. A more extensive adoption of system dynamics method in IS research and practice should be fruitful. To that direction, the chapter authors organized a Workshop with theme "Complex Information System Dynamics" in NYC on June 11 2008. They are also guest-editing a forthcoming *System*

Dynamics Review special issue on "Information Systems Dynamics", aiming to fuse a reinforcing feedback loop that will breed needed high-quality research on complex information systems dynamics.

REFERENCES

Abdel-Hamid, T. and Madnick, S. (1989). Lessons learned from modeling the dynamics of software development. *Communications of the ACM*, 32(12), 1426-1455.

Anthony, S. and Christensen, C. (2004). Forging innovation from disruption. *Optimize*, (Aug) issue 24.

Alfeld, L.E. and Graham, A. (1976). *Introduction to Urban Dynamics*. MIT Press, Cambridge MA. Reprinted by Productivity Press: Portland OR and currently available from Pegasus Communications: Waltham, MA.

Atkinson, G. (2004). Common ground for institutional economics and system dynamics modeling. *System Dynamics Review,* 20(4), 275-286.

Bower, J.L. and Christensen, C. (1995). Disruptive technologies: catching the wave. *Harvard Business Review* (Jan-Feb), 43-53.

Christensen, C.M. (1992). *The Innovator's Challenge: Understanding the Influence of Market Environment on Processes of Technology Development in the Rigid Disk Drive Industry.* Ph.D. Dissertation, Harvard Business School: Boston, MA.

Christensen, C.M. (1997). *The Innovator's Dilemma: When New Technologies Cause Great Firms to Fail.* Harvard Business School Press: Cambridge, MA.

Christensen, C.M., Johnson, M. & Dann, J. (2002). Disrupt and prosper. *Optimize* (Nov), 41-48.

Christensen, C.M. & Raynor, M.E. (2003). *The Innovator's Solution: Creating and Sustaining Successful Growth.* Harvard Business School Press: Boston MA.

Christensen, C.M., Raynor, M.E. & Anthony, S.D. (2003). Six Keys to Creating New-Growth Businesses. *Harvard Management Update* (Jan).

Dutta, A. and Roy, R. (2005). Offshore outsourcing: a dynamic causal model of counteracting forces. *Journal of Management Information Systems,* 22(2), 15-35.

Fontana, M. (2006). Simulation in economics: evidence on diffusion and communication. *Journal of Artificial Societies and Social Simulation,* 9(2) (http://jasss.soc.surrey.ac.uk/9/2/8.html).

Forrester, J.W. (1961). *Industrial Dynamics.* MIT Press: Cambridge, MA.

Forrester, J.W. (2003). Dynamic models of economic systems and industrial organizations. *System Dynamics Review,* 19(4), 331-345.

Forrester, J.W. & Senge, P.M. (1980). Tests for building confidence in system dynamics models. In AA Legasto Jr, JW Forrester and JM Lyneis (Eds), *TIMS Studies in the Management Sciences, Vol. 14: System Dynamics.* North-Holland: New York, NY, pp. 209-228.

Forrester, N. (1983). Eigenvalue analysis of dominant feedback loops. In *Plenary Session Papers Proceedings of the 1st International System Dynamics Society Conference*, Paris, France: 178-202.

Georgantzas, N.C. & Ritchie-Dunham, J.L. (2003). Designing high-leverage strategies and tactics. *Human Systems Management,* 22(1), 217-227.

Georgantzas, N.C. & Katsamakas, E. (2008). *Disruptive service-innovation strategy.* Working Paper, Fordham University, New York, NY.

Gharajedaghi, J. (1999). *Systems Thinking: Managing Chaos and Complexity: A Platform for Designing Business Architecture*. Butterworth-Heinemann: Boston MA.

Gonçalves, P., Lerpattarapong, C. and Hines, J.H. (2000). Implementing formal model analysis. In *Proceedings of the 18th International System Dynamics Society Conference*, August 6-10, Bergen, Norway.

Hill, C.W.L. & Jones,G.R. (1998). *Strategic Management: An Integrated Approach*. Houghton Mifflin: Boston, MA.

Kampmann, C.E. (1996). Feedback loops gains and system behavior. In *Proceedings of the 12th International System Dynamics Society Conference*, July 21-25, Cambridge, MA.

Kanungo, S. (2003). Using system dynamics to operationalize process theory in information systems research. *Proceedings of the* 24th *International Conference on Information Systems*, 450-463.

Katsamakas, E. & Georgantzas, N. (2008). *Open source disruptive innovation strategies*. Working Paper, Fordham University, New York, NY.

Lyytinen, K. & Rose, G. (2003a). The disruptive nature of Information Technology innovations: the case of internet computing in systems development organizations. *MIS Quarterly,* 27(4), 557-595.

Lyytinen, K. & Rose, G. (2003b). Disruptive information system innovation: the case of internet computing. *Information Systems Journal*, 13, 301-330.

Meadows, D.H. (1989). System dynamics meets the press. *System Dynamics Review,* 5(1), 68-80.

Mojtahedzadeh, M.T. (1996). *A Path Taken: Computer-Assisted Heuristics for Understanding Dynamic Systems*. Ph.D. Dissertation. Rockefeller College of Public Affairs and Policy, SUNY: Albany NY.

Mojtahedzadeh. M.T., Andersen, D. & Richardson, G.P. (2004). Using *Digest*® to implement the pathway participation method for detecting influential system structure. *System Dynamics Review,* 20(1), 1-20.

Morecroft, J.D.W. (1985). Rationality in the analysis of behavioral simulation models, *Management Science,* 31, 900-916.

Oliva, R. (2004). Model structure analysis through graph theory: partition heuristics and feedback structure decomposition. *System Dynamics Review,* 20(4), 313-336.

Oliva, R. (1994). *A Vensim Module to Calculate Summary Statistics for Historical Fit*. MIT System Dynamics Group D-4584.

Oliva, R. & Mojtahedzadeh, M.T. (2004). Keep it simple: a dominance assessment of short feedback loops. In *Proceedings of the 22nd International System Dynamics Society Conference*, July 25-29, Keble College, Oxford University, Oxford UK.

Oliva, R., Sterman, J.D. & Giese, M. (2003). Limits to growth in the new economy: exploring the 'get big fast' strategy in e-commerce. *System Dynamics Review,* 19(2), 83-117.

Paich, M. & Sterman, J.D. (1993). Boom, bust and failures to learn in experimental markets. *Management Science,* 39(12), 1439-1458.

Raynor, M.E. (2007). *The Strategy Paradox*. Currency-Doubleday: New York, NY.

Repenning, N.P. (2002). A simulation-based approach to understanding the dynamics of innovation implementation. *Organization Science,* 13(2), 109-127.

Repenning, N.P. (2003). Selling system dynamics to (other) social scientists. *System Dynamics Review,* 19(4), 303-327.

Richardson, G.P. (1991). *Feedback Thought in Social Science and Systems Theory.* University of Pennsylvania Press: Philadelphia, PA.

Richardson, G.P. (1995). Loop polarity, loop prominence, and the concept of dominant polarity. *System Dynamics Review,* 11(1), 67-88.

Richmond, B. (1993). Systems thinking: critical thinking skills for the 1990s and beyond. *System Dynamics Review,* 9(2), 113-133.

Richmond. B. et al. (2006). *iThink® Software* (*version* 9). iSee Systems™: Lebanon NH.

Sastry, M.A. (1997). Problems and paradoxes in a model of punctuated organizational change. *Administrative Science Quarterly,* 42(2), 237-275.

Senge, P. et al.(1994). *The Fifth Discipline Fieldbook*, Currency-Doubleday: New York, NY.

Sterman, J.D. (1989). Modeling managerial behavior: misperceptions of feedback in a dynamic decision making experiment. *Management Science*, 35(3), 321-339.

Sterman, J.D. (1994). Beyond training wheels. In *The Fifth Discipline Fieldbook*, Senge P. et al, Currency-Doubleday: New York, NY.

Sterman, J.D. (2000). *Business Dynamics: Systems Thinking and Modeling for a Complex World.* Irwin McGraw-Hill: Boston, MA.

Sterman, J.D. (1984). Appropriate summary statistics for evaluating the historical fit of system dynamics models. *Dynamica,* 10(Winter), 51-66.

Theil, H. (1966). *Applied Economic Forecasting.* Elsevier Science (North Holland): New York, NY.

Tirole, J. (1988). *The Theory of Industrial Organization.* MIT Press: Cambridge, MA.

Tushman, M.L. & Anderson, P. (1986). Technological discontinuities and organizational environments. *Administrative Science Quarterly,* 31, 439-465.

Unsworth, K. (2001). Unpacking creativity. *Academy of Management Review,* 26, 289-297.

Veryzer, R.W. (1998). Discontinuous innovation and the new product development process. *Journal of Product Innovation Management,* 15(2), 136-150.

APPENDIX

Table 1. Hard-disk (HD) makers' population and users' jobs-to-do sector equations

Stock or Level (State) Variable ({·} = comments and/or units)	***Equation #***
*HD Makers(t) = HD Makers(t - dt) + (enter - exit) * dt*	(1)
INIT HD Makers = 18 {unit: firm}	(1.1)
*Jobs To Do(t) = Jobs To Do(t - dt) + (new jobs – done jobs) * dt*	(2)
INIT Jobs To Do = TIME / job articulation fraction {unit: job}	(2.1)
Flows or Rate Variables	
*done jobs = jobs delivery delay effect * jobs sought* {unit: job / year}	(3)
*enter = ROUND (STEP (HD Makers * empirical growth fraction * annual shortage of jobs effect, TIME))* {unit: firm / year}	(4)
*exit = ROUND (STEP (HD Makers * exit fraction, TIME))* {unit: firm / year}	(5)
*new jobs = 1 - job articulation fraction * (Jobs To Do - done jobs) / TIME* {unit: job / year}	(6)
Auxiliary Parameters and Converter Variables	
empirical growth fraction = 0.1385 {unit: 1 / year}	(7)
*exit fraction = (1.048 - jobs delivery delay effect * annual shortage of jobs effect)* {unit: 1 / year}	(8)
jobs delivery delay = Jobs To Do / jobs sought {unit: year}	(9)
jobs fraction = 0.103 {unit: 1 / year}	(10)
jobs sought per firm per year = 29.3 {unit: job / firm / year}	(11)
shortage of jobs ratio = done jobs / jobs sought {unit: unitless}	(12)
*jobs sought = HD Makers * jobs sought per firm per year* {unit: job / year}	(13)
year = 1 {Data time interval (i.e., unit: year)}	(14)
actual HD Makers = GRAPH(TIME {Christensen's (1992) HD Makers data}) (1973, 18.0), (1974, 20.0), (1975, 22.0), (1976, 24.0), (1977, 26.0), (1978, 28.0), (1979, 27.0), (1980, 26.0), (1981, 23.0), (1982, 20.0), (1983, 17.0), (1984, 14.0), (1985, 11.0), (1986, 10.4), (1987, 9.75), (1988, 9.12), (1989, 8.50), (1990, 7.88), (1991, 7.25), (1992, 6.62), (1993, 6.00)	(15)
annual shortage of jobs effect = GRAPH(shortage of jobs ratio / year {unit: 1 / year}) (0.00, 0.00), (0.1, 0.06), (0.2, 0.14), (0.3, 0.255), (0.4, 0.395), (0.5, 0.535), (0.6, 0.685), (0.7, 0.825), (0.8, 0.92), (0.9, 0.98), (1, 1.00)	(16)
jobs delivery delay effect = GRAPH(jobs fraction * jobs delivery delay {unit: unitless}) (0.00, 0.00), (0.1, 0.06), (0.2, 0.14), (0.3, 0.255), (0.4, 0.395), (0.5, 0.535), (0.6, 0.685), (0.7, 0.825), (0.8, 0.92), (0.9, 0.98), (1, 1.00)	(17)
job articulation fraction = GRAPH(TIME {unit: 1 / year}) (1973, 0.197), (1974, 0.221), (1975, 0.237), (1976, 0.259), (1977, 0.287), (1978, 0.325), (1979, 0.369), (1980, 0.416), (1981, 0.468), (1982, 0.527), (1984, 0.593), (1985, 0.667), (1986, 0.75), (1987, 0.844), (1988, 0.949), (1989, 1.07), (1990, 1.20), (1991, 1.35), (1992, 1.52), (1993, 1.71)	(18)

Table 2. Behavior reproduction testing sector equations

Stock or Level (State) Variable ({·} = comments and/or units)	*Equation #*
*Est HD Makers(t) = Est HD Makers(t - dt) + (in - out) * dt; INIT Est HD Makers = 18* {unit: firm}	(19)
*∑ee(t) = ∑ee(t - dt) + (add ee) * dt; INIT ∑ee = 0*	(20)
*∑x(t) = ∑x(t - dt) + (add x) * dt; INIT ∑x = 0* {Cumulative sum of the actual data}	(21)
*∑xx(t) = ∑xx(t - dt) + (add xx) * dt; INIT ∑xx = 0* {Cumulative sum of the squared actual data}	(22)
*∑xy(t) = ∑xy(t - dt) + (add xy) * dt; INIT ∑xy = 0* {Cumulative sum of the xy product}	(23)
*∑y(t) = ∑y(t - dt) + (add y) * dt; INIT ∑y = 0* {Cumulative sum of the simulated data}	(24)
*∑yy(t) = ∑yy(t - dt) + (add yy) * dt; INIT ∑yy = 0* {Cumulative sum of the squared simulated data}	(25)
*n(t) = n(t - dt) + (add n) * dt; INIT n = 1e-9* {The current count n of data points}	(26)
Flows or Rate Variables	
add ee = e: residuals^2 / DT {Adds to the sum of squared errors between actual and simulated data}	(27)
add n = sample / DT {Increments n, i.e., adds one to the number of observations}	(28)
add x = x / DT {Adds to the cumulative sum of the actual data}	(29)
add xx = x^2 / DT {Adds to the sum of the squared actual data}	(30)
*add xy = x * y / DT* {Adds to the cumulative sum of the xy product of actual and simulated data}	(31)
add y = y / DT {Adds to the cumulative sum of the simulated data}	(32)
add yy = y^2 / DT {Adds to the cumulative sum of the squared simulated data}	(33)
in = STEP(2, 1973) - STEP(2, 1978) {unit: firm / year}	(34)
out = STEP(1, 1978) - STEP(1, 1980) + STEP(3, 1980) - STEP(3, 1985) + STEP(0.625, 1985) - STEP(0.625, 1993) {unit: firm / year}	(35)
Auxiliary Parameters and Converter Variables	
bias TIS = ((∑x / n) - (∑y / n))^2 / (1e-9 + MSE) {The unequal bias Theil inequality statistic (TIS) is the MSE fraction caused by unequal means of the actual and simulated data}	(36)
covariance TIS = (2 * s x * s y * (1 - r)) / (1e-9 + MSE) {The unequal covariance Theil inequality statistic (TIS) is the MSE fraction caused by imperfect correlation between actual and simulated data}	(37)
e: residuals = x – y {The difference between sampled actual and simulated data}	(38)
MSE = ∑ee / n {The mean squared error between actual and simulated data}	(39)
*r = ((∑xy / n) - (∑x / n) * (∑y / n)) / (s x * s y + 1e-9)* {The correlation between x and y}	(40)
RR = r^2 {The coefficient of determination R^2 is the square of the correlation coefficient}	(41)
s x = SQRT ((∑xx / n) - (∑x / n)^2) {The standard deviation of x}	(42)
s y = SQRT ((∑yy / n) - (∑y / n)^2) {The standard deviation of y}	(43)
sample = PULSE (DT, year 1973, year) * (STEP (1, year 1973) - STEP (1, year 1993 + DT / 2)) {Sterman (2000, Ch. 21 + CD) suggests sampling once a year between in order to compare actual and simulation data only where actual data exist}	(44)
variance TIS = (s x - s y)^2 / (1e-9 + MSE) {The unequal variance Theil inequality statistic (TIS) is the MSE fraction caused by the unequal variance of actual and simulated data}	(45)
*x = sample * Est HD Makers* {The actual data sampled}	(46)
*y = sample * HD Makers* {The simulated data sampled}	(47)
year 1973 = 1973 {The data start time}	(48)
Year 1993 = 1993 {The data end time}	(49)
Zero = 0 {This plots a horizontal line at the origin of the y axis in the time domain}	(50)

Chapter XIV
Modeling Customer-Related IT Diffusion

Shana L. Dardan
Susquehanna University, USA

Ram L. Kumar
University of North Carolina at Charlotte, USA

Antonis C. Stylianou
University of North Carolina at Charlotte, USA

ABSTRACT

This study develops a diffusion model of customer-related IT (CRIT) based on stock market announcements of investments in those technologies. Customer-related IT investments are defined in this work as information technology investments made with the intention of improving or enhancing the customer experience. The diffusion model developed in our study is based on data for the companies of the S&P 500 and S&P MidCap 400 for the years of 1996-2001. We find empirical support for a sigmoid diffusion model. Further, we find that both the size and industry of the company affect the path of CRIT diffusion. Another contribution of this study is to illustrate how data collection techniques typically used for financial event studies can be used to study information technology diffusion. Finally, the data collected for this study can serve as a Bayesian prior for future diffusion forecasting studies of CRIT.

INTRODUCTION

Customer-Related IT (CRIT) investments are defined as information technology investments made with the intention of improving or enhancing the customer experience. CRIT investments are specifically chosen because of the customer-focus employed by many companies, and the overwhelming need for companies in general to increase customer satisfaction. Technologies that make the customer's experience with the company better include among others CRM software, wireless technology, and data mining-enabled profiles for e-Commerce. Given that our intent is to study the broad phenomenon of investing IT dollars to improve the customer experience, we believe that, as found by Fichman (2001), studying an aggregated set of innovations would lead to more robust and generalizable results. Our reasoning is also consistent with other lines of research that have studied the diffusion of broad phenomena or aggregated technologies, such as IT outsourcing (e.g., Loh and Venkatraman, 1992; Hu et al., 1997) and telecommunication technologies (e.g., Grover and Goslar, 1993).

We propose that, as companies see for themselves how IT can benefit their relationship with their customers, they tend to invest more in IT-related technologies. Early adopters depend more heavily on the media, which is the communications channel for the external model (Rogers, 1995). Since we primarily studied the investment into "relatively" newer technologies for the period studied (e.g., Internet, CRM, etc), it is reasonable to deduce that firms investing into CRIT are early adopters. Therefore, this work hypothesizes that the diffusion of customer-related IT investments follows an external influence sigmoidal (or logistics) curve. This is consistent with recent work done by Ranganathan et al (2004), who used an external influence curve to model SCM adoption between companies.

According to Rogers (1995), the size of a company is also positively related to innovator characteristics and thus diffusion influence. Tornatzky and Fleisher (1990) further suggest that the size of a company is not a determinant for innovativeness, so much as it (size) is a proxy for other constructs that are positively related with innovativeness. These variables include wealth, specialization and slack resources. Indeed, according to Hunter (2003), larger firms tend to purchase innovative technologies earlier and "force" smaller companies to also invest in the technology for survival. If this is true, then characteristics such as size, innovativeness, and financial stability should change the diffusion path for those companies. This research tested whether the investment in Customer-Related Information Technologies follows a diffusion path, and whether that path is affected by industry type and firm size.

The study has additional importance in that its data set can serve as a Bayesian prior longitudinal data set that will enable technology companies to better forecast how and when other investments would be made into customer-related information technologies (Sultan et al., 1990).

BACKGROUND

Technology innovation and the investment into technologies by firms have been touted as a driving force in organizational competitiveness and even as the key driver of future competitive capability (Fichman, 1999). The diffusion of CRIT is affected both by the characteristics of the technology and by the characteristics of the firm using it (Rogers, 1995 and Fichman, 1999). Diffusion models are attitude change models, and the basis of these types of models is that consumers follow a rational decision-making or problem-solving approach in their actions that is not always linear (Robertson, 1970). Examples of diffusion models are the Sigmoidal Curve (or Logistics Curve), the Bass Model and the Survival Curve (Bass, 1969; Bauer, 1964; and Pindyck and Rubinfeld, 1998). Based on different assumptions about communication channels or influence sources, diffusion models have been classified into three fundamental types: internal, external, and mixed (Mahajan and Peterson, 1985).

Recent literature on technology diffusion and the effect of firm characteristics on that diffusion process has shown that technology investment follows a diffusion path and is affected by such things as market share, economic health, and consumer loyalty (Kreamer et al., 2002). E-commerce, for example, was found to follow a diffusion path designated by the Bass model and the process of diffusion was found to be affected by such things as policy, the overall technology environment, and the imitation coefficient (Akura and Kemal, 2002). Diffusion of information technology in general was found to be affected by the freedom of goods and capital as well as country and regional specifics (Forman et al., 2002; Kraemer et al., 2002; Kshetri and Dholakia, 2002). As noted in Table 1 (adapted from Shih et al., 2002, and Foreman et al., 2002), recent literature has found that use of technologies over time follows the diffusion pattern.

Customer-Related IT Investments

A CRIT investment is defined in this work as an information technology investment made with the intention of improving or enhancing the customer experience. This definition is intentionally broad as it is possible to enhance the customer experience in many ways. Each technology chosen to be included has been referenced in prior research as a technology that improves the customer experience in some way.

HYPOTHESES

This work proposes that the announcements of customer-related IT investments, which reflect the demand for those investments, will follow a logistics curve over time. However, it is intuitive that firms that are structurally different will invest in IT at different rates. This difference is due to the need and capability of investing in large CRIT projects.

We study the impact of two specific firm differentiators: size and core competency to determine the impact those factors have on the diffusion path. We expect that firms with a core competency of customer service will be driven to invest in customer-related technologies more quickly than manufacturing firms. For customer

Table 1. Recent technology innovation diffusion studies

Study	Item	Diffusion Path
Shih et al. (2002)	IT Investment	varies by country
Forman et al. 2002	Internet use	varies by industry and region
Kraemer et al. (2002)	e-commerce	varies by the technology environment and policy
Cenk (2002)	Electronic Market Pricing	varies by loyalty of customer
Green et al. (2002)	Technology	affected by economic freedom, but not human capital
Akura and Kemal (2002)	B2B, B2C e-commerce	varies significantly by imitation, but not by innovation
Wolfgang (2002)	Technological knowledge spillovers	varies by language and distance
Kshetri and Dholakia (2002)	B2B e-commerce:	varies by the determinants of : freedom of movement of goods, capital, etc. and country specifics
Hu et al. (1997)	IT Outsourcing	mixed influence.
Loh and Venkatraman (1992)	IT Outsourcing	mixed influence.

service oriented firms, customer-related IT can provide a competitive advantage when introduced quickly, and before competitors have had a chance to acquire the technology. Manufacturing firms, on the other hand, are expected to make the CRIT investments later in the development cycle, since customer service is not a primary focus.

We also propose that there will be a difference in the timing of investments into CRIT between large and midsize companies. This difference in investing is due to the inherent structural and financial differences between large and mid-sized companies, and thus the perception of the value of the investment. The larger and more financially stable the firm, the less risky an IT investment. That is, a firm's capitalization may affect the timing of a CRIT investment merely by its ability to make the more risky early investment into CRIT. Although there was some disagreement in literature about the effect of firm size on IT adoption, larger firms will be more likely to adopt IT due to their financial resources and risk tolerance (Patterson et al, 2003; Lee 2006).

Hypothesis 1: Announcements of customer-related IT investments will follow a logistic diffusion path.

Hypothesis 2: The rate and intercept of the logistic diffusion path for the news announcements of customer-related IT investments will vary between large and midsize firms.

Hypothesis 3: The rate and intercept of the logistic diffusion path for the news announcements of customer-related IT investments will vary between firms in the manufacturing sector and firms in the service sector.

Figure 1A shows two diffusion curves with different intercepts and Figure 1B shows curves with different slopes.

We use the Mithas et al (2002) definition of service firms as those that conduct customer-related businesses in the hospitality, airline, and financial services sectors; and manufacturing firms are defined as those that create durable and non-durable goods. This division of firms as manufacturing or service follows that of the American Consumer Satisfaction Index (ACSI) maintained and researched by the University of Michigan. For the purpose of differentiating between midsize and large firms, we utilize the Standard and Poor and define the midsize firm as a publicly traded firm within the S&P MidCap

Figure 1. Diffusion path

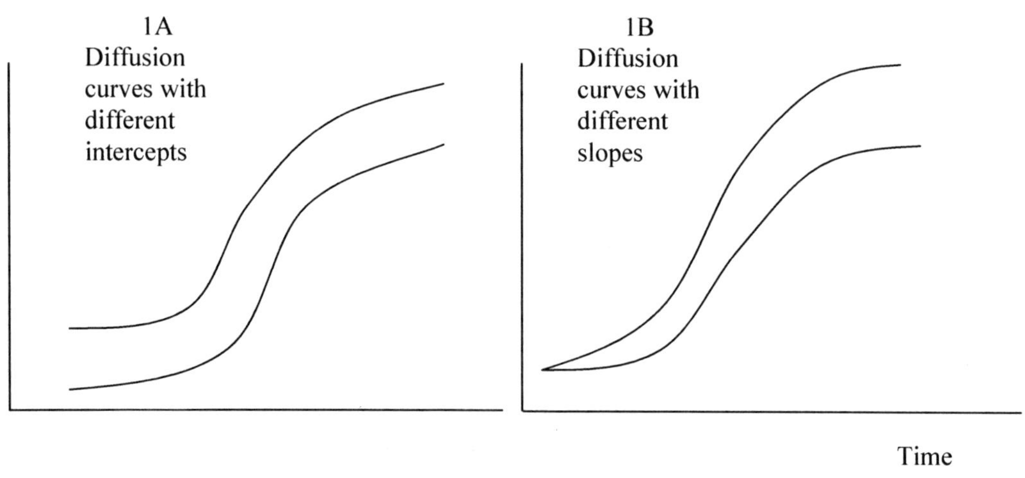

400 and a large firm as a publicly traded company listed in the S&P 500. The Standard and Poor differentiates between these two lists by market capitalization.

METHODOLOGY

Data

Firms were chosen for this study from both the S&P 500 and the S&P MidCap 400 due to the diversity of firm size and characteristics inherent in the group, as well as the fact that these firms are all traded in United States equity markets. Furthermore, the large sampling associated with 500 large firms and 400 mid-sized firms ensures a uniquely complex and complete data set. CRIT investment announcements were gathered from the period of January 1996 through December 2001, a time frame that enabled the capture of the significant rising and falling market trends in our analysis. The news announcements of CRIT investments were used as a surrogate for actual investment in customer-related information technologies. The data set consists of 24 longitudinal (quarterly) data points over the period of six years. The diversity of the firms contained in this data set, as depicted in Table 2, enables generalization and inference ability from the results. This study examined these firms' announcements of IT investments used to enhance customer service. This examination was done by gathering announcements published in the business news media using all news sources (e.g., PR Newswire and Business Wire) within the LexisNexis academic search engine.

The search string was developed following the structure used by Hu at al. (1997), Loh and Venkatraman (1992), Im et al. (2001) and Dardan and Stylianou (2001). The structure of these search strings contains the company name, the company ticker symbol, the verb representing the action of the announcement, and the noun of the technology being discussed. In addition, we included the noun: "customer" to ensure that the customer-focus was captured. This search string was then checked using the companies: Bank of America, Alcoa, AT&T, and Intel to ensure that all expected announcements were returned by the search string. The final string is shown in Figure 2.

The search string was applied to each of the S&P 500 and S&P MidCap 400 firms for the years of 1996-2001. This process yielded thousands of announcements. In classifying news announcements as CRIT investments events, we sorted the announcements by the individuals who initiated the announcements. An announcement was included in the study if it was made by the firm or its public relations company, acting as agent. Following Dardan and Stylianou (2001), announcements were not included in the study if they were made by another company. Then, each announcement was read in its entirety to confirm that it met the definition of a CRIT investment (i.e., IT investment made with the intention of enhancing the customer experience).

Hu at al. (1997) and Loh and Venkatraman (1992) also used keywords to search databases of IT outsourcing articles/announcements. The data collection procedure used in this study is distinguished by (a) the use of a more comprehensive and generally accepted data base of announcements, i.e., NexisLexis; and (b) the use of a rigorous and sophisticated method of developing the search string and validating the search results, which can be used to collect data on relatively complex phenomena.

This method of data collection can be considered a surrogate for obtaining primary (self reported) data through an interview or questionnaire. As a result of the direct data source, we can have a higher level of confidence about the accuracy of the data. The use of firm announcements of investment into a CRIT is offered as an innovative alternative to, and as a surrogate for, actual demand data. It is used in this work because the actual demand data for the S&P 500

Table 2. Customer-related IT announcements

Quarter	Number of MidCap Firm Announcements (30 firms)	Number of Large Firm Announcements (80 firms)	Number of Service Firm Announcements (58 firms)	Number of Manufacturing Firm Announcements (52 firms)	Total Number of Announcements (110 firms)
q1 1996	1	10	7	4	11
q2 1996		7	6	1	7
q3 1996	4	2	2	4	6
q4 1996		3	0	3	3
q1 1997		6	3	3	6
q2 1997		5	1	4	5
q3 1997		5	4	1	5
q4 1997		8	5	3	8
q1 1998	1	6	4	3	7
q2 1998		8	3	5	8
q3 1998		6	4	2	6
q4 1998	1	9	6	4	10
q1 1999	3	6	6	3	9
q2 1999	1	18	11	8	19
q3 1999	5	9	7	7	14
q4 1999	5	23	15	13	28
q1 2000	5	18	9	14	23
q2 2000	4	27	21	10	31
q3 2000	8	23	15	16	31
q4 2000	6	25	20	11	31
q1 2001	2	14	9	7	16
q2 2001	5	15	15	5	20
q3 2001	4	10	8	6	14
q4 2001	2	17	12	7	19
Column Totals	51	280	193	144	337

Figure 2. Search string

(([Company Name] launches) **OR** ([Company Name] announces) **OR** ([Company Name] invests) **OR** ([Company Name] installs) **OR** ([Company Name] develops)) **AND** (Customer) **AND** (Information Technology **OR** Information System **OR** Data **OR** Customer Relationship Management **OR** Supply Chain Management **OR** Demand Chain Management **OR** Decision Support System **OR** Expert Information System **OR** Expert System **OR** Enterprise Resource Planning **OR** Internet **OR** Intranet **OR** Client-Server System **OR** Broadband **OR** Pocket PC **OR** Database **OR** Datamining OR Wireless OR Mobile) **AND** (NYSE **OR** NASDAQ **OR** AMEX **OR** OTC) and S&P MidCap 400 firms may be difficult or expensive to obtain. While this method has limitations, namely that we are aware of investments only if the company publicly announces them, the method is robust in its availability and in its use in financial research such as event studies.

The final data sample consisted of 337 announcements made by 110 firms. The number of announcements per period per adopter group studied is outlined in Table 2.

Model

This research hypothesizes that the investment path of CRIT investments will vary by types of manufacturing and service industries and firm size. The regression model used is a standard nonlinear logistics curve, which enables the forecast of how these and similar future technologies will be purchased.

The model for Innovation Diffusion follows an S-Curve, or a Sigmoidal Curve, represented mathematically by the Logistics Curve (Rogers, 1995; and Pindyck and Rubinfeld, 1998). This model is given by:

$$y_t = e^{k_1 - (k_2/t)}$$

where k_1 and k_2 are parameters, and t is time (Pindyck and Rubinfeld, 1998).

The benefit in using this S-curve model is that it can easily be transformed into a linear model using a logarithmic function. Having linear parameters allows the estimation of the model using standard regression techniques. Therefore:

$$\ln y_t = k_1 - \frac{k_2}{t}$$

Based on Rogers (1995), earlier adopters depend more heavily on the media, which is the communications channel for the external model. Since we primarily studied the investment into "relatively" newer technologies (e.g., Internet, CRM, etc), it is reasonable to consider that our firms are early adopters. Therefore, we used an external influence diffusion model, i.e., the diffusion process is driven primarily by external media communications. This model estimation is limited if there are substantial internal communication channels. The comparison of an internal/external model with this is left as future research.

MODEL ESTIMATION AND RESULTS

A visual test for outliers in the data was done, following Maddala (1992), through a data plot of each data set. There were no outliers observed in the data plot. Table 3 contains the estimation of the model parameters without adjusting for autocorrelation.

Heteroskedasticity

An initial test for heteroskedasticity (the violation of the assumption that the error variances are constant) was done through a visual test of the residual plots. This initial analysis follows Maddala (1992). As there was evidence of a systematic pattern within the residuals, White's test was performed on each of the regression models. Table 4 shows the p-value of the chi-square statistic associated with White's test of the hypothesis of homoskedasticity. In each of the cases, the assumption of homoskedasticity was not rejected. In keeping with econometric tradition, the White's adjusted standard errors are also displayed in Table 4.

Autocorrelation

Autocorrelation, or the violation of the assumption that error terms are independent, was tested using the Augmented Dickey-Fuller test and confirmed through a visual test of the Partial Autocorrelations. Evidence of white noise autocorrelation was prevalent throughout all of the models (p-value of

Table 3. Model estimation: Unadjusted for autocorrelation

Regression	Model Estimation	Adjusted R-Square	F Statistic	P-Value	DW
Full	$\hat{y}_t = e^{5.03-(3.616/t)}$	0.5576	29.84	1.73 x 10^{-05}	0.2121
MidCap	$\hat{y}_t = e^{3.042-(4.135/t)}$	0.519	25.79	4.35 x 10^{-05}	0.3935
Large	$\hat{y}_t = e^{4.88-(3.56/t)}$	0.5574	29.97	1.68 x 10^{-05}	0.2145
Service	$\hat{y}_t = e^{4.436-(3.57/t)}$	0.554	29.56	1.84 x 10^{-05}	0.1842
Manufacturing	$\hat{y}_t = e^{4.24-(3.94/t)}$	0.6248	39.30	2.61 x 10^{-06}	0.3735
All Parameter Estimates Significant to 99% on a Two-Tail Test.					

Table 4. White's test for heteroskedasticity

Model	Intercept Estimate (White's Adjusted Se)	1/t Estimate (White's Adjusted Se)	White's Test p-value
Full	5.03 (0.1723)	3.616 (0.87304)	0.6229
MidCap	3.04 (0.2156)	4.135 (1.02)	0.3082
Large	4.879 (0.1676)	3.56 (0.8703)	0.5599
Service	4.436 (0.1676)	3.57 (0.8207)	0.6442
Manufacturing	4.24 (0.1655)	3.94 (0.9717)	0.219

0.0001 for each of the Chi-Square values). This finding rejects the null hypothesis of no autocorrelation in the residuals. Following Dickey (2002), the white noise autocorrelation was corrected using the PROC AUTOREG procedure in SAS with the back-step initialized at lag six. In all models, either the Augmented Dickey-Fuller Unit Root test or a visual test of the Partial Autocorrelation function found a significant trend lag at lag one. These models were differenced using the Hindreth-Lu procedure as outlined by Pindyck and Rubinfeld (1998). Upon differencing the Manufacturing model, the PROC AUTOREG did not require the addition of a residual lag for adjustment for white noise. The resulting ρ (rho) value for each of the models is noted in Table 5.

The three hypotheses were tested after the models were adjusted for autocorrelation.

Announcements of CRIT investments were found to follow a sigmoidal diffusion curve. Further, the diffusion path was found to vary by type of firm and firm size, and each of the hypotheses was supported.

Hypothesis #2 stated that the rate and intercept of the logistic diffusion path for the news announcements of customer-related IT investments would vary between large and midsize firms. A standard t-test for the stability of means of the rate of diffusion on time was used to analyze the moderating effect of firm size. In a one-tail test, *this hypothesis was accepted* at 99% after the Hindreth-Lu transformation and estimation. It was further found that *the intercepts for the*

Table 5. Hindreth-Lu and PROC AUTOREG model estimation

Regression Estimates	Intercept (Se)	1/t (Se)	Residual Lag (Se)	Total Adjusted R-Square
Full (ρ = 0.4)	3.3597*** (0.1382)	6.9218*** (1.1489)	-0.8409*** (0.121)	0.9737
MidCap (ρ = 0.2)	3.359*** (0.4011)	8.6527*** (1.537)	-0.8618*** (0.11343)	0.9283
Large (ρ = 0.4)	3.389*** (0.1218)	12.2*** (1.706)	-0.732*** (0.1523)	0.9631
Service (ρ = 0.4)	3.1686*** (0.1333)	12.806*** (1.9437)	-0.6563*** (0.1687)	0.9405
Manufacturing (ρ = 0.3)	3.666*** (0.1097)	18.2635*** (1.7177)	No Lag	0.8433
*** = *99% significance*				

Figure 3. Regression estimate of all customer-related IT investments

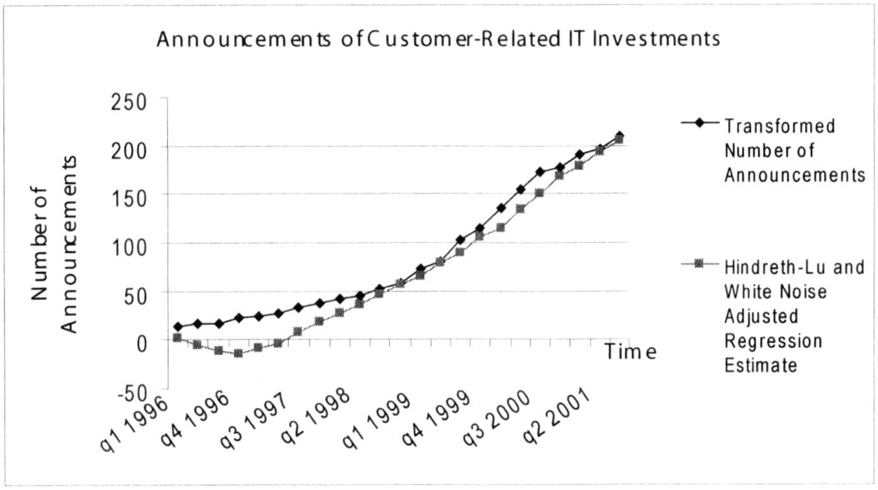

large companies were statistically greater than mid-sized companies to 99%. Figure 3 contains the data plots of both the Hindreth-Lu transformed regression estimate, and of the actual data for the entire sample of CRIT investment announcements. Figure 4 shows the data and regression estimate plots for the large and midsize firms.

Hypothesis #3 stated that the rate and intercept of the logistic diffusion path for the news announcements of customer-related IT investments would vary between firms in the manufacturing sector and firms in the service sector. A standard t-test for the stability of means of the rate of diffusion on time was used to analyze the moderating effect of firm type. After transformation, in a two-tail test, *both the intercept and the rate of diffusion were found to be significantly different between service and manufacturing firms* at a significance of 99%. It was also found that *manufacturing firms had both a greater intercept and a greater rate of diffusion than did service firms.* This is consistent with research done by Zhao et al. (2002), who found that increased competition

Figure 4. Regression estimates by firm size

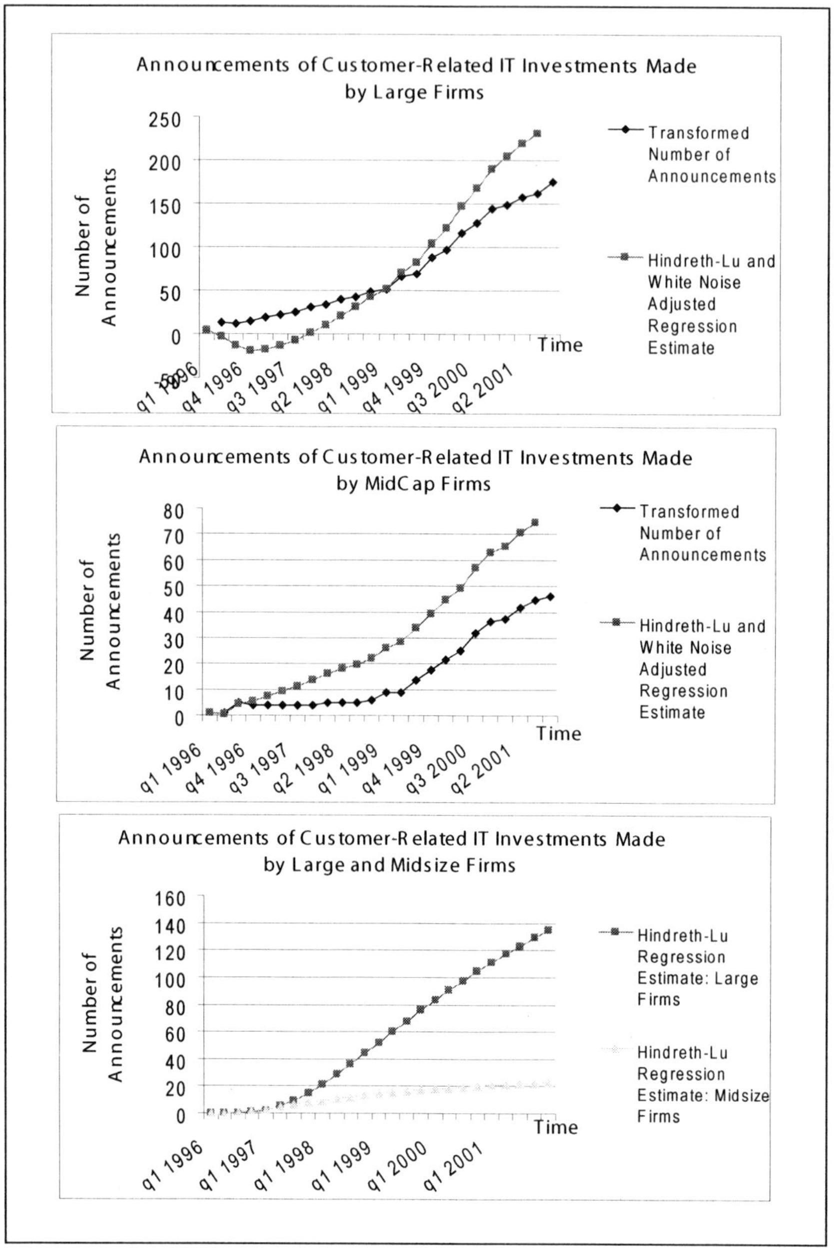

among manufacturing firms was driving the push for better customer service.

While the use of public announcements of information technology investment is a good surrogate for demand data, there is a possible limitation of a self-selection bias inherent in the methodology. That is, the only investment choices that we are aware of are those that the company chooses to disclose. It is possible that larger companies are more predisposed to making public announcements in general, and possibly specifically to an announcement that reflects the expenditure of a significant amount of money on an information technology. Further, the size of a

Figure 5. Regression estimates by industry

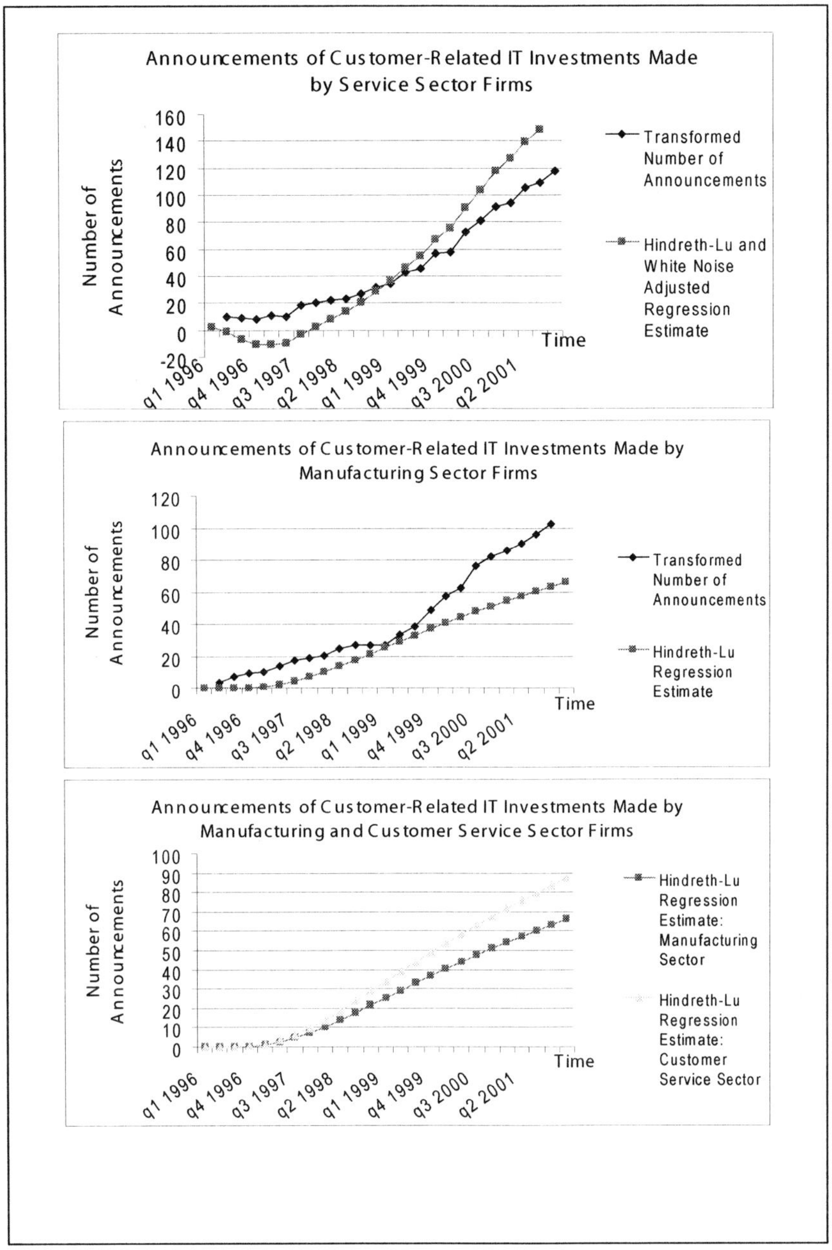

firm was designated through the Standard and Poor measures. Had we used a more detailed assessment of company size and moderated for such things as IT department size and funding, it is possible that we may have found a more complex understanding of the impact of firm size on adoption behavior. Figure 5 shows the data and regression estimate plots by industry.

CONCLUSION

This study has used announcement data to estimate the diffusion path of customer-related IT investments. A broad range of customer related technologies were studied over a six-year period. We find empirical support for a sigmoid diffusion model. Further, we find that both the size and industry of the company affect the path of CRIT diffusion. . It is important to realize that B2B diffusion is a more global phenomenon, while B2C diffusion could include country-specific factors (Gibbs et al. 2003). While this research explored CRIT diffusion in one country, future studies could be done in a multi-country setting. These findings suggest that investment in IT, specifically those that support the customer experience, will be made at differing rates depending on the industry and size of the company. We propose that this information can be used in a variety of ways. This understanding of purchasing behavior can be used by companies that sell these technologies to better forecast when their targeted market will invest into the technologies and to better understand the factors that drive the timing of their customers' purchases.

REFERENCES

Akura, T., and Altinkemer, K. (2002). Diffusion Models for B2B, B2C, and P2P Exchanges and E-Speak. *Journal of Organization Computing and Electronic Commerce*, 12(3), 243-261.

Bass, F.M. (1969). A New Product Growth Model for Consumer Durables. *Management Science*, 15, 215-227.

Bauer, R.A. (1964). The Obstinate Audience: the Influence Process From the Point of View of Social Communication. *American Psychologist*, 19, 319-328.

Cenk, K. (2002). Evolution of Prices in Electronic Markets Under Diffusion of Price-Comparison Shopping. *Journal of Management Information Systems*, 19(3), 99-119.

Dardan, M., and Stylianou, A.C. (2001). The Impact of Fluctuating Financial Markets on the Signaling Effects of E-Commerce Announcements Through Firm Valuation. *Proceedings of the International Conference on Information Systems.*

Fichman, R., (1999). Book Chapter: *Framing the Domains of IT Management: Projecting the Future Through the Past.* Cincinnati, OH: Pinnaflex Educational Resources.

Fichman, R., (2001). The Role of Aggregation in the Measurement of IT-Related Organizational Innovation. *MIS Quarterly,* 25(4), 427-456.

Forman, C., Goldfarb, A., and Greenstein, S. (2002). The Digital Dispersion of Commercial Internet Use: A Comparison of Industries and Countries. *Proceedings of the WISE Conference.*

Gibbs J., Kraemer K.L., and Dedrick J. (2003). Environment and Policy Factors Shaping Global E-Commerce Diffusion: A Cross-Country Comparison. *The Information Society*, 19(1), 5-18.

Green, S., Melnyk, A., and Powers, D. (2002). Is Economic Freedom Necessary for Technology Diffusion? *Applied Economic Letters*, 9(14), 907-910.

Grover, V., and Goslar, M.D. (1993). The Initiation, Adoption and Implementation of Telecommunications Technologies in U.S. Organizations. *Journal of Management Information Systems,* 10(1), 141-163.

Ha, S.H., Bae, S.M., and Park, S.C. (2002). Computer's Time-Variant Purchase Behavior and Corresponding Marketing Strategies: An Online Retailer's Case. *Computers and Industrial Engineering,* 43(4), 801-820.

Hu, Q., Saunders, C., and Gebelt, M. (1997). Research Report: Diffusion of Information Systems Outsourcing: A Reevaluation of Influence Sources. *Information Systems Research*, 8(3), 288-301.

Hunter, S. D. (2003). Information Technology, Organizational Learning, and the Market Value of the Firm. *JITTA: Journal of Information Technology Theory and Application;* Hong Kong 5(1), 1-28.

Im, K., Dow, K., and Grover, V. (2001). Research Report: A Reexamination of IT Investment and the Market Value of the Firm: an Event Study Methodology. *Information Systems Research* 12(1), 103-117.

Kraemer, K., and Dedrick, J. (1994). Payoffs from Investment in Information Technology: Lessons from the Asia-Pacific Region. *World Development,* 22(12), 1921-1931.

Kraemer, K., Gibbs, J., and Dedrick, J. (2002). Environment and Policy Factors Shaping E-Commerce Diffusion: A Cross-Country Comparison. *Proceedings of the International Conference of Information Systems.*

Kshetri, N., and Dholakia, N. (2002). Determinants of the Global Diffusion of B2B E-Commerce. *Electronic Markets,* 12(2), 120-129.

Lee, G. and Xia W. (2006) Organizational Size and IT Adoption: A Meta-Analysis. *Information and Management.* 43, 975-985

Loh, L., and Venkatraman, N. (1992). Diffusion of Information Technology Outsourcing: Influence Sources and the Kodak Effect. *Information Systems Research,* 3(4), 334-358.

Maddala, G.S. (1992). *Introduction to Econometrics.* Prentice Hall, NJ.

Mahajan, V., and Peterson, R.A. (1985). *Models for Innovation Diffusion.* Sage Publications, Beverly Hills, CA

Mithas, S., Krishnan, M.S., and Fornell, C. (2002). Effect of IT Investments on Customer Satisfaction: An Empirical Analysis. *Proceedings of the WISE Conference.*

Patterson, K. Grimm, C., and Corsi, T. (2003). Adopting New Technologies for Supply Chain Management. *Transportation Research Part E,* pp.95-121.

Pindyck, R., and Rubinfeld, D. (1998). *Econometric Models and Economic Forecasts.* Boston, MA.: McGraw-Hill Companie.

Ranganathan, C. Dhaliwal, J. and Thompson, T. (2004). Assimilation and Diffusion of Web Technologies in Supply-Chain Management: An Examination of Key Drivers and Performance Impacts. *International Journal of Electronic Commerce.* 9(1), 127-161.

Robertson, T. (1970). *Consumer Behavior.* Glenview, Ill.: Scott Foresman.

Rogers, E.M. (1995). *Diffusion of Innovations.* New York: The Free Press.

Shih, C.F., Kraemer, K.L., and Dedrick, J. (2002). *Determinants of Information Technology Spending in Developed and Developing Countries.* Center for Research on Information Technology and Organizations. Forthcoming, UC Irvine

Sultan, F., Farley, J., and Lehmann, D. (1990). A Meta-Analysis of Applications of Diffusion Models. *Journal of Marketing Research,* 27, 70-77.

Tornatzky, L.G. and Fleisher, M. (1990). *The Process of Technological Innovation.* Lexington.

Wolfgang, K. (2002). Geographical Localization of International Technology Diffusion. *American Economic Review,* 91(1), 120-142.

Zhao, X., Yeung, J., and Zhou, Q. (2002). Competitive Priorities of Enterprises in China. *Total Quality Management,* 13(3), 285-300.

Chapter XV
The Impact of Computer Self-Efficacy and System Complexity on Acceptance of Information Technologies

Bassam Hasan
The University of Toledo, USA

Jafar M. Ali
Kuwait University, Kuwait

ABSTRACT

The acceptance and use of information technologies by target users remain a key issue in information systems (IS) research and practice. Building on past research and integrating computer self-efficacy (CSE) and perceived system complexity (SC) as external variables to the technology acceptance model (TAM), this study examines the direct and indirect effects of these two factors on system eventual acceptance and use. Overall, both CSE and SC demonstrated significant direct effects on perceived usefulness and perceived ease of use as well as indirect effects on attitude and behavioral intention. With respect to TAM's variables, perceived ease of use demonstrated a stronger effect on attitude than that of perceived usefulness. Finally, attitude demonstrated a non-significant impact on behavioral intention. Several implications for research and practice can be drawn from the results of this study.

INTRODUCTION

In today's highly competitive and global markets, businesses continue to make considerable investments in information systems (IS) and computer technologies as means to increase productivity, maintain their competitiveness, and provide their customers with better and faster service. However, the achievement of these benefits is contingent, in part, on the extent to which users are willing to accept and utilize the systems to perform their daily tasks. While much research has addressed systems acceptance, reported results have been mixed and inconclusive. As a result, there is a need for additional research to provide further insights into factors that can facilitate or hinder an individual's decisions to accept or reject information systems (Chau, 2001; Agarwal & Prasad, 1999).

Among the various theoretical models utilized in IS acceptance research, the technology acceptance model (TAM) (Davis, 1989; Davis, Bagozzi, & Warshaw, 1989) has enjoyed widespread recognition over other models (Mathieson, 1991). TAM models IS acceptance behavior as a function of users' beliefs about the usefulness and ease of use of a target system. Replication and review studies of TAM have confirmed its robustness and reliability to predict and explain IS acceptance behavior (Legris, Ingham, & Collerette, 2003; Mahmood, Hall, & Swanberg, 2001; Ma & Liu, 2004). TAM was successfully used across a wide range of computer systems and user groups and continues to be used studying newer technologies such Internet and wireless technologies (Hsu & Lin 2008; Liu et al., 2008).

While TAM provides a basis for capturing the effects of external factors on users' internal beliefs of usefulness and ease of use (Davis, 1989), the impact of external factors on TAM's core variables received little research attention in past research (Hu, Chau, Sheng, & Tam, 1999; Thong, Hong, & Tam, 2002) and most studies of external factors in the context of TAM have lacked a clear pattern with respect to the choice of external variables (Legris et al., 2003). Accordingly, several researchers have suggested that further research is needed to study additional external variables and examine their effects on TAM's constructs and acceptance behavior (Agarwal & Prasad, 1999; Legris et al., 2003; Thong et al., 2002; Venkatesh & Davis, 1996).

This study aims to fill the aforementioned void and aims to examine the impact of external variables on TAM and IS acceptance. Specifically, study attempts to extend prior research by incorporating two factors, namely perceptions of computer self-efficacy and perceived system complexity, as external variables affecting TAM's core constructs. Thus, the present study hypothesizes and empirically tests relationships among the following variables: computer self-efficacy, perceived system complexity, perceived usefulness, perceived ease of use, attitude, and behavioral intention to use a target system.

RESEARCH MODEL

The research model underlying the present study (Figure 1) was based on the technology acceptance model (TAM) and relevant research. The research model incorporates computer self-efficacy (CSE) and perceived system complexity, in a single study, as direct determinants of user beliefs about usefulness and ease of use. Moreover, consistent with TAM, the research model suggests indirect relationships among the two external factors, attitude, and behavioral intention.

Computer Self-Efficacy

Self-efficacy refers to people's judgments about their capabilities to organize and execute courses of action necessary to perform a given task. Self-efficacy influences what people choose to perform, how much effort they are ready to exert, and how long they will persist to overcome obstacles (Bandura, 1986; Gist, 1987). Self-efficacy was introduced by Bandura (1986) as is a key concept in the social cognitive theory (SCT). According to SCT, individuals with stronger efficacy beliefs are believed to expend more effort and tend to be more persistent in their efforts than those with lower efficacy beliefs.

The concept of self-efficacy has been extended to various domains such as mathematics, sports, and computing. Adapted from the general concept

Figure 1. TAM and research model

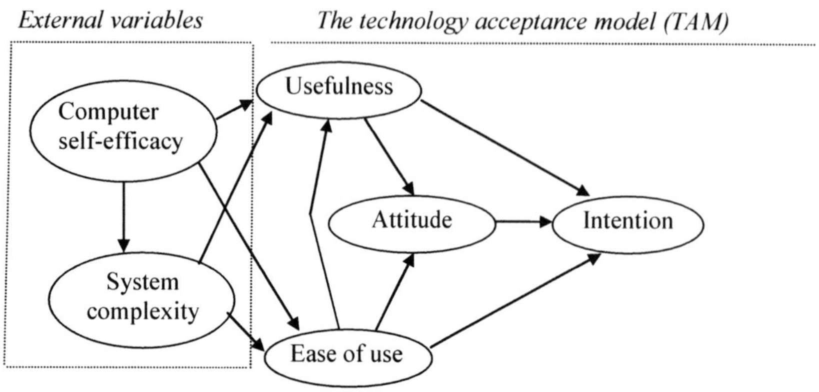

of self-efficacy, computer self-efficacy (CSE) refers to people's judgments about their abilities to use a computer system successfully (Compeau & Higgins, 1995). Perceptions of CSE have been found to influence various computer-related behaviors and outcomes. For instance, CSE demonstrated a negative effect on computer anxiety and positive impacts on affect toward computers, performance outcome expectations, personal outcome expectations, and actual systems usage (Compeau & Higgins, 1995). Likewise, Hsu and Chiu (2004) found that CSE had positive effects on computer usage attitudes and intentions.

Although a direct link between CSE and perceived usefulness has been suggested in the literature (Davis, 1989; Mathieson, 1991), very little research has examined this purported relationship and results have been mixed (Ma & Liu, 2005). For instance, while some studies found a positive relationship between CSE and perceived usefulness (Hung & Liang, 2001; Ong et al., 2004), other studies reported a negative, non-significant relationship between the two constructs (Chau, 2001). Yet, a non-significant relationship between perceived CSE and usefulness has also been reported in the literature (Igbaria & Iivari, 1995).

The relationship between CSE and perceived ease of use has been examined in many studies (Chau, 2001; Ma &Liu, 2005, Thong et al., 2002; Venkatesh & Davis, 1996). For example, Hu, Clark, and Ma (2003) found that CSE had a positive effect on perceived ease of use before and after subjects received training on the target technology. In a recent study of acceptance of an e-learning system among 140 engineers, CSE was found to have a significant positive effect on perceived ease of use (Ong, Lai, & Wang, 2004). Hence, consistent with these findings, CSE is expected to have a positive effect on perceived ease of use.

Task complexity is conceptualized as an interaction between a task (e.g., using a system) and the task-doer (e.g., user) (Campbell, 1986). Thus, a person who doubts his/her ability to perform a given task may view the task in question to be very complex, whereas an individual with high confidence in his/her capabilities may view the same task as less complex. Despite the theoretical relationship between self-efficacy and perceived complexity (Bonner, 1994; Campbell, 1986), very few studies have examined the relationship between IS contexts. In their study, Teo and Pok (2003) investigated self-efficacy and system complexity as parallel determinants of attitude, subjective norms, and perceived behavioral control and Igbaria et al. (1996) found that system complexity had a negative correlation with prior computer experience and organizational support.

As SCT suggests that prior experience, encouragement, and social support are determinants of self-efficacy, we posit that CSE will have a negative effect on perceived system complexity.

Perceived System Complexity

Perceived system complexity (PSC) refers to the degree to which a computer system is perceived to be difficult to learn or use (Moore & Benbasat, 1991). Thus, PSC focuses on perceptions of using a system rather than perceptions of the system itself or the difficulty of using a system. Given critical role that PSC plays in shaping users' beliefs toward using a system, most models of IS acceptance have identified PSC as a major barrier to individuals' acceptance and utilization of a computer system.

An inverse relationship between PSC and acceptance and usage behavior has been established in the literature. For example, Igbaria et al. (1996) found that PSC had a negative impact on perceived usefulness, social pressure, and perceived fun/enjoyment. Moreover, PSC was found to have a negative impact on utilization of personal computers (Thompson, Higgins, & Howell, 1991), user satisfaction with ERP implementation (Bradford & Florin, 2003), and behavioral intention to use a groupware technology (Van Slyke, Lou, & Day, 2002).

As a task (e.g., using a system) is perceived to be more complex, achieving the outcomes associated with the task becomes more distal and less likely (Chen, Casper, & Cortina, 2001). Accordingly, individuals who perceive a system to be complex to use or learn are likely to doubt their abilities and skills to use the system successfully. This is expected to have negative effects on judgments about the usefulness and ease of use of the system. Accordingly, PSC is posited to have negative effects on perceptions of usefulness and ease of use.

METHODOLOGY

Participants and Procedure

The participants in this study were undergraduate students enrolled in two information systems courses at a four-year public university in the USA. Participation in the study was completely voluntary and anonymous, and no credit was given in exchange for participation. A total of 121 subjects were given a seventy-minute behavioral-modeling training presentation on the use of pico (a Unix-based text editing application). A total of 102 questionnaires were collected, 96 of which were complete and used for data analysis. Of the 96 participants, females were 21.9 percent (n = 21) and males were 78.1 percent (n = 75). The mean age of participants was 23.78 years (SD = 4.84).

Measurements

Seven items from the widely-used and highly reliable instrument developed by Compeau and Higgins (1995) were used to measure CSE. Perceived system complexity was measured by three items adapted from the instrument developed by Thompson et al. (1991). Perceived ease of use (3 items), perceived usefulness (4 items), and attitude (3 items) were measured based on the work by Davis et al. (1989). Finally, behavioral intention was measured by three items from the work of Agarwal and Karahanna (2000).

Items on the CSE instrument asked respondents to indicate their confidence in their ability to use unfamiliar software to complete an unidentified computing task, and responses were recorded on a 10-point interval scale ranging from (1) *not at all confident* to (10) *totally confident*. Items on the remaining instruments asked subjects to indicate the extent to which they agree or disagree with statements pertaining to the measured construct, and responses to these items were recorded on a 7-point Likert-type scale with endpoints being (1) *strongly disagree* and (7) *strongly agree*.

RESULTS

This study used path analysis to empirically test the research model and assess its direct and indirect relationships. Path analysis provides quantitative estimates of proposed relationships between sets of variables by using multiple-regression to test explicitly formulated causal models (Billings & Wroten, 1978). That is, standardized regression coefficients (betas) are used to determine the strength and direction of relationships among independent and dependent variables. Therefore, it is important to assess correlations among the study variables to assess the possibility of multicollinearity. The correlations, presented in Table 1, are within the acceptable range ($r < 0.80$), indicating that multicollinearity was not suspected (Bryman & Cramer, 1994). In addition Table 1 presents means, standard deviations, a internal consistency reliability estimates of the study variables.

Path analysis results for PSC, ease of use, and usefulness are presented in Table 2. The results indicate that CSE has significant effects on perceived ease of use, perceived usefulness, and PSC. While the impacts of CSE on perceived ease of use (beta = 0.454, $p < .001$) and perceived system complexity (beta = -0.297, $p < .001$) are in the hypothesized directions, its impact on perceived usefulness (beta = -0.345, $p < .001$) is in the opposite (i.e., negative) direction. In addition, CSE demonstrated substantial indirect effects on attitude and intention through its direct effects on PSC, perceived usefulness, and perceived ease of use.

PSC demonstrated significant effects on both perceived ease of use (beta = -0.196, $p < 0 .05$) and perceived usefulness (beta = -0.434, $p < 0.01$). PSC and CSE explained approximately 29.7 percent of the variance in perceived ease of use. PSC demonstrated a substantial indirect, negative effect on behavioral intention through

Table 1. Descriptive statistics and correlations

	Mean	SD	α	PSC	CSE	PEOU	PU	Attitude	Intention
PSC	11.86	4.79	0.92	1.00	-0.327**	-0.294**	-0.478*	-0.323**	-0.343**
CSE	47.07	14.88	0.94		1.00	0.512**	0.008	0.266**	0.347**
PEOU	15.81	4.40	0.89			1.00	0.356**	0.569**	0.642*
PU	18.27	6.11	0.94				1.00	0.464**	0.409**
Attitude	11.97	2.55	0.83					1.00	0.437**
Intention	12.47	5.45	0.82						1.00
	** $p < 0.01$; * $p < 0.05$								

Table 2. Results of path analysis

	PSC			**PEOU**			**PU**		
	Direct	Indirect	Total	Direct	Indirect	Total	Direct	Indirect	Total
CSE	-0.297**		-0.297	0.454**	0.057	0.511	-0.345**	0.151	0.194
PSC				-0.196*		-0.196	-0.434**	-0.078	-0.512
PEOU							0.406**		0.405
R^2		0.088			0.297			0.357	
** $p < 0.01$; * $p < 0.05$									

Table 3. Results of path analysis

	Attitude			Behavioral intention		
	Direct	Indirect	Total	Direct	Indirect	Total
CSE		0.194	0.194		0.280	0.280
PSC		-0.016	-0.016		-0.214	-0.214
PEOU	0.463**	0.121	0.583	0.555**	0.110	0.665
PU	0.299**		0.299	0.198*	0.008	0.205
Attitude				0.029		0.029
R^2		0.402			0.450	
** $p < 0.01$; * $p < 0.05$						

Table 4. Predictors of intention (excluding attitude)

	B	T	Sig T
Perceived ease of use	0.568	6.909	0.000
Perceived usefulness	0.206	2.509	0.013
R^2	0.449		

its direct effects on perceived ease of use and perceived usefulness. Perceived ease of use had significant effects on perceived usefulness (beta = 0.406, $p < 0.01$), attitude (beta = 0.463, $p < 0.01$), and intention (beta = 0.555, $p < 0.01$). The combination of CSE, PSC, and perceived ease of use explained around 35.7 percent of the variance in perceived usefulness.

The results of path analysis for attitude and behavioral intention are presented in Table 3. The results show that perceived usefulness has a significant effect on attitude (beta = 0.299, $p < 0.01$) and behavioral intention (beta = 0.197, $p < 0.05$). Moreover, perceived ease of use demonstrated a positive indirect effect on attitude. Approximately 40.2 percent of the variance in attitude was explained by perceived ease of use and perceived usefulness. Contrary to expectations, the impact of attitude on intention is not statistically significant (beta = 0.029, $p = 0.773$). The amount of variance in intention that was explained by perceived ease of use, perceived usefulness, and attitude was about 45 percent.

To further examine the nonsignificant relationship between attitude and behavioral intention, a regression model comprising perceived ease of use and perceived usefulness (excluding attitude) as predictors of behavioral intention was tested. The regression results (Table 4) show that the amount of variance explained by this model is about 44.9%. These results indicate that amount of explained variance in intention is virtually unchanged whether attitude is included or excluded from the model. A summary of path coefficients and results is presented in Figure 2.

DISCUSSION AND IMPLICATIONS

The present study examined the direct and indirect effects of two external factors, computer self-efficacy and perceived system complexity

Figure 2. Results of path analysis

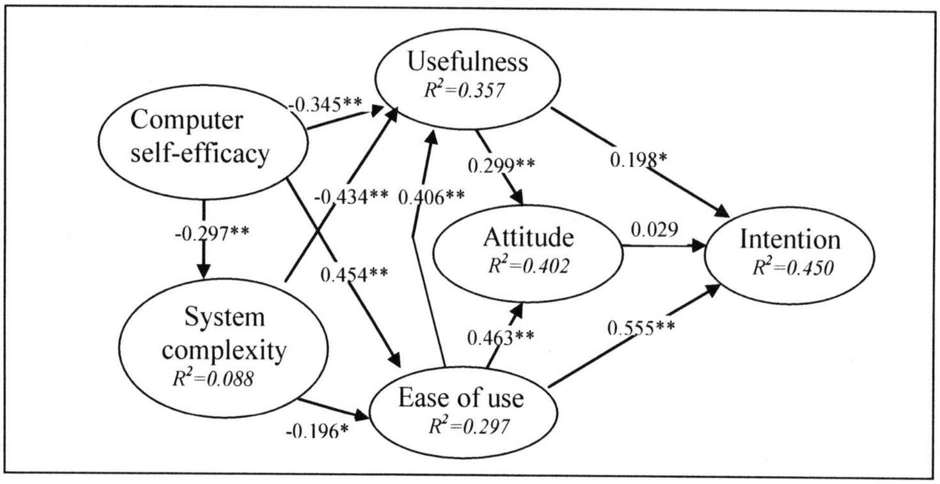

on determinants of IS acceptance behavior in the context of TAM. The results provide a strong support for the proposed model and provide better understanding of the relationships among the two external variables as determinants of acceptance behavior.

CSE demonstrated a positive direct effect on perceived ease of use and a considerable indirect effect on attitude and behavioral intention, providing support for the suggestion that TAM provides a basis for tracking the effects of external factors (Davis, 1989). Given the relative complexity of the examined technology, the strong indirect effects of CSE on perceptions of ease of use and usefulness corroborate the notion that the self-efficacy demonstrates stronger effects in complex behaviors (Chen et al., 2001).

The impact of CSE on perceived usefulness was significant but in the opposite (negative) direction (beta = -0.345). One explanation for this finding may be that individuals with high efficacy beliefs perhaps are able to see the limitations of an application that may not be immediately obvious to those with low efficacy beliefs (Chau, 2001) or can determine whether there is a technology-task fit (Goodhue & Thompson, 1995). Another plausible explanation may be that individuals with low self-efficacy cannot form an accurate mental model of usefulness about the system because they are more concerned about their ability to learn and use the system (Kuo et al., 2004).

Perceived system complexity demonstrated negative effects on perceived ease of use and perceived usefulness. These findings support recent research findings. For example, Ramamuthy et al. 92008) found that the perceived complexity of a data warehousing (DW) technology was negatively related relative advantage. They also maintain that complex technologies demand development of new skills which instigates challenges in understanding and using the technology.

Hover, our deviated from previous technology acceptance research findings in two notable aspects: (1) ease of use demonstrated stronger effects on attitude and intention than did usefulness, and (2) attitude had a non-significant effect on intention. A plausible explanation for these findings may relate to the timeframe in which perceptions of usefulness become fully-developed and matured. Davis (1989) suggests that perceptions of usefulness take longer to develop as users need more time to gain detailed knowledge about the system and learn how the system can improve their work. Thus, given the relatively short time in which perceptions of usefulness were measured in this study, it is possible that this period of time was not long enough for subjects to gain detailed knowledge about the system and its potential benefits to them. Another possible explanation pertains to the unfamiliarity of the technology. Because the effect of ease of use is more powerful than that of usefulness in the case of difficult technologies (Davis, 1989), the technology examined in this study might have been more complex compared to the more user-friendly and common window-based applications examined in past research. Likewise, Ramamurphy et al. (2008) contend that complex technologies demand the development of significantly new skill sets and additional competencies which require some time to build these skills.

The non-significant effect of attitude on behavioral intention is consistent with prior studies which examined complex technologies and appears to provide further support for excluding attitude as a determinant of acceptance behavior (Jackson et al., 1997). However, the correlation between attitude and intention ($r = 0.409, p < 0.001$) was positive suggesting that when other variables and paths are factored in, the direct relationship between attitude and intention may weaken and may become statistically nonsignificant.

This study makes valuable contributions to IS research and practice. From a research standpoint, the current study expanded TAM-related research by incorporating CSE and PSC as external factors affecting IS acceptance. Given that TAM provides a framework for tracing the indirect effects of external factors on IS acceptance behavior, this study provides further evidence to support TAM's ability to mediate the influence of external factors. Furthermore, TAM was expanded to examine the acceptance of unfamiliar, command-based technology. Since most prior studies have focused on familiar and common technologies such as Microsoft Word and Excel and there is evidence to suggest that perceived ease of use and perceived usefulness are invariant to these types of applications (Doll, Hendrickson, & Deng, 1998), the present study investigated the acceptance of a fundamentally different technology. Finally, as described below, the results of this study uncovered promising areas for future research to enhance understanding of IS acceptance behavior.

From practice, the results provide a foundation upon which effective courses of action to enhance users' beliefs about a target system and, ultimately, improve their acceptance and utilization of the system can be built. Since CSE demonstrated substantial direct and indirect effects on IS acceptance behavior, organizational attempts to boost users' self-efficacy beliefs toward a target system could be instrumental in improving their perceptions of ease of use and usefulness and reducing perceptions of system complexity.

The results indicated that the effect of ease of use on intention was stronger than that of usefulness. Given that subjects had little experience with the target technology, the findings suggest that focusing on usefulness, especially in the early stages of system introduction or when users have little experience with the technology, may not be very effective in influencing users' beliefs and usage intention. Rather, increased focus on ease of use and emphasizing the simplicity of a target system may yield more favorable beliefs and intentions toward the system. Providing user support mechanisms such as internal and external training (Igbaria et al., 1996) and other individual and organizational help resources (Mathieson, Peacock, & Chinn, 2001) could be useful in boosting users' perceptions of ease of use.

LIMITATIONS AND FUTURE RESEARCH

This study is not without limitations that should be pointed out and recognized when interpreting the results. The use of student subjects to test the research model represents the first limitation.

Although the use of student subjects in studies of this nature is extensive in the literature, it is vital that more diverse samples in organizational settings to enhance generalizing the results to other user groups are used in future research. Furthermore, the fact that the research model was tested against one data set concerning one technology represents another potential limitation. Although the technology examined here differed substantially from most of the technologies investigated in prior research, it remains essential that the research model be tested against other technologies. Finally, this study attempted to predict and explain behavioral intention to use rather than actual usage. While this approach is consistent with prior studies (e.g. Van Slyke et al., 2002), examining actual usage behavior is necessary to enhance validity of the results.

Several interesting areas for future research have emerged from this study. First and foremost, we focused on examining the impact of only two external factors, CSE and PSC and the results revealed that only 45% of the variance in intention was explained by the research model. This suggests that other factors not included in the research model play an important role in shaping users' beliefs and intentions to use a technology. Hence, investigating other factors as antecedent to IS acceptance is much needed to provide better understanding and prediction of behavioral intention and system acceptance behavior.

Undoubtedly the relationship between attitude and behavioral intention needs further investigation. As noted earlier, although attitude and intention were positively correlated, attitude demonstrated a nonsignificant effect on intention. This suggests that other variables may moderate the relationship between attitude and intention. Therefore, a promising area for future research would be to identify some of those moderating variables and examine how they impact the relationship between attitude and intention in IS settings. For instance, Mathieson et al. (2001) found that the impact of attitude on intention dropped substantially when perceived user recourses were introduced into the research model. More recently, Yang and Yoo (2004) examined the impact of attitude as a bidimensional construct and found that only cognitive attitude but not affective attitude had a significant effect on intention. These studies offer good starting points for future investigations of the relationship between attitude and intention.

The results demonstrated that the effect of usefulness on attitude and behavioral intention was weaker than that of ease of use. Since the beliefs about usefulness require more time to develop and take effect, this finding was attributable in part, to the fact that perceived usefulness was measured in a relatively short period of time. Thus, future research aimed at examining the timeframe in which perceptions of usefulness are fully developed and more reliable to predict attitude and intention is warranted.

REFERENCES

Agarwal, R. & Karahanna, E (2000). Time flies when you're having fun: Cognitive absorption and beliefs about information technology usage. *MIS Quarterly*, 24(4), 665-694.

Agarwal, R. & Prasad, J. (1999). Are individual differences germane to the acceptance of new information technologies?. *Decision Sciences*, 30(2) 361-401.

Bandura, A. (1986). *Social foundations of thought and action: A social cognitive theory*. Englewood, NJ: Prentice-Hall.

Billings, R. & Wroten, S. (1978). Use of path analysis in industrial/organizational psychology: Criticism and suggestions. *Journal of Applied Psychology*, 63, 677-688.

Bonner, S.E. (1994). A model of the effects of audit task complexity. *Accounting, Organizations and Society*, 19(3), 213-234.

Bradford, M. & Florin, J. (2003). Examining the role of innovation diffusion factors on the implementation success of enterprise resource planning systems. *International Journal of Accounting Information Systems*, 4(3), 205-225.

Bryman, D. & Cramer, D. (1994). *Quantitative data analysis for social scientists.* New York: Routledge.

Campbell, D.J. (1988). Task complexity: A review and analysis. *Academy of Management Review*, 13(1) 40-52.

Chau, P.Y.K. (2001). Influence of computer attitude and self-efficacy on IT usage behavior. *Journal of End User Computing*, 13(1), 26-33.

Chen, G., Casper, W.J., & Cortina, T J.M. (2001). The roles of self-efficacy and task complexity in the relationships among cognitive ability, conscientiousness, and task performance: A meta-analytic examination. *Human Performance*, 14(3), 209-230.

Cheung, W., Chang, M.K., Lai, V.S. (2000). Prediction of Internet and World Wide Web usage at work: A test of an extended Triandis model. *Decision Support Systems*, 30(1), 83-100.

Compeau, D.R. & Higgins, C.A. (1995). Computer self-efficacy: Development of a measure and initial test. *MIS Quarterly*, 19(2), 189-211.

Davis, F.D. (1993). User acceptance of information technology: System characteristics, user perceptions and behavioral impacts. *International Journal of Man-Machine Studies*, 38(3), 475-487.

Davis, F.D. (1989). Perceived usefulness, perceived ease of use, and user acceptance of information technology. *MIS Quarterly*, 13(3), 319-340.

Davis, F.D., Bagozzi, R.P., & Warshaw, P.R. (1989). User acceptance of computer technology: A comparison of two theoretical models. *Management Science*, 35(8), 982-1003.

Dishaw, M. T., & Strong, D. M. (1999). Extending the technology acceptance model with Task-technology fit constructs. *Information and Management, 36*(1), 9-21

Doll, W.J., Hendrickson, A., & Deng, X. (1998). Using Davis's perceived usefulness and ease-of-use instruments for decision making: A confirmatory and multigroup Invariance Analysis. *Decision Sciences*, 29(4), 840-869.

Gist, M.E. (1987). Self-efficacy: Implications for organizational behavior and human resource management. *Academy of Management Review*, 12(3), 472-485.

Goodhue, D.L. & Thompson, R.L. (1995). Task-technology fit and individual performance. *MIS Quarterly* 19(2), 1995, 213-236.

Hong, W.H., Thong, J.Y.L., Wong, W.M., & Tam, K.Y. (2001-2002). Determinants of user acceptance of digital libraries: An empirical examination of individual differences and system characteristics. *Journal of Management Information Systems*, 18(3), 97-124.

Hsu, M.H. & Chiu, C.M. (2004). Internet self-efficacy and electronic service acceptance. *Decision Support Systems*, 38(3), 369-381.

Hsu, C. & Lin, J. C.C. (2008) Acceptance of blog usage: The roles of technology acceptance, social influence and sharing motivation. *Information & Management*, 41(3), 65-74.

Hu, P.J., Chau, P.Y.K., Sheng, O.R.L., & Tam, K.Y. (1999). Examining the technology acceptance model using physician acceptance of telemedicine technology. *Journal of Management Information Systems*, 16(2), 91-112.

Hu, P.J.H., Clark, T.H.K., & Ma, W.W. (2003). Examining technology acceptance by school teachers: A longitudinal study. *Information & Management*, 41(2), 227-241.

Hung, S.Y. & Liang, T.P. (2001). Effect of computer self-efficacy on the use of executive support systems. *Industrial Management and Data Systems*, 101(5), 227-237.

Igbaria, M. & Iivari, J. (1995). The effects of self-efficacy on computer usage. *Omega International Journal of Management Science*, 23(6), 587-605.

Igbaria, M., Parasuraman, S., & Baroudi, J. (1996). A motivational model of microcomputer usage. *Journal of Management Information Systems*, 13(1), 127-143.

Jackson, C.M., Chow, S., & Leitch, R.A. (1997). Towards an understanding of the behavioral intention to use an information system. *Decision Sciences*, 28(2), 357-389.

Kuo, F.Y., Chu, T.H., Hsu, M.H., & Hsieh, H.S. (2004). An investigation of effort–accuracy trade-off and the impact of self-efficacy on Web searching behaviors. *Decision Support Systems*, 37(3), 331-342.

Legris, P., Ingham, J., & Collerette, P. (2003). Why do people use information technology? A critical review of the technology acceptance model. *Information & Management*, 40(3), 191-204.

Lu, J., Liu, C., Yu, C.S., & Wang, K. (2008). Determinants of accepting wireless mobile data services in China. *Information & Management*, 45(1), 52-64.

Ma, Q. & Liu, L. (2005). The role of Internet self-efficacy in the acceptance of web-based electronic medical records. *Journal of Organizational and End User Computing*, 17(1), 38-57.

Ma, Q. & Liu, L. (2004). The technology acceptance model: A meta-analysis of empirical findings. *Journal of Organizational and End User Computing*, 16(1), 59-72.

Mahmood, M.A., Hall, L., & Swanberg, D.L. (2001). Factors affecting information technology usage: A meta-analysis of the empirical literature. *Journal of Organizational Computing & Electronic Commerce*, 11(2), 107-130.

Mathieson, K. (1991). Predicting user intentions: Comparing the technology acceptance model with the theory of planned behavior. *Information Systems Research*, 2(3), 173-191.

Mathieson, K., Peacock, E., & Chinn, W.C. (2001). Extending the technology acceptance model: The influence of perceived user resources. *The Data Base for Advances in Information Systems*, 32(3), 86-112.

Moore, G.C. & Benbasat, I. (1991). Development of an instrument to measure the perceptions of adopting an information technology innovation. *Information Systems Research*, 2(3), 192-222.

Ong, C.S., Lai, J.Y., & Wang, Y.S. (2004). Factors affecting engineers' acceptance of asynchronous one e-learning systems in high-tech companies. *Information & Management*, 41(6), 795–804.

Ramamurphy, K., Sen, A., & Sinha, A. (2008). An empirical investigation of key determinants of data warehouse adoption. *Decision Support Systems*, 44(1), 817-841.

Teo, T.S.H. & Pok, S.H. (2003). Adoption of WAP-enabled mobile phones among Internet users. *Omega International Journal of Management Science*, 31(6), 483-498.

Thompson, R.L., Higgins, C.A., & Howell, J.M. (1991). Personal computing: Toward a conceptual model of utilization. *MIS Quarterly*, 15(1), 125-143.

Thong, J.Y.L, Hong, W.H., & Tam, K.R. (2002). Understanding user acceptance of digital libraries: What are the roles of interface characteristics, organizational context, and individual differences?. *International Journal of Human-Computer Studies*, 57(3), 215-242.

Van Slyke, C., Lou, H., & Day, J. (2002). The impact of perceived innovation characteristics on intention to use groupware. *Information Resource Management Journal*, 15(1), 5-12.

Venkatesh, V. & Davis, F.D. (1996). A model of the antecedents of perceived ease of use: Development and test. *Decision Sciences*, 27(3), 451-481.

Yang, H.D. & Yoo, Y. (2004). It's all about attitude: Revisiting the technology acceptance model. *Decision Support Systems*, 38(1), 19-31.

Chapter XVI
Determining User Satisfaction from the Gaps in Skill Expectations Between IS Employees and their Managers

James Jiang
University of Central Florida, USA

Gary Klein
University of Colorado, USA

Eric T.G. Wang
National Central University, Taiwan

ABSTRACT

The skills held by information system professionals clearly impact the outcome of a project. However, the perceptions of just what skills are expected of information systems (IS) employees have not been found to be a reliable predictor of eventual success in the literature. Though relationships to success have been identified, the results broadly reported in the literature are often ambiguous or conflicting, presenting difficulties in developing predictive models of success. We examine the perceptions of IS managers and IS employees for technology management, interpersonal, and business skills to determine if their perceptions can serve to predict user satisfaction. Simple gap measures are dismissed as inadequate because weights on the individual expectations are not equal and predictive properties low. Exploratory results from polynomial regression models indicate that the problems in defining a predictive model extend beyond the weighting difficulties, as results differ by each skill type. Compound this with inherent problems in the selection of a success measure, and we only begin to understand the complexities in the relationships that may be required in an adequate predictive model relating skills to success.

INTRODUCTION

Past studies on information system skills focused on the identification of the ideal skill set for information system (IS) personnel. From this slant, the viewpoints of different stakeholders have been explored (Lee, Trauth, & Farwell, 1995; Trauth, Farwell, & Lee, 1993). It should not surprise one that there exists a significant difference of thought among stakeholders (users, IS managers, and IS employees) in their expectations on skill sets. Depending on the stakeholder, some studies argue technical skill is most important (Duncan, 1995; Todd, McKeen, & Gallupe, 1995), while other studies argue that business and interpersonal skills are more important (Leitheiser, 1992). One fundamental assumption of these IS skill studies is that there is a positive link between skills expectation and success measures. However, this fundamental assumption has never been fully established in the literature (Jiang, Klein, Van Slyke, & Cheney, 2003).

Studies found that satisfaction of any stakeholder is likely determined by the gaps between their own perceived skill expectation and skill proficiency (***within*** a stakeholder) (Byrd & Turner 2001). These studies, however, tend to apply equal weights to expectations and performance. Other empirical IS skill studies show there to be expectation gaps among different stakeholders (Klein, Jiang, & Sobol, 2001). These studies naturally lead to question if the interaction of expectations ***among*** stakeholders will impact the final outcomes, such as user satisfaction. More specifically, can the existence of this skill expectation gap *between* two (or more) stakeholders serve as a predictor of user satisfaction?

Some researchers have argued that a "shared vision" of skill requirements among stakeholders is necessary to achieve success (Trauth et al., 1993). An understanding of how skill expectation gaps among stakeholders (between IS managers and IS employees in this study) impact user satisfaction ratings is crucial, as user satisfaction ratings are often used in organizations as the basis for IS employee promotions, terminations, transfers, and reward distributions. In addition, ratings that are obtained as part of job analyses can be used to specify the skills required of a job incumbent. Such ratings require judgment of the relative importance of skills by IS employees and IS managers (Wexley & Latham, 1991). This evaluation often is used concurrently in personnel and human resource decisions such as personnel planning, training needs analysis, employee selection, and the design and administration of compensation programs. In spite of its importance, to our best knowledge, research on IS skills has not explored the impacts of the perceived skill expectation gap between IS employees and IS managers to determine if these measures may be at all predictive of user satisfaction.

The purpose of this study is, therefore, to investigate the relationship of the expectation gap between IS managers and IS personnel and user satisfaction. Social interaction theory provides the foundation for examining the relative weights on IS managers' expectation and IS personnel's expectation on determining user satisfaction. The results of this study will provide knowledge in two areas: 1) the existence of skill expectation gaps between IS employees and IS managers; and 2) the impact of gaps in these expectations to user satisfaction allowing for the components of the gaps to vary in weight.

HYPOTHESIS DEVELOPMENT

There is considerable agreement among IS skill researchers and practitioners concerning generalized job requirements and the associated job skill categories that are required of IS professionals. A commonly accepted group of IS professional skills includes (1) technology management skills, (2) business functional skills, and (3) interpersonal skills (Byrd & Turner, 2001). It is established that the skills of the IS employees can impact the satisfaction of the users (Ramasubbu, Mithas and Krishnan, 2008). Studies, however, show there are gaps in the levels of expected proficiency for each skill among the different stakeholders (Klein & Jiang, 2001). The explanations for these gaps include different organizational environments, the changing roles of IS, the changing technologies, and varying project complexity (Guimaraes, 1986; Kelley, 1994; Lee and Heiko, 1994; McCann, 1992; Parsons, 1982). Studies show that a difference in expectations among stakeholders is an indicator of potential problems, and possibly an early indicator of potential failure in IS development (Bridges, Johnston & Sagar, 2007; Ginzberg, 1981).

Social interaction theorists have long suggested a model such that expectations may elicit the very behaviors that are expected (Merton, 1948). Our own behavior also may be affected by others' expectations; we may conform to others' visions of who we are, perhaps not even realizing that our own self-presentations have been influenced by the expectations of others (Rosenthal, 1974). Social interaction theory has been demonstrated in empirical investigations in which one person (the perceiver), having adopted beliefs about another person (the target), acts in ways that cause the behavior of the target to appear to confirm these beliefs (Hilton & Darley, 1991). Early work on behavioral confirmation demonstrated that these phenomena exist, and this has been documented in diverse domains. Teachers, led to expect particular levels of performance from students in their classrooms, act in ways that elicit performances that confirm initial expectations (Rosenthal, 1974; Rosenthal, 1993; Rosenthal, 1994). Related studies have demonstrated confirmation in organizational settings (Dougherty, Turban, & Calledder, 1994; Dvir, Eden & Banjo, 1995). Many studies, however, default to a condition that assumes equal weights in the components of the gaps studied.

Other researchers point out the power differences inherent in the roles of perceiver and target – the perceiver with greater power and the target with lesser power (Snyder, 1995). These differences in power between perceivers and the dependent targets of their expectations may, even in a negative expectation situation, place targets in a situation where it is difficult to disconfirm such expectations (Swann, 1983) – as targets are often in low-power roles and therefore they may not be able to take sufficient charge of their interactions to disconfirm the negative expectations held by powerful perceivers. Moreover, targets in positions of low power may fear possible recriminations and avoid contradicting those holding more power (Stukas & Snyder, 1995). Because of outcome dependency, the targets are often responsive to cues given off by their perceivers (Geis, 1993). From the theory of social interaction and related empirical studies, we propose the following hypothesis:

Ho: The levels of IS managers' skill expectation and the levels of IS employees' skill expectation have an equal weight on predicting user satisfaction.

Ha: IS mangers' expectations have a higher weight than the IS employees' expectations on predicting user satisfaction.

RESEARCH METHODOLOGY

Sample

Any meaningful consideration of expectation differences from the various IS stakeholders' points of view will require paired comparisons of the IS employees and their managers. Therefore, for each observation, a member of the IS employees and an IS manager who worked on a specific IS project together were asked to complete the survey instruments. In order to measure user satisfaction, a user involved on a project with each IS staff member/IS manager pair was also identified. A list of contacts was developed from an industry council for an IS program at a major southwestern university. Corporate members of the council were from Texas, Arkansas, and Louisiana. The council represented both service and manufacturing concerns and included small businesses, Fortune 500 companies, and government operations.

Initial contact with participants was made in one of two ways: (1) by contacting IS department directors or (2) by contacting a IS staff member. When the initial contact was with the IS department director, the purpose of the study and the survey instruments were described to the IS director. IS directors who agreed to participate were asked to distribute survey instruments to an IS manager, an IS employee, and a user who worked on the same project. When initial contact was made with IS staff person, the initial participant was asked to distribute the survey instruments to the IS manager and a user participating in the same project. All the respondents were assured that their responses would be kept confidential. Self-addressed return envelopes for each participant were provided to the subjects. A total of 232 completed surveys were returned. Eighteen surveys were discarded due to missing observations for either the IS staff member or the IS manager. From the remaining sample, a total of 107 complete matched observations were presented and used for the data analysis. The demographic characteristics of the sample respondents are shown in Table 1.

Constructs

IS skill: The IS skill construct asks respondents to indicate their perception of the importance of each identified skill as well as their satisfaction with the indicated skill level (Lee et al., 1995). Each response was scored using a 5-point scale ranging from 1 (unimportant/unsatisfied) to 5 (very important/very satisfied). All items were presented such that the greater the score, the greater the importance/satisfaction of/with the skill. The items are listed in Table 2.

To examine the reliability and validity of the skill measure, we conducted a confirmatory factor analysis (CFA). When conducting a CFA, if the model provides a reasonably good approximation to reality, it should provide a good fit to the data. Goodness of fit indices considered included (1) root mean square residual (RMR); (2) chi-square value / degrees of freedom; (3) Bentler's Comparative Fit Index (CFI); and (4) Bollen's Non-Normed Fit Index (NNFI) (Bentler, 1990; Bentler & Bonett, 1980; Bollen, 1989). The CFA for the IS skill/knowledge measure resulted in an RMR of .04 (<= .10 recommended), chi-square/d.f. of 1.67 (<= 5 recommended), a CFI of .93 (>= .90 recommended), and an NNFI of .93 (>= .90 recommended). Thus, the measures represent a good fit for the measurement model. To verify that the measurement model applies for the various subsets of data, two separate CFAs were conducted

Table 1. Demographics

	IS Managers	IS Employees	IS Users
Average Work Experience (years):	19	8	13
Average Age:	49	38	45
Percent Male:	68	72	47
Degreed %:			
Graduate	16	11	8
Bachelor	53	57	41

on the skills inventory: (1) IS employees' expectation and (2) IS managers' expectation. The results in Table 3 indicate that the measurement model holds for both groups.

Once the measures had been determined, further tests of validity followed. Convergent validity is when different instruments are used to measure the same construct, and scores from these different instruments are strongly correlated. Convergent validity was demonstrated by t-tests on the factor loadings and hold accordingly (Anderson & Gerbing, 1988). Discriminant validity was examined with the confidence interval test described in Anderson and Gerbing (1988). Homogeneity of the items was established by the reliability scores of Cronbach (1951). The Cronbach alpha value for the technology management, business functions, and interpersonal/management skills constructs were .84, .91, and .84, respectively, which exceeds the recommended level of .70.

User satisfaction: Baroudi and Orlikowski's (1988) 13-item scale was used to measure user

Table 2. Convergent validity and reliability of skills

Item	Loading	T-value
Technology Management (F1) (Cronbach's α = .84)		
Ability to learn new technologies	.77	15.04*
Ability to focus on technology as a means, not an end	.85	16.99*
Ability to understand technological trends	.78	15.29*
Business Functions (F2) (α = .91)		
Ability to learn about business functions	.88	19.53*
Ability to interpret business problems & develop technical solutions	.79	16.41*
Ability to understand the business environment	.90	20.31*
Knowledge of business functions	.87	18.95*
Interpersonal/Management Skills (F3) (α = .84)		
Ability to work in a collaborative environment	.67	12.51*
Ability to deal with ambiguity	.69	13.08*
Ability to maintain productive user/client relationships	.52	9.07*
Ability to accomplish assignments	.66	12.32*
Ability to teach others	.61	11.21*
Ability to be self-directed and proactive	.69	13.06*
Ability to be sensitive to the organization's culture/politics	.67	12.45*
	* significant at .05	

Table 3. Fit measures for the subgroups

	IS Manager Skill Expectation	IS Employees' Skill Expectation
RMR (< .10)	.07	.04
Chi-square / d.f. (<5)	2.91	1.67
CFI (>= .90)	.90	.93
NNFI (>= .90)	.90	.93

Table 4. Descriptive statistics of study metrics

		Interpersonal Skill Expectation	Technology Management Expectation	Business Skill Expectation	User Satisfaction
IS Users	Mean				4.19
	Std dev				.68
IS Managers	Mean	4.41	4.38	4.30	
	Std dev	.57	.74	.77	
IS Employees	Mean	4.34	4.25	4.19	
	Std.	.55	.73	.90	

satisfaction. Though used frequently in published studies, a CFA was conducted to validate the quality of the metric for the collected user sample. The fit indices for the CFA indicate that the measures have an acceptable level of fit with the data, with a root mean square residual of .06 (<= .10 recommended), a chi-square to degree of freedom ratio of 2.89 (<= 3 recommended), a comparative fit index of .92 (>= .90 recommended), and a non-normed fit index (NNFI) of .90 (>= .90 recommended). Internal reliability was also acceptable with a Cronbach alpha value of 0.85. The descriptive statistics of examined constructs are shown in Table 4.

Threats to external validity could occur if the samples indicated other systematic biases in terms of demographics, such as an IS employee's (or IS manager's) age, gender, and position. A multiple regression analysis was conducted by using user satisfaction as the dependent variable against each demographic category (independent dummy variables) appearing in Table 1. The results did not indicate any significant relationship with user satisfaction indicating probable lack of undue bias on the part of the demographics.

DATA ANALYSIS AND RESULTS

To test the hypothesis, regression coefficients, with the dependent variable user satisfaction, should be equal for IS managers' skill expectations and IS employees' skill expectations. Three separate polynomial regressions were conducted (Edwards & Parry, 1993). First, the measures were centered by averaging the relevant items and subtracting the scale midpoint, producing scores that could range from -2 to + 2. Such scaling reduces multicollinearity (Cronbach, 1987). The polynomial regression equation is the following:

$$Z = b_0 + b_1X + b_2Y + b_3X^2 + b_4XY + b_5Y^2 + \varepsilon$$

Table 5. Polynomial regression analysis

Skills	b_0	X (b_1)	Y (b_2)	X^2 (b_3)	XY (b_4)	Y^2 (b_5)
Interpersonal	4.18	-.20	-.49	-.10	.28	.06
Technology Management	3.78	-.01	-.33	-0.08	.08	.17
Business	3.56	-.21	.23	.04	.11	-.09
Where: X = IS employee expectation, Y = IS manager expectation						

where X = IS employee expectation, Y = IS manager expectation.

In this case, the b1 and b2 terms represent concepts similar to linear regression, but the remaining terms account for a wide variety of shapes in the relationships. The regression coefficients appear in Table 5.

The results indicate that all the "IS employee expectation" do not always differ in sign from the "IS manager expectation". Additionally, the magnitude of the coefficients of IS employee skill expectations and IS managers' skill expectations for each dimension is not equal. These results imply that user satisfaction is indeed predicted by both stakeholders instead of IS employee expectation alone; however, the exact gap functions may not be linear. In sum, the results failed to support the null hypothesis that the levels of IS managers' perceived skill importance and the levels of IS employees' perceived skill importance have an equal weight on predicting IS employees' job performance in favor of the alternate. In this way, the evidence questions models that test gaps applying equal weights, such as those of difference scores employing linear models. Interpretation of the results is often easier to explore using graphs, shown in Figure 1.

For interpersonal skill expectations (Figure 1a), the graphed surface is highest along the Y=X line, indicating that user satisfaction is slightly higher under congruence (when the IS employee expectation matches the IS manager expectation). Though relatively flat, the surface is curved downward from that line. This case is when user satisfaction is maximized along the line of perfect congruence as argued by certain researchers (Tesch, Jiang, & Klein, 2003). In other words, a higher level of user satisfaction is associated with "congruence" between the IS manager and IS employees with respect to expectations of interpersonal skills. One interpretation of this result is that IS managers and IS employees emphasize interpersonal skills to a similar extent, the level not being significant but the projection of agreement being important in pleasing the user.

For technology management skill expectations (Figure 1b), the surface has a high value when managers have lower skill expectations and is flat regardless of the level of IS employee expectations. This indicates the expectations of the managers dominate the prediction of user satisfaction. Unexpectedly, lower expectations relate to higher satisfaction. One possible explanation of this result is that users tend to derive greater satisfaction from a project that shields them from technology considerations while relying on the skills of the IS employees, or perhaps even being too naïve to be concerned with the technology skills of the IS employees. When IS managers recognize this and communicate their expectations, the users are better satisfied.

For business skills (Figure 1c), the curve similarly indicates that user satisfaction is best predicted by the expectations of IS management, but here the relation is such that user satisfaction is higher when the IS manager's expectation is higher. Since user needs are business based rather than technology based, this reversal from the technology dimension should not surprise. As with technology skills, the curve is only slightly

Figure 1. Response surfaces for interpersonal, technology management, and business skills

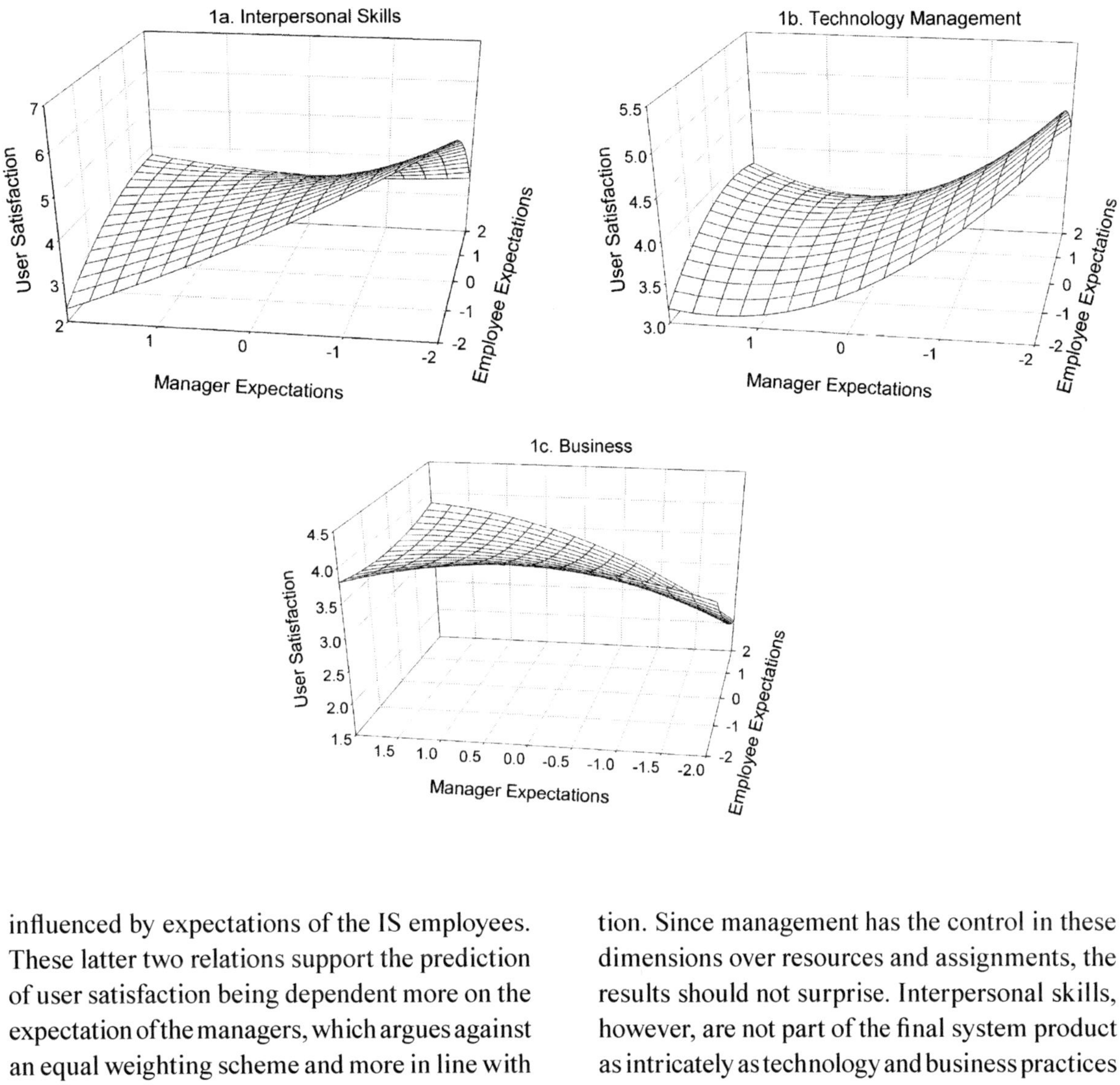

influenced by expectations of the IS employees. These latter two relations support the prediction of user satisfaction being dependent more on the expectation of the managers, which argues against an equal weighting scheme and more in line with social interaction theory. The case where IS employee expectations would dominate, as would be suggested by previous researchers (Ginzberg, 1981), was not found in this data set.

This analysis does not allow examination of particular causes of greater user satisfaction. But clearly, the IS manager's expectations are better predictors of user satisfaction than the IS employees. In particular, a lack of emphasis of technology skills and a push for business skills by IS management led to higher levels of satisfaction. Since management has the control in these dimensions over resources and assignments, the results should not surprise. Interpersonal skills, however, are not part of the final system product as intricately as technology and business practices but are an important part of the process arriving at the final product. As such, they are not as fully under the control of management, leading to highest satisfaction when the two stakeholders agree.

DISCUSSION

A lack of skills in the IS function of an organization is known to create problems in successful delivery of an information system. Understanding relationships between potential predictive variables and eventual success is essential if we are ever to be able to predict system outcomes. Here, we examined how two major stakeholders, IS employees and IS managers, view the required skill. These views were used as possible predictors of user satisfaction in a polynomial regression. The results indicate that, for interpersonal skills, when managers and their employees had similar views, user satisfaction was highest. For these skills, a gap measure may be an appropriate predictor of user satisfaction.

On the other hand, for technology management skills, the results indicated that user satisfaction is positively associated with lower levels of IS manager expectations, with little or no weight on the level of IS employee expectations. This indicates that IS managers' expectations on technology management played a much more critical role in predicting the final user satisfaction than those of IS employees. The heavier influence of managers was not unexpected, according to social interaction explanations. However, managers who tend to view technology management skills as less important are associated with projects with higher user satisfaction. This result may be due to the use of user satisfaction as the independent variable. In such a case, users may not be concerned with the ability of the IS function to handle the changing technology landscape but only with the final software product. Managers who understand this lack of concern are better in tune with the users. However, a different measure of success, say one that measures satisfaction of the IS personnel, may produce a different response surface (Bridges, Johnston & Sagar, 2007).

Finally, for business skills, user satisfaction is also mostly determined by the levels of IS managers' expectations; however, opposite to technology management skill, the higher the managers' business skill expectations, the higher the user satisfaction. In this case, the managers again dominate the predictive power of user satisfaction, as would be expected under social interaction theory. In this case, the direction is as expected, perhaps due to the nature of business skills and the criteria applied by users to the final product. The relations shown in these predictive equations would lead one to push the business skills in the IS staff.

The analysis is limited by the data scope. First, other stakeholders exist that need to be considered in this context. The results demonstrate the variation that can occur just across two of the many stakeholders involved in a system. Users and owners have a major stake in the development of any system and should be considered in further gap studies. Second, only user satisfaction is evaluated. Though user satisfaction is an important and often adopted measure of system success in the IS literature, it is not representative for all stakeholders and only presents one dimension of success. Lastly, the skill sets measured are of a general nature. The ability to draw specific conclusions or draw specific plans to counter the gaps is curtailed by the lack of granularity. The results show how limited the analysis in previous studies has been. It becomes evident that skills, stakeholders, and success metrics are not interchangeable in the analysis of IS skill importance. Researchers and managers alike must view these interchanges in a more micro fashion.

In general, the results of this study confirm the applicability of social interaction theory to this setting because of the power differences inherent in the roles of perceiver and target. Hence, IS managers' expectations usually have a much greater weight in determining final user satisfaction levels than IS employee expectations. The results of this study also provide additional insight to explain the inconsistent findings of skill importance in the IS literature. Some studies argue technical skills are more important (Duncan, 1995; Todd et al., 1995), while other studies argue that business and interpersonal skills are more important (Leitheiser, 1992).

Instead of arguing one skill is more important than others, the results of this study imply that the importance of any particular skill may be associated with the roles of the IS personnel. Do IS managers have the social power to dominate the prediction of success? Is this power the result of personnel decisions, their closeness to the user community, their maturity in an organization, or other factor explored (or not) in the vast skill literature? What is important to address is how these expectations may come to be set. If users are more satisfied when IS managers and IS employees are in agreement about interpersonal skills, are there approaches that help strike this balance? In turn, would altering the expectations of IS employees to be in agreement on the other dimensions further improve user satisfaction? In gathering requirements for the design phase of system development, it is common practice to interview and observe the behaviors of a random sample of users from the intended user population. This practice should be extended to establish their expectations and used to shape those of the IS managers and staff.

REFERENCES

Anderson, J. C., & Gerbing, G. W. (1988). Structural equation modeling in practice: A review and recommended two-step approach. *Psychological Bulletin, 103*(3), 411-423.

Baroudi, J. J., & Orlikowski, W. J. (1988). A short-form measure of user information satisfaction: A psychometric evaluation and notes on use. *Journal of Management Information Systems, 4*(4), 44-59.

Bentler, P. M. (1990). Comparative fit indexes in structural models. *Psychological Bulletin, 107*(2), 238-246.

Bentler, P. M., & Bonett, D. G. (1980). Significance tests and goodness of fit in the analysis of covariance structures. *Psychological Bulletin, 88*(3), 588-606.

Bollen, K. A. (1989). *Structural equations with latent variables*. New York: Wiley.

Bridges, E., Johnston, H. H., & Sager, J. K. (2007). Using model-based expectations to predict voluntary turnover. *International Journal of Research in Marketing, 24*(1), 65-76.

Byrd, T. A., & Turner, D. E. (2001). An exploratory analysis of the value of the skills of IT personnel: Their relationship to IS infrastructure and competitive advantage. *Decision Sciences, 32*(1), 21-54.

Charette, R. N. (1989). *Software engineering risk analysis and management*. New York: Multiscience Press, Inc.

Cronbach, L. J. (1951). Coefficient Alpha and the internal structure of tests. *Psychometrica, 16*, 297-334.

Cronbach, L. J. (1987). Statistical tests for moderator variables: Flaws in analyses recently proposed. *Psychological Bulletin, 102*, 414-417.

Dougherty, T. W., Turban, D. B., & Calledder, J. C. (1994). Confirming first impressions in the employment interview: A field study of interviewer behavior. *Journal of Applied Psychology, 79*, 659-665.

Duncan, N.B. (1995). Capturing flexibility of information technology infrastructure: A study of resource characteristics and their measure. *Journal of Management Information Systems, 12*(2), 37-57.

Dvir, T., Eden, D., & Banjo, M. L. (1995). Self-fulfilling prophecy and gender: Can women be Pygmalion and Galatea. *Journal of Applied Psychology, 80*, 253-270.

Edwards, J. R., & Parry, M. E. (1993). On the use of polynomial regression equations as an alternative to difference scores in organizational research. *Academy of Management Journal, 36*, 1577-1613.

Geis, F. L. (1993). Self-fulfilling prophecies: A social-psychological view of gender. In A. E. Beall & R. J. Sternberg (Eds.), *The psychology of gender*. New York: Guilford Press.

Ginzberg, M. J. (1981). Early diagnosis of MIS implementation failure: Promising results and unanswered questions. *Management Science, 77*(4), 459-478.

Guimaraes, T. (1986). Human resources needs to support and manage user computing activities in large organizations. *Human Resource Planning, 9*(2), 69-80.

Hilton, J. L., & Darley, J. M. (1991). The effects of interaction goals on person perception. In M. P. Zanna (Ed.), *Advances in experimental social psychology*. Orlando, FL: Academic Press.

Jiang, J. J., Klein, G., Van Slyke, & Cheney, P. (2003). A note on interpersonal and communication skills for IS professionals: Evidence of positive influence. *Decision Sciences, 34*(4), 799-812.

Kelley, M. R. (1994). Productivity and information technology: The elusive connection. *Management Science, 40*(11), 1406-1425.

Klein, G., & Jiang, J. J. (2001). Seeking consonance in information systems. *Journal of Systems and Software, 56*(2), 195-202.

Klein, G., Jiang, J. J., & Sobol, M. G. (2001). A new view of IS personnel performance evaluation. *Communications of the ACM, 44*(6), 95-101.

Lee, D. M. S., & Heiko, L.(1994). Innovative design practices and product development performance. In *Proceedings of International Conference of Product Development*, 127-152.

Lee, D. M. S., Trauth, E. M., & Farwell, D. (1995). Critical skills and knowledge requirements of IS professionals: A joint academic/industry investigation. *MIS Quarterly, 19*(3), 313-340.

Leitheiser, R. L. (1992). MIS skills for the 1990s: A survey of MIS managers' perceptions. *Journal of Management Information Systems, 9*(1), 69-91.

McCann, S. (1992). Want to succeed? Get out of IS for awhile. *CIO, 26*(44), 107.

Merton, R. K. (1948). The self-fulfilling prophecy. *Antioch Review, 8*, 193-210.

Parsons, G. (1982). Information technology: A new competitive weapon. *Sloan Management Review, 25*(1), 3-14.

Ramasubbu, N. Mithas, S., & Krishnan, M. S. (2008). High tech, high touch: The effect of employee skills and customer heterogeneity on customer satisfaction with enterprise system support services. *Decision Support Systems, 44*(2), 509-523.

Rosenthal, R. (1974). *On the social psychology of the self-fulfilling prophecy: Further evidence for Pygmalion effects and their mediating mechanisms*. New York: MSS Inf. Corp. Modul. Publishers.

Rosenthal, R. (1993). Interpersonal expectations: Some antecedents and some consequences. In P. D. Blanck (Ed.), *Interpersonal expectations: Theory, research, and applications* (3-24). London: Cambridge University Press.

Rosenthal, R. (1994). Interpersonal expectancy effect: A 30-year perspective. *Current Directions in Psychology Science, 3*, 176-179.

Snyder, M. (1995). Power and the dynamic of social interaction. In *Proceedings of 8th Annual Conference on Advers,* Amherst, MA.

Stukas, A. A., & Snyder, M. (1995). Individuals confront negative expectations about their personalities. In *Proceedings of Annual Meeting of the American Psychology Society*, New York.

Swann, W. B., Jr. (1983). Self-verification: Bringing social reality into harmony with the self. In J. Suls & A. G. Greenwald (Eds.), *Psychological perspectives on the self, vol. 2* (33-66). Hillsdale, NJ: Erlbaum.

Tesch, D. J., Jiang, J. J., & Klein, G. (2003). The impact of information personnel skill discrepancies on stakeholder satisfaction. *Decision Sciences, 34*(1), 107-130.

Todd, P. A., McKeen, J. D., & Gallupe, R. B. (1995). The evolution of IS job skills: A content analysis of IS job advertisements from 1970 to 1990. *MIS Quarterly, 19*(1), 1-27.

Trauth, E., Farwell, D. W., & Lee, D. (1993). The IS expectation gap: Industry expectations versus academic preparation. *MIS Quarterly, 13*(3), 293-307.

Wexley, K. N., & Latham, G. P. (1991). *Developing and training human resources in organizations, 2nd ed.* New York: Harper Collins.

Chapter XVII
The Impact of Missing Skills on Learning and Project Performance

James Jiang
University of Central Florida, USA

Gary Klein
University of Colorado in Colorado Springs, USA

Phil Beck
Southwest Airlines, USA

Eric T.G. Wang
National Central University, Taiwan

ABSTRACT

To improve the performance of software projects, a number of practices are encouraged that serve to control certain risks in the development process, including the risk of limited competences related to the application domain and system development process. A potential mediating variable between this lack of skill and project performance is the ability of an organization to acquire the essential domain knowledge and technology skills through learning, specifically organizational technology learning. However, the same lack of knowledge that hinders good project performance may also inhibit learning since a base of knowledge is essential in developing new skills and retaining lessons learned. This study examines the relationship between information system personnel skills and domain knowledge, organizational technology learning, and software project performance with a sample of professional software developers. Indications are that the relationship between information systems (IS) personnel skills and project performance is partially mediated by organizational technology learning.

INTRODUCTION

The importance of technical and business skills and knowledge for information systems personnel has been advocated in the IS literature for decades (Cheney & Lyons, 1980; Jiang, Klein, Van Slyke, & Cheney, 2003). In spite of the recognized importance, empirical investigations that examine IS project performance focus too much on the tools rather than employee competence (Rose, Pedersen, Hosbond & Kraemmergaard, 2007). Partly, this is due to an inability to model this lack of skill such that a link becomes evident (Byrd & Turner, 2001). Why should empirical studies contradict experience? Possibly the relationships in an organization where IS personnel skills are applied have too many complexities to be modeled accurately. Could there be a mediating variable between IS personnel skills and IS project performance that further explains how to overcome this essential lack? Perhaps the intervention of certain learning abilities is essential in the ability to apply competences to new projects.

Researchers have observed that activities during information system development and implementation offer an opportunity for organizational technology learning, or the ability and practice of bringing new skills and knowledge into the organization related to IS development and the application of IS tools to business domains (Ko, Kirsch, & King, 2005; Stein & Vandenbosch, 1996). For a successful IS implementation, skills must be brought to bear from the application domain and technical domains, which can best happen when the organization encourages the learning of newer skills and knowledge, and has practices to incorporate these newly acquired assets into current and future projects. In short, organizational technology learning is a critical factor for predicting final IS project performance, and a base of knowledge and skills in the IS project team are a necessary condition for organizational technology learning to occur. This suggests that organizational technology learning is a mediator between IS skills and knowledge and the performance of the IS project. Unfortunately, no empirical study has attempted to validate this reasoning.

The focus of this study is, therefore, to examine the relationship from IS staff development skills and domain knowledge to project performance with organizational technology learning as a mediator. A positive result of this study will provide additional insights on IS skill research and provide an alternative explanation to the unsolved IS skills puzzle of Byrd and Turner (2001). From a survey sample of 212 Institute of Electrical and Electronics Engineers Computer Society members, the results indicate that the lack of system development skills and knowledge in the application domain have a direct negative impact on organizational technology learning and project performance. Furthermore, organizational technology learning has a significant positive impact on final project performance, showing that the impact of IS personnel skill levels on project performance is partially mediated by organizational technology learning.

HYPOTHESIS DEVELOPMENT

Broad categories of critical IS personnel skills are identified, including (1) technical specialties/technology management skills and (2) business domain knowledge and skills (Jiang et al., 2003). Unfortunately, given decades of emphasis, these IS skills were still not linked to IS project performance (Byrd & Turner, 2001). This may be due to the lack of an intervening variable similar to an established relationship between IS staff competency and firm performance where learning is a mediator (Tippins & Sohi, 2003). This study investigates the possibility of a variation on learning as a mediating variable in the project context between IS personnel knowledge and skills and IS project success.

This research considers learning from the perspective of general technology skills acquired by the firm in the project context (Cooprider & Henderson, 1990). Organizational technology learning is an organization's furthered understanding of its operational business procedures and information system technology capabilities (Lee & Choi, 2003). The IS application development process itself can be viewed as an intensive activity of skill learning and knowledge acquisition (Rus & Lindvall, 2002). Such learning results in associations, cognitive systems, and memories that are developed and shared by members of an organization. These learned skills can then be used to enhance the performance of a software project and, thus, the organization. From concept generation to implementation, integration of skills and knowledge to achieve a desired product can be viewed as the central theme of the software development process. IS projects require such an in-depth set of skills and knowledge of application domains (Badaracco, 1991).

Various project stakeholders (e.g., IS developers and end-users) bring different repositories of expertise, skills, knowledge, and perspectives to the project teams. This potential pool of skills held collectively by project stakeholders represents *embedded* knowledge (Schramer, 2000). The delivered system represents *embodied* (i.e., learned) knowledge – referring to how the technical knowledge and knowledge of application domain is formalized and incorporated in the design, functionality, policies, and features of a system. Okhuysen & Eisenhardt (2002) indicated that the successful integration and learning of embedded knowledge into embodied knowledge is the key to successful product and service developments. The information system development process is a process of converting embedded knowledge into embodied knowledge (Robillard, 1999). Proposed organizational practices to achieve this conversion can be found in various literatures on knowledge management, organizational learning, and employee education (Chiva & Alegre, 2005; Kayes, Kayes & Kolb, 2005). In particular, practices have been proposed to enhance knowledge management via information systems, promote learning during development, and educating through training (Majchrzak, Beath, Lim, & Chin, 2005; Olfman, Bostrom, & Sein, 2003; Sher & Lee, 2004). As a result, a relatively stable and accessible body of embedded knowledge that exists within the project team may become a necessary condition for an occurrence of organizational technology learning and improved project performance.

The notion of organizational entities, like project teams as vehicles for integrating fragmented knowledge, is the core of knowledge-based theory (Grant, 1996). Some knowledge is codified in documents or embodied in procedures and policies, and much is held tacitly in the minds of individuals. The development of new products and services require combining both tacit and explicit knowledge held by many individuals (Kogut & Zander, 1992). Many of the "run-away" IS projects can be related to either embedded customer or technical knowledge that are difficult to be embodied in a system: vague requirements, new technologies/methods, new development methodologies, new ideas, and changing user needs. To be successful, technical knowledge and knowledge about user functions and needs must be learned by the organization and embodied in the system design and implementation. Based upon the above discussion, we propose the following research model (see Figure 1). We propose that the lack of system development technical knowledge and the lack of application domain knowledge will negatively impact organizational technology learning, and, in turn, negatively impact final project outcomes.

For learning to occur, it is accepted that certain conditions must be in place in the organization. One seeming catch-22 is that existing knowledge must be in place for learning to occur (Cohen & Levinthal, 1990). In this instance, learning is not merely the sum of the basic knowledge and skills of the individuals, but the structure in place to

Figure 1. Research model of risk impact on learning and performance

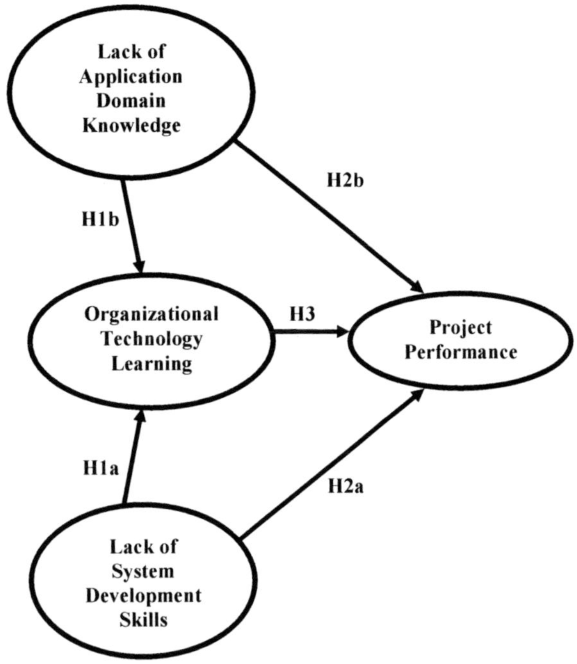

retain and transfer knowledge throughout the organization (Schulz, 2001). This by itself indicates that individual knowledge is not sufficient to guarantee that organizational technology learning will take place. Knowledge and skills must be the collective of a project team that can be directed to accomplish the goals of a software development project (Schulz, 2001).

Absorptive capacity is a theory-based explanation of this phenomena (Cohen & Levinthal, 1990). The basic premise of absorptive capacity is that the IS project team must have prior related knowledge and skills to assimilate and utilize the new knowledge. Research in other fields supports this premise. Memory development research suggests that an accumulation of prior knowledge improves the ability to store new knowledge and the ability to recall and use knowledge as skills (Bower & Hilgard, 1981). Furthermore, lack of knowledge in the appropriate context limits the ability to make new knowledge intelligible (Lindsay & Norman, 1977). New knowledge must be exploitable as skills and depends upon the transfer of knowledge within the organization (Sarin & McDermott, 2003). Essentially, a lack of knowledge blocks organizational access to further knowledge and the ability to utilize the skills derived from the knowledge. A previous knowledge base is important to the rapid dissemination and assimilation of the knowledge required to exploit technology and adopt new technology into productive domain applications (Ko et al., 2005). In addition, diversity of knowledge is important for further learning in order to place new knowledge in a corporate context (Fichman & Kemerer, 1997). Based upon absorptive capacity theory and existing studies demonstrating the importance of previous knowledge, we expect:

> **H1a:** There is a negative relationship between the lack of system development skills and organizational technology learning.
> **H1b:** There is a negative relationship between the lack of application domain

knowledge and organizational technology learning.

Risk-based software engineering describes why software project uncertainties have an adverse impact on performance (Boehm, 1991). According to this theory, project uncertainties can be viewed as risk drivers that increase the performance risk of the project. The purpose of software engineering is to manage the particular sources of project risks and lead to a successful project development. If this holds, then project performance depends upon the reduction or control of the various risks in place, including those associated with knowledge deficiencies on the part of the IS development staff. Research based upon the analysis of risk in project environments supports this notion (Jiang & Klein, 2000). Researchers and practitioners have indicated that the lack of knowledge on the part of the IS staff is a significant project risk that could negatively impact a project's outcome (Schmidt, Lyytinen, Keil, & Cule, 2001). In the IS skill literature, Jiang et al. (2003) found that the lack of skills was correlated with project failures. Based upon the risk management theory and above discussion, we expect that:

H2a: There is a negative relationship between the lack of system development skills of IS staff and project performance.
H2b: There is negative relationship between the lack of application domain knowledge of IS staff and project performance.

Various learning models incorporate the concept of feedback (Argyris, 1999). Single-loop learning is defined as matching expected consequences to those incurred from action and correcting the actions when a match is not present. Double-loop learning occurs when the mismatch causes a reflection on the underlying rules and principles of the system. This mechanism is similar to the feedback and control mechanisms of cybernetic (control) theory (Henderson & Lee, 1992). In projects, when expectations are not met, this creates feedback that is then used in a learning process to prevent the errors in the future. Thus, when organizational technology learning occurs, subsequent errors in the software development projects are reduced through either corrective action or reformulation of the principles of practice.

Performance improvement by learning is a general assumption in learning research (Lee & Choi, 2003; Sarin & McDermott, 2003). A study on shared knowledge has found positive relationships to group performance (Nelson & Cooprider, 1996). Project teams pursuing project goals are usually defined to be groups along the lines of those whose performance can be improved by shared knowledge (Klein, 1991). Organizations benefit from knowledge management practices implanted during system development and completed system projects (Fedor, Ghosh, Caldwell, Maurer, & Singhal, 2003; Sher & Lee, 2004). This process of sharing knowledge is considered one form of learning (Schulz, 2001). Thus, based on limited empirical results and the adaptive learning model, we expect support for:

H3: There is a positive relationship between organizational technology learning and project performance.

RESEARCH METHODS

Sample

Questionnaires were mailed to 1,000 randomly selected IEEE Computer Society members. The letter salutation was directed to software engineers. This sample is likely familiar with software development activities and, thus, appropriate for study. Instructions in the letter told the targets to consider their responses in light of their most recently completed software development project.

From the initial mailing and a follow-up, 221 responses were received. Nine questionnaires were eliminated due to missing data, leaving a final sample of 212 used in the data analysis. Demographic features of the sample population are in Table 1.

Non-response bias occurs when the opinions and perceptions of the survey respondents do not accurately represent the overall sample to which the survey was sent. One test for non-response bias is to compare the demographics of early versus late respondents to the survey (Armstrong & Overton, 1977). T-tests on the means of key demographics (work experience, gender, recent project duration, and team sizes) to examine whether significant differences existed between early and late respondents in the first mailing, and from those received in the first mailing to those in the follow-up mailing, found no significant differences.

Since all independent and dependent variables were collected from the same subject at the same time, common method bias was assessed using Harman's one-factor test (Podsakoff & Organ, 1986). Two models, a single factor model and a four-factor model, were created and tested in EQS. The model fit indices of single factor model (GFI=0.514, CFI=0.564, Chi-Square = 1343.264, df =152, RMR=0.231, and RMSEA=0.193) are worse than the model fit indices of three factors

Table 1. Demographic information

1. Gender	
Male	189
Female	23
2. Position:	
IS Manager	55
Project Leader	71
IS Professional	75
Others	8
3. The industry type of your company:	
Service	110
Manufacturing	78
Education	12
Others 6	
4. Average IS project duration in your organization:	
1 years and under	85
1 – 2 years	75
2 – 3 years	23
3 – 5 years	11
6 or more years	13
5. Average size of IS project teams in your organization:	
7 and under	113
8 – 15	69
16 – 25	13
26 and over	13

model (GFI = 0.849, CFI = 0.928, Chi-Square = 343.6, df =146, RMR=0.068, RMSEA=0.08) indicating that common method bias will not be a potential problem in the following analysis.

Constructs

Project performance is a comprehensive view that includes meeting project goals, budget, schedule, user requirement, and operational efficiency considerations. This is also reflected in the information systems literature in terms of meeting system budget, meeting delivery schedule, fulfilling user requirements, the amount of work produced, the quality of work produced, and an ability to meet project goals (Jones & Harrison, 1996). The items used in this study were adopted from a previous study (Henderson & Lee, 1992). The questionnaire asked respondents' satisfaction with the project team performance when developing information systems. The specific items are listed in Table 2. Each item was scored using a five-point scale ranging from criterion not met at all (1) to criterion fully met (5). All items were presented such that the greater the score, the greater the satisfaction of the particular item.

Organizational technology learning describes the technology knowledge being acquired by the firm (Cooprider & Henderson, 1990). This instrument was applied in previous studies involving organizational technology learning (Cooprider & Henderson, 1990). Three items were used to measure this construct and are shown in Table 2. Respondents were asked to indicate the extent of the items typically incurred when developing IS applications in their organization. Each item was scored using a five-point scale ranging from never occurring (1) to always occurring (5). All items were presented such that the greater the score, the greater the extent of the particular item occurred during the system development.

Lack of application domain knowledge relates to the IS staff's knowledge of the new application areas. *Lack of system development skills* is the IS staff's overall lack of expertise of the development methods used during system development. These two risks are all based on items proposed in earlier studies (Barki, Rivard, & Talbot, 1993; Jiang, Klein, & Means, 2000). The items associated with each of these risks are in Table 2. All items were presented such that the greater the score, the greater the extent of the particular item present during the system development projects.

Analytical Procedures

The analysis followed a two-step procedure. In the first step, confirmatory factor analysis (CFA) was applied to develop a measurement model describing the nature of the relationship between a number of latent factors and the manifest indictor variable that measures those latent variables. In step two, the measurement model serves to test the theoretical model of interest. The indicators used to present the latent variables in the theoretical model tested are identical to those presented in the measurement model. This analysis step may be described as a path analysis with latent variables. The path model consists of the unobservable constructs and the theoretical relationships among them (the paths). It evaluates the explanatory power of the model and the significance of paths in the structural model, which represent hypotheses to be tested. The estimated path coefficients indicate the strength and the sign of the theoretical relationships.

Three important assumptions associated with path analysis are: 1) normal distribution of the variables examined; 2) absence of multicollinearity among the variables; and 3) a limit on the maximum number of variables in the model. To test for normality, Mardia's multivariate kurtosis and normalized multivariate kurtosis tests were conducted. No violation was found. Multicollinearity is present when one or more variables exhibit very strong correlations with one another.

Table 2. Measurement model – confirmatory factor analysis

Construct Indicators	*Loadings*	*T-value*
Project Performance (α=.90)		
Ability to meet project goals	.79	12.64*
Expected amount of work completed	.76	11.98*
High quality of work completed	.82	13.43*
Adherence to schedule	.75	11.87*
Adherence to budget	.71	10.30*
Efficient task operations	.76	12.09*
Organizational Technology Learning (α=.80)		
Knowledge is acquired by your organization about use of key technologies	.86	13.31*
Knowledge is acquired by your organization about use of development techniques	.83	12.69*
Knowledge is acquired by your organization about supporting users' business	.57	7.95*
Lack of System Development Skills (α=.87)		
Lack of expertise in the development methodology used in projects	.84	13.86*
Lack of expertise in the development support tools used in projects (e.g., DFD, flowcharts, ER model, CASE tools)	.90	15.41*
Lack of expertise in the project management tools used in projects (e.g., PERT charts, Gantt diagrams, walkthroughs, project management software)	.79	12.68*
Lack of expertise in the implementation tools used in projects (e.g., programming languages, data base inquiry languages, screen generators)	.62	9.03*
Lack of Application Domain Knowledge (α=.86)		
The members of the development team are unfamiliar with the application types	.68	10.25*
Insufficient knowledge of organizational operations	.89	14.97*
Lack of knowledge of the functioning of user departments	.95	14.04*
Lack of expertise in the specific application areas of new systems	.71	10.71*

The correlations between variables (see Table 3) were all less than .80, thus no present (Anderson & Gerbing, 1988).

When conducting a CFA, if the model provides a reasonably good approximation to reality, it should provide a good fit to the data. The CFA for the measurement model resulted in a root mean square residual of .07 (<= .10 is recommended), a chi-square/degree of freedom ratio of 2.41 (<= 3 is recommended), a comparative fit index of .90 (>= .90 recommended), and a non-normed fit index of .89 (>= .90 recommended) using the SAS CALIS procedure. The recommended values are based on research traditions and established authors in the field of structural equation modeling (Bentler, 1990). The measurement model was adequate for the data set.

Convergent validity is demonstrated when different instruments are used to measure the same construct, and scores from these different instruments are strongly correlated. Convergent validity can be assessed through t-tests on the fac-

Table 3. Descriptive analysis and correlations of measures

	Organizational Technology Learning	*Lack of Development Skills*	*Lack of Application Knowledge*	*Project Performance*
Mean	3.64	2.64	2.47	3.52
Std. Dev.	.83	.93	.8	.75
Median	3.67	2.75	2.50	3.67
Skewness	-.34	.09	.07	-.51
Kurtosis	-.26	-.56	-.50	.22
Correlations				
Lack of Development Skills	-.36 (.0001)			
Lack of Application Knowledge	-.37 (.0001)	.64 (.0001		
Project Performance	.54 (.0001)	-.46 (.0001)	-.36 (.0001)	

tor loadings, such that the loadings are greater than twice their standard error (Anderson & Gerbing, 1988). The t-tests for the loadings of each variable are in Table 2. The results show that the constructs demonstrate a high convergent validity since all t-values are significant at the .05 levels. In addition, the reliability of each construct is examined by the Cronbach alpha value, all of which exceeded the recommend level of .70 (Nunnally, 1978).

A threat to external validity occurs if the sample shows systematic biases in terms of demographics. An ANOVA was conducted by using project performance as the dependent variable against each demographic category (as independent variables). Results did not indicate any significant relationship to project performance. Similar results were found for the remaining variables in the model. The external validity of the findings is also threatened if the sample is systematically biased – for example, if the responses were generally from projects that are more successful. Table 3 shows the descriptive statistics for the construct. The responses had a good distribution for project performance since the mean and median were similar, skewness was less than two, and kurtosis was less than five (Ghiselli, Campbell, & Zedeck, 1981). Similar results held for the remaining variables. Lastly, external validity is improved if the measures are similar to those found in other studies. In our case, the project performance measure matches within 2% to two other studies (Henderson & Lee, 1992; Jones & Harrison, 1996).

Discriminant validity is demonstrated when different instruments are used to measure different constructs and the correlations between the measures of those different constructs are relatively weak. Discriminant validity is accessed by using the confidence interval test (Anderson & Gerbing, 1988). A confidence interval test involves calculating a confidence interval of plus or minus two standard errors around the correlation between factors and determining whether this interval includes 1.0 (or -1.0). If the interval (for each pair of constructs) does not include 1.0, discriminant validity is demonstrated. No violations were found.

Results

The theorized model in Figure 1 fit the data reasonably well, with a root mean square residual of .08, a chi-square/degree of freedom fit of 2.47, a comparative fit index of .88, and a non-normed fit index of .86. Hypotheses H1a, H1b, H2a, H2b, and H3, were all supported at the .05 significance level. The high R-square value (.49) indicated that the independent variables included in this model were all critical to the project performance. The strengths of these relationships, path coefficients, are on Figure 2.

DISCUSSION

The importance of system development skills and business domain knowledge for IS personnel has been advocated in the IS literature for decades. However, empirical examinations that investigated the relationship between these skills and system success provided conflicting results (Byrd & Turner, 2001). To provide an alternative explanation of the IS skill puzzle in the literature, this study proposed that organizational technology learning is a mediator between the lack of system development technical skills and application domain knowledge and project performance. Results indicate that risk of lack of skills and knowledge adversely impacts IS software development projects and interferes with the organizational technology learning required to help overcome the risks. Furthermore, organizational technology learning was found to promote project performance.

Figure 2. Research model path coefficients

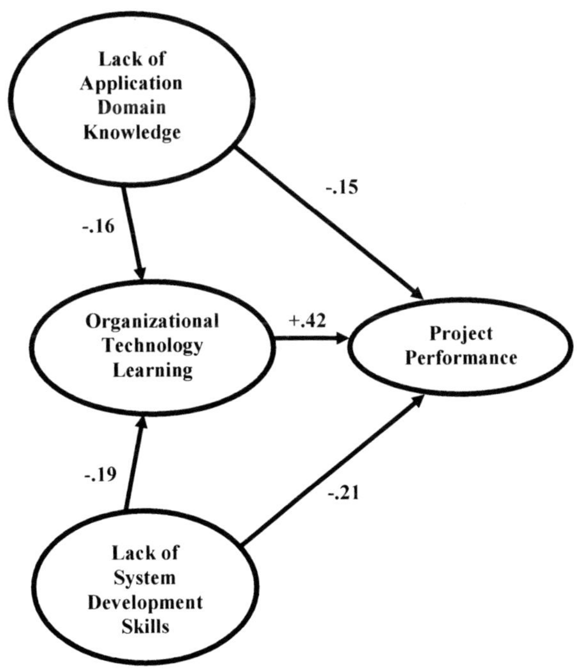

For researchers, this study complements existing literature in several respects. First, learning does not take place unless a set of knowledge and skills is in place to use as a foundation (Cohen & Levinthal, 1990). This result has specific consequences to the limited framework of the study but also puts forth the idea that risks thought to be associated with project performance may impact other organizational processes and remedies. Second, lack of knowledge and skills is shown to be a large risk to the performance of projects. This study confirms the IS skill literature that a lack of skills does have a *negative* impact on project performance. Third, the *positive* relationship between IS skills and project performance may be explained by the mediator -- organizational technology learning. This extends the mediation results found in the organizational setting to the project environment (Tippins & Sohi, 2003). It provides an alternative explanation for a lack of positive relationships between IS skills and project performance in previous studies. Some natural actions to promote learning of the technology may be needed for the newer developments (Schulz, 2001). Additionally, a direct link between organizational technology learning and the performance of IS projects is established. This goes beyond the literature that considers success limited to the completion of learning, the dissemination of new ideas, or the adoption of new methodologies.

For practitioners, the results encourage management to seek ways to overcome risks associated with knowledge deficiencies. The IS personnel literature contains studies of composing teams that have a variety of knowledge and skills (Jiang, Klein & Balloun, 1998). This goes along with a need for a diversity of knowledge and skills. The knowledge management literature supports this knowledge diversity through examples of loyalty in personnel and cross-fertilization of specialties (Nonaka & Takeuchi, 1995). A set of knowledge must be present in order to acquire more knowledge and must be present in the individuals in order for the organization to acquire and utilize the knowledge as applied skills (Cohen & Levinthal, 1990). Hiring practices must be set to ensure the requisite variety and background in the organization as a whole and in the individual expected to grow the knowledge and skills of the organization.

Organizational policies or practice may also contribute to the ability to overcome lack of knowledge and skills. Training is still an effective tool in the preparation of employees; however, the organization must appropriately target the training. Employees, or groups of employees, with limited background may not gain as much as employees with a stronger background. Employees with a broad technical, business, and liberal arts background have a larger learning set to grow from than do employees with strictly a technical background. Appropriate structures that promote growth of knowledge should serve to leverage existing knowledge (Nonaka & Takeuchi, 1995). Knowledge systems within an organization serve to distribute the knowledge more widely (Davenport & Prusak, 2000). Each of these techniques must be carefully weighed to determine their value in overcoming deficiencies. Just as importantly, the correct knowledge must be targeted. Application knowledge is crucial to the development of a system as well as in the satisfaction of clients (Ramasubbu, Mithas & Krishnan, 2008).

The study is limited by its scope, which is narrowly defined to include only certain skill components, and only learning that occurs about technology application. However, it does confirm existing learning theory. A bigger limitation is on the risks considered. Risks are not isolated and are often interrelated. The control of one risk factor may lead to an associated increase in another. Key learning elements, however, can assist in the management of risk and uncertainty (Perminova, Gustafsson & Wikstrom, 2008). As such, establishing learning as a priority can be an important part of a risk management plan. Continuing to follow the procedures associated with learning can thus become an important element in project success.

REFERENCES

Anderson, J. C., & Gerbing, G. W. (1988). Structural equation modeling in practice: A review and recommended two-step approach. *Psychological Bulletin, 103*(3), 411-423.

Argyris, C. (Ed.). (1999). *On organizational learning* (Second ed.). Malden: Blackwell Publishers, Inc.

Armstrong, J. S., & Overton, T. S. (1977). Estimating non-response bias in mail surveys. *Journal of Marketing Research, 14*, 396-402.

Badaracco, J. (1991). *The knowledge link: How firms compete through strategic alliances*. Boston, MA: Harvard Business School Press.

Barki, H., Rivard, S., & Talbot, J. (1993). Toward an assessment of software development risk. *Journal of Management Information Systems, 10*(2), 202-223.

Bentler, P. M. (1990). Comparative fit indexes in structural models. *Psychological Bulletin, 107*(2), 238-246.

Boehm, B. W. (1991). Software risk management: Principles and practice. *IEEE Software*, 32-41.

Bower, G. H., & Hilgard, E. R. (1981). *Theories of learning*. Englewood Cliffs, NJ: Prentice-Hall.

Byrd, T. A., & Turner, D. E. (2001). An exploratory analysis of the value of the skills of IT personnel: Their relationship to IS infrastructure and competitive advantage. *Decision Sciences, 32*(1), 21-54.

Cheney, P. H., & Lyons, N. R. (1980). Information systems skill requirements: A survey. *MIS Quarterly, 4*(1), 35-43.

Chiva, R., & Alegre, J. (2005). *Organizational learning* and *organizational* knowledge: Towards the integration of two approaches. *Management Learning, 36*(1), 49-68.

Cohen, W. M., & Levinthal, D. A. (1990). Absorptive capacity: A new perspective on learning and innovation. *Administrative Science Quarterly, 35*, 128-152.

Cooprider, J. G., & Henderson, J. C. (1990). Technology-process fit: Perspectives on achieving prototyping effectiveness. *Journal of Management Information Systems, 7*(3), 67-87.

Davenport, T. H., & Prusak, L. (2000). *Working knowledge*. Boston: Harvard University Press.

Fedor, D. B., Ghosh, S., Caldwell, S. D., Maurer, T. J., & Singhal, V. R. (2003) The effects of knowledge management on team members' ratings of project success and impact. *Decision Sciences, 34*(3), 513-539.

Fichman, R. G., & Kemerer, C. F. (1997). The assimilation of software process innovations: An organizational learning perspective. *Management Science, 43*(10), 1345-1363.

Fiol, C. M., & Lyles, M. A. (1985). Organizational learning. *Academy of Management Review, 10*(4), 803-813.

Green, G. I. (1989). Perceived importance of systems analysts' job skills, roles, and non-salary incentives. *MIS Quarterly, 13*(2), 115-133.

Harlow, H. F. (1949). The formation of learning sets. *Psychological Review, 56*, 51-65.

Henderson, J. C., & Lee, S. (1992). Managing IS design teams: A control theory perspective. *Management Science, 38*(6), 757-777.

Jiang, J. J., & Klein, G. (1999). Risks to different aspects of system success. *Information & Management, 36*, 263-272.

Jiang, J. J., & Klein, G. (2000). Software development risks to project effectiveness. *Journal of Systems and Software*, *52*, 3-10.

Jiang, J. J., Klein, G., & Balloun, J. (1998). Systems analysts' attitudes toward information systems development. *Information Resources Management Journal*, *11*(4), 5-10.

Jiang, J. J., Klein, G., & Means, T. (2000). Project risk impact on software development team performance. *Project Management Journal*, *31*(4), 19-26.

Jiang, J. J., Klein, G., Van Slyke, C., & Cheney, G. (2003). A note on interpersonal and communication skills for IS professionals: Evidence of positive influence. *Decision Sciences*, *34*, 4, 1-15.

Jones, M. C., & Harrison, A. W. (1996). IS project team performance: An empirical assessment. *Information & Management*, *31*(2), 57-65.

Kayes, A. B., Kayes, D. C., & Kolb, D. A. (2005). Experiential learning in teams. *Simulation & Gaming*, *36*(3), 330-354.

Klein, H. (1991). Further evidence on the relationship between goal setting and expectancy theories. *Organizational Behavior and Human Decision Processes*, *49*, 230-257.

Ko, D., Kirsch, L., & King, W. (2005). Antecedents of knowledge transfer from consultants to clients in enterprise system implementations. *MIS Quarterly*, *29*(1), 59-85.

Kogut, B., & Zander, U. (1992). Knowledge of the firm, competitive capabilities, and the replication of technology. *Organization Science 3*, 383-397.

Lee, H., & Choi, B. (2003). Knowledge management enablers, processes, and organizational performance: An integrative view and empirical examination. *Journal of Management Information Systems*, *20*(1), 179-228.

Lindsay, P. H., & Norman, D. A. (1977). *Human information processing*. Orlando, FL: Academic Press.

Majchrzak, A., Beath, C. M., Lim, R. A., & Chin, W. W. (2005). Managing client dialogues during information system design to facilitate client learning. *MIS Quarterly*, *29*(4), 653-672.

Nelson, K. M., & Cooprider, J. G. (1996). The contribution of shared knowledge to IS group performance. *MIS Quarterly*, *20*(4), 409-432.

Nonaka, I., & Takeuchi, H. (1995). *The knowledge-creating company: how Japanese companies create the dynamics of innovation*. Oxford: Oxford University Press.

Nunnally, J. C. (1978). *Psychometric theory (2nd ed.)*. New York: McGraw-Hill.

Okhuysen, G., & Eisenhardt, K. (2002). Integrating knowledge in groups: How formal interventions enable flexibility. *Organization Science* *13*(4), 370-386.

Olfman, L., Bostrom, R. P., & Sein, M. K. (2003). A best-practice model for information technology learning strategy formulation. In *Proceedings of the 2003 SIGMIS Conference on Computer Personnel Research*, ACM Digital Library, 75-86.

Perminova, O., Gustafsson, M., & Wikstrom, K. (2008). Defining uncertainty in projects – a new perspective. *International Journal of Project Management, 26,* 73-79.

Podsakoff, P. M., & Organ, D. W. (1986). Self-reports in organizational research: Problems and prospects. *Journal of Management, 12,* 531-544.

Ramasubbu, N., Mithas, S., & Krishnan, M. S. (2008). High tech, high touch: The effect of employee skills and customer heterogeneity on customer satisfaction with enterprise system support services. *Decision Support Systems, 44,* 509-523.

Robillard, R. (1999). The role of knowledge in software development. *Communications of the ACM*, *42*(1), 87-92.

Rose, J., Pedersen, K., Hosbond, J. H., & Kraemmergaard, P. (2007). Management competences, not tools and techniques: A grounded examination of software project management at WM-data. *Information & Software Technology, 49,* 605-624.

Rus, L., & Lindvall, M. (2002). Knowledge management in software engineering. *IEEE Software*, 26-38.

Sarin, S., & McDermott, C. (2003). The effect of team leader characteristics on learning, knowledge application, and performance of cross-functional new product development teams. *Decision Sciences*, *34*(4), 707-739.

Schmidt, R. C., Lyytinen, K., Keil, M., & Cule, P. E. (2001). Identifying software project risks: An international Delphi study. *Journal of Management Information Systems*, *17*(4), 5-36.

Schramer, C. (2000). Organizing around not-yet-embedded knowledge. In G. Von Krogh, I. Nonaka, & T. Nishiguchi (Eds.), *Knowledge creation: A source of wealth* (pp. 36-60). London: Palgrave MacMillan.

Schulz, M. (2001). The uncertain relevance of newness: Organizational learning and knowledge flows. *Academy of Management Journal*, *44*(4), 661-681.

Sher, P. J., & Lee, V. C. (2004). Information technology as a facilitator for enhancing dynamic capabilities through knowledge management. *Information & Management*, *41*(8), 933-945.

Stein, E. W., & Vandenbosch, B. (1996). Organizational learning during advanced system development: Opportunities and obstacles. *Journal of Management Information Systems*, *13*(2), 115-136.

Tippins, J., & Sohi, R. (2003). IT competency and firm performance: Is organizational learning a missing link. *Strategic Management Journal*, *24*, 745-761.

Chapter XVIII
Beyond Development:
A Research Agenda for Investigating Open Source Software User Communities

Leigh Jin
San Francisco State University, USA

Daniel Robey
Georgia State University, USA

Marie-Claude Boudreau
University of Georgia, USA

ABSTRACT

Open source software has rapidly become a popular area of study within the information systems research community. Most of the research conducted so far has focused on the phenomenon of open source software development, rather than use. We argue for the importance of studying open source software use and propose a framework to guide research in this area. The framework describes four main areas of investigation: the creation of OSS user communities, their characteristics, their contributions and how they change. For each area of the framework, we suggest several research questions that deserve attention.

INTRODUCTION

In recent years, the open source software (OSS) development movement has captured the attention of both information systems practitioners and researchers. The "open community model" is one that involves the development and support of software by volunteers with no or limited commercial interest. This model differs from proprietary software development, and with other open source business models such as corporate distribution, sponsored open source and second-generation open source (Watson, Boudreau, York, Greiner, & Wynn, in press). The open community model is appealing to many because of its application of community principles of governance over commercial activities (Markus, Manville, & Agres, 2000; von Hippel & von Krogh, 2003). By describing open source as a "movement," we reflect the broader excitement about the implications of community governance processes in a knowledge economy (Adler, 2001).

Open source has rapidly become a popular area of study within the information systems (IS) research community, as evidenced by the appearance of special tracks for OSS within conferences and special issues of journals. For example, the Americas Conference on Information Systems sponsored an "Open Source Adoption and Use" minitrack, and the Hawaii International Conference on System Sciences offered a minitrack on "Open Source Software Development." On the journal side, *Management Science* invited submissions to a special issue on "Open Source Software" in 2004. Also, *Journal of Database Management* announced a special issue on "Open Source Software."

Although these calls for OSS research do not limit contributions, the vast majority of the research conducted so far has focused on OSS development rather than use (Fitzgerald & Kenny, 2003). The interest in open community development reflects a desire to explain the counterintuitive practice of treating commercially valuable products as public goods rather than proprietary products for sale. Likewise, the development and maintenance of complex software products by communities of expert volunteers has piqued interest into the incentives for developers. As a consequence of the primary focus on OSS development, little research has yet been conducted on OSS use, especially by non-technical users.

The neglect of OSS use may be attributed to two false assumptions about OSS projects. First, it is known that people often become OSS developers because they intend to use the product being developed. To echo Raymond's (2001) frequently quoted expression, OSS developers are users with an "itch to scratch," so they are willing to devote time and expertise to develop software solutions to their own problems as users. Thus, it is commonly assumed that there is no distinction between OSS developers and users (Feller & Fitzgerald, 2000). Following this line of argument, we might conclude that no special research agenda for OSS use is needed because OSS use is redundant with OSS development.

However, this argument and its underlying assumption can be challenged on the grounds that OSS use by technically experienced developers differs from OSS use by technically naïve users. Verma, Jin, and Negi (2005) argued that technical developers and non-technical users have very different interpretations of OSS's ease of use. Non-technical users may experience difficulty in using OSS products because OSS developers are motivated to improve functionality rather than usability (Nichols & Twidale, 2003). Thus, even though all OSS developers are likely also to be users, the distinction between developers and non-technical users remains important.

The assumption can also be challenged by statistics showing the rapid rise in the number of OSS users, the vast majority of whom have no interest or capability to contribute to modifications of the source code (Fitzgerald & Kenny, 2003). For widely distributed OSS such as Linux, it makes no sense to assume that more than a small percentage of users could possibly become developers (von Hippel & von Krogh, 2003). Clearly, users vastly outnumber developers in larger OSS projects. As OSS development becomes increasingly targeted toward productivity and entertainment applications, the relative proportion of non-technical users can be expected to increase.

The second assumption dissuading research on OSS use is that the OSS movement is unique solely because of the way software is developed, but that its use is similar to any other type of software. Given the abundance of IS research that is focused on the adoption and use of software applications, one might assume that no special research program is needed for OSS use.

This assumption can be challenged by examining some differences between OSS and proprietary software. Users of OSS are typically confronted by a fundamentally different type of technical support than that found with proprietary software. Rather than relying on a vendor's customer support, users of OSS generally need to search for community resources for help for installing, learning and using their freely acquired software. OSS users are likely to receive such help through participation in user groups or mailing lists that are supported by volunteers, similar to the communities supporting OSS development (Golden, 2005; Lakhani & von Hippel, 2003; Raymond, 2001). Given these distinctive features of OSS products and support, we do not agree with the assumption that OSS use is the same as proprietary software use.

These arguments justify research into OSS use. In this article, we adopt a community perspective on OSS use, which is explained in the following section. We then present a framework that includes four main areas of investigation: *creation* of OSS user communities, their *characteristics*, their *contributions* and how they *change*. For each element of the framework we pose several research questions.

A COMMUNITY PERSPECTIVE ON OSS USE

The term "community" was introduced into the English language in the 14th century from Latin to refer to a group of people living in a common geographical location. Between the 17th and 19th centuries the meaning of community was extended to describe people who shared common characteristics, interests or identities – even if they were not geographically close (Cole, 2002; Williams, 1973). As the 21st century begins, people have grown more accustomed to participating in virtual communities that are enabled by Internet technology and the World Wide Web (Rheingold, 2000). Virtual communities differ from colocated communities by offering a wider range of options for participation and by allowing community size to grow, unconstrained by physical space. As Cole (2002) noted, virtual communities can be more heterogeneous: "each [community] is unique in the combination of institutional arrangements, educational content, forms of Internet communication, and participant goals that it embodies" (p. xxvi). Moreover, individual members may tailor their virtual communities to satisfy personal preferences (Wellman, 2001).

The power of collaboration within geographically dispersed communities is demonstrated by the making of the first edition of the *Oxford English Dictionary*, one of the earliest examples of an open community project (Watson, Boudreau, Greiner, Wynn, York & Gul, 2005). The dictionary, which took about 70 years to complete, was compiled primarily from definitions submitted by thousands of volunteers fluent in the English language. In his book, *The Professor and the Madman,* Winchester (1998) reported that an insane American prisoner became the most prolific contributor to the original compilation of the *Oxford English Dictionary.* This story illustrates two principles that also sustain modern OSS communities: everyone is welcome to contribute regardless of personal circumstance, and value can be produced through community effort.

OSS development largely depends upon the ability of developers to contribute as members of virtual communities (Markus et al., 2000; Lakhani & von Hippel; 2003; Raymond, 2001). Given that much OSS development transpires in online communities, we expect that OSS use also relies on virtual communities for software acquisition, implementation, maintenance and support. For example, Lakhani and von Hippel (2003) suggested that successful OSS projects were capable of delivering high quality field support

– mundane but necessary tasks – to users through voluntary effort. Field support primarily involves experienced users answering questions posted by novice users through an archived mailing list. Indeed, a highly organized system of OSS user groups has grown around major OSS products. Taking Linux user groups (LUGs) as an example, in July 2005 there were 846 registered LUGs in 108 countries, including 299 in the United States (http://www.linux.org/groups).

Despite the importance of electronically mediated interaction within OSS communities, we do not assume that OSS user communities are exclusively virtual. Indeed, one of the naïve assertions about OSS development is that software can be developed by a community of complete strangers who interact only through electronic media. To the contrary, experienced OSS participants have opportunities to attend conferences and regular meetings held in physical places. For example, the O'Reilly Open Source Convention and LinuxWorld Conferences are popular venues for OSS developers to meet and exchange ideas. Research on Linux user groups (Jin, Robey, & Boudreau, 2006) reveals that the Silicon Valley LUG holds face-to-face meetings at least monthly and organizes InstallFests, where new users can bring in their computers and allow experienced volunteers to install Linux, diagnose problems and repair configurations. The LUG of Davis, California, sponsors a Linux Emergency Relief Team, staffed with experts who may even travel to users' homes to service their Linux systems (Jin et al., 2006). According to Moen (2003), LUGs are vital to the Linux movement, taking on many of the same roles that a regional office does for a large organization:

LUGs' role in Linux advocacy cannot be overestimated, especially since wide-scale commercial acceptance of Linux is only newly underway. While it is certainly beneficial to the Linux movement each and every time a computer journalist writes a positive review of Linux, it is also beneficial every time satisfied Linux users brief their friends, colleagues, employees, or employers.

The following research agenda focuses on questions about the creation, characteristics, contributions and change in OSS user communities. There is no direct empirical rationale for dividing the agenda into these four categories because research on OSS user communities is just beginning. Rather, the research agenda reflects a progression through different phases of an OSS community over its life cycle. Creation is the beginning, characteristics describe the makeup of the community, contribution describes the major functions performed, and change describes later growth. The four phases are associated with different kinds of issues, which we offer as researchable topics. Because the life of a community is not biologically limited, our agenda shows that communities may repeat the cycle as they change.

The agenda is proposed at a high level due to the novelty of the phenomenon and the paucity of existing research efforts. By restricting our attention to a community perspective, we purposefully omit consideration of individual and organizational influences on OSS use. However, we believe that a community perspective on OSS research is valuable because it has played such a prominent role in research on OSS development.

A RESEARCH AGENDA

Figure 1 identifies the four main areas where research into OSS user communities should be undertaken: creation (C1), characteristics (C2), contributions (C3) and change (C4). As shown, these areas are related sequentially, beginning with creation. It is also shown that change not only completes the cycle but potentially begins a new cycle.

Figure 1. Research areas

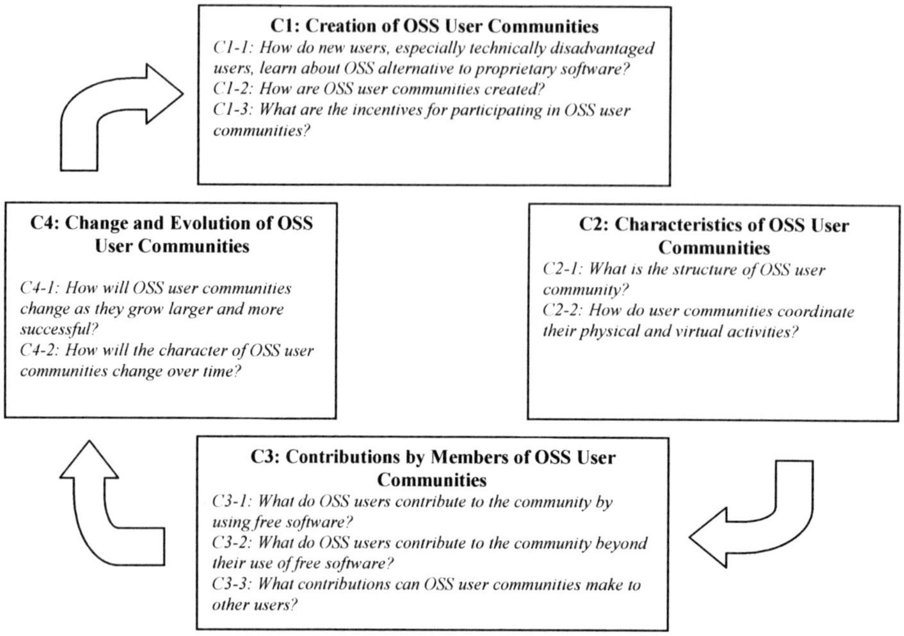

C1: Creation of OSS User Communities

The creation of an OSS user community requires potential members to learn about OSS as an alternative to proprietary software and in-house development, to engage in community activities and to respond to incentives for starting or joining a user community. The research questions below address these three important issues.

C1-1: How do new users, especially technically disadvantaged users, learn about OSS alternatives to proprietary software?

This issue is interesting because, compared to proprietary software, open-community software projects lack specialized teams to market the product and to promote it through mass media. Although the notion of gift culture is well established within the OSS development community, users are likely to be suspicious of the opportunity to receive software as a free gift. Although OSS has made news headlines and gained immense exposure on the Internet, a nontechnical user would still be expected to have difficulty installing and using a new operating system such as Linux. Indeed, many new users are introduced to OSS through personal friends, whom they trust and rely upon for support when they encounter problems. The role of the broader OSS user community in introducing new users to OSS products stands as an important research question.

C1-2: How are OSS user communities created?

Creating and sustaining a software user community requires resources such as meeting places, newsletters, and Web hosting services. Traditional software user groups are often sponsored by vendors, who provide considerable benefits to both users and themselves (Buckner, 1996). On the one hand, users may benefit from discounted prices negotiated with the vendors and the chance to suggest improvements in the software's next release. On the other hand, vendors receive a low cost marketing opportunity and obtain feedback on the usability of their products.

Because software vendors are rarely involved in open-community OSS user groups, their creation depends on a group of enthusiasts sharing the same passion for the software. These enthusiasts may be among the original developers, motivated to increase the software's user base. Alternatively, these enthusiasts may be pure users who believe in the principles behind OSS, therefore promoting its use and maximizing the benefits of their own use. Large companies may also be the principal instigators of OSS user groups. If an OSS product is used extensively within a company, creation of a user group for that product provides free training opportunities for the company's employees. Large technology companies with a stake in an OOS product may also support OSS user groups indirectly by providing meeting space or donating Web hosting services. Companies providing such support may enhance their reputations within the OSS community, which in turn may improve their opportunities to recruit talented new members.

Although we acknowledge that OSS user groups are important components of OSS communities, the creation of other community components should not be overlooked. Special interest groups and forums may be established by universities, government agencies and other organizations. Although their activities may be less visible to the public, they may generate additional resources, such as training provided by the sponsoring organizations.

C1-3: What are the incentives for participating in OSS user communities?

Because users may obtain OSS freely, with no obligation to contribute to development, their use of the software is likely to be based primarily on cost and quality considerations (Fitzgerald & Kenney, 2003). The incentives for community participation, however, differ from the incentives for using OSS (Wang, 2005). For developers who incur substantial private costs by investing their own resources into development, incentives include not only the ability to use the software but also benefits related to reputation and learning. It is conceivable that users may also obtain such benefits, gaining reputations as skilled implementers who are helpful to novice users.

It has been argued that the true benefit for using open source software goes beyond its low initial cost and involves a user's long-term control over information technology. By contrast, users of proprietary software become dependent on software that remains inside the vendor's black box. With no ability to change the source code, users of proprietary software lose control and subject themselves to a monopoly relationship with their vendor (Moen, 2000). OSS may provide an incentive by restoring the user's control.

It is also likely that OSS user groups offer more value than user groups organized by proprietary software vendors. Vendor-sponsored user groups often charge membership fees and use their meetings to promote new products. These commercial interests may interfere with the activities of OSS user groups. For the more technically inclined, OSS user groups offer solutions in the form of code modifications that address specific problems of individual users. By contrast, vendors are more likely to avoid solutions involving code modification and focus on software configuration or settings, which may or may not solve the user's problems. As stated by Moen (2003), OSS user groups are ready and willing to modify source code on the spot:

Traditional groups must closely monitor what software users redistribute at meetings. While illegal copying of restricted proprietary software certainly occurred, it was officially discouraged –for good reason. At LUG meetings, however, that entire mindset simply does not apply: Far from being forbidden, unrestricted copying of Linux should be among a LUG's primary goals.

Outside geopolitical forces could also provide powerful incentives for OSS user community participation. When a U.S. company refused to develop a Portuguese language version of its software for a company studying rain forest biodiversity in Brazil, the Brazilians turned to an inexpensive OSS solution. The OSS software not only delivered the functionality that the company needed, but also provided all prompts in the Portuguese language (Hall, 2002). Consequently, the Brazilian government became a strong advocate of the OSS movement, as explained by a Brazilian representative at the LinuxWorld 2004 conference:

The question is . . . how the universities can have better tools to teach their students, how government can save millions or billions of dollars each year and still be able to use all kinds of technology. Our government decided that OSS is a good idea; it is something to be supported. In fact, we are the biggest user of OSS in Latin America. We have something around now, eight or ten million users of OSS.

Understanding the creation of OSS user communities requires attention to many issues pertaining to users learning about OSS products; the creation of specific mechanisms, such as user groups, to support user activities, and incentives for wide participation. Because these issues are raised at the community level of analysis, answers cannot be obtained by looking at individual decisions to join and contribute to user communities. Studies of OSS user communities may draw insights from OSS development communities, but it should not be assumed that use is the same as development. For these reasons, our research agenda focuses specifically on the creation of OSS user communities.

C2: Characteristics of OSS User Communities

Like all communities, OSS user communities are likely to be differentiated by the roles that different members play. It is also important to recognize the relationships between user and developer communities. Indeed, it may be desirable to consider users and developers as subcommunities within an OSS project. The questions below address issues related to the characteristics of OSS user communities.

C2-1: What is the structure of an OSS user community?

An OSS community is built around a specific OSS project, with shared interests of improving and using the software. As more people become interested in using the software, the community grows and differentiates into various roles. For example, Ye, Kishida, Nakakoji, and Yamamoto (2002) defined eight roles in OSS communities: (1) project leader, (2) core members, (3) active developers, (4) peripheral developers, (5) bug fixers, (6) bug reporters, (7) source code readers and (8) passive users.

Although helpful in defining the characteristics of an OSS community, the roles defined by Ye et al. (2002) appear most suitable as a description of an OSS development-oriented community (Jin, Verma, & Negi, 2005). Of the eight roles identified, only the last three include users, while the first seven describe developers. According to Jin et al. (2005), an OSS development-oriented community is "exclusively dedicated to develop, support, and maintain a single or multiple open source project(s)" (p. 16522). An OSS user-oriented community, by contrast, is typically created by users for users to "promote the use of OSS products" (Jin et al., 2005, p. 16523). The primary activities of OSS user-oriented communities are attracting new members to adopt OSS products and educating existing members about the best use practices for OSS products. Linux user groups are excellent examples of OSS user-oriented communities. Other examples include the perl mongers community, BSD User Groups, and MYSQL User Groups. While developers could be involved in an OSS user-oriented community, the roles that its members play would differ from those played in an OSS development-oriented community. Based on our participation in various LUGs, the following roles of OSS user oriented community are evident: (1) founder/officer, (2) meeting and facilities coordinator, (3) public relations officer, (4) Installfest coordinator, (5) mailing list/Web site administrator, (6) face-to-face meeting attendees and (7) mailing list subscribers.

Depending on the size of a particular user-oriented community, some of these roles could be combined and performed by one person. An important issue deserving research attention is the way members assume these roles and the relationships among the various roles. Such research could contribute to more effective designs for community structure.

C2-2: How do user communities coordinate their physical and virtual activities?

Given that OSS development communities operate both physically and virtually, it is an important question to understand how they use these different arenas of community life. Theories of virtual organizing have pointed to the possibility for virtual and physical activities to reinforce, complement, compensate and produce synergies with each other (Robey, Schwaig & Jin, 2003). At one level, OSS virtual activities allow developers to access and modify source code, access necessary archives, and interact through mailing lists, Internet Relay Chat channels, and Web logs. At another level, OSS physical activities are important for forging social ties and clarifying communications (Jin et al., 2006). Moen (2003) emphasized that LUGs' socializing function was effective for members to become acculturated into the Linux user community:

By "socializing", here I mean primarily sharing experiences, forming friendships, and mutually-shared admiration and respect. In other words, acculturation turns you from "one of them" to "one of us." ... LUGs are often much more efficient at this task than are mailing lists or newsgroups, precisely because of the former's greater interactivity and personal focus.

Besides the socializing benefit from face-to-face meetings, physical activities like InstallFests can be effective for advanced users to tailor their help to new users' particular needs. Because new users bring their computers to InstallFests, OSS experts can demonstrate software installation, diagnose problems, and even conduct hands-on training individually with new users.

Understanding the characteristics of OSS user communities requires attention to the roles played by members and the mechanisms for coordinating community action. Again, such matters cannot be undertaken from an individual or even small group perspective. The virtual nature of OSS user communities makes their potential size practically unlimited. Yet, research on the characteristics of OSS communities needs to understand their virtual nature without losing sight of the importance of their face-to-face, physical activities.

C3: Contributions by Members of OSS User Communities

In the OSS development literature, much is made of the voluntary gifts donated by skilled designers for the creation of a public good (Fitzgerald & Kenney, 2003). Indeed, communities are likely to fail if such contributions are not made. The following questions are posed with the same issue in mind for the OSS user community.

C3-1: What do OSS users contribute to the community by using free software?

If contributions are not made by users, OSS users assume the status of free riders who simply take from the community without paying back. Paradoxically, free ridership by OSS users is actively encouraged rather than discouraged. Because the number of OSS users is a measure of a project's success, users are not pressured to contribute as developers do (von Hippel & von Krogh, 2003). Indeed, their most important contribution may simply be their use of the OSS product.

For example, one of the goals of the Firefox team (a popular OSS Internet browser) is to acquire ten percent of the browser market share. According to one of the team's leaders, "It really doesn't matter how great your technology is. If nobody's using it, then you are not achieving that mission of bringing back choice" (personal communication, 2005). Although most users may never contribute toward product improvement, they are valuable to the success of the Firefox project because their usage adds to Firefox's market share. Indeed, some software projects have found an OSS strategy to be an effective solution for acquiring a customer base before pursuing more commercial objectives. Onetti and Capobianco (2005) found a positive correlation between the number of downloads generated on a Sourceforge OSS project site and the number of new clients interested in purchasing the product's commercial license. As more users download and use an OSS product, the more credible and successful the project becomes, potentially attracting even more new users.

C3-2: What do OSS users contribute to the community beyond their use of free software?

As Raymond (2001) pointed out, some of the most successful OSS projects are created by the most talented software developers. Because the OSS community tends to attract people with extensive technical backgrounds, there is a risk that resulting products would reflect the "geek" culture and be less useful to ordinary users. For example, the user interfaces of OSS tend to be command-line driven, making their installation and configuration technically demanding. It is conceivable that less technical users might contribute to development by making OSS projects easier to install, configure, use and maintain.

In the case of the Firefox browser project, project leaders not only encouraged contributions from nontechnical users but also valued them as vital assets to the project's success. Instead of contributing code, nontechnical users contributed artistic skills to design the logo and images, marketing skills to help spread the word about Firefox, and even monetary contributions to help place an advertisement in *The New York Times* (McHugh, 2005). Whether such participation would be welcomed on other projects remains uncertain, so the issue presents a good research opportunity to study the impact of less technical users on the development process.

C3-3: What contributions can OSS user communities make to other users?

Fitzgerald and Kenney (2003) reported an interesting case of an Irish hospital using OSS software for a number of internal operations. Although the hospital's IT staff had no intention of ever contributing modifications to the software's source code, they had begun to offer the applications, which they had tailored for themselves, to other health care organizations free of charge. In this manifestation of community spirit, one user was giving back to the community of other users. The study suggests that users may add further value by making OSS programs fit specific industry needs. While these contributions may not earn great reputations, they may provide value for the user community. Future research is warranted on the practice of users making vertical applications more useful for other users, in contrast to the traditional focus in OSS development on horizontal infrastructure systems (Fitzgerald & Kenny, 2003).

Studying contributions is important because communities are held together by such contributions. The research questions posed above guide these potential research opportunities.

C4: Change and Evolution of OSS User Communities

It is clear that OSS user communities are new phenomena that have only become significant economically in the last half decade. We expect the nature of OSS communities to change, perhaps rapidly, as software development and use practices evolve. This, in turn, will affect the creation of new communities, as our cyclical representation in Figure 1 suggests. The following questions address the evolution and change of OSS user communities.

C4-1: How will OSS user communities change as they grow larger and more successful?

Although core developers initiate and contribute the major portion of source code (e.g., 80% in the case of the Apache project (Mockus, Fielding, & Herbsleb, 2002)), the largest growth in community size comes from supporting roles like bug fixers, bug reporters and users. Core developers may even recede in importance as a project stabilizes and does not require major revision. Thus, users may assume more prominent stature in mature communities, partly from their endorsement of a particular OSS project.

Communities are sensitive in the longer run to the free ridership phenomenon because attempts to control free ridership involve increased monitoring costs that eventually outweigh the rewards from contributions (von Hippel & von Krogh, 2003). Because free ridership is viewed positively in OSS development communities, it would be useful to study whether growth will strengthen the community or whether growth can ultimately erode feelings of community solidarity. In other words, will the trust that characterizes a community form of governance (Adler, 2001) disappear as community size increases?

One could also argue that size may not be the most important factor promoting community change. The expansion of low cost communication channels allows OSS users to reach out globally and stay connected. Thus, the cost of monitoring members could remain low despite growth. In addition, increasing user community size could distribute monitoring costs across more members. Simultaneously, community trust could be reinforced at more local levels through the events and social activities discussed earlier. These potential effects of changing size could be studied as part of a research program on community change.

C4-2: How will the character of OSS user communities change over time?

As OSS communities grow and prosper, commercial interests may be expected to appear and taint the gift culture characterizing open communities. Firms such as RedHat emerged quickly to create value by improving software distribution and by adding supplementary services such as installation, support and training. JBoss promoted its application server software as "professional open source," charging users for the expertise and services of key developers (Watson et al., 2006). User groups associated with these and other commercial open source companies may come to resemble proprietary software user groups more than the open communities described earlier. Such changes would potentially affect the character of OSS user communities currently operating under volunteer arrangements.

Although user communities affected by commercial open source companies may lose free access to developer expertise, ultimately less experienced users may benefit more from subscribing to paid services at different levels of support. In addition, companies like JBoss have operated community forums in which independent developers can still contribute free advice. In such cases, commercial and noncommercial interests co-exist in the community. One benefit to the commercial interest is that community forums become fertile recruiting grounds for new developers. As a JBoss representative at the JavaOne 2005 conference explained:

There are individuals on our forums that don't work for us. They answer questions. We actually try to get a ranking system of who answer the most questions, so it gives us an idea of who we can hire for support. So the forums might turn into a recruiting ground for us.

As the interests of commercial software developers and open source communities become reconciled, the line between the OSS user community and closed source user communities may blur. As more enterprises adopt Linux, for example, users have become more interested in running both Linux and Windows platforms (Adelstein, 2004). The OSS user community could attend to the needs of these ambidextrous users by addressing issues related to usability, hardware and software compatibility.

Alternatively, OSS user communities may try to preserve their character to some degree. For example, although the Firefox team had little marketing budget, they tapped into the resources of the OSS community to launch a promotional campaign. They were able to raise $200,000 from about 10,000 donors in 10 days to pay for a two-page print advertisement in *The New York Times*. In addition, the Firefox team worked closely with international OSS communities to achieve the simultaneous launch of Firefox in 14 languages. Firefox's experience illustrates that communities can remain powerful without having to co-opt commercial interests.

Although the nature and direction of change in OSS user communities cannot be predicted with certainty, it seems inevitable that changes will come, probably rapidly. However, there are probably no easily identifiable drivers of community change. Researchers investigating change in OSS user communities should approach this area with an appreciation for the complexity of organizational and institutional change. This recommendation lies beyond our present scope, but it remains an important consideration.

CONCLUSION

The framework offered in this article is designed to stimulate a new direction in OSS research, one that focuses primarily on software use rather than software development. Although development has attracted the bulk of research interest to date, many important issues pertain to OSS use. OSS users far outnumber OSS developers, and as OSS products become more popular, the number of OSS users will continue to increase. We have identified many of the issues that make OSS different from the use of proprietary and in-house developed software and posed our research questions accordingly. Our research agenda emphasizes the community perspective that has attracted such interest in OSS development research. We believe that many valuable insights can be generated by a focus on OSS user communities.

Beyond the present agenda, we may speculate on the impact of OSS user communities as a model for industries besides software. Although market research and customer relationship management are time-honored ways for companies to feel the pulse of their customers, the phenomenon of OSS user communities suggests that a more active role for customers might be valuable. For example, Threadless.com holds a weekly competition, in which anyone who wishes can upload T-shirt artwork to the company's Web site. Online shoppers can then vote for their favorite designs. Threadless.

com prints the winning graphics on limited-edition t-shirts, which are available for purchase at the Web site. Winners are awarded cash or store credits. By 2005, threadless had attracted over 40,000 design submissions (Luman, 2005). This experience offers innovative ideas for community participation in electronic commerce.

In conclusion, the study of OSS user communities offers the potential to learn not only about OSS projects but also about communities in general. The research agenda proposed in this article suggests many avenues for investigating OSS user communities. Given that there is little extant research on any of the questions raised in this article, our objective is to stimulate thinking about important research areas rather than to summarize findings. Hopefully, the IS research community will begin systematic investigation of the research questions posed here.

REFERENCES

Adler, P. (2001). Market, hierarchy, and trust: The knowledge economy and the future of capitalism. *Organization Science 12*(2), 215-234.

Adelstein, T. (2004). Desktop linux: New linux users changing the face of community. Retrieved July 27, 2006, from http://www.desktoplinux.com/articles/AT3791991696.html

Buckner K. (1996). Computer user groups: The advantage of successful partnership. *International Journal of Information Management, 16*(3), 195-204.

Cole, M. (2002) Virtual communities for learning and development – A look to the past and some glimpses into the future. In K. Ann Renninger & W. Shumar (Eds.), *Building virtual communities: Learning and change in cyberspace*. Cambridge: Cambridge University Press.

Feller, J., & Fitzgerald, B. (2000). A framework analysis of the OpenSource software development paradigm. In *Proceedings of the International Conference of Information Systems* (pp. 21, 58-69).

Fitzgerald, B., & Kenny, T. (2003). OpenSource software the trenches: Lessons from a large-scale OSS implementation. In *Proceedings of the International Conference on Information Systems* (pp. 24, 316-326).

Golden, B. (2005). *Succeeding with OpenSource.* Boston: Addison-Wesley.

Hall, J. (2002, September 6). Free software in Brazil. *Linux Journal, 101.*

Jin, L., Robey, D., & Boudreau, M. C. (2006). Exploring the hybrid community: Intertwining virtual and physical representations of Linux user communities. In *Proceedings of the Administrative Science Association of Canada,* Banff, Canada.

Jin, L., Verma, S., & Negi, A. (2005). Profiling OpenSource: A use perspective across OpenSource communities in the US and India. In *Proceedings of the 36th Annual Meeting of the Decision Sciences Institute,* San Francisco, California.

Lakhani, K. R., & von Hippel, E. (2003). How OpenSource software works: "Free" user-to-user assistance. *Research Policy, 32*(6), 923.

Luman, S. (2005, June). OpenSource Software. *Wired Magazine,* p. 68.

Markus, M. L., Manville, B., & Agres, C. E. (2000). What makes a virtual organization work? *Sloan Management Review, 42*, 13-26.

McHugh, J. (2005, February). The Firefox explosion. *Wired Magazine*, pp. 92-96.

Mockus, A., Fielding, R. T., & Herbsleb, J. D. (2002). Two case studies of OpenSource software development: Apache and Mozilla. *ACM Transactions on Software Engineering and Methodology, 11*(3), 309-346.

Moen, R. (2000). Eric Raymond's tips for effective OpenSource advocacy. Retrieved July 28, 2006, from http://www.itworld.com/AppDev/344/LW-D000913expo00/pfindex.html

Moen, R. (2003). Linux user group HOW TO. Retrieved July 28, 2006, from http://www.linux.org/docs/ldp/howto/User-Group-HOWTO.html

Nichols, D. M., & Twidale, M. B. (2003).The usability of OpenSource software. *First Monday, 8*(1).

Onetti, A., & Capobianco, F. (2005). OpenSource and business model innovation: The Funambol case. In M. Scotto & G. Succi (Eds.), In *Proceedings of the 1st International Conference on Opens Source Systems* (pp. 224-227).

Raymond, E. (2001). *The cathedral and the bazaar: Musings on Linux and OpenSource by an accidental revolutionary.* Sebastopol, CA: O'Reilly & Associates.

Rheingold, H. (2000). *Virtual community: Homesteading on the electronic frontier.* Cambridge: The MIT Press.

Robey, D., Schwaig, K., & Jin, L. (2003). Intertwining material and virtual work. *Information and Organization, 13*(2), 111-129.

Verma, S., Jin, L., & Negi, A. (2005). OpenSource adoption and use: A comparative study between groups in the US and India. In *Proceedings of the 11th Annual Americas Conference on Information Systems* (pp. 960-972).

von Hippel, E., & von Krogh, G. (2003) OpenSource software and the "private-collective" innovation model: Issues for organization science. *Organization Science, 14*(2), 209-223.

Wang, J. (2005). The role of social capital in OpenSource software communities. In *Proceedings of the 11th Annual Americas Conference on Information Systems* (pp. 937-943).

Watson, R. T., Boudreau, M. C., Greiner, M., Wynn, D., York, P., & Gul, R. (2005). Governance and global communities. *Journal of International Management, 11,* 125-142.

Watson, R. T., Boudreau, M. C., York, P., Greiner, M., & Wynn, D. (in press). The business of OpenSource. *Communications of the ACM.*

Wellman, B. (2001). Physical place and cyberplace: The rise of personalized networking. *International Journal of Urban and Regional Research, 25*(2), 227-252.

Williams, R. (1973). *Keywords.* Oxford: Oxford University Press.

Winchester, S. (1998). *The professor and the madman: A tale of murder, insanity, and the making of the Oxford English Dictionary.* New York: HarperCollins.

Ye, Y., Kishida, K., Nakakoji, K., & Yamamoto, Y. (2002). Creating and maintaning sustainale OpenSource software communities. In *Proceedings of International Symposium on Future Software Technology 2002 (ISFST '02),* Wuhan, China.

This work was previously published in the Information Resources Management Journal, Vol. 20, Issue 1, edited by M. Khosrow-Pour, pp. 68-80, copyright 2007 by IGI Publishing, formerly known as Idea Group Publishing (an imprint of IGI Global).

Chapter XIX
Electronic Meeting Topic Effects

Milam Aiken
University of Mississippi, USA

Linwu Gu
Indiana University of Pennsylvania, USA

Jianfeng Wang
Indiana University of Pennsylvania, USA

ABSTRACT

In the literature of electronic meetings, few studies have investigated the effects of topic-related variables on group processes. This chapter explores the effects of an individual's perception of topics on process gains or process losses using a sample of 110 students in 14 electronic meetings. The results of the study showed that topic characteristics variables, individual knowledge, and individual self-efficacy had a significant influence on the number of relevant comments generated in an electronic meeting.

INTRODUCTION

An **electronic meeting system** (EMS), otherwise known as a **group support system** (GSS), is "an information technology-based environment that supports group meetings, which may be distributed geographically and temporally" (Dennis, George, Jessup, Nunamaker, & Vogel, 1988). In these automated meetings, groups perform negotiation, conflict resolution, systems analysis and design, and other collaborative group activities. Often during traditional, verbal meetings, some group members might not be able to participate because others are talking, and some might be apprehensive about saying what they think (Nunamaker, Dennis, Valacich, Vogel, & George, 1991), but using an EMS, most of these problems are alleviated. People in **electronic meetings** often participate more, save more time, and are more satisfied than those in traditional meetings (McLeod, 1992).

Many variables can affect the processes and outcomes of electronic meetings, however, including group size, individual typing speed, the idea generation technique used, and the **topic** of the meeting (Aiken & Paolillo, 2000; Aiken & Vanjani, 2002; Benbasat & Lim, 1993). Much EMS research has focused on the impacts of group structure, task characteristics of the technology, and context (Zak, 1994), but the choice of discussion topic can be a major influence on meeting process gains (e.g., more information, synergy, and learning) and process losses (e.g., free riding, evaluation apprehension, information overload, and conformance pressure). Relatively few studies have investigated the effects of topic choice on meeting outcomes (Briggs, Nunamaker, & Sprague, 1998; Pervan, 1998).

One earlier study (Reinig, Briggs, & Nunamaker, 1997) showed that uninteresting **topics** brought more "**flaming**" (i.e., hostile, obscene, or inappropriate comments). In addition, group member participation can vary with the meeting topic (Cornelius & Boos, 2003; Pinsonneault, Barki, Gallupe, & Hoppen, 1999). Finally, group members' knowledge of the topic and judgments of the importance of the problem and their influence over the final decision can affect the number of comments in a discussion (Aiken, 2002; Aiken & Waller, 2000; Tyran, Dennis, Vogel, & Nunamaker, 1992). Thus, inappropriate topic selection has the potential to produce flaming, less participation, and fewer useful comments in a meeting. The purpose of this chapter is to advance our understanding of topic choice further by investigating the relationships of multiple characteristics including ambiguity, difficulty, and self-efficacy on outcomes such as group cohesion, effectiveness, participation, and number of comments generated.

RESEARCH MODEL

The research model (shown in Figure 1) includes many variables not used in prior studies of topic

Figure 1. Research model of topic effects on electronic meetings

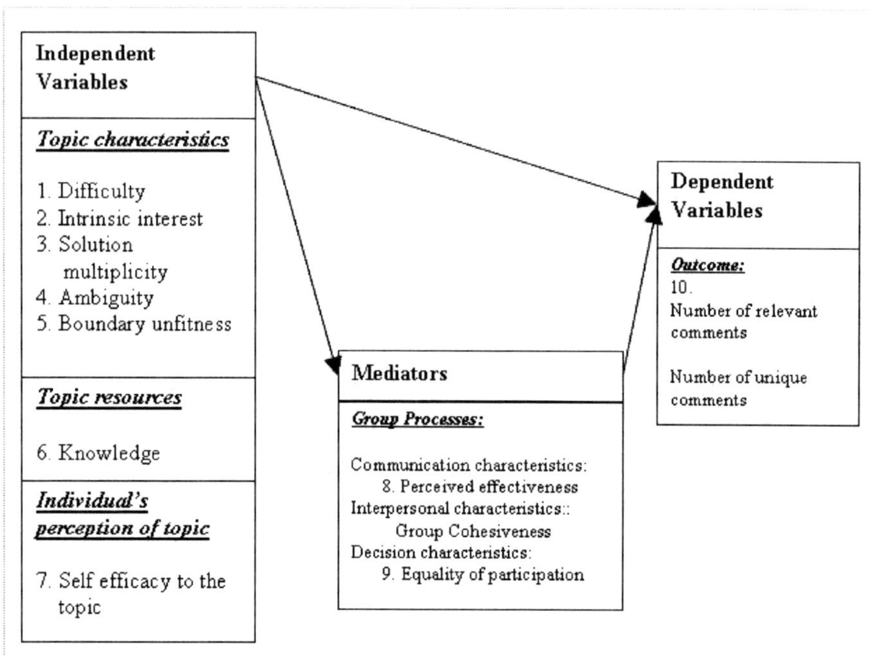

effects, and these variables are described below along with their associated hypotheses.

Difficulty

Topic difficulty is defined as "the amount of effort required to complete the task. For example, time to solve, number of errors, or failures to complete, etc. would be measures of difficulty" (Shaw, 1976). A task is difficult not because it is always complex, but because it may require a large amount of effort, and the more difficult a task is, the more time a group requires for a solution. Previous studies indicate that the degree of task difficulty is related to the amount of effort required to complete the task, to the degree of group member involvement and presentation, and to the speed of a group member's reaction (Hackman, 1968). Task demands, self-esteem, and conformity are all related to task difficulty, and task difficulty influences group effectiveness and performance (Griffin, Neale, & Neale, 2000). Thus, difficult topics can affect group involvement, perceived effectiveness, and the number of comments generated during a meeting.

Based on these previous studies, we have the following hypotheses:

> $\mathbf{H_{1a}}$: Topic difficulty decreases the number of relevant comments.
> $\mathbf{H_{1b}}$: Topic difficulty decreases the number of unique comments.
> $\mathbf{H_{1c}}$: Topic difficulty decreases group cohesiveness.
> $\mathbf{H_{1d}}$: Topic difficulty decreases perceived effectiveness.
> $\mathbf{H_{1e}}$: Topic difficulty decreases equality of participation.

Intrinsic Interest

Intrinsic interest is defined as "the degree to which the task in and of itself is interesting, motivating, or attractive to the group members" (Shaw, 1976). One study (Aiken, 2002) showed that more relevant comments were generated if group members thought that the topic was more important. Group members in a meeting are more motivated when the topic that they discuss is interesting, involving, and challenging.

Thus, we have the following hypotheses:

> $\mathbf{H_{2a}}$: Topic intrinsic interest increases the number of relevant comments.
> $\mathbf{H_{2b}}$: Topic intrinsic interest increases the number of unique comments.
> $\mathbf{H_{2c}}$: Topic intrinsic interest increases perceived effectiveness.
> $\mathbf{H_{2d}}$: Topic intrinsic interest increases group cohesiveness.
> $\mathbf{H_{2e}}$: Topic intrinsic interest increases equality of participation.

Solution Multiplicity

Solution multiplicity is defined as more than one correct solution to the task or more than one possible course of action to attain a goal (Campbell & Gingrich, 1986). Solution multiplicity increases information overload, and the number of desired outcomes of a task is related to the degree of complexity. If a topic has multiple solutions but none can be proved to be the sole correct answer, the topic is controversial and can affect the number of relevant comments (Aiken, 2002). Therefore, we have the following hypotheses:

> $\mathbf{H_{3a}}$: Topic solution multiplicity decreases the number of relevant comments.
> $\mathbf{H_{3b}}$: Topic solution multiplicity decreases the number of unique comments.
> $\mathbf{H_{3c}}$: Topic solution multiplicity decreases perceived effectiveness.
> $\mathbf{H_{3d}}$: Topic solution multiplicity decreases group cohesiveness.
> $\mathbf{H_{3e}}$: Topic solution multiplicity decreases equality of participation.

Topic Ambiguity

Ambiguity is defined as the potential for multiple and possibly conflicting interpretations of a symbol or message (Huber & Daft, 1987) and can be a feature of an unstructured or ill structured task (Turoff , Hiltz, Bahgat, & Rana, 1993). Further, task ambiguity can result in solution uncertainty, i.e., uncertainty about whether a given solution could lead to a desired outcome. Many factors can add to the level of ambiguity, such as incompleteness, conflicting task objectives, and inconsistent task inputs, and a large solution space can make the task more ill-structured or unstructured. Therefore, problems arise when the meaning of a topic is ambiguous or when the participants are unclear about what a topic means, and what the goal of the task is. Generally, ill-structured or unstructured topics can have a large potential solution space. In addition, ambiguous topics can generate inconsistent viewpoints that often cannot be readily resolved based on the information available. Thus, a group faced with an ambiguous topic frequently does not generate many relevant comments and individual participation can be limited.

Thus, we have the following hypotheses:

> **H_{4a}:** Topic ambiguity decreases the number of relevant comments.
> **H_{4b}:** Topic ambiguity decreases the number of unique comments.
> **H_{4c}:** Topic ambiguity decreases perceived effectiveness.
> **H_{4d}:** Topic ambiguity decreases group cohesiveness.
> **H_{4e}:** Topic ambiguity decreases equality of participation.

Boundary Unfitness

Boundaries are identified as "often imaginary lines that mark the edge or limit of something" (Espinosa, Cummings, Wilson, & Pearce, 2003), and boundary control of a topic is relative to the effectiveness of communication because it helps group interaction (Putnam & Stohl, 1990). The flow of information is restricted if the boundaries transcend any particular domain such as relationships, groups, privacy, etc. People usually like to establish the rules for disclosing private information, and group members' accessibility depends on boundary fit. The flow of information in exchanging the viewpoints of group members is determined by the communication rules such as those for privacy boundary and self-disclosure boundary (Petronio, Ellemers, Giles, & Gallois, 1998). Based on these studies, we propose the following hypotheses:

> **H_{5a}:** Topic boundary unfitness decreases the number of relevant comments.
> **H_{5b}:** Topic boundary unfitness decreases the number of unique comments.
> **H_{5c}:** Topic boundary unfitness decreases perceived effectiveness.
> **H_{5d}:** Topic boundary unfitness decreases group cohesiveness.
> **H_{5e}:** Topic boundary unfitness decreases equality of participation.

Knowledge

An individual's knowledge is a task resource that affects group productivity (Littlepage, Robison, & Reddington, 1997; Steiner, 1972), and people with task knowledge have more accurate judgment and are less biased than those without it (Smith & Kida, 1991). Further, prior experiences can affect the expectation of outcomes because a recursive relationship is found between knowledge and outcomes (Higgins, 1995). Group members' perceived expertise increases both their participation and their willingness to share their unique knowledge (Thomas-Hunt, Ogden, & Neale, 2003), and finally, the more topic knowledge an individual has, the less time he or she works on that topic, and the more relevant comments are generated (Aiken, 2002). Therefore, the hypotheses about knowledge are:

H_{6a}: Knowledge increases the number of relevant comments.
H_{6b}: Knowledge increases the number of unique comments.
H_{6c}: Knowledge increases perceived effectiveness.
H_{6d}: Knowledge increases group cohesiveness.
H_{6e}: Knowledge increases equality of participation.

Self-Efficacy

Self-efficacy is a belief in one's capability to execute a required action and outcome for a defined task (Wood, Atkins, & Tabernero, 2000), and is defined as "not an estimation of skills; rather it is a judgment about what one can do with one's skills that influence choice of activities, effort level, and persistence" (Feng, Chu, Hsu, & Hsieh, 2004). Self-efficacy beliefs have been found to be predictors of performance across tasks of varying complexity (Bandura, 1977). In addition, self-efficacy makes individuals have a perception that they can influence the topic's outcome, and it might determine the cognitive load that individuals believe they need in order to control the results. The following hypotheses are proposed:

H_{7a}: Self efficacy increases the number of relevant comments.
H_{7b}: Self efficacy increases the number of unique comments.
H_{7c}: Self efficacy increases perceived effectiveness.
H_{7d}: Self efficacy increases group cohesiveness.
H_{7e}: Self efficacy increases equality of participation.

Effectiveness and Group Cohesiveness

Cohesiveness is defined as attraction to group members or as the field of forces that keep members together (Shaw, 1976). Both cohesiveness and perceived effectiveness have significant effects on the number of comments generated (Gallupe, Dennis, Cooper, Valacich, Bassinette, & Nunamaker, 1992; Wong & Aiken, 2003), and highly cohesive groups are able to increase conformity, which may be helpful when deviance endangers the group or may be harmful when innovation and creativity are necessary. In general, groups with high levels of cohesion and perceived effectiveness are more effective in reaching desired outcomes. People who are members of cohesive or effective groups generally are more satisfied than those who are members of non-cohesive or ineffective groups. Further, group cohesion might reduce stress because members are more supportive to each other.

Equality of Participation

Equality of participation is widely used as a group process characteristic (Tung & Turban, 1998), and studies have shown that greater participation equality increases the number of comments and participant satisfaction (Mejias, Shepherd, Vogel, & Lazaneo, 1996-97) and reduces decision time (George, Easton, Nunamaker, & Northcraft, 1990). Further, one study (Tyran, Dennis, Vogel, & Nunamaker, 1992) showed that there are positive relationships between participation and information sharing and between participation and idea synthesis, and a negative relationship between participation and production blocking, i.e., difficulty in communication. However, other studies (e.g., McLeod & Liker, 1992; Turoff, Hiltz, Bahgat, & Rana, 1993) have found that there were no significant relationships between participation equality and outcomes.

Relevant and Unique Comments

While 44.5% of electronic meeting studies measure group satisfaction and 48.6% focus on decision quality as dependent variables (Fjermestad & Hiltz, 1998), a large number also focus on the number of comments generated (e.g., Aiken, 2002; Chidambaram & Jones, 1993). Here, we define the number of unique ideas as the number of total ideas minus the number of redundant ideas (Connolly, Jessup, & Valacich, 1990), and a relevant comment is defined as any comment related to the topic. The following hypotheses are suggested:

> **H_{8a}:** Perceived effectiveness increases the number of unique comments.
> **H_{8b}:** Perceived effectiveness increases the number of relevant comments.
> **H_{9a}:** Group cohesiveness increases the number of relevant comments.
> **H_{9b}:** Group cohesiveness increases the number of unique comments.

RESEARCH METHODOLOGY

A total of 72 junior and senior undergraduate Business students and 38 MBA students, aged 20 to 46, served as the subject pool for an experiment to investigate the proposed hypotheses. Most had part-time or full time working experience. The subjects were assigned randomly to 14 groups, each with seven to eight participants, because it has been suggested that the minimum size needed for electronic meeting success is about seven (Aiken, Krosp, Shirani, & Martin, 1994). The subjects participated on a voluntary basis for extra credit.

This experiment used Web-based electronic meeting software developed locally that implemented the gallery writing technique (Aiken, Vanjani, & Paolillo, 1996), allowing each participant to post comments anonymously and simultaneously in a face-to-face environment (see Figures 2 and 3). At any time, all comments were available for viewing by the entire group.

At the beginning of the meeting, subjects were told the purpose of the study and were instructed

Figure 2. The online EMS system login screen

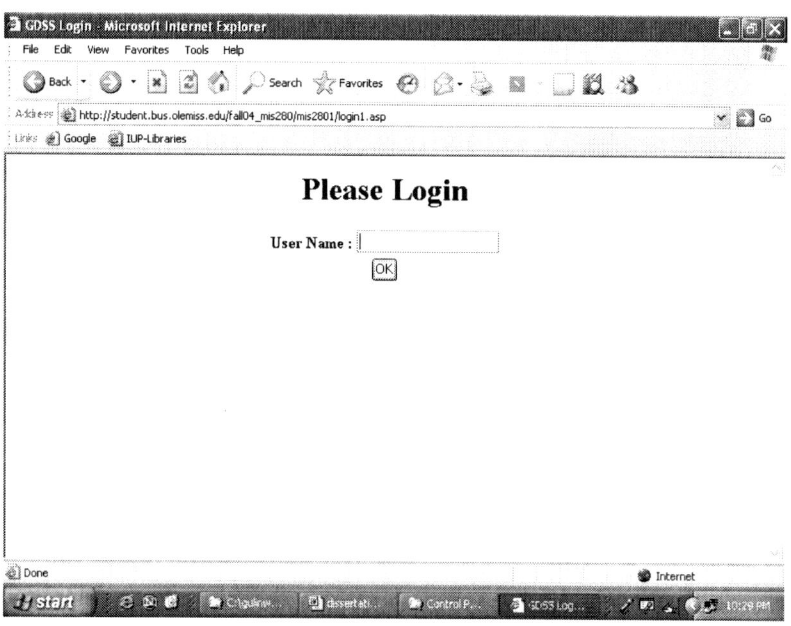

how to use the software. Each group typed comments about one of the topics shown in Table 1. While 20 minutes might be optimal for complex tasks with voting (Wong & Aiken, 2006), only 10 minutes is usually sufficient for topics such as those used in this experiment (Aiken, 2002). Therefore, each meeting was terminated after 10 minutes. Upon the completion of the electronic meeting, all subjects completed a self-assessed questionnaire.

Difficulty was measured using the method of Campbell and Gingrich (1986). The perceived difficulty included two items: "how much effort is required" and "how difficult is it," and the two items had an average Cronbach's α coefficient of .77. Intrinsic interest was measured in terms of individual preferences and interests via feelings and evaluations regarding topics, and ambiguity was measured using four items.

Solution multiplicity and boundary unfitness were measured using five items. Each participant was asked to rate on a seven-point Likert scale the solution multiplicity or boundary unfitness of the topic with response possibilities ranging from "no solution" to "many solutions" for solution multiplicity and from "do not access privacy boundary" to "highly access privacy boundary" for boundary unfitness.

Knowledge was measured by asking how much the participants knew about the topic, using a seven-point Likert scale. Self-efficacy was measured using a scale modified from those of Bandura (1995) and Feng, Chu, Hsu, & Hsieh (2004). The perceived self-efficacy was measured against levels of topics. Group members were asked to judge their abilities to generate ideas and solve problems. The group members were asked "how sure" they were of their perceived efficacy in solving cognitive problems on a seven-point scale, ranging from "cannot do" to "certainly can do."

Perceived effectiveness was measured using the methods of Wong and Aiken (2003) and the

Figure 3. The online EMS system comment screen

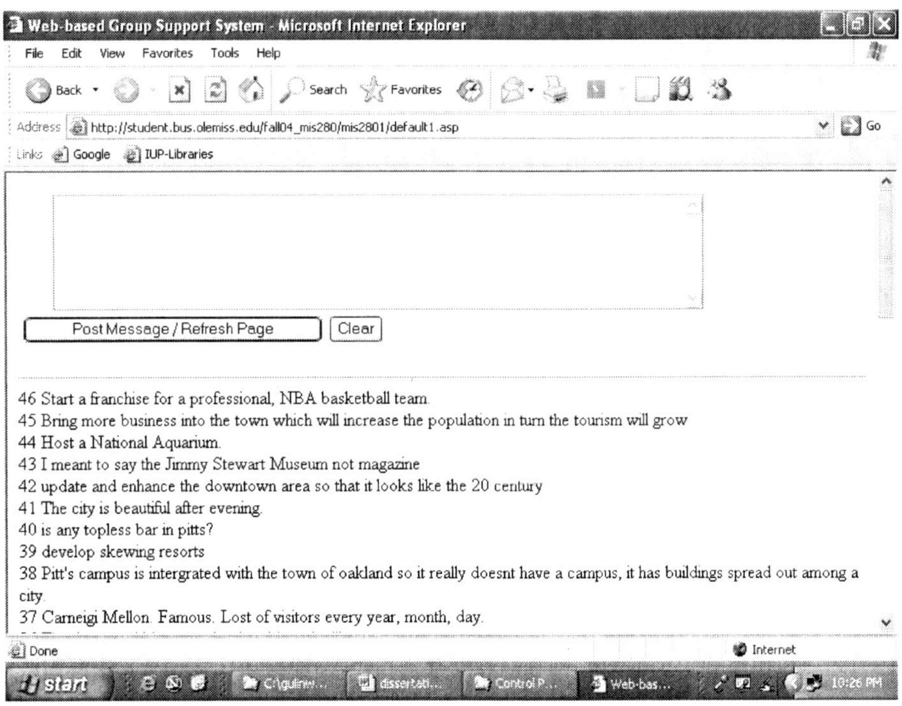

reliability of the construct using Cronbach's alpha was 0.85. Cohesiveness was measured using the Seashore (1954) index of group cohesiveness and showed a Cronbach's alpha of 0.89. Equality of participation was measured using a scale with three items combined from Zmud, Mejias, Reinig, & Martinez-Martinez (2001) with a Cronbach's alpha is 0.80.

The final two dependent measures in this experiment were the number of relevant comments and unique comments. Objective raters counted the number of relevant and unique comments from each of the 14 groups using the coding rules defined by Bouchard & Hare (1970).

The reliabilities of all 10 variables were all over 0.7, indicating adequate construct reliability.

RESULTS

The numbers of relevant comments and unique comments, the corresponding topics, and the percentages of comments are listed in Table 1, and Figure 4 summarizes the relationships among the experimental variables.

Table 1. Number of relevant and unique comments at each meeting

Meeting	Topics	Relevant Comments	Unique Comments	Relevant %	Unique %
1	What makes for success in our culture?	34	14	67	27
2	How can we improve the parking problem on campus?	46	11	84	20
3	How can the spread of AIDS be reduced?	36	16	63	28
4	How can we encourage more tourists to visit the city?	31	17	74	40
5	How can we improve the parking problem on campus?	54	19	77	27
6	How can the spread of AIDS be reduced?	47	18	81	31
7	What makes for success in our culture?	49	10	89	18
8	Do you have some ideas about how to make a class more interesting?	35	15	73	31
9	Do you fear that Iraq is slowly becoming another Vietnam?	49	9	66	12
10	Do you fear that Iraq is slowly becoming another Vietnam?	59	23	87	34
11	Do you have some ideas about how to make a class more interesting?	26	15	68	39
12	What type of soft drink should be in the vending machines on campus?	79	19	78	19
13	What type of soft drink should be in the vending machines on campus?	85	14	73	12
14	How can we encourage more tourists to visit the city?	28	13	54	25

The effects of topic variables on the number of relevant comments were all significant; therefore, H1a, H2a, H3a, H4a, H5a, H6a, and H7a were all supported by the statistical analyses. Topic interest and topic ambiguity influenced the number of unique comments, so H2b and H4b also were supported. Topic interest and topic ambiguity significantly influenced both group process effectiveness and group process cohesiveness, therefore, H2c, H2d, H4c, and H4d were supported. The experimental results also showed the effects of topic knowledge on the group process cohesiveness and topic boundary unfitness were significant. Therefore, H5e and H6d were supported. The effects of group process effectiveness on both the number of relevant comments and the number of unique comments were significant. Therefore, H8a and H8b were supported.

Following the approach of Baron and Kenny (1986) of testing mediating effects, we found that perceived effectiveness and group cohesiveness are two significant mediators between topic ambiguity and unique comments.

CONCLUSION

Results of experiments with 14 groups and varying topics showed that topic interest, solution multiplicity, knowledge, and individual self-efficacy

Figure 4. Significant topic and group process effects

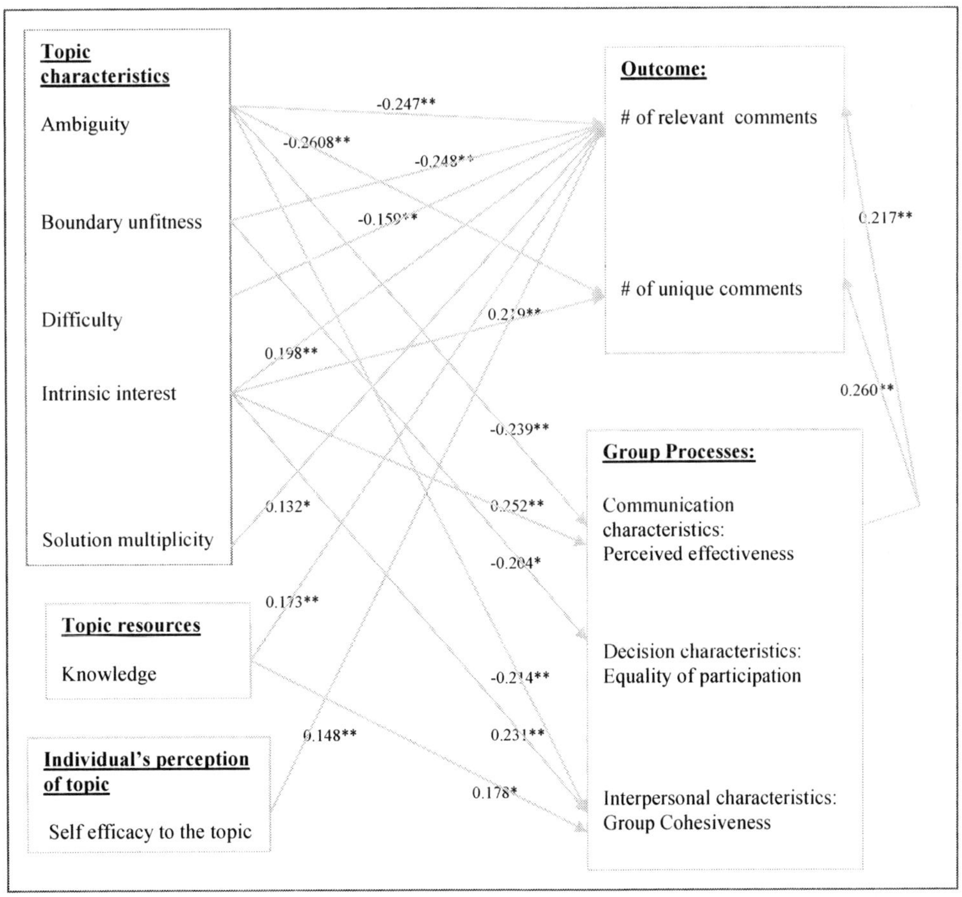

*$p < 0.05$. **$p < 0.10$

enhances the productivity of electronic meetings by increasing the number of relevant comments generated. However, topic ambiguity, difficulty, and boundary unfitness decreases the number of relevant comments. Our findings also indicate that topic interest improves group process perceived effectiveness while topic ambiguity reduces it. Group process cohesiveness is enhanced by topic interest and topic knowledge; however, it is lowered by topic ambiguity.

In order to increase the productivity of electronic meetings, facilitators should try to include participants who have knowledge of and interest in the problem and who are able to implement the group decision. If the topic is too difficult, perhaps the problem can be broken down into smaller discussions. In addition, assumptions should be defined before the meeting to reduce ambiguity.

A major limitation of the study is the use of only seven topics in the experiment. Although we believe these topics covered a wide gamut of variation in ambiguity, boundary unfitness, difficulty, intrinsic interest, solution multiplicity, knowledge, and self efficacy, other meeting problems might yield different results.

Although the use of students in one-time, ad-hoc meetings might be considered by some as a limitation (Gordon, Slade, & Schmitt, 1988), that is not the case here. Many meetings in organizations are one-time and ad-hoc. Further, we believe undergraduate university students have the same thought and decision-making processes as those in businesses or other organizations when faced with unfamiliar, difficult, meeting topics. In fact, most, if not all of the students had already participated in such meetings at some point in their lives. Finally, in only a few years, many of these students will be participating in business meetings.

Future studies should examine how other variables interact with topic choice on process gains and losses in electronic meetings. For example, prior studies have shown that time pressure and group size can affect the number of relevant comments generated. Larger groups with more time faced with an interesting topic and multiple solutions could contribute many more unique, quality ideas. In addition, there could be interactions among topic characteristics, individuals' topic knowledge, and self-efficacy. Solution multiplicity might be negatively related with topic boundary, and both solution multiplicity and self-efficacy could be positively linked with topic interest and knowledge. Boundary unfitness might negatively interact with topic interest and knowledge, but positively interact with ambiguity and topic difficulty. Topic interest could be related to topic difficulty, and topic knowledge could be negatively related with topic ambiguity and difficulty. The interaction of the topic characteristics, topic knowledge, and individual self-efficacy is interesting and should be addressed in a further study.

REFERENCES

Aiken, M. (2002).Topic effects on electronic meeting comments, *Academy of Information and Management Sciences*, 5(1/2), 115-126.

Aiken, M., Krosp, J., Shirani, A., & Martin, J. (1994). Electronic brainstorming in small and large groups. *Information and Management*, 27, 141-149.

Aiken, M. & Paolillo, J. (2000). An abductive model of group support systems. *Information and Management*, 37, 87-94.

Aiken, M. & Vanjani, M. (2002). A mathematical foundation for group support system research. *Communications of the International Information Management Association,* 2(1), 73-83.

Aiken, M., Vanjani, M. & Paolillo, J. (1996). A comparison of two electronic idea generation techniques. *Information and Management*, 30(2), 91-99.

Aiken, M. & Waller, B. (2000). Flaming among first-time group support system users. *Information and Management*, 37, 95-100.

Bandura, A. (1977). Self-efficacy: Toward a Unifying Theory of Behavioral Change. *Psychology Review*, 84(2), 191-215.

Bandura, A. (1995). *Manual for the construction of self-efficacy scales*. Stanford University, Department of Psychology

Baron, R. & Kenny, D. (1986). The moderator-mediator variable distinction in social psychological research: conceptual, strategic, and statistical considerations. *Journal of Personality and Social Psychology*, 51(6), 1173-1182.

Benbasat, I. & Lim, L. (1993). The effects of group, task, context, and technology variables on the usefulness of group support systems: A meta-analysis of experimental studies. *Small Group Research* 24, 430-462.

Bouchard, T. and Hare, M. (1970). Size, performance and potential in brainstorming groups. *Journal of Applied Psychology*, 54, 51–55.

Briggs, R., Nunamaker, J., & Sprague, R. (1998). 1001 unanswered research questions in GSS. *Journal of Management Information Systems*, 14(3), 3-21.

Campbell, D. & Gingrich , K. (1986). The interactive effects of task complexity and participation on task performance: A field experiment. *Organizational Behavior and Human Decision Processes*, 38, 162-180.

Chidambaram, L. & Jones, B. (1993). Impact of communication medium and computer support on group perceptions and performance: A comparison of face-to-face and dispersed meetings. *MIS Quarterly* 17(4), 465-491.

Connolly, T., Jessup, L., & Valacich, J. (1990). Effects of anonymity and evaluative tone on idea generation in computer-mediated groups. *Management Science*, 36(6), 689-703.

Cornelius, C. & Boos, M. (2003). Enhancing mutual understanding in synchronous computer-mediated communication by training: Trade-offs in judgmental tasks. *Communication Research*, 3(2), 147-177.

Dennis A., George J., Jessup L., Nunamaker J., & Vogel D. (1988). Information technology to support electronic meetings. *MIS Quarterly*, 12(4), 591-615.

Espinosa, J., Cummings, J., Wilson, J., & Pearce, R. (2003). Team boundary issues across multiple global firms. *Journal of Management Information System*, 19(4), 157-190.

Feng, Y., Chu, T., Hsu, M., & Hsieh, H. (2004). An investigation of effort–accuracy trade-off and the impact of self-efficacy on Web searching behaviors. *Decision Support Systems*, 37, 331– 342.

Fjermestad, J & Hiltz S. (1998-99). An assessment of group support systems experimental research: Methodology and results. *Journal of Management Information System*, 15(3), 7-149.

Gallupe, B., Dennis, A., Cooper, W., Valacich, J., Bassinette, L., & Nunamaker, J. (1992). Electronic brainstorming and group size. *The Academy of Management Journal*, 35(2), 350–369.

George, J., Easton, G., Nunamaker, J., & Northcraft, G., (1990). A study of collaborative group work with and without computer-based support. *Information Systems Research*, 1(4), 394-415.

Gordon, M., Slade, A., and Schmitt, N. (1988). Student guinea pigs: Porcine predictors and particularistic phenomena. *Academy of Management Review*, 12:1, 160-163.

Griffin, M., Neal, A., & Neale, M. (2000). The contribution of task performance and contextual performance to effectiveness: Investigating the role of situational constraints. *Applied Psychology: An International Review*, 49(3), 517-534.

Hackman, J. (1968). Effects of task characteristics on group products. *Journal of Experimental Social Psychology*, 4, 162-187.

Higgins, C. (1995). Application of social cognitive theory to training for computer skills. *Information Systems Research* 6(2), 118–143.

Huber, G. & Daft, R. (1987). The information environments of organization. In F. Jablin, L. Putman, K. Roberts, and L. Porter (Eds.), *Handbook of organization communication.* Beverly Hills, CA: Sage.

Littlepage, G., Robison, W., & Reddington, K. (1997). Effects of task experience and group experience on group performance, member ability, and recognition of expertise. *Organizational Behavior Human Decision Processes,* 69, 133–147.

McLeod, P. (1992). An assessment of the experimental literature on electronic support of group work: Results of a meta-analysis. *Human Computer Interaction* 7, 257-280.

McLeod, P., & Liker, J. (1992). Electronic meeting systems: Evidence from a low structure environment. *Information Systems Research,* 3(3), 195-223.

Mejias, R., Shepherd, M., Vogel, D., & Lazaneo, L. (1996-97). Consensus and satisfaction levels: A cross-cultural comparison of GSS and non-GSS outcomes within and between the United States and Mexico. *Journal of Management Information Systems,* 13(3), 137-161.

Nunamaker, J., Dennis, A., Valacich, J, Vogel, D., & George, J. (1991). Electronic meeting systems to support group work. *Communications of the ACM,* 34(7), 40-61.

Pervan, G. (1998). A review of research in group support systems: Leaders approaches and directions. *Decision Support Systems*, 23, 149-159.

Petronio, S., Ellemers, N., Giles, H., & Gallois, C. (1998). (Mis)communicating across boundaries: Interpersonal and inter-group considerations. *Communication Research,* 25(6), 571-595.

Pinsonneault, A., Barki, H., Gallupe,R., & Hoppen, N. (1999). Electronic brainstorming: The illusion of productivity. *Information Systems Research.* 10(2), 110 – 133.

Putnam, L. & Stolh, C. (1990). Bona fide groups: A reconceptualization of groups in context. *Communication Studies,* 41, 248-265.

Reinig, B., Briggs, R., & Nunamaker, J. (1997). Flaming in the electronic classroom. *Journal of Management Information System,* 14(3), 45-59.

Seashore, S. (1954). *Group cohesiveness in the industrial work group,* Ann Arbor: University of Michigan, Institute for Social Research.

Shaw, M. (1976). *Group dynamics: The psychology of small group behavior* (2nd ed.), McGraw-Hill.

Smith, J. & Kida, T. (1991).Heuristics and biases: Expertise and task realism in auditing. *Psychological Bulletin,* 109, 472–489.

Steiner, I. (1972). *Group process and productivity.* New York: Academic Press.

Thomas-Hunt, M., Ogden, T. & Neale, M. (2003). Who's really sharing? Effects of social and expert status on knowledge exchange within groups. *Management Science,* 49(4), 464–477.

Tung, L. & Turban, E. (1998). A Proposed research framework for distributed group support systems. *Decision Support Systems.* 23, 175-188.

Turoff, M., Hiltz, S., Bahgat, A., & Rana, A. (1993). Distributed group support systems. *MIS Quarterly*, 17(4), 1054-1060.

Tyran, C., Dennis, A., Vogel, D., & Nunamaker, J. (1992). The application of electronic meeting technology to support strategic management. *MIS Quarterly,* 16(3), 313-334.

Wong, Z. & Aiken, M. (2003). Automated facilitation of electronic meetings. *Information & Management,* 41, 125–134.

Wong. Z. & Aiken, M. (2006). The effects of time on computer-mediated communication group meetings: An exploratory study using an evaluation task. *International Journal of Information Systems and Change Management,*1(2), 138-158.

Wood, R., Atkins, P., & Tabernero, C. (2000). Self-efficacy and strategy on complex tasks. *Applied Psychology: An International Review,* 49(3), 430-447.

Zak, M. (1994). Electronic messaging and communication effectiveness in an ongoing work group. *Information & Management,* 26, 231-241.

Zmud, R., Mejias, R., Reinig, B., & Martínez-Martínez, I. (2001). *Participation equality: Measurement within collaborative electronic environments: A three country study.* University of Oklahoma.

Chapter XX
Mining Text with the Prototype-Matching Method

A. Durfee
Appalachian State University, USA

A. Visa
Tampere University of Technology, Finland

H. Vanharanta
Tampere University of Technology, Finland

S. Schneberger
Appalachian State University, USA

B. Back
Åbo Akademi University, Finland

ABSTRACT

Text documents are the most common means for exchanging formal knowledge among people. Text is a rich medium that can contain a vast range of information, but text can be difficult to decipher automatically. Many organizations have vast repositories of textual data but with few means of automatically mining that text. Text mining methods seek to use an understanding of natural language text to extract information relevant to user needs. This article evaluates a new text mining methodology: prototype-matching for text clustering, developed by the authors' research group. The methodology was applied to four applications: clustering documents based on their abstracts, analyzing financial data, distinguishing authorship, and evaluating multiple translation similarity. The results are discussed in terms of common business applications and possible future research.

INTRODUCTION

It can be argued that computers are now used more for storing and retrieving data than computing data. Organizational computer systems are used for maintaining inventory, production, marketing, financial, sales, accounting, personnel, customer, and other types of data. With enterprise systems, vast amounts of corporate data can be stored digitally and made available to employees when and where needed. Data mining software is often used to further glean information from corporate databases.

A lot of transactional corporate data is numeric but not all of it. Indeed, it's often stated that about 80% of corporate information is textual or unstructured information (for example, see Chen, 2001, and Robb, 2004). An entire information systems specialty—knowledge management—includes collecting, storing, organizing, evaluating, and using textual data such as prevalent with consulting agencies in vast repositories of written reports.

The World Wide Web provides access to planetary-wide databases of textual data for corporate users. Just one of hundreds of online article databases (Education Resources Information Center, or ERIC) has more than 1.2 million citations and 110,000 full text articles. Another, HighWire Press, has more than 1.3 million full text articles. Internal and external data sources offer extensive decision support for managers in dynamic, complex, and demanding business environments. But how can managers, decision makers, and knowledge workers find appropriate textual content among billions of words in internal and external document repositories when it's virtually impossible to do so manually? Seventy-five percent of managers spend more than an hour per day just sorting their e-mails, according to a Gartner Group survey (Marino, 2001).

Compounding the problem is that text, by its very nature, can have multiple meanings and interpretations. The structure of text is not only complex but also not always directly obvious. Even the author of a text might not know the extent of what might be interpreted from the text. These features of text make it a very rich medium for conveying a wide range of meanings but also very difficult to manage, analyze, and mine using computers (Nasukawa & Nagano, 2001). Therein lies the conundrum: There is too much internal and external text to mine manually, but it's problematic for computer software to correctly interpret let alone create knowledge from text.

Text mining (TM) looks for a remedy of that problem. TM seeks to extract high-level knowledge and useful patterns from low-level textual data. Text mining tools seek to analyze and learn the meaning of implicitly structured information automatically (Dorre, Gerstl, & Seiffert, 1999). There are two broad categories of textual mining: *text categorization* and *text clustering.*

Text categorization analyzes text using pre-determined structures or words (i.e., keywords). It is a framework-driven approach, usually based on earlier analysis or expectations. Authors, readers, and librarians may introduce and use keywords, indexes, or mark-ups to outline the main ideas, concepts and themes within a text to make textual searches easier for computers (Anderson, 1999; Chieng, 1997; Lahtinen, 2000; Salton, 1989; Weiss, White, Apte, & Damerau, 2000). However, authors and textual information users can assign different keywords to the same text, or even ascribe different meanings to the same keywords—possibly defeating the speed and accuracy of computer-based textual keyword searches. Readers need only consider their own wayward searches using keyword-based online search engines to understand the depth and breadth of the problem.

Text clustering, on the other hand, differs from keywords or pre-determined structural searches. Text clustering discovers latent groupings of text, where the textual similarities within a group are maximized while similarities among groups are minimized. Effective text clustering uses the characteristics of textual meanings, structure, syntax, and semantics to find commonality and group similar text. The resulted clusters-groups can then be used to efficiently search and analyze textual documents. Text clustering is a textual data-driven, not dependent on the accuracy and meaning of pre-conceived keywords or structure approach.

The key to gaining knowledge from internal and external textual repositories, therefore, may be to exploit computers for processing the vast amounts of textual data with text mining software using text clustering to discover intrinsic knowledge within documents.

This paper seeks to present a new text clustering methodology developed by the authors' research group, position it among other text mining approaches, and empirically test it in four different applications. In the next section, this article examines related text mining research, approaches, and problems. Then the paper closely explains the process and research methodologies used by the new methodology, analyzes the results of testing it against four applications, and then discusses the general business applicability of it. Finally, the paper examines further text mining research opportunities.

RELATED WORK

The Nature of Text

Text, as a written form of spoken natural language, provides one of the most effective communication bridges among people. Text has a complicated and ambiguous multilevel structure; it is highly multidimensional with tens of thousands of dimensions (Fayyad, Piatetsky-Shapiro, & Smyth 1996). Structure exists in word formation (the morphology of language), in sentence grammar (syntax), and meaning (semantics). Moreover, the three components of text (word usage, grammatical construction, and meaning) vary considerably within every individual language.

The authors and readers of text often represent the same semantics using different words (synonymy) or describe different meanings using words that have various meanings (polysemy). For example, in human-system communication, two people favor the same term with a probability of less than 20%, consequently resulting in 80-90% failure rates in communication (Furnas, Landauer, Gomez, & Dumais, 1987).

This characteristic of natural language words as the basic units of text can confuse text handling technologies such as document management systems, automatic thesauruses, and search engines. These technologies are primarily based on keywords, indexes, or a text property (such as author, subject, type, word count, printed page count, and time last written). These approaches are less effective working with natural language text because of the ambiguity, polesymy, synonymy, syntactic complexity, and multi-variance of interpretations. Text mining users should be able to categorize, prioritize, and compare documents not only by pre-defined keywords but also understand and utilize the meaning of any particular document without having to manually browse, read, and analyze them.

Text Mining Challenges

To some extent, a language is merely a fixed stock of words that can be arranged in seemingly endless variations. Additionally, words can interact in many ways; some words are more likely to occur near certain other words, for example, while others modify the meanings of words nearby. The product of the frequency of words and their relative importance is, therefore (according to Zipf's law) approximately constant (Zipf, 1972). This can allow some textual analysis based on word occurrence and placement.

A more fundamental reason for a language being more than a simple word stock is that natural language expressions have syntactic structural significance.[1] This is the fundamental problem

Table 1. A classification of text mining approaches, adapted from Kroeze et al. (2003)

Non-novel investigation finding/ retrieving already existing and known information	*Semi-novel investigation* patterns/trends already exist in the data but are unknown	*Novel investigation* creating new knowledge outside of the data collection itself
Information retrieval uses exact or best matching (e.g., finds full texts or abstracts of papers)	*Standard text mining* uses mainly statistical and computational methods (e.g., discovers lexical and syntactic features; finds beginnings of new themes; categorizes text into preexisting classes; summarizes text; and groups text into clusters with shared qualities)	*Intelligent text mining* uses interaction between investigator and a computerized tool (e.g., which business decision is implied; how can linguistic features of text be used to create knowledge about the outside world)

with text categorization using keywords; finding keywords does not necessarily equate to finding meaning. Different individuals may describe the same meaning with different (key)words because of word synonymy. In natural language, there is no one-to-one correspondence between word strings and syntactic structure or between syntactic structure and meaning.

According to Pullum and Scholz (2001), other features of natural languages that confuse automated systems are the unlimited complexity of natural language expressions and syntax variability. Even by omitting some words from context, a reader or listener is usually able to infer the meaning from ill-structured text. A speaker or writer who constructs textual expressions to deliver certain information to a listener or reader naturally allows some degree of personal preference and background to determine textual structure—giving the literary world its vast range of writing styles. The same exact features that allow us to accept different structural styles and ill-structured expressions only handicap automated text mining software.

Text Mining

Text mining (TM) methods and tools strive to search, organize, browse, and analyze text collections automatically looking for patterns (Kroeze, Matthee, & Bothma, 2003). TM can be simply defined, according to Witten, Bray, Mahoui, and Teahan (1998), as the process of analyzing text to extract information useful for particular purposes. Hearst (1999) introduces TM as a step toward discovering or creating knowledge from a collection of documents. TM as a knowledge management technique identifies patterns and unexpected relationships in text previously unknown and to its users (Albrecht & Merkl, 1998). Kroeze et al. (2003), expand TM terminology and offers the parameters of non-novel, semi-novel, and novel investigation to differentiate between full-text information retrieval, standard text mining, and intelligent text mining. This terminology framework is represented in Table 1.

Understanding textual data can be supported by specific mathematical operations: *categorization, clustering, feature extraction, thematic indexing* and *information retrieval by content*

(Hand, Mannila, & Smyth, 2001; van Rijsbergen, 1979). *Categorization* assigns documents to pre-existing categories, called "topics" or "themes." Text categorization applications include indexing text to support document retrieval and data extraction (Lewis, 1992). *Clustering* partitions a given collection of items into a number of previously unknown groups with similar content. Clustering can discover unknown or previously unnoticed links in a subset of words, sentences, paragraphs, or documents. *Feature extraction* extracts particular items from a collection of items to provide a representative sample of the overall content. Distinctive vocabulary items found in a document can be assigned to different categories by measuring the importance of those items to the document content. *Thematic indexing* identifies significant items in a particular collection. Textual indexing can identify a given document or query text by a set of weighted or un-weighted terms often referred to as index terms or keywords (most commonly or rarely used). *Information retrieval* locates a subset of a collection deemed to be relevant to a posed query based on a preconceived classification system. Traditionally, textual information retrieval systems are query-based, and it is assumed that users can describe their information needs explicitly and adequately in a parsable query. Text categorization and clustering are the most prevalent text mining methodologies. This chapter focuses on text clustering.

Text Clustering

There are number of text mining clustering techniques based on statistical clustering (Slonim & Tishby, 2000; Zamir & Etzioni, 1998) and neural networks, often in the form of self-organizing maps (SOM) (Chieng, 1997; Lagus, 2000). WebSOM, for example, applies SOM to cluster and visualize text content (Kohonen, 1997; Lagus, 2000; Toivonen, Visa, Vesanen, Back, & Vanharanta, 2001). WebSOM is based less on subjective perceptions of the authors and more on organizing or "visualizing" document content. Another statistical approach is based on fuzzy semantic typing to draw up a complete fuzzy affect lexicon of free text as introduced by Subasic and Huettner (2000). Gedeon, Sing, Koczy, and Bustos (1996) apply fuzzy importance measures to retrieve significant "concepts" from documents using the entire document as a query vector. The hyperlink vector voting method of indexing and retrieving hypertext documents uses the content of hyperlinks pointing to a document to rank its relevance to the query terms (Li, 1998).

A new methodology for text clustering—the prototype matching method (PMM)—is introduced and discussed in the next section. PMM statistically analyzes natural language text as a digital array to understand semantic meaning hidden in the text (Visa, Back, & Vanharanta, 1999). The method is free from human preconceptions about the text such as with text categorization techniques such as markups, indexes, or keywords.

RESEARCH METHODOLOGY

PMM text mining methodology could be applied to various real-world problems finding hidden patterns in textual information (Visa et al., 1999). The starting point was to provide a mechanism enabling computers to retrieve pieces of text semantically relevant to each other. The PMM can be thought of as a type of document matching, which matches a new document to old documents and ranking the new document by assigning a score or relevance (Weiss et al., 2000). The proposed methodology was implemented in a prototyping software package called GILTA-3.

GILTA-3, using PMM, seeks similarities between the document-prototype and the closest-matching subject documents. For every prototype, there are two clusters created: one cluster of documents that are similar in some specific way, and another cluster of documents that are different from the prototype in some specific way.

Figure 1. Comparing documents based on extracted histograms of words and sentences

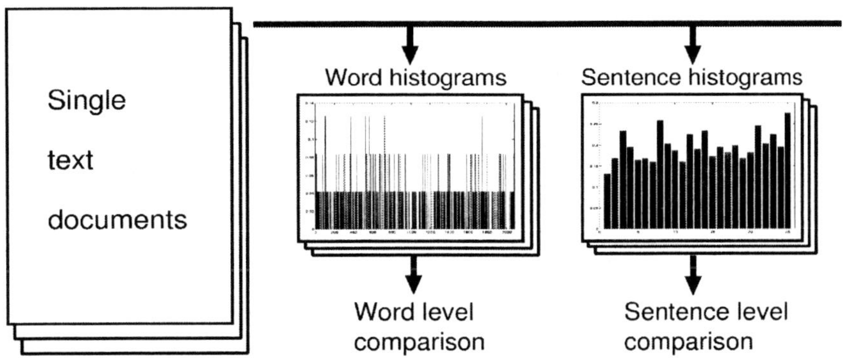

The method constructs a ranked list for every document-prototype and creates clusters from the first hits on the ranked list. A cluster of similar documents is formed from documents that "fire," or appear as the closest matches at the top of a ranked list (in ascending order) of the distances between the prototype and the other documents. The cluster of documents different from the prototype shares few or no patterns with the prototype. The documents in this cluster fire at the farthest distance in a ranked list to the prototype.

It should be noted that clustering is the most challenging task, since there is no pre-existing set of categories created by human experts. Similarly, clustering results can be difficult to evaluate. The patterns that combine or separate documents into clusters may not be obvious to a user, and therefore evaluating the results can become tricky. Figure 1 below schematically depicts the process of comparing documents from a collection of documents.

Document Preprocessing and Encoding

Automated text mining using statistical methods can be aided by preprocessing every textual line in a document. Preprocessing rounds numbers, separates punctuation marks with extra spaces, and excludes extra carriage returns, mathematical signs, and dashes. Abbreviation, synonym, and compound word files are used to perform synonym and compound word filtering. Preprocessing does not omit words or perform word stemming, to keep as much initial information and structure in the preprocessed documents as possible since word order, their combinations, concurrences, and conjunctions can convey important insights.

After preprocessing, every document is encoded. Every word w in a document is transformed into a unique number according to the formula:

$$y = \sum_{i=0}^{L} k^i \times c_{L-i} \qquad (1)$$

where L is the length of a word as a string of characters; c_i is the ASCII encoding value of every character within a word w, and k is a constant. Since the eight-bit ACSII character set was used, $k = 256$. The encoding algorithm produces a unique number for each word disregarding word stems, capitalization, and synonyms; only the exact same words have equal y values. Since punctuation marks also have unique ASCII values, they are also encoded. Resulting values of every word and punctuation mark from every document become word vectors. These vectors can then be statistically processed.

Figure 2. Example of a sentence distribution

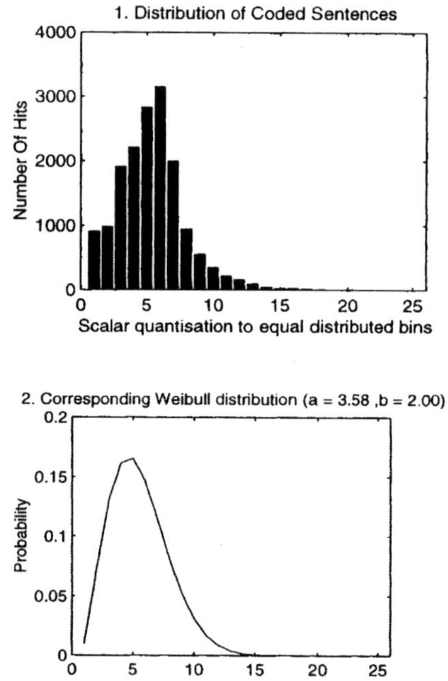

Document Processing

PMM is based on the frequency distribution of all words compared to a training set, often comprised of the entire text collection as the initial training set. Word and sentence histograms, which allow the comparison of different documents to each other, may rely heavily on the frequency distributions of words or sentences from an entire document collection. The same processing and analysis can be performed for document paragraphs if they are sufficiently lengthy to provide good distributions. Processing begins by examining the distribution of the coded word numbers.

Word Quantization

From a set of word codes from equation (1), the minimal and maximal values are identified for the entire document collection. The distribution of the codes is then examined using a Weibull distribution. The Weibull distribution is a highly adaptable distribution that can take on the characteristics of other types of distributions based on the value of shape parameters (ReliaSoft Corporation, 2002). The range between the minimal and maximal values is divided into N_w logarithmically equal bins, where N_w is the total number of words in the text collection. The word frequency of each bin is calculated and further normalized according to N_w.

Using a selected precision, Weibull distributions are then calculated. The best-fitting Weibull distribution corresponding to the textual data is determined by examining the cumulative distribution. Every estimated Weibull distribution is compared with the code distribution by calculating the cumulative distribution function (CDF) according to:

$$CDF = 1 - e^{\left(\left(-2.6 \times \log(y / y_{\max})\right)^{b}\right) \times a} \qquad (2)$$

where minimum a and maximum b define the shape of the Weibull distribution. The ratio y/y_{max} is the actual portion of the total density mass. The only way to compare distributions is to use cumulative functions that are the same as the integrated probability distributions. Comparing estimated Weibull distributions and the cumulative code number distribution is performed in terms of the smallest square sum.

Repetitively, the best-fitting Weibull distribution is divided into N_w bins of equal sizes, and every word is assigned to a bin. Every word is eventually represented as the number of the bin of the distribution in which it belongs.

Sentence Quantization

In the same manner as words, every sentence is converted to a representational number. After every word in a sentence is changed to a bin number (bn_i), the whole encoded sentence is considered a sampled signal (vector). Since not all sentences contain the same number of words, sentence vector lengths vary. To compensate for this, a discrete fourier transformation (DFT) converts every sentence vector from a collection into an input signal. The input signal is a vector (bn_1, bn_2 ... bn_m), where m is the word's placement number in a sentence. The output signals from DFT are the coefficients B_i (i= 0 ... n). The coefficient B_1 is then selected to further represent the sentence.

After every sentence has been converted into numbers, a cumulative distribution is created from the sentence data set using coefficients (B_1) in the same way as on the word level. The range between the minimal and maximal parameters of the sentence code distribution is divided into N_s equally sized bins, where N_s is the length of the histogram vector. The frequency of sentences belonging to each bin is calculated. Then the bin counts are normalized in accordance with N_s. Finally, the best-fitting Weibull distribution corresponding to the sentence distributions is found. A graphical representation of sentence quantization from Back, Toivonen, Vanharanta, and Visa (2001) is shown in Figure 2.

Individual Histograms

Finally, every document in a collection is reprocessed to create individual word and sentence level histograms. After each word is quantified using word quantization, a word histogram A_w is created for each word. The histograms A_w are then normalized according to the length of the histogram vectors. Similarly, the histograms on the sentence level for every document in a collection are created and normalized

Document Matching and Ranking

The individual word and sentence level histograms of all documents in a collection can then be compared with a histogram corresponding to a document-prototype (or sample document). This analysis is called document matching. Matching is done by first calculating simple Euclidian distances among the histograms; the documents closest to a document-prototype in terms of Euclidian distance form a document cluster. This matching is done for word and sentence histograms.

In the ranking phase, the documents with the smallest distances to a document-prototype are chosen from the top of the ranked list. The system creates a proximity table of all distances among the documents in a collection. The documents from the top of the proximity table for a given document-prototype are presented to a user within a specified recall window. The recall window is the quantity of closest-matching documents that a user wants to retrieve and consider for further analysis.

Empirical Validation

The prototype-matching text mining methodology was validated in four applications: clustering scientific articles, analyzing financial data, authorship attribution, and translation accuracy.

Scientific Article Clustering

Scientific research articles are published in the tens of thousands each year in hundreds of different academic fields. Their topics similarly range in the thousands, yet may overlap to some degree. A marketing research paper, for example, may investigate segmentation using a new information systems technology, or a biology paper may examine ant colonies in terms of economic theories. How can one best mine scientific research papers when there may be significant topical overlap? At present, most papers (including this one) include keywords for text categorization techniques, but text clustering may offer much more efficient and effective text mining. Similar problems can be found in business, when many cross-related reports need to be mined for specific topics.

For this paper, the prototype-matching tool was applied to 444 scientific abstracts obtained from The Hawaii International Conference on System Science 2001 (HICSS-34). The scientific papers were organized by conference track chairs into nine major thematic tracks with further subdivision into 78 mini-tracks. Furthermore, the track chairs attempted to identify six themes that ran across the tracks. They outlined six cross-track themes featuring 134 papers in 26 mini-tracks.

Using GILTA-3 software based on PMM, the authors sought to justify the conference's chosen tracks' themes based on theme published in the papers. The full text of every abstract was encoded into an array of 2,080 text distribution bins based on common word histograms. Sentence histograms of size 25 were generated for every abstract.

There were mixed results comparing what GILTA-3 found versus how conference chairs allocated papers. With a recall window set at 25, for example, 26% of the data-mining papers clustered with the papers from the data mining mini-track theme. Only 12% of papers from the e-commerce development track clustered with papers discussing e-commerce issues. For other cross-track themes, such as knowledge management, collaborative learning, workflow, and e-commerce development, the number of papers that fired as the closest ones to the papers within a theme was less than 10%.

Qualitative Financial Data

Traditionally, corporate financial performance is analyzed using quantitative financial ratio data (such as stock price per earnings ratio). However, some valuable financial descriptive data can be found in the textual portions of corporate reports such as annual reports. Manually reading thousands of long annual reports to get a complete financial picture of companies, however, is not practical. Can automated text mining methods be applied to glean financial information from corporate reporting text?

Using a database of 234 annual reports by 50 pulp companies from 1985-1989, the text was evaluated using PMM. The textual mining results were compared with the results of the quantitative analysis conducted for the same companies in Kloptchenko et al. (2004). The comparison highlighted some discrepancies between the qualitative and quantitative performance results in the reports. While the discrepancies may be partly explained by a possible tendency to overstate actual financial status in textual reports, the analysis appeared to support the notion that PMM text mining can be used to analyze qualitative, textual, and financial data.

Another effort was made to cluster textual quarterly reports from the leaders of telecommunications sector, Ericsson, Motorola, and Nokia, from the years 2000-2003 (Back et al., 2001). It was found that annual or quarterly textual reports contain messages about company future prospects, not just past performance. This explained the dissimilarities in clustering qualitative and quantitative data by the phenomena that exists in qualitative and quantitative parts of every quarter/annual report obtained in Kloptchenko et al., (2004).

Both results suggest differences in the clustering of quantitative and qualitative data from the reports. Moreover, it was observed how fluctuations in quantitative financial performances influenced the qualitative parts of reports within some existing time lag. Moreover, time lag varies by company; for Ericsson, it lasts about one quarter, while for Motorola it can last two quarters.

Authorship Attribution

When digitized text can so easily be found through the Internet and copied directly into documents, can PMM be used to identify when text is significantly different from other text?

Two tests were made to check how the clustering methodology can find divergences in text written by different authors. Three texts from classical authors (William Shakespeare, Edgar Alan Poe, and George Bernard Shaw) were examined (Visa, Toivonen, Back, & Vanharanta, 2000). After the preprocessing, vector quantization, and histograms were created for the texts on word and sentence levels. Bin sizes were set to 2080 on the word level and 25 on the sentence level. Each text piece was treated one-by-one as a prototype, matching it against consolidated text from all sources.

The results of author divergence were extremely good on the word level. The closest matches occurred among the text pieces written by the same author. On the sentence level, the results were good in general, except for one mismatch from Shaw's *Mrs. Warren's Profession* and Poe's *The Assignation*. PMM appeared to have significant potential to recognize and distinguish author styles based on peculiarities of sentence structuring by different authors.

Translation Authenticity

In a global business environment, textual documents are routinely translated into many languages. Since language fluency is too often a specialty, business managers often have to take it on faith that translations are accurate. Can PMM be used to evaluate different translations of the same underlying text?

To evaluate this possibility, Bible versions in Greek, Latin English, and two in Finnish from the years 1933 and 1938 were chosen as test materials. They were assumed to be very accurate translations of significant cultural and religious meanings. Word-, sentence-, and paragraph-level histograms were created using the procedures outlined previously. All the books in the Bible were used as the prototype for the different versions of the Bible (Toivonen et al., 2001). A recall window of the closest-matching documents of 10 was chosen to compare identical passages in different translations. The assumption was that if books in different languages were similar, it was evidence that PMM could be used to verify translations (Visa, Toivonen, Vanharanta, & Back, 2001).

PMM found that an average of 6 books out of 10 appeared to be identical, that is, within the same bins. There were, on average, 4.52 books within the same bins in English and Finnish versions based on the word map, 7.94 books based on the sentence map, and 5.56 books based on the paragraph maps. Mathematically, a random sample would have had only two similar books in a bin. The results therefore appear to support the notion of using PMM text mining to compare translation accuracy. As a side note, comparing translations appears to work best at the sentence level than the word or paragraph level.

Discussion

In spite of the multidimensional and complex nature of natural language, statistical methods

Table 2. Potential business applications of PMM text mining

Area	Filtering	Searching	Managing
Uses	e-mails mail routing news monitoring push publishing	automated indexing genre classification authorship attribution survey coding e-mails corporate reports social network analysis business intelligence	knowledge management corporate learning leveraging expertise legal document retention compliance

such as prototype-matching appear to be suitable for mining text in terms of text clustering. Given the enormous range and amount of text available in digital text files within and without companies, this can present a number of potentially valuable automated applications.

In particular, three areas may provide the greatest return: text filtering, searches, and management, as shown in Table 2. These applications appear to be useful across a corporate value chain but perhaps most useful in marketing and finance where textual news and reports can be mined for indications of future trends. Moreover, the applications appear to be worthwhile working in different languages for global business operations.

The authors believe that the GILTA tool using PMM goes beyond information retrieval as an intelligent text mining tool since it uncovers semi-novel information and creates knowledge from knowledge. Furthermore, the authors believe the GILTA-3 software can be implemented as a module either into an existing enterprise support system or into individual decision support systems such as financial analysis or marketing tools.

Research Opportunities

Given the depth and breadth of digitally available text and the range of business opportunities presented in Figure 2, there appear to be considerable opportunities for refining PMM and its application.

PMM formulas might be refined to be more accurate yet more flexible to natural text variations and different native languages. The constant parameters and the encoding methods might be improved. Appropriate bin sizes can be determined for different applications. Algorithms specifically for filtering text streams can be designed and tested. Search engines may be able to use PMM techniques to improve the efficacy of search results. In particular, search engines could use entire paragraphs or documents to search with instead of just keywords.

Testing the applicability of PMM text clustering to the uses in Figure 2 may present huge opportunities for research and refinement. And it's possible that research into PMM uses will uncover even more applications where automated text mining can contribute to business success.

ACKNOWLEDGMENT

The financial support of TEKES (grant number 40887/97) and the Academy of Finland is gratefully acknowledged.

REFERENCES

Albrecht R. & Merkl D. (1998). *Knowledge discovery in literature data bases. Library and information services in astronomy III*, ASP Conference Series, Vol. 153.

Anderson, M. (1999). A tool for building digital libraries. *Journal Review*, 5(2).

Back, B., Toivonen, J., Vanharanta, H., & Visa, A. (2001). Comparing numerical data and text information from annual reports using self-organizing maps. *International Journal of Accounting Information Systems, 2.*

Chen, (2001). *Knowledge management systems: A text mining perspective*. Tucson, AZ: Knowledge Computing Corporation.

Chieng, L. (1997). PAT-tree-based keyword extraction for Chinese information retrieval. In *Proceedings of Special Interest Group on Information Retrieval*, SIGIR'97, ACM, Philadelphia.

Dörre, J., Gerstl, P., & Seiffert, R. (1999). Text mining: Finding nuggets in mountains of textual data. In *Proceedings of the KDD-99, Fifth ACM SIGKDD International Conference on Knowledge Discovery and Data Mining*, San Diego.

Fayyad, U., Piatetsky-Shapiro, G., & Smyth, P. (1996). Knowledge discovery and data mining: Towards a unifying framework. In *Proceedings of The Second International Conference on Knowledge Discovery and Data Mining* (KDD-96), Portland, OR.

Furnas, G. W., Landauer, T. K., Gomez, L. M., & Dumais, S. T. (1987). The vocabulary problem in human-system communication. *Communications of the ACM, 30*(11), 964-971.

Gedeon, T., Sing, S., Koczy, L., & Bustos, R. (1996). Fuzzy relevance values for information retrieval and hypertext link generation. In *Proceedings of the EUFIT-96, Fourth European Congress on Intelligent Techniques and Soft Computing,* Aachen, Germany.

Hand, D., Mannila, H., & Smyth, P. (2001). *Principles of data mining.* Boston: The MIT Press.

Hearst, M. (1999). Untangling text data mining. In *Proceedings of 37th Annual Meeting of the Association for Computational Linguistics* (ACL'99), MD.

Kloptchenko, A., Eklund, T., Back, B., Karlsson, J., Vanharanta, H, & Visa, A. (2004). Combining data and text mining techniques for analyzing financial reports. *International Journal of Intelligent Systems in Accounting, Finance, and Management, 12*(1), 29-41

Kohonen, T. (1997). *Self-organizing maps.* Springer-Verlag.

Kroeze, J., Matthee, M., & Bothma, J. (2003). Differentiating data and text mining terminology. In *Proceedings of SAICSIT*, 93-101.

Lagus, K. (2000). *Text mining with WebSOM.* Unpublished doctoral dissertation, Espoo, Finland.

Lahtinen, T. (2000). *Automatic indexing: An approach using an index term corpus and combining linguistic and statistical methods.* Unpublished doctoral dissertation, University of Helsinki, Finland.

Lewis, D. (1992). Feature selection and feature extraction for text categorization. *Speech and Natural Language Workshop.*

Li, Y. (1998). Toward qualitative search engine. *IEEE Internet Computing*, July-August.

Marino, G. (2001). *Workers mired in e-mail wasteland.* Retrieved from CNetNews.com.

Nasukawa T., & Nagano T., (2001). Text analysis and knowledge mining systems. *IBM Systems Journal 40*(4), 967-984.

Pullum, G., & Scholz, B. (2001). More than words. *Nature, 413*, 367.

ReliaSoft Corporation (2002). *Reliability glossary.* ReliaSoft Corporation.

Robb, D. (2004). Text mining tools take on unstructured data. *ComputerWorld,* June 21.

Salton, G. (1989). *Automatic text processing.* Addison-Wesley.

Slonim, N., & Tishby, N. (2000). Document clustering using word clusters via information Bootleneck method. In *Proceedings of SIGID 2000,* New York: ACM Press.

Subasic, P., & Huettner, A. (2000). Calculus of fuzzy semantic typing for qualitative analysis of text. In *Proceedings of KDD-2000 Workshop on Text Mining, Sixth ACM SIGKDD International Conference on Knowledge Discovery and Data Mining,* Boston.

Toivonen, J., Visa, A., Vesanen, T., Back, B., & Vanharanta, H. (2001). Validation of text clustering based on document contents. In *Proceedings of MLDM'2001, International Workshop on Machine Learning and Data Mining in Pattern Recognition,* Leipzig, Germany.

van Rijsbergen, C. (1979). *Information retrieval* (2nd ed.). London: Butterworths.

Visa, A., Back, B., & Vanharanta, H. (1999). Toward text understanding: Comparison of text documents by sentence map. In *Proceedings of the EUFIT'99, 7th European Congress on Intelligent Techniques and Soft Computing,* Aachen, Germany.

Visa, A., Toivonen, J., Back, B., & Vanharanta, H. (2000). Toward text understanding: Classification of text documents by word map. In *Proceedings of AeroScience 2000, SPIE 14th Annual International Symposium on Aerospace/Defense Sensing,* Simulating and Controls, Orlando, FL.

Visa, A., Toivonen, J., Vanharanta, H., & Back, B. (2001). Prototype-matching: Finding meaning in thee books of the Bible. In *Proceedings of HICSS-34, Hawaii International Conference on System Sciences,* Maui, Hawaii.

Weiss, S., White, B., Apte, C., & Damerau, J. (2000). Lightweight document matching for help-desk applications. *IEEE Intelligent Systems,* March/April.

Witten, I., Bray Z., Mahoui, M., & Teahan, B. (1998). Text mining: A new frontier for lossless compression. In *Proceedings of Data Compression Conference '98, IEEE.*

Zamir, O., & Etzioni, O. (1998). Web document clustering: A feasibility demonstration. In *Proceedings of Conference of Information Retrieval (SIGIR'98),* ACM Press.

Zipf, G. K. (1972). *Human behavior and the principle of least effort: An introduction to human ecology.* New York: Hafner.

ENDNOTE

1 "Mohammed will come to the mountain" and "The mountain will come to Mohammed" have, of course, completely different meanings although they use the exact same words.

This work was previously published in the Information Resources Management Journal, Vol. 20, Issue 3, edited by M. Khosrow-Pour, pp. 19-31, copyright 2007 by IGI Publishing, formerly known as Idea Group Publishing (an imprint of IGI Global).

Chapter XXI
A Review of IS Research Activities and Outputs Using Pro Forma Abstracts

Francis Kofi Andoh-Baidoo
State University of New York at Brockport, USA

Elizabeth White Baker
Virginia Military Institute, USA

Santa R. Susarapu
Virginia Commonwealth University, USA

George M. Kasper
Virginia Commonwealth University, USA

ABSTRACT

Using March and Smith's taxonomy of information systems (IS) research activities and outputs and Newman's method of pro forma abstracting, this research mapped the current space of IS research and identified research activities and outputs that have received very little or no attention in the top IS publishing outlets. We reviewed and classified 1,157 articles published in some of the top IS journals and the ICIS proceedings for the period 1998–2002. The results demonstrate the efficacy of March and Smith's (1995) taxonomy for summarizing the state of IS research and for identifying activity-output categories that have received little or no attention. Examples of published research occupying cells of the taxonomy are cited, and research is posited to populate the one empty cell. The results also affirm the need to balance theorizing with building and evaluating systems because the latter two provide unique feedback that encourage those theories that are the most promising in practice.

INTRODUCTION

The information systems' literature is diverse. Some applaud this expansive scope while others consider it indicative of a lack of discipline. This research investigates the scope of IS literature using a taxonomy proposed by March and Smith (1995) and a classification method developed by Newman (1994). This offers a different and richer view of the literature landscape than that provided by citation analysis and one that is independent of epistemological and methodological partisanship. The authors approach IS research from the perspective of juxtaposing research activities and research outputs, leading to 16 different classifications of IS research products. Being able to move away from dichotomous classification systems and toward a richer lens through which to view IS research, IS researchers can take a broader view of the underrepresented areas in the field and surgically address those research voids in the IS research quilt.

At the first International Conference on Information Systems (ICIS), Keen (1980) warned IS researchers of the need to develop a cumulative research tradition, to build upon each other's and their own work; to develop shared definitions, topics and concepts; to ensure that journals in the field have a clear focus; and to build orthodoxy without dissuading novelty. Since then, several researchers have considered IS's progress toward this goal (Banville & Landry, 1989; Benbasat & Weber, 1996; Weber, 1987, 1999). Baskerville and Myers (2002) for example, stated, "[i]t is our opinion that IS has been singularly successful in developing its own research perspective and its own tradition" (p. 3). Likewise, Culnan (1987) stated that IS has "made significant progress toward a cumulative research tradition" (p. 341). Others, however, such as Vessey, Ramesh and Glass (2002) suggested that a cumulative research tradition has not yet been achieved because of a lack of focus on *theory,* "[o]ur data leads us to the conclusion that IS research does not demonstrate reliance on a single theory, or a set of theories, even in what we may regard as well-defined subareas of the discipline" (pp. 166–167). Benbasat and Zmud (2003) also concluded that there is a lack of cumulative research tradition in IS, but they argue that this is a result of a failure to focus on the *artifact.*

The state of IS cumulative research remains unclear, and whether this confusion is a result of a lack of focus on theory or artifact may be both a contributor and a result of this confusion, a chicken-and-egg argument. In other words, any meaningful assessment of the state of IS cumulative research must (a) categorize theory and artifact research, (b) consider the impact of the theory-artifact mix on cumulative knowledge, and (c) identify and encourage research programs that fill-in gaps and have the greatest potential impact on IS cumulative knowledge. To our knowledge, these relationships have not collectively been considered in past empirical reviews of IS literature.

Others have recognized that development of IS cumulative knowledge requires a symbiotic give-and-take between artifact design research, building and evaluating systems, and behavioral science research, theorizing and justifying systems (Hevner, March, Park, & Ram, 2004; Lee, 1991; March & Smith, 1995; Newman, 1994; Simon, 1996; Walls, Widmeyer, & El Sawy, 1992). The behavioral science paradigm is well established in the IS literature. Although introduced to IS researchers in the early 1990s (Walls et al., 1992), the design science paradigm is only recently beginning to gather momentum (Walls, Widmeyer, & El Sawy, 2004). Moreover, Simon (1996) asserts that design science research is the *foundation* of all professional disciplines.

Everyone designs who devises courses of action aimed at changing situations into preferred ones. The intellectual activity that produces material artifacts is no different fundamentally from the one that prescribes remedies for a sick patient or the one that devises a new sales plan for a company or a social welfare policy for a state. Design, so construed, is the core of all professional training; it is the principal mark that distinguishes the professions from the sciences. Schools of engineering, as well as schools of architecture, business, law, and medicine, are all centrally concerned with the process of design. (Simon, 1996, p. 111)

Describing the landscape of IS research requires mapping the content of individual papers onto a collective scheme that captures the mix of theory and artifact research. In this regard, March and Smith (1995) proposed an integrative, comprehensive taxonomy for classifying IS research that recognizes distinctions of design and behavioral science activities as well as multiple research outputs. In order to utilize this taxonomy or any other, some means of classification is needed. Newman (1994) provides such an instrument. Newman's pro forma abstracts are frames into which the results of specific research are "slotted" according to the research method utilized and research product generated.

Using Newman's method of pro forma abstracting, the research reported here mapped articles published in some of the top IS journals and the ICIS proceedings over the period 1998-2002 into an updated version of March and Smith's (1995) taxonomy. Specifically, each paper was read and classified using terms found in the paper into the appropriate and distinct pro forma abstract template. The results demonstrate the efficacy of the taxonomy and provide a view of both the numbers and mix of IS theory and artifact research over the 5 years studied. Moreover, the results identify research activities and outputs in need of attention by IS researchers.

The article begins with a review of previous works that have considered the state of IS cumulative research. Next, the research methodology used in this study is detailed. The results of the study are then reported. Based on these results, IS research in general and publishing outlets in particular are characterized. Publishing patterns of the reviewed IS journals and ICIS proceedings are summarized, and the potential benefits of a more diversified portfolio of research both within and across design and behavioral science research is discussed.

BACKGROUND

Several research studies have investigated the body of IS research, some focusing on the overall field (e.g., Chua et al., 2002; Culnan, 1986; Culnan & Swanson, 1986; Palvia, Leary, Pinjani, & Midha, 2004), and others have focused on specific subdisciplines of IS such as DSS (Arnott & Pervan, 2005), and e-commerce (Urbaczewski, Jessup, & Wheeler, 2002). Vessey et al. (2002) described the article by Alavi, Carlson, and Brooke (1989) as the main work that really sought to study cumulative research tradition in IS. Alavi and her co-authors applied two classifications to IS articles: (a) the Barki-Rivard-Talbot (1988) scheme consisting of nine top-level categories, each with several subcategories and (b) a binary classification of empirical or nonempirical methodology. Using these two classifications, Alavi et al. (1989) found that the three most popular research topics were (a) IS management (including IS evaluation, planning and management); (b) information systems (including types of information systems, IS application areas, and IS characteristics); and (c) IS development and operations (including IS life-cycle activities, IS development strategies, and IS implementation). They also reported that 46.5% of the articles published between 1968 and 1988 were empirical and concluded that "the field has taken major steps towards establishing a cumulative tradition of research necessary for providing scientific and valid guidelines for practice and research" (Alavi et al., p. 398). Similarly, Baskerville and Myers (2002) concluded that IS has progressed and matured to where it need not look to other disciplines for reference; it has developed to where it can serve as a reference discipline in its own right to other fields. Indeed, they argue that discussions regarding proper reference disciplines discourage IS from standing on its own merits.

In related work that investigated products of computer–human interaction (CHI) research, Newman (1994) stated that the "primary value [of CHI research] lies in its contributions to the practice of interactive computer systems development ... of simplifying theory into practical models, which are the tools for designers to apply the theory" (p. 279). Looking to engineering as a successful model, Newman found that as much as 90% of the engineering literature reported enhancements to and evaluations of existing techniques, solutions, and tools, what he called "normal" engineering science (design science in IS); the remaining 10% positing new theory and concepts.

Commenting on his pro forma abstracting methodology, Newman concluded that by differentiating research products, pro forma abstracts were invaluable for categorizing publications. "Pro forma abstracts are templates, written in the style of normal abstracts, into which the results of research can be 'slotted' according to the category of method followed and research product generated" (Newman, 1994, p. 279). In the research reported here, a pro forma abstract template was developed for each cell in the updated March and Smith's taxonomy.

Shown as Figure 1, March and Smith's updated taxonomy consists of two dimensions: research activity and research output. The research output dimension encompasses IS scholarly output defined as: a construct, a model, a method, or an instantiation of an information system. The research activities dimension is split in March and Smith's original paper (1995) into design science activities and natural science activities. Later, Hevner et al. (2004) relabeled natural science to behavioral science. We use the term *behavioral science* in the remainder of this article to include March and Smith's "natural" science.

The behavioral science paradigm seeks to develop and verify theories that predict and explain human and organizational capabilities by creating new and innovative artifacts; whereas in design science, knowledge and understanding are advanced in the building and application of the artifact (Hevner et al., 2004). "Rather than producing general theoretical knowledge, design scientists produce and apply knowledge of tasks or situations in order to create effective artifacts" (March & Smith, 1995, p. 253). While behavioral scientists seek to use theory to explain a phenomenon, design scientists make instrumental use of theory to build efficient and effective systems (Lee, 2000). March and Smith (1995) argued

Figure 1. Framework for classifying IS research products

		Research Activities			
		Design Science		**Behavioral Science**	
		Build	Evaluate	Theorize	Justify
Research Outputs	Constructs				
	Model				
	Method				
	Instantiation				

Note. Adapted from March and Smith (1995) and Hevner et al. (2004)

that their framework provides an integrative and comprehensive classification scheme to evaluate the IS publishing portfolio.

Beginning the description of Figure 1 with Design Science activities, "Build refers to the construction of the artifact demonstrating that such an artifact can be constructed" (March & Smith, 1995, p. 254). In Evaluate, metrics or criteria are developed and used to test the artifact for the purpose it was designed. In the Behavioral Science columns, Theorize involves explaining why and how the effects came about; that is, why and how the constructs, models, methods, and instantiations work. The Theorize colulmn attempts to unify the known data into viable theory and includes developing ideas with which to theorize about constructs, models, methods and instantiations. Justify uses evidence to refute or fail to refute research constructs, models, methods, and instantiations (March & Smith, 1995).

Turning to the Research Output categories, "[c]onstructs or concepts form the vocabulary of a domain. They constitute a conceptualization used to describe problems within the domain and specify solutions" (March & Smith, 1995, p. 256). Model is a set of propositions or statements expressing relationships among constructs. Methods define a set of steps (an algorithm or heuristic) used to perform a task. "Instantiation refers to the realization of an artifact in its environment"

Table 1. March and Smith classifications, Newman pro forma abstract, and example journal article

March & Smith Classification	Pro Forma Abstract Template	Example Journal Abstract
Build Construct	New/Existing construct (s) in/for <IT artifact type> has/have been proposed/developed/enhanced.	New constructs for secure RPC frameworks for information service creation on future high-speed ATM-based open-architectured Internet have been proposed (Kuo & Lin, 1998)
Build Model	New/Existing model for/in <IT artifact-type> has been proposed/ developed/enhanced.	A model for knowledge evolution system within virtual communities has been proposed (Bieber et al., 2002)
Build Method	New/Existing method/algorithm/ technique/approach for building <IT artifact-type> has been proposed/developed/enhanced.	New approach for building databases that address inferential disclosure of confidential views in multidimensional categorical databases has been developed (Chowdhury, Duncan, Krishnan, Roehrig, & Mukherjee, 1999)
Build Instantiation	New <IT artifact-type> has been developed. This <IT artifact-type> presents a solution to/for <environment-type> and/or <user-type.>	New case base reasoning (CBR) DSS tool has been developed. This tool presents a solution for storing the process by which the decision maker arrived at their solution (Angehrn & Dutta, 1998)
Evaluate Construct	The <IT construct-type> for building <IT artifact-type> has been evaluated using <performance measuring metrics>. The paper shows/fails to show that the <IT construct-type> has better/favorable <performance-type> than/to existing constructs.	The security requirement for building effective perturbation methods of protecting confidential data has been evaluated by statistical methods. The paper shows that the new security requirement has better security standard than that defined in prior study (Muralidhar, Sarathy, & Parsa, 2001)

continued on following page

Table 1. continued

Evaluate Model	New/Existing model (s) for/in <IT artifact type> has/have been evaluated using <performance measuring metrics>. The paper shows/fails to show that the model provides a more comprehensive representation and captures more of the <IT tasks> than existing models.	Existing access control models for developing secured web applications have been evaluated using security requirement metrics. The paper shows that the model (RBAC) presents a more comprehensive representation and captures more security requirements than existing models (Joshi, Aref, Ghafoor, & Spafford, 2001)
Evaluate Method	<Method-type> for building <IT artifact-type> has/have been evaluated using <performance measuring metrics>. The paper shows/fails to show that this method is effective and/efficient. In addition, this method presents a complete and or/consistent/and or/easy to use/and or high quality features when applied in <environment-type.>	Three emerging web standards - HTML, XML, and CSS have been evaluated as standards for building Multipurpose publishing. The paper shows that these standards provide high quality features (device independence, content reuse and network-friendly encoding) in delivering content on the Web (Lie & Saarela, 1999)
Evaluate Instantiation	<IT artifact-type> has been evaluated using <performance measuring metrics>. The paper shows/fails to show that the <IT artifact-type> presents a better/comparable solution than/to and or in <user-type> and or <environment-type.>	UML has been evaluated using International standard metrics. The paper shows that the UML 1.3 presents a better product to other products including previous versions of UML and future revisions and factors that have contributed to the success and expectation in future versions have been presented (Kobryn, 1999)
Theorize Construct	New/Existing construct (s) has /have been developed/enhanced to explain/study/measure <IT phenomena>. The paper shows/fails to show that this/these construct (s) is/are valid and reliable.	Cognitive absorption construct has been developed to explain users' behavior towards information technology use. The paper shows that this construct is valid and reliable (Agarwal & Karahanna, 2000)
Theorize Model	New/Existing theoretical framework/model for studying/explaining the relationship between <constructs>/ factors that influence <IT phenomena> has been developed/ enhanced. The paper shows/fails to show that model/framework effectively represents/explains <IT phenomena> <in an environment-type.>	New theoretical model for explaining the factors that influence the assimilation of web technologies has been developed. The paper shows that this model effectively explains assimilation of web technologies in the eCommerce environment (Chatterjee, Grewal, & Sambamurthy, 2002)
Theorize Method	New/Existing method/approach for <IT phenomena> doing <IT task> has been developed/enhanced. The paper shows/fails to shows using <IT-artifact> or <participants> that this framework/method/approach is effective <in/or> <environment/ situation.>	New approach for conducting and evaluating Interpretive field studies in Information Systems has been developed. The paper shows using existing IS research papers that this approach is effective for interpretive case studies of hermeneutic in nature (Klein & Myers, 1999)

continued on following page

Table 1. continued

Theorize Instantiation	New/Existing theory for explaining <information technology type> has been developed/enhanced. The paper shows/fails to show that this theory effectively explains how/ why the <IT artifact-type> works <in environment-type.>	New theory has been developed for explaining virtual-cross-value-chain, creative collaborative team. The paper shows that this theory effectively explains how virtual-cross-value-chain, creative collaborative teams work (Malhotra, Majchrzak, Carman, & Lott, 2001)
Justify Construct	A/An empirical and or theoretical research has been performed to validate <IT construct-type>. The paper shows/fails to show that this/these construct (s) underlies/underlie <IT theory>, /is/are <useful/critical/influence> <for studying> <IT phenomena> <and that the construct (s) is/are valid, reliable and useful/ not valid and reliable.>	An empirical and theoretical research has been performed to validate means objective and fundamental objectives constructs. The paper shows that these constructs influence Internet shopping and that the constructs are valid, reliable and useful. (Torkzadeh & Dhillon, 2002)
Justify Model	A/An empirical and theoretical research has been performed to validate <IT model-type>. The paper shows/fails to show that this theoretical <model-type> effectively represents the <IT phenomena> or explains how/why the <IT phenomena> works.>	An empirical and theoretical research has been performed to validate Media Richness Theory. It has been shown that the Media Richness Theory is not supported in the new media environment (Dennis & Kinney, 1998)
Justify Method	A/An empirical and or theoretical research has been performed to validate <IT method-type> for doing <IT task>. The paper shows/fails to show that that the <IT method type> is effective This method is effective and/efficient in doing <IT task.]	An empirical and theoretical research has been performed to validate techniques for doing IS research. The paper shows that the IS research techniques are ineffective in the validation of the instruments used (Boudreau, Gefen, & Straub, 2001)
Justify Instantiation	A/An empirical and theoretical research has been done for studying <IT artifact-type> /explaining how/why <IT artifact-type> works. The paper shows/fails to show that this theory effectively explains how/why <IT artifact-type> works. The <IT artifact-type> presents a better/comparable solution to/and or in <user-Type>/and or <environment-type.>	No examples found.

(March & Smith, 1995, p. 258). This realization ranges from installation (e.g., migrating an application from development to production environment) to institutionalization, implementation that actually achieves the intended business value (Murphy, 2002).

RESEARCH METHODOLOGY

Some reviews of the IS literature use bibliographic assessment, in particular citation analysis (Culnan, 1986; Culnan & Swanson, 1986; Larsen & Levine, 2005). Citation analysis can show the web of reference interconnects among publications, addressing Keen's (1980) concern of building upon our own and each other's work; it does not consider content, nor does it address the publication landscape. Indeed, the limitations of citation analysis in this regard are well documented (Osareh, 1996). Similarly, the Barki-Rivard-Talbot categorization used by Alavi et al. (1989) is a keyword classification and not a prescriptive taxonomy.

The study reported here uses Newman's pro forma abstract method to classify journal articles and populate March and Smith's taxonomy. One of the authors developed a distinct pro forma abstract template for each cell of March and Smith's taxonomy. These 16 pro forma abstract templates are listed in column 2 of Table 1.

Column 1 of Table 1 lists the 16 March and Smith classifications, and column 3 cites a specific article taken from the papers read for this study as an example of the abstract template and classification. Column 2 shows the pseudo code form used to assign each article to its cell in the taxonomy. The selected examples shown in column 3 will be discussed in aggregate in the following section.

Publication Outlet Selection

Publications from six journals and ICIS proceedings were gathered for this research. The six journals are *Communications of the ACM* (CACM), *Decision Sciences* (DS), *Journal of Management Information Systems* (JMIS), *Information Systems Research* (ISR), *Management Science* (MS) and *MIS Quarterly* (MISQ). These journals were selected because (a) all six journals are well recognized as among the top journals in the field (Larsen & Levine, 2005; Lowry, Romans, & Curtis, 2004; Vessey et al., 2002); (b) they have been used in earlier studies (Alavi et al., 1989); (c) despite their collective interests in computing, their core audiences and perspectives differ; and (d) both within and without the IS academic community, these journals are pointed to as leading outlets for quality IS research and publishing. No claim is made that publications in these journals represent the whole field of IS research and writing; however, these journals have historically been included in analyses of IS publications. For many both within and without IS, articles in these journals serve as bellwethers of IS research and writing.

Data Collection

All IS articles for the period 1998–2002 were collected from each journal and ICIS proceedings. A 5-year window was selected because it is consistent with earlier reviews of the IS literature and because it provided a large enough longitudinal timeframe to minimize aberrations in the types of research published by each outlet. All articles were collected from JMIS, ISR, MISQ and the ICIS proceedings, whereas only the IS articles were gathered from CACM, DS and MS. All IS and information technology (IT) articles in DS and MS were included in the sample. CACM articles were included if the IT artifact reported in the article was discussed within the context of an organizational system or organizational aspects of IS.

Next, one of the authors read each randomly assigned article and matched statements in the article to those in a pro forma abstract template

Table 2. Classification of articles into March and Smith's and Hevner, et al.'s taxonomy across journals and ICIS proceedings

		Research Activities			
		Design Science		Behavioral Science	
		Build	Evaluate	Theorize	Justify
Research Outputs	Constructs	6 (0.5)	1 (0.1)	55 (4.8)	4 (0.3)
	Model	32 (2.8)	3 (0.3)	744 (64.3)	20 (1.7)
	Method	138 (11.9)	45 (3.9)	55 (4.8)	4 (0.3)
	Instantiation	38 (3.3)	9 (0.8)	3 (0.2)	0 (0.0)
	Totals	214 (18.5)	58 (5.0)	857 (74.1)	28 (2.4)

from the pool of 16 pro forma abstracts listed in Table 1. There was little difficulty identifying the appropriate pro forma abstract that closely matched the wording used in each article, and all articles were classified.

To ensure the consistency and accuracy of the coding overall, one of the researchers experienced with using this classification method, read the articles over the period of two semesters. A second researcher independently classified a subset of the articles using the same pro forma abstracts methodology to assess reliability. This second reader classified 11% of the sample (131 of the 1,157 articles). Interrater reliability was computed using Cohen's kappa (Cohen, 1960), which adjusts the raw agreement to account for the possibility of agreement occurring by chance. The raw agreement was 89% (116 out of 131), resulting in a kappa calculation of 0.84. According to Landis and Koch (1977), kappa values equal to or greater than 0.81 are regarded as almost perfect. When disagreements occurred between the coders, or if the focus of the paper was ambiguous, the papers almost always included multiple research outputs and activities. For example, a paper may have included both theorizing a model and justifying a model. When this occurred, the two raters met and assigned the article to the classification coinciding with their agreement on the primary focus of the paper.

RESULTS

Table 2 shows the pro forma results for the 1,157 articles reviewed in this study within the updated March and Smith taxonomy pooled across the journals. Raw counts and their corresponding percents, given in parentheses, are presented in each cell.

It is clear that a preponderance of IS research activity is in Behavioral Science. The data in Table 2 show that the Behavioral Science research activity of Theorize constituted 74.1% of all IS research activity published in the journals and ICIS proceedings included in this study over the period 1998–2002, and only 2.4% of publishing was categorized as Justify Behavioral Science research. Table 2 also shows that Build Design Science research activity accounted for 18.5 percent of all IS research activity, and 5.0% of publications were Evaluate Design Science research activity.

Table 3. Classification of articles into March and Smith's updated taxonomy by journal

	Journal/Conference							
	MISQ	**ISR**	**JMIS**	**DS**	**MS**	**CACM**	**ICIS**	**Total**
Build/ Construct	-	-	-	-	-	4(0.8)	2(0.9)	6 (0.5)
Build/ Model	-	6(5.8)	5(2.9)	-	2(9.1)	13(2.5)	6(2.9)	32 (2.8)
Build/ Method	1(1.1)	4(3.9)	12(7.1)	-	5(22.7)	100(19.5)	16(7.6)	138 (11.9)
Build/ Instantiation	-	-	3(1.8)	2(4.1)	-	30(5.8)	3(1.4)	38 (3.3)
All Build	1(1.1)	10(9.7)	20(11.8)	2(4.1)	7(31.8)	147(28.7)	27(12.9)	214 (18.5)
Evaluate/ Construct	-	-	-	1(2.0)	-	-	-	1 (0.1)
Evaluate Model	-	-	-	1(2.0)	-	2(0.4)	-	3 (0.3)
Evaluate/ Method	-	1(1.0)	1(0.6)	2(4.1)	-	38(7.4)	3(1.4)	45 (3.9)
Evaluate/ Instantiation	-	-	-	-	-	9(1.8)	-	9 (0.8)
All Evaluate	-	1(1.0)	1(0.6)	4(8.2)	-	49(9.5)	3(1.4)	58 (5.0)
Total Design Science	1(1.1)	11(10.7)	21(12.4)	6(12.2)	7(31.8)	196(38.2)	30(14.3)	272(23.5)
Theorize/ Construct	17(18.9)	4(3.9)	9(5.3)	2(4.1)	1(4.5)	6(1.2)	16(7.6)	55 (4.8)
Theorize/ Model	60(66.7)	76(73.8)	126(74.1)	28(57.1)	11(50.0)	290(56.5)	153(72.9)	744 (64.3)
Theorize/ Method	2(2.2)	6(5.8)	14(8.2)	8(16.3)	3(13.6)	19(3.7)	3(1.4)	55 (4.8)
Theorize/ Instantiation	2(2.2)	-	-	-	-	-	1(0.5)	3 (0.2)
All Theorize	81(90.0)	86(83.5)	149(87.6)	38(77.5)	15(68.2)	315(61.4)	173(82.4)	857 (74.1)
Justify/ Construct	-	2(1.9)	-	1(2.0)	-	1(0.2)	-	4 (0.3)
Justify/ Model	6(6.7)	4(3.9)	-	4(8.2)	-	1(0.2)	5(2.4)	20 (1.7)
Justify/ Method	2(2.2)	-	-	-	-	-	2(0.9)	4 (0.3)
Justify/In-stantiation	-	-	-	-	-	-	-	0 (0.0)
All Justify	8(8.9)	6(5.8)	-	5(10.2)	-	2(0.4)	7(3.3)	28 (2.4)
Total Behav-ioral Science	89(98.9)	92(89.3)	149(87.6)	43(87.8)	15(68.2)	317(61.8)	180(85.7)	885(76.5)
Total	90(7.8)	103(8.9)	170(14.7)	49(4.2)	22(1.9)	513(44.3)	210(18.2)	1157

Of particular interest is the Instantiation row where there is little activity beyond the Instantiation/Build cell and no activity in the Instantiation/Justify cell. This may confirm March and Smith's (1995) statement:

"[T]here is little argument that novel constructs, models, and methods are viable research results, there is less enthusiasm in the information technology literature for novel instantiations. Novel instantiations, it is argued, are simply extensions of novel constructs, models, or, methods. Hence, we should value the constructs, models, and methods, but not the instantiations...instantiations that apply known constructs, models, or methods to novel tasks may be of little significance" (p. 260).

However, much of computer science and engineering realizes that what works "in theory" may not work in practice (March & Smith, 1995). We'll discuss this in more detail below.

Reviewing results within each outlet, Table 3 presents the research outputs nested in research activities for each journal and the ICIS proceedings. A review of this data shows dramatic differences across journals in the distribution of articles by classifications. Publication of Design Science research ranges from 1.1% in MISQ to 14.3% in ICIS, to over 30% in MS and CACM. In fact, these results show that only one Design Science article appeared in MISQ from 1998–2002. At the other extreme, CACM published 196 articles categorized as Design Science. Conversely, the data show that 90% of the publications in MISQ theorized a Behavioral Science construct, model, method or instantiation, but 77 of these 81 articles fell into two categories: Construct and Model theorizing. At the other extreme, only three Theorize/Instantiation articles were published in these IS outlets between 1998 and 2002; two appeared in MISQ and one appeared in the ICIS proceedings. Likewise, the four Justify/Method publications were evenly split between the MISQ and the ICIS proceedings. Somewhat surprising, almost 99% of the publications in MISQ are Behavioral Science, whereas they account for only about 85% of work in ICIS proceedings. Across all six journals and the ICIS proceedings, 74.1%, or 857 articles, were categorized as Behavioral Science Theorize pieces. The two categories with the fewest number of publications were Evaluate with 58 pieces, or 5%, and Justify with 28, or 2.4%.

Discussion

One motivation for mapping a discipline's research is to identify topics in need of investigation and development—holes in the research fabric of a discipline—that may leave the portfolio less than balanced. The mapping reported here highlights the need for Justify/Instantiation research. One reason for the dearth of research on IS instantiations is the feeling that these artifacts are already built and in use, and there is no motivation for justifying these specific artifacts per se in a journal article. Instead of justifying an instantiation, authors are more inclined to justify models, which would lead ultimately to justifying instantiations. However, much of the business-organization context of IS centers effectively integrating instantiations into an organization so as to achieve the hoped for holistic performance and business value. In other words, much might be learned by investigating successful instantiations and looking backwards toward their inception to posit the nature of their success.

That theory does not always coincide with practice is well known to anyone that has to actually do the work. Former President Ronald Reagan quipped that "economists are people who see something that works in practice and wonder if it would work in theory." ("Ronald Reagan," 2004). The history of computing, particularly IS, is replete with discrepancies between theory and practice. Perhaps we should be looking at things that work in practice and seeing if they also work in theory. Methodology exists to conduct such research, and such research has been conducted, but it is not being published in the premier IS journals.

CONCLUSION

This study mapped articles published in some of the top IS journals and the ICIS proceedings over the period 1998–2002 into an updated version of March and Smith's taxonomy of IS research activities using Newman's method of pro forma abstracting. The results show that publication in these IS outlets is almost exclusively behavioral science; design science activities, research that builds and evaluates systems, is negligible. The proportion of design science to behavioral science publications ranges from a low of one article of 90, or 1.1%, for MISQ to a high of 196 articles out of 513, or 38.2%, for CACM. Some of these differences may be attributed to differences in intended audiences. For example:

institutional issues have had, and continue to have, an important impact on the IS field's evolution. In other words, the field's evolution depends on various institutional stakeholders, not just intrinsic characteristics of IS as a scientific or applied field.(Alter, 2003, p. 620)

The institutional arrangements in business schools that determine promotion, tenure and rewards have a part to play to increase the amount of design science research and publication in IS. As sponsored research makes greater inroads into the culture of business schools, greater emphasis will be placed on design science research. As in engineering, this is likely to result in more publication of design science research activities and outputs. Similarly, few, if any, IS doctoral programs consider design science. Obviously, if design science is to become a methodology known to researchers and properly used in the IS research community, nascent scientists must be introduced to the methodology. IS Ph.D. students must be introduced to design science in much the same way that most doctoral programs now include qualitative research methods. Development of design science research and methodology is beyond the scope of this article. However, the reader interested in knowing more about design sciences should review Vaishnavi and Kuechler (2004) and Hevner et al. (2004).

Based on these results, we join the increasing number of IS researchers calling for an increase in design science research and publication to advance IS cumulative research. Building and evaluating systems provides unique feedback that advances those ideas that are the most promising in practice. March and Smith (1995) and Hevner et al. (2004) also conclude that IS research must include a proper mix of both design science and behavioral science research activities and outputs. "Progress is achieved ... when existing technologies are replaced by more effective ones (which could only be done if existing technologies [are] part of the cumulative tradition)" and are subjected to scientifically rigorous procedures and methods (March & Smith, 1995, p. 254). In other words, IS cumulative tradition is diminished as opposed to strengthened by a disproportionate, in this case almost exclusive, focus on behavioral science in relation to design science research. An increase in design science research and publication will enhance rather than diminish both IS practice and scholarship.

As is the case in all scholarly endeavors, IS researchers recognize theory development and theory testing as critical parts of their discipline. However, IS researchers must also be involved in building and evaluating artifacts that instantiate theory. This integrative, proof-of-concept process is critical, especially in professional disciplines such as IS (Brooks, 1996; Hevner et al., 2004; Iivari, Hirschheim, & Klein, 1998; Lee, 1991; March & Smith, 1995; Simon, 1996).

The authors feel compelled to echo Hevner et al. (2004) by emphasizing that it would be counterproductive to embark on design science research program without a proper appreciation for rigor. Because design science is practice oriented, it is relevant by definition. It is the rigor of design science that often must be defended. This can be a challenge because for many IS artifacts their "proof" is confirmed within environments that are heavily influenced by factors that raise very compelling competing hypotheses questions, making it almost impossible to differentiate cause and effect relations.

The obvious limitation of this work is the sample of IS outlets. Other IS outlets may publish much more design science research. However, even if this is the case, it does not diminish the conclusion that many of the most prestigious and most recognized IS outlets publish very little design science research, and that it would add to the visibility and credibility of design science to have more quality design science papers published in these recognized IS journals. As was discussed in the Research Methodology section, another limitation of this research results from the individual research outputs which appeared to fall into two template categories. While the authors chose to classify the article based on its primary focus, it is possible that by ignoring the other aspects of each of these papers that the overall distribution of IS research outputs might be distorted.

Last, this study integrated and applied a classification and coding scheme based on pro forma abstracts rather than using key words, abstracts or citations. This methodology provides a level of detail in assessing content heretofore not used in evaluating cumulative IS research.

Chua et al. (2002) divide a large breadth of journal outlets into different baskets, of which the selection of journals that the authors used in this study would be one basket. The future direction of this research stream is to expand the research publication outlets covered by using different journal baskets identified in Chua et al. (2002). To achieve this end, future studies using pro forma abstracts to cover the IS cumulative research tradition would use different baskets than the one used in this study. This might have significant ramifications in determining what types of research outputs are published and in what journals. Also, it is important to classify articles of a more recent vintage. The 5-year time period that was chosen for this study, 1998-2002, would need to be updated to cover the next 5-year time period of 2003–2007 to see if there is any perceptible shift in the focus of IS research from the current study.

REFERENCES

Agarwal, R., & Karahanna, E. (2000). Time flies when you're having fun: Cognitive absorption and beliefs about information technology usage. *MIS Quarterly, 24*(4), 665-694.

Alavi, M., Carlson, P., & Brooke, G. (1989). The ecology of MIS research: A twenty year status review. In J. I. DeGross, J. Henderson, & B. Konsynsky (Eds.), *Proceedings of the tenth international conference on information systems* (pp. 363-375). New York: ACM Press.

Alter, S. (2003). The IS core-XI: Sorting out issues about the core, scope, and identity of the IS field. *Communications of the AIS, 12*, 607-628.

Angehrn, A., & Dutta, S. (1998). Case-based decision support. *Communications of the ACM, 41*(5es), 157-165.

Arnott, D., & Pervan, G. (2005). A critical analysis of decision support systems research. *Journal of Information Technology, 20*, 67-87.

Banville, C., & Landry, M. (1989). Can the field of MIS be disciplined? *Communications of the ACM, 32*(1), 48-60.

Barki, H., Rivard, S., & Talbot, J. (1988). An Information systems keyword classification scheme. *MIS Quarterly, 34*(3), 299-322.

Baskerville, R., & Myers, M. D. (2002). Information systems as a reference discipline. *MIS Quarterly, 26*(1), 1-14.

Benbasat, I., & Weber, R. (1996). Rethinking "diversity" in information systems research. *Information Systems Research, 7*(4), 389-399.

Benbasat, I., & Zmud, R. W. (2003). The identity crisis within the IS discipline: Defining and communicating the discipline's core properties. *MIS Quarterly, 27*(2), 183-194.

Bieber, M. P., Engelbart, D., Furuta, R., Hiltz, S. R., Noll, J., Preece, J., et al. (2002). Toward virtual community knowledge evolution. *Journal of Management Information Systems, 18*(4), 11-36.

Boudreau, M., Gefen, D., & Straub, D. W. (2001). Validation in information systems research: A state-of-the-art assessment. *MIS Quarterly, 25*(1), 1-16.

Brooks, F. (1996). The computer scientist as toolsmith II. *Communications of the ACM, 39*(3), 61-68.

Chatterjee, D., Grewal, R., & Sambamurthy, V. (2002). Shaping up for e-commerce: Institutional enablers of the organizational assimilation of Web technologies. *MIS Quarterly, 26*(2), 65-89.

Chowdhury, S. D., Duncan, G. T., Krishnan, R., Roehrig, S. F., & Mukherjee, S. (1999). Disclosure detection in multivariate categorical databases: Auditing confidentiality protection through two new matrix operators. *Management Science, 45*(12), 1710-1723.

Chua, C., Cao, L., Cousins, K., Mohan, K., Straub, D. W., & Vaishnavi, V. (2002). IS bibliographic repository (ISBIB): A central repository of research information for the IS community. *Communications of the AIS, 8*, 392-412.

Cohen, J. A. (1960). Coefficient of agreement for nominal scales. *Educational and Psychological Measurement, 20*(1), 37-46.

Culnan, M. J. (1986). Mapping the intellectual structure of MIS, 1972-1982: A co-citation analysis. *Management Science, 32*(2), 156-172.

Culnan, M. J. (1987). Mapping the intellectual structure of MIS, 1980-1985: A co-citation analysis. *MIS Quarterly, 11*(3), 341-350.

Culnan, M. J., & Swanson, E. B. (1986). Research in management information systems, 1980-1984: Points of work and reference. *MIS Quarterly, 10*(3), 289-301.

D'Aubeterre, F., Palvia, P., & Stevens, J. (2005). *A meta-analysis of current global information systems research.* Paper presented at the Americas Conference on Information Systems, Omaha, NE.

Dennis, A. R., & Kinney, S. T. (1998). Testing media richness theory in the new media: The effects of cues, feedback, and task equivocality. *Information Systems Research, 3*(9), 256-274.

Hevner, A. R., March, S. T., Park, J., & Ram, S. (2004). Design science in information systems research. *MIS Quarterly, 28*(1), 75-105.

Iivari, J., Hirschheim, R., & Klein, H. K. (1998). A paradigmatic analysis contrasting information systems development approaches and methodologies. *Information Systems Research, 9*(2), 164-193.

Joshi, J. B. D., Aref, W. G., Ghafoor, A., & Spafford, E. H. (2001). Security models for Web-based applications. *Communications of the ACM, 44*(2), 38-44.

Keen, P. G. W. (1980). *MIS research: Reference disciplines and a cumulative tradition.* Paper presented at the First International Conference on Information Systems, Philadelphia, PA.

Klein, H. K., & Myers, M. D. (1999). A set of principles for conducting and evaluating interpretive field studies in information systems. *MIS Quarterly, 23*(1), 67-94.

Kobryn, C. (1999). UML 2001: A standardization odyssey. *Communications of the ACM, 42*(10), 29-37.

Kuo, G., & Lin, J. (1998). New design concepts for an intelligent Internet. *Communications of the ACM, 41*(11), 93-98.

Landis, J. R., & Koch, G. G. (1977). The measurement of observer agreement for categorical data. *Biometrics, 33*(1), 159-174.

Larsen, T. J., & Levine, L. (2005). Searching for MIS: Coherence and change in the discipline. *Information Systems Journal, 15*, 357-381.

Lee, A. S. (1991). Architecture as a reference discipline for MIS. In H.-E. Nissen, H. K. Klein & R. Hirschheim (Eds.), *Information research: Contemporary approaches and emergent traditions* (pp. 573-592). Amsterdam: North-Holland.

Lee, A. S. (2000). Irreducibly sociological dimensions in research and publishing: Editor's comments. *MIS Quarterly, 24*(4), v-vii.

Lie, H. W., & Saarela, J. (1999). Multipurpose Web publishing using HTML, XML, and CSS. *Communications of the ACM, 42*(10), 95-101.

Lowry, P. B., Romans, D., & Curtis, A. (2004). Global journal prestige and supporting disciplines: A scientometric study of information systems journals. *Journal of the AIS, 5*(2), 29-77.

Malhotra, A., Majchrzak, A., Carman, R., & Lott, V. (2001). Radical innovation without collocation: A case study at Boeing-Rocketdyne. *MIS Quarterly, 25*(2), 229-249.

March, S. T., & Smith, G. F. (1995). Design and natural science research on information technology. *Decision Support Systems, 15*(4), 251-266.

Muralidhar, K., Sarathy, R., & Parsa, R. (2001). An improved security requirement for data perturbation with implications for e-commerce. *Decision Sciences Journal, 32*(4), 683-698.

Murphy, T. (2002). *Achieving business value from technology: A practical guide for today's executive.* Hoboken, NJ: Gartner Press, Wiley.

Newman, W. (1994). *A preliminary analysis of the products of HCI research, using pro forma abstracts.* Paper presented at the Human Factors in Computing Systems, Boston, MA.

Osareh, F. (1996). Bibliometrics, citation analysis, and co-citation analysis: A review of literature. *Libri, 46*(4), 217-225.

Palvia, P., Leary, T., Pinjani, P., & Midha, V. (2004). *A meta-analysis of MIS research.* Paper presented at the Americas Conference on Information Systems, New York, NY.

Ronald Reagan: The early years. (2004, June 6). *San Francisco Chronicle,* A-24.

Simon, H. (1996). *The Sciences of the artificial* (3rd ed.). Cambridge, MA: MIT Press.

Torkzadeh, G., & Dhillon, G. (2002). Measuring factors that influence the success of Internet commerce. *Information Systems Research, 13*(2), 187-204.

Urbaczewski, A., Jessup, L. M., & Wheeler, B. (2002). Electronic commerce research: A Taxonomy and synthesis. *Journal of Organizational Computing and Electronic Commerce, 12*(4), 263-305.

Vaishnavi, V., & Kuechler, W. (2004). Design research in information systems online working paper. Retrieved May 7, 2007, from http://www.isworld.org/Researchdesign/drisISworld.htm

Vessey, I., Ramesh, V., & Glass, R. L. (2002). Research in information systems: An empirical study of diversity in the discipline and its journals. *Journal of Management Information Systems, 19*(2), 129-174.

Walls, J. G., Widmeyer, G. R., & El Sawy, O. A. (1992). Building an information system design theory for vigilant EIS. *Information Systems Research, 3*(1), 36-59.

Walls, J. G., Widmeyer, G. R., & El Sawy, O. A. (2004). Assessing information systems design theory in perspective: How useful was our 1992 initial rendition? *Journal of Information Technology Theory and Application, 6*(2), 43-58.

Weber, R. (1987). Toward a theory of artifacts: A paradigmatic base for information systems research. *Journal of Information Systems, 1*(2), 3-19.

Weber, R. (1999). *The information systems discipline: The need for and nature of the foundational core.* Paper presented at the Information Systems Foundation Workshop: Ontology, Semiotics, and Practice, Macquarie University.

This work was previously published in the Information Resources Management Journal, Vol. 20, Issue 4, edited by M. Khosrow-Pour, pp. 65-79, copyright 2007 by IGI Publishing, formerly known as Idea Group Publishing (an imprint of IGI Global).

Compilation of References

Aastrup, J. (2002). *Networks producing intermodal transport.* Unpublished doctoral dissertation, Copenhagen Business School.

Abdel-Hamid, T. and Madnick, S. (1989). Lessons learned from modeling the dynamics of software development. *Communications of the ACM*, 32(12), 1426-1455.

Abdel-Hamid, T., & Madnick, S. E. (1991). *Software project dynamics: An integrated approach.* Englewood Cliffs, NJ: Prentice Hall.

Abell, A. (2000). Creating corporate information literacy: 1-3. *Information Management Report*(April-June): 1-3, 1-3, 1-4.

Ackermann, F., Walls, L., Meer, R. v. d., & Borman, M. (1999). Taking a strategic view of BPR to develop a multidisciplinary framework. *Journal of the Operational Research Society, 50*(1999), 195-204.

Ackoff, R. (1960). Systems, organizations and interdisciplinary research. *General System Yearbook, 5*, 1-8.

Ackoff, R. (1971). Towards a system of systems concepts. *Management Science, 17*(11), 661-671.

Ackoff, R. (1973). Science in the systems age: Beyond IE, OR and MS. *Operations Research, 21*(3), 661-671.

Ackoff, R. (1981). *Creating the corporate future.* New York: John Wiley & Sons.

Ackoff, R. (1981). The art and science of mess management. *Interfaces, 11*(1), 20-26.

Ackoff, R. (1993, November). From mechanistic to social systems thinking. In *Proceedings of Systems Thinking Action Conference*, Cambridge, MA.

Ackoff, R., Gupta, S., & Minas, J. (1962). *Scientific method: Optimizing applied research decisions.* New York: Wiley.

Adam, F., & Fitzgerald, B. (2000). The status of the information systems field: Historical perspective and practical orientation. *Information Research, 5*(4), 1-16.

Adamides, E.D. and Karacapilidis N., (2006). A knowledge centred framework for collaborative business process modeling. *Business Process Management Journal*, 12(5), 557-575.

Adelstein, T. (2004). Desktop linux: New linux users changing the face of community. Retrieved July 27, 2006, from http://www.desktoplinux.com/articles/AT3791991696.html

Adler, P. (2001). Market, hierarchy, and trust: The knowledge economy and the future of capitalism. *Organization Science 12*(2), 215-234.

Agarwal, R. & Prasad, J. (1999). Are individual differences germane to the acceptance of new information technologies?. *Decision Sciences*, 30(2) 361-401.

Agarwal, R. & Karahanna, E (2000). Time flies when you're having fun: Cognitive absorption and beliefs about information technology usage. *MIS Quarterly*, 24(4), 665-694.

Aiken, M. & Paolillo, J. (2000). An abductive model of group support systems. *Information and Management*, 37, 87-94.

Aiken, M. & Vanjani, M. (2002). A mathematical foundation for group support system research. *Communications of the International Information Management Association, 2*(1), 73-83.

Aiken, M. & Waller, B. (2000). Flaming among first-time group support system users. *Information and Management*, 37, 95-100.

Aiken, M. (2002).Topic effects on electronic meeting comments, *Academy of Information and Management Sciences*, 5(1/2), 115-126.

Aiken, M., Krosp, J., Shirani, A., & Martin, J. (1994). Electronic brainstorming in small and large groups. *Information and Management*, 27, 141-149.

Aiken, M., Vanjani, M. & Paolillo, J. (1996). A comparison of two electronic idea generation techniques. *Information and Management*, 30(2), 91-99.

Akura, T., and Altinkemer, K. (2002). Diffusion Models for B2B, B2C, and P2P Exchanges and E-Speak. *Journal of Organization Computing and Electronic Commerce*, 12(3), 243-261.

Aladwani, A. M., & Palvia, P. (2002). Developing and validating an instrument for measuring user-perceived Web quality. *Information & Management, 39*, 467-476.

Alavi, M., Carlson, P., & Brooke, G. (1989). The ecology of MIS research: A twenty year status review. In J. I. DeGross, J. Henderson, & B. Konsynsky (Eds.), *Proceedings of the tenth international conference on information systems* (pp. 363-375). New York: ACM Press.

Albrecht R. & Merkl D. (1998). *Knowledge discovery in literature data bases. Library and information services in astronomy III*, ASP Conference Series, Vol. 153.

Aldrich, H. (1999). *Organizations evolving*. Thousand Oaks, CA: Sage.

Alfeld, L.E. and Graham, A. (1976). *Introduction to Urban Dynamics*. MIT Press, Cambridge MA. Reprinted by Productivity Press: Portland OR and currently available from Pegasus Communications: Waltham, MA.

Al-Humaidan, F., & Rossiter, N. (2004). Business process modeling with OBPM combining soft and hard approaches. *1st Workshop on Computer Supported Activity Coordination (CSAC)*. Retrieved 13 October 2006, from http://computing.unn.ac.uk/staff/CGNR1/porto%20april%202004%20bus%proc.rtf

Alter, S (2006). *The work system method: Connecting people, processes, and IT for business results*. Larkspur CA: Work System Press.

Alter, S. (2001). Are the fundamental concepts of information systems mostly about work systems? *CAIS*, 5(11), 1-67.

Alter, S. (2002). The work system method for understanding information systems and information system research. *Communications of the AIS, 9* (6), 90-104.

Alter, S. (2003). 18 reasons why IT-reliant work systems should replace the IT artifact as the core subject matter of the IS field. *Communications of the AIS, 12* (23), 365-394.

Alter, S. (2003). The IS core-XI: Sorting out issues about the core, scope, and identity of the IS field. *Communications of the AIS, 12*, 607-628.

Alter, S. (2005). Architecture of Sysperanto - A model-based ontology of the IS field. *Communications of the AIS, 15* (1), 1-40.

Alter, S. (2006). *The work system method: Connecting people, processes and IT for business results*. Larkspur, CA: Work System Press.

Alter, S. (2007). *Service responsibility tables: A new tool for analyzing and designing systems*. Paper presented at the 13th Americas Conference on Information Systems, Keystone, CO.

Alter, S. (2008). Service system fundamentals: work system, value chain, and life cycle. *IBM Systems Journal*, 47(1), 2008, 71-85. Available at http://www.research.ibm.com/journal/sj/471/alter.html

Alvesson, M. (2003). *Understanding organizational culture*. London, Sage.

Amabile, T. M., Conti, R., et al. (1996). Assessing the work environment for creativity. *Academy of Mangement Journal 39*(5): 1154-1184.

Ambler, S. (2005). Quality in an agile world. *Extreme Programming Series, 7*(3), 34-40.

American Management Association (AMA) (2004) *Workplace E-Mail and Instant Messaging Survey.* New York, USA.

Amit, R. & Schoemaker, P. J. H. (1993). Strategic assets and organizational rent. *Strategic Management Journal 14*: 33-46.

Anderson, J. C., & Gerbing, G. W. (1988). Structural equation modeling in practice: A review and recommended two-step approach. *Psychological Bulletin, 103*(3), 411-423.

Anderson, M. (1999). A tool for building digital libraries. *Journal Review*, 5(2).

Andreau, R. & Ciborra, C. (1995). Organisational learning and core capabilities development: the role of IT. *Journal of Strategic Information Systems 5*: 111-127.

Angehrn, A., & Dutta, S. (1998). Case-based decision support. *Communications of the ACM, 41*(5es), 157-165.

Angelou, G. and Economides A. (2007) Controlling Risks in ICT investments with Real Options thinking. *11th Panhellenic Conference in Informatics (PCI 2007)*, May 18-20, 2007, University of Patras, Patras, Greece

Angelou, G. and Economides, A. (2005). Flexible ICT investment analysis using Real Options. *International Journal of Technology, Policy and Management*, 5(2), 146–166

Angelou, G. and Economides, A. (2006). Broadband investments as growth options under competition threat. *FITCE 45th Congress 2006*, Athens, Greece.

Angelou, G. and Economides, A. (2008) A Real Options approach for prioritizing ICT business alternatives: A case study from Broadband Technology business field. *Journal of the Operational Research Society*, Forthcoming.

Angelou, G. and Economides, A. (2008) A decision analysis framework for prioritizing a portfolio of ICT infrastructure projects. *IEEE Transactions on Engineering Management.*

Anthony, S. and Christensen, C. (2004). Forging innovation from disruption. *Optimize*, (Aug) issue 24.

Archer, M. (1995). *Realist social theory: The morphogenetic approach.* Cambridge: Cambridge University Press.

Argyris, C. (1993). *On organizational learning.* Cambridge, MA: Blackwell.

Argyris, C. (Ed.) (1999). *On organizational learning* (Second ed.). Malden: Blackwell Publishers, Inc.

Arkes, H. R., & Blumer, C. (1985). The psychology of sunk cost. *Organizational Behavior and Human Decision Processes 35*, 124-140.

Arkes, H. R., & Hutzel, L. (2000). The role of probability of success estimates in the sunk cost effect. *Journal of Behavioral Decision Making 13*(3), 295-306.*

Armstrong, J. S., & Overton, T. S. (1977). Estimating non-response bias in mail surveys. *Journal of Marketing Research, 14*, 396-402.

Arnott, D., & Pervan, G. (2005). A critical analysis of decision support systems research. *Journal of Information Technology, 20*, 67-87.

Ashby, R. (1956). *An introduction to cybernetics.* London: Chapman & Hall Ltd.

Atkinson, G. (2004). Common ground for institutional economics and system dynamics modeling. *System Dynamics Review*, 20(4), 275-286.

Attaran, M. (2000). Managing Legal Liability of the Net: A Ten Step Guide for IT Managers. *Information Management and Computer Security*, 8, 2, 98-100.

Back, B., Toivonen, J., Vanharanta, H., & Visa, A. (2001). Comparing numerical data and text information from annual reports using self-organizing maps. *International Journal of Accounting Information Systems, 2.*

Backström, T., Eijnatten, F. M. van, & Kira, M. (2002). A complexity perspective on sustainable work systems. In P. Docherty, J. Forslin, & A. B. Shani, (Eds.), *Creating sustainable work systems: Emerging perspectives and practice.* London: Routledge.

Bacon, J., & Fitzgerald, B. (2001) A systemic Framework for the Field of Informaiton Systems. *The DATA BASE for Adavances in Informaion Systems, 32(2)*, 46-67.

Badaracco, J. (1991). *The knowledge link: How firms compete through strategic alliances.* Boston, MA: Harvard Business School Press.

Bandura, A. (1977). Self-efficacy: Toward a Unifying Theory of Behavioral Change. *Psychology Review*, 84(2), 191-215.

Bandura, A. (1986). *Social foundations of thought and action: A social cognitive theory.* Englewood, NJ: Prentice-Hall.

Bandura, A. (1995). *Manual for the construction of self-efficacy scales.* Stanford University, Department of Psychology

Banville, C., & Landry, M. (1989). Can the field of MIS be disciplined? *Communications of the ACM, 32*(1), 48-60.

Barber, K D; Dewhurst, F W; Burns, R L D H; Rogers, J B B (2003). Business-process modeling and simulation for manufacturing management: a practical way forward. *Business Process Management Journal,* 9(4), 527-543.

Barkhi, R., & Sheetz, S. (2001). The state of theoretical diversity of information systems. *CAIS, 7*(6), 1-19.

Barki, H., Rivard, S., & Talbot, J. (1988). An Information systems keyword classification scheme. *MIS Quarterly, 34*(3), 299-322.

Barki, H., Rivard, S., & Talbot, J. (1993). Toward an assessment of software development risk. *Journal of Management Information Systems, 10*(2), 202-223.

Barney, J. (1991). Firm resources and sustained competitive advantage. *Human Resource Management 36*(1): 39-47.

Baron, R. & Kenny, D. (1986). The moderator-mediator variable distinction in social psychological research: conceptual, strategic, and statistical considerations. *Journal of Personality and Social Psychology,* 51(6), 1173-1182.

Baroudi, J. J., & Orlikowski, W. J. (1988). A short-form measure of user information satisfaction: A psychometric evaluation and notes on use. *Journal of Management Information Systems, 4*(4), 44-59.

Bart, Y., Shankar, V., Sultan, F., & Urban, G. L. (2005). Are the drivers and role of online trust the same for all Web sites and consumers? A large-scale exploratory empirical study. *Journal of Marketing, 69*(4), 133-152.

Baskerville, R., & Myers, M. D. (2002). Information systems as a reference discipline. *MIS Quarterly, 26*(1), 1-14.

Bass, F.M. (1969). A New Product Growth Model for Consumer Durables. *Management Science*, 15, 215-227.

Bauer, R.A. (1964). The Obstinate Audience: the Influence Process From the Point of View of Social Communication. *American Psychologist*, 19, 319-328.

Beer, S. (1959). *Cybernetics and management.* London: The English University Press.

Beer, S. (1966). *Decision and control.* Chichester: Wiley.

Beer, S. (1979). *The heart of enterprise.* Chichester: Wiley.

Beer, S. (1981). *Brain of the firm*, 2nd ed. Chichester, UK and New York: John Wiley.

Beer, S. (1985). *Diagnosing the system for organisations.* Chichester: Wiley.

Begg, C. B. (1994). Publication bias. In H. Cooper and L. V. Hedges, *The handbook of research synthesis* (pp. 399-409). New York: Russell Sage Foundation.

Belanger, F., Hiller, J. S., & Smith, W. J. (2002). Trustworthiness in e-commerce: The role of privacy, security, and site attributes. *Journal of Strategic Information Systems, 11,* 245-270.

Bellman, S., Lohse, G., & Eric, J. (1999). Predictors of online buying behavior. *Communications of the ACM, 42*(12), 32-38.

Benaroch, M. (2001). Option-based management of technology investment risk. *IEEE Transactions on Engineering Management*, 48(4), 428-444.

Benaroch, M. (2002). Managing information technology investment risk: A real options Perspective. *Journal of Management Information Systems*, 19(2), 43-84.

Benbasat, I. & Lim, L. (1993). The effects of group, task, context, and technology variables on the usefulness of group support systems: A meta-analysis of experimental studies. *Small Group Research* 24, 430-462.

Benbasat, I., & Weber, R. (1996). Rethinking "diversity" in information systems research. *Information Systems Research, 7*(4), 389-399.

Benbasat, I., & Zmud, R. W. (2003). The identity crisis within the IS discipline: Defining and communicating the discipline's core properties. *MIS Quarterly, 27*(2), 183-194.

Bennet, S., McRobb, S., & Farmer, R. (2006). *Object-oriented systems analysis and design* (3rd ed.). Berkshire: McGrawHill.

Bentler, P. M. (1990). Comparative fit indexes in structural models. *Psychological Bulletin, 107*(2), 238-246.

Bentler, P. M., & Bonett, D. G. (1980). Significance tests and goodness of fit in the analysis of covariance structures. *Psychological Bulletin, 88*(3), 588-606.

Bertalanffy, L. von. (1950). An outline of general systems theory. *British Journal of the Philosophy of Science, 1*, 134-164 (reprinted in Bertalanffy (1968)).

Bertalanffy, L. von. (1951). The theory of open systems in physics and biology. *Science, 111*, 23-29.

Bertalanffy, L. von. (1968). *General systems theory – foundations, developments, applications.* New York: G. Brazillier.

Bertalanffy, L. von. (1972). The history and status of general systems theory. *Academy of Management Journal, December*, 407-426.

Bhaskar, R. (1975). *A realist theory of science.* Sussex: Harvester Press.

Bhaskar, R. (1979). *The possibility of naturalism.* Hemel, Hempstead: Harvester Wheatsheaf.

Bhaskar, R. (1986). *Scientific realism and human emancipation.* Verso: London.

Bhaskar, R. (1989). *Reclaiming reality: A critical introduction to contemporary philosophy.* London: Verso.

Bhaskar, R. (1991). *Philosophy and the idea of freedom.* Oxford: Blackwell.

Bieber, M. P., Engelbart, D., Furuta, R., Hiltz, S. R., Noll, J., Preece, J., et al. (2002). Toward virtual community knowledge evolution. *Journal of Management Information Systems, 18*(4), 11-36.

Billings, R. & Wroten, S. (1978). Use of path analysis in industrial/organizational psychology: Criticism and suggestions. *Journal of Applied Psychology*, 63, 677-688.

Blackler, F. (1995). Knowledge, knowledge work and organizations. *Organization Studies 16*(6): 1021-1046.

Blanchette, S. (2005). *U.S. Army acquisition – The program executive officer perspective*, (Special Report CMU/SEI-2005-SR-002). Pittsburgh, PA: Software Engineering Institute.

Boehm, B. (2006). Some future trends and implications for systems and software engineering processes. *Systems Engineering*, 9(1), 1-19.

Boehm, B. W. (1991). Software risk management: Principles and practice. *IEEE Software*, 32-41.

Boehm, B., & Lane, J. (2006). 21st century processes for acquiring 21st century systems of systems. *CrossTalk, 19*(5), 4-9.

Boehm, B., Abt, C., Brown, A., Chulani, S., Clark, & et al. (2000). *Software cost estimation with COCOMO II.* Upper Saddle River, NJ: Prentice Hall.

Boehm, B., Valerdi, R., Lane, J., & Brown, A. (2005). COCOMO suite methodology and evolution. *CrossTalk, 18*(4), 20-25.

Boer, P. F. (1999). *The valuation of technology: business and financial issues in R&D.* Hoboken, NJ: Wiley.

Boer, P. F. (2002). *The real options solution: finding total value in a high-risk world*. Hoboken, NJ: Wiley.

Boer, P. F. (2004). *Technology valuation solutions*. Hoboken, NJ: Wiley.

Bollen, K. A. (1989). *Structural equations with latent variables*. New York: Wiley.

Bonner, S.E. (1994). A model of the effects of audit task complexity. *Accounting, Organizations and Society*, 19(3), 213-234.

Boonthanom, R. (2003). Information technology project escalation: Effects of decision unit and guidance. In *Proceedings of 24th International Conference on Information Systems*.*

Bouchard, T. and Hare, M. (1970). Size, performance and potential in brainstorming groups. *Journal of Applied Psychology*, 54, 51–55.

Boudreau, M., Gefen, D., & Straub, D. W. (2001). Validation in information systems research: A state-of-the-art assessment. *MIS Quarterly, 25*(1), 1-16.

Boulding, K. (1956). General systems theory – the skeleton of the science. *Management Science, 2*(3), 197-208.

Boulding, K. (1964). General systems as a point of view. In J. Mesarovic (Ed), *Views on general systems theory*. New York: John Wiley.

Bourne, M., Neely, A., et al. (2003). Implementing performance measurement systems: A literature review. *International Journal of Business Performance Management, 5*(1), 1-24.

Bower, G. H., & Hilgard, E. R. (1981). *Theories of learning*. Englewood Cliffs, NJ: Prentice-Hall.

Bower, J.L. and Christensen, C. (1995). Disruptive technologies: catching the wave. *Harvard Business Review* (Jan-Feb), 43-53.

Bradford, M. & Florin, J. (2003). Examining the role of innovation diffusion factors on the implementation success of enterprise resource planning systems. *International Journal of Accounting Information Systems*, 4(3), 205-225.

Bräutigam, J., and Esche, C. (2003). *Uncertainty as a key value driver of real options*. European Business School, Schloss Reichartshausen, Oestrich-Winkel, Germany Anett Mehler-Bicher University of Applied Science, Mainz, Germany. Working paper, University of Applied Science, 7th Annual Real Options Conference.

Bridges, E., Johnston, H. H., & Sager, J. K. (2007). Using model-based expectations to predict voluntary turnover. *International Journal of Research in Marketing, 24*(1), 65-76.

Briggs, R., Nunamaker, J., & Sprague, R. (1998). 1001 unanswered research questions in GSS. *Journal of Management Information Systems*, 14(3), 3-21.

Briscoe, B., Odlyzko, A., & Tilly, B. (2006). Metcalfe's Law is wrong. *IEEE Spectrum*, July, 26-31.

Brockner, J. (1992). The escalation of commitment to a failing course of action. *Academy of Management Review 17*(1), 39-61.

Brooks, F. (1975). *The Mythical Man-Month*. Reading, MA: Addison Wesley.

Brooks, F. (1996). The computer scientist as toolsmith II. *Communications of the ACM, 39*(3), 61-68.

Brooks, F. P. (1975). *The mythical man-month: Essays on software engineering*. Reading, MA: Addison-Wesley

Bryman, D. & Cramer, D. (1994). *Quantitative data analysis for social scientists*. New York: Routledge.

Brynjolfsson, E., & Smith, M. D. (2000). Frictionless commerce? A comparison of Internet and conventional retailers. *Management Science, 46*(4), 563-585.

Buckner K. (1996). Computer user groups: The advantage of successful partnership. *International Journal of Information Management, 16*(3), 195-204.

Burgess, A., Jackson, T. & Edwards, J. (2005) Email Training Significantly Reduces Email Defects. *International Journal of Information Management*, 25, 1, 71-83.

Burns, T., & Klshner, R. (2005, October 20 -22, 2005). *A cross-collegiate analysis of software development course content.* Paper presented at the SIGITE'05, Newark, NJ, USA.

Burroughs, R. E., & Sabherwal, R. (2002). Determinants of retail electronic purchasing: A multi-period investigation. *INFOR, 40*(1),.

Bustard, D. W., He, Z., & Wilkie, F. G. (2000). Linking soft systems and use-case modeling through scenarios. *Interacting with Computers,* 13(2000), 97-110.

Byrd, T. A., & Turner, D. E. (2001). An exploratory analysis of the value of the skills of IT personnel: Their relationship to IS infrastructure and competitive advantage. *Decision Sciences, 32*(1), 21-54.

Campbell, D. & Gingrich , K. (1986). The interactive effects of task complexity and participation on task performance: A field experiment. *Organizational Behavior and Human Decision Processes,* 38, 162-180.

Campbell, D.J. (1988). Task complexity: A review and analysis. *Academy of Management Review*, 13(1) 40-52.

Carlsson, S. (2003). Advancing information systems evaluation (research): A critical realist approach. *Electronic Journal of Information Systems Evaluation, 6*(2), 11-20.

Carlsson, S. (2003, June 16-21). Critical realism: A way forward in IS research. In *Proceedings of the ECIS 2003 Conference* Naples, Italy.

Cenk, K. (2002). Evolution of Prices in Electronic Markets Under Diffusion of Price-Comparison Shopping. *Journal of Management Information Systems*, 19(3), 99-119.

Champion, D., Stowell, F., & O'Callaghan, A. (2005). Client-led information system creation (CLIC): Navigating the gap. *Information Systems Journal,* (15), 213-231.

Chang, M. K., Cheung, W., & Lai,V. S. (2005). Literature derived reference models for the adoption of online shopping. *Information & Management, 42*(4), 543-559.

Charette, R. N. (1989). *Software engineering risk analysis and management.* New York: Multiscience Press, Inc.

Chatterjee, D., Grewal, R., & Sambamurthy, V. (2002). Shaping up for e-commerce: Institutional enablers of the organizational assimilation of Web technologies. *MIS Quarterly, 26*(2), 65-89.

Chau, P.Y.K. (2001). Influence of computer attitude and self-efficacy on IT usage behavior. *Journal of End User Computing*, 13(1), 26-33.

Checkland, P. (1981). *Systems thinking, systems practice.* Chichester: John Wiley.

Checkland, P. (1983). O.R. and the systems movement: mappings and conflicts. *Journal of the Operational Research Society, 34*(8), pp. 661-675.

Checkland, P. (1999). *Systems thinking, systems practice.* West Sussex, England: Wiley.

Checkland, P. (2000). Soft systems methodology: A thirty year retrospective. *Systems Research and Behavioral Science, 17*, S11–S58.

Checkland, P., & Holwell, S. (1995). Information systems: What's the big idea? *Systemist, 7*(1), 7-13.

Checkland, P., & Holwell, S. (1998). *Information, systems and information systems: Making sense of the field.* West Sussex, England: John Wiley and Sons Ltd

Checkland, P., & Scholes, J. (1999). *Soft systems methodology in action.* Chichester: John Wiley and Sons Ltd.

Chen, (2001). *Knowledge management systems: A text mining perspective.* Tucson, AZ: Knowledge Computing Corporation.

Chen, G., Casper, W.J., & Cortina, T J.M. (2001). The roles of self-efficacy and task complexity in the relationships among cognitive ability, conscientiousness, and task performance: A meta-analytic examination. *Human Performance*, 14(3), 209-230.

Chen, P. Y., & Hitt, L. M. (2002). Measuring switching costs and the determinants of customer retention in Internet-enabled businesses: A study of the online brokerage industry. *Information Systems Research, 13*(3), 255-274.

Cheney, P. H., & Lyons, N. R. (1980). Information systems skill requirements: A survey. *MIS Quarterly, 4*(1), 35-43.

Cheung, W., Chang, M.K., Lai, V.S. (2000). Prediction of Internet and World Wide Web usage at work: A test of an extended Triandis model. *Decision Support Systems*, 30(1), 83-100.

Chidambaram, L. & Jones, B. (1993). Impact of communication medium and computer support on group perceptions and performance: A comparison of face-to-face and dispersed meetings. *MIS Quarterly* 17(4), 465-491.

Chieng, L. (1997). PAT-tree-based keyword extraction for Chinese information retrieval. In *Proceedings of Special Interest Group on Information Retrieval*, SIGIR'97, ACM, Philadelphia.

Chiva, R., & Alegre, J. (2005). *Organizational learning* and *organizational* knowledge: Towards the integration of two approaches. *Management Learning, 36*(1), 49-68.

Choi, B. & Lee, H. (2003). An Empirical Investigation of KM Styles and Their Effect on Corporate Performance. *Information & Management 40*: 403-417.

Choo, C. W. (2001). Environmental scanning as information seeking and organizational learning. *Information Research: an International Electronic Journal 7*(1).

Chou, T. C., Dyson, R. G. & Powell, P. L. (1998). An empirical study of the impact of information technology intensity in strategic investment decisions. *Technology Analysis & Strategic Management 10*(3): 325-39.

Chowdhury, S. D., Duncan, G. T., Krishnan, R., Roehrig, S. F., & Mukherjee, S. (1999). Disclosure detection in multivariate categorical databases: Auditing confidentiality protection through two new matrix operators. *Management Science, 45*(12), 1710-1723.

Christensen, C.M. & Raynor, M.E. (2003). *The Innovator's Solution: Creating and Sustaining Successful Growth*. Harvard Business School Press: Boston MA.

Christensen, C.M. (1992). *The Innovator's Challenge: Understanding the Influence of Market Environment on Processes of Technology Development in the Rigid Disk Drive Industry*. Ph.D. Dissertation, Harvard Business School: Boston, MA.

Christensen, C.M. (1997). *The Innovator's Dilemma: When New Technologies Cause Great Firms to Fail.* Harvard Business School Press: Cambridge, MA.

Christensen, C.M., Johnson, M. & Dann, J. (2002). Disrupt and prosper. *Optimize* (Nov), 41-48.

Christensen, C.M., Raynor, M.E. & Anthony, S.D. (2003). Six Keys to Creating New-Growth Businesses. *Harvard Management Update* (Jan).

Chu, W., Choi, B., & Song, M. R. (2005). The role of on-line retailer brand and infomediary reputation in increasing consumer purchase intention. *International Journal of Electronic Commerce, 9*(3) 115-127.

Chua, C., Cao, L., Cousins, K., Mohan, K., Straub, D. W., & Vaishnavi, V. (2002). IS bibliographic repository (ISBIB): A central repository of research information for the IS community. *Communications of the AIS, 8*, 392-412.

Churchman, C. W. (1979). *The design of inquiring systems: Basic concepts of systems and organizations*. New York, Basic Books.

Clegg, B. (2006), Business process orientated holonic (PrOH) modeling, *Business Process Management Journal*, 12(4), 410-432

Cockburn, A. (2001). *Writing effective use cases*. Boston: Addison-Wesley.

Cockburn, A. (2002). *Agile software development*: Pearson Education, Inc.

Cockburn, A. (2002). Agile software development joins the "would-be" crowd. *The Journal of Information Technology Management*, 15(1), 6-12.

Codington, S. & Wilson, T. D. (1994). Information system strategies in the UK insurance industry. *International Journal of Information Management 14*(3): 188-203.

Cohen, J. (1977). *Statistical power analysis for the behavioral sciences*. New York: Academic Press.

Cohen, J. (1988). *Statistical power analysis for the behavioral sciences (2nd ed.).* Hillsdale, NJ: Erlbaum.

Cohen, J. A. (1960). Coefficient of agreement for nominal scales. *Educational and Psychological Measurement, 20*(1), 37-46.

Cohen, W. M., & Levinthal, D. A. (1990). Absorptive capacity: A new perspective on learning and innovation. *Administrative Science Quarterly, 35*, 128-152.

Cole, M. (2002) Virtual communities for learning and development – A look to the past and some glimpses into the future. In K. Ann Renninger & W. Shumar (Eds.), *Building virtual communities: Learning and change in cyberspace*. Cambridge: Cambridge University Press.

Collier, A. (1994). *Critical realism: An introduction to the philosophy of Roy Bhaskar.* London: Verso.

Compeau, E. R., & Higgins, C. A. (1995). Computer self-efficacy: Development of a measure and initial test. *MIS Quarterly, 19*(2), 189-211.

Conlon, D. E., & Garland, H. (1993). The role of project completion information in resource allocation decisions. *Academy of Management Journal 38*(2), 402-413.

Connolly, T., Jessup, L., & Valacich, J. (1990). Effects of anonymity and evaluative tone on idea generation in computer-mediated groups. *Management Science*, 36(6), 689-703.

Cooper, H. & Hedges, L. V. (1994). The handbook of research synthesis. New York: Russell Sage Foundation.

Cooprider, J. G., & Henderson, J. C. (1990). Technology-process fit: Perspectives on achieving prototyping effectiveness. *Journal of Management Information Systems*, *7*(3), 67-87.

Cornelius, C. & Boos, M. (2003). Enhancing mutual understanding in synchronous computer-mediated communication by training: Trade-offs in judgmental tasks. *Communication Research,* 3(2), 147-177.

Correia, Z. & Wilson, T. D. (1997). Scanning the business environment for information: a grounded theory approach. *Information Research: an International Electronic Journal 2*(4).

Cronbach, L. J. (1951). Coefficient Alpha and the internal structure of tests. *Psychometrica, 16*, 297-334.

Cronbach, L. J. (1987). Statistical tests for moderator variables: Flaws in analyses recently proposed. *Psychological Bulletin, 102*, 414-417.

Cronin, B. & Davenport, E. (1993). Social intelligence. *Annual Review of Information Science and Technology 28*: 3-44.

Culnan, M. J. (1986). Mapping the intellectual structure of MIS, 1972-1982: A co-citation analysis. *Management Science, 32*(2), 156-172.

Culnan, M. J. (1987). Mapping the intellectual structure of MIS, 1980-1985: A co-citation analysis. *MIS Quarterly, 11*(3), 341-350.

Culnan, M. J., & Swanson, E. B. (1986). Research in management information systems, 1980-1984: Points of work and reference. *MIS Quarterly, 10*(3), 289-301.

Curry, A. & Moore, C. (2003). Assessing information culture - an exploratory model. *International Journal of Information Management 23*: 91-110.

D'Aubeterre, F., Palvia, P., & Stevens, J. (2005). *A meta-analysis of current global information systems research.* Paper presented at the Americas Conference on Information Systems, Omaha, NE.

Dardan, M., and Stylianou, A.C. (2001). The Impact of Fluctuating Financial Markets on the Signaling Effects of E-Commerce Announcements Through Firm Valuation. *Proceedings of the International Conference on Information Systems.*

Davenport, T. H. (2000). *Mission critical: Realizing the promise of enterprise systems.* Boston, MA: Harvard Business School Press.

Davenport, T. H., & Prusak, L. (2000). *Working knowledge*. Boston: Harvard University Press.

Davis, F.D. (1989). Perceived usefulness, perceived ease of use, and user acceptance of information technology. *MIS Quarterly*, 13(3), 319-340.

Davis, F.D. (1993). User acceptance of information technology: System characteristics, user perceptions and behavioral impacts. *International Journal of Man-Machine Studies*, 38(3), 475-487.

Davis, F.D., Bagozzi, R.P., & Warshaw, P.R. (1989). User acceptance of computer technology: A comparison of two theoretical models. *Management Science*, 35(8), 982-1003.

Davis, G. (1974). *Management information systems: Conceptual foundations, structure and development*. New York: McGraw-Hill.

De Wulf, K., Schillewaert, N., Muylle, S., & Rangarajan, D. (2006). The role of pleasure in Web site success. *Information & Management, 43*(4), 434-446.

DeLone, W. H., & McLean, E. R. (1992). Information systems success: The quest for the dependent variable. *Information Systems Research 3*(1), 60-95.

DeLone, W. H., & McLean, E. R. (2002). Information systems success revisited. *Proceedings of the 35th Hawaii International Conference on System Sciences*, Hawaii.

Dennis A., George J., Jessup L., Nunamaker J., & Vogel D. (1988). Information technology to support electronic meetings. *MIS Quarterly*, 12(4), 591-615.

Dennis, A. R., & Kinney, S. T. (1998). Testing media richness theory in the new media: The effects of cues, feedback, and task equivocality. *Information Systems Research, 3*(9), 256-274.

Dewhirst, H. D. (1971). Influence of perceived information-sharing norms on communication channel utilization. *Academy of Management Journal 14*(3): 305-315.

Dhillon, G. (1999). Managing and Controlling Computer Misuse. *Information Management and Computer Security*, 7, 4, 171-175.

Dinev, T., & Hart, P. (2005–2006). Internet privacy concerns and social awareness as determinants of intention to transact. *International Journal of Electronic Commerce, 10*(2), 7-29.

Dishaw, M. T., & Strong, D. M. (1999). Extending the technology acceptance model with Task-technology fit constructs. *Information and Management, 36*(1), 9-21

Dixon, J. R., Arnold, P., et al. (1994). Business process reengineering: improving in new strategic directions. *California Management Review 36*(4): 93-108.

Dobson, P. (2001). The philosophy of critical realism -- An opportunity for information systems research. *Information Systems Frontiers, 3*(2), 199-210.

Dobson, P. (2002). Critical realism and information systems research: Why bother with philosophy? *Information Systems Research, 7*(2). Retrieved from http://InformationR.net/ir/7-2/paper124,html.

Dobson, P. (2003). The SoSM revisited – A critical realist perspective. In Cano, J. (Ed). *Critical reflections of information systems: A systemic approach* (pp. 122-135). Hershey, PA: Idea Group Publishing.

Doll, W.J., Hendrickson, A., & Deng, X. (1998). Using Davis's perceived usefulness and ease-of-use instruments for decision making: A confirmatory and multigroup Invariance Analysis. *Decision Sciences*, 29(4), 840-869.

Dörre, J., Gerstl, P., & Seiffert, R. (1999). Text mining: Finding nuggets in mountains of textual data. In *Proceedings of the KDD-99, Fifth ACM SIGKDD International Conference on Knowledge Discovery and Data Mining*, San Diego.

Dougherty, T. W., Turban, D. B., & Calledder, J. C. (1994). Confirming first impressions in the employment interview: A field study of interviewer behavior. *Journal of Applied Psychology, 79*, 659-665.

Downes S. (1998) *The future of Online Learning.* http://www.downes.ca/future/index.htm

Doyle, C. S. (1995). Information literacy in an information society. *Emergency Librarian 22*(4): 30-32.

Duncan, N.B. (1995). Capturing flexibility of information technology infrastructure: A study of resource characteristics and their measure. *Journal of Management Information Systems*, *12*(2), 37-57.

Dutta, A. and Roy, R. (2005). Offshore outsourcing: a dynamic causal model of counteracting forces. *Journal of Management Information Systems,* 22(2), 15-35.

Dvir, T., Eden, D., & Banjo, M. L. (1995). Self-fulfilling prophecy and gender: Can women be Pygmalion and Galatea. *Journal of Applied Psychology, 80*, 253-270.

Eastlick, M., Lotz, S. L., & Warrington, P. (2006). Understanding online B-to-C relationships: An integrated model of privacy concerns, trust, and commitment. *Journal of Business Research, 59*(8), 877-886.

Economides, N. (1996), The economics of networks. *International Journal of Industrial Organization, 14*(6), 673-699.

Economides, N. (2001). The Microsoft antitrust case. *Journal Of Industry, Competition And Trade: From Theory To Policy, 1*(1), 7-39.

Economides, N., & Himmelberg, C. (1994). Critical mass and network evolution in telecommunications. *Proceedings of Telecommunications Policy Research Conference, 1-25*, Retrieved from http://ww.stern.nyu.edu/networks/site.html.

Economides, N., & White, L., J. (1996). One-way networks, two-way networks, compatibility, and antitrust. In D. Gabel & D. Weiman (Eds.), *The regulation and pricing of access.* Kluwer Academic Press.

Edwards, C., Braganza, A., & Lambert, R. (2000). Understanding and managing process initiatives: a framework for developing consensus. *Knowledge and process management, 7*(1), 29-36.

Edwards, J. R., & Parry, M. E. (1993). On the use of polynomial regression equations as an alternative to difference scores in organizational research. *Academy of Management Journal, 36*, 1577-1613.

Electronic Industries Alliance. (1999). EIA Standard 632: Processes for engineering a system.

Eriksson, H. E., & Penker, M. (2000). *UML business patterns at work.* New York: John Wiley & Sons Inc.

Esichaikul, V. (2001). Object oriented business process modeling: A case study of a port authority. *Journal of Information Technology: Cases and Applications,* 3(2), 21-41.

Espejo R., Bowling, D., & Hoverstadt, P. (1999). The viable system model and the viplan software. *Kybernetes*, (28) Number 6/7, 661-678.

Espejo, R, and Reyes, A. (2000). Norbert Wiener. In Malcom Warner (ed), *The international encyclopedia of business and management: The handbook of management thinking.* London: Thompson Business Press.

Espejo, R. (1989). A cybernetic method to study organisations. In Espejo, R. and Harnden, R. (eds), *The viable system model: interpretations and applications of Stafford Beer's VSM.* Chichester: Wiley.

Espejo, R. (1992). Cyberfilter: A management support system. In Holtham, C.(ed.), *Executive information systems and decision support.* London: Chapman.

Espejo, R. (1993). Strategy, structure and information management. *Journal of Information Systems*, (3), 17-31.

Espejo, R. (1994). ¿What is systemic thinking? *Systems Dynamics Review*, (10), Nos. 2-3 (Summer-Fall), 199-212.

Espinosa, J., Cummings, J., Wilson, J., & Pearce, R. (2003). Team boundary issues across multiple global firms. *Journal of Management Information System,* 19(4), 157-190.

Ethier, J., Hadaya, P., Talbot, J., & Cadieux, J. (in press). B2C Web site quality and emotions during online shopping episodes: An empirical study. *Information & Management.*

Everard, A., & Galletta, D. F. (2005). How presentation flaws affect perceived site quality, trust, and intention to purchase from an online store. *Journal of Management Information Systems, 22*(3), 55-95.

Farhoomand, A. (1987). Scientific progress of management information systems. *Database, Summer*, 48-57.

Farhoomand, A., & Drury, D. (2001). Diversity and scientific progress in the information systems discipline. *CAIS, 5*(12), 1-22.

Farrell, J., & Katz, M. (2001). Competition or predation? Schumpeterian rivalry in network markets. (Working Paper No. E01-306). University of California at Berkeley. Retrieved from http://129.3.20.41/eps/0201/0201003.pdf

Fayyad, U., Piatetsky-Shapiro, G., & Smyth, P. (1996). Knowledge discovery and data mining: Towards a unifying framework. In *Proceedings of The Second International Conference on Knowledge Discovery and Data Mining* (KDD-96), Portland, OR.

Fedor, D. B., Ghosh, S., Caldwell, S. D., Maurer, T. J., & Singhal, V. R. (2003) The effects of knowledge management on team members' ratings of project success and impact. *Decision Sciences, 34*(3), 513-539.

Feller, J., & Fitzgerald, B. (2000). A framework analysis of the OpenSource software development paradigm. In *Proceedings of the International Conference of Information Systems* (pp. 21, 58-69).

Feng, Y., Chu, T., Hsu, M., & Hsieh, H. (2004). An investigation of effort–accuracy trade-off and the impact of self-efficacy on Web searching behaviors. *Decision Support Systems,* 37, 331– 342.

Fichman, R. G., & Kemerer, C. F. (1997). The assimilation of software process innovations: An organizational learning perspective. *Management Science, 43*(10), 1345-1363.

Fichman, R., (1999). Book Chapter: *Framing the Domains of IT Management: Projecting the Future Through the Past.* Cincinnati, OH: Pinnaflex Educational Resources.

Fichman, R., (2001). The Role of Aggregation in the Measurement of IT-Related Organizational Innovation. *MIS Quarterly,* 25(4), 427-456.

Fiol, C. M., & Lyles, M. A. (1985). Organizational learning. *Academy of Management Review, 10*(4), 803-813.

Fitzgerald, B., & Howcroft, D. (1998). Towards dissolution of the IS research debate: From polarization to polarity. *Journal of Information Technology, 13*, 313-326.

Fitzgerald, B., & Kenny, T. (2003). OpenSource software the trenches: Lessons from a large-scale OSS implementation. In *Proceedings of the International Conference on Information Systems* (pp. 24, 316-326).

Fjermestad, J & Hiltz S. (1998-99). An assessment of group support systems experimental research: Methodology and results. *Journal of Management Information System,* 15(3), 7-149.

Flavin, C., Guinaliu, M., & Gurrea, R. (2006). The role played by perceived usability, satisfaction, and consumer trust on Web site loyalty. *Information & Management, 43*(1), 1-14.

Fleetwood, S. (Ed.) (1999). *Critical realism in economics: Development and debate.* London: Routledge.

Flood, L. (2003). Close Monitoring Provides Protection. *Sunday Business Post.* IRL. Feb 9.

Flood, R., & Jackson, M. (1991). *Creative problem solving: Total systems intervention.* New York: Wiley.

Flood, R., & Romm, N. (Eds). (1996) *Critical Systems Thinking.* New York: Plenum Press.

Fontana, M. (2006). Simulation in economics: evidence on diffusion and communication. *Journal of Artificial Societies and Social Simulation,* 9(2) (http://jasss.soc.surrey.ac.uk/9/2/8.html).

Forman, C., Goldfarb, A., and Greenstein, S. (2002). The Digital Dispersion of Commercial Internet Use: A Comparison of Industries and Countries. *Proceedings of the WISE Conference.*

Forrester, J. (1958). Industrial dynamics – A major breakthrough for decision makers. *Harvard Business Review, 36*, 37-66.

Forrester, J. (1971). Counterintuitive Behavior of Social Systems. *Technology Review, 73* (3), January.

Forrester, J. (1991). *Systems dynamics and the lessons of 35 years.* (Tech. Rep. D-4224-4). Retrieved from http://sysdyn.mit.edu/sd-group/home.html

Forrester, J.W. & Senge, P.M. (1980). Tests for building confidence in system dynamics models. In AA Legasto Jr, JW Forrester and JM Lyneis (Eds), *TIMS Studies in the Management Sciences, Vol. 14: System Dynamics*. North-Holland: New York, NY, pp. 209-228.

Forrester, J.W. (1961). *Industrial Dynamics*. MIT Press: Cambridge, MA.

Forrester, J.W. (2003). Dynamic models of economic systems and industrial organizations. *System Dynamics Review*, 19(4), 331-345.

Forrester, N. (1983). Eigenvalue analysis of dominant feedback loops. In *Plenary Session Papers Proceedings of the 1st International System Dynamics Society Conference*, Paris, France: 178-202.

Frickel, S., & Gross, N. (2005). A general theory of scientific/intellectual movements. *American Sociological Review, 70*, 204-232.

Furnas, G. W., Landauer, T. K., Gomez, L. M., & Dumais, S. T. (1987). The vocabulary problem in human-system communication. *Communications of the ACM, 30*(11), 964-971.

Galliers, R. (2004). Change as crisis or growth? Toward a trans-disciplinary view of information systems as a field of study: A response to Benbasat and Zmud's call for returning to the IT artifact. *JAIS, 4*(7), 337-351.

Galliers, R. D. (1994). Information systems, operational research and business reengineering. *International Transactions in Operations Research,* 1(2), 159-167.

Gallupe, B., Dennis, A., Cooper, W., Valacich, J., Bassinette, L., & Nunamaker, J. (1992). Electronic brainstorming and group size. *The Academy of Management Journal,* 35(2), 350–369.

Gamba, A. and Trigeorgis, L., (2001). *A Log-transformed Binomial Lattice Extension for Multi-Dimensional Option Problems*. Paper presented at the 5th Annual Conference on Real Options, Anderson School of Management, UCLA, Los-Angeles.

Gardner, C. (2000). *The valuation of information technology: A guide for strategy, development, valuation, and financial planning*. Hoboken, NJ: Wiley.

Garland, H. & Conlon, D. E. (1998). Too close to quit: The role of project completion in maintaining commitment. *Journal of Applied Psychology 28*(22), 2025-2048.*

Garland, H. (1990). Throwing good money after bad: The effect of sunk costs on the decision to escalate commitment to an ongoing project. *Journal of Applied Psychology 75*(6), 728-731.*

Garland, H., & Newport, S. (1991). Effects of absolute and relative sunk costs on the decision to persist with a course of action. *Organizational Behavior and Human Decision Processes 48,* 55-69.

Garland, H., Sandefur, C.A., & Rogers, A.C. (1990) De-escalation of commitment in oil exploration: When sunk costs and negative feedback coincide, *Journal of Applied Psychology 75*(6), 721-727.

Garrett, S. & Caldwell, B. (2002). Describing functional requirements for knowledge sharing communities. *Behaviour & Information Technology 21*(5): 359-364.

Gedeon, T., Sing, S., Koczy, L., & Bustos, R. (1996). Fuzzy relevance values for information retrieval and hypertext link generation. In *Proceedings of the EUFIT-96, Fourth European Congress on Intelligent Techniques and Soft Computing,* Aachen, Germany.

Gefen, D. (2000). E-commerce: The role of familiarity and trust. *Omega, 28*(6), 725-737.

Gefen, D., & Straub, D. W. (2004). Consumer trust in B2C e-commerce and the importance of social presence: Experiments in e-products and e-services. *Omega, 32*(6), 407-425.

Gefen, D., Karahanna, E., & Straub, D. W. (2003). Trust and TAM in online shopping: An integrated model. *MIS Quarterly, 27*(1), 51–90.

Geis, F. L. (1993). Self-fulfilling prophecies: A social-psychological view of gender. In A. E. Beall & R. J. Sternberg (Eds.), *The psychology of gender*. New York: Guilford Press.

Gellner, E. (1993). What do we need now? Social anthropology and its new global context. *The Times Literary Supplement, 16*, July, 3-4.

Gelman, O., & Garcia, J. (1989). Formulation and axiomatization of the concept of general system. *Outlet IMPOS (Mexican Institute of Planning and Systems Operation), 19*(92), 1-81.

Gelman, O., Mora, M., Forgionne, G., & Cervantes, F. (2005). M. Khosrow-Pour (Ed.) Information Systems and Systems Theory. In *Encyclopedia of Information Science and Technology* (1491-1496). Hershey, PA: IGR.

Georgantzas, N.C. & Katsamakas, E. (2008). *Disruptive service-innovation strategy.* Working Paper, Fordham University, New York, NY.

Georgantzas, N.C. & Ritchie-Dunham, J.L. (2003). Designing high-leverage strategies and tactics. *Human Systems Management,* 22(1), 217-227.

George, J., Easton, G., Nunamaker, J., & Northcraft, G., (1990). A study of collaborative group work with and without computer-based support. *Information Systems Research,* 1(4), 394-415.

Gharajedaghi, J. (1999). *Systems Thinking: Managing Chaos and Complexity: A Platform for Designing Business Architecture.* Butterworth-Heinemann: Boston MA.

Gibbs J., Kraemer K.L., and Dedrick J. (2003). Environment and Policy Factors Shaping Global E-Commerce Diffusion: A Cross-Country Comparison. *The Information Society,* 19(1), 5-18.

Gigch, van J., & Pipino, L. (1986). In search of a paradigm for the discipline of information systems. *Future Computer Systems, 1*(1), 71-97.

Ginzberg, M. J. (1981). Early diagnosis of MIS implementation failure: Promising results and unanswered questions. *Management Science, 77*(4), 459-478.

Gist, M.E. (1987). Self-efficacy: Implications for organizational behavior and human resource management. *Academy of Management Review,* 12(3), 472-485.

Glass, G. V. (1976). Primary, secondary, secondary, and metaanlaysis. *Educational Researcher 5*, 3-8.

Golden, B. (2005). *Succeeding with OpenSource.* Boston: Addison-Wesley.

Gonçalves, P., Lerpattarapong, C. and Hines, J.H. (2000). Implementing formal model analysis. In *Proceedings of the 18th International System Dynamics Society Conference*, August 6-10, Bergen, Norway.

Goodhue, D.L. & Thompson, R.L. (1995). Task-technology fit and individual performance. *MIS Quarterly* 19(2), 1995, 213-236.

Gordon, M., Slade, A., and Schmitt, N. (1988). Student guinea pigs: Porcine predictors and particularistic phenomena. *Academy of Management Review,* 12:1, 160-163.

Graff, J. (2002) Building Email: Economy, Resilience and Business Value. *Gartner Group*, 22nd March, Note Number LE-15-6155. Advanced Search of Archived Research. Located At Http://www.Gartner.com

Graff, J. (2002) Building a High Performance Email Environment. *Gartner Group*, 21st March, Note Number M-15-8182. Advanced Search of Archived Research. Located At Http://www.Gartner.com

Gray and Grey (2002) Email And IM As Essential Platform Components in 2002. *Gartner Group*, 13th December, Note Number SPA-15-0931. Located at Http://www.gl.iit.edu/gartner2/research/103200/103210/103210.html.

Green, G. I. (1989). Perceived importance of systems analysts' job skills, roles, and non-salary incentives. *MIS Quarterly, 13*(2), 115-133.

Green, S., Melnyk, A., and Powers, D. (2002). Is Economic Freedom Necessary for Technology Diffusion? *Applied Economic Letters*, 9(14), 907-910.

Gregory, W. (1996). Dealing with diversity. In R. Flood & N. Romm (Eds.), *Critical Systems Thinking* (37-61). New York: Plenum Press.

Griffin, M., Neal, A., & Neale, M. (2000). The contribution of task performance and contextual performance to effectiveness: Investigating the role of situational constraints. *Applied Psychology: An International Review,* 49(3), 517-534.

Grover, V., and Goslar, M.D. (1993). The Initiation, Adoption and Implementation of Telecommunications Technologies in U.S. Organizations. *Journal of Management Information Systems,* 10(1), 141-163.

Guimaraes, T. (1986). Human resources needs to support and manage user computing activities in large organizations. *Human Resource Planning, 9*(2), 69-80.

Ha, S.H., Bae, S.M., and Park, S.C. (2002). Computer's Time-Variant Purchase Behavior and Corresponding Marketing Strategies: An Online Retailer's Case. *Computers and Industrial Engineering,* 43(4), 801-820.

Habermas, J. (1978). Knowledge and human interests. London: Heinemann.

Hackman, J. (1968). Effects of task characteristics on group products. *Journal of Experimental Social Psychology,* 4, 162-187.

Hair, J. F., Anderson, R. E., Tatham, R. L., & Black, W. C. (1998). *Multivariate data analysis* (5th ed). Upper Saddle River, NJ: Prentice Hall.

Hall, J. (2002, September 6). Free software in Brazil. *Linux Journal, 101.*

Hammer, M., & Champy, J. (1993). *Re-engineering the corporation.* London: Harper Business.

Hand, D., Mannila, H., & Smyth, P. (2001). *Principles of data mining.* Boston: The MIT Press.

Hansen, M. T., Nohria, N. & Tierney, T. (1999). What's your strategy for managing knowledge. *Harvard Business Review* (March-April): 106-116.

Harlow, H. F. (1949). The formation of learning sets. *Psychological Review, 56,* 51-65.

Harris, S. E. & Katz, J. L. (1991). Organizational performance and IT investment intensity in the insurance. *Organization Science 2*(3): 263-95.

Hearst, M. (1999). Untangling text data mining. In *Proceedings of 37th Annual Meeting of the Association for Computational Linguistics* (ACL'99), MD.

Heath, C. (1995). Escalation and de-escalation of commitment in response to sunk costs: The role of budgeting in mental accounting. *Organizational Behavior and Human Decision Processes 62*(1), 38-54.

Hedges, L. V. (1982). Estimating effect size from a series of independent experiment. *Psychological Bulletin, 92,* 490-499

Hedges, L. V., & Olkin, I. (1985), *Statistical methods for meta-analysis.* Orlando, FL: Academic Press

Hedges, L. V., & Vevea, J. L. (1998). Fixed- and random-effects models in meta-analysis. *Psychological Methods 3,* 486-504.

Hedström, P., & Swedberg, R. (1998). Social mechanisms: An introductory essay. In P. Hedström & R. Swedberg (Eds.), *Social mechanisms: An analytical approach to social theory* (pp. 1-31). Cambridge University Press, New York.

Heijden, H. V. D. (2003). Factors Influencing the usage of Websites: The case of a generic portal in the Netherlands. *Information & Management, 40*(6), 541-549.

Heijden, H. V. D., Verhagen, T., & Creemers, M. (2003). Understanding online purchase intentions: Contributions from technology and trust perspectives. *European Journal of Information Systems, 12*(1), 41-49.

Heims, S. (1991). *The cybernetics group.* Cambridge, MA: MIT Press.

Henderson, J. C., & Lee, S. (1992). Managing IS design teams: A control theory perspective. *Management Science, 38*(6), 757-777.

Heng, C. S., Tan, B. C. Y., & Wei, KK. (2003). De-escalation of commitment in software projects: Who matters? What matters? *Information and Management 41,* 99-110.*

Herath, H. and Park, C. (2002). Multi-Stage Capital Investment Opportunities as Compound Real Options. *The Engineering Economist,* 47(1), 1-27.

Herzum, P., & Sims, O. (2000). *Business component factory.* New York: John Wiley & Sons, Inc.

Hevner, A. R., March, S. T., Park, J., & Ram, S. (2004). Design science in information systems research. *MIS Quarterly, 28*(1), 75-105.

Hew, K. F. & Hara, N. (2007). Knowledge sharing in online environments: a qualitative case study. *Journal of the American Society for Information Science and Technology 58*(14): 2310-2324.

Higgins, C. (1995). Application of social cognitive theory to training for computer skills. *Information Systems Research* 6(2), 118–143.

Hill, C.W.L. & Jones,G.R. (1998). *Strategic Management: An Integrated Approach.* Houghton Mifflin: Boston, MA.

Hilton, J. L., & Darley, J. M. (1991). The effects of interaction goals on person perception. In M. P. Zanna (Ed.), *Advances in experimental social psychology.* Orlando, FL: Academic Press.

Hirschheim, R., & Klein, H. (2003). Crisis in the IS field? A critical reflection on the state of the discipline. *JAIS, 4*(10), 237-293.

Hodson, T.J., Englander, F. and Englander, V. (1999). Ethical, Legal and Economic Aspects of Monitoring of Employee Email. *Journal of Business Ethics*, 19, 99-108.

Hoffer, J., George, J., & Valachi, J. (1996). *Modern systems analysis and design.* Menlo Park, CA: Benjamin/Cummings.

Hofstede, G. (1991). *Kulturer og organisationer: overlevelse i en graensoverskridende verden.* Kobenhavn, Schultz.

Holmqvist, M. (2003). Intra- and interorganisational learning processes: an empirical comparison. *Scandinavian Journal of Management 19*: 443-466.

Hong, W.H., Thong, J.Y.L., Wong, W.M., & Tam, K.Y. (2001-2002). Determinants of user acceptance of digital libraries: An empirical examination of individual differences and system characteristics. *Journal of Management Information Systems*, 18(3), 97-124.

Hsu, C. & Lin, J. C.C. (2008) Acceptance of blog usage: The roles of technology acceptance, social influence and sharing motivation. *Information & Management*, 41(3), 65-74.

Hsu, M.H. & Chiu, C.M. (2004). Internet self-efficacy and electronic service acceptance. *Decision Support Systems*, 38(3), 369-381.

Hu, P.J., Chau, P.Y.K., Sheng, O.R.L., & Tam, K.Y. (1999). Examining the technology acceptance model using physician acceptance of telemedicine technology. *Journal of Management Information Systems*, 16(2), 91-112.

Hu, P.J.H., Clark, T.H.K., & Ma, W.W. (2003). Examining technology acceptance by school teachers: A longitudinal study. *Information & Management,* 41(2), 227-241.

Hu, Q., Saunders, C., and Gebelt, M. (1997). Research Report: Diffusion of Information Systems Outsourcing: A Reevaluation of Influence Sources. *Information Systems Research*, 8(3), 288-301.

Huber, G. & Daft, R. (1987). The information environments of organization. In F. Jablin, L. Putman, K. Roberts, and L. Porter (Eds.), *Handbook of organization communication.* Beverly Hills, CA: Sage.

Huizingh, E. (2000). The content and design of Web sites: An empirical study. *Information & Management, 37*(3), 123-134.

Hung, S.Y. & Liang, T.P. (2001). Effect of computer self-efficacy on the use of executive support systems. *Industrial Management and Data Systems*, 101(5), 227-237.

Hunter, J. E., & Schmidt, F. L. (1990). *Methods of meta-analysis, correcting error and bias in research findings.* Sage Publications.

Hunter, S. D. (2003). Information Technology, Organizational Learning, and the Market Value of the Firm. *JITTA: Journal of Information Technology Theory and Application;* Hong Kong 5(1), 1-28.

Huotari, M.-L. (1998). Human resource management and information management as a basis for managing knowledge. *Swedish Library Research* (3-4): 53-71.

Huysman, M. & de Wit, D. (2002). *Knowledge sharing in practice.* Dordrecht, Kluwer.

Hwang, M. I. (1996). The use of meta-analysis in MIS research: Promises and problems. *The Data Base for Advances in Information Systems 27*(3), 35-48.

Hyldegård, J. (2004). Collaborative information behaviour - exploring Kuhlthau's Information Search Process model in a group-based educational setting. *Information Processing & Management,* in press.

Iatropoulos A., Economides A. and Angelou G., (2004). Broadband investments analysis using real options methodology: A case study for Egnatia Odos S.A.. *Communications and Strategies*, No 55, 3rd quarter 2004, 45-76.

Igbaria, M. & Iivari, J. (1995). The effects of self-efficacy on computer usage. *Omega International Journal of Management Science*, 23(6), 587-605.

Igbaria, M., Parasuraman, S., & Baroudi, J. (1996). A motivational model of microcomputer usage. *Journal of Management Information Systems*, 13(1), 127-143.

Iivari, J., Hirschheim, R., & Klein, H. K. (1998). A paradigmatic analysis contrasting information systems development approaches and methodologies. *Information Systems Research, 9*(2), 164-193.

Im, K., Dow, K., and Grover, V. (2001). Research Report: A Reexamination of IT Investment and the Market Value of the Firm: an Event Study Methodology. *Information Systems Research* 12(1), 103-117.

Ingwersen, P. (1992). *Information retrieval and interaction.* London, Tyler.

Ives, B., Hamilton, S., & Davis, G. (1980). A framework for research in computer-based management information systems. *Management Science, 26*(9), 910-934.

Iwaarden, J. V., & Wiele, T. V. D. (2003). Applying SERVQUAL to Web sites: An exploratory study. *International Journal of Quality, 20*(8), 919-935.

Iwaarden, J. V., Wiele, T. V. D., Ball, L., & Millen, R. (2004). Perceptions about the quality of Websites: A survey amongst students at Northeastern University and Erasmus University. *Information & Management, 41*(8), 947–959.

Jackson, C.M., Chow, S., & Leitch, R.A. (1997). Towards an understanding of the behavioral intention to use an information system. *Decision Sciences*, 28(2), 357-389.

Jackson, M. (2000). *Systems approaches to management.* New York: Kluwer.

Jackson, M. C. (1995). Beyond the fads: Systems thinking for managers. *Systems Research,* 12(1), 25-42.

Jackson, M. C. (2003). *Systems thinking, creative holism for managers.* Chichester: Wiley.

Jackson, T.W., Dawson, R. and Wilson, D. (2000). The Cost of Email Within Organisations. *Proceedings of the IRMA 2000*, Anchorage, Alaska, May.

Jacobson, I. (2002). A resounding "yes" to agile processes - but also to more. *The Journal of Information Technology Management,* 15(1), 18-24.

Jamshidi, M. (2005). System-of-systems engineering - A definition. *Proceedings of IEEE System*, Man, and Cybernetics (SMC) Conference. Retrieved January 29, 2005 from http://ieeesmc2005.unm.edu/SoSE_Defn.htm

Jarvenpaa, S. L., Tractinsky, N., & Vitale, M. (2000). Consumer trust in an Internet store. *Information Technology and Management, 1*(2), 45-71.

Jiang, J. J., & Klein, G. (1999). Risks to different aspects of system success. *Information & Management, 36*, 263-272.

Jiang, J. J., & Klein, G. (2000). Software development risks to project effectiveness. *Journal of Systems and Software, 52*, 3-10.

Jiang, J. J., Klein, G., & Balloun, J. (1998). Systems analysts' attitudes toward information systems development. *Information Resources Management Journal, 11*(4), 5-10.

Jiang, J. J., Klein, G., & Means, T. (2000). Project risk impact on software development team performance. *Project Management Journal, 31*(4), 19-26.

Jiang, J. J., Klein, G., Van Slyke, & Cheney, P. (2003). A note on interpersonal and communication skills for IS professionals: Evidence of positive influence. *Decision Sciences, 34*(4), 799-812.

Jin, L., Robey, D., & Boudreau, M. C. (2006). Exploring the hybrid community: Intertwining virtual and physical representations of Linux user communities. In *Proceedings of the Administrative Science Association of Canada,* Banff, Canada.

Jin, L., Verma, S., & Negi, A. (2005). Profiling Open-Source: A use perspective across OpenSource communities in the US and India. In *Proceedings of the 36th Annual Meeting of the Decision Sciences Institute,* San Francisco, California.

Johnson, R., Kast, F., & Rosenzweig, J. (1964). Systems theory and management. *Management Science, 10*(2), 367-384.

Jones, M. (1992). SSM and information systems. *Systemist,* 14(3), 12-125.

Jones, M. C., & Harrison, A. W. (1996). IS project team performance: An empirical assessment. *Information & Management, 31*(2), 57-65.

Joshi, J. B. D., Aref, W. G., Ghafoor, A., & Spafford, E. H. (2001). Security models for Web-based applications. *Communications of the ACM, 44*(2), 38-44.

Kahneman, D., & Tversky, A. (1979). Prospect theory: An analysis of decisions under risk. *Econometrica, 47,* 263-291

Kampmann, C.E. (1996). Feedback loops gains and system behavior. In *Proceedings of the 12th International System Dynamics Society Conference,* July 21-25, Cambridge, MA.

Kanter, R. M. (1996). When a thousand flowers bloom: Structural, collective, and social conditions for innovation in organizations. In P. S. Myers (Ed.), *Knowledge management and organizational design.* Newton, MA: Butterworth-Heinemann.

Kanungo, S. (2003). Using system dynamics to operationalize process theory in information systems research. *Proceedings of the* 24th *International Conference on Information Systems,* 450-463.

Katsamakas, E. & Georgantzas, N. (2008). *Open source disruptive innovation strategies.* Working Paper, Fordham University, New York, NY.

Kaufman, J. J., & Woodhead, R. (2006). *Stimulating innovation in products and services.* Hoboken, NJ: Wiley.

Kayes, A. B., Kayes, D. C., & Kolb, D. A. (2005). Experiential learning in teams. *Simulation & Gaming, 36*(3), 330-354.

Keen, P. G. W. (1980). *MIS research: Reference disciplines and a cumulative tradition.* Paper presented at the First International Conference on Information Systems, Philadelphia, PA.

Keil, M., Mann, J., & Rai, A. (2000a). Why software projects escalate: An empirical analysis and test of four theoretical models. *MIS Quarterly 24*(4), 631-664.

Keil, M., Mixon, R., Saarinen, T., & Tuunainen, V. (1995). Understanding runaway information technology projects. *Journal of Management Information Systems 11*(3), 65-85.*

Keil, M., Tan, B. C. Y., et al. (2000). A cross-cultural study on escalation of commitment behavior in software projects. *MIS Quarterly 24*(2), 299-325.

Keil, M., Truex, D., & Mixon, R. (1995). The effects of sunk cost and project completion on information technology project escalation. *IEEE Transactions on Engineering Management, 24*(4), 372-381.*

Kelley, M. R. (1994). Productivity and information technology: The elusive connection. *Management Science, 40*(11), 1406-1425.

Kettinger, W. J. (1997). Business process change: A study of methodologies, techniques, and tools. *MIS Quarterly,* (March), 55-79.

Kiely, T. (1997). The Internet: Fear and shopping in cyberspace. *Harvard Business Review, 75*(4), 13-14.

Kim, D. (1993). The Link between individual and organizational learning. *Sloan Management Review,* Fall, 37-50.

Klein, G., & Jiang, J. J. (2001). Seeking consonance in information systems. *Journal of Systems and Software*, *56*(2), 195-202.

Klein, G., Jiang, J. J., & Sobol, M. G. (2001). A new view of IS personnel performance evaluation. *Communications of the ACM*, *44*(6), 95-101.

Klein, H. (1991). Further evidence on the relationship between goal setting and expectancy theories. *Organizational Behavior and Human Decision Processes*, *49*, 230-257.

Klein, H. K., & Myers, M. D. (1999). A set of principles for conducting and evaluating interpretive field studies in information systems. *MIS Quarterly*, *23*(1), 67-94.

Kling, R. (1999). What is social informatics and why does it matter? *D-Lib Magazine* *5*(1).

Klir, G. (1969). *An approach to general systems theory*. New York: Van Nostrand.

Kloptchenko, A., Eklund, T., Back, B., Karlsson, J., Vanharanta, H, & Visa, A. (2004). Combining data and text mining techniques for analyzing financial reports. *International Journal of Intelligent Systems in Accounting, Finance, and Management*, *12*(1), 29-41

Ko, D., Kirsch, L., & King, W. (2005). Antecedents of knowledge transfer from consultants to clients in enterprise system implementations. *MIS Quarterly*, *29*(1), 59-85.

Kobryn, C. (1999). UML 2001: A standardization odyssey. *Communications of the ACM*, *42*(10), 29-37.

Koch, C. (2006, January). The ABCs of ERP, *CIO Magazine*.

Koenig, M. (1998). *Information Driven management concepts and Themes*. München, Saur.

Kogut, B., & Zander, U. (1992). Knowledge of the firm, competitive capabilities, and the replication of technology. *Organization Science* *3*, 383-397.

Kohonen, T. (1997). *Self-organizing maps*. Springer-Verlag.

Koufaris, M., & Hampton-Sosa, W. (2004). The development of initial trust in an online company by new customers. *Information & Management*, *41*(3), 377-397.

Kraemer, K., and Dedrick, J. (1994). Payoffs from Investment in Information Technology: Lessons from the Asia-Pacific Region. *World Development*, 22(12), 1921-1931.

Kraemer, K., Gibbs, J., and Dedrick, J. (2002). Environment and Policy Factors Shaping E-Commerce Diffusion: A Cross-Country Comparison. *Proceedings of the International Conference of Information Systems*.

Kroeze, J., Matthee, M., & Bothma, J. (2003). Differentiating data and text mining terminology. In *Proceedings of SAICSIT*, 93-101.

Krueger, R. A. (1988). *Focus groups: A practical guide for applied research*. Newbury Park, CA: Sage Publications.

Kshetri, N., and Dholakia, N. (2002). Determinants of the Global Diffusion of B2B E-Commerce. *Electronic Markets*, 12(2), 120-129.

Kuhn, T. (1970). *The structure of scientific revolutions*. Chicago: Chicago University Press.

Kumar, K., & Hillegersberg, V. J. (2000). ERP experiences and evolution. *Communications of the ACM*, 43(4), 23-41.

Kuo, F.Y., Chu, T.H., Hsu, M.H., & Hsieh, H.S. (2004). An investigation of effort–accuracy trade-off and the impact of self-efficacy on Web searching behaviors. *Decision Support Systems*, 37(3), 331-342.

Kuo, G., & Lin, J. (1998). New design concepts for an intelligent Internet. *Communications of the ACM*, *41*(11), 93-98.

Lagus, K. (2000). *Text mining with WebSOM*. Unpublished doctoral dissertation, Espoo, Finland.

Lahtinen, T. (2000). *Automatic indexing: An approach using an index term corpus and combining linguistic and statistical methods*. Unpublished doctoral dissertation, University of Helsinki, Finland.

Lakhani, K. R., & von Hippel, E. (2003). How Open-Source software works: "Free" user-to-user assistance. *Research Policy, 32*(6), 923.

Land, F., & Kennedy-McGregor, M. (1987). Information and information systems: Concepts and perspectives. In R. Galliers (Ed.), *Information analysis: Selected readings* (pp. 63-91). Sydney: Wesely.

Landis, J. R., & Koch, G. G. (1977). The measurement of observer agreement for categorical data. *Biometrics, 33*(1), 159-174.

Lane, C. (1998). *Methods for transitioning from soft systems methodology models to object oriented analysis developed to support the army operational architecture and an example of its application.* United Kingdom.: Hi-Q Systems Ltd, The Barn Micheldever Station Winchester S021 3AR.

Lane, J. (2005). *System of systems lead system integrators: Where do they spend their time and what makes them more/less efficient.* (Tech. Rep. No. 2005-508.) University of Southern California Center for Systems and Software Engineering, Los Angeles, CA.

Lane, J. (2006). *COSOSIMO Parameter Definitions.* (Tech. Rep. No. 2006-606). University of Southern California Center for Systems and Software Engineering, Los Angeles, CA.

Langenwalter, G. A. (2000). *Enterprise resource planning and beyond: Integrating your entire organization.* Boca Raton, FL: CRC Press, Taylor and Francis.

Larsen, T. J., & Levine, L. (2005). Searching for MIS: Coherence and change in the discipline. *Information Systems Journal, 15*, 357-381.

Larses, O., and El-Khoury, J. (2005). *Review of Skyttner (2001) in O. Larses and J. El-Khoury, "Views on General Systems Theory."* Technical Report TRITA-MMK 2005:10, Royal Institute of Technology, Stockholm, Sweden. Retrieved June 30, 2006 on the World Wide Web: http://apps.md.kth.se/publication_item/web.phtml?ss_brand=MMKResearchPublications&department_id='Damek'

Larson, T., & Levine, J. (2005). Serching for Management Information Systems: Coherence and Change in the Discipline. *Information Systems Journal, 15*, pp. 357-381.

Lawson, T. (1997). *Economics and reality.* Routledge: London.

Layder, D. (1993). *New strategies in social research: An introduction and guide.* Cambridge: Polity Press.

Lazlo, E., & Krippner, S. (1998). In J.S. Jordan (Ed.), *Systems theories and a priori aspects of perception* (47-74). Amsterdam: Elsevier Science.

Lazlo, E., & Lazlo, A. (1997). The contribution of the systems sciences to the humanities. *Systems Research & Behavioral Science, 14*(1), 5-19.

Leana, C. R. & Van Buren, H. J. (1999). Organizational Social Capital and Employes Practices. *Academy of Management Review 24*(3): 538-555.

Leavitt, H., & Whisler, T. (1958). Management in the 80's. *Harvard Business Review, 36*(6), 41-48.

Lee, A. S. (1991). Architecture as a reference discipline for MIS. In H.-E. Nissen, H. K. Klein & R. Hirschheim (Eds.), *Information research: Contemporary approaches and emergent traditions* (pp. 573-592). Amsterdam: North-Holland.

Lee, A. S. (2000). Irreducibly sociological dimensions in research and publishing: Editor's comments. *MIS Quarterly, 24*(4), v-vii.

Lee, D. M. S., & Heiko, L.(1994). Innovative design practices and product development performance. In *Proceedings of International Conference of Product Development*, 127-152.

Lee, D. M. S., Trauth, E. M., & Farwell, D. (1995). Critical skills and knowledge requirements of IS professionals: A joint academic/industry investigation. *MIS Quarterly, 19*(3), 313-340.

Lee, G. and Xia W. (2006) Organizational Size and IT Adoption: A Meta-Analysis. *Information and Management.* 43, 975-985

Lee, G., & Lin, H. (2005). Customer perceptions of e-service quality in online shopping. *International Journal of Retail & Distribution Management, 33*(2), 161-176.

Lee, H., & Choi, B. (2003). Knowledge management enablers, processes, and organizational performance: An integrative view and empirical examination. *Journal of Management Information Systems, 20*(1), 179-228.

Lee, M., & Turban, E. A. (2001). Trust model for consumer Internet shopping. *International Journal of Electronic Commerce, 6*(1), 75-91.

Legris, P., Ingham, J., & Collerette, P. (2003). Why do people use information technology? A critical review of the technology acceptance model. *Information & Management*, 40(3), 191-204.

Leitheiser, R. L. (1992). MIS skills for the 1990s: A survey of MIS managers' perceptions. *Journal of Management Information Systems, 9*(1), 69-91.

Lepkowska-White, E. (2004). Online store perceptions: How to turn browsers into buyers. *Journal of Marketing Theory and Practice, 12*(3), 36-48.

Lewis, D. (1992). Feature selection and feature extraction for text categorization. *Speech and Natural Language Workshop.*

Li, X. and Johnson, J. (2002). Evaluate IT Investment Opportunities Using Real Options Theory. *Information Resource Management Journal*, 15(3), 32-47.

Li, Y. (1998). Toward qualitative search engine. *IEEE Internet Computing*, July-August.

Liao, Z., & Cheung, T. (2001). Internet-based e-shopping and consumer attitudes: An empirical study. *Information & Management, 38*(5), 299-306.

Lie, H. W., & Saarela, J. (1999). Multipurpose Web publishing using HTML, XML, and CSS. *Communications of the ACM, 42*(10), 95-101.

Liebowitz, S. J. (2002). *Rethinking the networked economy: The true forces driving the digital marketplace.* New York: Amacom Press.

Liebowitz, S. J., & Margolis, S. E. (1994). *Network externality: An uncommon tragedy. Journal of Economic Perspectives, 19*(2), 219-234.

Liebowitz, S. J., & Margolis, S. E. (2002). *Winners, losers & Microsoft.* Oakland, CA: The Independent Institute.

Lin, H.-F. (2007). Knowledge sharing and firm innovation capability: an empirical study. *International Journal of Manpower 28*(3/4): 315-332.

Lindquist, C. (2000). You've Got Dirty Mail. *ComputerWorld*, 34, 11, 72-73.

Lindsay, P. H., & Norman, D. A. (1977). *Human information processing.* Orlando, FL: Academic Press.

Lipsey, M. W., & Wilson, D. B. (2001). *Practical meta-analysis.* Sage Publications.

Littlepage, G., Robison, W., & Reddington, K. (1997). Effects of task experience and group experience on group performance, member ability, and recognition of expertise. *Organizational Behavior Human Decision Processes,* 69, 133–147.

Liu, C., & Arnett, K. P. (2000). Exploring the factors associated with Web site success in the context of e-commerce. *Information & Management, 38*(1), 23-33.

Liyanage, J. P., & Kumar, U. (2003). Towards a value-based view on operations and maintenance performance management. *Journal of Quality in Maintenance Engineering, 9*(4), 1355-2511.

Locke, J. (1894). An essay concerning human understanding. In A. C. Fraser (Ed.), *vol. 1.* Oxford: Clarendon.

Loh, L., and Venkatraman, N. (1992). Diffusion of Information Technology Outsourcing: Influence Sources and the Kodak Effect. *Information Systems Research*, 3(4), 334-358.

Lohse, G. L., & Spiller, P. (1999). Internet retail store design: How the user interface influences traffic and sales. *Journal of Computer Mediated Communication, 5*(2). Retrieved from www.ascusc.org/jcmc/vol5/issue2/

Loiacono, E., Watson, R., & Goodhue, D. (2002). WebQual: A Web site quality instrument. *American marketing association. Winter Marketing Educators' Conference, Austin, TX,* 432-438.

Lopes, E., & Bryant, A. (2004). SSM: A Pattern and Objet Modeling overview. *ICT+ Conference*, from http://www.leedsmet.ac.uk/ies/redot/Euric%20Lopes.pdf

Lowry, P. B., Romans, D., & Curtis, A. (2004). Global journal prestige and supporting disciplines: A scientometric study of information systems journals. *Journal of the AIS, 5*(2), 29-77.

Lu, J., Liu, C., Yu, C.S., & Wang, K. (2008). Determinants of accepting wireless mobile data services in China. *Information & Management*, 45(1), 52-64.

Luman, S. (2005, June). OpenSource Software. *Wired Magazine*, p. 68.

Lyytinen, K. & Rose, G. (2003). The disruptive nature of Information Technology innovations: the case of internet computing in systems development organizations. *MIS Quarterly*, 27(4), 557-595.

Lyytinen, K. & Rose, G. (2003). Disruptive information system innovation: the case of internet computing. *Information Systems Journal*, 13, 301-330.

Ma, Q. & Liu, L. (2004). The technology acceptance model: A meta-analysis of empirical findings. *Journal of Organizational and End User Computing*, 16(1), 59-72.

Ma, Q. & Liu, L. (2005). The role of Internet self-efficacy in the acceptance of web-based electronic medical records. *Journal of Organizational and End User Computing*, 17(1), 38-57.

Maddala, G.S. (1992). *Introduction to Econometrics.* Prentice Hall, NJ.

Mahajan, V., and Peterson, R.A. (1985). *Models for Innovation Diffusion.* Sage Publications, Beverly Hills, CA

Mahmood, M.A., Hall, L., & Swanberg, D.L. (2001). Factors affecting information technology usage: A meta-analysis of the empirical literature. *Journal of Organizational Computing & Electronic Commerce*, 11(2), 107-130.

Maier, M. (1998). Architecting principles for systems-of-systems. *Systems Engineering, 1*(4), 267-284.

Majchrzak, A., Beath, C. M., Lim, R. A., & Chin, W. W. (2005). Managing client dialogues during information system design to facilitate client learning. *MIS Quarterly, 29*(4), 653-672.

Malhotra, A., Majchrzak, A., Carman, R., & Lott, V. (2001). Radical innovation without collocation: A case study at Boeing-Rocketdyne. *MIS Quarterly, 25*(2), 229-249.

Manicas, P. (1993). Accounting as a human science. *Accounting, Organizations and Society, 18*, 147- 161.

Mantzari, D. and Economides, A. (2004). Cost analysis for e-learning foreign languages. *European Journal of Open and Distance Learning*, November, issue 2, vol 1, http://www.eurodl.org

March, S. T., & Smith, G. F. (1995). Design and natural science research on information technology. *Decision Support Systems, 15*(4), 251-266.

Marino, G. (2001). *Workers mired in e-mail wasteland.* Retrieved from CNetNews.com.

Markus, L.M. (1994). Finding A Happy Medium: Explaining The Negative Effects Of Electronic Communication On Social Life At Work. *ACM Transactions On Information Systems, 12*, 2, Apr, 119-149.

Markus, M. L., Manville, B., & Agres, C. E. (2000). What makes a virtual organization work? *Sloan Management Review, 42*, 13-26.

Markus, M.L. and Mao, J.Y. (2004). Participation in development and implementation – updating an old, tired concept for today's IS contexts. *Journal of the Association for Information Systems, 5* (11: 14).

Martin, D. D., (1988). Technological Change and Manual Wiork. In D. Gallie (Ed.), *Employment in Britain* (102-127). Oxford: Basil Balckwell.

Mason, R., & Mitroff, I. (1973). A program of research on MIS. *Management Science, 19*(5), 475-485.

Mathiassen, L., & Nielsen, P. A. (2000). Interaction and transformation in SSM. *Systems Research and Behavioral Science,* (17), 243-253.

Mathieson, K. (1991). Predicting user intentions: Comparing the technology acceptance model with the theory of planned behavior. *Information Systems Research,* 2(3), 173-191.

Mathieson, K., Peacock, E., & Chinn, W.C. (2001). Extending the technology acceptance model: The influence of perceived user resources. *The Data Base for Advances in Information Systems*, 32(3), 86-112.

Mauldin, E., & Arunachalam, V. (2002). An experimental examination of alternative forms of Web assurance for business-to-consumer e-commerce. *Journal of Information Systems, 16,* 33-54.

McCann, S. (1992). Want to succeed? Get out of IS for awhile. *CIO, 26*(44), 107.

McDermott, R. & O'Dell, C. (2001). Overcoming cultural barriers to knowledge sharing. *Journal of Knowledge Management 5*(1): 76-85.

McDermott, R. (1999). Why information technology inspired but cannot deliver knolwedge management. *California Management Review 41*(4): 103-117.

McHugh, J. (2005, February). The Firefox explosion. *Wired Magazine*, pp. 92-96.

McKnight, H. D., Choudhury, V., & Kacmar, C. (2002). Developing and validating trust measures for e-commerce: An integrative typology. *Information Systems Research, 13*(3), 334-359.

McKnight, H. D., Choudhury, V., & Kacmar, C. (2002). The impact of initial consumer trust on intentions to transact with a Web site: A trust building model. *Journal of Strategic Information Systems, 11,* 297-323.

McLeod, P. (1992). An assessment of the experimental literature on electronic support of group work: Results of a meta-analysis. *Human Computer Interaction 7,* 257-280.

McLeod, P., & Liker, J. (1992). Electronic meeting systems: Evidence from a low structure environment. *Information Systems Research,* 3(3), 195-223.

Meadows, D.H. (1989). System dynamics meets the press. *System Dynamics Review,* 5(1), 68-80.

Mejias, R., Shepherd, M., Vogel, D., & Lazaneo, L. (1996-97). Consensus and satisfaction levels: A cross-cultural comparison of GSS and non-GSS outcomes within and between the United States and Mexico. *Journal of Management Information Systems,* 13(3), 137-161.

Merton, R. K. (1948). The self-fulfilling prophecy. *Antioch Review, 8,* 193-210.

Midgley, G. (1996). What is this thing called CST? In R. Flood & N. Romm (Eds.), *Critical systems thinking* (11-24). New York: Plenum Press.

Miles, M.B., And Huberman, M.A. (1994). *An Expanded Sourcebook Of Qualitative Data Analysis.* Sage Publications, California.

Miller, J. & Glassner, B. (1988). *The 'inside' and 'outside': finding realities in interviews. Qualitative Research.* D. Silverman. London, Sage: 99-112.

Miller, J. G. (1978). *Living systems.* New York: McGraw-Hill.

Miller, W. L., & Morris, L. (1999). *Fourth generation R& D: Managing knowledge, technology and innovation.* Hoboken, NJ: Wiley.

Mingers, J. (1992). SSM and Information Systems: An Overview. *Systemist,* 14(3), 82-87.

Mingers, J. (1995). *Using soft systems methodology in the design of information systems.* London: McGraw-Hill.

Mingers, J. (2000). The contributions of critical realism as an underpinning philosophy for OR/MS and systems. *Journal of the Operational Research Society 51,*1256-1270.

Mingers, J. (2001). Combining IS research methods: Towards a pluralist methodology. *Information Systems Research,* 12(3), 240-259.

Mingers, J. (2002). Realizing information systems: Critical realism as an underpinning philosophy for information systems. In *Proceedings Twenty-Third International Conference on Information Systems, 295-303.*

Mingers, J. (2003). A classification of the philosophical assumptions of management science methodologies. *Journal of the Operational Research Society, 54*(6), 559-570.

Mingers, J., & Brocklesby, J. (1997). Multimethodology: Towards a framework for mixing methodologies. *International Journal of Management Science,* 25(5), 489-509.

Mithas, S., Krishnan, M.S., and Fornell, C. (2002). Effect of IT Investments on Customer Satisfaction: An Empirical Analysis. *Proceedings of the WISE Conference.*

Mockus, A., Fielding, R. T., & Herbsleb, J. D. (2002). Two case studies of OpenSource software development: Apache and Mozilla. *ACM Transactions on Software Engineering and Methodology, 11*(3), 309-346.

Moen, R. (2000). Eric Raymond's tips for effective OpenSource advocacy. Retrieved July 28, 2006, from http://www.itworld.com/AppDev/344/LWD000913expo00/pfindex.html

Moen, R. (2003). Linux user group HOW TO. Retrieved July 28, 2006, from http://www.linux.org/docs/ldp/howto/User-Group-HOWTO.html

Mojtahedzadeh, M.T. (1996). *A Path Taken: Computer-Assisted Heuristics for Understanding Dynamic Systems.* Ph.D. Dissertation. Rockefeller College of Public Affairs and Policy, SUNY: Albany NY.

Mojtahedzadeh. M.T., Andersen, D. & Richardson, G.P. (2004). Using *Digest®* to implement the pathway participation method for detecting influential system structure. *System Dynamics Review,* 20(1), 1-20.

Monarch, I. (2000). Information science and information systems: Converging or diverging? In *Proceedings of the 28th Annual Conference of the Canadian Association in Information Systems*, Alberta.

Moon, H. (2001). Looking forward and looking back: Integrating completion and sunk cost effects within an escalation-of-commitment progress decision. *Journal of Applied Psychology 86*(1), 104-113.

Moon, M. (2000). Effective use of information & competitive intelligence. *Information Outlook 4*(2): 17-20.

Moore, G.C. & Benbasat, I. (1991). Development of an instrument to measure the perceptions of adopting an information technology innovation. *Information Systems Research*, 2(3), 192-222.

Mora, M. Gelman, O, Forgionne, G. Petkov D and Cano, J. Integrating the fragmented pieces in IS research paradigms and frameworks – a systems approach. *Information Resource Management Journal*, 20(2), 1-22.

Mora, M., Gelman, O., Cano, J., Cervantes, F., & Forgionne, G. (2006, July 9-14). Theory of systems and information systems research frameworks. In *Proceedings of the International Society for the Systems Sciences 50th Annual Conference*, Rohnert Park, CA.

Mora, M., Gelman, O., Cervantes, F., Mejia, M., & Weitzenfeld, A. (2003). A systemic approach for the formalization of the information system concept: why information systems are systems? In J. Cano (Ed), *Critical reflections of information systems: A systemic approach* (1-29). Hershey, PA: Idea Group Publishing.

Mora, M., Gelman, O., Cervantes, F., Mejía, M., and Weitzenfeld, A. (2002). A Systemic Approach for the Formalization of the Information Systems Concept: Why Information Systems are Systems. In J.J. Cano, (Ed.), *Critical reflections on information systems: A systemic approach.* Hershey, PA: Idea Group Publishing, 1-29.

Mora, M., Gelman, O., Forgionne, G., & Cervantes, F. (2004, May 19-21). Integrating the soft and the hard systems approaches: A critical realism based methodology for studying soft systems dynamics (CRM-SSD). In *Proceedings of the 3rd. International Conference on Systems Thinking in Management (ICSTM 2004)*, Philadelphia, PA.

Mora, M., Gelman, O., Forgionne, G., & Cervantes, F. (in press). Information Systems: a systemic view. M.

Khosrow-Pour (Ed.) In *Encyclopedia of information science and technology, 2nd ed.* Hershey, PA: IGR.

Morecroft, J.D.W. (1985). Rationality in the analysis of behavioral simulation models, *Management Science,* 31, 900-916.

Morgan, M. (2000). *Is distance learning worth it? Helping to determine the costs of online courses.* ED 446611, http://webpages.marshall.edu/~morgan16/onlinecosts/

Muchinsky, P. M. (1977). Organizational communication : relationships to organizational climate and job satisfaction. *Academy of Management Journal 20*(4): 592-607.

Mun, J. (2002) *Real Options Analysis: Tools and Techniques for Valuing Strategic Investments and Decisions.* Wiley Finance.

Mun, J. (2003) *Real Options Analysis Course: Business Cases and Software Applications.* Wiley Finance.

Muralidhar, K., Sarathy, R., & Parsa, R. (2001). An improved security requirement for data perturbation with implications for e-commerce. *Decision Sciences Journal, 32*(4), 683-698.

Murphy, T. (2002). *Achieving business value from technology: A practical guide for today's executive.* Hoboken, NJ: Gartner Press, Wiley.

Mutch, A. (1999). Critical realism, managers and information. *British Journal of Management, 10*, 323-333.

Mutch, A. (2000). Managers and information: Agency and structure. *Information Systems Review, 1.*

Mutch, A. (2002). Actors and networks or agents and structures: Towards a realist view of information systems. *Organization, 9*(3), 477-496.

Nahapiet, J. & Ghoshal, S. (1998). Social Capital, Intellectual Capital, and the Organizational Advantage. *Academy of Management Review 23*(3): 242-266.

Nasukawa T., & Nagano T., (2001). Text analysis and knowledge mining systems. *IBM Systems Journal 40*(4), 967-984.

Nelson, K. M., & Cooprider, J. G. (1996). The contribution of shared knowledge to IS group performance. *MIS Quarterly, 20*(4), 409-432.

Newman, F. and Couturier, L., (2002). Trading Public Good in the Higher Education Market. *Futures Project: Policy for Higher Education in a Changing World.* January. The observatory on borderless higher education, John Foster House, London UK.

Newman, M., & Sabherwal, R. (1996). Determinants of commitment to information systems development: A longitudinal investigation. *MIS Quarterly 20*(1), 23-54.

Newman, W. (1994). *A preliminary analysis of the products of HCI research, using pro forma abstracts.* Paper presented at the Human Factors in Computing Systems, Boston, MA.

Nichols, D. M., & Twidale, M. B. (2003).The usability of OpenSource software. *First Monday, 8*(1).

Nicholson, N., Rees, A. & Brookes-Rooney, A. (1990). Strategy, innovation, and performance. *Journal of Management Studies 27*(5): 511-534.

Nolan, R., & Wetherbe J. (1980). Toward a comprehensive framework for MIS research. *MIS Quarterly, June*, 1, 1-20.

Nonaka, I. (1994). Dynamic theory of organisational knowledge creation. *Organization Science 5*(1): 14-37.

Nonaka, I., & Takeuchi, H. (1995). *The knowledge-creating company: how Japanese companies create the dynamics of innovation.* Oxford: Oxford University Press.

Northcraft, G.B., & Neale, M.A. (1986) Opportunity costs and the framing of resource allocation decisions. *Organizational Behavior and Human Decision Processes* 37(3). 348-356.

Nunamaker, J., Dennis, A., Valacich, J, Vogel, D., & George, J. (1991). Electronic meeting systems to support group work. *Communications of the ACM,* 34(7), 40-61.

Nunnally, J. C. (1978). *Psychometric theory (2nd ed.).* New York: McGraw-Hill.

Nuseibeh, B., & Easterbrook, S. (2000). Requirements engineering: A roadmap. *Communications of the ACM,* 35(9), 37-45.

Odlyzko, A. (2001). Internet growth: Myth and reality, use and abuse. *Journal of Computer Resource management, 102*, Spring, pp. 23-27.

Okhuysen, G., & Eisenhardt, K. (2002). Integrating knowledge in groups: How formal interventions enable flexibility. *Organization Science 13*(4), 370-386.

Olfman, L., Bostrom, R. P., & Sein, M. K. (2003). A best-practice model for information technology learning strategy formulation. In *Proceedings of the 2003 SIGMIS Conference on Computer Personnel Research*, ACM Digital Library, 75-86.

Oliva, R. & Mojtahedzadeh, M.T. (2004). Keep it simple: a dominance assessment of short feedback loops. In *Proceedings of the 22nd International System Dynamics Society Conference*, July 25-29, Keble College, Oxford University, Oxford UK.

Oliva, R. (1994). *A Vensim Module to Calculate Summary Statistics for Historical Fit.* MIT System Dynamics Group D-4584.

Oliva, R. (2004). Model structure analysis through graph theory: partition heuristics and feedback structure decomposition. *System Dynamics Review,* 20(4), 313-336.

Oliva, R., Sterman, J.D. & Giese, M. (2003). Limits to growth in the new economy: exploring the 'get big fast' strategy in e-commerce. *System Dynamics Review,* 19(2), 83-117.

Onetti, A., & Capobianco, F. (2005). OpenSource and business model innovation: The Funambol case. In M. Scotto & G. Succi (Eds.), In *Proceedings of the 1st International Conference on Opens Source Systems* (pp. 224-227).

Ong, C.S., Lai, J.Y., & Wang, Y.S. (2004). Factors affecting engineers' acceptance of asynchronous one e-learning systems in high-tech companies. *Information & Management*, 41(6), 795–804.

Oravec, J.A (2002) Constructive Approaches To Internet Recreation In The Workplace. *Communications Of The ACM*, 45, 1, 60-63.

Orlikowski, W., & Iacono, S. (2001). Desperately Seeking the IT in IT research. *Information Systems Research, 7*(4), 400-408.

Orlikowski, W.J. (1991). Integrated Information Environment or Matrix of Control?: The Contradictory Implications of Information Technology. *Accounting, Management and Information Technology*, 1, 1, 9-42.

Ormerod, R. (1995). Putting soft OR to work: Information systems strategy development at Sainsbury's. *Journal of the Operational Research Society,* 46, 277-293.

Orna, E. (2004). *Information strategy in practice.* Aldershot, Gower.

Osareh, F. (1996). Bibliometrics, citation analysis, and co-citation analysis: A review of literature. *Libri, 46*(4), 217-225.

Oslington, P. (2004). The impact of Uncertainty and irreversibility on Investments in Online Learning. *Distance Education*, vol 25, No. 2.

Osterwalder, A., Pigneur, Y., & Tucci, I. C. (2005). Clarifying business models: Origins, present, and future of the concept. *Communications of the Association for Information Systems,* 16, 1-25.

Outhwaite, W. (1987). *New philosophies of social science: Realism, hermeneutics, and critical theory.* New York: St. Martin's Press.

Overton, R. C. (1998). A comparison of fixed-effects and mexed (random-effects) models for meta-analysis tests of moderator variable effects. *Psychological Methods 3*, 354-379.

Owens, I. & Wilson, T. D. (1997). Information and business performance : a study of information systems and services in high-performing companies. *Journal of Librarianship and Information Science 29*(1): 19-28.

Paich, M. & Sterman, J.D. (1993). Boom, bust and failures to learn in experimental markets. *Management Science,* 39(12), 1439-1458.

Palvia, P., Leary, T., Pinjani, P., & Midha, V. (2004). *A meta-analysis of MIS research.* Paper presented at the Americas Conference on Information Systems, New York, NY.

Parsons, G. (1982). Information technology: A new competitive weapon. *Sloan Management Review, 25*(1), 3-14.

Patterson, K. Grimm, C., and Corsi, T. (2003). Adopting New Technologies for Supply Chain Management. *Transportation Research Part E*, pp.95-121.

Pavlou, P. A. (2003). Consumer acceptance of electronic commerce integrating trust and risk with the technology acceptance model. *International Journal of Electronic Commerce, 7*(3), 101-134.

Pawson, R., Greenhalgh, T., Harvey G., & Walshe K. (2004). *Realist synthesis: An introduction* (RMP Methods Paper 2/2004). Manchester, ESRC Research Methods Programme, University of Manchester.

Pawson, R., Greenhalgh, T., Harvey, G., & Walshe K. (2005). Realist review – A new method of systematic review designed for complex policy interventions. *Journal of Health Services Research & Policy 10*(1), 21–34.

Pechtl, H. (2003). Adoption of online shopping by German grocery shoppers. *The International Review of Retail, Distribution and Consumer Research, 13*(2), 145-159.

Pedreira, O., Piattini, M., Luaces, M. R., & Brisaboa, N. R. (2007). A systematic review of software process tailoring. *ACM SIGSOFT Software Engineering Notes,* 32(3), 1-6.

Peppard, J., & Rowland, P. (1995). *The essence of business process re-engineering.* New York: Prentice Hall.

Perminova, O., Gustafsson, M., & Wikstrom, K. (2008). Defining uncertainty in projects – a new perspective. *International Journal of Project Management, 26,* 73-79.

Pervan, G. (1998). A review of research in group support systems: Leaders approaches and directions. *Decision Support Systems*, 23, 149-159.

Petkov, D. , Petkova, O., Andrew T. and Nepal T. (2007). Mixing multiple criteria decision making with soft systems thinking techniques for decision support in complex situations. *Decision Support Systems,* (43), 1615-1629.

Petkov, D., Edgar-Nevill, D., Madachy, R. and O'Connor, R., (2008). Information systems, software engineering and systems thinking – challenges and opportunities. *International Journal on Information Technologies and Systems Approach*, 1(1), 62-78.

Petkova, O., & Roode, D., R. (1999). A pluralist systemic framework for evaluation of the factors affecting software development productivity. *South African Computer Journal*, 24, 26-32.

Petronio, S., Ellemers, N., Giles, H., & Gallois, C. (1998). (Mis)communicating across boundaries: Interpersonal and inter-group considerations. *Communication Research,* 25(6), 571-595.

Pindyck, R., and Rubinfeld, D. (1998). *Econometric Models and Economic Forecasts.* Boston, MA.: McGraw-Hill Companie.

Pinsonneault, A., Barki, H., Gallupe,R., & Hoppen, N. (1999). Electronic brainstorming: The illusion of productivity. *Information Systems Research.* 10(2), 110 – 133.

Podsakoff, P. M., & Organ, D. W. (1986). Self-reports in organizational research: Problems and prospects. *Journal of Management, 12*, 531-544.

Polanyi, M. (1958). *Personal knowledge: towards a post-critical philosophy.* Chicago, University of Chicago Press.

Porter, M. E. & Millar, V. E. (1985). How information gives you competitive advantage. *Harvard Business Review 64*(4): 149-160.

Porter, M. E. (1980). *Competitive strategy: techniques for analysing industries and competitors.* New York, Free Press.

Porter, M. E. (1990). *The Competitive Advantage of Nations.* New York, Free Press.

Pratt, A. (1995). Putting critical realism to work: The practical implications for geographical research. *Progress in Human Geography 19*(1), 61-74.

Pressman, J., & Wildavsky, A. (1973). *Implementation: How great expectations in Washington are dashed in Oakland.* Oakland, CA: University of California Press.

Pullum, G., & Scholz, B. (2001). More than words. *Nature, 413*, 367.

Putnam, L. & Stolh, C. (1990). Bona fide groups: A reconceptualization of groups in context. *Communication Studies,* 41, 248-265.

Ramamurphy, K., Sen, A., & Sinha, A. (2008). An empirical investigation of key determinants of data warehouse adoption. *Decision Support Systems*, 44(1), 817-841.

Ramasubbu, N. Mithas, S., & Krishnan, M. S. (2008). High tech, high touch: The effect of employee skills and customer heterogeneity on customer satisfaction with enterprise system support services. *Decision Support Systems, 44*(2), 509-523.

Ranganathan, C. Dhaliwal, J. and Thompson, T. (2004). Assimilation and Diffusion of Web Technologies in Supply-Chain Management: An Examination of Key Drivers and Performance Impacts. *International Journal of Electronic Commerce*. 9(1), 127-161.

Ranganathan, C., & Ganapathy, S. (2002). Key dimensions of business-to-consumer Web sites. *Information & Management, 39*(6), 457-465.

Rapoport, A. (1968). Systems Analysis: General systems theory. *International Encyclopedia of the Social Sciences, 14*, 452-458.

Raymond, E. (2001). *The cathedral and the bazaar: Musings on Linux and OpenSource by an accidental revolutionary.* Sebastopol, CA: O'Reilly & Associates.

Raynor, M.E. (2007). *The Strategy Paradox*. Currency-Doubleday: New York, NY.

Reich, B. H. & Kaast-Brown, M. L. (2003). Creating Social and Intellectual Capital Through IT Career Transitions. *Journal of Strategic Information Systems 12*: 91-109.

Reinig, B., Briggs, R., & Nunamaker, J. (1997). Flaming in the electronic classroom. *Journal of Management Information System,* 14(3), 45-59.

ReliaSoft Corporation (2002). *Reliability glossary.* ReliaSoft Corporation.

Repenning, N.P. (2002). A simulation-based approach to understanding the dynamics of innovation implementation. *Organization Science,* 13(2), 109-127.

Repenning, N.P. (2003). Selling system dynamics to (other) social scientists. *System Dynamics Review,* 19(4), 303-327.

Rheingold, H. (2000). *Virtual community: Homesteading on the electronic frontier.* Cambridge: The MIT Press.

Richardson, G.P. (1991). *Feedback Thought in Social Science and Systems Theory.* University of Pennsylvania Press: Philadelphia, PA.

Richardson, G.P. (1995). Loop polarity, loop prominence, and the concept of dominant polarity. *System Dynamics Review,* 11(1), 67-88.

Richmond, B. (1993). Systems thinking: critical thinking skills for the 1990s and beyond. *System Dynamics Review,* 9(2), 113-133.

Richmond. B. et al. (2006). *iThink® Software (version* 9). iSee Systems™: Lebanon NH.

Robb, D. (2004). Text mining tools take on unstructured data. *ComputerWorld*, June 21.

Robertson, T. (1970). *Consumer Behavior.* Glenview, Ill.: Scott Foresman.

Robey, D., & Markus, M.L. (1984). Ritual in information systems design. *MIS Quarterly, 8*, 5-15

Robey, D., Schwaig, K., & Jin, L. (2003). Intertwining material and virtual work. *Information and Organization, 13*(2), 111-129.

Robillard, R. (1999). The role of knowledge in software development. *Communications of the ACM, 42*(1), 87-92.

Rogers, E.M. (1995). *Diffusion of Innovations*. New York: The Free Press.

Romme, G. & Dillen, R. (1997). Mapping the landscape of organizational learning. *European Management Journal 15*(1): 68-78.

Ronald Reagan: The early years. (2004, June 6). *San Francisco Chronicle*, A-24.

Rose, J., Pedersen, K., Hosbond, J. H., & Kraemmergaard, P. (2007). Management competences, not tools and techniques: A grounded examination of software project management at WM-data. *Information & Software Technology, 49*, 605-624.

Rosenberg, D., & Scott, K. (2004). *Use case driven object modeling with UML*. New York: Addison Wesley.

Rosenthal, R. (1974). *On the social psychology of the self-fulfilling prophecy: Further evidence for Pygmalion effects and their mediating mechanisms*. New York: MSS Inf. Corp. Modul. Publishers.

Rosenthal, R. (1993). Interpersonal expectations: Some antecedents and some consequences. In P. D. Blanck (Ed.), *Interpersonal expectations: Theory, research, and applications* (3-24). London: Cambridge University Press.

Rosenthal, R. (1994). Interpersonal expectancy effect: A 30-year perspective. *Current Directions in Psychology Science, 3*, 176-179.

Rosenthal, R., &Rubin, D. B. (1982) Comparing effect sizes of independent studies, *Psychological Bulletin, 92*, 500-504

Rouse, W. B. (1992). *Strategies for innovation: Creating successful products, systems and organizations*. Hoboken, NJ: Wiley.

Rouse, W. B. (2001). *Essential challenges of strategic management*. Hoboken, NJ: Wiley.

Rouse, W. B. (2005). A theory of enterprise transformation. *Systems Engineering, 8*(4) 279-295.

Rouse, W. B. (Ed.). (2006). *Enterprise transformation: Understanding and enabling fundamental change*. Hoboken, NJ: Wiley.

Rudy, I.A. (1996). A Critical Review of Research on Email. *European Journal of Information Systems*, 4, 4, 198-213.

Ruggeri, G. Stevens and McElhill, J. (2000). A Qualitative Study and Model of the Use of EMail in Organisations. *Internet Research, Special Issue on Electronic Networking Applications and Policy*, 10, 4, 271.

Rus, L., & Lindvall, M. (2002). Knowledge management in software engineering. *IEEE Software*, 26-38.

Ryan, S., & Porter, S. (1996). Breaking the boundaries between nursing and sociology: A critical realist ethnography of the theory-practice gap. *Journal of Advanced Nursing, 24*, 413-420.

Sadler-Smith, E. (1998). Cognitive style: some human resource implications for managers. *The International Journal of Human Resource Management 9*(1): 185-199.

Sage, A. P. (1995). *Systems management for information technology and software engineering*. Hoboken, NJ: John Wiley & Sons.

Sage, A. P. (2000). Transdisciplinarity perspectives in systems engineering and management. In M. A. Somerville & D. Rapport (Eds.) *Transdisciplinarity: Recreating integrated knowledge* (158-169), Oxford, U.K.: EOLSS Publishers Ltd.

Sage, A. P. (2006). The intellectual basis for and content of systems engineering. *INCOSE INSIGHT, 8*(2) 50-53.

Sage, A. P., & Rouse, W. B. (Eds.). (1999). *Handbook of systems engineering and management*. Hoboken, NJ: John Wiley and Sons.

Sage, A., and Cuppan, C. (2001). On the systems engineering and management of systems of systems and federations of systems. *Information, Knowledge, and Systems Management 2*, 325-345.

Salaun, Y., & Flores, K. (2001). Information quality: Meeting the needs of the consumer. *International Journal of Information Management, 21*, 21-37.

Salton, G. (1989). *Automatic text processing*. Addison-Wesley.

Samuels, A. R. & McClure, C. R. (1983). Utilization of information decision making under varying organizational climate conditions in public libraries. *Journal of Library Administration 4*(3): 1-20.

Sarin, S., & McDermott, C. (2003). The effect of team leader characteristics on learning, knowledge application, and performance of cross-functional new product development teams. *Decision Sciences, 34*(4), 707-739.

Sastry, M.A. (1997). Problems and paradoxes in a model of punctuated organizational change. *Administrative Science Quarterly,* 42(2), 237-275.

Sayer, A. (1985). Realism in geography. In R. J. Johnston (Ed.), *The future of geography* (pp. 159-173). London: Methuen.

Sayer, A. (2000). *Realism and social science*. London: Sage Publications Ltd.

Sayer, R. A. (1992). *Method in social science: A realist approach*. Routledge: London.

Scarbrough, H., & Corbett, J. M. (1992). *Technology and organization: Power, meaning and design*. Routledge: London.

Schlosser, A. E., White, T. B., & Lloyd, S. M. (2006). Converting Web site visitors into buyers: How Web site investment increases consumer trusting beliefs and online purchase intentions. *Journal of Marketing, 70*(2), 133-148.

Schmidt, R. C., Lyytinen, K., Keil, M., & Cule, P. E. (2001). Identifying software project risks: An international Delphi study. *Journal of Management Information Systems, 17*(4), 5-36.

Schramer, C. (2000). Organizing around not-yet-embedded knowledge. In G. Von Krogh, I. Nonaka, & T. Nishiguchi (Eds.), *Knowledge creation: A source of wealth* (pp. 36-60). London: Palgrave MacMillan.

Schulz, M. (2001). The uncertain relevance of newness: Organizational learning and knowledge flows. *Academy of Management Journal, 44*(4), 661-681.

Scott Morton, M. S. (1991). *The Corporation of the 1990s: Information Technology and Organisational Transformation.* Oxford University Press: New York.

Seashore, S. (1954). *Group cohesiveness in the industrial workgroup,* Ann Arbor: University of Michigan, Institute for Social Research.

Senge, P. (1994). *The Fifth Discipline: the Art and Practice of Learning Organization.* New York, Currency Doubleday.

Senge, P. et al.(1994). *The Fifth Discipline Fieldbook,* Currency-Doubleday: New York, NY.

Shapiro, C., & Varian, H. R. (1999). *Information rules – A strategic guide to the network economy.* Boston, MA: Harvard Business School Press.

Shaw, M. (1976). *Group dynamics: The psychology of small group behavior* (2nd ed.), McGraw-Hill.

Sher, P. J., & Lee, V. C. (2004). Information technology as a facilitator for enhancing dynamic capabilities through knowledge management. *Information & Management, 41*(8), 933-945.

Shih, C.F., Kraemer, K.L., and Dedrick, J. (2002). *Determinants of Information Technology Spending in Developed and Developing Countries.* Center for Research on Information Technology and Organizations. Forthcoming, UC Irvine

Shih, H. P. (2004). An empirical study on predicting user acceptance of e-shopping on the Web. *Information & Management, 41*(3), 351-368.

Silver, M., Markus, M., & Beath, C. (1995) The Information Techonlogy Interation Model: a Foundation of the MBA Course. *MIS Quarterly, 19(3)*, pp. 361-369.

Simmers, C.A. (2002) Aligning Internet Usage With Business Priorities. *Communications Of The ACM*, 45, 1, 71-74.

Simon, H. (1996). *The Sciences of the artificial* (3rd ed.). Cambridge, MA: MIT Press.

Simonson, I., & Nye, P. (1992) The effect of accountability on susceptibility to decision errors. *Organizational Behavior and Human Decision Processes (51)*, 416-446.

Sipior, J.C. and Ward, B.T. (2002). A Strategic Response to the Broad Spectrum of Internet Abuse. *Information Systems Management*, Fall, 71-79.

Sipior, J.C., Ward, B.T. and Rainone, S.M. (1996). The Ethical Dilemma of Employee Email Privacy in the US. *Proceedings of European Conference on Information Systems (ICIS).*

Skyttner, L, (1996). General systems theory: Origin and hallmarks. *Kybernetes, 25* (6), 16, 7 pp.

Skyttner, L. (2001). *General systems theory.* Singapore: World Scientific Publishing

Slonim, N., & Tishby, N. (2000). Document clustering using word clusters via information Bootleneck method. In *Proceedings of SIGID 2000*, New York: ACM Press.

Small, C. T., & Sage, A. P. (2006). Knowledge management and knowledge sharing: A review. *Information, knowledge, and systems management. 5*(6) 153-169.

Smit H. and Trigeorgis L., (2004). Quantifying The Strategic Option Value of Technology Investments. In *Proceedings of the 8th annual conference in Real Options.* Montréal Canada, June 17-19. (http://www.realoptions.org/papers2004/SmitTrigeorgisAMR.pdf).

Smith, J. & Kida, T. (1991).Heuristics and biases: Expertise and task realism in auditing. *Psychological Bulletin,* 109, 472–489.

Smith, M. L. (1980). Publication bias and meta-analysis. *Evaluation in Education 4*, 22-24.

Smith, M. L. (2005). *Overcoming theory-practice inconsistencies: Critical realism and information systems research.* Unpublished manuscript, Department of Information Systems, London School of Economics and Political Science, working paper 134.

Snyder, M. (1995). Power and the dynamic of social interaction. In *Proceedings of 8th Annual Conference on Advers,* Amherst, MA.

Software Engineering Institute (2001). *Capability maturity model integration* (CMMI) (Special report CMU/SEI-2002-TR-001). Pittsburgh, PA: Software Engineering Institute.

Solomon, P. (2002). Discovering information in context. *Annual Review of Information Science and Technology 36*: 229-264.

Sommer, R. (2002). Why is middle management in conflict with ERP? *Journal of International Technology and Information Management,* 11(2), 19-28.

Sonnenwald, D. H. & Pierce, L. G. (2000). Information behavior in dynamic group work contexts: interwoven situational awareness, dense social networks and contested collaboration in command and control. *Information Processing & Management 36*: 461-479.

Spasser, M. A. (2002). Realist activity theory for digital library evaluation: Conceptual framework and case study. *Computer Supported Cooperative Work, 11*, 81-110.

Spiller, P., & Lohse,G. L. (1997). A classification of Internet retail stores. *International Journal of Electronic Commerce, 2*(2), 29-56.

Sproull, L. and Kiesler, S. (1991). *Connections: New Ways of Working in the Networked Organisation.* Cambridge, Massachusetts: MIT Press.

Srikantaiah, T. K. (2000). Knowledge Management: a faceted overview. In T. K. Srikantaiah & M. Koenig (Eds.), *Knowledge Management for the information professional.* Medford, NJ, Information Toady: 1-17.

Stanton, J.M. and Stam, K.R. (2003). Information Technology, Privacy and Power within Organisations: A View from Boundary Theory and Social Exchange Perspectives. *Surveillance & Society*, 1, 2, 152-190.

Staw, B. M., & Ross, J. (1987). Behavior in escalation situations: antecedents, prototypes, and solutions. In B. M. Staw and L. L. Cummings, *Research in organizational behavior* (pp. 39-78). Greenwich, CT: JAI Press Inc.

Stein, E. W., & Vandenbosch, B. (1996). Organizational learning during advanced system development: Opportunities and obstacles. *Journal of Management Information Systems, 13*(2), 115-136.

Steiner, I. (1972). *Group process and productivity.* New York: Academic Press.

Steinfield, C.W. (1990). Computer-Mediated Communications in the Organisation: Using Email at Xerox. In *Case Studies in Organisational Communication*, 282-294, Guilford Press.

Sterman, J.D. (1984). Appropriate summary statistics for evaluating the historical fit of system dynamics models. *Dynamica,* 10(Winter), 51-66.

Sterman, J.D. (1989). Modeling managerial behavior: misperceptions of feedback in a dynamic decision making experiment. *Management Science*, 35(3), 321-339.

Sterman, J.D. (1994). Beyond training wheels. In *The Fifth Discipline Fieldbook*, Senge P. et al, Currency-Doubleday: New York, NY.

Sterman, J.D. (2000). *Business Dynamics: Systems Thinking and Modeling for a Complex World.* Irwin McGraw-Hill: Boston, MA.

Stewart, T. A. (1998). *Intellectual Capital: the new wealth of organizations.* London, Brealey.

Stones, R. (1996). *Sociological reasoning: Towards a past-modern sociology.* MacMillan.

Stowell, F. (1995). *Information systems provision - the contribution of soft systems methodology.* United Kingdom: McGraw-Hill Publishing Co.

Stowell, F. (1997). *Information systems: An emerging discipline?* United Kingdom: McGraw-Hill Publishing Co.

Stowell, F., & Mingers, J. (1997). Introduction. In J. Mingers, & F. Stowell (Eds.), *Information systems: An emerging discipline?* London: McGraw-Hill.

Stukas, A. A., & Snyder, M. (1995). Individuals confront negative expectations about their personalities. In *Proceedings of Annual Meeting of the American Psychology Society*, New York.

Subasic, P., & Huettner, A. (2000). Calculus of fuzzy semantic typing for qualitative analysis of text. In *Proceedings of KDD-2000 Workshop on Text Mining, Sixth ACM SIGKDD International Conference on Knowledge Discovery and Data Mining*, Boston.

Suh, B., & Han, I. (2003). The impact of customer trust and perception of security control on the acceptance of electronic commerce. *International Journal of Electronic Commerce, 7*(3), 135-161.

Sultan, F., Farley, J., and Lehmann, D. (1990). A Meta-Analysis of Applications of Diffusion Models. *Journal of Marketing Research,* 27, 70-77.

Swann, W. B., Jr. (1983). Self-verification: Bringing social reality into harmony with the self. In J. Suls & A. G. Greenwald (Eds.), *Psychological perspectives on the self, vol. 2* (33-66). Hillsdale, NJ: Erlbaum.

Talja, S. (2002). Information sharing in academic communities: types and levels of collaboration in information seeking and use. *New Review of Information Behaviour Research 3*: 143-159.

Tarafdar, M., & Zhang, J. (2005). Analyzing the influence of Web site design parameters on Web site usability. *Information Resources Management Journal, 18*(4), 62-80.

Teo, T.S.H. & Pok, S.H. (2003). Adoption of WAP-enabled mobile phones among Internet users. *Omega International Journal of Management Science*, 31(6), 483-498.

Tesch, D. J., Jiang, J. J., & Klein, G. (2003). The impact of information personnel skill discrepancies on stakeholder satisfaction. *Decision Sciences, 34*(1), 107-130.

Theil, H. (1966). *Applied Economic Forecasting.* Elsevier Science (North Holland): New York, NY.

Thomas-Hunt, M., Ogden, T. & Neale, M. (2003). Who's really sharing? Effects of social and expert status on knowledge exchange within groups. *Management Science,* 49(4), 464–477.

Thompson, R.L., Higgins, C.A., & Howell, J.M. (1991). Personal computing: Toward a conceptual model of utilization. *MIS Quarterly*, 15(1), 125-143.

Thong, J.Y.L, Hong, W.H., & Tam, K.R. (2002). Understanding user acceptance of digital libraries: What are the roles of interface characteristics, organizational context, and individual differences? *International Journal of Human-Computer Studies*, 57(3), 215-242.

Tippins, J., & Sohi, R. (2003). IT competency and firm performance: Is organizational learning a missing link. *Strategic Management Journal, 24*, 745-761.

Tirole, J. (1988). *The Theory of Industrial Organization.* MIT Press: Cambridge, MA.

Todd, P. A., McKeen, J. D., & Gallupe, R. B. (1995). The evolution of IS job skills: A content analysis of IS job advertisements from 1970 to 1990. *MIS Quarterly, 19*(1), 1-27.

Toivonen, J., Visa, A., Vesanen, T., Back, B., & Vanharanta, H. (2001). Validation of text clustering based on document contents. In *Proceedings of MLDM'2001, International Workshop on Machine Learning and Data Mining in Pattern Recognition*, Leipzig, Germany.

Torkzadeh, G., & Dhillon, G. (2002). Measuring factors that influence the success of Internet commerce. *Information Systems Research, 13*(2), 187-204.

Tornatzky, L.G. and Fleisher, M. (1990). *The Process of Technological Innovation.* Lexington.

Trauth, E., Farwell, D. W., & Lee, D. (1993). The IS expectation gap: Industry expectations versus academic preparation. *MIS Quarterly, 13*(3), 293-307.

Trigeorgis L. (1996). *Real Options: Managerial Flexibility and Strategy in Resource Allocation.* The MIT Press.

Trigeorgis, L. (1993). The nature of options interactions and the valuation of investments with multiple real options. *Journal of Financial and Quantitative Analysis.* 28(1), 1-20.

Trigeorgis, L., (1999). Real Options: A Primer". In James Alleman and Eli Noam, (Eds), *The New Investment Theory of Real Options and its Implication for Telecommunications Economics.* Kluwer Academic Publishers, Boston, pp. 3-33.

Tsang, E., & Kwan, K., (1999). Replication and theory development in organizational science: A critical realist perspective, Academy of Management Review (24:4), 759-780

Tung, L. & Turban, E. (1998). A Proposed research framework for distributed group support systems. *Decision Support Systems.* 23, 175-188.

Turoff, M., Hiltz, S., Bahgat, A., & Rana, A. (1993). Distributed group support systems. *MIS Quarterly,* 17(4), 1054-1060.

Tushman, M.L. & Anderson, P. (1986). Technological discontinuities and organizational environments. *Administrative Science Quarterly,* 31, 439-465.

Tyran, C., Dennis, A., Vogel, D., & Nunamaker, J. (1992). The application of electronic meeting technology to support strategic management. *MIS Quarterly,* 16(3), 313-334.

United States Air Force Scientific Advisory Board (2005). *Report on system-of-systems engineering for Air Force capability development.* (Public Release SAB-TR-05-04). Washington, DC: HQUSAF/SB.

Unsworth, K. (2001). Unpacking creativity. *Academy of Management Review,* 26, 289-297.

Urbaczewski, A. and Jessup, L.M. (2002). Does Electronic Monitoring of Employee Internet Usage Work? *Communications of the ACM*, 45, 1, 80-83.

Urbaczewski, A., Jessup, L. M., & Wheeler, B. (2002). Electronic commerce research: A Taxonomy and synthesis. *Journal of Organizational Computing and Electronic Commerce, 12*(4), 263-305.

Urban, G. L., Sultan, F., & Qualls, W. J. (2000). Placing trust at the center of your Internet strategy. *Sloan Management Review, 42*(1), 39-48.

Vaishnavi, V., & Kuechler, W. (2004). Design research in information systems online working paper. Retrieved May 7, 2007, from http://www.isworld.org/Researchdesign/drisISworld.htm

Valerdi, R (2005). *The constructive systems engineering cost model (COSYSMO).* Unpublished doctoral dissertation, University of Southern California, Los Angeles.

Van Den Hooff, B. (1997). *Incorporating Email: Adoption, Use and Effects of Email in Organisations*. Universite IT van Amsterdam. ISBN 90-75727-72-0.

van Rijsbergen, C. (1979). *Information retrieval* (2nd ed.). London: Butterworths.

Van Slyke, C., Lou, H., & Day, J. (2002). The impact of perceived innovation characteristics on intention to use groupware. *Information Resource Management Journal*, 15(1), 5-12.

Vatanasombut, B., Stylianou, A.C., & Igbaria, M. (2004). How to retain online customers. *Communications of the ACM, 47*(6), 64-70.

Venkatesh, V. & Davis, F.D. (1996). A model of the antecedents of perceived ease of use: Development and test. *Decision Sciences*, 27(3), 451-481.

Verma, S., Jin, L., & Negi, A. (2005). OpenSource adoption and use: A comparative study between groups in the US and India. In *Proceedings of the 11th Annual Americas Conference on Information Systems* (pp. 960-972).

Verner, J. M., Overmyer, S. P. & McCain, K. W. (1999). In the 25 years since The Mythical Man-Month what we have learned about project management? *Information and Software Technology 41*: 1021-1026.

Veryzer, R.W. (1998). Discontinuous innovation and the new product development process. *Journal of Product Innovation Management,* 15(2), 136-150.

Vessey, I., Ramesh, V., & Glass, R. L. (2002). Research in information systems: An empirical study of diversity in the discipline and its journals. *Journal of Management Information Systems, 19*(2), 129-174.

Vickers, G. (1965). *The art of judgment*. London: Chapman & Hall.

Vijayasarathy, L. R. (2004). Predicting consumer intentions to use on-line shopping: The case for an augmented technology acceptance model. *Information & Management, 41*(6), 747-762.

Visa, A., Back, B., & Vanharanta, H. (1999). Toward text understanding: Comparison of text documents by sentence map. In *Proceedings of the EUFIT'99, 7th European Congress on Intelligent Techniques and Soft Computing,* Aachen, Germany.

Visa, A., Toivonen, J., Back, B., & Vanharanta, H. (2000). Toward text understanding: Classification of text documents by word map. In *Proceedings of AeroScience 2000, SPIE 14th Annual International Symposium on Aerospace/Defense Sensing,* Simulating and Controls, Orlando, FL.

Visa, A., Toivonen, J., Vanharanta, H., & Back, B. (2001). Prototype-matching: Finding meaning in thee books of the Bible. In *Proceedings of HICSS-34, Hawaii International Conference on System Sciences,* Maui, Hawaii.

von Hippel, E., & von Krogh, G. (2003) OpenSource software and the "private-collective" innovation model: Issues for organization science. *Organization Science, 14*(2), 209-223.

Wad, P. (2001, August 17-19). *Critical realism and comparative sociology.* Draft paper for the IACR conference.

Wainwright, S. P. (1997). A new paradigm for nursing: The potential of realism. *Journal of Advanced Nursing, 26*, 1262-1271

Walls, J. G., Widmeyer, G. R., & El Sawy, O. A. (1992). Building an information system design theory for vigilant EIS. *Information Systems Research, 3*(1), 36-59.

Walls, J. G., Widmeyer, G. R., & El Sawy, O. A. (2004). Assessing information systems design theory in perspective: How useful was our 1992 initial rendition? *Journal of Information Technology Theory and Application, 6*(2), 43-58.

Wan, H. A. (2000). Opportunities to enhance a commercial Website. *Information & Management, 38*(1), 15-21.

Wand, Y., & Weber, R. (1990). An ontological model of an information system. *IEEE Transactions on Software Engineering, 16*(11), 1282-1292.

Wang, J. (2005). The role of social capital in OpenSource software communities. In *Proceedings of the 11th An-*

nual Americas Conference on Information Systems (pp. 937-943).

Watson, R. T., Boudreau, M. C., Greiner, M., Wynn, D., York, P., & Gul, R. (2005). Governance and global communities. *Journal of International Management, 11*, 125-142.

Watson, R. T., Boudreau, M. C., York, P., Greiner, M., & Wynn, D. (in press). The business of OpenSource. *Communications of the ACM.*

Webb, H. W., & Webb, L. A. (2004). SiteQual: An integrated measure of Web site quality. *Journal of Enterprise Information Management, 17*(6), 430-440.

Weber, R. (1987). Toward a theory of artifacts: A paradigmatic base for information systems research. *Journal of Information Systems, 1*(2), 3-19.

Weber, R. (1999). *The information systems discipline: The need for and nature of the foundational core.* Paper presented at the Information Systems Foundation Workshop: Ontology, Semiotics, and Practice, Macquarie University.

Weber, R. (2004). The Grim Reaper: The Curse of Email. Editor's Comments. *MIS Quarterly*, Vol. 28, No.3, iii-xiii, September.

Weiss, P. (1971). *Hierarchically organized systems in theory and practice.* New York: Hafner.

Weiss, S., White, B., Apte, C., & Damerau, J. (2000). Lightweight document matching for help-desk applications. *IEEE Intelligent Systems,* March/April.

Wellman, B. (2001). Physical place and cyberplace: The rise of personalized networking. *International Journal of Urban and Regional Research, 25*(2), 227-252.

Wentling T., Waight C., Gallaher J., Fleur J., Wang C., and Kanfer A., (2000). *E-learning - A Review of Literature.* Knowledge and Learning Systems Group, NCSA, University of Illinois at Urbana-champaign, p.5. http://learning.ncsa.uiuc.edu/papers/elearnlit.pdf

Weston, R. (1999). Model-driven, component-based approach to reconfiguring manufacturing software systems. *International Journal of Operations & Production Management,* 19(8), 834-855.

Wexley, K. N., & Latham, G. P. (1991). *Developing and training human resources in organizations, 2nd ed.* New York: Harper Collins.

Whalen T. and Wright D.,(1999). Methodology for Cost-Benefit Analysis of Web-based Tele-learning: Case Study of the Bell online Institute. *The American Journal of Distance* Education, 13(1), 26.

Whyte, G. (1993). Escalating commitment in individual and group decision making: A prospect theory approach. *Organizational Behavior and Human Decision Processes 54*, 430-455.

Widén-Wulff, G. & Ginman, M. (2004). Explaining knowledge sharing in organizations through the dimensions of social capital. *Journal of Information Science 30*(5): 448-458.

Widén-Wulff, G. & Suomi, R. (2003). Building a knowledge sharing company: evidence from the Finnish insurance industry. *The 36th Hawaii International Conference on System Sciences (HICSS-36)*, Big Island, Hawaii.

Widén-Wulff, G. (2001). *Informationskulturen som drivkraft i företagsorganisationen.* Åbo, Åbo Akademi University Press.

Widén-Wulff, G. (2003). Information as a resource in the insurance business: the impact of structures and processes on organisation information behaviour. *New Review of Information Behaviour Research 4*: 79-94.

Widén-Wulff, G. (2005). Business information culture: a qualitative study of the information culture in the Finnish insurance industry. In E. Maceviciute & T. D. Wilson (Eds), *Introducing Information Management: an Information Research reader.* London, Facet: 31-42.

Widén-Wulff, G. (2007). *Challenges of Knowledge Sharing in Practice: a Social Approach.* Oxford, Chandos Publishing.

Wiener, N. (1948). *Cybernetics: Or control and communication in the animal and the machine.* New York: Wiley.

Williams, R. (1973). *Keywords.* Oxford: Oxford University Press.

Wilson, F. (1999). Flogging a dead horse: The implications of epistemological relativism within information systems methodological practice. *European Journal of Information Systems, 8*(3), 161-169.

Wilson, T. D. (2002). The nonsense of 'knowledge management'. *Information Research: an International Electronic Journal 8*(1).

Winchester, S. (1998). *The professor and the madman: A tale of murder, insanity, and the making of the Oxford English Dictionary.* New York: HarperCollins.

Witten, I., Bray Z., Mahoui, M., & Teahan, B. (1998). Text mining: A new frontier for lossless compression. In *Proceedings of Data Compression Conference '98, IEEE.*

Wixom, B. H., & Watson, H. J. (2001). An empirical investigation of the factors affecting data warehousing success. *MIS Quarterly, 25*(1), 17-41.

Wolfgang, K. (2002). Geographical Localization of International Technology Diffusion. *American Economic Review,* 91(1), 120-142.

Wong, Z. & Aiken, M. (2003). Automated facilitation of electronic meetings. *Information & Management,* 41, 125–134.

Wong. Z. & Aiken, M. (2006). The effects of time on computer-mediated communication group meetings: An exploratory study using an evaluation task. *International Journal of Information Systems and Change Management,*1(2), 138-158.

Wood, R., Atkins, P., & Tabernero, C. (2000). Self-efficacy and strategy on complex tasks. *Applied Psychology: An International Review,* 49(3), 430-447.

Yang, H.D. & Yoo, Y. (2004). It's all about attitude: Revisiting the technology acceptance model. *Decision Support Systems,* 38(1), 19-31.

Yang, J. (2007). Individual attitudes and organisational knowledge sharing. *Tourism Management 29*: 345-353.

Ye, Y., Kishida, K., Nakakoji, K., & Yamamoto, Y. (2002). Creating and maintaning sustainale OpenSource software communities. In *Proceedings of International Symposium on Future Software Technology 2002 (ISFST '02),* Wuhan, China.

Yetton, P. (1997). *Managing the Introduction of Technology in the Delivery and Administration of Higher Education.* Evaluations and Investigations Program; Higher Education Division, Department of Employment, Education, Training and Youth Affairs, Australia. Available at: http://www.dest.gov.au/archive/highered/eippubs/eip9703/front.htm

Yin, R. K. (1989). *Case study research: Design and methods (vol. 5).* Beverley Hills, CA: SAGE Publications Ltd.

Yoh, E., Damhorst, M. L., Sapp, S., & Laczniak, R. (2003). Consumer adoption of the Internet: The case of apparel shopping. *Psychology & Marketing, 20*(12), 1095–1118.

Zak, M. (1994). Electronic messaging and communication effectiveness in an ongoing work group. *Information & Management,* 26, 231-241.

Zamir, O., & Etzioni, O. (1998). Web document clustering: A feasibility demonstration. In *Proceedings of Conference of Information Retrieval (SIGIR'98),* ACM Press.

Zhang, X., Prybutok, V. R., & Koh, C. E. (2006). The role of impulsiveness in TAM-based online purchasing behavior. *Information Resources Management Journal, 19*(2), 54-68.

Zhao, X., Yeung, J., and Zhou, Q. (2002). Competitive Priorities of Enterprises in China. *Total Quality Management,* 13(3), 285-300.

Zipf, G. K. (1972). *Human behavior and the principle of least effort: An introduction to human ecology.* New York: Hafner.

Zmud, R., Mejias, R., Reinig, B., & Martínez-Martínez, I. (2001). *Participation equality: Measurement within collaborative electronic environments: A three country study.* University of Oklahoma.

Zviran, M., Glezer, C., & Avni, I. (2006). User satisfaction from commercial Web sites: The effect of design and use. *Information & Management, 43*(2), 157-178.

About the Contributors

Mehdi Khosrow-Pour, DBA, received his Doctorate in Business Administration (DBA) from the Nova Southeastern University (FL, USA). Dr. Khosrow-Pour taught undergraduate and graduate information system courses at the Pennsylvania State University – Harrisburg for 20 years where he was the chair of the Information Systems Department for 14 years. He is currently president and publisher of IGI Global, an international academic publishing house with headquarters in Hershey, PA and an editorial office in New York City (www.igi-global.com). He also serves as executive director of the Information Resources Management Association (IRMA) (www.irma-international.org), and executive director of the World Forgotten Children's Foundation (www.world-forgotten-children.org). He is the author/editor of over twenty books in information technology management. He is also the editor-in-chief of the Information Resources Management Journal, the Journal of Cases on Information Technology, the Journal of Electronic Commerce in Organizations, and the Journal of Information Technology Research, and has authored more than 50 articles published in various conference proceedings and journals.

Milam Aiken is a professor and chair of management information systems in the School of Business Administration at the University of Mississippi. He has published over 100 articles in journals including Information & Management; ACM Transactions on Information Systems; IEEE Transactions on Man, Machines, and Cybernetics; International Journal of Knowledge Engineering and Software Engineering; and Decision Support Systems, and he has been rated as the leading researcher in group support systems in terms of article count.

Steven Alter is professor of information systems at the University of San Francisco. He earned a PhD from MIT and extended his thesis into one of the first books on decision support systems. After teaching at the University of Southern California he served for eight years as vice president of Consilium, a manufacturing software firm that went public in 1989 and was acquired by Applied Materials in 1998. His research for the last decade has concerned developing systems analysis concepts and methods that can be used by typical business professionals and can support communication with IT professionals. His latest book, The Work System Method: Connecting People, Processes, and IT for Business Results, is a distillation and extension of ideas in four editions of his information system textbook. His articles have been published in Harvard Business Review, Sloan Management Review, MIS Quarterly, IBM Systems Journal, European Journal of Information Systems, Decision Support Systems, Interfaces, Communications of the ACM, Communications of the AIS, CIO Insight, and many conference proceedings.

Georgios N. Angelou was educated at Democritus University of Thrace and received a diploma degree in electrical engineering, in 1995. He also received a MSc in communications & radio engineering from

King's College London in 1997 and a MSc in techno-economic systems – management of technology systems from the National Technical University of Athens in 2002. He worked in telecommunication industry, in companies Siemens and Nokia, for four years as a technical consultant. He is currently a PhD candidate in information systems at the University of Macedonia, Thessaloniki. His current research interests are ICT business analysis, real options & game theory applications in technology investments evaluation. He has publications in various journals, related to the current work, including Journal of the Operational Research Society, Information Resources Management Journal and IEEE Trans. on Engineering Management. He is a member of TEE (Technical Chamber of Greece).

Phil Beck works in the optimization solutions group Southwest Airlines. Previously, he served as director of the Center for Information Technologies Management at the University of Texas at Arlington. Prior to joining UTA he worked in industry for over eighteen years and held a variety of positions including: consultant, project manager, manager of financial analysis, director of financial planning and analysis, and director of aircraft maintenance system implementation. He received a PhD in management science from the University of Texas at Austin. His publications have appeared in journals such as Journal of Systems and Software, International Journal of Innovation and Learning, Decision Sciences, ACM Transactions on Mathematical Software, MIS Quarterly, Journal of Management Information Systems, Communications in Statistics, Naval Research Logistics, Operations Research Letters and Mathematical Programming.

Shana Dardan holds a PhD from the University of North Carolina at Charlotte in information technology. Currently, she is conducting research in the area of IT investment valuations and digital healthcare for UCDMC, Sutter Health and Geisinger medical center. Shana has been an invited member of the WiSac and Pennsylvania Broadband task forces. Previous corporate research includes notable companies such as Intel Corp, where she conducted research for Doug Busch, VP and CIO. She speaks at industry events on investment strategies, IT security, and outsourcing. Shana joined Susquehanna University in 2006, where she teaches systems analysis and design as well as IT strategy.

Aidan Duane holds an MSc from University College Cork (UCC). At present he is following the PhD program at UCC at the Department of Accounting, Finance and Information Systems. He also currently lectures in information systems and electronic business at Waterford Institute of Technology (WIT), Ireland. His research interests include electronic business, electronic communication systems, electronic monitoring, and IS ethical issues. His research has been published in leading IS journals and conferences including The Information Systems Journal, The International Journal of E-Business Research, ICIS, ICEC and IRMA.

Anastasios A. Economides was educated at Aristotle University of Thessaloniki and received a diploma degree in electrical engineering, in 1984. After receiving a Fulbright and a Greek State Fellowship, he continued for graduate studies at the United States. He received a MSc and a PhD degree in computer engineering, from the University of Southern California, Los Angeles, in 1987 and 1990 respectively. He is a professor of computer networks and vice-chairman of the Information Systems Department at the University of Macedonia, Thessaloniki. He is also the director of CONTA (COmputer Networks and Telematics Applications) Laboratory. His research interests are in the area of multimedia high speed networks, e-commerce, tele-education and telematic Web applications. He has publications in various journals, related to the current work, including Journal of the Operational Research Society and Information Resources Management Journal. He is a member of IEEE Computer Society, IEEE Communications Society, TEE (Technical Chamber of Greece).

Patrick Finnegan holds a PhD in information systems from the University of Warwick, and is currently a senior lecturer in management information systems at University College Cork. His research interests include electronic business and IS strategy. He has published his research in a number of international journals and conferences including The International Journal of Electronic Commerce, IT& People, Database, Electronic Markets, The Information Systems Journal, ECIS, ICIS and AMCIS.

Nicholas Constantine Georgantzas is professor, management systems, and director, system dynamics consultancy, Fordham University Business Schools. An associate editor, System Dynamics Review, he is also consultant to senior management, specializing in simulation modeling for learning in strategy, production and business process (re) design. Author of Scenario-Driven Planning (Greenwood 1995), Dr. Georgantzas has published over 80 articles in refereed scholarly journals, conference proceedings and edited books. His publications include articles in systems thinking, knowledge technology and strategy design, focusing on the necessary theory and tools for learning in and about the dynamic systems in which we all live.

Linwu Gu is an associate professor of management information systems at Indiana University of Pennsylvania. Her research interests include group support systems, strategic information systems, and information security.

Bassam Hasan is an assistant professor of management information systems at The University of Toledo. He holds a PhD in MIS from The University of Mississippi and MBA in CIS from Missouri State University. His research interests include end-user computer training and management of information systems. His reserach has been published in several IS journals and presented at various regional and national IS conferences.

James Jiang is professor of management information systems at the University of Central Florida. He is also the honorary Jin-Ding professor at the National Central University in Taiwan. His PhD in information systems was granted by the University of Cincinnati. His research interests include IS project management, IS human resources management, and IS service quality management. He has published over 100 academic articles in these areas in journals such as JMIS, DS, CACM, IEEE SMC, IEEE Engineering Management, IEEE Professional Communications, JAIS, and MIS Quarterly. He teaches programming, project management, and software engineering courses.

Evangelos Katsamakas is assistant professor, information systems, Fordham University Business Schools. He holds a PhD (2004) from the Stern School of Business, New York University and a MSc from the London School of Economics. Professor Katsamakas research has been published in Management Science, Information Resources Management Journal and other major journals and international conference proceedings. Dr. Katsamakas research focuses on strategic aspects of open source software, electronic markets, technology platforms and disruptive innovation. His research interests include economics and game theory modeling and analysis, system dynamics and simulation of complex systems.

Gary Klein is the Couger professor of information systems at the University of Colorado in Colorado Springs. He obtained his PhD in management science from Purdue University. Before that time, he served with the company now known as Accenture in Kansas City and was director of the information systems department for a regional financial institution. His research interests include project management, technology transfer, and mathematical modeling with over 100 academic publications in these areas. In addition to being an active participant in international conferences, he has made professional presentations on decision support systems in the US and Japan where he once served as a guest professor to Kwansei Gakuin University.

Ram L. Kumar is a professor in Belk College of Business Administration, UNC-Charlotte. He received his PhD in information systems from the University of Maryland. He worked for major multinational corporations such as Fujitsu before entering academics. His research has been funded by organizations such as the U.S. Department of Commerce, and organizations in the financial services and energy industries. His current research interests include techniques for evaluating and managing portfolios of IT investments, service science, and knowledge management. His research has been published in Communications of the ACM, Computers and Operations Research, Decision Sciences, Information Resource Management Journal, International Journal of Electronic Commerce, International Journal of Production Research, Journal of MIS, and others.

Doncho Petkov is a professor in IS at Eastern Connecticut State University, USA. He has taught at university level since 1987: in Zimbabwe (till 1991); South Africa (1991-01.2002) and USA (since 2002). Prior to that, he worked in the IT industry for nine years. He is a deputy editor (USA) for Systems Research and Behavioral Science, a senior area editor for IJITSA, co-editor of IJCSS and a member of the editorial boards of Scientific Inquiry, Information Systems Education Journal and The International Journal of Decision Support System Technology. His publications have appeared in the Journal of Systems and Software, Decision Support Systems, IRMJ, Telecommunications Policy, JITTA, International Journal on Technology Management, IJITSA, JITCAR, Kybernetes, ISEDJ and elsewhere.

Alfonso Reyes is a physicist and a systems engineer from Los Andes University in Colombia. He has an MSc in computer science from the University of Maryland at College Park (USA) and a PhD in management cybernetics from the University of Humberside in England. He did also postdoctoral studies in organizational learning with professor Raúl Espejo at the University of Lincoln in Englad. He has worked for the last twenty years in addressing organisational problems in the public sector especially in the administration of justice. He is a former adviser of the Ministry of Justice in Colombia and was the chairman of a governmental committee proposing normative recommendations to improve the administration of justice to be included in the Colombian Constitution in 1991. He has been an international consultant for the Interamerican Development Bank and the Agency for International Development (USA) in the area of applied management cybernetics to the public sector. He is actually an associate professor at the Department of Industrial Engineering at Los Andes University in Colombia. He has published several papers about individual learning, organisational learning and self-regulation from the point of view of second-order cybernetics.

Kosheek Sewchurran is a senior lecturer at the University of Cape Town in South Africa, and a research associate of Center for IT And National Development in Africa (CITANDA). He has been at the

University of Cape Town(UCT) since 2006. Prior to UCT he worked in the IT industry for approximately twelve years in various capacities; and lectured at the University of Kwa-Zulu Natal on a part-time basis. His research interests are: project managment practice and education; action research in the modes of action learning and reflexive learning; organisational culture and information systems.

Antonis C. Stylianou has over 20 years of experience in computer information systems. Currently, he is professor of management information systems and a member of the graduate faculty at the University of North Carolina at Charlotte. His industry experience includes an appointment in the information management department at Duke Energy. Dr. Stylianou has published numerous research articles in the Communications of the ACM, Management Science, Decision Sciences, Information & Management, and other journals. He is a frequent presenter on the management of information systems, and serves as a consultant to organizations. He is currently a senior editor of the Database for Advances in Information Systems journal.

Reima Suomi is professor of information systems science at Turku School of Economics, Finland since 1994. He is docent for the universities of Turku and Oulu, Finland. Years 1992-93 he spent as a "Vollamtlicher Dozent" in the University of St. Gallen, Switzerland, where he led a research project on business process re-engineering. Currently he concentrates on topics around management of telecommunications, including issues such as management of networks, electronic and mobile commerce, virtual organizations, telework and competitive advantage through telecommunication-based information systems. Also different governance structures applied to the management of IS and the application of information systems in health care belong to his research agenda. Reima Suomi has together over 300 publications, and has published in journals such as Information & Management, Information Services & Use, Technology Analysis & Strategic Management, The Journal of Strategic Information Systems and Behaviour & Information Technology. For the academic year 2001-2002 he was a senior researcher at the Academy of Finland. With Paul Jackson he has published the book "Virtual Organization and workplace development" at Routledge, London.

Eric T.G. Wang is dean and professor of school of management at National Central University, Taiwan (R.O.C.). He received the PhD degree in business administration, specialized in computer & information systems, from the William E. Simon Graduate School of Business Administration, University of Rochester. His research interests include electronic commerce, supply chain management, outsourcing, organizational economics, and organizational impact of information technology. His research has appeared in Information Systems Research, Management Science, Decision Support Systems, Information & Management, European Journal of Information Systems, Information Systems Journal, Omega, European Journal of Operational Research, International Journal of Information Management, International Journal of Project Management and others.

Jianfeng Wang is an associate professor of management information systems in Indiana University of Pennsylvania. His research areas include the economics of information technology, group support systems, and database technology.

Gunilla Widén-Wulff is professor of information studies at Åbo Akademi University, Finland where she has been appointed as teacher and researcher since 1996. She holds a PhD in information science from 2001. She is teaching in knowledge organization, information seeking, and information management. During the winter of 2004–2005 she was a visiting researcher at School of Computing, Napier University, Edinburgh. Her research fields concern information and knowledge management in business organizations, and aspects of social capital and knowledge sharing in groups and organizations. She is also project leader of a larger research project financed by the Academy of Finland called *Library 2.0 - a new participatory context*, looking at various aspects of library 2.0 and web 2.0 and social media.

Index